Bernd Engler & Oliver Scheiding (Eds.)

A Companion to American Cultural History:

From the Colonial Period
to the End of the 19th Century

A Companion to American Cultural History

From the Colonial Period
to the End of the 19th Century

Bernd Engler & Oliver Scheiding (Eds.)

wvt Wissenschaftlicher Verlag Trier

A Companion to American Cultural History:
From the Colonial Period to the End of the 19th Century
Bernd Engler / Oliver Scheiding (eds.)
Trier: WVT Wissenschaftlicher Verlag Trier, 2009
   ISBN 978-3-86821-112-2

Cover illustration: Detail from Fanny F. Palmer.
Across the Continent – Westward the Course of Empire Takes Its Way (Lithograph).
New York: Currier & Ives, 1868.
Courtesy Library of Congress.

Cover Design: Brigitta Disseldorf

© WVT Wissenschaftlicher Verlag Trier, 2009
ISBN 978-3-86821-112-2

Alle Rechte vorbehalten
Nachdruck oder Vervielfältigung nur mit
ausdrücklicher Genehmigung des Verlags

WVT Wissenschaftlicher Verlag Trier
Postfach 4005, D-54230 Trier
Bergstraße 27, D-54295 Trier
Tel. (0651) 41503, Fax (0651) 41504
Internet: http://www.wvttrier.de
E-Mail: wvt@wvttrier.de

CONTENTS

TO THE READER .... vii–xi

OLIVER SCHEIDING
  Mapping America
  and the Colonial Imagination 1

MARGIT PETERFY
  Images of Native Americans 27

CLEMENS SPAHR
  Puritanism in the New World 55

FRANK OBENLAND
  Providential Thought in the
  Puritan Historiography of New England 87

JAN STIEVERMANN
  Interpreting the Role of America in
  New England Millennialism, 1640 to 1800 121

FRANK KELLETER
  The Great Awakening and the Enlightenment 163

GERD HURM
  Founding Dissent: Revolutionary Discourse
  and the Declaration of Independence 191

DENNIS HANNEMANN / ULRICH ESCHBORN
  The Early Republic and the Rites of Memory 219

GESA MACKENTHUN
  Expansionism 245

GÜNTER LEYPOLDT
  The Transcendental Turn in
  Nineteenth-Century New England 275

ISABELL KLAIBER
  Women's Roles in American Society:
  Difference, Separateness, and Equality 303

MELANIE FRITSCH
  Slavery and Racial Thought in
  American Cultural History 331

WOLFGANG HOCHBRUCK
  Civil War and Reconstruction 363

TIM LANZENDÖRFER
  The Gilded Age:
  The Emergence of Modern America 385

LIST OF KEY CONCEPTS 421

INDEX 423

TO THE READER

This volume is designed as a companion piece to the anthology *Key Concepts in American Cultural History: From the Colonial Period to the End of the 19th Century*, which was first published in 2005 and has, within two years, reached a second edition. This fact illustrates that a comprehensive source book providing essential documents of American cultural history fulfills the needs of American Studies programs in Germany and Europe. Several years of using the anthology as a textbook have also shown, however, that both students and scholars still consider a companion and study guide to American cultural history a desideratum. The collection of essays at hand responds to this obvious need for an introduction to the major developments in US intellectual history. For this purpose, it seeks to position the documents presented in the anthology within the major ideological formations in which they originally operated and developed their political and social impact.

Although a multiplicity of voices has defined America's cultural development since the colonial period, the conceptualization of America as a distinct nation has evolved from a relatively small number of pervasive concepts. Such key concepts served as ideological blueprints and mental signposts in the process of building a common basis for a society which – with respect to gender, class, ethnicity, and religion – had an extremely diversified origin.

In accordance with the editorial policies that guided the selection of documents in the anthology, this volume foregrounds concepts which have transcended their original historical contexts to become crucial factors in the forging of a uniquely American cultural identity. Given this particular focus, the essays investigate the cultural logic that allowed certain basic ideas not only to gain prominence at a specific historic moment, but to establish themselves as forces which reached wide social currency and, by implication, exerted a fundamental, long-term ideological impact. As Terry Eagleton has pointed out in his seminal study on *Ideology* (London: Verso 1991, 5-6), the cultural logic at work in "*promoting* beliefs and values" (original emphasis) usually appears to be "some unspoken but systematic logic" that tends to naturalize or universalize such beliefs as if they came into being through an evolutionary process. By evolving in a seemingly natural way, this cultural logic obscures not only the very constructedness of such beliefs, but also hides the highly debatable nature of their claims to authority. As the following essays point out, ideological blueprints are foremost constructs that, for various reasons, succeeded in obtaining and securing their validity in the public domain. They accomplished this validity by answering particular communal needs at the moment of their origin and then proved to be adaptable enough to the evolving needs of an ever-changing society. The fact that ideological blueprints achieve plausibility through their own "systematic logic," thus becoming cultural essentials themselves, results from a perfect interaction of a set of ideas that was already dominant during the formative period of colonial society in America.

The assumption of such a cultural logic throughout this volume seems to imply, at first glance, that American culture is far less diversified than is commonly supposed, when American intellectual history is considered as an ever variable configuration of an extremely heterogeneous set of beliefs and values. However, the individual essays are far from regarding the constant re-articulation of a relatively small number of ideological blueprints as an indicator of a reductive or repressive cultural system. The repetition of concepts in diverse cultural contexts and the ensuing formation of a reputedly homogeneous archive of central ideas that seem to represent a culture in a pars pro toto fashion cannot at all be considered a result of mental streamlining. Instead, as the essays collected in this volume reveal, a mere repetition of ideas is never possible, since repetition always enforces an awareness of the different contexts in which it takes place. Thus, only by analyzing continuities within American cultural history can one expose the fundamental discontinuities that such a cultural logic always produces. We can only observe the gradual transformation of key concepts by means of a diachronic study of a particular set of ideas and their re-articulation over time. Instead of catering to the essentialist assumption that long-established concepts form the 'natural foundations' of a culture because of their longevity, this volume claims that the long-term social acceptance of such concepts is the very result of their enormous adaptability to changing cultural needs. A student of American cultural history who concludes from the mere re-appearance of a particular piece of vocabulary (for instance, 'manifest destiny' as it is used in both colonial and mid-nineteenth century texts) that it conveys the same idea, would completely miss the major transformations in the meaning and ideological uses of the term. Identical terms employed in different cultural contexts evoke different meanings, and they often refer to entirely different "ways of world-making" (Nelson Goodman, Indianapolis 1978), as re-articulation takes place within new ideological formations or responds to particular political and social situations.

One prominent example for this transformation of ideas is the notion of a special national mission, which was circulated throughout American history with various intentions and ideological connotations. Originally advertised in the late sixteenth century by English promoters of emigration to the New World, it soon transformed into a means of justifying the large-scale colonization of foreign territory and, as a consequence, also as a means of offering moral support to frustrated colonists questioning the godliness of their mission. The 'errand' into an all-too-obvious wilderness, inhabited by 'savage Indians' and wild beasts had to be transformed into an errand into a promised land sanctified by God in the form a 'New Covenant' for His chosen people. As the editors have already pointed out in *Key Concepts in American Cultural History*, the concept of America's particular mission thus "served as a means of moral sustenance in times of distress" (*KC*, xvi). When the concept was then re-employed during the Great Awakening and later on by nineteenth-century reform movements, it was already attached to a different set of values as well as social and political agendas, which had little to do with the original implications.

*

As a companion piece to *Key Concepts in American Cultural History*, this volume mirrors the overall design of the original collection of documents. But while the collection of documents could only offer limited introductory explanations of the hidden continuities as well as the transformations of the key concepts embedded in the documents, the essays of this volume analyze the ideological trajectories of those concepts in depth. Instead of reading the documents as mere re-articulations of invariable concepts, the focus will be on investigating how these concepts emerged in and responded to a specific historical moment. While the editors selected the documents based on their employment of essential concepts such as providentialism and expansionism within different historical contexts, the analytical essays in this volume explore how those concepts originally gained cultural momentum and acceptance, how they were re-articulated and re-configured in ever-changing new contexts, and how they then became cultural determinants, which not only described a culture, but also shaped all the processes in its formation.

As this volume of essays serves a double purpose, i.e., both offering a close reading of processes of cultural formation and serving as a study guide for students and an instructional guide for teachers of American Studies, the editors have decided to supplement the analytical essays with sections focusing on classroom issues and self-study strategies. Following the anthology's intention "to encourage cross-segmental and diachronic readings that make the student aware of the continuities and discontinuities of ideological 'formations'" (*KC*, xvi), the study guide section of each essay provides the reader with

I.   the various concepts and major themes defined and renegotiated in the historical documents (cf. "I. Key Concepts and Major Themes"),
II. information on how various concepts functioned and interacted in ever-changing ideological formations (cf. "II. Comparison – Contrasts – Connections"),
III. basic questions every reader should keep in mind when studying the documents (cf. "III. Reading and Discussion Questions"),
IV. essential tools for further study in the form of an annotated bibliography of recommended reading and additional reading suggestions (cf. "Resources").

*

The editors are grateful to all those who have made the publication of this study guide possible through their unfailing dedication and by generously investing their time in reading drafts and supplying criticism at crucial stages: first of all, those who shared their expertise and knowledge by providing contributions – Ulrich Eschborn, Melanie Fritsch, Dennis Hannemann, Wolfgang Hochbruck, Gerd Hurm, Frank Kelleter, Isabell Klaiber, Tim Lanzendörfer, Günter Leypoldt, Gesa Mackenthun, Frank Obenland, Margit Peterfy, Clemens Spahr, Jan Stievermann –, then all those who expended their invaluable energy and proficiency by editing and proof-reading the essays, and preparing this companion for publication – notably Sara Duke, Timor Hwa, Tim Lanzendörfer, Martin Peter, and Thomas Smyth (PhD). Our special thanks go to Christina Kühnel for her perceptive and efficient copy-editing.

Mainz and Tübingen   Oliver Scheiding
January 2009   Bernd Engler

Cross-referencing within this volume

Internal cross-referencing is intended to help the reader overcome common "mental compartmentalizations" and the confines imposed by analyzing ideological patterns in isolation. Cross-sectional comparisons of major themes and notions provide guidance on the complex interrelatedness of key concepts.

Parenthetical references to documents published in the anthology *Key Concepts in American Cultural History* will be abbreviated "doc." with document number added, or "*KC*" with page number. If not otherwise indicated, italics and capitalization in quotations reproduce the original document's emphasis.

Further illustrations and e-Texts

Reproductions of additional illustrations and documents cited in the text, but not printed in the anthology, can be downloaded from the anthology's web site: http://www.amerikanistik.uni-mainz.de/key. Illustrations and documents available on the web site are in the public domain and may be used in the classroom. The web site also contains short biographical entries on the documents' authors.

Copyright and other restrictions which apply to publication and other forms of distribution of images

The images reproduced in this publication are presented for educational and research purposes only. For those images not in the public domain, we have attempted to obtain permission from copyright holders or commercial stock image suppliers. Transmission or reproduction of protected items beyond that permitted by fair use requires the written permission of the copyright owners and may be subject to copyright fees and other legal restrictions.

OLIVER SCHEIDING

Mapping America and the Colonial Imagination

> Not only has this navigation confounded many affirmations of former writers about terrestrial things, but it has also given some anxiety to interpreters of the Holy Scriptures.
> Francesco Guiccardini
> (in Elliott 1970, 28-9)

> I will confute those blind geographers
> That make a triple region of the world,
> Excluding regions which I mean to trace
> Christopher Marlowe (1998, 59)

I. Themes and Arguments

This chapter will discuss conceptualizations of America that evolved in late sixteenth-century English promotional literature and maps. It will investigate the intersections between geography, religion, and historiography, as they have been outlined in the first segment of documents, "Early Conceptualizations of America," in the anthology. Explaining the ways in which mapping and storytelling complement each other, this chapter demonstrates how the expansion of England brought about geohistories that shaped the colonial imagination of British America.

Contrary to postcolonial studies that frequently omit the sixteenth century in order to reconstruct the rise of the colonial imagination during the eighteenth century and the Enlightenment (cf. Mignolo 2000, 62), this chapter will address the formation of global designs and imperial concepts in early Protestant England.[1] The chapter contends that, to avoid the risk of telling only one story about

---

[1] Early Americanist and Atlantic historians call for a more overtly transatlantic approach to the period before 1800. Such an approach emphasizes the role that crossing the Atlantic plays in the conception, production, distribution, and reception of seventeenth- and eighteenth-century Anglophone literature and culture. Recent studies conceive of early American culture as an active and dynamic factor in an emerging British American transatlantic system. Culture does not merely flow outward from England to the colonies,

the colonial past, it is necessary to go beyond the eighteenth century and to readdress conceptualizations of America within the expanding boundaries of Christian geography beyond the Old World and into the American hemisphere. The transformation of the geography of salvation, as this chapter will show, fosters the colonial imagination of British America and serves as a point of departure for understanding the global dynamics of empire building.

This chapter will focus on the writings of Richard Hakluyt the Younger, as well as a group of associate promoters of English expansion overseas. Hakluyt's compilations of archival materials and cartographic sources on North America contain an immense body of geographical and historical knowledge. In his *The Principall Navigations, Voiages and Discoveries of the English Nation Made by Sea or Over Land, to the Most Remote and Farthest Distant Quarters of the Earth at any Time Within the Compasse of these 1500. yeeres* (1589), Hakluyt synthesizes maps, historical documents, and voyage narratives into a monumental history that marks the threshold of American colonization.[2]

The following chapter is divided into three parts. The first deals with the transformation of the geography of salvation in the late sixteenth century. It will discuss Hakluyt's *Discourse of Western Planting* (doc. 7) to show how, in this text, key concepts emerge that have helped to 'locate' America within traditional Christian cosmography. The second part illustrates how geographical and religious discourses complement each other and, in so doing, 'remap' America in terms of England's westward expansion. The final part examines the formation of the colonial imagination in local histories of geography that were promulgated by Hakluyt.

---

there translating into local forms, but is produced in a process of intra-imperial cultural exchanges (cf. Kupperman 1995; Warner 2000; Schueller and Watts 2003; Vickers 2003; Bailyn 2005; Hornsby 2005; Mancall 2007b; Brückner 2006; Brückner and Hsu 2007).

[2] In the 1580s, Hakluyt received financial support from the clothworkers' company in London, which was directly involved in trade with Spain and the Mediterranean. In an attempt to counter the dominant influence of cross-Channel commerce, the clothworkers encouraged Hakluyt's efforts to publicize longer-distance trades. Hakluyt championed the colonization efforts of Sir Humphrey Gilbert in New-Foundland and of Sir Walter Raleigh in Virginia. In 1589, a year after the defeat of the Spanish Armada, he published his massive epic of English colonization overseas, *The Principall Navigations*. During the same years, various promotional tracts and eyewitness accounts of exploration and settlement also appeared. Among these was Thomas Hariot's *A Briefe and True Report of the New Found Land of Virginia* (doc. 10), an eyewitness account of Sir Walter Raleigh's second voyage to Virginia (Roanoke), which included compelling descriptions of North Carolina Algonquian native culture. These accounts, as well as accompanying maps, illustrations, and ship's logbooks, marked the beginning of what has been called the "imperial archive" (Richards 1993), a fund of knowledge that helped shape England's expansion overseas (cf. Taylor 1934, 1-66; Helgerson 1992, 151-2; Mancall 2007a).

II. Locating America and the Geography of Salvation

According to medieval cosmography, the world consisted of three continents: Europe, Asia, and Africa. The idea of a triple world was so embedded in European thought that it was still in use long after the discovery of America. Furthermore, according to biblical world order, the descendants of Noah peopled the three parts of the world. In most maps from the fifteenth and sixteenth centuries, Europe belonged to the sons of Japheth, Africa to Ham's, and Asia to Shem's.[3] The tripartite Christian division of the world mirrored the *orbis terrarum* already known to classical geographers. America, the new fourth continent, was therefore difficult to assimilate (cf. Scheiding 2008).

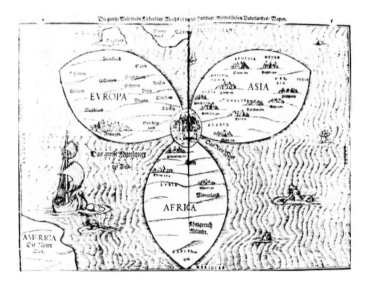

Fig. 1: Heinrich Bünting. "Die gantze Welt in ein Kleberblat" *Itinerarium Sacræ Scripturæ. Das ist Ein Reisebuch, Uber die gantze heilige Schrifft*: in zwey Bücher getheilt. Das Erste Theil Begreifft alle Reisen der lieben Patriarchen Richter Könige Propheten Fürsten. Das Ander gehet auff das Newe Testament und zeiget an wie die Jungfraw Maria Joseph die Weisen aus Morgenlannd der Herr Jesus Christus und die lieben Apostel gereiset haben. Aus den glaubwirdigsten und fürnembsten Büchern zusamen gezogen und Geometrischerweise ausgerechnet. Helmstedt 1581.

---

[3] See Hartmann Schedel's *Das Buch der Chronicken und Geschichten* (doc. 1). Schedel's incunabula world map is a remarkable record of late medieval cartography (cf. Wolff 1992), as it combines the outdated concepts of Claudius Ptolemy (the geocentric worldview) with the biblical tradition that depicts the world divided between the three sons of Noah. The border vignettes contain fabled mythical beasts and creatures believed to exist outside Christendom; for medieval myths about the New World, see Mandeville's *Travels* (doc. 22), and for animals on maps Sebastian Münster's *Typus Cosmographicus Universalis* (doc. 2; cf. George 1969).

A good case in point is Heinrich Bünting's map, "Die gantze Welt in ein Kleberblat," published in 1581 (doc. 5). Bünting's map builds the world around Jerusalem, which is the spiritual center of the earth. Excluding America, the map arranges the continents of Europe, Asia, and Africa like the three parts of a clover leaf, surrounding the Holy Land. America's peripheral location in the geography of salvation results from earlier assumptions about the New World as a place of devilish creatures.[4]

Since the Middle Ages, geographical limits coincided with the boundaries of humanity. Outlandish creatures with two heads, three arms, and the like were supposed to inhabit the regions beyond the known geographical boundaries. The first account of America that appeared in England, for instance, described the New World as the land of cannibals. As such, the people of America had no capacity for Christianity, and there was, therefore, never any possibility that they might achieve salvation. However, while incorporating North America into the geographical understanding of Englishmen, Hakluyt and his associate promoters drew a dividing line between the cannibals that inhabited 'America' – a name initially used to describe the southern regions of Spain's dominion in the New World – and the savages who occupied its northern portion.[5] While the mental and social worlds of the cannibals were the outcome of the Devil's busy handiwork, the northern Indians were intelligent and would thus welcome the achievements of the English nation.

In his *Discourse of Western Planting* (doc. 7), Hakluyt "traces" the English region of North America in terms of England's prominent role in the history of salvation.[6] The first chapter heading already claims "[t]hat this westerne discoverie will be greatly for thinlargement of the gospell of Christe," and the following argument ensues:

---

[4] Similar to Martin Waldseemüller's well-known globe gores of 1507, on Lorenz Fries's world map (1525) "America" refers to South America. In addition, it contains illustrations of Brazilian Indians as cannibals (cf. doc. 2, 24), and the western hemisphere resembles a dragon that arises out of Asia. Dragons were widely used on maps to denote dangerous and unexplored territories, but they could also refer to the medieval legend of the apocalyptic tribes of Gog and Magog who inhabited Asia as recorded in the *Alexander Romance* (cf. Westrem 1998).

[5] George Peckham (doc. 9) claims that the northern native people are descendants from a Welsh prince who had sailed to the New World in 1160 (cf. Williams 1987). Accordingly, he concludes that "[the Indians] shalbe defended from the cruelty of their tyrannicall & blood sucking neighbors, the *Canniballes*, wherby infinite number of their lives shalbe preserved. And lastly, by this meanes many of their poore innocent children shalbe preserved from the bloody knife of the sacrificer, a most horrible and detestable custome in the sight of God & man, now and ever heeretofore used amongst them" (*KC*, 15).

[6] Two years earlier, Hakluyt had published a compilation of various documents relating to discoveries in the New World, entitled *Divers Voyages Touching the Discoverie of America, and the Ilands Adiacent unto the Same Made First of all by Our Englishmen* (1582). "For the Plainer Understanding of the Whole Matter," as the title has it, Hakluyt annexed two maps. The maps by Thomas Thorpe and Michael Lok depict the greater North-Atlantic region (cf. *KC* web site).

> Nowe yf they [the Spaniards] in their superstition by meanes of their plantinge in those partes have don so greate things in so shorte space, what may wee hope for in our true and syncere Relligion, proposinge unto our selves in this action not filthie lucre nor vaine ostentation as they in deede did, but principally the gayninge of the soules of millions of those wretched people, the reducinge of them from darkenes to lighte, from falshoodde to truthe, from dombe Idolls to the lyvinge god, from the depe pitt of hell to the highest heavens. [...] Even so wee whiles wee have soughte to goo into other Contries (I woulde I mighte say to preache the gospell) God by the frustratinge of our actions semeth to forbydd us to followe those courses, and the people of America crye oute unto us their nexte neighboures to comme and helpe them, and bringe unto them the gladd tidinges of the gospell. (*KC*, 11)

Hakluyt interprets English expansion and colonization overseas in providential terms.[7] He explains the failed attempts of earlier ventures as positive signs that God had finally singled out North America to be occupied by the descendants of the "True Church." Carrying the light of the "True Church" into the vast regions of the northern continent implies that it has remained in darkness for such a long time because it was God's plan to open North America for English expansion only at the beginning of the Reformation.[8]

Hakluyt rearranges Bünting's triple division of the world. While Bünting moved America and England to the margins and conceived of America in terms of Rome's global legacy – on the map, Rome is to the west of Jerusalem – Hakluyt moved the spiritual center to the north. Since the sons of Japheth, as the sons of "true and syncere Relligion," now occupy England, Hakluyt's tract rearticulates the idea of an enlargement of Japheth in terms of England's westward extension. He relocates the center of salvation by interpreting the discovery of America in light of the progressive course of Reformation history. Hakluyt creates a 'christianography' that opens a space in which the various national projects or geographical fictions could be played out.

---

[7] In his *Hakluytus Posthumus, or Purchas His Pilgrimes* (1625), Samuel Purchas, who became Hakluyt's successor in compiling multivolume accounts of geographical exploration, compared the English discoveries in the New World to "Salomon's Discoveries," which by God's "Revelation were aimed to prepare us for that holy Jerusalem, descending out of Heaven from God, having the Glory of God" (4-5; cf. Taylor 1934, 53-66; Bauer 2003, 78-117).

[8] At the end of the seventeenth century, Cotton Mather (doc. 81) defends America's role in the history of salvation. He supports Hakluyt's argument by pointing out that the "concealing of America" is part of God's "over-ruling *Providence.*" While the "discovering" of America coincides with the "*Reformation* of *Religion*," it is obvious that "*Geography* must now find work for a *Christianography* in Regions far enough beyond the Bounds wherein the *Church* of God had thro' all former Ages been circumscribed" (*KC*, 182-3). Next in the line of colonial writers who transform the concealment of the western hemisphere into America's exceptionalism is Thomas Paine. In *Common Sense* (doc. 130), he argues that "[t]he Reformation was preceded by the discovery of America; As if the Almighty graciously meant to open a sanctuary to the persecuted in future years, when home should afford neither friendship nor safety" (*KC*, 300).

III. Mapping America and Modern Cartography

Hakluyt uses geography to supply spatiotemporal evidence for his providentialist reading of American colonization.[9] The "modern" and "most accurate" maps used by Hakluyt complement the information given in the voyage narratives. The verbal and the visual determine and redefine geographic space in terms of an English perspective; both also relate America to the progressive course of Reformation history. While reprinting Abraham Ortelius's "Typus Orbis Terrarum" (1570) for the first edition of his *The Principall Navigations* (1589), Hakluyt offers the reader geographical facts for a Protestant vision of American colonization.

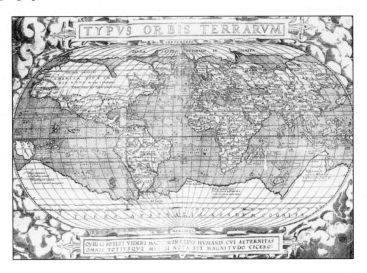

Fig. 2: Abraham Ortelius. "Typus Orbis Terrarum," as the legend reads; folded engraved map, included in the first edition of Richard Hakluyt the Younger, *The Principall Navigations*. London 1589. The map was copied from Abraham Ortelius's *Theatrum Orbis Terrarum* (1570).

---

[9] Hakluyt echoes Ortelius's statement that "geography is the eye of history" (in Armitage 1995, 57), thus acknowledging the study of cartography and its importance for English land claims in the New World. In his *Divers Voyages Touching the Discoverie of America* (1582), an early attempt to promote English coloniziation, Hakluyt had included the first English map of the New World by Robert Thorne the Younger. The map depicts the northern parts of America in close proximity to England and Protestant northern Europe. Along the Atlantic coastline, one reads in Latin: "Terra heac ab Anglis primum fuit inventa" (cf. Hakluyt 1582, n. p.) The inscription refers to the landfall of John Cabot who had sailed under the flag of England's Henry VII to the New World in 1496. English promoters claimed that the discovery of the northern continent had actually taken place two years before Columbus reached the mainland of Central America in 1498; see also Edward Hayes "A Report of the Voyage and Successe Thereof" (doc. 8).

The Principall Navigations pays special attention to the westward voyage of the English nation: In the first period, England begins adventuring on the seas, with voyages to the Canaries; consequently, a greater naval power develops, capable of mounting battles with Spain and Portugal, and finally permanent overseas bases are created within the bounds of what is to become an empire.

To provide geographical proof for England's expansion, Hakluyt inserts maps and documents that demonstrate England's priority in 'planting' North America. English writers had made frequent references to the most "scientific" cartographers of their time. Some, for instance, referred to Gerhard Mercator's general map, since it gave evidence that the countries of North America "stretche out itselfe towards England onelie" (*KC*, 14). English writers left out the earlier fabulous cosmographies with their emblematic representations of the globe and their zones, poles, and regions as projections of the celestial sphere.[10] Instead, they replaced earlier cartographic productions with "modern" maps, whose longitudinal lines bring into being undiscovered lands and thus spell out a spatial reality for the progressive course of English history. Likewise, the division of the world into the New and Old World – *Occidens* and *Oriens* – tabulated by meridians, parallels, and the line of zodiac, structures the world.

Ortelius's cartographic projections of the world mark a shift in European map production. He departs from earlier collections of maps – frequently assembled to suit the needs of individual customers – by addressing a wide audience with a new form of map presentation. Ortelius's *Theatrum Orbis Terrarum* (1570) consists of a single-sized compilation of maps, historical narratives, and source references. It is the first true atlas in the modern sense, and, at the same time, an encyclopedic depiction of the world.[11]

Likewise, in Hakluyt's work, maps and narratives complement each other. The world map illustrates Hakluyt's theme of England's expansion overseas. Given the minor role of America and England on Bünting's world map, the "Typus Orbis Terrarum" (doc. 4) verifies the existence of a huge northern con-

---

[10] See the oval map of the world *Typus Cosmographicus Universalis* (doc. 2) and the cordiform map of the world *Charta Cosmographica, cum Ventorum Propria Natura et Operatione by Petrus Apianus* (doc. 3).

[11] In contrast to earlier representations of the world in terms of an *imago mundi*, Ortelius's "Typus Orbis Terrarum" (doc. 4) highlights the model character of his map and expresses the spreading cartographic literacy in Europe. The Ciceronian quotation from *Tusculan Disputations* and the decoration of the map are interrelated and unfold an image of the earth that can be read in terms of a divine sanctification of Europe's religious, economic, and political expansion. Furthermore, the atlas opens with an allegorical title page which depicts the four continents of Europe, Asia, Africa, and America as native goddesses (cf. *KC* web site). Ortelius's hierarchy of the continents heralds Europe's global dominion over the other parts of the earth. Although the atlas is dedicated to Philip II, King of Spain and the Netherlands, the allegedly exact distribution of the continents and the different sizes of the two parts of America also allow for a reading of the map in terms of a Protestant vision of westward expansion.

tinent that is close to England. Like England, eastern North America belongs to the temperate zone of the middle Atlantic. Moreover, as all attempts by the French and the Spanish have failed to establish permanent settlements in eastern North America, England now has the chance to possess this land that stretches in her direction.[12] In comparison to earlier maps, Ortelius also features a vast and empty landmass that extends further to the west and is without mountains in the interior. Given Hakluyt's intention to reinterpret the geography of salvation, the deformation of the southern continent marks a paradigmatic shift in Christian global designs that began with the Reformation. As the "True Church" moved from the Catholic south to the Protestant nations of the north in the course of the sixteenth century, the diminished southern hemisphere demonstrates the decline of papal dominion in the New World. Hakluyt's conclusion that Spain's role in America is "out of date" reverses a widespread interpretation of the course of history developed by the Italian humanist Peter Martyr, who had argued that those who seek fortune should bend their way towards the south, not towards the "frozen north" (1555, 184-6).

Furthermore, in one of his prefatorial notes, Ortelius had announced Europe's historic mission of world conquest. Accordingly, the inhabitants of Europe had always surpassed all other people in intelligence and physical dexterity. These attributes naturally qualified Europeans to govern the other parts of the world. However, as Hakluyt contends, Spain had disqualified itself from playing a leading role in the western hemisphere. In his *Discourse of Western Planting*, he asserts that Spain had "dispeopled" its lands, only to add that the Spanish "[r]ealmes [...] unto this present day remain in a wilderness and utter desolation" (*KC*, 11). Hakluyt's argument recalls the concept of improvement that had made an early appearance in Thomas More's *Utopia* (1516).[13] More had stated that those who keep the land idle forfeit legal possession of it. Hakluyt couples this concept with ideas of cultural development that had found their way to England in the 1580s. While the most lurid information about Spanish conduct in the New World was circulating Europe, Hakluyt imagined Protestant England as a vanguard of mankind as it advanced along the road of civilization. He advertised an idea of progress that viewed all peoples as being in different stages of development, ranging from the stage of primitive beginnings to the highest stage attained by fully civilized nations, which are illuminated by Evangelical Law.

---

[12] Hakluyt was familiar with Las Casas's *Brief Narration of the Destruction of the Indes, by the Spaniards* (doc. 26) that was translated into English in the 1580s and had been used by many English writers to demonstrate how Spanish colonization had utterly failed. Hakluyt copies the exact numbers of Indians who have been killed by the Spaniards since 1520 (cf. *KC*, 42; Peterfy in this vol., 35-7).

[13] In the chapter "Of their Traffick," More holds: "[b]ut if the Natives refuse to conform themselves to their Laws, they drive them out for themselves, and use Force if they resist. For they account it a very just Cause of War, for a Nation to hinder others from possessing a Part of that Soil, of which they make no use, but which is suffered to lie idle and uncultivated" (1751, 73).

Progress from the first savage stage common to all nations to a higher stage was made through the agency of great teachers who emerged within a group, or came from other lands, and taught men social intercourse as well as the utility of law and government. Therefore, Hakluyt's statement that English planting does not seek "filthie lucre nor vain ostentations as [the Spaniards] did," but rather intends to "gain" people from "darknes to lighte," conceptualizes America in terms of the advancements of English civilization.

As the empty space to the west of England shows an empire in decay and another in ascent, English writers openly voiced the progressive conviction that North America was meant for England. In a co-authored pamphlet, Edward Hayes and Christopher Carleill conclude that

> Onto thys infallible prediction of Christ, I wyll drawe a probable conjecture allso from the Revolution of Gods word, which hytherto hath moved Cyrcularly.
>
> For lyke as the same begann in the East in paradice, And moved westwards in[to] Palestina, And at length into Europe. thear beginning in the East also proceded by South into the west, and spredd afterwards North: Even from Europe it hath contynewed hys Revolution west into America, wh[ile] it begann East: proceded South & west. And may happely more purely [be] preached also in the North by us. Unto which tyme (thys being the last of the last Age of the world:) we are now arryved. And therfore may ho[pe] by so muche the more, of our good success in thys Action now. Seing the last dayes are come upon us. And that now or never theyr conversion is to [be] expected. (*KC*, 19)

According to both authors, geography and religion reveal the gradual westward course of civilization. Like Hakluyt, they endow America with the ideal of a mission and cherish the idea of an empire in the west.

IV. Relating America and the Colonial Imagination

By compiling, translating, and editing a mass of documents from the discovery, exploration, and settlement of the New World, Richard Hakluyt was a prime agent in the gradual association of the American experience with the colonial imagination. Hakluyt reprinted many early English and non-British reports, and he even wrote narratives himself, based on eyewitness accounts. A good case in point is Thomas Hariot's *A Briefe and True Report of the New Found Land of Virginia* (doc. 10). Hariot's promotional pamphlet was the first published book about America by an English explorer. For many critics, Hariot's report marks the beginning of American literature, in which Virginia is staged as an earthly paradise and a second Eden. The pamphlet stirs the reader's fantasies of everything being "farre greater" in the New than in the Old World. As the first edition, however, turned out to be a failure, it was taken up by Hakluyt in his *The Principall Navigations* and passed on by him to the Dutch illustrator and Frankfurt publisher Theodor de Bry. When de Bry republished Hariot's account in 1590, he included many of his own engravings that were based on the watercolors of John White, an artist who was sent to the Roanoke colony by Sir Walter Raleigh to paint Natives and natural commodities of America. De Bry also designed two maps of Virginia that frame Hariot's report. While the opening map serves as a visual accompaniment to de Bry's foundational tale that describes "The Englishmen's Arrival in Virginia," the closing map supports Hariot's observations that Virginia is waiting for English colonization. Hariot's *A Briefe and True Report* also contains one of the first visualizations of native culture in English literature and evokes spatial fantasies through which England declares its presence in the New World.

John White produced a remarkable set of pictures of Indians and their daily life (cf. Sloan 2007). Meticulous in his effort to render an exact likeness, his Indians are tanned, they assume postures which are ungainly to Western eyes, and their faces are somewhat Oriental, with low foreheads and straight black hair. These watercolors were, however, not known publicly until the twentieth century. What the contemporary English public did see were the engravings of Indians done by de Bry and his assistants, based on White's watercolors. Thomas Hariot, who had worked with White at Roanoke, had published his account of the Natives and commodities of Virginia immediately after his return to England in 1588. In his report, Hariot refers to his plan to include the graphic material both men had collected in Virginia. De Bry's edition, which was put to press in 1590 at the urging of Richard Hakluyt and the cooperation of Hariot, reprinted *A Briefe and True Report* and presented de Bry's engravings of White's watercolors with notes on the pictures written by Hariot. De Bry's engravings retained White's meticulous attention to dress, hair style, and body decoration, but changed the appearance of the Indians to look more European.

Fig. 3: John White. "Indian Woman and Young Girl" (created 1585/6).

Much has been written about the ways in which de Bry "dramatized" the Indians by transforming their faces, postures, and bodies; for example, the new edition made the Indians resemble classical figures in the German engraving tradition.[14] A closer look at the illustrated version of Hariot's account, however, shows that the authors have created a densely interwoven tissue of texts and

---

[14] See the *Costume Book* (*Trachtenbuch*, 1529) of the artist traveller Christoph Weiditz, in which Aztec Indians brought to Spain by Hernán Cortés were sketched from life.

drawings that frames White's earlier sketches of Algonquian life within numerous maps and landscape views.

One of the framing illustrations, de Bry's drawing of "Adam and Eve" that opens the book, adds the scriptural (as well as legal) rationale for appropriating native lands. The opening illustration follows the perspectival arrangements of Renaissance engravings. It consists of three distinct pictorial layers. The foreground refers to the prelapsarian state of mankind with animals (panther, lion, hare, mouse) alluding to the peaceable kingdom as it is described in Isa. 11.6-8. The middleground portrays mankind's fall, with the demon-serpent entwined around the center of the tree of knowledge, while Adam gazes guilelessly heavenward. The background alludes to the postlapsarian state of mankind: Adam tills the soil while Eve mothers Cain in a makeshift shelter. The illustration has been frequently read as Europe's hope that North America would prove a new Eden of peace and a land of plenty.[15]

Fig. 4: Theodor de Bry. "Adam and Eve." In: Thomas Hariot. *A Briefe and True Report of the New Found Land of Virginia*. Frankfurt/M. 1590.

---

[15] See John Smith, *A Description of New England* (doc. 15) and Francis Higginson, *New Englands-Plantation* (doc. 18).

Moreover, in light of the religious ideas that fueled English colonization, the illustration contains a more subtle message. In unfolding a prospective view of scriptural prophecies, it reassesses mankind's fall in light of a second, 'profitable' Eden that awaits English settlers in the New World. Contrary to exhortative readings of man's fall, the engraving heralds the remunerative opportunities that lie in "planting and building a foundation for his Posteritie, gotte from the rude earth, by Gods blessing & and his own industrie" in Virginia (*KC*, 23-4). The illustration envisions Genesis and the most popular biblical quotation in the English occupation of the New World, "*Gen.* 1.28. *Multiply, and replenish the earth, and subdue it.*" This phrase has been described by many ministers as the "grand Charter" given to Adam's sons and their posterity (*KC*, 26). In his sermon *Gods Promise to His Plantation* (doc. 16), which outlines the policies and ordinances of the Puritan settlement in the New World, John Cotton draws upon examples from the Bible to justify the dispossession of the Indians:

> Thirdly, when hee makes a Country though not altogether void of Inhabitants, yet void in that place where they reside. Where there is a vacant place, there is liberty for the sonnes of *Adam* or *Noah* to come and inhabite, though they neither buy it, nor ask their leaves. *Abraham* and *Isaac*, when they sojourned amongst the *Philistins*, they did not buy that land to feede their cattle, because they said There is roome enough. And so did *Iacob* pitch his Tent by *Sechem*, *Gen.* 34.21. [...] but admitteth it as a Principle in Nature, That in a vacant soyle, hee that taketh possession of it, and bestoweth culture and husbandry upon it, his Right it is. And the ground of this is from the grand Charter given to *Adam* and his posterity in Paradise, *Gen.* 1.28. *Multiply, and replenish the earth, and subdue it.* If therefore any sonne of *Adam* come and finde a place empty, he hath liberty to come, and fill, and subdue the earth there. This Charter was renewed to *Noah*, *Gen.* 9.1. *Fulfill the earth and multiply*: So that it is free from that comon Grant, for any to take possession of vacant Countries. Indeed no Nation is to drive out another without speciall Commission from heaven, such as the *Israelites* had, unlesse the Natives do unjustly wrong them, and will not recompence the wrongs done in peaceable sort, & then they may right themselves by lawfull war, and subdue the Countrey unto themselves. (*KC*, 25-6)

God's commandment to fill the earth and subdue it unites the concept of vacant land (*vacuum domicilium*) with the concept of improvement, and as such it found entry into political and legal writings (cf. Mackenthun in this vol., 249-51).[16] As culturally specific as the understandings of these actions were,

---

[16] John Locke summed up the characteristic English understanding of the scriptural concept of replenishment: "God and his Reason commanded him to subdue the Earth [...]. He that in Obedience to this Command of God, subdued, tilled, and sowed any part of it, thereby annexed to it something that was his Property" (1698, 189). The same idea appeared earlier as well: "When God had made man after his own Image, in a perfect state, and would have him to represent himself in authoritie, tranquilitie and pleasure upon the earth, he placed him in Paradise. What was Paradise? but a Garden and Orchard of trees and herbs, full of all pleasure: and nothing but delights" (Lawson 1618, 56). English faith and planting practices guaranteed a legitimate title to the land and granted English settlers the right to pos-

their absence was used to deny indigenous peoples of the New World possession of their lands. Robert Cushman, who was one of the leading figures among the nonconformist Puritans, argued that New England was a "vast and empty chaos" (*KC*, 29):

> This then is a sufficient reason to prove our going thither to live, lawfull: their land is spacious and void, & there are few and doe but run over the grasse, as doe also the Foxes and wilde beasts: they are not industrious, neither have art, science, skill or facultie to use either the land or the commodities of it, but all spoiles, rots, and is marred for want of manuring, gathering, ordering, &c. (*KC*, 29)

The notion of taking possession frequently relates to bestowing "Culture and husbandrie" upon the land (*KC*, 15). In his *A True Report, of the Late Discoveries and Possession, Taken in the Right of the Crowne of England* (doc. 9), George Peckham asserts that "being brought from brutish ignoraunce, to civility and knowledge, and made them [the Indians] to understand how the tenth part of their land may be so manured and emploied, as it may yeeld more commodities to the necessary use of mans life, then the whole now dooth" (*KC*, 15).[17]

In addition to the notion of bestowing culture and husbandry, Peckham also alludes to the idea of replenishing (i.e., enriching the soil of) and subduing the land. Likewise, Hariot points out in his report that the Indians never "fatten" the ground "with mucke, dounge or any other thing, neither plow nor digge it as we in England" (1590, 14). Collecting animal manure as fertilizer appears to have been a distinctive English agricultural technique and was, for instance, referred to with great disgust by medieval Frenchmen. The verb *manure* in sixteenth-century English meant "to own," "to cultivate" by hand as well as "to enrich land with manure." Peckham as well as the garden-variety engravings of Indians in Hariot's report therefore evoke a colonial imagination that results from distinct English methods of working the soil and were closely related to the concept of improvement.

Depicting the New World as a garden thus denied Indian land rights because it implied that by working the soil the English could legally take possession of it. This can be seen on the map that concludes the illustrated edition of de Bry. The closing map looks at the region from an imperial point of view. The royal coat of arms claims English dominion of the land.

---

sess the New World. In the anonymously published tract *Brief and True Narration* (1675), the writer states that "by their great industry, [the Puritans had] of a howling Wilderness improved those Lands into Cornfields, Orchards, enclosed Pastures, and Towns inhabited; which hath considerably advanced the values of the Lands" (1675, 3).

[17] "Culture" here does not mean language or laws or rules, rather it has a quite different meaning: farming, cultivating fruits, and planting gardens were part of husbandry, which was itself the key to maintaining the world. Planting the garden involved neither simple physical exertion nor mere aesthetic enjoyment; it was an act of taking possession of the New World for England. It was not a law that entitled Englishmen to possess the New World, but an action which established their rights.

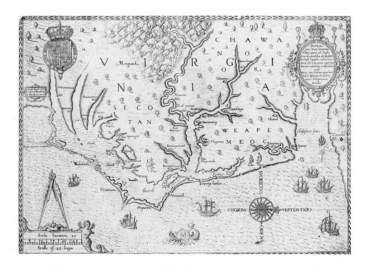

Fig. 5: Theodor de Bry. "America, pars, nunc Virginia." In: Thomas Hariot. *A Briefe and True Report of the New Found Land of Virginia.* Frankfurt/M. 1590.

The map endows the land with a particular story that is closely related to Hariot's account. Hariot describes the geography, climate, vegetation, wildlife, and the "manners" of the "natural inhabitants" of Virginia. He takes his reader on a journey from the east to the west and then into the interior of the newly found country. He concludes his journey by calling the reader's attention to the vistas of the west:

> As we have reason so to gather by the difference we found in our travails; for although all which I have before spoken of, have bin discovered & experimented not far from the sea coast where was our abode & most of our travailing: yet somtimes as we made our iourneies farther into the maine and countrey; we found the soyle to bee fatter; the trees greater and to growe thinner; the grounde more firme and deeper mould; more and larger champions; finer grasse and as good as ever we saw any in England; in some places rockie and farre more high and hillie ground; more plentie of their fruites; more abundance of beastes [...].
>
> Why may wee not then looke for in good hope from the inner parts of more and greater plentie, as well of other things, as of those which wee have alreadie discovered? Unto the Spaniardes happened the like in discovering the maine of the West Indies. The maine also of this countrey of *Virginia*, extending some wayes so many hundreds of leagues, as otherwise then by the relation of the inhabitants wee have most certaine knowledge of, where yet no Christian Prince hath any possession or dealing, cannot but yeeld many kinds of excellent commodities, which we in our discoverie have not yet seene. (*KC*, 16)

Hariot's report of his actual experience in Virginia translates Ortelius's projection of a void and empty land into a narrative of westward expansion. In so doing, he familiarizes the reader with objects that the New World keeps in store. The voyage brings forward commodities which the English reader knows – for instance, silk and flaxe – but also unknown items, such as "Wapeih" (Hariot 1590, 8), a kind of healing clay, "Uppówoc" (1590, 16), which is tobacco, and Indian corn (cf. Knapp 1993, 282-90). While commodities such as "Worme Silke" reveal the future greatness of Virginia (1590, 7-8), the 'transplanting' to the New World signals the fall of eastern empires like Persia and Spain that were formerly associated with this product. Moreover, the description of Indian corn as a "graine of marveilous great increases" evokes biblical prophecies (1590, 13), such as the parable of the sower (cf. Matt. 13.31; Mark 4.30-3), and implies that its prophetic promises refer to America. The descriptions of Old and New World products mentioned in the report represent the four continents. Since Asia, Africa, and Europe encompass earlier stages of growth and development, America is left as the good ground that will prove more fruitful. Other New World commodities, such as tobacco, support the idea of a progressive movement of empires and religion from the east to the west. While Virginia's products "preserveth the body from obstructions" (1590, 16), as Hariot notes, the commodities of the East, such as sugar and liquor, are often the cause of degradation and derangement. Conversely, the commodities of America stimulate the senses. Given the attempts to redefine the role of America within the history of salvation, Hariot's catalogue of native goods contains an ironic twist on the exclusion of the New World in Christian cosmography, since it becomes obvious that the fourth continent, which once was the devil's corner, now regenerates the Old World.

The map's imperial language and its symbolic decoration minimize the Indians. The representations of the Indians, whose bodily shape resembles pictures of Picts and Ancient Britons (cf. Fig. 6, 7), fit into the progressive scheme mapped out by Richard Hakluyt and the group of English promoters.

Fig. 6, 7: Theodor de Bry's engravings of an ancient Pict and Indian warrior. In: Thomas Hariot. *A Briefe and True Report of the New Found Land of Virginia*. Frankfurt/M. 1590.

De Bry's engraving of an ancient Pict warrior reminded readers of Hariot's account that the "Virginia" Indians were not culturally inferior to the colonists' own ancestors. Likewise, John Smith compared the "salvages" to the "seede of *Abraham*" (*KC*, 24) as he considered the northern "salvages" as grand-children of the Old World, who lived in a state of infancy. The voyage to the west was thought of as a journey into the past, as he maintains that "[e]ven wee our selves, had at this present beene as Salvage, and as miserable as the most barbarous Salvage yet uncivilized" (*KC*, 24). English promotional writers frequently considered the Indians as what all men had once been before they became civilized.

Virginia is not the land of cannibals, and therefore its "natural inhabitants" do have the capacity for Christianity. Moreover, de Bry's illustrations of Indians as well as the Indian names on the map support assumptions that the Ancient Britons are the progenitors of North America's Indians.[18] Thus, the map suggests that Indians are the descendants of Noah who have only forgotten social virtues as they turned into hunters over time.

Finally, the numerous English ships signal the country's future destiny as a center of commerce, immigration, and religion. England's technological superiority is symbolized by the nautical instrument and the compass. The map thus contrasts the busy highways of the Atlantic sea with the empty space of North America, whose broad waterways open to the west and invite English settlers to enter the void to improve it. As native attributes (i.e., bows and arrows) demonstrate, Indians are at a lower stage of civilization; since they keep the land idle and do not cultivate it, it is only natural – according to the concept of improvement – that they will be dispossessed in the course of history.

Additionally, through naming, space is transformed symbolically into a place with an imperial history. The Latin inscription, which claims that Virginia was first discovered by the English, summarizes an imperial project of permanent possession. Furthermore, Virginia's newly evolving history is narrowed down to one actor. Raleigh descends from the mythic line of English heroes whose great deeds are collected by Hakluyt (cf. doc. 13). In discovering and settling Virginia, Raleigh exemplifies the divine law that governs English history. The compass ultimately emblematizes the progressive course of British America: It is the west that turns into a field of futurity.

---

[18] For the legend of Prince Madoc and the fable of a Welsh-speaking tribe of Indians, cf. George Peckham's *A True Report, of the Late Discoveries and Possession* (doc. 9; Axtell 1992). According to Peckham, Madoc sailed west, landing in the New World at an unknown spot. In his report, Peckham quotes Montezuma's later speech to Hernán Cortés, in which the Aztec emperor refers to his own peoples' alleged Welsh ancestors: "You ought to have in remembraunce, that eyther you have heard of your Fathers, or else our divines have instructed you that we are not naturallie of this Countrie, nor yet our Kingdome is durable, because our Forefathers came from a farre countrie and their King and Captaine who brought them hither, returned againe to his natural countrie, saying, that he would sende such as should rule and governe us, if by chaunce he himself returned not" (in Williams 1987, 42).

Accordingly, ideas of progress and manifest destiny, which fueled the colonial imagination of Puritanism and the revolutionary period, originate in the rearticulation of Christian global designs during the sixteenth century.[19] Colonial critics such as Walter Mignolo therefore question the "chronological frontier" of the modern colonial world system. Contrary to postcolonial studies, which set the formation of a Western style for dominating, restructuring, and having authority over the globe in the eighteenth century, Mignolo reexamines the emergence of Western conceptualizations of America in the colonial horizon of the sixteenth century and the Renaissance. He contends that

> The Occident [...] was never Europe's Other but the difference within sameness: [...] America, contrary to Asia and Africa, was included as part of Europe's extension and not as its difference. Occidentalism was a transatlantic construction precisely in the sense that the Americas became conceptualized as the expansion of Europe, the land occupied by the descendants of Japheth. (2000, 58)

Thus, to further explore the "cartography of American uniqueness" (Amy Kaplan 1993, 4), it is necessary to go beyond the "chronological frontier" established by postcolonial critics and to reexamine the formation of imperial cultures as well as their continuities in the texts of America's colonial past.

Instructional Strategies and Classroom Issues

I. Key Concepts and Major Themes

1. Transformation of the triple world order (docs. 1-8; cf. further cartographic documents on the *KC* web site)
   The transformation of the triple world order expands the limits of the world and of humanity and moves America into the center of the geography of salvation. Furthermore, it challenges European thought, as America has to be incorporated into the cosmographical, geographical, and anthropological conceptions of Europeans.

2. Westward expansion (docs. 7-13)
   The call for an enlargement of the realm of Japheth remaps North America as an extension of England into the west. The reinterpretation of the

---

[19] See, for instance, the following texts: Samuel Sewall, *Phaenomena Quaedam Apocalyptica* (doc. 79); Nicholas Noyes, *New Englands Duty and Interest* (doc. 80); Cotton Mather, "A General Introduction [to *Magnalia Christi Americana*]" (doc. 70); Cotton Mather, "Venisti tandem? Or Discoveries of America" (doc. 81); Jonathan Edwards, "Some Thoughts Concerning the Present Revival in New-England" (doc. 82); Samuel Sherwood, "The Church's Flight into the Wilderness" (doc. 85); Jedidiah Morse, *The American Geography* (doc. 154); John Quincy Adams, *An Oration Delivered at Plymouth, December 22, 1802* (doc. 149); Anonymous, "The Destiny of the Country" (doc. 178); Josiah Strong, "The Anglo-Saxon and the World's Future" (doc. 318).

medieval *orbis terrarum* and the reterritorialization of spiritual centers bring about the invention of a new Protestant global design.

3. America as a Second Eden (docs. 6, 11, 13, 15, 18)
   America as land of plenty leads to the idea of settling the continent in terms of a secular venture of exploration and appropriation of the land. John Smith's emphasis on building and planting a plantation by God's blessing and one's own industry (doc. 15) anticipates the rhetoric of opportunity that later characterizes the ideology of the American Dream.

4. America's providential role (docs. 14, 19-20)
   The inclusion of North America into eschatological schemes brings about the progressive conviction of America's manifest destiny as a land of universal freedom. America fulfills a providential role in the history of salvation; cf. Alexander Whitaker: "[T]he finger of God hath been the onely true worker heere" (*KC*, 21).

5. Transfer of imperial power, religion, and culture (docs. 12, 21)
   The projection of *translatio imperii, religionis et studii* unto America results in the creation of the Atlantic circuit with British America at its center.

6. Concept of improvement (docs. 16-7)
   Conceptualizing North America as a vast and empty space (*vacuum domicilium*) to be improved by English settlers justifies possession of the land. The notion of an empty land also fuels missionary plans to convert the Indians.

7. Concept of 'savage' (doc. 15)
   The northern indigenous peoples have been considered descendants of the Old World, who live in a state of infancy. In light of missionary endeavors, English writers argue that the Indian savages are the same as Englishmen have once been before becoming civilized.

II. Comparison – Contrasts – Connections

Example: Docs. 5, 58, 107, 131, 134, 150, 291-2

The study unit opens with a reading of the cover illustration (doc. 292) from the anthology's last segment of documents ("Gilded Age: Problems at Home and Abroad"). The illustration promotes the centennial exposition that was held in Philadelphia in 1876. It was part of a profusely illustrated collection of eight hundred plates and fold-outs printed by the publishers of the popular and widely read *Frank Leslie's Illustrated Newspaper* (1855-1922). The document belongs to America's history of pictorial journalism that started during the Civil War (1860-1865; cf. Hochbruck in this vol., 363-83). As photography had not yet found its way into publications, books and newspapers were illustrated with woodcuts and engravings to dramatize current events.

After the Civil War and the closing years of the Reconstruction period, the centennial exhibition was a showcase for America's technological and civil advancement. The Philadelphia fairground was turned into a site that brought forth the "manifest designs of Providence" (*KC*, 652). In his Fourth of July oration for the centennial ceremonies, William M. Evarts (doc. 291) assured his audience that

> we are met, on the spot and on the date of the great Declaration, to compare our age with that of our fathers, our structure with their foundation, our intervening history and present condition with their faith and prophecy. [...] We have taken no steps backward, nor have we needed to seek other paths in our progress than those in which our feet were planted at the beginning. (*KC*, 652-3)

Aside from the exuberant ceremonial rhetoric aimed at concealing the political and social rifts of the post-Civil War period, most foreign visitors were deeply impressed by America's industrial progress. Even Americans themselves felt, as writer and critic William Dean Howells observed, that "no one can now see the fair without a thrill of patriotic pride" (1876, 107). The centennial exhibition ushered in an era of modern industrialization as America moved from agriculturalism to an age of steam and electricity.

The illustration refers to earlier conceptualizations of America in terms of a hierarchy of continents that can be seen on Heinrich Bünting's world map, as well as in allegorical illustrations that foreshadow America's future role as an empire of reason and commerce (cf. doc. 150). The cover advertisement of the *Historical Register of the Centennial Exposition* depicts the four continents as women standing on a cliff that provides them with a bird's-eye view over the Atlantic coastline and allows them to glimpse the country's western lands. The elevated position alludes to proleptic images frequently used in post-revolutionary vision poems which predict America's future greatness (cf. doc. 107). The *topos* of the 'high place' derives from Deut. 34.1, which tells the story of Moses's climbing onto Mount Pisgah, from which he sees the promised land of Canaan (cf. *KC*, 113).

At the center of the cover illustration (doc. 292) is Columbia, who appears as Minerva, the Roman goddess of war and wisdom. Instead of the traditional breastplate, she wears a gown tailored from a star-spangled banner, and her high-crested and plumed helmet indicates strength and prowess (cf. doc. 134). Next to her stands Britannia, leaning on a shield that shows the three lions of England. The olive branch she is holding signals the peaceful relationship of the two leading trading nations. In light of the subordinated role the other women play, British-American sisterhood foreshadows the Anglo-Saxon supremacy that is to crown the world.

The accompanying maidens, Asia and Africa, appear in descending order. Asia's richly embroidered silk garment signals an advanced state of civilization, while the kneeling, half-naked Nubian figure as well as the crouching Indian occupy lower stages of civilization. Early depictions of the hierarchy of the four continents can be found on Ortelius's title page which introduces his atlas (cf. *KC* web site). In contrast to Europe's global dominion, Ortelius positions America on the lowest stage of human progress. Likewise, on Bünting's Christo-centric world map, America possesses only a fairly liminal place in the history of salvation.

The cover illustration reverses traditional global hierarchies as it envisions the transfer of power, religion, and knowledge (cf. *translatio imperii*) to the New World. "Europe," as it appears on the globe in the dimly lit background of the cover illustration, disappears into the dark, while the shining light of a rising American empire illuminates the western sphere. The shrinking brightness of the Old World underscores the shift of eschatological centers from the east to the west. America is the new promised land, as signaled by Columbia's inviting gesture that points to the west. She makes the other nations see America's unhampered advancement from the time of the first settlements in the New World to the present. America's universal values, which are summarized by *The Declaration of Independence* (doc. 131), derive from and are symbolized by major American buildings and institutions that can be seen below the cliff. Despite British success in being the first to build a Crystal Palace for the world exhibition of 1851, America's achievements lie in democracy (Capitol), religious freedom (colonial church building), commerce (sailing ships and steamboats), as well as modern technology and communication (transcontinental railway and telegraph posts). The cover advertisement serves to prepare Americans for changes to come and for a wider international role (cf. Lanzendörfer in this vol., 385-419).

Additional indigenous maps may be used to problematize the discovery, conquest, and settlement of America from a non-Western perspective:
- Medieval maps and maps of ancient Mexico.
- The Cortés map of Tenochtitlan (1524) and the codex Mendoza map of Tenochtitlan (1542).
- Guman Poma de Ayala's *Pontifical Mundo* (*Pontifical World*) for Incan world maps (c. 1615).
- Leslie Marmon Silko's map of conquest in *Almanac of the Dead* (1991).

III. Reading and Discussion Questions

1. Discuss the transformation of the world order from the Middle Ages to the late sixteenth century (docs. 1-8). Explain the changing locations of America and discuss how the new continent is assimilated into the existing division of the world.

2. Read Christopher Columbus's *Journal of the First Voyage to America* (doc. 6). Consider how Columbus describes the New World and compare this text to

John Smith's *A Description of New England* (doc. 15). Explain the differences between their conzeptualizations of America.

3. Read the poems (doc. 13, 19-21) contained in the section and consider the schemes for justifying and "planting" the New World. Discuss the objectives and concepts applied by the writers to promote English colonization and the various images of America used to underscore the importance of the new continent.

4. Discuss the changing role of Indians (doc. 8, 15, 17) in English promotional literature and sermons. Examine the ways in which the writers justify possession of the land and the role conversion plays in appropriating native land.

IV. Resources

a. Recommended Reading

John H. Elliott. *The Old World and the New, 1492-1650*. Cambridge: Cambridge University Press, 1970. Elliott's book is a foundational work in transatlantic studies. Its strength lies in his informative analysis of the reorientation of European thought (historiography, geography, religion, and anthropology) caused by the discovery of America and its people. Elliott's book is particularly strong as a comparative study of how America was integrated into the Renaissance mind.

Hans Galinsky. *Geschichte amerikanischer Kolonialliteratur: Multinationale Wurzeln einer Weltliteratur in Entwicklungslinien und Werkinterpretationen (1542-1722)*. Darmstadt: Wissenschaftliche Buchgesellschaft, 1991. Galinsky's three-volume collection is a good starting point into the field of colonial literature. Through mostly comparative analysis and close readings of texts, it surveys the literatures of the Americas from a bifocal point of view that takes into account European literary traditions and their American modifications as caused by the changing nature of New World realities.

Stephen Greenblatt. *Marvelous Possessions: The Wonder of the New World*. Oxford: Clarendon Press, 1991. The book reconsiders the medieval tradition of the marvelous and how it has been used for colonial appropriations. It thus examines early European responses to the New World in light of an existing representational system and a "symbolic technology" that Europeans projected unto non-European peoples in order to take possession of the New World.

Walter D. Mignolo. *Local Histories/Global Designs: Coloniality, Subaltern Knowledges, and Border Thinking*. Princeton: Princeton University Press, 2000. Mignolo looks at the articulation of the modern/colonial world system in its diverse local histories. Contrary to earlier world system studies, he argues that the colonial world system is not only the outcome of economic transactions and networks, but also of its imaginary writings. He delineates the rise of Occidentalism prior to the eighteenth century and challenges positions held in postcolonial theory, especially in Edward Said's study on *Orientalism*.

Anthony Pagden. *European Encounters with the New World: From Renaissance to Romanticism*. New Haven: Yale University Press, 1993. Pagden delineates the European gaze and the ways in which it confers existence upon the New World. He describes in great detail the changing role of Indians as "savages" in European thinking from the colonial period to the nineteenth century.

David B. Quinn, ed. *New American World: A Documentary History of North America to 1612*. London: Macmillan, 1973. This is one of the most comprehensive and extensive collections of promotional documents, travel accounts, and maps available to students of English exploration and settlement. The maps collected by Quinn show Europe's increasing cartographic knowledge of the New World and the ways in which it was used by English writers to foster colonization projects.

Seymour I. Schwartz and Ralph E. Ehrenberg, eds. *The Mapping of America*. New York: Harry N. Abrams, 1980. The book contains one of the most extensive collections of maps of the New World, which range from the first tentative chartings, to woodcuts, engravings, and nineteenth-century lithographs. In highly perceptive interpretations, the authors offer a cultural history of mapmaking that demonstrates the ways in which mapping America has informed the colonial imagination of the Old World.

Robert Blaire St. George, ed. *Possible Pasts: Becoming Colonial in Early America*. Ithaca: Cornell University Press, 2000. This collection of essays unites articles by leading scholars in the field of colonial studies (such as Peter Hulme, Michael Warner, and Karen Ordahl Kupperman). The essays in this volume reassess colonial studies in terms of the "middle ground." The term was coined by Richard White (1991) and refers to an exchange of rites, negotiations, customs, and conceptions that emerged neither from European nor from Indian culture but from local interactions. The contributors delineate the changing function of the colonial imagination in Anglo-American culture and its restructuring within the greater paradigm of Atlantic history.

b. Works Cited and Reading Suggestions

Akerman, James R. (2006). *Cartographies of Travel and Navigation*. Chicago: University of Chicago Press.
Andrews, Kenneth R., et al., eds. (1978). *The Westward Enterprise: English Activities in Ireland, the Atlantic, and America, 1480-1650*. Liverpool: Liverpool University Press.
Anon. (1675). *A Brief and True Narration of the Late Wars Risen in New-England Occasioned by the Quarrelsom Disposition and Persidious Carriage of the Barbarous, Savage and Heathenish Natives There*. London: Printed for J. S.

Armitage, David (1995). "The New World and British Historical Thought." *America in European Consciousness, 1493-1750*. Ed. Karen Ordahl Kupperman. Chapel Hill: University of North Carolina Press, 52-78.

Armitage, David, and Michael J. Braddick (2002). *The British Atlantic World, 1500-1800*. Basingstoke: Palgrave Macmillan.

Axtell, James (1992). *Beyond 1492: Encounters in Colonial North America*. New York: Oxford University Press.

Bailyn, Bernard (2005). *Atlantic History: Concept and Contours*. Cambridge: Harvard University Press.

Baker, Emerson W. (1994). *American Beginnings: Exploration, Culture, and Cartography in the Land of Norumbega*. Lincoln: University of Nebraska Press.

Bauer, Ralph (2003). *The Cultural Geography of Colonial America: Empire, Travel, Modernity*. Cambridge: Cambridge University Press.

Bowen, Margarita (1981). *Empiricism and Geographical Thought: From Francis Bacon to Alexander von Humboldt*. Cambridge: Cambridge University Press.

Brückner, Martin (2006). *The Geographic Revolution in Early America: Maps, Literacy, and National Identity*. Chapel Hill: University of North Carolina Press.

Brückner, Martin, and Hsuan L. Hsu, ed. (2007). *American Literary Geographies: Spatial Practice and Cultural Production, 1500-1900*. Newark: University of Delaware Press.

Ehrenberg, Ralph E., ed. (2006). *Mapping the World*. Washington: National Geographic Society.

Elliott, John H. (1970). *The Old World and the New, 1492-1650*. Cambridge: Cambridge University Press.

Galinsky, Hans (1991). *Geschichte amerikanischer Kolonialliteratur: Multinationale Wurzeln einer Weltliteratur in Entwicklungslinien und Werkinterpretationen (1542-1722)*. Darmstadt: Wissenschaftliche Buchgesellschaft.

George, Wilma (1969). *Animals and Maps*. Berkeley: University of California Press.

Gordon, Andrew, and Bernhard Klein, eds. (2001). *Literature, Mapping, and the Politics of Space in Early Modern Britain*. Cambridge: Cambridge University Press.

Greenblatt, Stephen (1991). *Marvelous Possessions: The Wonder of the New World*. Oxford: Clarendon Press.

Gruzinski, Serge (1993). *The Conquest of Mexico: The Incorporation of Indian Societies into the Western World, 16th-18th Centuries*. Cambridge: Polity Press.

Hakluyt, Richard (1582). *Divers Voyages Touching the Discoverie of America, and the Ilands Adiacent unto the Same Made First of all by our Englishmen, and Afterward by the Frenchmen and Britons: and Certaine Notes of Advertisements for Observations, Necessarie for such as shall Heereafter Make the Like Attempt, with two Mappes Annexed Heereunto for the Plainer Understanding of the Whole Matter*. London: By Thomas Dawson.

– (1589). *The Principall Navigations, Voiages and Discoveries of the English Nation Made by Sea or Over Land, to the Most Remote and Farthest Distant Quarters of the Earth at any Time Within the Compasse of these 1500. yeeres: Devided into Three Severall Parts, According to the Positions of the Regions Wherunto They Were Directed.* [...] *Whereunto Is Added the Last Most Renowmed English Navigation, Round About the Whole Globe of the Earth*. London: George Bishop and Ralph Newberie.

Hariot, Thomas (1590). *A Briefe and True Report of the New Found Land of Virginia of the Commodities and of the Nature and Manners of the Natural Inhabitants*. Frankfurt/M.: Theodor de Bry, Sigismund Feirabend.

Harisse, Henry (1892). *The Discovery of North America: A Critical, Documentary and Historic Investigation, with an Essay on the Early Cartography of the New World, Including Descriptions of Two Hundred and Fifty Maps or Globes, Existing or Lost, Constructed before the Year 1536*. London: H. Stevens.

Harley, J. B. (2001). *The New Nature of Maps: Essays in the History of Cartography*. Ed. Paul Laxton. Baltimore: Johns Hopkins University Press.

Helgerson, Richard (1992). *Forms of Nationhood: The Elizabethan Writing of England*. Chicago: University of Chicago Press.

Honour, Hugh (1975). *The New Golden Land: European Images of America from the Discoveries to the Present Time*. New York: Pantheon Books.

Hornsby, Stephen J. (2005). *British Atlantic, American Frontier: Spaces of Power in Early Modern British America*. Hanover: University Press of New England.

Howells, William Dean (1876). "A Sennight of the Centennial." *Atlantic Monthly* July, 92-107.

Kaplan, Amy (1993). "Left Alone with America: The Absence of Empire in the Study of American Culture." *Cultures of United States Imperialism*. Ed. Amy Kaplan and Donald E. Pease. Durham: Duke University Press, 3-21.

Karrow, Robert Jr. (1993). *Mapmakers of the Sixteenth Century and Their Maps*. Chicago: Speculum Orbis Press.

Knapp, Jeffrey (1993). "Elizabethan Tobacco." *New World Encounters*. Ed. Stephen Jay Greenblatt. Berkeley: University of California Press, 273-312.

Knorr, Klaus E. (1963). *British Colonial Theories, 1570-1850*. London: Frank Cass.

Kupperman, Karen Ordahl, ed. (1995). *America in European Consciousness, 1493-1750*. Chapel Hill: University of North Carolina Press.

Lawson, William (1618). *A New Orchard and Garden, or, The Best Way for Planting, Grafting, and to Make any Ground Good, for a Rich Orchard*. Printed in London by Bar: Alsop for Roger Iackson.

Lestringant, Frank (1994). *Mapping the Renaissance World: The Geographical Imagination in the Age of Discovery*. Cambridge: Polity Press.

Locke, John (1698). *Two Treatises of Government in the Former the False Principles and Foundation of Sir Robert Filmer and His Followers are Detected and Overthrown; the Latter Is an Essay Concerning the True Original, Extent, and End of Civil-Government*. London: Printed for Awnsham and John Churchill.

Lorant, Stefan (1946). *The New World: The First Pictures of America Made by John White and Jacques LeMoyne and Engraved by Theodore De Bry*. New York: Duell, Sloan, Pearce.

Mancall, Peter C. (2007a). *Hakluyt's Promise: An Elizabethan's Obsession for an English America*. New Haven: Yale University Press.
– (2007b). *The Atlantic World and Virginia, 1550-1624*. Chapel Hill: University of North Carolina Press.
Marlowe, Christopher (1998). *Tamburlaine the Great, Part I*. 1590. The Complete Works of Christopher Marlowe. Vol. 5: *Tamburlaine the Great, Parts I and II*. Ed. David Fuller. Oxford: Clarendon Press. 3-77.
Marshall, Peter J., and Glyndwr Williams (1982). *The Great Map of Mankind: British Perceptions of the World in the Age of Enlightenment*. London: J. M. Dent.
Martyr, Peter [Pietro Martire d'Anghiera] (1555). *The Decades of the Newe Worlde or West India Conteynyng the Nauigations and Conquestes of the Spanyardes, with the Particular Description of the Moste Ryche and Large Landes and Ilandes lately Founde in the West Ocean Perteynyng to the Inheritaunce of the Kinges of Spayne. Wrytten in the Latine tounge by Peter Martyr of Angleria, and translated into Englysshe by Rycharde Eden*. London: William Powell.
Mignolo, Walter D. (2000). *Local Histories/Global Designs: Coloniality, Subaltern Knowledges, and Border Thinking*. Princeton: Princeton University Press.
More, Thomas (1751). *Utopia: Containing an Impartial History of the Manners, Customs, Polity, Government, &c. of that Island*. 1519. Oxford: Newbery.
Mundy, Barbara E. (1996). *The Mapping of New Spain: Indigeneous Cartography and the Maps of the relaciones geográficas*. Chicago: University of Chicago Press.
Pagden, Anthony (1993). *European Encounters with the New World: From Renaissance to Romanticism*. New Haven: Yale University Press.
– (1995). *The Lords of all the World: Ideologies of Empire in Spain, Britain and France, c.1500-c.1800*. New Haven: Yale University Press.
Penrose, Boise (1952). *Travel and Discovery in the Renaissance, 1420-1620*. Cambridge: Harvard University Press.
Pratt, Mary Louise (1993). *Imperial Eyes: Studies in Travel Writing and Transculturation*. London: Routledge.
Purchas, Samuel (1625). *Hakluytus Posthumus, or Purchas His Pilgrimes*. Vol. 1. London: William Stransby.
Quinn, David B. (1979a). *America from Concept to Discovery: Early Exploration of North America*. London: Macmillan.
–, ed. (1979b). *New American World: A Documentary History of North America to 1612*. Vol. 3: *English Plans for North America*. London: Macmillan.
– (1990). *Explorers and Colonies*. London: Hambledon Press.
Richards, Thomas (1993). *The Imperial Archive: Knowledge and the Fantasy of Empire*. London: Verso.
Rowse, Alfred L. (1955). *The Expansion of Elizabethan England*. New York: Harper and Row.
Sauer, Carl O. (1971). *Sixteenth Century North America: The Land and the People as Seen by Europeans*. Berkeley: University of California Press.

Scheiding, Oliver (2008). "Kartographie: Wissenspraxis und Raumvorstellungen in der Neuzeit." *Gewusst wo! Wissen schafft Räume. Die Verortung des Denkens im Spiegel der Druckgraphik*. Ausstellungskatalog Gutenberg-Museum Mainz. Ed. Katharina Bahlmann, Elisabeth Oy-Marra, and Cornelia Schneider. Berlin: Akademie-Verlag, 38-50, 186-211.

Schueller, Malini Johar, and Edward Watts, eds. (2003). *Messy Beginnings: Postcoloniality and Early American Studies*. New Brunswick: Rutgers University Press.

Schwartz, Seymour I., and Ralph E. Ehrenberg, eds. (1980). *The Mapping of America*. New York: Harry N. Abrams.

Sheehan, Bernard W. (1980). *Savagism and Civility: Indians and Englishmen in Colonial Virginia*. Cambridge: Cambridge University Press.

Shirley, Rodney W. (1983). *The Mapping of the World: Early Printed World Maps 1472-1700*. London: Holland Press.

Sloan, Kim (2007). *A New World: England's First View of America*. Chapel Hill: University of North Carolina Press.

St. George, Robert Blaire, ed. (2000). *Possible Pasts: Becoming Colonial in Early America*. Ithaca: Cornell University Press.

Taylor, Eva G. R. (1934). *Late Tudor and Early Stuart Geography, 1583-1650*. London: Methuen.

Vickers, Daniel, ed. (2003). *A Companion to Colonial America*. Oxford: Blackwell.

Wagner, Henry R. (1968). *The Cartography of the Northwest Coast of America to the Year 1800*. 1937. 2 vols. Berkeley: University of California Press.

Warner, Michael (2000). "What's Colonial about Colonial America?" *Possible Pasts: Becoming Colonial in Early America*. Ed. Robert Blaire St. George. Ithaca: Cornell University Press, 49-72.

Weber, David J. (1992). *The Spanish Frontier in North America*. New Haven: Yale University Press.

Westrem, Scott D. (1998). "Against Gog and Magog." *Text and Territory: Geographical Imagination in the European Middle Ages*. Ed. Sylvia Tomasch and Sealy Giles. Philadelphia: University of Pennsylvania Press, 54-75.

White, Richard (1991). *The Middle Ground: Indians, Empires, and Republics in the Great Lakes Region, 1650-1815*. Cambridge: Cambridge University Press.

Williams, Gwyn A. (1987). *Madoc: The Making of a Myth*. Oxford: Oxford University Press.

Wolff, Hans, ed. (1992). *America: Early Maps of the New World*. München: Prestel.

Wright, Louis B., ed. (1966). *The Elizabethans' America: A Collection of Early Reports by Englishmen on the New World*. Cambridge: Harvard University Press.

Zakai, Avihu (1992). *Exile and Kingdom: History and Apocalypse in the Puritan Migration to America*. Cambridge: Cambridge University Press.

MARGIT PETERFY

Images of Native Americans

I. Themes and Arguments

Academic study of Native American history and culture in the twenty-first century takes place in complex and often contested circumstances. This has several causes, two of which seem particularly important. First, Native Americans and their cultures suffered, and to a considerable extent still suffer, under the various consequences of colonization, expropriation, even attempted genocide by white intruders, whether 'European' or 'American.'[1] Second, the indigenous cultures of the North American continent on the one hand, and the imposed European cultures on the other, have traditionally operated under different epistemological assumptions.[2] At the same time, the claim of "pure" or "disinterested" research in Western scholarship often turned out to be centered solely around the interests of the white researchers. Native Americans have thus become suspicious of scholarly approaches to their culture. Anthropology and ethnography are especially distrusted as continued violations of indigenous dignity and cultural integrity (cf. Deloria 1969 and Biolsi 1997). Today, after centuries of having been stereotyped and objectified by outsiders, Native Americans are intent on controlling their own representations.

Furthermore, the great diversity of Native American languages and cultures, together with the fact that this diversity had long been transmitted orally and is further complicated by cross-cultural translation, renders any textual analysis of Native American cultures methodologically challenging.[3] Recent

---

[1] Historians and political activists today nevertheless wish to emphasize that Native Americans should not just be seen as victims but also as successful and active members of their communities who, often against great odds, have succeeded in leading fulfilling lives on their own terms (cf. Iverson 1998, 3).

[2] Arnold Krupat describes this issue in *Ethnocriticism: Ethnography, History, Literature*: "Native modes of knowing and understanding are not well known [...]. Traditional Indian expression has many stories about stories, about aspects of language, about various words and phrases. But there are no traditional essays on the nature of language, no rule-governed explicit definitions" (Krupat 1992, 44).

[3] At the time of first contact in the fifteenth century, there were an estimated five hundred languages. Today, fewer than two hundred are spoken (cf. Porter 2005, 42).

archaeological findings, which have greatly increased our knowledge of the culture of pre-contact America, show the additional importance of interdisciplinary approaches (cf. Salisbury 1996).

The current anthology investigates, in Robert F. Berkhofer's terminology, the "white man's Indian" (1978), by presenting original historical documents with the aim of highlighting culturally and ideologically interlinked topics across time. Thus, the anthology's emphasis is on the representational strategies that the culture of the colonizers and later Republican imperialists employed when they depicted Native Americans, or Indians. The importance of existing Native American testimonies cannot be emphasized enough (cf. Nabokov 1992), but the majority of politically and culturally influential early documents from the sixteenth and seventeenth centuries originated with Europeans such as traders, soldiers, agents, missionaries, and ethnographers *avant la lettre*. Today's interpretations of these sources must be aware of a complex set of determining influences, which implies that the images in these documents are, as a rule, distorted. Nevertheless, as Wilcomb E. Washburn writes, "early reporting from the New World reflects also a substantial amount of accurate description that later historians must be ready to respect, even while identifying and discarding the accretions and distortions of myth, ignorance, special interest and the like" (1976, 336). Accordingly, any discussion of the representation of Native Americans has to invest substantial analytical effort into the identification and evaluation of these influences to discern more clearly both the truly indigenous elements and the various motives of the white authors.

This chapter moves in three thematic sections through the centuries up to 1900, showing how certain representational patterns were dominant in specific historical situations and which alternatives were possible. Although particular circumstances and details vary, one aspect has remained constant throughout the centuries: the tendency to simplify and generalize. For a long time many white observers overlooked not just the cultural diversity of Native America but also the different motives of the imperialists, who created representations of 'the Indian' that fit their own theological, economic, and military convictions and interests.

II. What is an 'Indian'? – Racial Essentialism from the 'Golden Age' to the 'Vanishing Indian'

From classical antiquity through the Middle Ages to the Renaissance, Europeans felt secure about their central position in the universe. The discovery of an unexpected continent did not upset this world view; rather "America" was contextualized within existing frameworks of knowledge (cf. Scaglione 1976, 65). America's inhabitants, in turn, became a means to be used for European ends, whether material or spiritual. At the same time, a profound fascination with the rumors and reports from the newly discovered lands fueled the imaginations of artists and writers. Initially, conceptualizations were rooted in classical and Judeo-

Christian traditions, and further influenced by medieval ideas. The first visual representations of Native Americans relied on a range of sources and inspirations, from legendary (e.g. Mandeville; doc. 22) to accurate observation (John White; cf. Scheiding in this vol., 9-11). Established rules of composition affected the representation of posture and the human body in its naked or scantily clad form was mostly known from classical sculpture, which was then reproduced in Renaissance drawing (cf. docs. 28-31; Sturtevant 1976, 419; Fig. 8).[4]

Painters and engravers also used elements of European iconography in this early period. The parrot, for example, appears both as naturalistic detail and as a symbol in allegorical representations of America. The parrots of South and Central America were, among other birds, the sources for the magnificent feather capes and ornaments brought to Europe and put on display. But in medieval bestiaries (i.e., allegorical-theological compendia of real and fantastic animal descriptions) parrots, though obstinate, were also believed to be able to learn how to speak. They could be allegorically equated with the native population, who as 'savages' were also expected to learn the language of culture and civilization. Further, according to Pliny, parrots came from India, which means that when Columbus first saw the birds he may very well have taken them as another proof of his having reached the Asian subcontinent (cf. Weckmann 1951, 131).

Fig. 8: Louis Hennepin. *A New Discovery of a Vast Country in America, Extending Above Four Thousand Miles between New France and New Mexico with a Description of the Great Lakes, Cataracts, Rivers, Plants, and Animals: Also the Manners, Customs, and Languages of the Several Native Indians, and the Advantage of Commerce with those Different Nations: With a Continuation, Giving an Account of the Attempts of the Sieur De la Salle upon the Mines of St. Barbe &c., the Taking of Quebec by the English: With the Advantages of a Shorter Cut to China and Japan.* London 1698.

---

[4] Additionally, artists, lacking appropriate models, often assumed that all non-Europeans resembled each other: Brazilian Indians appear in Mexico, Florida Indians hold Brazilian clubs, Natchez Indians in Louisiana use a North Carolinian temple, and Pocahontas wears a Tupinamba feather costume (cf. Sturtevant 1976, 418).

Since the native population of the Americas was obviously not Christian, the first discoverers and conquerors looked for points of reference in other known non-Christian cultures for their comparisons. Preconceptions from classical antiquity included myths of happy and far away islands (e.g. Atlantis, Island of the Phaeacians), travels of discovery (the Argonauts), monsters (the Hydra), and the tales by Hesiod and Ovid of a golden age when humankind lived without worries and did not have to work for sustenance (cf. Klarer 1999, 390). Descriptions of legendary riches in exotic kingdoms seemed to have foreshadowed Montezuma's treasures, examples of which the Aztec king sent in 1519 as presents to the emperor Charles V. The gold and silver artifacts, which deeply impressed those Europeans who saw them, including Albrecht Dürer, were taken to corroborate theories of a legendary land of gold (cf. Jantz 1976, 94), thus reducing the shock of the 'New World' and turning it into evidence for existing European beliefs. Traces of these can be identified in many visual documents, for example in the etching "Allegory of America" (doc. 27), in which the artist shows several figures obviously at ease in the foreground. Three smaller figures in the background are standing in a river panning for gold. Similarly, the "Discovery of America" (doc. 31) shows a naked woman rising from a hammock as a fully clad Amerigo Vespucci steps on shore. Vespucci is holding an astrolabe as a symbol of the preeminence of his technology, while behind him a flag with the cross symbolizes the 'superiority' of Christian civilization. This 'superiority' is further emphasized by the cannibalistic 'barbecue' depicted in the background.[5]

Although the age of discoveries is traditionally identified with the Renaissance, medieval influences still ran strong, especially with the first Spanish expeditions. Travel accounts, or texts masquerading as such, above all John Mandeville's influential medieval collection *Mandeville's Travels* from 1356 (doc. 22), paved the way for later communally shared and widely circulated perceptions of Native Americans. Despite the fact that 'Mandeville' did not exist in the way his early readers imagined him, and certainly had not traveled to Sumatra (or "Lamory"), his descriptions seeped into the popular imagination, which was captivated by his sensational claims of cannibalism among primitive tribes: "[T]hey have an yll custume they ete gladlyer mans flesshe than other. Theder brynge marchauntes their children to sell and those that are fatte they ete theym" (*KC*, 36). The existence of such accounts not only laid the ground for apparently similar reports from the New World, but, even more importantly, influenced travelers' perceptions.

One of the best examples of how preconceptions shaped new impressions is Sir Walter Raleigh's *Discoverie of the Large, Rich and Bewtiful Empyre of Guiana* (1596), in which he writes about headless creatures. His description harks back

---

[5] Michel de Certeau reads the image also as an allegory of a new age of historical writing in the West: "What is really initiated here is a colonization of the body by the discourse of power. This is writing that conquers. It will use the new world as if it were a blank, a 'savage' page on which Western desire will be written" (1988, xxv).

to rumors about the Blemmyae, a race that had formerly been thought to have lived in Ethiopia or India and had been described by Pliny and Herodotus. The title page of the 1599 German publication of Raleigh's *Discoverie* (doc. 29), by the Nuremberg printer Levinus Hulsius, features a print inspired by these Blemmyae. In his original text from 1596, Raleigh provides first a purely descriptive version of the customs of the Ypurugoto, who, he claims, liked to raise their shoulders unusually high ("a nation of people, whose heades appeare not above their shoulders," 69), but later he insists that the existence of these legendary creatures does not belong in the realm of fable, but

> it is true, because every child in the provinces *Arromaia* and *Canuri* affirm the same: they are called *Ewaipanoma*: they are reported to have their eyes in their shoulders, and their mouths in the middle of their breasts, & that a long train of hair groweth backward between their shoulders. (70)

Similarly, women who had probably been described by some Native American informants simply as being without husbands or living alone, became in the telling female warriors, i.e., Amazons with bow and arrow (cf. Heinen and Zent 1996, 340). Such Amazons can also be seen in the etchings "Allegory of America" and "America" (docs. 27, 28).

Medieval and Renaissance cartographers had moved the home of these legendary warrior-women to different outskirts of the known world, from Asia to Africa, until they were finally placed in South America. Eyewitness accounts of women fighting against *conquistadores* may have supported such theoretical efforts to reconcile existing belief with new empirical data (cf. Baumgärtner 2002, 74). The former centrality of the concept lives on in the names of the Amazon River and the state of California, which the Spanish christened after 'Queen Calafia,' who was said to live on an island populated only by women (cf. Weckmann 1951, 133).

Concerns with the female 'savage,' and its special prominence in the early history of European cultural engagement with America, can also be seen in the fascination of almost every sailor or conqueror with American women, and in particular in Amerigo Vespucci's 1504 letter (in fact a book-length report) to Piero Soderini (doc. 23; cf. the erotic component of doc. 31). Vespucci's "letter" was widely disseminated and significantly influenced the representation of Native Americans.[6] Vespucci describes Native American women as physically attractive and without inhibitions or sexual taboos. The reported promiscuity of these women corresponds to the educated European conviction that limited sexual contact, i.e., monogamous relationships, were a sign of a higher civilization, and, inversely, that freely practiced sexuality was a sign of a primitive society (cf. Baumgärtner 2002, 78). Vespucci's final condemnation is, however, clothed in

---

[6] By the nineteenth century, historians started to question the authenticity of Vespucci's text, including his claims of first-hand experience. Nevertheless, the text's initial reception secured its relevance for early European conceptions of Native Americans (cf. Fernández-Arnesto 2006).

theological terms: "They are worse than heathen; because we did not see that they offered any sacrifice, nor yet did they have [any] house of prayer. I deem their manner of life to be Epicurean" (*KC*, 37).⁷ Vespucci's distinction is noteworthy because it prefigures the controversy about whether Native Americans could be converted to Christianity. An 'Epicurean' philosophy implies an attitude that is hostile to any kind of religion, whereas with 'heathens' one could hope to replace 'wrong' gods with the 'right' one.

Europeans found tales of Native American cannibalism both fascinating and repellent. Stories of cannibalism or cannibalistic rites in the New World were not without foundation,⁸ but it should be emphasized that such activities were neither common to all indigenous American tribes, nor did they imply a preferred diet, as suggested by Mandeville. The recurrent theme of Europeans simplifying and homogenizing Native American cultures thus finds a conspicuous starting point in the notion that 'Indians' equaled 'cannibals' – a term first used by Columbus which subsequently came to replace the earlier 'anthropophage' (cf. Klarer 1999, 391). In this vein, Johan Froschauer's woodcut from 1505 (doc. 24), which is the earliest European picture of Native Americans and which purports to show the "people and the island that were lately discovered by the Christian king of Portugal or his subjects" (*KC*, 37), includes details such as human body parts hanging from a beam above a fire, in the process of being smoked, and a native gnawing on an obviously human arm. The caption provides an explicit description of the scene.⁹

Cannibalism was an early element of the ideological construct that Roy Harvey Pearce would later define as 'savagism' (Pearce 1965). Such stereotypical perceptions of Native Americans as 'Wild Men,' 'ravenous beasts,' etc., often went hand in hand with the destruction policy of later colonizers and conquerors. Vilifying the people in whose land one was interested made it easier to justify their expulsion and even extermination. Certain theoretical frameworks, such as Puritan millennialism and the belief in the providential role of their settlement in 'New England,' further encouraged conceptualizations which cast any kind of Native American resistance as Satan's work, "acted by the Devil to engage in some early and bloody Action, for the Extinction of a Plantation so contrary to his Interests" (*KC*, 55; cf. docs. 32-3).

---

⁷ As Vespucci emphasized, he lived with an Indian tribe for 27 days, with the explicit purpose of learning about their rites, language, and general way of life. The length of this period of an early case of ethnographic fieldwork is already telling: First, it implies that the 27 days were considered a comparatively long period, and second, we may safely assume that these four weeks were not sufficient to learn much of the language (cf. Berkhofer 1978, 200).

⁸ There is no scholarly consensus about the occurrence of cannibalism in North America, while the Aztecs undoubtedly practiced human sacrifice and certain Central American tribes practiced ritualistic cannibalism (cf. Turner 1999; Dongoske, Martin, Ferguson 2000.)

⁹ In 1557, the German adventurer Hans Staden published an account of his captivity among a cannibalistic tribe in Brazil. This surely helped the creation of a receptive climate for similar representations (cf. Fig. 9; Jantz 1976).

Fig. 9: Hans Staden. *Warhaftig Historia und Beschreibung eyner Landschafft der Wilden, Nacketen, Grimmigen, Menschenfresser Leuthen, in der Newenwelt America gelegen.* Marburg 1557.

However, the ideology of savagism had already been challenged from the times of the earliest encounters, not just individually but also generally. The notion of the Noble Savage was the obverse essentialist theory of Native Americans (cf. White 1976, 125). Not all positive descriptions of Native Americans should be read as examples of the stereotype of the Noble Savage, but whenever Native Americans are primarily used to critisize European civilization, and when they are seen as arrested in time, i.e., as purely historical participants, one should be wary of such generalizations. The term Noble Savage originated with Jean-Jacques Rousseau's *Discours sur l'origine et les fondements de l'inégalité parmi les hommes* (1755), but the concept goes back further. Michel de Montaigne (doc. 25) can be seen as one of the earliest theorists of the Noble Savage, as well as a proponent of anthropological cultural relativism. His positive description emphasizes European misconduct in order to defend the seemingly barbarous behavior of Native Americans: the European practice of torturing humans to death is accordingly much more "barbarous" than the eating of people when they are already dead. Montaigne's opinion is based on some, mostly second-hand, empirical observation and theoretical deduction. He also looks back nostalgically to the golden age of classical antiquity, which he equates with the world of the "savages" as they live in the America of his day (cf. Scaglione 1976, 64; Klarer 1999, 396). Eric Cheyfitz sees the relevance of Montaigne's document as a theoretical treatment (and deconstruction) of the contrast "barbarous vs. civilized" (1991, 142-57), revealing this dichotomy as an imperialist strategy. Nevertheless, the repeated criticism of European life in Montaigne's account verges on a functionalization and objectification of "the Cannibal." In this sense, Montaigne can indeed be seen as an early proponent of the Noble Savage ideology, as laying the first stepping stone towards Rousseau's elaboration of the normative theory that man in a pure state of nature was *necessarily* more virtuous and "authentic" than in so-called civilized society. But, tellingly, neither Rousseau nor other philosophers wanted to abandon European civilization, no matter how critical they were of it, for the actual life of the Noble Savage (cf. Berkhofer 1978, 77).

In North America, beginning in the Early Republic and continuing throughout the nineteenth century, the idea of the Noble Savage also contributed to the development of the concept of the Vanishing Indian. The conflation of these two generalizations operated on the assumption that Native Americans could not be properly civilized because once they met with Europeans they only adopted the vices of civilization and turned into ignoble savages. According to this logic, whereas it might have been just about worthwhile to try to save them in their original "noble" state, the effort became pointless and impossible once Native Americans had been "corrupted" by white habits (cf. Dippie 1970). Thus, the Vanishing Indian and the Noble Savage became, in practice, synonyms in much of North American discourse. Even Margaret Fuller, who not only described Chippewa and Ottowa Indians sympathetically but also harshly criticized white missionaries, traders, and the US government, seemed to think that the "speedy extinction" of the "first born of the soil" (*KC*, 458) was inevitable. Unequivocal rejection of the providential logic behind the ideology of the Vanishing Indian was seldom clearly expressed, William Ellery Channing in 1837 being one of the very few exceptions:

> It is sometimes said that nations are swayed by laws, as unfailing as those which govern matter; that they have their destinies; that their character and position carry them forward irresistibly to their goal; [...] that the Indians have melted before the white man, and the mixed, degraded race of Mexico must melt before the Anglo-Saxon. Away with this vile sophistry! There is no necessity for crime. There is no Fate to justify rapacious nations, any more than to justify gamblers and robbers, in plunder. (*KC*, 384-5)

Most of Channing's contemporaries discussing the Vanishing Indian shared the habitual racism of the white population. Nevertheless, some were able to see more clearly, e.g. Washington Irving, who considered Native Americans unjustly persecuted "intellectual beings" (*KC*, 60), as well as Margaret Fuller who deplored the "hatred felt by the white man for the Indian" (*KC*, 457). The socially approved rule, however, was defined by cultural and legal restrictions such as, for example, the anti-miscegenation law of 1705 in Massachusetts, which forbade ministers to marry Native Americans to whites. In 1768, the Mohegan minister Samson Occom complained that a white missionary was paid more for the same work than a Native American.[10] Similarly, more than half a century later, William Apess, political activist and self-educated Christian minister, bitterly accused his white contemporaries in 1833: "Now let me ask you, white man, if it is a disgrace for to eat, drink and sleep with the image of God, or sit, or walk and talk with them?" (Apess 1992, 158). Apess later identifies the values of the whites as, literally, being "skin-deep," i.e., as superficial (in today's terminology, racist) categories. Thus, between the dominant stereotypes of the "savage," the Noble Savage, and the Vanishing Indian, there was only highly limited conceptual space for Native American individuals to negotiate for themselves a fully realized membership in nineteenth-century US-American society.

III. Christian Mission and Indian Captivity: Contact Zones in Colonial Times

In an era dominated by the rift between Catholicism and Protestantism, the discovery of a new continent and its subsequent incorporation into the political world order was unavoidably under the influence of religious and theological conflicts. The first encounters, under Christopher Columbus's leadership, between Christians and indigenous Americans had already combined the central issues of theology and race in a fatal nexus of violent conquest and physical appropriation: Since Columbus could only sell as slaves those Indians who had not been baptized as Catholics, he regularly hindered missionaries from baptizing willing Indios (cf. Varela 2006). An ensuing investigation led to Columbus's losing his position as viceroy, which shows that even within the seemingly homogeneous group of colonizers conflicts existed, some of them being based on moral issues. By the beginning of the sixteenth century, there were pronounced differences in opinion over whether Native Americans were essentially human and thus capable of Christian conversion and salvation. The Archives of the Council of the Indies in Sevilla contain divergent testimonies on the nature of "the Indians" (cf. Hanke 1976, 367). In 1537, Pope Paul III declared Native Americans "truly men" and held Satan responsible for the notion that they were created for the service of the white man. The best-known arguments in favor of Native Americans were made by the Dominican Bartholomew de Las Casas (doc. 26). In 1552, he published his influential *Brevísima relación de la destrucción de las Indias occidentales*. Las Casas emphasizes the Indians' predisposition towards Christianity: "They have their understanding very pure and quicke, being teachable and capable of all good learning, verye apt to receive our holy Catholique faith [...] and

---

[10] "So I am ready to Say, they have used me thus, because I Can't Influence the Indians so well as other missionaries; but I can assure them I have endeavored to teach them as well as I know how; – but I must say, 'I believe it is because I am a poor Indian.' I Can't help that God has made me So; I did not make my self so" (Occom 1982, 735). Occom's statement is so revealing because it is one of the first documents by a Native American showing that it was not specific behavior that provoked unfair treatment by whites, but the simple fact that Occom belonged to a certain race.

are so enflamed, ardent, and importune to knowe and understand the matters of faith after they have but begunne once to taste them" (*KC*, 41-2). But even Las Casas, who was a most sympathetic observer, could only conceive of indigenous cultures and religions in terms of his own Christian theological understanding. Moreover, he compares the Indios to children, "such sorte as the very children of Princes and Noble men brought up amongst us" (*KC*, 41), a benevolent but paternalistic attitude that relegates Native Americans to the position of proto-humans, in line with the then accepted notions of childhood.

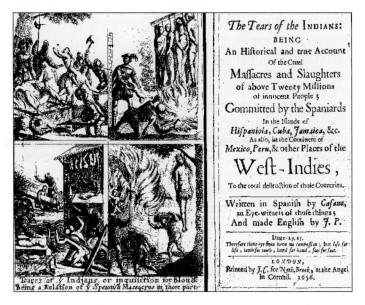

Fig. 10: Bartholomew de las Casas. *The Tears of the Indians Being an Historical and True Account of the Cruel Massacres and Slaughters of above Twenty Millions of Innocent People, Committed by the Spaniards in the Islands of Hispaniola, Cuba, Jamaica, &c.: As also, in the Continent of Mexico, Peru, & Other Places of the West-Indies, to the Total Destruction of those Countries*. London 1656.

Las Casas's *A Briefe Narration*, in particular in its various English editions with detailed engravings of the horrors of Spanish conquest, became influential as a source of anti-Spanish propaganda, the so-called 'Black Legend' (cf. Fig. 10; Parry 1976, 289). Thus, the European religious conflict generated by the Reformation was carried over into the New World, not just in terms of empire building, but also as an expression of theological conviction. Whether this conviction was truly felt or was merely 'cant' to hide the Europeans' hunger for land can only be answered, if at all, by examining individual cases.[11]

---

[11] The term "cant" was first used in this context by Francis Jennings, in his influential book *The Invasion of America: Indians, Colonialism, and the Cant of Conquest* (1976).

When the Elizabethan projectors Edward Hayes and Christopher Carleill discuss the "Speedy Advauncement of a State" in "Discourse Concerning a Voyage Intended for the Planting of Chrystyan Religion and People in the North West Regions of America" (doc. 12), they emphasize their spiritual mission and explicitly allude to the competition between the two faiths: "Our adversaries have noted thys to be a veary great deffect in our Churche, that we have not Converted Infidells unto the fayth. [...] So now agayn in thys latter are to travayll in sowyng the Seed of pure Religion in those exceeding large & popolus Nations lyeng to the Northwest of America and to sett them free from the Captivetie of the dyvell" (*KC*, 19). Virtually all early British texts concerning colonization contain at least a token paragraph dealing with Indian missionizing, such as John Smith's promotional tract (doc. 15), Robert Cushman's deliberations from 1622 about the lawfulness of settling in North America (doc. 17), or John Cotton's farewell sermon to the settlers of the Massachusetts Bay Colony in 1630 (doc. 16).

Once the British settlers arrived in America, however, their missionary zeal abated, and it was only in the 1640s, following John Eliot's initiative, that Indian missionizing was again seriously pursued, both in the colonies and the metropolis. Eliot's so-called "Indian Tracts," a series of reports about the progress of the missionizing efforts amongst the Indians in New England, played an influential part in the foundation in 1649 of the Society for the Propagation of the Gospel, better known as the New England Company (cf. Kellaway 1961; Kelleter 2000). It was also Eliot who in 1651 established the first of fourteen villages for "Praying Indians," i.e., for Native American converts to Christianity. His, John Sassomon's, and Job Nesuton's translation of the Bible into the Massachusetts language (1661-1663) was the first complete Bible printed in the colonies.

The motivation to convert Native Americans was connected in these decades with the so-called 'lost tribe theory,' which proposed that Native Americans were descendants of one of the ten lost tribes of Israel and therefore of Semitic origin. Some Puritan theologians found this idea particularly attractive because it could further be connected to millennialist readings of American history. According to the biblical books of Daniel and Revelation, the conversion of the Jews – now in New England in their re-incarnation as 'Indians' – would be a sign of the approaching millennium (cf. Wyss 2000, 162). John Eliot also believed this theory to be true, an opinion which was also given serious consideration by Samuel Sewall in 1697 (doc. 79), thus identifying New England with New Jerusalem.

For Cotton Mather, however, the Indians' ancestral connection to one of the lost tribes was just a "guess" or a "wish" (*KC*, 54). In his description of Eliot's life (doc. 34), he highlights the virtues and achievements of the missionary by emphasizing the depravity of the Natives, who are depicted as "forlorn, [...] doleful Creatures [...], the veriest *Ruines of Mankind*," and as "abject," "shiftless," and "*slothful*" (*KC*, 52-3). Mather uses the contrast between the "Eminent Christian" Eliot (*KC*, 55) and the "stupid" Native Americans (*KC*, 54) to elevate Eliot's achievement, which by 1702 had become an achievement of the past. The outbreak of hostilities in 1675, which would develop into King Philip's War (1675-1676), brought a decisive turn in racial relationships. In consequence, the general colonial Indian policy moved from "assimilation to extermination" (Bross 2004, 195).

The change of policy and attitudes of whites towards Native Americans, in particular towards the so-called praying Indians, and the prospective neglect of Indian missionizing becomes evident also in Mary Rowlandson's captivity narrative *The Soveraignty and Goodness of God* (doc. 33). Rowlandson interprets her captivity in her retrospective account in typological terms as God's affliction to punish her previous slack religious conduct and to test her faith. In the initial scene of her narrative, which describes the attack on Lancaster, she presents almost all Native Americans as evil, hellish "savages," relying on a startling array of lexical variation: "murderous wretches," "bloody heathens," "merciless infidels," "hell-hounds," "ravenous beasts," "barbarous creatures," and "black creatures" (*KC*, 50-2). In spite of the explicitly stated function of the text as a theological treatise, her narrative offers psychological, even ethnographic realism, providing a fascinating account of her experiences and of her captors' lives. Rowlandson's primary ideological opponents are Christian Indians who present a special threat because of their ambiguous, liminal position between the "waste and howling wilderness" (*KC*, 128) and the 'civilization' of the white settlers. She uses her individual experiences with some 'praying Indians' as the basis for an argument against all baptized Native Americans, leading to a general condemnation of conversion. Thus, for her first readers, Rowlandson's account had a clear political topicality: It participated in the debates about the cohesion of the Puritan community and the continuity of the 'New England Way'; but it also contributed to the persecution and destruction of New England's Native American communities (cf. Salisbury 1997; Wyss 2000).[12]

IV. The "Great Father" in Washington: Republican Imperialists

The theological and typological systematization of Native Americans as representatives of the 'devil' waned together with the dominance of Puritanism at the end of the eighteenth and beginning of the nineteenth century. Violent conflicts on the frontier continued, however, aggravated by the War of Independence, in which Native Americans fought mostly as allies of the British. At the same time, as a result of the growing influence of religious groups (e.g. the Quakers, Methodists, and others) and also of the spread of Enlightenment thought, politicians seemed to begin to develop a more humane approach to Native Americans. Thomas Jefferson, for example, argues in his *Notes on the State of Virginia* (doc. 251) for the possibility of civilizing and assimilating them. He sees this potential exemplified by Native American oratory skills, "such as prove their reason and

---

[12] The political topicality of Rowlandson's narrative is further emphasized by Increase Mather's preface and his involvement in the first publication of the narrative (cf. Salisbury 1997).

sentiment strong, their imagination glowing and elevated" (*KC*, 559). Nevertheless, for Jefferson, too, Native Americans always remained merely instrumental in his efforts to build his "Empire of Liberty" (cf. Wallace 1999).

In his dealings with Native American tribes he continued the colonial traditions established by the British. One of the most important formal characteristics of British and later US-American relations with Native Americans was the reliance on treaties. The treaty system between Europeans and Native peoples in the United States was singular in the history of American colonization. Far fewer treaties were made in Canada, and none in Latin America (cf. Harring 1995). With the introduction of such a ritual of mutual agreement, British settlers and authorities tried to follow up on their claim that their effort of colonization would be "fairer" and more just than the Spanish and Portuguese policies. John Cotton's farewell sermon to the colony under the leadership of John Winthrop in 1630 (doc. 16) is an example of an early effort at such legalistic justification built on theological foundations. Cotton's main theological argument of *vacuum domicilium* ("That in a vacant soyle, hee that taketh possession of it, and bestoweth culture and husbandry upon it, his Right it is," *KC*, 26) went hand in hand with the colonizers' wish to live beyond the reach of the Anglican establishment. That epidemics had decimated the native population just before the arrival of the Pilgrims in 1620 was taken as an additional sign of divine providence.

The early treaties were, however, also evidence for the fear and the precarious situation of the English in the first century of settlement. Since English colonization, unlike that sponsored by other European powers, was not subsidized or guaranteed by the government or the monarch, all the ventures had to be financed privately, mostly by joint-stock companies. If these companies ever felt that they were not getting a return on their investment, they could back out any time. As a consequence, all written material about the North American colonies reaching Britain carried the subtext "Do not withdraw your support" (Kupperman 2000, 3), when reporting Native American consent or even cooperation.

However, the treaty system was from its inception tainted by cultural and political misunderstandings. The English developed it on the basis of several faulty assumptions: one, that land ('the wilderness') was unlimited, two, that 'Indians' would readily adopt Christianity and the European way of living, and, three, that the native population represented a monolithic racial and cultural unity. The colonists probably became rapidly aware of all these mistakes, but they continued the practice, nevertheless, because it gave a semblance of legitimacy to their actions. A further problem was the notion, or pretense, that there were only two well-defined parties involved: Native Americans and whites. Regarding whites, this view did not acknowledge the anarchic element represented by pioneers, settlers, and squatters on the frontier, who continuously encroached on Native American territory in spite of treaties signed by state or federal authorities. On the Native side, cultural and hierarchical conflicts between tribes also upset supposed agreements. When it came down to it, white racial solidarity dominated in almost all cases over treaty obligations.

Native American leaders openly criticized the system from the beginning, but explicit white criticism was rare. Among the first white commentators to address this hypocrisy in print was Washington Irving (doc. 37), who wrote about such treaties in 1814: "It may be said that the soil was originally purchased by the settlers; but who does not know the nature of Indian purchases?" (*KC*, 61). Irving's statement does not just make his own position clear, but also the fact that the morally questionable nature of Indian treaties was widely known.[13]

Nevertheless, agents of the United States continued to 'buy' land from Native Americans and to use the treaty system as the legal arm of their expansion policy. Lewis Cass, Governor of Michigan Territory from 1813 to 1831, and a self-proclaimed expert on Native Americans, exerted a weighty influence on the nation's Indian policy (cf. Dippie 1970, 44-5).[14] His "Remarks on the Policy and Practice of the United States in Their Treatment of the Indians" (doc. 161) are a defense of US actions against British accusations. His argument rests on the validity of the treaty system in dealing with Native Americans: If Indians did not manage to live according to the provisions of these treaties, this was not the fault of the whites but had to be ascribed to various flaws in "the Indian constitution," such as his "baleful passions," his "indolence," and his "fatuity" (*KC*, 373). Although Cass is careful in his choice of words, he also gives voice to the ideology of the Vanishing Indian in his text: "But perhaps he [the Indian] is destined to disappear with the forests" (*KC*, 373).

The legal and moral flaws of the treaty system became a national issue in the 1820s with the conflict between Georgia and the so-called Five Civilized Tribes, i.e., Cherokee, Creek, Seminole, Choctaw, and Chickasaw. The situation in Georgia, where Native American land was coveted by the state and private investors, was almost a "case study in the dilemma of American Indian policy" (Dippie 1970). The inherent logical absurdity lay in the fact that the Indian tribes, on the one hand, were considered sovereign tribes or nations, but, on the other hand, the American government and official policy treated even the "civilized tribes" paternalistically as minors. President Jackson (1829–1837) claimed to have the interest of the tribes in mind when he proposed to "open the eyes of those children in the forest to their true condition, and by a speedy removal to relieve them from all the evils, real and imagery, present or prospective, with which they may be supposed to be threatened" (*KC*, 376). Jackson secured the passing of the Removal Bill in 1830 in spite of strong opposition to his plans throughout

---

[13] Irving can be counted among the first historians morally aware of Native Americans. "It is painful to perceive," he writes, "how the footsteps of civilization in this country may be traced in the blood of the original inhabitants; how easily the colonists were moved to hostility by the lust of conquest; how merciless and exterminating was their warfare" (*KC*, 60).

[14] Cass was also Secretary of War under Andrew Jackson and thus directly involved in the Indian removal.

the Republic, especially in the Northeast. The bill passed by quite a narrow margin: 102 to 97 in the House, 28 to 19 in the Senate (cf. Herschberger 1999, 30). The Cherokees' effort to protect themselves against white encroachment within the framework of the legal provisions of the Constitution, through their 1831 appeal to the Supreme Court, was rejected on grounds of white racial preconceptions, or in Chief Justice John Marshall's words:

> At the time the constitution was framed, the ideal of appealing to an American court of justice for an assertion of right or a redress of wrong, had perhaps never entered the mind of an Indian or of his tribe. Their appeal was to the tomahawk, or to the government. This was well understood by the statesmen who framed the constitution of the United States. (*KC*, 378)

According to this logic, since Indians had not been expected by the original framers of the Constitution to argue their case in legal terms, tribes were not supposed to do it in 1831 either (cf. doc. 163). As a final consequence of the conflict, the forceful removal of the tribes beyond the Mississippi began, culminating in 1837 in the Trail of Tears, during which thousands of Cherokees died (cf. Maddox 1991).

The further settlement of the west almost automatically initiated frontier violence due to the flawed treaty system and the anarchic, often criminal, behavior of white squatters, adventurers, and traders. This was no secret, and already in 1832 an anonymous writer warned prospective settlers of the dangers expecting them in Oregon:

> Do they know that their path is directly in the track of the no less barbarous than brave Blackfeet, who, when Captain Lewis killed two of their tribe (in an attempt to steal his horses) made a vow never to spare an American, and have religiously kept it ever since? Do they know that all the Indians of that region justly hold the very name of an American in abhorrence? (*KC*, 381)

In spite of the writer's sympathy for the Natives, whose resistance he even calls "just," his description contributes to the dissemination of the notion of Indian "savagery." In 1893, the influential historian Frederick Jackson Turner (doc. 185) moved the issue to the center of American national mythology: "The frontier is the outer edge of the wave – the meeting point between savagery and civilization. [...] The frontier is the line of most rapid and effective Americanization. The wilderness masters the colonist. It takes him from the railroad car and puts him in the birch canoe. [... H]e shouts the war cry and takes the scalp in orthodox Indian fashion" (*KC*, 415). In Turner's theory, Native Americans occupy a transitory place between "geology" and "civilization," showing the way for the white settlers. The "Indian trails," formerly buffalo trails, are now transformed into railroads; Indian villages "suggested by nature," into cities. Turner characterizes the development as the "steady growth of a complex nervous system for the originally simple, inert continent" (*KC*, 417; cf. doc. 183). Native Americans are here considered part of the wilderness, and although their encounter is supposed to have an effect on white settlers, the outcome is the triumph of civilization over nature. Richard Slotkin identified this psychological pattern of historiographic explanation as a "regeneration through violence" in his influential study of the same title (cf. Slotkin 1974).

By the end of the nineteenth century, when it became clear that Native Americans would not vanish, efforts at 'civilizing' them again became more pronounced. Since the history of Indian-white relations is full of the "cant of conquest" (Jennings 1976), it is difficult to assess the intentions behind these programs. Many so-called "benefactors" certainly had other motives in mind than the well-being of Indians. Others may truly have believed that they were being helpful when they suggested the cultural deracination of Native Americans as a solution to their problems.[15]

Simultaneously with Indian education programs, however, scientific racism and social Darwinism joined forces to position the Anglo-Saxon race at the pinnacle of human evolution (docs. 171, 177; cf. Berkhofer 1978, 33-69). As part of a providential reading of American history, the "extinction of inferior races," i.e., of Native Americans, "certainly appears probable," Josiah Strong wrote in 1885 (*KC*, 710). Such racial arguments stood in logical contradiction to educational programs – a 'double-bind' that had devastating cultural, psychological, and economical consequences for America's native peoples. Only towards the end of the twentieth century is it possible to identify a true, i.e., sincere, reversal in federal attitude towards Native Americans, made widely visible by the opening of the National Museum of the American Indian on the Washington Mall in 2004.

Instructional Strategies and Classroom Issues

I. Key Concepts and Major Themes

1. Savage (docs. 23-4, 32-4, 164)
   The view of Native Americans as 'savages,' i.e., as barbaric, violent, and lawless, has its roots in the European failure to understand Native cultures (docs. 23-4). Europeans saw the later resistance of (mostly) North American indigenous population against the encroachment of white settlers as proof of "Indian savagery" (cf. docs. 32-3, 163)

2. Noble Savage (docs. 25, 161, 201)
   This stereotype is based on the notion that European culture is degenerate and thus inferior to the 'natural' or 'pre-civilized' state in which Native Americans were thought to be living. Although the Noble Savage may

---

[15] In *A Century of Dishonor* (1881), for example, Helen Hunt Jackson summarized the governmental injustice in the treatment of Native Americans. Nevertheless, "periods that have been presented in almost entirely negative terms, such as the Americanization from the 1880s through the 1920s or the 'termination' era from the mid-1940s through the 1960s yielded mixed, instead of entirely unhappy consequences" (Iverson 1998, 3).

seem at first sight a positive concept, in practice, it has restricted the sphere of influence and political power of Native Americans. The inversion 'ignoble savage' explicitly rejects the existence of the Noble Savage as a Romantic phantasy.

3. Vanishing Indian (docs. 162, 164, 169, 170, 177-8, 315)
   In a North American context, the concept is closely related to the idea of the Noble Savage. The pure and authentic Noble Savage was perceived as being without defenses against the inevitable expansion (cf. 'manifest destiny') of the much more vital European civilization. Upon contact with the superior force of Europeans, mostly of Anglo-Saxon stock, Indians would necessarily "melt away" (cf. doc. 170). By the end of the nineteenth century, this notion had become invalidated by the obvious presence of Native Americans and by the growing awareness of hybrid identities.

4. Typological Indian (docs. 33, 79)
   Providential interpretations of American history give Native Americans a place in God's plan by equating them with Satan and identifying parallels to their conduct in the Bible as prefigurations. This typological view of Native Americans is most prominent in captivity narratives, such as in Mary Rowlandson's account of her captivity, in which Native Americans are seen as God's tools, sent to punish the author's unobservant religious conduct. In more positive typological terms, some theologians saw Native Americans as one of the ten lost tribes of Israel, whose conversion would signify the approaching millennium.

5. *Vacuum domicilium* or vacant and uncultivated land (docs. 16-7, 315)
   The biblical theory of "empty" or uncultivated land was embraced by religiously motivated British settlers to legitimate their move to North America: "[Jacob] admitteth it as a Principle in Nature, That in a vacant soyle, hee that taketh possession of it, and bestoweth culture and husbandry upon it, his Right it is" (*KC*, 26). The concept is equivalent to expropriation, especially in the case of Native American tribes with migratory cultures.

6. Indian Convert or Praying Indian (docs. 33-4, 36)
   These terms for converted Native Americans denote their liminal (transcultural) position in New England. Since Protestantism was based on scriptural literacy, Indian missions by Puritans demanded the acculturization of their converts as opposed to Catholic missionary work: "[T]hey must be *civilized* [ere] they could be *Christianized*" (doc. 34; *KC*, 54). Praying Indians were not integrated into white settlements but lived in Praying Towns. Their social acceptance in general, both by Natives and whites, was low (doc. 36).

7. Wilderness (docs. 65, 85, 279)
   In Puritan terminology, 'wilderness' denoted the habitation of Native Americans. The term referred not only to a physical or natural wilderness as found in primeval forests but also to a spiritual one, as belonging to the realm of Satan. Nature is a "waste and howling wilderness" (*KC*, 128) that has to be subdued and purged. The farmer and cultivator of land is not just providing sustenance, but also fighting a spiritual battle against the devil.

8. Indian Treaties (docs. 37, 161-3)
   The acquisition of land by British colonizers, and later US-American imperialists, was regulated by treaties between native tribes and appointed governmental agents. The use of this legal framework was unique to North America and has had long-reaching consequences for the relationship between Native Americans and the dominant political powers. It was also characteristic of the hypocritical position towards Native Americans: While treaties acknowledged the fundamental equality between Indians and whites, the agreements were nevertheless regularly violated by white settlers. Almost all conflicts were, in the end, decided in favor of white interests. The treaty system was officially ended by Congress in 1871.

9. Domestic dependent nation (docs. 161-3)
   The term coined by Chief Justice John Marshall in 1831 (*KC* 378), described the legal status of Native American tribes within the US. It was an effort to reconcile two aims of US-American policy towards Native Americans in the nineteenth century: On the one hand, the tribes were granted the right to self-government, which, however, also meant their exclusion from the rights of a US citizen. On the other hand, the tribes were expected to respect the fact that they lived on territory which belonged to the United States. The concept thus was the legal underpinning of the forceful removal (i.e., ethnic cleansing) of tribes to reservations, most prominently the removal of the so-called "Five Civilized Tribes" from Georgia and Florida to Indian Territory (today Oklahoma) in 1836.

II. Comparison – Contrasts – Connections

Example: Docs. 14-5, 26, 251, 308, 319

At the height of the Gilded Age, Andrew Carnegie, the millionaire industrialist, wrote his essay "Wealth" (doc. 308), in which he expounded his theory about the responsibility of rich men towards society. As if pre-empting criticism from anybody who might possibly share, for example, August Spies's ideas that "capitalism expropriates the masses for the benefit of the privileged class" (*KC*, 690), he starts his essay by praising social inequality as a sign of social progress. His example of a backward society, recognizable as such because equal social conditions prevail, is the Sioux, where the chief's wigwam is "just like others in external appearance, and even within, the difference was trifling between it and those of the poorest of his braves" (*KC*, 692). Carnegie's example relies on the well-known and generally accepted contemporary theory that different "races" are understood to be at different ages of their development: "The Indians are to-day where civilized man then [in former days] was" (*KC*, 692).

Carnegie does not seem to find it impolite or disrespectful to take the hospitality and openness of the Sioux as an opportunity to belittle them, writing without the least sense that they could object to being used as the primitive counterexample to progressive white America. He repeats the reductive approach of countless white observers, beginning with early travelers such as Vespucci, who treated the Native Americans he met not as equal human beings but as objects of study (doc. 23).[16] Carnegie is also not aware of the meaning of certain features of Sioux culture. His interpretation disregards an aspect observed by an early seventeenth century English traveler: "They [Native Americans] love not to be encumbered with too many utensils," which is a cultural characteristic in itself, not just a lack of imagination or ambition (in Boyer 1996, 17). For Carnegie, however, the manifestation of social standing necessarily goes hand in hand with the possession of material objects,[17] whereas in Native American gift exchange economies, valuables were socially most useful when they were given away as presents to ensure others' obligation (cf. Salisbury 1996). The nature of Native American gift giving stood as a source of possible cultural misunderstanding at the very beginning of Indian-white encounters in North America: the Mayflower Pilgrims accepted the Wampanoags' gifts without realizing what kind of social ties the presents were supposed to forge.

Carnegie simply assumes that all cultures develop in well-defined, identical stages, and that they can exist in these different stages side by side. In this, he is drawing on a long tradition of seeing Native American cultures as "childlike." This categorization goes back to the earliest conceptualizations of Native American cultures and can be divided further into two subcategories: The first sees individual Natives as still being in the lower stage of childhood, i.e., as morally and intellectually not fully formed, dependent, and weak. The second subcategory functions on a metaphorical level in which indigenous cultures are compared to

---

[16] Several contemporary Native American spokesmen place modern anthropologists and ethnographers in the same tradition, as people who make careers out of the lives of Native Americans. Consequently, anthropological research today has to get the approvement of tribal councils (cf. Krupat 1992; King 1998; Sanner 2000).

[17] The importance of 'property' has been traditionally one of the pillars of US-American national ideology, starting with John Locke's idea of government and then moving on to the problem of slavery and property. Jefferson's efforts to "civilize" Native Americans also included the strategy to make property attractive to them: "When once you have property, you will want laws and magistrates to protect your property and persons, and punish those among you who commit crimes. You will find that our laws are good for this purpose" (Jefferson to the Delawares, in White 1991, 474).

the 'childhood' of European civilization, i.e., either to classical antiquity or the cultures of the former "barbaric" fringes of the Greek and Roman Empires, such as the Picts or Celts. Both of these conceptualizations presume the potential for development, while the first emphasizes the need for help and protection. The pleading of a Native American on the Great Seal of the Massachusetts Bay Colony (1629) – "Come over and help us" – is an expression of this categorization, which has a clear biblical precursor in St. Paul's dream (Acts 16.9-10; cf. Bross 2004).[18]

By the sixteenth century, the idea of infantile primitives is well documented. In *A Brief Narration of the Destruction of the Indes, by the Spanyardes* (doc. 26), Bartholomew de Las Casas looks upon Native Americans as "the very children of Princes and Noble men brought up amongst us" (*KC*, 41). While this is meant as a compliment, it also emphasizes the vulnerability and immaturity of the Natives.[19] Other contemporary Spanish advocates share Las Casas's view, for example the influential Dominican priest and one of the founders of international law, Francisco de Vitoria, who wrote in his *De Indis et de iure belli relectiones*: "Those people are not unintelligent, but primitive; they seem incapable of maintaining a civilized State [...] their government, therefore, should be entrusted to people of intelligence and experience, as though they were children" (in Parry 1976, 292). More than three hundred years later, at the end of the nineteenth century, US-American politicians still conceive of "savages" as constitutionally unable to form governments, which gives them the rights of parental authority:

> We [the United States] govern the Indians without their consent, we govern our territories without their consent, we govern our children without their consent. [...] Would not the people of the Philippines prefer the just, humane, civilizing government of this Republic to the savage, bloody rule of pillage and extortion from which we have rescued them? (*KC*, 711)

Thus asks Albert Beveridge in 1898 in "The March of the Flag" (doc. 319), in justifying the imperial ambitions of the United States.

The second, metaphorical parallel between childhood and Native American cultures was used to emphasize the 'primitive' population's capability for 'advancement.' In promotional tracts such as Alexander Whitaker's 1613 *Good Newes from Virginia* (doc. 14), in which the minister of an American colony gathers arguments to convince the Virginia Company back in London to continue its support of the colony, he emphasizes that the "savages" are actually promising candidates for Christianity because their status resembles the cultural infancy of the colonizing powers: "Oh remember (I beseech you) what was the state of

---

[18] "And a vision appeared to Paul in the night; there stood a man of Macedonia, and prayed him, saying, Come over into Macedonia, and help us. And after he had seen the vision, immediately we endeavoured to go into Macedonia, assuredly gathering that the Lord had called us for to preach the gospel unto them" (Acts 16.9-10).

[19] It is of further interest to note the parallel to the later concept of the Noble Savage: the Indios may be children, but they are the children of *noblemen*.

England before the Gospell was preached in our Countrey? How much better were we then, and concerning our soules health, then these now are?" (*KC*, 22). Three years later, in *A Description of New England*, John Smith uses the same argument (doc. 15).

The Enlightenment belief in the perfectibility and unity of man led, then, to a conceptual placing of Native Americans in the vicinity of proto-Greeks or proto-Romans. Joseph-François Lafitau's *Moers des sauvages amériquains* (1724) was the first systematic comparison between Native American cultures and classical antiquity. In American texts, the connection was primarily created through Native American oratory skills; for example in Jefferson's *Notes on the State of Virginia* (doc. 251): "[Indians] astonish you with strokes of the most sublime oratory" (*KC*, 559). Of the Mingo Chief Logan's speech from 1774, Jefferson even claimed that "we may challenge the whole orations of Demosthenes and Cicero, and of any more eminent orator, if Europe has furnished more eminent, to produce a single passage, superior to the speech of Logan" (1982, 62).[20] Margaret Fuller, in her sympathetic travel narrative *Summer on the Lakes* (doc. 201), admires the aesthetic sense of the Natives in their choice of habitation and is reminded of "Greek splendor, a Greek sweetness." She can believe "that an Indian brave, accustomed to ramble in such paths, and be bathed by such sunbeams, might be mistaken for Apollo" (*KC*, 455).[21]

Visual representations also reflected the notion that Native Americans were to be found on a 'lower' level of civilization. Whenever 'Indians' were not the main subject, but their presence was felt to be necessary, they are placed at the bottom of compositions, often kneeling, as in John James Barralet' engraving *Apotheosis of Washington* (doc. 137) or on the cover illustration of *Frank Leslie's Historical Register of the Centennial Exposition* in Philadelphia (doc. 292; cf. doc. 12). Thus, when Carnegie in his essay "Wealth" classified the Sioux as a "race" on a lower stage of civilization, he relied on a number of long-established common assumptions that were more or less unchallenged in mainstream American culture until the end of the nineteenth century.

---

[20] Jefferson's comparison is based, however, not entirely on disinterested facts, but was written in response to Comte du Buffon's *Les Époques de la nature* (1778), which claimed that "savages" were deficient in intellect, and also Europeans living in America would degenerate with time (cf. Golden and Golden 1999, 82).

[21] William Rounsville Alger, popular actor Edwin Forrest's biographer, who modeled his melodramatic performance of Metamora on the Choctaw chief Push-ma-ta-ha, uses the same comparison: "The young chief, without a word, cast aside his Choctaw garb and stepped forth with a dainty tread, a living statue of Apollo in glowing bronze" (in Roach 1998, 354).

III. Reading and Discussion Questions

1. Compare the portrayal of Native Americans in Whitaker's text (doc. 14) with their portrayal in Cotton Mather's (doc. 34). Analyze the differences between the representational strategies displayed. In particular, how do the texts' respective genres influence the representation of Native Americans?

2. Identify passages in the texts that argue for the humanity of Native Americans. List explicit and implicit arguments separately (docs. 14-5, 201).

3. In what way does Puritan American historiography incorporate Native Americans into its scheme of history? Think about providential and millennial aspects (docs. 16-7, 35, 49).

4. Compare the Puritan striving for subduing the 'wilderness' to later transcendental notions of Nature. How do these ideologies affect the status of Native Americans (docs. 16, 65, 279)?

5. Comment on Washington Irving's and Margaret Fuller's representations of Native Americans. Think in particular about the way both authors incorporate aesthetic aspects into their arguments (docs. 37, 201).

IV. Resources

a. Recommended Reading

James Axtell. *Beyond 1492: Encounters in Colonial North America*. Oxford: Oxford University Press, 1992. Collection of essays from an ethnohistorical vantage point, dealing with the history of first and second encounters from the perspectives of both Native Americans and Europeans, with additional discussions of representations of Native Americans in contemporary textbooks.

Robert F. Berkhofer, Jr. *The White Man's Indian: Images of the American Indian from Columbus to the Present*. New York: Random House, 1978. This book traces the historical development of stereotypical representations of Native Americans. Berkhofer identifies and interprets in particular the origins of prejudices. He also discusses the ensuing misconceptions that were used as the foundation for political and cultural strategies against Native Americans.

Kristina Bross. *Dry Bones and Indian Sermons: Praying Indians in Colonial America*. Ithaca: Cornell University Press, 2004. A bifocal, transatlantic approach to the writings of John Eliot, placing the publications of this Puritan missionary in the context of both colonial and metropolitan debates about millennial readings of Protestant English history.

Philip Joseph Deloria. *Playing Indian*. New Haven: Yale University Press, 1998. A historical overview of US-Americans' fascination with Native Americans, and the way "Indians" have been used as symbols and metaphors in mainstream American culture. Deloria argues that there is a generally unacknowlegded presence of "the Indian" at the core of American national identity.

Francis Jennings. *The Invasion of America: Indians, Colonialism, and the Cant of Conquest*. New York: Norton, 1976. Controversial but highly influential revisionist study of the motives behind Puritan (and later) colonization of New England. Jennings questions the sincerity of Puritan attitudes, even on their own terms, towards Native Americans during the conquest and settlement.

C. Richard King. *Colonial Discourses, Collective Memories, and the Exhibition of Native American Cultures and Histories in the Contemporary United States*. New York: Garland, 1998. A representative collection of essays on current issues in Native American studies: exhibition in museums, questions of Native American identity, revitalization of tribal structures, languages and traditions.

Karen Ordahl Kupperman. *Indians and English: Facing Off in Early America*. Describes the first encounters (ca. 1600-1650) between English settlers and Native American tribes and documents the actual vulnerability of the early colonists in direct contradiction to their providential rhetoric. Analyzes the strategies on both sides, i.e., Native American and European, to control their encounters and further dealings with each other.

David Murray. *Forked Tongues: Speech, Writing, and Representation in North American Indian Texts*. London: Pinter, 1991. Analyzes how representations of Native Americans create a set of connected discourses which fulfill particular strategic and ideological functions within white society. The analyses are based on linguistic and philosophical readings, making use of literary theory. Murray focuses on translation, on the relationship between oral and written discourses, and on the function of dialogic representation.

Francis Paul Prucha. *The Great Father: United States Government and the American Indians*. 2 vols. Lincoln: University of Nebraska Press, 1984. An extensive historical study of the attitudes of the US-American federal government towards Native Americans.

Wilcomb E. Washburn, ed. *History of Indian-White Relations*. Washington: Smithsonian Institution, 1988. Indispensable collection of historical essays by leading scholars on Indian-white relations. It contains more than fifty essays on all aspects of the topic, such as the national policies of European colonial powers, the military situation, political, economic and religious relations as well as conceptual relations.

Richard White. *The Middle Ground: Indians, Empires, and Republics in the Great Lakes Region, 1650-1815*. Cambridge: Cambridge University Press, 1991. A historical study that documents the contact between Native Americans and whites outside the realm of Puritan settlements and describes examples of peaceful coexistence. Identification of cultural patterns was to be found on this "middle ground" before the rise of the US as a dominant imperial nation put an end to such negotiations.

b. Works Cited and Reading Suggestions

Apess, William (1992). "An Indian's Looking-Glass for the White Man." 1833. *On Our Own Ground: The Complete Writings of William Apess, a Pequot*. Ed. Barry O'Connell. Amherst: University of Massachusetts Press, 154-161.
Axtell, James (1985). *The Invasion Within: The Contest of Cultures in Colonial North America*. New York: Oxford University Press.
– (1992). *Beyond 1492: Encounters in Colonial North America*. New York: Oxford University Press.
Baumgärtner, Ingrid (2002). "Biblische, mythische und fremde Frauen: Zur Konstruktion von Weiblichkeit in Text und Bild mittelalterlicher Weltkarten." *Chloe: Beihefte zu Daphnis*. Ed. Xenia von Ertzdorff and Gerhard Giesemann. Amsterdam: Rodopi, 31-86.
Berkhofer, Robert F., Jr. (1978). *The White Man's Indian: Images of the American Indian from Columbus to the Present*. New York: Random House.
Biolsi, Thomas (1997). *Indians and Anthropologists: Vine Deloria, Jr. and the Critique of Anthropology*. Tucson: University of Arizona Press.
Bitterli, Urs (1976). *Die 'Wilden' und die 'Zivilisierten': Grundzüge einer Geistes- und Kulturgeschichte der europäisch-überseeischen Begegnung*. München: Beck.
Boyer, Paul S., et al., eds. (1996). *The Enduring Vision: A History of the American People*. 3rd ed. Lexington: Heath.
Bross, Kristina (2004). *Dry Bones and Indian Sermons: Praying Indians in Colonial America*. Ithaca: Cornell University Press.
Certeau, Michel de (1988). *The Writing of History*. 1975. New York: Columbia University Press.
Cheyfitz, Eric (1991). "Eloquent Cannibals." *The Poetics of Imperialism: Translation and Colonization from* The Tempest *to* Tarzan. New York: Oxford University Press, 142-172.
Cogley, Richard W. (1986/87). "John Eliot and the Origins of the American Indians." *Early American Literature* 21.3, 210-225.
Deloria, Vine Jr. (1969). *Custer Died for Your Sins: An Indian Manifesto*. New York: Macmillan.
Derounian-Stodola, Katherine and James Levernier (1993). *The Indian Captivity Narrative, 1550-1900*. New York: Twayne.
Dippie, Brian W. (1970). "The Vanishing American: Popular Attitudes and American Indian Policy in the Nineteenth Century." Diss. University of Texas, Austin.
Dongoske, Kurt E., Debra L. Martin, and T. J. Ferguson (2000). "Critique of the Claim of Cannibalism at Cowboy Wash." *American Antiquity* 65.1, 179-190.

Elliott, John H. (1970). *The Old World and the New, 1492-1650*. Cambridge: Cambridge University Press.
Elton, Geoffrey R. (1963). *Reformation Europe 1517-1559*. London: Collins.
Fernández-Arnesto, Felipe (2006). *Amerigo: The Man Who Gave His Name to America*. London: Weichfeld and Nicholson.
Golden, James L., and Joanne M. Golden (1999). "Logan's Speech: A Social Semiotic Perspective on a Rhetorically Significant Text." *Semiotica* 126.1-4, 75-95.
Greenblatt, Stephen (1991). *Marvellous Possessions: The Wonder of the New World*. Chicago: University of Chicago Press.
Hanke, Lewis (1976). "The Theological Significance of the Discovery of America." *First Images of America: The Impact of the New World on the Old*. Vol. 1. Ed. Fredi Chiappelli. Berkeley: University of California Press, 363-374.
Hariot, Thomas (1931). *A Briefe and True Report of the New Found Land of Virginia*. 1588. Ann Arbor: Edwards Brothers.
Harring, Sidney L. (1995). *Crow Dog's Case: American Indian Sovereignty, Tribal Law, and United States Law in the Nineteenth Century*. Cambridge: Cambridge University Press.
Heinen, H. Dieter, and Stanford Zent (1996). "On the Interpretation of Raleigh's Discoverie of Guiana: A View from the Field." *Current Anthropology* 37.2, 339-341.
Herschberger, Mary (1999). "Mobilizing Women, Anticipating Abolition: The Struggle Against Indian Removal in the 1830s." *The Journal of American History* 86.1, 15-40.
Iverson, Peter (1998). *"We Are Still Here": American Indians in the Twentieth Century*. Wheeling: Harlan Davidson.
Jackson, Helen H. (2003). *A Century of Dishonor: The Classic Exposé of the Plight of the Native Americans*. 1881. Mineola: Dover.
Jantz, Harold (1976). "Images of America in the German Renaissance." *First Images of America: The Impact of the New World on the Old*. Vol. 1. Ed. Fredi Chiappelli. Berkeley: University of California Press, 91-106.
Jefferson, Thomas (1982). *Notes on the State of Virginia*. 1787. Ed. William Peden. Chapel Hill: University of North Carolina Press.
Jennings, Francis (1976). *The Invasion of America: Indians, Colonialism, and the Cant of Conquest*. New York: Norton.
Kellaway, William (1961). *The New England Company, 1649-1776*. London: Longman.
Kelleter, Frank (2000). "Puritan Missionaries and the Colonization of the New World: A Reading of John Eliot's *Indian Dialogues* (1671)." *Early America Re-Explored: New Readings in Colonial, Early National, and Antebellum Culture*. Ed. Klaus H. Schmidt and Fritz Fleischmann. New York: Lang, 71-106.
King, C. Richard (1998). *Colonial Discourses, Collective Memories, and the Exhibition of Native American Cultures and Histories in the Contemporary United States*. New York: Garland.

Klarer, Mario (1999). "Cannibalism and Carnivalesque: Incorporation as Utopia in the Early Image of America." *New Literary History* 30.2, 389-410.

Konkle, Maureen (2004). *Writing Indian Nations: Native Intellectuals and the Politics of Historiography, 1827-1863*. Chapel Hill: University of North Carolina Press.

Krupat, Arnold (1992). *Ethnocriticism: Ethnography, History, Literature*. Berkeley: University of California Press.

Kupperman, Karen Ordahl (2000). *Indians and English: Facing Off in Early America*. Ithaca: Cornell University Press.

Maddox, Lucy (1991). *Removals: Nineteenth-Century American Literature and the Politics of Indian Affairs*. New York: Oxford University Press.

Nabokov, Peter, ed. (1992). *Native American Testimony: A Chronicle of Indian-White Relations from Prophecy to the Present, 1492-1992*. New York: Penguin.

Occom, Samson (1982). "A Short Narrative of My Life." 1786. *The Elders Wrote: An Anthology of Early Prose by Native American Indians, 1768-1931*. Ed. Bernd Peyer. Berlin: Reimer, 12-18.

Parry, John H. (1976). "A Secular Sense of Responsibility." *First Images of America: The Impact of the New World on the Old*. Vol. 1. Ed. Fredi Chiappelli. Berkeley: University of California Press, 287-304.

Pearce, Roy Harvey (1965). *Savagism and Civilization: A Study of the Indian and American Mind*. Baltimore: Johns Hopkins University Press.

Peyer, Bernd C. (1997). *The Tutor'd Mind: Indian Missionary-Writers in Antebellum America*. Amherst: University of Massachusetts Press.

Porter, Joy (2005). *The Cambridge Companion to Native American Literature*. Cambridge: Cambridge University Press.

Pratt, Mary Louise (1993). *Imperial Eyes: Studies in Travel Writing and Transculturation*. London: Routledge.

Prucha, Francis Paul (1976). *American Indian Policy in Crisis: Christian Reformers and the Indian, 1895-1900*. Norman: University of Oklahoma Press.

– (1984). *The Great Father: United States Government and the American Indian*. 2 vols. Lincoln: University of Nebraska Press.

– (1994). *American Indian Treaties: The History of a Political Anomaly*. Berkeley: University of California Press.

Raleigh, Sir Walter (1596). *Discoverie of the Large, Rich and Bewtiful Empire of Guiana, with a Relation of the Great and Golden Citie of* Manoa *(which the Spanyards call El Dorado) and the Provinces of Emeria, Arromaia, Amapaia, and Other Countries, with Their Rivers, Adjoining, Performed in the Year 1595*. London: Robert Robinson.

Roach, Joseph (1998). "The Emergence of the American Actor." *The Cambridge History of American Theatre*. Vol 1. Ed. Don B. Wilmeth and Christopher Bigsby. Cambridge: Cambridge University Press, 338-372.

Rogin, Michael (1975). *Fathers and Children: Andrew Jackson and the Subjugation of the American Indian*. New York: Knopf.

Salisbury, Neal (1996). "The Indians' Old World: Native Americans and the Coming of Europeans." *The William and Mary Quarterly* 53, 435-459.
- (1997). "Mary Rowlandson and Her Removes." Introduction. *The Sovereignty and Goodness of God. Together with the Faithfulness of His Promises Displayed: Being a Narrative of the Captivity and Restoration of Mrs. Mary Rowlandson and Related Documents*. Ed. Neal Salisbury. Boston: Bedford, 1-60.
Sanner, Hans-Ulrich (2000). "Confessions of the Last Hopi Fieldworker." *Mirror-Writing: (Re)Constructions of Native American Identity*. Ed. Thomas Claviez and Maria Moss. Glienicke/Berlin: Galda and Wilch, 41-66.
Scaglione, Aldo (1976). "Montaigne and the Humanist Tradition." *First Images of America: The Impact of the New World on the Old*. Vol. 1. Ed. Fredi Chiappelli. Berkeley: University of California Press, 63-70.
Sekora, John (1993). "Red, White, and Black: Indian Captivities, Colonial Printers, and the Early African-American Narrative." *A Mixed Race: Ethnicity in Early America*. Ed. Frank Shuffleton. New York: Oxford University Press, 92-104.
Sewell, David (1993). "'So Unstable and Like Mad Men They Were': Language and Interpretation in American Captivity Narratives." *A Mixed Race: Ethnicity in Early America*. Ed. Frank Shuffleton. New York: Oxford University Press, 39-55.
Slotkin, Richard (1974). *Regeneration through Violence: The Mythology of the American Frontier, 1600-1860*. Middletown: Wesleyan University Press.
Sturtevant, William C. (1976). "First Visual Images of Native America." *First Images of America: The Impact of the New World on the Old*. Vol. 1. Ed. Fredi Chiappelli. Berkeley: University of California Press, 417-454.
Turner, Christy (1999). *Man Corn: Cannibalism and Violence in the Prehistoric American Southwest*. Salt Lake City: University of Utah Press.
Varela, Consuelo (2006). *La caida de Cristóbal Colón. El juicio de Bobadilla*. Ed. and trans. Isabel Aguirre. Madrid: Marcial Pons Historia.
Wallace, Anthony F. C. (1999). *Jefferson and the Indians: The Tragic Fate of the First Americans*. Cambridge: Belknap Press.
Washburn, Wilcomb E. (1976). "The Clash of Morality in the American Forest." *First Images of America: The Impact of the New World on the Old*. Vol. 1. Ed. Fredi Chiappelli. Berkeley: University of California Press, 335-350.
- , ed. (1988). *History of Indian-White Relations*. Vol. 4: *Handbook of North American Indians*. Washington: Smithsonian Institution.
Weckmann, Luis (1951). "The Middle Ages in the Conquest of America." *Speculum* 26.1, 130-141.
White, Hayden (1976). "The Noble Savage Theme as Fetish." *First Images of America: The Impact of the New World on the Old*. Vol. 1. Ed. Fredi Chiappelli. Berkeley: University of California Press, 121-135.
White, Richard (1991). *The Middle Ground: Indians, Empires, and Republics in the Great Lakes Region, 1650-1815*. Cambridge: Cambridge University Press.
Wyss, Hilary E. (2000). *Writing Indians: Literacy, Christianity, and Native Community in Early America*. Amherst: University of Massachusetts Press.

CLEMENS SPAHR

Puritanism in the New World

I. Themes and Arguments

In 1917, H. L. Mencken published his essay "Puritanism as a Literary Force," in which he bitterly complained about the lasting influence of Calvinism. According to Mencken, Calvinism had turned theology into "a luxuriant demonology; even God himself was transformed into a superior sort of devil, ever wary and wholly merciless" (197). The Puritan's austere piety, his "utter lack of aesthetic sense, his distrust of all romantic emotion, his unmatchable intolerance of opposition, his unbreakable belief in his own bleak and narrow views, his savage cruelty of attack, his lust for relentless and barbarous persecution – these things have put an almost unbearable burden upon the exchange of ideas in the United States" (201). To be sure, the institutional structures of the New England colonies had long withered away. Newer religious and social ideas had displaced the dogmas of Calvinism. Only a few remnants survived into the twentieth century, as in "the barbaric doctrines of the Methodist and Baptists, particularly in the South" (197). At the same time, however, Mencken found that "[o]n the ethical side […] Calvinism is dying a much harder death, and we are still a long way from the enlightenment" (198). American culture needed to take up the fight against a stern Puritan morality which Mencken saw as the root of all cultural evil. Whatever the adequacy of his assessment, it is evident that the Puritans cast their long shadow over American history well into the twentieth century.

It is striking, however, that Mencken, in a manner that is typical for popular perceptions of New England Puritanism, assumes a homogeneity in the term 'Puritan' which simply does not exist. The ease with which we talk of 'the Puritans' is quite ironic, given that there was no such thing as a 'Puritan' denomination or sect. In fact, the Puritans received their name from their reviled opponents as a stigma rather than using it to consciously define themselves. Originally, the epithet 'Puritan' referred to those English Protestants attempting to purify the Anglican Church of the remnants of Roman Catholicism. The Puritans themselves, however, preferred to call themselves 'the godly.' Beyond these terminological troubles, the religion both in its English and colonial incarnations comprised such a variety of practices that it seems problematic to cling to a conception of Puritanism as a unified group of believers and a coherent theological system.[1]

Should we, then, discard the term 'Puritanism' and instead discuss smaller groups and their individualized religious practices? In fact, it seems more reasonable to use the word 'Puritanism' as a heuristic device. In this sense, Puritanism denotes a spectrum of religious answers to the same theological and sociohistorical problem. The Puritans were deeply rooted in the Calvinist tradition, or, more appropriately, in the dogma of the Reformed Church, and from this perspective they sought to understand the world. Their religion centered upon the key Calvinist tenets – the so-called 'five points' of Calvinism as exemplified by Cotton Mather (doc. 45) – and the belief that an omniscient God has determined the fate of the world. This sense of predetermination, however, created a number of troublesome questions. Who belonged to the elect? Had God chosen a particular community or nation to fulfil his will? Puritans disagreed over the answers to these conundra. How could the subjects know whether or not they were elected, given man's total depravity after the Fall? Could the individual relate to God directly? Did the ministers have the right to function as mediators between God and the individual? The answers, as we shall see, varied widely. If we speak of Puritanism, then, we should use the term not in Mencken's sense as referring to a unified group of believers, but rather as denoting a range of religious beliefs grounded in the Calvinist tradition.

Before we engage in the analysis of the varieties of New England Puritanism, we need to address the question why 'Puritanism in the New World' should be different from 'Puritanism in the Old World.' Prior to their experiment in the New World, the Puritans had been conceived as a homogenous group. 'The godly' were rooted in the dogma of Reformed Protestantism and all of them endeavored to find an appropriate sociopolitical expression of their theology. They carried these reformist impulses to the shores of the New World. Despite their close ties to England and their origin in the European Reformed tradition, once they had landed on the shores of America the New England Puritans started from very changed premises. In the New World, the Puritans encountered the unprecedented and unexpected opportunity to enact their theocratic model to a degree which would have been inconceivable in Europe. Here was a unique chance to build a society of saints, a chance that was not to be forfeited. This opportunity, however, also raised the question of what exactly a godly and pious society was.

This occasion appeared all the more precious to the reform-seeking Protestant groups as the history of English Puritanism had been one of tremendous failure. Having seen their hopes for a purer Protestantism disillusioned by Elizabeth I. (r. 1558-1603), they decided that England might not be the place where their version of the true church could be established after all. For the Puritans, the

---

[1] For the variety of religious practices that extend beyond New England Puritanism and denominations cf. Butler (1990 and 1993).

reign of Elizabeth marked a historical watershed, for it stood as the age which terminated their hopes for a truly reformed church and society. To understand the relevance of the Elizabethan Age for their eventual exodus, it is necessary to go back to Henry VIII (r. 1509-47), under whose reign the Church of England separated from the Catholic Church in the 1530s, a decision which opened the prospect of building a purer community of believers. His successor Edward VI (r. 1547-53) made every effort to propel the cause of Protestantism. During the subsequent reign of Mary Tudor (r. 1553-1558), however, Catholicism was restored, and about eight hundred Protestant subjects were sent into exile. John Foxe's *Book of Martyrs* (1563) memorialized those who were burnt at the stake. Together with the Geneva Bible, Foxe's epic work provided the foundation of Puritan self-conception and was well known by the colonial Puritans. When Elizabeth ascended the throne upon her sister's death in 1558, the radical Protestants' hopes that England would finally witness a dramatic shift toward a 'purer' church were raised. It was during this time that the term 'Puritan' was coined for the more extreme varieties of Protestantism. The radical reformers saw their opportunity to leave a path of suffering and martyrdom and to establish a truly pious theocracy. However, as it became progressively more obvious that Elizabeth was concerned with power politics rather than a purification of the church, those of a more radical reformist bent had to acknowledge that their vision of a pure church might be doomed in England.

Despite the fact that the Calvinist James I. (r. 1603-1625) had ascended the throne, in 1609 a large number of separatists (often called Brownists after Robert Browne, one of the first to advocate a break with the English church) moved to Holland, then one of the most liberal countries in Europe. Believing that the Church of England was just as corrupt and unworthy of God's grace as the Catholic Church, the separatists attempted to establish an ecclesiastical enterprise in opposition to and cut off from the Church of England. Nevertheless, the separatist Puritans did not find the freedom that they had hoped for in the Netherlands, and in 1620 one hundred of them set sail on the *Mayflower* with a charter from the Plymouth Company. Intending to arrive at Virginia, they accidentally landed west of Cape Cod, where they founded Plymouth Colony. In 1630, one year after the charter had been issued by the Massachusetts Bay Company, a large group of Congregationalists under the leadership of John Winthrop followed the separatist's example and embarked on the *Arbella* to voyage to New England. The Congregationalists believed that the most appropriate model of a true church could be realized in small 'congregations.' They held more moderate political and religious views than the separatists, still hoping, for instance, for a change in the English church. As opposed to the separatists, the Puritan settlers of Massachusetts Bay intended their community in the New World to be a model for the Old World, a thought elaborated in John Winthrop's speech on the *Arbella*, "A Modell of Christian Charity" (1630; doc. 62). It is safe to assert, however, that "rapidly the distinction between the Massachusetts Puritans and the Plymouth separatists lost its meaning, and the story of Plymouth and the Plymouth separatists became in large part that of Puritan New England" (Bremer 1995, 36). The emerging Puritanism produced complex dogmas that were subject to discussion. As we shall see, a change of emphasis could lead to dramatic theological and social consequences.

The Massachusetts Puritans, then, eventually came to be the dominant group of Puritans in the New World. Despite unprecedented political freedom, however, their model community did not develop as smoothly as they would have hoped. Warfare with Native Americans, diseases, and radical voices proposing alternative forms of Puritanisms posed serious hindrances for the Puritan leaders, who found themselves in situations in which they had to justify their vision of a successful Puritan theocracy. While Puritanism found itself in a constant struggle with its historical conditions, it is hardly surprising that the writings of those in power sought to gloss over these tensions, attempting to create a coherent version of Puritanism. *The New-England Primer* (1762; doc. 52) suggests that there is a monolithic Puritanism. Just as "Job feels the Rod, / Yet blesses GOD" (*KC*, 98), the Puritans were expected to be subjects in the truest sense of the word – subjected to God and faithful to Puritan doctrine. God had once established a covenant with humankind and promised eternal happiness. But after Adam and Eve broke the covenant – "In ADAM'S Fall, / We sinn'd all" (*KC*, 98) – there was no return to this original condition. *The New-England Primer* reminds its readers of the original sin committed by their ancestors and admonishes them to conduct their life in the knowledge of Adam's sin. The apodictic tone of this early spelling book is typical of the discipline and self-discipline which Puritan theology demanded. Puritanism was an elaborate theological system, and individuals were expected to succumb to this system and abide by its rules. On a more elaborate theological level than the *Primer*, the towering work of Puritan historiography, Cotton Mather's *Magnalia Christi Americana: Or, the Ecclesiastical History of New-England, from Its First Planting in the Year 1620. unto the Year of the Lord, 1698* (1702), elaborates central Calvinist tenets. It is notable, however, that just as *The New-England Primer*'s alphabet of faith conveyed the impression that all Puritans who arrived in the New World subscribed to a coherent thought-system, Mather's *magnum opus* self-confidently proclaims to stand as "*the* Ecclesiastical History" of New England (*KC*, 87; emphasis mine), and thus lays claim to the universal validity of the dominant institutionalized form of Puritanism.

While both works mention salient issues at the heart of the Puritan experience, they do not raise the question of who advanced these creeds and whether the dogmas were indeed unanimously accepted. True, Mather's history deals with the ecclesiastical development of Puritanism and thus limits the scope of his history to one area of the sociopolitical sphere, but he also takes the history of the central figures of New England Puritanism to be representative of the New World experience as a whole. This portrayal of Puritanism as a coherent system, however, has also dominated academic discourse in the twentieth century, most prominently embodied in Perry Miller's 'declension model,' which posited an essentially unified Puritan thought system that had to adapt to specific American circumstances in order to retain its essence. This assumption permitted him to delineate the history "of the accommodation to the American landscape of an imported and highly articulated system of ideas" (Miller 1953, x).[2] In fact, the conflicting conclusions that Puritans drew from reformed dogma in the Old and the New World contradict such a view. If we talk of 'the Puritans,' then, we should not posit a shared experience objectively codified in the documents we will examine. Rather we should conceive of Puritanism as a creed that revolved around a set of doctrines the exegesis of which could be taken to various extremes.

Before investigating further the problems of New England Puritanism, it is helpful to have a brief look at a Puritan text from the Old World. George Goodwin's poem *Automachia* displays a notion of the Puritan self that helps us understand some of the theological principles with which Puritans embarked on their voyage to the New World. We will then turn to Thomas Shepard's "The Autobiography," which bears witness to the fact that the Puritans' journey was a search for a place where they could ponder and eventually realize these principles. As an example of the dominant, institutionalized version of Puritanism in the New World, we will then engage in a reading of a chapter of Cotton Mather's *Magnalia Christi Americana*. Subsequently, we shall be concerned with a different, less systematic but nevertheless firmly religious form of writing, namely Puritan poetry. Here, Anne Bradstreet's poems "The Flesh and the Spirit" and "Upon the Burning of Our House" will serve as prime examples of how Puritans sought to

---

[2] Miller's approach has been subject to various forms of criticism. Charles L. Cohen insists that "[d]efining English Puritanism as primarily an intellectual movement fails to explain either its political vitality or its programmatic diversity, and its existence in tension with but not absolutely separate from the established [Anglican] church" (1993, 578). A number of recent works have offered important revisions of earlier conceptions of Puritanism. Philip Gura's *A Glimpse of Sion's Glory* (1984) supplies a history of Puritan dissidents, radical in both their theology and their social thought. In *Orthodoxies in Massachusetts* (1994), Janice Knight locates Puritan dissidents in the center of Puritan institutions. In John Cotton and his followers, Knight sees an "oppositional mode of piety [which] may have proved a ground from which to challenge orthodoxy from within" (32). David H. Hall's *Worlds of Wonder* (1989) emphasizes the importance of religious practice and attempts to reconstruct popular religious belief in the early colonial time. For Hall, "[r]eligion comprehends a range of actions and beliefs far greater than those described in a catechism or occurring within a sacred space: it was a loosely bound set of symbols and motifs that gave significance to rites of passage and life crises, that infused everyday events with the presence of the supernatural" (18). In *The Long Argument* (1991), Stephen Foster states that Puritanism can be understood only in relation to its English context. Foster shows that "English migrants continued to move to America at a steady rate throughout the decade of the 1630s, and though immigration had all but ceased by 1642, New Englanders remained acutely aware of developments at home through correspondence, remigration, and their participation in the fierce pamphlet wars over 'Independency'" (138). Finally, Patricia Bonomi's *Under the Cope of Heaven* (1986) provides a social history of colonial religion which demonstrates "the increasing interpenetration of religion and politics" in colonial America (8-9).

comprehend everyday life in the light of a divinely preordained course of history. In conclusion, a short outline of threats to Puritan orthodoxy will be sketched.

II. The Puritan Self

In his *Automachia* (1607; doc. 38), the English writer George Goodwin seems to disdain "[t]his wicked world" (*KC*, 67) and thus to renounce all earthly things. This rejection includes the human self, which, due to its fallen condition, can no longer appreciate God's beauty. Upon a closer look at Goodwin's poem, however, it becomes obvious that it does not suggest a linear movement from earth to heaven, but rather dwells on the tension created by the fact that the self longs for a heaven which it cannot reach, while at the same time being chained to the very place it wants to leave. The speaker tells us that "Vertue I love, I leane to Vice: I blame / This wicked World, yet I embrace the fame / I clime to Heaven, I cleave to Earth: I both / Too-love my Selfe, and yet my Selfe I loath: / Peacelesse, I Peace pursue: In Civill Warre, / With, and against my Selfe, I ioine, I iarre" (*KC*, 67). But his reflection upon this inescapable situation contains the solution to the problem: While the self is fundamentally corrupted, the very perception of this corruption is nonetheless the precise starting point for the self's elevating itself beyond its present state and for its search for hints of God's plan.[3] However, the civil war which the individual finds within himself should not be stopped. While "Concording Discord kils me," it is also true that "Discording Concord doth my life maintaine" (*KC*, 68). This opposition is not clearly resolvable by leaving all earthly matters behind – or by trying to do so – but rather constitutes what Puritans considered the essential human condition. The Puritan self is always aware of its depravity, of the fact that it is a descendent of Adam and thus sinful, and consequently finds itself in a painful relation to the world. At the same time, however, the individual conceives that through his bodily existence he is situated in a world that was created by God and is thus a world of potential bliss. The conclusion "I can not live with nor without my Selfe" (*KC*, 69) captures the Puritan condition of being situated between a world that is God's beautiful work, the beauty of which, however, cannot be perceived, and the heavenly sphere which promises the restoration of the sinful individual to a regenerate being. This salvation, in turn, is a rather vague promise for one's earthly toils, as the individual can never be sure about whether or not he belongs to the elect.

---

[3] Sacvan Bercovitch has called this concept of the subject "the archetypical Puritan protagonist-antagonist, 'my SELF'" (1975, 19). Bercovitch's reading of Goodwin's poem goes to the heart of the Puritan concept of selfhood. The self is constantly torn between a transcendent sphere it cannot reach and the exertion of its own corrupted powers. For Bercovitch, this dilemma throws the individual back on himself and therefore the poem for him is expressive of "the spirit of an age that was to be decisive in the development in Western individualism" (1975, 20).

Goodwin's poem, however, also gestures toward a larger context. The metaphor of the civil war within the individual captures the eternal struggle between good and evil. By the same token, this terminology opens up a historical dimension. In Goodwin's England, it became more and more obvious that the struggle between good and evil threatened to be decided in favor of evil.[4] The situation in which Puritans found themselves was highly problematic, for it did not permit the adequate practice of Puritan piety. Furthermore, England was increasingly perceived as a place too impious for the realization of a purer form of religion. These considerations contributed largely to the decision of those Puritans who left their country to find a more apt place for their project. What united English Puritans across all strata of society was "first, their own attainment of a sense of purpose, their forsaking of a life 'at randome,' and second their perception of how little church and state were doing to give that same sense to England as a whole" (Foster 1991, 9), a perception which partially accounts for the New England Puritans' obsession with social structures. In the New World, for the first time, they had found a ground on which their theocracy could be established. Even if this ground was contested by 'savages,' they could be subjected to the divine cause and given a positive interpretation as God's means of testing his chosen people.

With the settlements in Plymouth and Boston, the hope arose that it would be possible to build an institutional apparatus from scratch that could foster God's divine plan. John Winthrop's famous admonition captures this interrelation between faith and social structures:

> [W]ee must be knitt together in this worke as one man, wee must entertaine each other in brotherly Affeccion, wee must be willing to abridge our selves of our superfluities, for the supply of others necessities, wee must uphold a familiar Commerce together in all meekenes, gentlenes, patience and liberallity, wee must delight in eache other, make others Condicions our owne, reioyce together, mourne together, labour, and suffer together, allwayes haveing before our eyes our Commission and Community in the worke, our Community as members of the same body, soe shall wee keepe the unitie of the spirit in the bond of peace, the Lord will be our God and delight to dwell among us, as his owne people and will commaund a blessing upon us in all our wayes, soe that wee shall see much more of his wisdome power goodnes and truthe then formerly wee have beene acquainted with, wee shall finde that the God of Israell is among us, when tenn of us shall be able to resist a thousand of our enemies, when hee shall make us a prayse and glory, that men shall say of succeeding plantacions: the lord make it like that of New England: for wee must Consider that wee shall be as a City upon a Hill, the eies of all people are upon us; soe that if wee shall deale falsely with our god in this worke wee have undertaken and soe cause him to withdrawe his present help from us, wee shall be made a story and a by-word through the world, wee

---

[4] Thomas Shepard imparts the impression that England had become a hopeless place for God's cause when he relates that "I saw the Lord dep[ar]ting from England where Mr Hooker & Mr Cotton were gone, & I saw the h[e]arts of most of the godly set & bent that way & I did thinke I should feele many miseries if I stayd behind" (*KC*, 74).

shall open the mouthes of enemies to speake evill of the wayes of god and all professours for Gods sake. (*KC*, 121)

The New Englanders conceived of themselves as a community of saints, a beacon of faith for those firm believers that were prepared to follow God's will. Thomas Shepard in his autobiography exemplifies the desire to reconcile the private and the public realm that we have observed in Goodwin's poem and Winthrop's sermon. Once it became possible to realize true faith in a purified church, engagement in the social sphere was mandatory: "I saw it my duty to desire the fruition of all gods ordinances, which I could not enjoy in old England" (*KC*, 75). Furthermore, Shepard "saw no reason to spend my time privately when I might possibly exercise my talent publikely in N.E." (*KC*, 75). New England Puritanism, then, was an attempt to reconcile society and theology, a reconciliation which had been precluded by historical circumstances in Europe. The "Lord had opened a doore of escape" (*KC*, 75), and the Puritans were willing to cross the threshold into what promised to be a better future.

III. Puritan Doctrine

The question of saving faith was at the heart of Puritan doctrine. Man could be saved only if he believed in God. In fact, he could prepare himself for God's grace only through faith (*sola fide*), not through good works. However, even if the believer professed to be faithful and gave himself to the ways of God, the question of whether or not he belonged to the chosen few did not disappear. How could the Puritans establish whether they were chosen or doomed; how could they be sure of their destiny? What did God's will hold in store for them? The uncertainty resulting from these questions led to an experimental predestinarian tradition which advocated perseverance as a believer's main trait. Only his unflinching faith in God's benevolence could prepare him for his possible calling. In the face of the fundamental uncertainty of his own fate, the believer first had to accept his inability to penetrate God's will before he could hope to be saved by giving himself entirely to Christ.

Building the appropriate social and ecclesiastical structures that provided the opportunity to live a pious life was part of the colonial experiment. New England should become a place in which a faithful life would be possible. The settlers followed a distinct agenda, namely the advancement of what they considered the pure doctrine of faith: "They moved not so much for 'religious freedom' – certainly not for tolerating other faiths – as for setting up a holier, more disciplined community in the diaspora than England would allow" (Cohen 1993, 584). Increasingly, however, they came to see the diaspora as the center of religious history. Still largely ignored by the majority of English Protestants, the colonial Puritans conceived of New England as the appointed place for the erection of a purer Christian society. Wars with Native Americans and conflicts within the community were considered God's tests for his chosen people. New England was not only understood to be the providential place of salvation, but also an example for England and Europe. Thomas Shepard's reference to the situation in the Old World shows that New England Puritans were always aware of events happening in the Old World:

> The Lord thus afflicting yet continud peace to the c[o]untry that amazing mercy when all England & Europe are in a flame the Lord hath set me & my children aside from the flames of the fires in Yorkshire & Northumberland whence if we had not bin delivered, I had bin in great afflictions & temptations, very weake & unfit to be tossed up & down & to beare violent p[ro]secution; the Lord therefore hath shewed his tenderness to me & mine in carrying me to a land of peace tho a place of tryall; where the Lord hath made the savage Indians who conspired the death of all the English by Miantinomo. (*KC*, 77)

While Europe had still not transcended the stage of history from which the Puritans fled, America held out the promise of a challenging yet rewarding place for the saints.

This new geopolitical situation also opened up the opportunity to create institutional structures from scratch, as the Puritans considered both their theological agenda and their own role in history in a fresh light.[5] Despite these changed circumstances, however, even the New World could not alter the fact that humanity was no longer capable of seeing God's glory, so that the original sin and its consequences remained central to Puritan doctrine. The chapter "A Confession of Faith," from Cotton Mather's *Magnalia Christi Americana*, provides a valuable outline of the basic Calvinist tenets that Puritans attempted to reconcile with their New World experience. In this chapter, Mather reproduces almost verbatim the catechisms of the *Westminster Confession of Faith* (1647), a central document of English Calvinism.[6] According to Calvinist theology, God

---

[5] As Stephen Innes has pointed out, this historical constellation facilitated the development of a Puritan work ethic "in its most purely distilled form in the early modern world": "While in Geneva, Holland, and low-country Scotland, Calvinist divinity was always qualified by pre-existing practices, in New England doctrine was the foundation for practice. New England represents the only historical case in which Calvinistic, sectarian Protestantism was institutionalized at the very founding of the social order" (1995, 12).

[6] Being notoriously imprecise regarding the formulation of their doctrine, European Calvinists nevertheless held synods which attempted to provide guidelines for believers. The Westminster Assembly (1643-1649) was the most important of a number of assemblies attempting to hammer out Calvinist tenets. From 1618 to 1619, the Dutch Reformed Church held the synod of Dort in Dordrecht. Here, participants penned the five points or tenets of Calvinist soteriology (doctrine of salvation), in English referred to with the acronym TULIP: firstly, the assumption of a complete corruption of human nature due to Original Sin (Total depravity); secondly, the assumption that each individual was predestined to either salvation or damnation (Unconditional election); thirdly, the notion that only a limited number of persons – the elect – were redeemed by Christ's sacrifice (Limited atonement); fourthly, the fact that humans cannot refuse their being elected by God (Irresistible grace); and fifthly, the eternal righteousness and security of the Elected (Perseverance of the saints). In 1643, the English Parliament called for an assembly "for the vindicating and clearing of the Doctrine of the

considers it necessary to reveal himself time and again so that humanity can glimpse his glory:

> Although the Light of Nature, and the Works of Creation and Providence do so far manifest the Goodness, Wisdom and Power of God, as to leave Men inexcusable; yet are they not sufficient to give that knowledge of God and of his Will, which is necessary unto Salvation: Therefore it pleased the Lord, at sundry times, and in divers manners to reveal himself, and to declare that his Will unto his Church; and afterwards for the better Preserving and Propagating of the Truth, and for the more sure Establishment and Comfort of the Church against the Corruption of the Flesh, and the Malice of Satan, and of the World, to commit the same wholly to Writing: Which maketh the Holy Scripture to be most necessary; those former ways of God's revealing his Will unto his People being now ceased. (*KC*, 81)

God reveals himself in his creation, and before the fall of man, nature could serve as a source of discovering God's beauty. But with the fall humanity has become blind to the "Light of Nature" and "those former ways of God's revealing his Will unto his People" have become unavailable, so that from then on humankind has to rely on the scripture for at least limited access to God's truth. The most dramatic effect of original sin was to break with the covenant of works that God had established between himself and humanity:

> I. God having made a Covenant of Works and Life thereupon, with our First Parents, and all their Posterity in them, they being seduced by the Subtilty and Temptation of Satan, did wilfully transgress the Law of their Creation, and break the Covenant, in eating the forbidden Fruit.
>
> II. By this Sin, they and we in them, fell from Original Righteousness and Communion with God, and so became dead in Sin, and wholly defiled in all the Faculties and Parts of Soul and Body. (*KC*, 83)

The fall had serious consequences for the further history of humankind. Not only could humanity no longer perceive God's glory in his creation, but also it became impossible to work for one's salvation. The original covenant of works required man to behave adequately to preserve the perfect state in which he existed. As Cotton Mather has it, the "first Covenant made with Man was a Covenant of Works, wherein Life was promised to *Adam*, and in him to his Posterity, upon Condition of Perfect and Personal Obedience" (*KC*, 83). Yet Adam ate the forbidden fruit and thus violated the covenant. Due to the resulting corruption of man's nature, a chasm opened between God and man, and the individual was left disoriented since he could no longer be sure about his destiny within God's plan.

Church of England from all false Calumnies and Aspersions" (in Kendall 1979, 168). The divines assembled at Westminster produced the Westminster Confession, a shorter and a larger catechism, all of which were attempts to cast into a mold the Protestant creed (for a detailed analysis of the Westminster Confession, see Kendall 1979, 167-208). In 1648, the 'Cambridge Platform' endorsed the Confession of Faith, thus defining the 'New England Way.'

The original bond with God was severed. To assure one's salvation, one first had to address humanity's fundamental corruptness which prompted the sinner to a radical self-examination. God had withdrawn the possibility of bliss on earth since human beings had proved incapable of honoring their obligations. Yet, in his eternal benevolence God sent Jesus to communicate his glory: "Altho' the *Work* of *Redemption* was not actually wrought by Christ, till after his Incarnation, yet the Virtue, Efficacy and Benefits thereof, were communicated unto the Elect in all Ages successively from the beginning of the World" (*KC*, 83). While Christ did not usher in the millennium, his atonement for humanity's sins enabled a limited number of individuals to achieve salvation ('limited atonement'). By sending his son to this sin-stricken world, God had established a new covenant, the covenant of grace:

> Man by his Fall having made himself uncapable of Life by that Covenant, the Lord was pleased to make a Second, commonly call'd the Covenant of Grace; wherein he freely offereth unto Sinners Life and Salvation by Jesus Christ, requiring of them Faith in him, that they may be saved, and promising to give unto all those that are ordained unto Life, his Holy Spirit to make them willing and able to believe. (*KC*, 83)

Within this covenant, the precondition for achieving salvation was faith. In his *Institutes of Christian Religion*, John Calvin had defined faith as "a firm and certain knowledge of God's benevolence toward us, founded upon the truth of the freely given promise in Christ, both revealed to our minds and sealed upon our hearts through the Holy Spirit" (1960, 551). The individual sinner had to believe in Christ and take his life as a model. Yet, faith was of no avail if the sinner was not included among the elect. Instead of being able to work for his grace, the individual had to remain in a passive position, preparing for possible salvation: "This effectual Call is of God's Free and Special Grace alone, not from any thing at all foreseen in Man, who is altogether Passive therein, until being quickned and renewed by the Holy Spirit, he is thereby enabled to answer this Call and to embrace the Grace offered and conveyed in it" (*KC*, 84).[7]

Through his sacrifice on the cross, Jesus enabled some chosen individuals to experience God's grace. God decided "to chuse and ordain the Lord Jesus, his only begotten Son, according to a Covenant made between them both, to be the mediator between God and Man [...], and to be by him, in time, redeemed, called, justified, sanctified and glorified" (*KC*, 83). This Puritan *ordo salutis* (order of salvation), which is also known as 'morphology of conversion,' a standardized pattern that outlined the individual's gradual transformation from sinner to saint, stated that the sinner had to be chosen by God as one of the elect ("redeemed") before the Spirit offered him grace ("called"). Subsequently, the indi-

---

[7] John Winthrop inferred a renewed covenant between God and the New England Puritans in "A Modell of Christian Charity": "Noting parallels between the Puritans and the Old Testament Hebrews, Winthrop's sermon culminates in a vision of the sacred covenant between God and His saints for this divine enterprise" (Elliott 1994, 194).

vidual had to cooperate with the Spirit and turn to God. After his turning to God, the elect reached the stage of justification, that is, he understood his calling and thus his soul was redeemed and he was reborn ("justified"). Following this conversion experience, the pilgrim would regulate his actions according to received grace and thus act in a truly religious way (be "sanctified"). The saint, however, remained doubtful as to the true state of his election, but his faithful and pious deeds allowed him to conclude that he might be one of the elect. The final assurance would only come in the last stage of this process (being "glorified"), and Puritans hotly debated whether this stage could be reached in one's lifetime or only in the afterlife. But even more contested was the question of which stage marked the true moment in which the individual experienced his calling. If one put too much emphasis on justification – as some radical Puritans did – one might arrive at a doctrine that deified the human being regardless of his behavior, whereas if one insisted on the prerogative of sanctification too strenuously – as some of the ministers did – one might arrive at a doctrine perilously close to a covenant of works.

To meet the problems that arose with the establishment of the new covenant, the saints decided to seek glimpses of God's glory in two authoritative books 'written' by God – the Bible and the Book of Nature. The divine status of the Bible remained largely uncontested, and thus Mather's remarks can be taken to be paradigmatic for the Puritan discourse on Scripture:

> The whole Counsel of God concerning all things necessary for his own Glory, Man's Salvation, Faith and Life, is either expresly set down in Scripture, or by good and necessary Consequence may be deduced from Scripture; unto which nothing, at any time, is to be added, whether by new Revelations of the Spirit, or Traditions of Men. (*KC*, 81)

Mather insists on a literalist reading of the Bible: Nothing may be added, but the original sense of the words should be discovered to infer a transhistorical Christian creed. Since nature was created by God and thus divine, the Puritans saw it as another source of inspiration. Even though our perceptual faculties were corrupted, nature was not, and hence, to seek to rediscover the beauty of the world was far from mocking God. These sources of knowledge were especially relevant in the context of the Puritans' constant reexamination of their own self, as they constituted reassuring sources of hope. Even the saints after their sanctification could never be sure of their calling: "This Sanctification is throughout in the whole Man, yet imperfect in this Life; there abide still some Remnants of Corruption in every part, whence ariseth a continual and irreconcileable War, the Flesh lusting against the Spirit, and the Spirit against the Flesh" (*KC*, 85).

The war between the devilish body and the sanctified spirit was also central to Puritan poetic discourse. Anne Bradstreet faces the same problems that William Goodwin had to grapple with, but she examines these issues in a very different historical situation. In contrast to the dreadful circumstances in England, the journey to America offered an awe-inspiring glimpse of God's plan, as it could be interpreted as the path which the saints had to follow. The Puritans conceived their attempt to erect a society of saints in New England as evidence of a righteous life and one's partaking in this social enterprise as a glimpse of one's future salvation. The question, of course, remained, as to how precisely to shape this society. Religion and society were thus inextricably interlinked: in a society that set up as its goal the realization of a pure doctrine, the discussion of and struggle over particular tenets received an imminent political quality. We will address this question in the last part of this essay, but first we will turn to Puritan poetry as a way of confronting one's doubts and of reassuring oneself of one's place in God's plan.

IV. Heaven and Earth

Philip Pain pondered a central Puritan question when he asked, "I believe a Heaven there is; but this / The Question is, *Shall I enjoy that bliss*?" (*KC*, 69). In asking these sorts of questions and in uttering their doubts in poetic form, Puritans found a way to accommodate the uncertainties and contradictions of Calvinism. But Puritan poetry is more than a dry exercise in rhetoric. Rather, Puritans saw poetry as a mode of perceiving the beauty of the world. Robert Daly has shown that, due to the fact that the Puritans considered the world itself as symbolic, and thus as expressive of God's higher laws, poetry was an appropriate didactic means to disclose the beauty of the world.[8] Starting from this premise, the Puritans could imitate the world without recreating it, that is, without elevating the writer to the level of a second, god-like re-creator. If they reproduced nature's glory in the language of art, "their avowed task was simply to say, to utter, the metaphoric truth they saw" (Daly 1978, 80). In poetry, then, the Puritans found less a means of diverting their attention away from godly matters and onto earthly things, but rather a method "to use the figural value of this world to turn their attention and affections to the next" (81). Consequently, poetry constituted a reassuring spiritual orientation for individuals finding themselves in both a theologically and historically insecure situation.

Ichabod Wiswall's poem engages with theological issues in a manner emblematic of Puritan poetry. He makes use of the appearance of a comet to relate the news that "[t]hese flaming Lights which now appear, / Do shew the Judgment-Day draws near" (*KC*, 91). The comet foretells a bleak future as a warning for those people who have been led astray. For Wiswall, the enemy can be easily identified in "the *Pope*, the *Turk*, the *Devil*, / Grand Architects of all that's evil" (*KC*, 92). Behind this rather crude polemic, however, Wiswall's poem attempts to perceive particular everyday events in terms of God's providential scheme. But not every poet took this rather simplistic functional tack to establish the relation between God

---

[8] See Jonathan Edwards's early short work *Beauty of the World* (1725). And yet, as Daly points out, the Puritans already held the belief that it was possible to see the natural world as the image of a more significant world (cf. 1978, 69-70).

and the world. Despite the fact that Puritan poetry remained within a didactic and theological framework and should not be misconceived as based on a modern concept of artistic or aesthetic freedom, Anne Bradstreet and Edward Taylor went beyond the preconceived notions of Wiswall's poetry to develop a poetic form of spiritual meditation. These meditations sought to find solutions for the problematic nature of the relation between the earthly and the heavenly sphere.

As a typical poetic meditation, Anne Bradstreet's poem "The Flesh and the Spirit" lays down the theological premises of Puritanism. Whereas Wiswall's poem was more concerned with a particular attempt to both reject the corrupted versions of faith and affirm the truly faithful saints, Bradstreet's poem is an examination of the speaker's own mind and thus reminiscent of Goodwin's *Automachia*. Bradstreet's dialogue poem depicts the struggle between man's fleshly lust and his divine spirit, which are constantly fighting within and for man's soul. At the beginning of the poem, Flesh questions the poem's meditative dimension and thus its very *raison d'être*: "Sister, quoth Flesh, what / liv'st thou on / Nothing but Meditation? / Doth Contemplation feed thee so / Regardlessly to let earth goe? / Can Speculation satisfy / Notion without Reality?" (*KC*, 70). In fact, Flesh counteracts the notional reality of Spirit: "Earth hath more silver, pearls and gold, / Then eyes can see, or hands can hold. / Affect's thou pleasure? take thy fill, / Earth hath enough of what you will" (*KC*, 71). "To catch at shadowes which are not" (*KC*, 70) does not provide a sufficient reason for Flesh to absolve earthly pleasures.

Immediately, Spirit seeks to disperse the doubt that has been raised by Flesh. Spirit contends that while carnal desires originated with "old Adam," her origin "is from above" (*KC*, 71). And yet, Spirit acknowledges her proneness to fall for the lures of Flesh, for she remembers "[h]ow oft thy slave hast thou me made, / When I believ'd, what thou hast said" (*KC*, 71). But Spirit has discerned a higher truth, a "hidden Manna" (*KC*, 71) which is beyond all earthly aspirations and enables her to "pierce the heavens, and see / What is Invisible to thee" (*KC*, 72), so that she can rightfully claim "my ambition lyes above" (*KC*, 71). Consequently, the dichotomy between flesh and spirit reproduces a separation between earthly and heavenly spheres, so that for the "City where I hope to dwell / There's none on Earth can parallel" (*KC*, 72). Spirit ends her riposte with a vision of the New Jerusalem: "This City pure is not for thee, / For things unclean there shall not be: / If I of Heaven may have my fill, / Take thou the world, and all that will" (*KC*, 72). Yet, Spirit's victory consists in having the better argument, not in eradicating the presence of her counterpart. Flesh, after all, remains a sister of Spirit, that is, the carnal desires of the individual are essential to its constitution. By the same token, Spirit's account of human nature contains only one dimension of man's existence. The "setled heart," which Spirit claims for herself (*KC*, 71), is unattainable for human beings and would thus be considered a self-delusion. Indeed, Spirit herself acknowledges that she is wedded to her bodily sister: "Sisters we are, / ye twins we be, / Yet deadly feud 'twixt thee and me" (KC, 71). The human soul will always be torn between flesh and spirit; the question is which side the individual will opt for. Consequently, "The Flesh and the Spirit" assures readers that "doubt could spur their spiritual growth if they opposed it with the persistence modeled by Bradstreet's spirit" (Hammond 1993, 129). Bradstreet's poem does not lopsidedly favor spiritual aspirations but rather presupposes a situation of fundamental uncertainty created by the inner conflict at work within the self, a conflict which can be directed toward a divine aim by attempting to separate heavenly aspirations from carnal desires.[9]

Another fine specimen of the Puritan's oscillation between self-doubt and reassurance can be found in Bradstreet's poem "Upon the Burning of Our House," which attempts to find a providential meaning in even the most catastrophic events:

> In silent night when rest I took
> For sorrow near I did not look
> I wakened was with thund'ring noise
> And piteous shrieks of dreadful voice.
> That fearful sound of "Fire!" and "Fire!"
> Let no man know is my desire.
> I, starting up, the light did spy,
> And to my God my heart did cry
> To strengthen me in my distress
> And not to leave me succorless.
> Then, coming out, beheld a space
> The flame consume my dwelling place.
> And when I could no longer look,
> I blest His name that gave and took,
> That laid my goods now in the dust.
> Yea, so it was, and so 'twas just.
> It was His own, it was not mine,
> Far be it that I should repine;
> He might of all justly bereft
> But yet sufficient for us left.
> When by the ruins oft I past
> My sorrowing eyes aside did cast,
> And here and there the places spy
> Where oft I sat and long did lie:
> Here stood that trunk, and there that chest,
> There lay that store I counted best.
> My pleasant things in ashes lie,
> And them behold no more shall I.
> Under thy roof no guest shall sit,
> Nor at thy table eat a bit.

---

[9] What Anne Bradstreet rejects is the overemphasis on carnal desires which would lead the individual astray from its search for divine truth. Puritanism was not opposed to the body and the senses per se. In "A Letter to Her Husband, Absent upon Public Employment," she goes so far as to cast the erotic relation between herself and her husband in the terminology of the relation between the individual and God (cf. Daly 1978, 106-8).

> No pleasant talk shall e'er be told,
> Nor things recounted done of old.
> No candle e'er shall shine in thee,
> Nor bridegroom's voice e'er heard shall be.
> In silence ever shall thou lie,
> Adieu, Adieu, all's vanity.
> Then straight I 'gin my heart to chide,
> And did thy wealth on earth abide?
> Didst fix thy hope on mold'ring dust?
> The arm of flesh didst make thy trust?
> Raise up thy thoughts above the sky
> That dunghill mists away may fly.
> Thou hast an house on high erect,
> Framed by that mighty Architect,
> With glory richly furnished,
> Stands permanent though this be fled.
> It's purchased and paid for too
> By Him who hath enough to do.
> A price so vast as is unknown
> Yet by His gift is made thine own;
> There's wealth enough, I need no more,
> Farewell, my pelf, farewell, my store.
> The world no longer let me love,
> My hope and treasure lies above.
>
> (Bradstreet 1967, 292-3)

Being awakened by a "thund'ring noise," the speaker realizes that her house is on fire. God's providence seems strangely suspended, as there is no immediate insight into the plausibility of the event, so that she calls upon God to "strengthen me in my distress / And not to leave me succorless." Yet, this call for the reassuring presence of the divine will is immediately superseded by the renewed turn to the horrible sight of her burning house: "Then, coming out, beheld a space / The flame consume my dwelling place." We can observe this dialectic between the speaker's despair and her acknowledgment of divine providence in the lines that follow upon the sight of her burning house: "And when I could no longer look, / I blest His name that gave and took, / That laid my goods now in the dust. / Yea, so it was, and so 'twas just." The truly despairing sight is mitigated and rendered meaningful within God's providential plan, a shift of perspective that is paradigmatic of the New England Puritans' attempt to cope with what they considered tests sent by God. Events that were experienced as disastrous within the limited frame of one's life could be understood as meaningful within God's providential plan, a figure of thought that worked just as well for everyday events as for the attempt to deal with encounters with 'savages.'

Despite God's overarching providence, however, the speaker's doubt cannot be entirely subdued. While passing the ruins of her house some time after the burning, she recalls the fond images she still has: "Here stood that trunk, and there that chest, / There lay that store I counted best. / My pleasant things in ashes lie, / And them behold no more shall I." Her exclamation "Adieu, Adieu, all's vanity" sounds like a call of desperation rather than an accepted truth. But the speaker recalls that her "hope and treasure lies above," and she thus begins to chide her heart to abandon all earthly wealth for the promises of heaven. Again, this conveys a sense of the vanity of things, and again the speaker's doubt in the face of the calamitous scenario contradicts this apparently clear position. The poem figures, then, not so much as an assertion of immediate insight into God's providential scheme, but acknowledges that doubt plays an essential role not only with respect to one's own chosenness, but also with regard to everyday events.

Despite the doubts displayed in her poetry, or rather precisely because of them, Anne Bradstreet was a firmly orthodox Puritan. Articulating certain doubts about the workings of divine providence becomes less heretical if located in the context of the Puritans' occupation with the self. Doubt was an essential component of the Puritans' striving for salvation. George Goodwin is emblematic of the Puritans' alternation between loving and hating one's self, and their oscillation between a cultivation of faith and the acceptance of the unreachability of God's will. Reassurance was deadly and would lead to the sinful hubris that had been responsible for man's original sin.[10] Thus, the Puritans' writings sought to capture the indecisiveness of their fate. In doing so, the writers found a way of preparing for saving grace, aware of the uncertainty of their destiny.

V. Radical Voices

Having analyzed the institutionalized or orthodox versions of Puritanism, we can now proceed to have a look at more radical voices who conceived of themselves as even 'purer' than the established clergy of New England. Two particularly radical proponents of Puritanism were Anne Hutchinson and Roger Williams, who chal-

---

[10] Edmund S. Morgan comprehensively sums up the pattern of conversion narratives that came to figure as the official version of the Puritans' conversion experience. These narratives were essentially based on the alternation between doubt and reassurance: "The pattern is so plain as to give the experiences the appearance of a stereotype: first comes a feeble and false awakening to God's commands and a pride in keeping them pretty well, but also much backsliding. Disappointments and disasters lead to other fitful hearkenings to the word. Sooner or later true legal fear or conviction enables the individual to see his hopeless and helpless condition and to know that his own righteousness cannot save him, that Christ is his only hope. Thereafter comes the infusion of saving grace, sometimes but not always so precisely felt that the believer can state exactly when and where it came to him. A struggle between faith and doubt ensues, with the candidate careful to indicate that his assurance has never been complete and that his sanctification has been much hampered by his own sinful heart" (1963, 91). In fact, the conversion experience was eventually subject to an 'objective' examination by the church elders, which is why Morgan refers to the regenerate sinner as the "candidate," i.e., the applicant for admission whose conversion experience was now officially tested. This pattern continued to exert a pervasive influence, a fact to which Jonathan Edwards's modified version of the conversion narrative bears witness (cf. doc. 94).

lenged the institutionalized form of Puritanism and thus the organization of social life in New England. They attempted to reform Puritan society from within by stressing particular ideas so as to create what they considered an even godlier society. Puritanism could assume a quite different form if one stressed particular points. Even by assigning a dominant role to one of the stages in the *ordo salutis*, one could fundamentally change religion's consequences. The preparationism evinced by the majority of Puritans all over New England and displayed in Bradstreet's and Taylor's poetry was highly disturbing to Anne Hutchinson. Hutchinson accused the clergy of Arminianism, that is, of over-emphasizing sanctification as a sign of the individual's salvation and thus of advocating human works as a path to God's grace. Hutchinson herself was situated on the opposite side of the Puritan spectrum. As an Antinomian, she believed that grace, the Bible, and the conversion experience sufficed for a truly faithful life. This emphasis on justification rather than sanctification led her to reject the notion that deeds were an indicator of the individual's saintliness. Thus, however, a dramatic consequence arose. If justification were the most important aspect of true conversion, the clergy and the institutionalized church would, after all, become superfluous. The individual would communicate directly with God, not needing any mediation through the ministry. It is hardly surprising that the clergy considered these views heretical. The radical voices pushed several Puritan ideas to an extreme and thus constituted a peril to the dominant creed advocated by the ministers in power.[11]

Hutchinson made no secret of her beliefs. Her statements were even more perilous since at the time of the controversy Puritan society was still taking shape. As Francis J. Bremer observes, the "crablike progress toward consensus that marked the Bay's political evolution can be seen in the religious history of the 1630s as well. Just as the Puritans had no blueprint for civil government, so too their concepts of church order were imprecisely defined" (1995, 62-3). Taking into account that the Pequot War of 1637 added to the unsettling atmosphere in New England, religious radicals proved especially dangerous since they offered alternative ways to channel the social dynamic into a direction running completely counter to the course that orthodox Puritans envisioned for their community.

If they wanted to maintain their dominant role in the shaping of a still unstable Christian commonwealth, the ministers needed to dissolve the Antinomian threat. According to John Winthrop, Hutchinson observed that in New England there "*is a great stirre about graces and looking to hearts, but give mee Christ, I seeke not for graces, but for Christ, I seeke not for promises, but for Christ, I seeke not for sanctification, but for Christ, tell not mee of meditation and duties, but tell mee of Christ*" (Winthrop 1644, 19; original emphasis). Hutchinson emphasized the pri-

---

[11] As Philip Gura (1984) has demonstrated, Puritan radicalism figured as a dangerous alternative to institutionalized versions of Puritanism so that these dominant Puritan ideologies felt obliged to react to the dissidents. For a history of radical Protestants during the English Revolution, see Hill (1991).

macy of man's direct access to Christ and the relative unimportance of deeds and institutionalized religion. Thomas Shepard's "The Autobiography" testifies to the threat posed by these radical voices:

> No sooner were we thus set down & entred into church fellowship; but the Lord exercised us & the whole cuntry with the opinions of Familists; begun by Mistress Hutchinson raysed up to a great height by Mr. Vane too suddenly chosen governour, & mayntayned too obscurely by Mr. Cotton. & propagated too boldly by the members of Boston & some in other churches; by meanes of which division by these opinions, the ancient & received truth came to be darkened gods name to be blasphemed, the churches glory diminished, many godly greeved many wretches hardned deceiving & being deceived, growing woorse and worse. (1932, 385)

Shepard confesses that he was not immune to these radical ideas and admits that "I account it no small mercy to my selfe that the Lord kept me from that contagion, & gave me any hart or light to see thorow those devises of mens heads; altho I found it a most uncomfortable time to live in contention" (1932, 386). Nevertheless, "the Lord was graciously pleased by giving witnesse agaynst them to keepe this poor church spotles & cleare from them" (386) and finally "delivered the c[o]untry from war with Indians & Familists (who arose & fell together)" (*KC*, 76).[12]

In this climate, a meeting was called. Assembling at Newtown on 30 August 1637, a synod decided that calling the clergy into question should be prohibited – Hutchinson even doubted the ministers' electedness – and that private meetings held by persons such as Hutchinson should be discouraged. Two months later, Hutchinson was banished from Boston. Despite a sophisticated defense strategy, Hutchinson admitted that "the Lord brought to mee by immediate revelation" directions for her life (in Winthrop 1644, 38), a claim that constituted a profound heresy from the authority's perspective. But Hutchinson did not stop there. She went so far as to proclaim that God had told her that she would be delivered and that, because of this, earthly powers held no sway over her. Drawing a parallel between her own situation and that of the prophet Daniel, she states:

> And see this scripture fulfilled this day in mine eyes, therefore take heed what yee goe about to doe unto me, for you have no power over my body, neither can you doe me any harme, for I am in the hands of the eternall Jehovah my Saviour, I am at his appointment, the bounds of my habitation are cast in Heaven, no further doe I esteeme of any mortall man, then creatures in his hand, I feare none but the great Jehovah, which hath foretold me of these things; and I doe verily beleeve that hee will deliver me out of your hands, therefore take heed how you proceed against me; for I know that for this you goe about to doe to me, God will ruine you and your posterity, and this whole State. (Winthrop 1644, 38)

---

[12] Here, the term 'familists' should be understood to refer to any group of radical or dissenting believers deviating from the officially institutionalized form of Puritanism.

Eventually the elders banished her, and Hutchinson and her family moved to Rhode Island. After remaining there for five years, they went on to New York, where Hutchinson was eventually killed by Indians.

Anne Hutchinson's rebellion was highly dangerous for the ministers in a twofold respect. Not only was she simply taking one aspect of Puritan thought to an extreme and was thus able to adopt the posture of a 'true Puritan,' but she also transgressed her role as a Puritan woman. Bremer is right in stressing that the ensuing struggle between the authorities and Hutchinson "was not one over the principle of religious liberty as often represented, for Anne Hutchinson was every bit as intolerant as her enemies. The struggle was over which of two competing views would be crowned and enforced as New England orthodoxy" (1995, 67). Hutchinson's very different version of Puritanism, however, would have had a dramatic impact on the structure and role of the church, as the clergy would have been deprived of any legitimation, since the individual needed to merely look inside to find his salvation instead of relying on instruction and working for a theocratic commonwealth. The self would thus have been restored beyond all limitations imposed on it by original sin.

The other radical voice which challenged the New England orthodoxy at this time was that of Roger Williams. Williams had received a classical education at Cambridge University and his career was generally far from unorthodox. In fact, in Boston he was offered a position as a teacher, that is, as the second minister at a church, who was responsible less for preaching about "the Christian life and how to lead it" than for "the exposition of doctrines" (Bremer 1995, 109). Williams refused the position on the grounds of his strong separatist sympathies. Boston was not willing to renounce the Church of England, and hence Williams rejected the offer, settling for Plymouth, the harbor of separatists. Subsequently, Williams left for Salem and took up lay preaching. There, he was an unofficial assistant to Reverend Samuel Skelton, with whom he severely criticized New England's divines. By far his most acute critique, however, was leveled at the king's right to Massachusetts' land. For Williams, it was evident that the king had no right whatsoever to distribute land to the Puritans, for the land belonged to the Native Americans. Williams, who entertained relations with Native Americans, set forth his view in a treatise. He wanted to present his tract to the king, an attempt which was barred by the General Court's censure.

After Skelton's death, Williams followed him in the pulpit in 1634. Provided with an occasion to air his views, Williams attempted to alter ecclesiastical structures. He came to be known as the first and most radical champion of the separation between church and state, as expressed in *The Bloudy Tenent* (1644), a response to a letter John Cotton had published:[13]

---

[13] In fact, this exchange took place over a longer time-span. After Williams had answered Cotton's letter, Cotton responded to Williams's treatise in *The Bloudy Tenent, Washed, and Made White in the Bloud of the Lamb* (1647), which, in turn, provoked another response from Williams some years later in *The Bloudy Tenent Yet More Bloudy* (1652).

> Therefore, [...] there is a *Civill sword*, called the Sword of *Civill justice*; which being of a *materiall civill nature*, for the *defence* of *Persons*, *Estates*, *Families*, *Liberties* of a *City* or *Civill State*, and the *suppressing* of *uncivill* or injurious persons or actions by such civill punishment, It cannot according to its utmost reach and capacitie (now under *Christ*, when all *Nations* are meerly *civill*, without any such typicall holy respect upon them, as was upon *Israel* a *Nationall Church*) I say, cannot extend to *spirituall* and *Soul-causes*, Spirituall and Soule *punishment*, which belongs to that *spirituall sword* with two edges, the *soule-piercing* (in *soule-saving* or *soule-killing*) the Word of God. (Williams 1963, 160)

In the tradition of Luther, Williams asserts the distinction between two realms: "[T]he *government* of the *civill Magistrate* extendeth no further then over the *bodies* and *goods* of their *subjects*, not over their *soules*, and therefore they may not undertake to give *Lawes* unto the *soules* and *consciences* of men" (1963, 202). The 'sword' of the earthly realm must not extend beyond its sphere of influence, as it would be a hubristic effort to interfere with God's decisions: Church and state must remain distinct spheres.

The separation of the earthly and heavenly realm also informs Williams's concept of typology. The New England Puritans tended to see Old Testament types as foreshadowing current events. In his *The Figures or Types of the Old Testament* (1667-1668), Samuel Mather still uses the original, 'conservative' form of typology, which establishes an analogy between the Old and New Testament: "As the Deliverance out of *Egypt* and *Babylon*, if we read the History thereof in the Old Testament, and compare it with the Prophesies in the New Testament, concerning the Churches Deliverance from Antichristian Bondage, we shall clearly see, that it was a Type thereof" (*KC*, 89). The extended form of typology, then, placed the Israelites' errand in secular history, and saw the Puritans' Errand into the Wilderness as the antitype fulfilling this Old Testament type. It was precisely this connection which Williams deemed ungodly: For Williams, any typological reference to secular history was incommensurate with a strict exegesis of the Bible. This essentially conservative position necessarily entailed the rejection of the colony as the place where a New Jerusalem could be established. Williams poses the question "whether the Kings of Israel and Judah were not types of Civill Magistrates," only to decidedly reject this idea (1963, 353). For him, it is evident that

> those former *types* of the *Land*, of the *People*, of their *Worships*, were *types* and *figures* of a *spirituall Land*, *spirituall People*, and *spirituall Worship* under *Christ*. Therefore consequently, their *Saviours*, *Redeemers*, *Deliverers*, *Judges*, *Kings*, must also have their *spirituall Antitypes*, and so consequently not *civill*, but *spirituall Governours* and *Rulers*; lest the very *essential nature* of *Types*, *Figures* and Shadowes be overthrowne. (1963, 353)

In fact, New England cannot be the place where a true theocracy is to be set up, because only the "*spirituall Land*" is pristine and pure, or, vice versa, because "all the *Nations* of the *Earth* [are] alike uncleane, untill it pleaseth the *Father* of *mer-*

cies to call some out to the *Knowledge* and *Grace* of his Sonne, making them to see their *filthinesse* and strangenesse from the *Commonweale* of *Israel*, and to wash in the bloud of the Lambe of *God*" (Williams 1963, 327).

Williams was again far stricter than the clergy on the issue of unregenerate access to worship, since he deemed that true believers must not mingle with those who are not yet saved. In fact, Williams's radicalism consisted of his attempt to cling as closely as possible to God's word: He held radical beliefs precisely because he had a conservative understanding of Puritan doctrine. However, his religious conservatism led to political outlooks which were perilous to traditional hierarchies. Williams's demand for the restriction of the state's rights was grounded in the elevation of the individual. The communication between God and the self sufficed to ensure access to the divine and no additional regulation or guidance was needed. God's laws must not be corrupted by state interference, and thus, in turn, Williams repudiated any state attempt to meddle with church affairs. Naturally, Williams's doctrines were too challenging for the dominant Puritans, so the Massachusetts General Court banished him in 1635 and demanded that he return to England. Williams, however, fled to Rhode Island, where he founded Providence, which came to be known as a hotbed of Puritan radicalism. By 1640, Rhode Island "already had become what a later observer called the 'Sinke into which all the rest of the Colonyes empty their Heretickes'" (in Gura 1984, 59). In Providence, Williams lived with Native Americans, whose language he learned, and whose culture he sought to understand adequately. Williams was one of the first individuals who saw more in Native Americans than just savages. Even after his banishment, Williams exerted influence on the population, since for many the question of the church's authority that he had raised had not been adequately settled.[14]

What these alternative versions of Puritanism show is that other varieties existed alongside the official, institutionalized view, varieties to which those in power needed to react. The ministry "managed to balance opposing aspirations and ideals to sustain a society that was from the start fragmenting from internal affairs" (Elliott 1994, 183), but those in power were aware of the fact that many

---

[14] Another radical figure usually not included in standard histories is Samuel Gorton. Gorton arrived in New England in 1636/37, when the controversy surrounding Anne Hutchinson had reached its climax. After a brief stay in Boston, he went to Plymouth, where "the elders tried Gorton for religious and civil insubordination" (Gura 1984, 280), on account of his lay preaching which advocated the beauty of the world without paying sufficient attention to the divine sphere. Harboring strong sympathies for the Antinomians, Gorton roamed New England and wound up in Providence where he succeeded in annoying even Roger Williams. Eventually Gorton was sentenced to hard labor by the General Court, a sentence which, however, was soon overturned to allow Gorton to return to England, where he recorded his radical tenets. Gorton's view that "if the most honourable in the Church, receive his dignity in Christ the least in the house has the same honour, for whether male or female yee, are all one in him" (Gorton 1647, 2) was hardly reconcilable with the theocracy proposed by John Winthrop in his sermon "A Modell of Christian Charity."

of their subjects were prone to adopt more radical beliefs. Janice Knight (1994) has suggested that these Puritan voices might even have been part of the institutional version of faith. For Knight, John Cotton advanced a version of Puritanism that was opposed to John Winthrop's, one of the reasons why Cotton and his followers were eventually ousted from public offices. But New England was not only under pressure from radical ideas. Foster notes "the centrality of England to the development of Puritan America" when discussing New England Puritanism (1991, 189). Thus, besides having to establish and maintain the colony's social structures, New England Puritans constantly needed to respond to theological and political developments in England.

Initially, the lack of institutions in the New World allowed for the rapid growth and realization of a Puritan theocracy. Where the Puritans had found that in their mother country they could not realize several of their beliefs, New England opened up new possibilities. Faced with the opportunity of building a new society from scratch, New England Puritans struggled over what its founding principles would be. In this light, the ideas that can be traced in the documents of early New Englanders are especially relevant. In the New World, their ideas could thrive. The controversies that simmered under the surface of Puritan orthodoxy, however, testify to alternative versions of Puritanism that soon emerged. In due time, then, the emergent sociopolitical structures became challenged by inner-colonial voices of dissent and increasingly involved in imperial politics, so that the question arose how these structures should be shaped in the light of the developing challenges. If they wanted to figure as a light to the world, the colonial Puritans needed to deliver proof of their cultural and social development. The dominant form of Puritanism, as embodied in Cotton Mather's reproduction of the Westminster Confession, had found a fruitful ground for its prospering in the New World, and yet it constantly had to defend itself against various challenges from inside and outside the colony. Thus, the dogmatic and political questions that have been discussed above must not be misconstrued as mere exercises in theology, but rather as a pious response to changing social and political contexts both within and outside of New England.

Over time, the demands of an emerging market formed additional challenges to New England Puritanism, as they threatened to render commerce more important than spiritual self-examination and the observations of God's commandments. From the 1650s on, the growing mercantile class developed interests in international trade which were largely non-religious in their motivation. In 1663, John Higginson responded to this tendency by cautioning that it "is never to be forgotten, that *New-England is originally a plantation of Religion, not a plantation of Trade*. Let Merchants and such as are increasing *Cent per Cent* remember this, Let others that have come over since at several times understand this, that worldly gain was not the end and designe of the people of *New-England*, but *Religion*" (*KC*, 137). Also, the question of church membership displayed the inner ruptures of the New England churches. A year earlier, the so-called Half-Way Covenant had been adopted and in many ways signaled the waning authority of New England Puritanism. Reacting to dwindling church membership, the Boston Synod decided that even children of unregenerate parents could become members of the church, though they could not enjoy all the privileges of full membership. In adopting the Half-Way Covenant, the New England theocracy began to move away from a stricter orthodox conception of the church to secure its own survival.

Once exposed to the pressure of an increasingly complex economic and social situation at home and fundamental sociopolitical changes abroad – the Glorious Revolution in England, for instance, forced the colonists into conflict with the French Canadians – Puritanism had to confront and adapt to the changed realities of imperial politics. When in the wake of the Enlightenment, Jonathan Edwards tried to retain crucial Calvinist tenets, he had to find different ways of legitimizing his endeavor, for the Enlightenment had endowed the subject with the ability to understand God's ways through the scientific examination of nature. But even as Puritanism became involved in and eventually superseded by more secular economic and social matters, its legacy provided a touchstone for subsequent generations of New England intellectuals.

Instructional Strategies and Classroom Issues

I. Key Concepts and Major Themes

1. Salvation (docs. 38–41, 43)
   Although God had opened a path to salvation through establishing a covenant of grace, Puritans could never know for certain whether they belonged to the elect. Philip Pain's lines capture the essential predicament that results from the believer's inability to achieve certainty about his status: "Lord, I believe a Heaven there is; but this / The Question is, *Shall I enjoy that bliss?*" (*KC*, 69). While the believer was barred from knowing his fate, he nevertheless could put the uncertainty of his situation to productive use by constantly examining whether his own life conformed to God's commandments, thus preparing for potential redemption.

2. Typology (docs. 46, 64)
   Typology is a hermeneutical method which reads 'types' in the Old Testament as foreshadowing the coming of Christ in the New Testament (the 'antitype'). New England Puritans, however, extended typology to include historical events and figures, which allowed them to see their situation as the fulfillment of biblical prophecies (cf. doc. 64). The Puritans' exodus, for instance, was read as the antitype of the biblical exodus of the people of Israel, just as the colony was sometimes conceived to be the counterpart of the biblical New Jerusalem.

3. Everyday Experience and Predestination (docs. 47-8, 50)
   Puritans believed that God had ordained the course of the world. This included not just the broader lines of history, but also significant events in everyday life, as displayed in Anne Bradstreet's poem on the occasion of the burning of her house. Natural phenomena such as comets were interpreted as God's warnings that sought to point to particular shortcomings of his chosen people.

4. Transatlantic Puritanism (docs. 45, 62)
   The Puritans must be understood in their relation to the Old World. While they left the Old World to found a new Christian society, New England Puritans remained intimately related to the developments of European Protestantism, as Cotton Mather's reproduction of the Westminster Confession shows (doc. 45). Generally, the Congregationalists at Massachusetts Bay, who came to be the dominant strain of Puritanism in New England, did not separate their endeavor from the rest of the world, but rather hoped to establish an exemplary congregation that would function as a beacon to the world. The New England Puritans' religious and political orientation, then, was profoundly universalistic, a fact that is sometimes forgotten in distorted interpretations of their endeavor to found "a City upon a Hill" (*KC*, 20; Matt. 5.14).

II. Comparison – Contrasts – Connections

Example: Docs. 38, 94, 193, 198-200

The Puritan conception of the self had a serious impact on later generations of theologians and philosophers. A valid starting point to trace this influence would be Jonathan Edwards, who attempted to maintain some of the key tenets of Calvinism in the eighteenth century. In the wake of Enlightenment philosophy, Edwards had to react to an increasing secularization and disenchantment of the world so that his theology was developed under conditions very different from those that the New England Puritans had to face. Nevertheless, in Edwards's conversion narrative (doc. 94), we find many of the key features of Puritan self-examination that we have previously encountered in George Goodwin's *Automachia*, including the "inward Struggles and Conflicts, and Self-reflections" (*KC*, 218), which shall lead him to salvation. But as opposed to the fundamental impossibility in Puritanism to find out whether or not one is part of the elect, for Edwards the individual, even though still subjected to the authority of the church, can achieve certainty about his fate. Upon several struggles with himself, Edwards can assert that after his conversion experience he is able to see the divine glory of nature. He relates that while he "looked up on the Sky and Clouds; there came into my Mind, a sweet Sense of the glorious Majesty and Grace of GOD, that I know not how to express" (*KC*, 219). His senses have been fully restored from their corruption, and through his 'sense of the heart' he is able to perceive the world in its beauty.

An important development of Edwards's case for the subject's 'sense of the heart' can be found in Unitarian and Transcendentalist texts of the nineteenth century. William Ellery Channing, a Unitarian minister, saw humanity's faculties in a much more positive light than the Puritans. Rejecting any notion of innate depravity, Channing asserted that "man has a kindred nature with God, and may bear most important and ennobling relations to him" (*KC*, 431). Indeed, Channing inferred the quite extreme position that "We see God around us, because he dwells within us" (*KC*, 432). Deeply influenced by Enlightenment philosophy, Channing proclaimed man's ability to educate himself so as to perfect his human nature and thus he disposed of any remnants of the theorem of original sin. The Transcendentalists Ralph Waldo Emerson and Henry David Thoreau provide the *locus classicus* for a romanticized version of the self (docs. 198-200). Where Channing is still limited by institutional restrictions, Emerson and Thoreau promote a radicalized version of the individual which derives the authority of its thoughts from its own divinity. Here, the self has cast off all restrictions that Puritanism saw imposed upon it and, instead of being a corrupted source of false perception, comes to figure as the resource of truth.

III. Reading and Discussion Questions

1. Explain the main tenets of Puritanism as stated in Cotton Mather's *Magnalia* (doc. 45). What role does original sin play in covenant theory? Do the five tenets of Puritanism ('TULIP') form a coherent creed or can you find contradictions that arise from these tenets?

2. Read George Goodwin's *Automachia* (doc. 38), Philip Pain's *Daily Meditations* (doc. 39), Edward Taylor's "Meditation 26" (doc. 41), and Anne Bradstreet's "To My Dear Children" (doc. 43), and discuss their presentation of the Puritan self. How would you describe the speakers' development? Do the poems emphasize different aspects of Puritanism?

3. Discuss the Puritans' perception of particular events within a providential scheme (docs. 47-50). Explain how these documents propose an understanding of God's providence both similar to and different from the one we found in Anne Bradstreet's "Upon the Burning of Our House."

4. Read Thomas Shepard's "The Autobiography" (doc. 42) as a short version of the settlers' exodus from the Old into the New World. What reasons does Shepard give for leaving England? How does he conceive of the relation between private and public life?

IV. Resources

a. Recommended Reading

Sacvan Bercovitch. *The Puritan Origins of the American Self*. New Haven: Yale University Press, 1975. Bercovitch's seminal – and at times quite demanding – study of the Puritans' conception of the self analyzes the role that this understanding played in the emergence of the modern American self. Bercovitch traces this notion well into the nineteenth century and locates, for instance, Ralph Waldo Emerson and Nathaniel Hawthorne in this tradition.

Francis J. Bremer. *The Puritan Experiment: New England Society from Bradford to Edwards*. Rev. ed. Hanover: University of New England Press, 1995. Bremer provides a very accessible standard history of the Puritan experiment. The book also contains a very valuable chapter on the most important tenets of Puritanism (ch. 2), as well as a helpful chronology of events.

Charles L. Cohen. "Puritanism." *Encyclopedia of the North American Colonies*. Vol. 3. Ed. Jacob Ernest Cooke. New York: Scribner, 1993, 577-594. The single best introduction to New England Puritanism, which should be the starting point for an engagement with Puritanism for students and teachers alike. Cohen addresses all relevant theological notions and briefly delineates the major critical approaches as he goes along. Furthermore, Cohen points out the necessity of understanding New England Puritanism in its transatlantic context. Jon Butler's article on "Protestant Pluralism" may be consulted for supplementary information.

Robert Daly. *God's Altar: The World and the Flesh in Puritan Poetry*. Berkeley: University of California Press, 1978. Daly's book reevaluates Puritan poetry and advances the claim that Puritans were far from condemning earthly beauty as inferior. On the contrary, in their poetry they constantly had to remind themselves that despite its beauty the Book of Nature did not suffice to decipher God's glory.

Emory Elliott. "New England Puritan Literature." *The Cambridge History of American Literature*. Vol. 1: *1590-1820*. Ed. Sacvan Bercovitch. Cambridge: Cambridge University Press, 1994, 169-306. Elliott's highly readable introduction is concerned not only with New England Puritan literature, but also with the theological and social context of Puritan writers. Elliott's interpretation ranges from Puritan poetry through autobiography to historiography and thus constitutes the best overview of the main concepts in Puritan thought.

Philip F. Gura. *A Glimpse of Sion's Glory: Puritan Radicalism in New England, 1620-1660*. Middletown: Wesleyan University Press, 1984. In his revisionist study of Puritanism, Gura points to the fact that Puritan radicalism was not a mere fringe phenomenon. Radicals such as Anne Hutchinson and Roger Williams were representative of a larger phenomenon which appealed to a broad audience and repeatedly forced the predominant clergy to adapt their ideology to these forces.

Janice Knight. *Orthodoxies in Massachusetts: Rereading American Puritanism*. Cambridge: Harvard University Press, 1994. In her important contribution to revisionist studies of Puritanism, Knight argues that to speak of one 'orthodoxy' that absorbed and subsumed all dissident voices is misleading, as in fact more radical Puritan voices were located in the middle of orthodoxy itself. Her prime example is the important and still underrepresented John Cotton. Knight's study forms a crucial counterpoise to Miller and Bercovitch who – albeit from different angles – argue for the predominance of a more or less coherent Puritan orthodoxy.

Perry Miller. *Orthodoxy in Massachusetts, 1630-1650*. 1933. Repr., with a new preface, Boston: Beacon, 1959; *The New England Mind: The Seventeenth Century*. New York: Macmillan, 1939; *The New England Mind: From Colony to Province*. Cambridge: Harvard University Press, 1953. Miller's classical studies are concerned with the intellectual roots of New England Puritanism, while at the same time analyzing their political concepts. Miller asserts that the idea of Puritanism had to adapt to the changing circumstances of the New World. While this approach has been partially superseded by more recent studies, Miller's works still provide a good overview of the intellectual and political foundations of New England Puritanism.

b. Works Cited and Reading Suggestions

Bercovitch, Sacvan, ed. (1972). *Typology and Early American Literature*. Amherst: University of Massachusetts Press.
- (1975). *The Puritan Origins of the American Self*. New Haven: Yale University Press.
- (1978). *The American Jeremiad*. Madison: University of Wisconsin Press.
Bonomi, Patricia U. (1986). *Under the Cope of Heaven: Religion, Society, and Politics in Colonial America*. New York: Oxford University Press.
Bozeman, Theodore Dwight (1988). *To Live Ancient Lives: The Primitivist Dimension in Puritanism*. Chapel Hill: University of North Carolina Press.
Bradstreet, Anne (1967). *The Works of Anne Bradstreet*. Ed. Jeannine Hensley. Cambridge: Harvard University Press.
Bremer, Francis J. (1995). *The Puritan Experiment: New England Society from Bradford to Edwards*. Rev. ed. Hanover: University of New England Press.
Brumm, Ursula (1970). *American Thought and Religious Typology*. Trans. John Hooglund. New Bunswick: Rutgers University Press.
Butler, Jon (1990). *Awash in a Sea of Faith: Christianizing the American People*. Cambridge: Harvard University Press.
- (1993). "Protestant Pluralism." *Encyclopedia of the North American Colonies*. Vol. 3. Ed. Jacob Ernest Cooke. New York: Scribner, 609-631.

Caldwell, Patricia (1983). *The Puritan Conversion Narrative*: *The Beginnings of American Express*. Cambridge: Cambridge University Press.
Calvin, John (1960). *Institutes of the Christian Religion*. Ed. John T. McNeill. Trans. Ford Lewis Battles. 2 vols. Philadelphia: Westminster Press.
Cohen, Charles Lloyd (1986). *God's Caress*: *The Psychology of Puritan Religious Experience*. New York: Oxford University Press.
– (1993). "Puritanism." *Encyclopedia of the North American Colonies*. Vol. 3. Ed. Jacob Ernest Cooke. New York: Scribner, 577-594.
Cressy, David (1987). *Coming Over*: *Migration and Communication between England and New England in the Seventeenth Century*. Cambridge: Cambridge University Press.
Daly, Robert (1978). *God's Altar*: *The World and the Flesh in Puritan Poetry*. Berkeley: University of California Press.
Delbanco, Andrew (1989). *The Puritan Ordeal*. Cambridge: Harvard University Press.
Elliott, Emory (1975). *Power and Pulpit in Puritan New England*. Princeton: Princeton University Press.
– (1979). *Puritan Influences in American Literature*. Urbana: University of Illinois Press.
Foster, Stephen (1971). *Their Solitary Way*: *The Puritan Social Ethic in the First Century of Settlement in New England*. New Haven: Yale University Press.
– (1991). *The Long Argument*: *English Puritanism and the Shaping of New England Culture, 1570-1700*. Chapel Hill: University of North Carolina Press.
Gildrie, Richard P. (1975). *Salem, Massachusetts, 1626-1683*: *A Covenant Community*. Charlottesville: University Press of Virginia.
Gilmore, Michael T. (1980). *Early American Literature*: *A Collection of Critical Essays*. Englewood Cliffs: Prentice Hall.
Gorton, Samuel (1647). *An Incorruptible Key Composed of the CX. Psalme, wherewith You May Open the Rest of the Holy Scriptures*. London: n. p.
Gura, Philip F. (1984). *A Glimpse of Sion's Glory*: *Puritan Radicalism in New England, 1620-1660*. Middletown: Wesleyan University Press.
Hall, David D. (1989). *Worlds of Wonder, Days of Judgment*: *Popular Religious Belief in Early New England*. New York: Knopf.
–, ed. (1990). *The Antinomian Controversy, 1636-1638*: *A Documentary History*. 2nd ed. Durham: Duke University Press.
Hambrock-Stowe, Charles (1982). *The Practice of Piety*: *Puritan Devotional Disciplines in Seventeenth-Century New England*. Chapel Hill: University of North Carolina Press.
Hammond, Jeffrey (1993). *Sinful Self, Saintly Self*: *The Puritan Experience of Poetry*. Athens: University of Georgia Press.
Hill, Christopher (1991). *The World Turned Upside Down*: *Radical Ideas During the English Revolution*. 1972. London: Penguin.
– (2002). *The Century of Revolution, 1603-1714*. 1961. London: Routledge.

Holstun, James (1987). *A Rational Millennium: Puritan Utopias of Seventeenth-Century England and America*. New York: Oxford University Press.
Innes, Stephen (1995). *Creating the Commonwealth: The Economic Culture of Puritan New England*. New York: Norton.
Jehlen, Myra (1994). "The Literature of Colonization." *The Cambridge History of American Literature*. Vol. 1: *1590-1820*. Ed. Sacvan Bercovitch. Cambridge: Cambridge University Press, 11-168.
Kendall, R. T. (1979). *Calvin and English Calvinism to 1649*. New York: Oxford University Press.
Knight, Janice (1994). *Orthodoxies in Massachusetts: Rereading American Puritanism*. Cambridge: Harvard University Press.
Lang, Amy Schrager (1987). *Prophetic Woman: Anne Hutchinson and the Problem of Dissent in the Literature of New England*. Berkeley: University of California Press.
Leverenz, David (1980). *The Language of Puritan Feeling: An Exploration in Literature, Psychology, and Social History*. New Brunswick: Rutgers University Press.
Lockridge, Kenneth A. (1985). *A New England Town: The First Hundred Years, Dedham, Massachusetts, 1636-1736*. Exp. ed. New York: Norton.
Lowance, Mason I. (1980). *The Language of Canaan: Metaphor and Symbol in New England from the Puritans to the Transcendentalists*. Cambridge: Harvard University Press.
Mencken, H. L. (1917). "Puritanism as a Literary Force." *A Book of Prefaces*. New York: Knopf, 197-283.
Meserole, Harrison T., ed. (1968). *Seventeenth-Century American Poetry*. New York: New York University Press.
Middlekauff, Robert (1999). *The Mathers: Three Generations of Puritan Intellectuals, 1596-1728*. 1971. Berkeley: University of California Press.
Miller, Perry (1956). *Errand into the Wilderness*. Cambridge: Harvard University Press.
Morgan, Edmund S. (1958). *The Puritan Dilemma: The Story of John Winthrop*. Boston: Little Brown.
– (1963). *Visible Saints: The History of a Puritan Idea*. Ithaca: Cornell University Press.
– (1966). *The Puritan Family: Religion and Domestic Relations in Seventeenth-Century New England*. Rev. ed. New York: Harper and Row.
Morison, Samuel Eliot (1956). *The Intellectual Life of Colonial New England*. 2nd ed. New York: New York University Press.
Noll, Mark A. (2002). *America's God: From Jonathan Edwards to Abraham Lincoln*. Oxford: Oxford University Press.
Pope, Robert G. (1969). *The Half-Way Covenant: Church Membership in Puritan New England*. Princeton: Princeton University Press.
Porterfield, Amanda (1992). *Female Piety in Puritan New England: The Emergence of Religious Humanism*. New York: Oxford University Press.

Robinson, David M. (1994). "The Cultural Dynamics of American Puritanism." *American Literary History* 6.4, 738-755.

Scheick, William J. (1992). *Design in Puritan American Literature*. Lexington: University Press of Kentucky.

Schweitzer, Ivy (1991). *The Work of Self-Representation*: *Lyric Poetry in Colonial New England*. Chapel Hill: University of North Carolina Press.

Shepard, Thomas (1932). "The Autobiography of Thomas Shepard." *Publications of the Colonial Society of Massachusetts*. Vol. 27: *Transactions 1927-1930*. Boston: The Colonial Society of Massachusetts, 352-400.

Smolinski, Reiner (1990). "Israel Redivivus: The Eschatological Limits of Puritan Typology in New England." *New England Quarterly* 63.3, 357-395.

Stout, Harry S. (1986). *The New England Soul*: *Preaching and Religious Culture in Colonial New England*. New York: Oxford University Press.

Vaughan, Alden T., and Francis J. Bremer, eds. (1979). *Puritan New England*: *Essays on Religion, Society, and Culture*. New York: St. Martin's.

Walzer, Michael (1965). *The Revolutions of the Saints*: *A Study in the Origins of Radical Politics*. Cambridge: Harvard University Press.

White, Peter, ed. (1985). *Puritan Poets and Poetics*: *Seventeenth-Century American Poetry in Theory and Practice*. University Park: Pennsylvania State University Press.

Williams, Roger (1963). *The Complete Writings of Roger Williams*. Vol. 3: *The Bloudy Tenent of Persecution*. 1644. Ed. Samuel L. Caldwell. New York: Russell and Russell.

Winthrop, John (1644). *A Short Story of the Rise, Reign, and Ruine, of the Antinomians, Familists & Libertines that Infected the Churches of New England*. London: Ralph Smith.

– (1931). "A Modell of Christian Charity." *Winthrop Papers*. Vol. 2: *1623-1630*. Boston: Massachusetts Historical Society, 282-295.

Zakai, Avihu (1992). *Exile and Kingdom*: *History and Apocalypse in the Puritan Migration in America*. Cambridge: Cambridge University Press.

Ziff, Larzer (1973). *Puritanism in America*: *New Culture in a New World*. New York: Viking.

FRANK OBENLAND

Providential Thought in the Puritan Historiography of New England

> Any history written on Christian principles will be of necessity universal, providential, apocalyptic, and periodized.
> R. G. Collingwood (1961, 49)

I. Themes and Arguments

Divine providence plays a prominent role in early American literature and in the seventeenth-century Puritan conceptualization of history. Defined as a deity's active intervention in human affairs, providence established a comprehensive structure of explanation that anchored the meaning of historical events in the divine order of the universe. Providential thought and its tendency to subsume any aspect of human experience under its explanatory framework appeared to most Puritan writers as an infallible instrument in explaining the meaning of human history in general and American colonial history in particular. Puritan historians found providential theories attractive as they allowed them to invest human affairs with a divine presence. Historical events, like the Reformation in Europe, the Puritan migration to the New World, or violent conflicts with Native Americans, evinced a divine plan for a universal history, while natural phenomena such as storms and earthquakes were seen as "illustrious providences" or direct interventions of a supernatural power in earthly affairs. These "special" or "illustrious" providences were either interpreted as the deity's merciful intervention on behalf of the elect, an assurance of God's maintenance of the cosmic order, portents of future calamities, or divine judgments for past sinful behavior. In this sense, providentialism denotes the belief in a theocentric universe and a cosmic plan, which could be understood through the observation of natural signs.

Providentialism thus invests human history with an immediate divine presence and combines a deterministic theory of history with the possibility of divine intervention in current affairs. Although providentialism was theologically based on biblical passages that emphasize God's omnipotence and loving care for his elect, providential thought is primarily concerned with detecting alternative, extra-biblical sources for discerning God's will in human history. Moreover, it insists on the existence of extra-biblical forms of divine revelation available in the recordings of natural phenomena and historical events that occurred in New England. Not primarily relying on biblical sources or the correlation of worldly and salvational history, popular notions of providentialism presuppose the possibility of direct revelations and immediate communication between the worldly and the heavenly spheres. Yet, despite the popularity of providential ideas in Puritan folk religion, providentialism also raised intricate theological problems for Puritan ministers. How can the deterministic outlook of a providential world view be reconciled with the free will of human beings? How can the providential character and supernatural causation of particular events be securely established? And how can the existence of evil be explained in the face of an overruling divine providence? Despite these quandaries, providentialism remained a popular belief that also inflected Puritan historical narratives. Early modern providential thought is central to the "worlds of wonders" inhabited by seventeenth-century Puritans (Hall 1989).

This chapter proposes to read Puritan historical narratives within the larger framework of a providential world view. Whereas typological readings of history strive to locate human history within God's plan for the ultimate redemption of mankind, as outlined in the Scriptures, providential thought relates the universe to the continual presence of a divine will in human history.[1] Providential beliefs emphasize a divine presence and agency within history, allowing Puritan writers to apply the Christian periodization of creation, fall, and restoration to their experience of historical time. Despite its paradoxical forms and often circular logic, providential thought provides the framework for central themes in Puritan historical thought, such as covenant theology or the jeremiad, which are all based on the premise of an effective divine presence in the observable world.

This essay will first trace the theological roots of providentialism in the theological debates about the nature of God and the doctrine of divine providence, and illustrate the transformations and adaptations of these providential ideas in early modern literary genres. It will then discuss the influence of these more popular conceptualizations of providential thought on the earlier lay historians of the Puritan colonies, focusing particularly on the historical vision of William Bradford and John Winthrop. The last part will show how later generations of Puritan theologians, most notably Increase and Cotton Mather, embraced "special providences" to defend the authority of Puritan magistrates and the Puritan world view against challenges from within and without.

---

[1] In describing a providential world view that reads historical and natural phenomena as manifestations of a divine will as fundamentally allegorical, I follow Ursula Brumm's proposal to read providentialism as a distinct strategy of symbolization, similar to typology, that is patterned on a specific allegorical hermeneutics of the Scriptures as a source of divine revelation (cf. 1963, 14-6).

II. Providentialism in Seventeenth-Century Puritan Thought and Culture

The growing significance of divine providence and "special providences" in Puritan literature resulted from larger changes in the idea of history and the historical consciousness of early modern Protestantism (cf. Zakai 1987, 300-6).[2] In contrast to a more secular tradition of Renaissance historiography on the continent, the Puritans espoused a theocentric philosophy of history that followed John Calvin in dismissing the humanistic allegorizations of *Fate* and *Fortuna* as pagan personifications of historical changes or personal misfortunes. They denied the general efficacy of chance, fortune, and contingency as explanatory premises for historical narratives. Instead, Puritan historians maintained the possibility of supernatural interventions through "special providences" in history as well as the notion of an overriding purpose of historical events. This had important consequences for their understanding of the relationship between history and the historian. Positing God as the author both of history in general and of individual events, Puritan historians assumed the role of the "Lord's Remembrancers," the devout and exact recorders of God's deeds in history.[3] Since it was incompatible with divine intentions, Puritan ministers diminished the significance of human volition and agency and attributed acts by individuals and prominent historical figures to a divinely ordained plan of history. This represented a significant change from the medieval understanding of history.

In the course of the Reformation in Europe, Protestant historical thought remodeled the traditional Christian philosophy of history codified in Augustine of Hippo's *De civitate Dei* (413–26). Presenting a dualistic philosophy of history that distinguished between the two spheres of the heavenly and profane cities, Augustine attributes the true meaning of human history not to the history of the phenomenal world but to the history of salvation that began with the fall of Adam and that will consummate in the Last Judgment and the renovation of fallen creation at the end of time. Introducing divine providence as the framework of an early modern theocentric philosophy of history, Protestant historiography diminished the differentiation between a hidden divine plan for salvation and secular history by emphasizing the interconnectedness of the worldly and heavenly spheres. Instead of separating profane from redemptive history, Protestants re-

---

[2] For a comprehensive survey of the contours of Protestant historical thought in the early modern period, see Thompson 1942, 520-645.

[3] The epithet about the historians' function "to be the Lords *Remembrancers* or *Recorders*" was coined by Urian Oakes in his election sermon *New-England Pleaded With* (1673): "[I]t is our great duty to be the Lords *Remembrancers* or *Recorders*, Isa. 62.6. that the mercies of the Lord (that hath allured us into this wilderness, spoken comfortably to us and dealt bountifully with us therein) may be faithfully registered in our hearts, and remembered by us. It is a desirable thing, that all the loving kindnesses of God, and his singular favours to this poor and despised outcast might be Chronicled and communicated (in the History of them) to succeeding Ages; that the memory of them may not dy and be extinct with the present generation" (Oakes 1673, 23; cf. Gay 1968, 55).

lied on the notion of a providential deity as the primary agent at the center of the universe (cf. Zakai 1987, 302-3). Puritan historians of the New World not only embraced the traditional genres of ecclesiastical history, as in Cotton Mather's *Magnalia Christi Americana* (cf. docs. 34-5, 70, 73), or turned to the biblical prophecy of the apocalypse, but they relied on a providential world view to invest profane history with meaning by invoking the active presence of God in their own time.

In contrast to lay articulations of providentialism, Puritan ministers framed their theories of divine providence in response to a pre-Reformation heritage of theological doctrines and the doctrinal teachings of continental Protestant reformers, especially the writings of John Calvin.[4] In Calvin's theological comments on divine providence, the notion of God's sovereignty and absolute government over his creation and everything that exists in time and space, also referred to as the doctrine of *gubernatio*, is supplemented by the notion of a supreme deity that continually intervenes in this world and sustains its continued existence:

> God claims, and would have us grant him, omnipotence – not the empty, idle and almost unconscious sort that the Sophists imagine, but a watchful, effective, active sort, engaged in ceaseless activity. (Calvin 1960, 200)[5]

Calvin argues that contrary to philosophical theories God's role as creator surpasses the idea of a divine architect. Only the continual emanation of divine power through the universe preserves the cosmological order. God appears as an "everlasting Creator and Preserver" who "sustains, nourishes, and cares for, everything he has made, even to the last sparrow" (1960, 197-8). While God's benevolence for his creation is exhibited through his "fatherly favor" which he also bestows through his grace upon the world in spiritual terms (cf. Calvin 1960, 198), Calvin also comments on a common theological degradation of different aspects of providence that distinguishes between "universal" or "general" providence, a more particular "special providence," and an intimate connection between God and individual human beings through "most special providences" (cf. Wendel 1968, 154). General or universal providence pertains to God's ordering of the creation as a whole. "Special providences" exceed the stable and divinely ordained "order of nature" (cf. Calvin 1960, 218-9). Special providences thus describe God's concern for every individual, whether good or evil. God's "most special providence" and care, however, is primarily directed toward his church

---

[4] Drawing from a philosophical-theological line of thought extending from Augustine (354-430) to the medieval philosophers Boëthius (c. 480-524) and Thomas Aquinas (1225-1274), Puritan divines elaborated on the early medieval and scholastic doctrines of a divine providence formulated by these authorities. Langford provides a more detailed discussion of the ancient and medieval sources of Protestant providentialism (cf. 1981, 39-55). Further valuable accounts of the theological debates on providence include an early essay by Vander Molen (1978) and the introductory survey on the doctrine of providence in the Reformed tradition provided by McGrath (cf. McGrath 1988, 86-93).

[5] By "Sophists," Calvin usually means scholastic thinkers (cf. 1960, 200).

which "he deigns to watch more closely" than the remainder of his creation and toward those individuals upon whom God dispenses his saving grace for eternal salvation (Calvin 1960, 210; cf. Wendel 1968, 154). Along with his insistence on the importance of God's particular benevolent providential care for those predestined for salvation, Calvin voiced the conviction that God's omnipotence would allow for either supernatural interventions into the material universe or for providence to effect events through instruments that are part of the natural order (1960, 210).[6]

Calvin's teachings also introduced a paradoxical discrepancy between providences that pertained to God's general government of the world and particular divine interventions. Whereas Calvin aligns his doctrine of predestination with the doctrine of *gubernatio*, he bridges the divide between the transient and permanent by introducing the concept of "most special providences" that are commensurate with God's dispensation of supernatural grace on the individual.[7] This ambiguous structure resulted in a complication of the notion of divine providence that Perry Miller describes as the difficulty of differentiating between the two aspects of natural order and divine grace as two modes of divine emanation (cf. 1954, 33). While "most special providences" also imply the possibility of communicating directly with the deity, Puritan ministers struggled to maintain the distinction between God's natural powers and his supernatural grace in order to avoid a pantheistic conflation of God with his creation (cf. Miller 1954, 32). At the same time, however, providentialism not only presented a comprehensive framework of history that extended from the distant past to the present and into the future, but also interrelates the sphere of secular history with the history of salvation and individual regeneration.[8]

---

[6] While Calvin thus draws on a common distinction between mediate and immediate channels of God's agency – a distinction which follows the differentiation between primary and secondary causes, he does not consistently distinguish between general and special providences and even claims that this distinction should not be made with regard to natural phenomena. At one point, Calvin refuses to delimit the regularity of the changes between night and day and between the seasons of the year to a 'universal' providence. From the biblical account of divine miracles, Calvin deduces that "the sun does not daily rise and set by a blind instinct of nature but that he himself, to renew our remembrance of his fatherly favor toward us, governs its course. Nothing is more natural than for spring to follow winter; summer, spring; and fall, summer – each in turn. Yet in this series one sees such great and uneven diversity that it readily appears each year, month, and day is governed by a new, a special, providence of God" (1960, 199).

[7] In the earlier editions of the *Institutes* between 1539 and 1554, Calvin treats the issue of predestination in the same chapter in which he also outlines his understanding of an overruling divine providence. In later editions, these two aspects are separated and the discussion of predestination is moved to a section in which Calvin discusses the workings of the Holy Spirit (cf. 1960, 197). For an outline of the connection between providence and predestination, see Winship (1996, 12-6).

[8] In *The Puritan Origins of the American Self*, Sacvan Bercovitch has argued that the Augustinian distinction between the City of God and the City of Man correlates with the distinction

A second paradoxical aspect of Calvin's theory of providence maintains the impossibility of discerning ultimate causes for worldly occurrences. In his explanation of adverse occurrences, Calvin endorses the view that successful or disastrous events do not occur randomly and that everyday experiences should not be attributed to the general contingency of historical events but that "all events are governed by God's secret plan" which is not immediately understandable for human beings (1960, 198). Calvin illustrates the sense of uncertainty this belief entails through the exemplary narrative of the violent death of an itinerant merchant (cf. 1960, 208-9). The seemingly fortuitous calamity that befalls an anonymous merchant is attributed to the workings of a heavenly decree. The story maintains that the events narrated have been previously known and preordained by an omniscient and omnipotent God. The seemingly accidental events are thus salvaged from the operations of chance and contingency, but remain inexplicable as the imposition of a divine providence forestalls the possibility of recognizing more than its operation, and even this might be questionable. As the story asserts that future and past events remain indeterminate and their meaning continues to be "uncertain to us" (1960, 209), Calvin's doctrine of providence constricts the sphere of human knowledge, especially the possibility of prophecy and divination. Although Calvin regularly cautioned his followers against the inclination to divine God's will through a reading of natural or historical occurrences, he nevertheless laid the foundation for a perception of the world in which natural or historical events potentially assume the character of signs that indicates God's will as well as the invisible and transcendent order of the universe.

Popular adaptations and modifications of Calvin's doctrine in the late seventeenth century gave rise to the belief that historical events as well as natural phenomena could indeed be identified as special or 'particular' providences (cf. Vander Molen 1978). Providentialism became the prime means of examining history and nature for the revelation of God's will. The belief in the readability of the universe in which providentialism assumes the function of a "semiological system" circulated widely through early modern print culture and was also adopted by American ministers and laymen (cf. Walsham 2003, 13, 19-20, 70; Winship 1996, 15, 158).[9] The use of providence as an explanatory device was widespread and collectors of popular anthologies especially used short didactic tales and narratives in order to stress man's dependence on God's mercy and

---

of "figural providences" and "secular providences" and that providential readings of history consign historical causation to God and refrain from implicating the history of salvation with secular history (cf. 1975, 40-1). While Bercovitch turns to the exegetical strategy of typology to explain the conflation of sacred and secular history in American Puritanism, the paradoxical structure of Puritan providentialism did also allow for a similar conflation through its distinction between "special" and "most special providences."

[9] Stein has suggested that Puritan providentialism even exceeds the significance of the idea of the millennium as a defining characteristic of early modern Protestant culture (cf. Stein 1978/79, 263).

judgment. The overlapping genres of the early modern judgment book, the sensational compilations of cautionary tales, and providential histories provide ample proof of the popular assumption that a transcendent providential design manifests itself in the visible world.[10] This was especially true for the genre of the cautionary tale that related stories about the punishment of offenders against communal religious morals and norms.[11] The general sense of the readability of God's providence in the material universe was especially conducive to intervention in divisive political issues and served the purpose of illustrating the necessity for fostering social order and morality. While cautionary tales often framed their marvelous accounts of adversities as an expression of a wrathful God punishing the sinful, polemicists and pamphleteers turned to providential explanations as appealing rhetorical instruments in the sectarian conflicts between concurring religious denominations and beliefs. The popular and influential historical account of the persecution of the Puritan saints during the reign of Queen Mary in John Foxe's *Actes and Monuments* (1563), for example, concludes with vivid accounts of God's retributive judgment laid on the persecutors of the faithful. In a similar vein, Thomas Beard's *The Theatre of God's Judgements* (1597) amassed sensational cautionary tales that reported God's immediate punishment of the sinful and wicked.

Providentialism was, however, not only a distinct attribute of sensational popular anthologies of cautionary tales; it was also a prominent feature of early modern English historiography. In Foxe's *Actes and Monuments*, the boundaries between secular history and the sacred history of redemption were blurred by his presentation of English history as the history of the Reformation of the Church of England (cf. Zakai 1992, 33-6). While the exemplary role of England within providential history was ultimately challenged by Puritan critics who questioned the sufficiency of the reforms in the Church of England, the more secular genres of historical writings retained the notion of a providential design visible in the course of history.[12] Providentialism thus informed the universal history of Sir Walter Raleigh, published in 1614. The connection between secular historical thought and providentialism is graphically illustrated by the frontispiece of the 1617 edition of Sir Walter Raleigh's *History of the World* (doc. 57). Uplifting and sustaining the world from death and oblivion, the allegorization of history as *magistra vitae* presents a combination that is characteristic of

---

[10] On the importance of the genre of cautionary tales, see Thomas (1980, 90-132); Hall (1989, 73-91); Walsham (2003, 65-96).
[11] Propagating moral norms of behavior – chastisements of drunkards and Sabbath-breakers were two favorite features of these tales – cautionary tales appropriated medieval narrative forms and combined them with a providential world view.
[12] For a succinct outline of the changes in the Puritan perception of England's role in the context of the history of salvation, see Zakai's account of early modern Protestant historiography in England (1992, 59-60).

the understanding of historiography during the Renaissance (cf. "Comparison – Contrasts – Connections," 111-3).[13]

Later in the seventeenth century, Puritan divines and historians of the Restoration Period and the early Enlightenment responded more systematically to theological and lay articulations of providential creeds and doctrines. Written at a time when an emerging mechanistic view of the universe and efforts by Anglican theologians to marginalize Calvinistic precepts threatened ministerial authority, the Puritan divines Increase Mather and Urian Oakes penned two theological surveys that maintained the notion of "special providences" as a source of divine revelation.[14] Writing from within a Calvinistic tradition, Increase Mather's systematic treatise *The Doctrine of Divine Providence Opened and Applied* (doc. 68) and Urian Oakes's *The Soveraign Efficacy of Divine Providence* (doc. 67) share a fundamentally deterministic outlook on the human role in history. Their providential theory echoes the Calvinistic doctrine of *gubernatio* and claims that "the decrees and wills of man" are subsumed to the immanentist notion that "all Events of Providence are the issues and executions of an Ancient, Eternal, Unchangeable decree of Heaven" (*KC*, 140). Far from presenting a fossilized doctrine of divine providence, however, Urian Oakes alleviates the deterministic aspects of Calvin's conception of the doctrine by deducing from God's abundant goodness that the divinity bestows "causal power and virtue to his Creatures" and elevates human beings into "*Co-workers* with Himself" (*KC*, 138). For Oakes, God remains the "Absolute First Cause" (*KC*, 138), but he concedes causal agency to human beings without violating the doctrine of God's unlimited sovereignty. While this adaptation of the doctrine does not offer a sufficient solution to the question of theodicy, or an explanation for the existence of evil, Oakes's theory presupposes that providence guarantees a harmonious relationship between primary (i.e., divine and supernatural) and secondary (i.e., human or natural) causes. Oakes refers to the doctrine of *concursus* and points out that God usually works through secondary causes as "He ordinarily concurreth with Second Causes according to the Law given and the Order set" (*KC*, 139). Not having abdicated from his "absolute Sovereignty and Dominion," God thus "reserves a Liberty to Himself to interpose, and to Umpire matters of Success and Event, contrary to the Law and common Rule of Second Causes" (*KC*, 139). God retains for himself the right to intervene directly. Both Oakes and Mather thus insist not so

---

[13] For a lucid discussion of Raleigh as historian and author of one of the first English universal histories, see Hill (1980, 118-200). For a discussion of his philosophy of history in relation to providential beliefs, see especially 162-3.

[14] Despite the consistency of the notion of special providences in Puritan theology, earlier references to special providences rather imply the existence of a providential cosmic design for the universe in observing seemingly trivial occurrences, whereas later accounts of special providences tend to be less concerned with general providence and divine predetermination than with the insistence on the efficacy of a transcendent divine will in the temporal world (cf. Miller 1954, 229-30; Rumsey 1986, 12).

much on the benevolent and protective aspects of a universal providence, as in earlier conceptualizations of the doctrine, but they rather accentuate the efficacy of special providences in the observable, temporal world (cf. Rumsey 1986, 12; Engler and Scheiding 1998, 14-21).

Increase Mather accordingly adopted the strategy of the earlier compilers of the cautionary tales and built a comprehensive collection of special providences that he published as an anthology of "illustrious providences" in 1684. Fostering the notion that nature provides a direct channel of communication between God and humanity, Mather's *An Essay for the Recording of Illustrious Providences* chronicled supposedly supernatural occurrences and heavenly interventions such as thunderstorms and marvelous apparitions in the skies, which he read as portents of future disasters or imminent divine retributions for sins committed in the past. As these assembled texts demonstrate, Mather insisted on the efficacy of divine providence and its powerful interventions to shape the material world at a time when the new science of the Royal Society propagated empirical research instead of theological speculation in natural philosophy. With regard to the providential readings of American history, Oakes and Mather agree that the history of the Puritan colonies manifests a historical development in harmony with God's providential plan. While this makes the Puritan experiment also conceivable in the context of salvation history, providential history is not reduced to a teleological movement toward Judgment Day, but provides a source for reassuring the community of God's protection and of His ability to intervene immediately in the life of both the community and the individual despite the experience of hardships and adversities.

III. Providential Thought and the Beginnings of New England Historiography

In the opening years of the seventeenth century, the more secular genres of early modern English literature rarely explicated the tenets of providentialism as a collective set of religious beliefs. However, the circulation and popularization of an early modern providential world view also included the nascent discipline of Protestant historiography. Early modern Protestant historiography and the Puritan historians in the New World adopted tenets of providentialism from its theological and popular articulations in Protestant print culture. Eschewing the secularization of historical thought characteristic of European humanism, providential thought provided the source for a justification of the Puritan emigration and supported the claim of God's special protection of the Puritan settlement in the New World. The notion of a covenant between God and His chosen people, for example, presupposes a providential world view that allows for a direct communication between the divine and worldly sphere. Early historians of New England strove to integrate this presupposition into their historical narratives.

Throughout "Of Plymouth Plantation" (1629-1646) – a historical chronicle of the group of separatists that migrated to New England in 1620 – William

Bradford refrains from developing a monolithic providential theory of history. He concentrates on singular and exemplary events that assume the status of special providences directed at individual members of the community. Exhibiting a separatist reticence against conflating providential and typological interpretations of history,[15] he largely eschews the elaborate typological rhetoric characteristic of contemporary non-separatist historians like Winthrop and Johnson, who present the beginnings of the history of the Massachusetts Bay colonies as an act of Christ's direct and active intervention in the process of history (cf. Anderson 2003, 163-5).[16] In the narrative, historical change and causation are only indirectly linked to supernatural influences. In his account of the separatists' decision to emigrate to the New World, for example, Bradford minutely details the considerations of the decision and the discussion of the "sundrie weightie and solid reasons" for the Pilgrims' migration from the Netherlands (cf. *KC*, 110-1). Instead of conceiving of historical agency and causation in strictly deterministic terms, Bradford provides a detailed outline of the discussion within the group on the advantages and disadvantages of migrating to the New World. The misgivings of those opposed to the endeavor are finally overcome by the invocation of the belief that all obstacles might be overcome through "providente care" [sic] and "the Lord's help," as well as "by fortitude and patience" and "the use of good means" (*KC*, 112).

Avoiding a narrow providential interpretation, Bradford resolves the quandary of how to relate transcendent causes and worldly history by constructing his narrative according to an eternal struggle between the forces of good and evil. The flight from England, first to the Netherlands and then to New England, is attributed to the supernatural operations of Satan's scheming and vexations in Old England. As a consequence, Bradford, who also served as a governor of Plymouth Plantation, exhibits the concern of a separatist Puritan about maintaining the distinction between the general unregenerate state of the world and the purity of the community of the saints. Beginning with the opening chapters of "Of Plymouth Plantation," Bradford upholds the exemplary "primitive order, liberty and bewtie" of early Christianity. The historian articulates his expectation of a renovation of the church according to the pristine model of the first Christian communities in the first century to which the Puritan churches

---

[15] Similar to Bradford, whose providential history does not present a typological interpretation of the separatists' migration, Robert Cushman, another separatist, explicitly denies the efficacy of divine providence in the separatists' decision to emigrate: "[W]hereas God of old did call and summon our Fathers by predictions, dreames, visions, and certaine illuminations to goe from their countries [...] according to his will and pleasure. Now there is no such calling to be expected for any matter whatsoever" (*KC*, 27-8). This position is consistent with the Reformed tenet that direct communication between God and his creation through miracles had ended with the apostolic period (cf. Holifield 2003, 37).

[16] In the course of his narrative, Bradford obviates "any conflict between Providential and natural causes" (Levin 1972, 16) and does not consistently distinguish between first and second causes.

should revert (*KC*, 109; cf. Bozeman 1988).¹⁷ While Bradford's history expresses a retrospective orientation in the separatist vision of history, Bradford's historical account insists that God's special care for his people also harbingers the danger of God's retributive punishments for "wickedness" or "sundrie notorious sins" (*KC*, 114). Despite the increased vigilance against backsliding in the Puritan colonies, Bradford observes that God's special care might quickly translate into God's corrective justice and the devil's "greater spite against the churches of Christ and the gospel hear" (*KC*, 114). Thus, Satan's "ancient strategemes, used of old against the first Christians," like sowing dissension and effecting "bloody and barbarous persecutions" (*KC*, 109), not only indicate the communal dangers waiting for the Pilgrims, they also support Bradford's argument of an institutional and spiritual continuity between the Puritan churches and the ancient Christian church.¹⁸

Observations of particular providences predominate in his narrative, and Bradford continually stresses the status of the believer as a fallen creature. God is presented as regularly meting out his punishments through providential interventions in order to exhort his chosen people to keep on the right path. In one instance, Bradford includes an account of divine retributive justice in which the travelers notice the effect of "the just hand of God" against "a proud and very profane yonge man" who curses the sick and wretched on the vessel and is consequently stricken with sickness and dies in "a dreadful manner" (*KC*, 112-3). While God ostensibly punishes the wicked, Bradford pays particular attention to providence's preserving interventions, as in the case of the migrants' deliverance from dangers at sea and his observation that God allows the founding fathers to live to old age (cf. *KC*, 113, 115). These special providences do not explicitly demarcate the Puritans' location within the framework of salvation history, but Bradford's narrative emphasizes the general exhortatory and preservative aspect of God's admirable and "marvelous providence" (*KC*, 115). In the case of his account of the life and death of Elder Brewster, the historian indirectly assures the

---

[17] Bradford's frantic embrace of millennial beliefs in an appendix to his history has been interpreted as the result of an increasing insecurity as to whether the separatist experiment in New England was still under God's favor and whether the center of providence's attention had not shifted back to Old England (cf. Rosenmeier 1991, 86-7). These fears of declension and degeneration are linked with the separatist call for a return to the pure and primitive Christianity of the apostles at the beginning of Bradford's narrative.

[18] Although Bradford's history was not published in print until 1856, the manuscript was available to numerous historians who made use of it in their own narratives. Histories that culled material from Bradford's "Of Plymouth Plantation" include Nathaniel Morton's *New England's Memoriall* (1669), William Hubbard's *Narrative of the Troubles with the Indians* (1677) and *General History of New England* (1682), Cotton Mather's *Magnalia Christi Americana* (1702), Thomas Prince's *Chronological History of New England, in the Form of Annals* (1736), and Thomas Hutchinson's *History of the Colony of Massachusetts Bay* (1764). For a detailed discussion of the editorial history of Bradford's history, see Anderson (2003) and Sargent (1992).

Pilgrims of a special relationship with God.[19] As a separatist, Bradford refrains from reading American history typologically or in terms of redemptive history, therefore his narrative moves from individual examples to the assumption of a benevolent general providence (cf. *KC*, 115). The history of the beginnings of the Puritan colony at Plymouth thus gestures towards a providential course of history, without, however, fully explicating the separatists' significance for the history of redemption.[20]

Within the non-separatist tradition of Puritan New England, John Winthrop and Edward Johnson wrote historical narratives in which they explicitly recurred to early modern providentialism in order to defend the Congregational orthodoxy of New England. While the first edition of Johnson's *Wonder Working Providence of Sions Saviour in New England*, published in London as *A History of New England* in 1654, circulated widely among Puritan readers, John Winthrop's journal of the Massachusetts Bay Colony's first twenty years remained unpublished during the seventeenth century and exerted its influence primarily as a desk reference for subsequent historians. Serving as governor for most of the period he covers in his journal, Winthrop penned a manuscript that remains one of the most important sources on the political and social history of the colonies. Emerging from his writings as the chief opponent of Anne Hutchinson during the Antinomian Crisis, Winthrop also released a shorter historical treatise in 1644, in which he denounces various groups dissenting from the Congregationalist communities. Judging from his various public statements, it might be safe to assume that he intended his journal to be more than a spiritual autobiography. During its composition the manuscript evolved more and more into a precise record of contemporary events, and in the second half of his narrative, Winthrop inserts chapter headings into his narrative that identify his manuscript as the annalistic history of New England.[21] Winthrop's historical thought exceeds Bradford's history in its reliance on federal theology and on the notion of "a speciall Commission" (*KC*, 120) or covenant between God and the Puritan colonies in order to frame the Puritan experiment as part of God's providential

---

[19] Emphasizing God's special care for the Puritan separatists, Bradford's narrative has also been read as invigorating a triumphant strain of church history that goes back to Eusebius of Caesarea (cf. Daly 1973, 556-60).

[20] For a more detailed discussion of this point, see David Levin's seminal discussion of Bradford's history (1972). More recently, David Read has argued that the differences between the first and second half of Bradford's journal indicate that the historian had completely abandoned an earlier providentialist theory of history, and that Bradford instead attempted to foment a collective Puritan identity in more secular terms (cf. 2005, 47-53). However, it is more convincing that Bradford had intended the second part as "the necessary prelude for understanding God's will in the present" and thus remained within a providential framework, although Bradford did not push through to unravel the "true meaning of Plymouth's history" (Wenska 1978, 157).

[21] For a discussion of the problem of how to describe the journal according to generic categories, see Dunn (1984, 186).

plan, but Winthrop generally abstains from explicating an exhaustive providential theory of history in his narrative.[22] However, he regularly takes notice of seemingly minor details and remains "alert for the ways current events, and the connections between them, may themselves have symbolic significance" (Moseley 1992, 139). Contrary to Bradford, though, Winthrop's view of history is more optimistic about the perfectionist potential inherent in the unfolding of New England history. Nevertheless, this optimism is balanced by a strain in early modern providentialism that is concerned with the maintenance of social control and the regulation of individual moral behavior.

Concerned about the maintenance of clerical and magisterial authority, as his political writings attest (docs. 62-3), Winthrop primarily invokes history as the theater of God's judgments in order to monitor social order and stability. The covenant between God and his elect becomes the cornerstone for his vision of an organic Christian community bound by brotherly love, as formulated in his speech "Modell of Christian Charity" (doc. 62). The providential world view underlying Winthrop's political thinking manifests itself most prominently at the beginning of his sermon when he argues from the authority of God's "most holy and wise providence" in order to acknowledge the social differences between rich and poor, on the one hand, and those "highe and eminent in power and dignitie" and those "meane and in subieccion" (*KC*, 119) on the other.[23] Invoking the ideal of a stable social order modeled on Christian love as the "bond of perfection" (*KC*, 119), Winthrop elaborates on this worldly notion of social order and develops a millennial strain of reasoning that prefigures the ultimate perfection of humanity at the end of time.[24] This prophetic quality of Winthrop's historical vision remains influential within the historiographical tradition of New England and enunciates the uneasiness of being caught between the past and the future. At the same time, Winthrop's writings attest to a polemical strain within the Puritans' providential histories which is echoed in later histories written in New England (cf. Arch 1994, 20).

Historical narratives by non-separatist writers habitually inflect their partisan character and their polemical tone with a providential world view that allows positing events in an explicitly moral framework. Edward Johnson's *Wonder-Working Providence* (1654), one of the most popular histories in early New

---

[22] In his study on John Winthrop, James G. Moseley has argued that Winthrop avoids "organiz[ing] the Puritan experience along the lines of a predetermined plan" (1992, 137).

[23] See Winthrop's appeals to "a speciall overruleing providence" that creates a "mutual consent" and secures the divine favor for the colonies (*KC*, 120).

[24] In his assessment of Winthrop's view of history, Arch has suggested that Winthrop thus intended to diminish inherent tensions within the group of Puritan emigrants and that his text captures the precarious sense of being caught between declension and degeneration in Old England and the possibility of attaining "the millennial restoration of man's prelapsarian goodness" in the New World (1994, 10). Thus Winthrop simultaneously articulates "an idealistic, even sacred vision of society" that is balanced with a rhetoric that operates as "a practical, far-sighted mechanism of social control" (1994, 17).

England, has been especially noted for its openly partisan defense of Boston's Congregationalist orthodoxy embracing a strong millenarian point of view and an aggressively militaristic diction.[25] As the running title of Johnson's volume already attests, his historical vision is firmly grounded in a providential world view that amounts to a "divine metahistory" presenting history as "the secret workings of God behind the masks and movements of the world" (Kemp 1991, 125). This point is illustrated by Johnson's description of the pecuniary preparations for the Great Migration in 1630 that differs considerably from Bradford's narrative of New England's beginnings. The historian broaches the idea that the Puritans' migration was part of a divine plan of cosmic history and that God actively intervened to unfold his intentions by divine interposition. According to Johnson, for example, the emigrants were only able to muster the money for their relocation to the New World through a "memorable providence of Christ for his *New England* Churches" (1654, 29), although the historian does not reveal through which precise means, i.e., primary or secondary causes, divine agency manifests itself in history.

In its overtly polemical and aggressively justificatory tone, Edward Johnson's history also introduces considerable alterations from Bradford's and Winthrop's conceptualizations of New England's history. In his assessment of the transcendent meaning of the discovery and settlement of New England, Johnson's providential history recasts the separatist perspective developed by Bradford, who concentrates on the Pilgrims' flight from persecution, and chronicles the "history of Christ's militant triumph over his enemies" (Kemp 1991, 122). Johnson presents the migration to the New World as a divinely ordained mission to seek a tactical retreat where the Puritan saints should prepare for a renewed engagement in the European struggle for the Puritan Reformation of the Church of England (cf. Gallagher 1970, 46). In *Wonder-Working Providence*, Johnson's greater reliance on a providential view of history – compared to his predecessor in "Of Plymouth Plantation" – coincides with making free use of a typological understanding of history that connects the divine care for the guidance of the individual into paradise with divine guidance for the Puritans into a glorious future. Exceeding Bradford's use of typological readings of historical phenomena, Johnson thus more resembles Winthrop, who concludes his speech "Modell of Christian Charity" by comparing his leadership to that of Moses during the Exodus from Egypt (*KC*, 121).

---

[25] Although Johnson's narrative was originally published under the title *A History of New England*, I follow the common practice of referring to this volume by its common title. In *Loss of Mastery*, Peter Gay dismissed Johnson's history as "a naïve military bulletin reporting Christ's victories against Satan in America" (1968, 53). Later criticism has salvaged Johnson from this diminishing criticism and has called attention to the complexity of his narrative and its affinities to Puritan typology and spiritual autobiography (cf. Gallagher 1970 and 1975; Bercovitch 1968; Rosenmeier 1991). Arguably, Nathaniel Ward's satire *The Simple Cobbler of Agawam* joins Johnson's defense of the New England Way (cf. Arch 1994, 66).

More explicitly than either Winthrop or Bradford, Johnson combines a typological interpretation of historical events with his providential vision of the history of New England Puritanism. The emphasis has shifted from Bradford's invocation of a benevolent general providence to an invocation of typology that allows Johnson to establish an analogy between the Israelites and the Puritans. In providential terms, Johnson addresses the "Lord Christ" as author of the Great Migration to New England at the beginning of his narrative and emphasizes the providence and special care of Christ who actively intervenes in history to salvage His chosen people from an erring England. Thus, Johnson establishes the "New England Way" within a continuum of progressive history that originates with the sacred history of the Old Testament but also comprises more recent historical events, without abandoning the millennial promise that New England "is the place where the Lord will create a new Heaven and a new Earth in new Churches and a new Common-wealth together" (Johnson 1654, 3). Presenting the New England Way and its codification in the Cambridge Platform of 1648 as part of this divine plan of history, Johnson joins Winthrop's defense of the Congregationalist orthodoxy against the background of a providential world view (cf. Gallagher 1970, 40). Winthrop's and Johnson's use of typology as a heuristic technique for reading God's messages for humanity shares the belief that God's symbols, either types or miraculous providences, approximate the terrestrial, physical world with the heavenly sphere, and thus God's divine providence accounts for an unbroken chain of past, present, and future events (cf. Winship 1996, 17; Kemp 1991, 122-4).[26]

IV. Providential Thought in the Late Seventeenth Century

During the second half of the seventeenth century, the historical thought of Puritan divines introduced decisive transformations in their responses to current historical events as well as refigurations of providential history. Puritan divines were confronted with the challenge of accommodating their providential conceptualization of history to precarious changes in the colonies' political situation after the Stuart Restoration (1660-1688). Decisive challenges comprised the growing strength of the Anglican Church, the emerging dissension within the Puritan community over the Half-Way Covenant, the violent military conflicts with New England's native inhabitants, and ultimately the Salem witch hunt. For most Puritan ministers these events were symptomatic of a spiritual and institutional crisis of the New England Way. These setbacks were attributed to the corrosion of public morality and the increasing worldly orientation of public life. Against these 'backsliding' tendencies, Puritan ministers began to explain the meaning of historical events and processes in the form of the jeremiad, a particu-

---

[26] The significance of typology for the epistemology and aesthetics of American Puritans is the subject of a long scholarly discussion. Contrasting influential discussions are included in Brumm (1963); Bercovitch (1972 and 1978); Lowance (1980); Engler (2006).

lar form of sermon used to redress the precarious spiritual situation of the colonies and to call for a renewal of the colonies' religious zeal.[27] Developing their sermons into a collective ritual to stabilize a faltering sense of social and religious cohesion in their congregations, ministers assured their audiences of the continued efficacy of divine providence in the history of the colonies. In their laments over spiritual declension, they not only resorted to traditional warnings about God's wrath against the sinful but also offered the historical example of the founding fathers to the "rising generation."

The filiopietistic veneration of the founding fathers that began to dominate public discourse in the second half of the seventeenth century also had important consequences for Puritan historiography. Reassessing the historical consciousness in the vein of the jeremiads led to a mythologization of the first generation that contrasted starkly with the failings of the present generation (cf. Scobey 1984, 22-3). The jeremiad also questioned the sense of newness that was accorded to the Puritan experiment to distinguish the New World from Europe, while the lionizing of the founders fostered the need for writing a "domestic history" of the colonies. Whereas the founding generation created a usable past out of typological readings of the sacred history recorded in the Old Testament, the official historical consciousness of the colonies after the Half-Way Covenant in 1662 blurred the distinction between secular and sacred history by emphasizing analogies between eminent founders and a register of biblical heroes.

The spiritualization of the first generation of American Puritans in the context of the more pervasive changes in the conceptualization of New England's place in history also reverberated in the genre of the historical narrative that simultaneously retained its didactic and exhortatory function. Nathaniel Morton's *New England's Memoriall* concluded with an explicit "advice to his readers" in which the historian exhorted his audience to follow the example of the founding fathers to forego the degeneration of the New England garden into a spiritual wilderness (cf. Holifield 1989, 55-6; Morton 1979, 197-8). The growing significance of the idealization of historical beginnings and of the filiopietistic veneration of the founding fathers culminated in Cotton Mather's *Magnalia Christi Americana* (1702) and its compilation of biographies of eminent Puritans that should reassure its American readers about New England's place in God's providential design.

No longer exclusively turning to medieval and classical subjects for his historical narratives, Cotton Mather and other Puritan historians increasingly understood the New World as being invested with a local history of its own and attempted to frame this history within the context of the history of salvation. These larger shifts in the Puritan historical imagination, however, did not result in the eclipse of a his-

---

[27] The question whether the ministerial jeremiads about a general degeneration of the Puritan experiment were warranted by factual observations of the historical changes in the colonies has been the subject of various historical studies. Scobey (1984) has given an outline of the complex interrelationship between the jeremiad as a rhetorical form and the more pervasive changes in Puritan historical thought in the seventeenth century.

torical theory based on a providential world view. The exhortative character of the jeremiads proved to be consistent with the appellative and disciplinary aspects of early modern providentialism as well as with the ideological definition of the Congregationalist New England Way (cf. Miller 1954, 229). Puritan ministers like Increase and Cotton Mather remained committed to the tenets of an early modern providential world view that also shaped the Puritan conceptualization of history until the beginnings of the eighteenth century (cf. Winship 1996, 138-9).

The validity of applying a providential theory of history to the military conflict with the Native Americans, which commenced in 1675 and is commonly referred to as "King Philip's War," became the object of a historiographical and ideological controversy over the providential character of this event.[28] In his declensionist interpretation of the causes and the significance of this cataclysmic conflict and its catastrophic effects on the majority of Puritan settlements in New England, Increase Mather judged the conflict to be God's providential interposition and adamantly persisted in claiming that the war should be understood as a divine punishment meted out for the colonies whose backsliding had incited God's wrath. While the jeremiad served Increase Mather's purpose of citing the war as proof of the need for moral and spiritual regeneration in the colonies, Mather shares with earlier Puritan historians the tendency to judge contemporary events from a providential perspective. Similar to his compilations of cautionary tales about God's punishment for backsliders, Mather regularly reverted to locating the causes for the colonies' adversities in the war to the retributive intervention of a divine providence (cf. Hall 1989, 104-5).

A similar view of the war is perceptible in Mary Rowlandson's account of her captivity among the Native Americans, for which Increase Mather wrote the prefatorial note.[29] Reflecting on "remarkable passages of providence" during her captivity among the Native Americans (*KC*, 144), Rowlandson first locates a mysterious transcendent meaning of the war in God's "own holy ends" that "should be marvelous in our eyes" (*KC*, 144). Then Rowlandson proceeds by identifying a "won-

---

[28] For a succinct summary of the controversy, see Elliott's substantial introductory chapter in *The Cambridge History of American Literature* (1994, 221-4). For an evaluation of this debate in the larger context of the development of American historical thought, see Engler and Scheiding (1998, 18-20). A detailed textual analysis of Hubbard's history and a convincing argument for the importance of Hubbard as a genuine historical thinker in the Puritan tradition is provided by Perry (1994) and Nelson (1970). Perry notes that Hubbard refers to "occasional providential interventions" almost exclusively in "positive terms," presenting not a wrathful deity but "God helping, but never undermining the colonists" (Perry 1994, 170-1). For a convincing contextualization of Hubbard in the providential world view of the late seventeenth century, see Michael Winship's assessment of the Hubbard-Mather controversy (1996, 20-4).

[29] The criticism on Rowlandson's narrative is too vast to be discussed in detail here. A good starting point for students of Rowlandson's is Tara Fitzpatrick's essay "The Figure of Captivity: The Cultural Work of the Puritan Captivity Narrative" (1991; cf. Slotkin 1978; Derounian 1988; Breitwieser 1990; Davis 1992; Burnham 1993; Derounian-Stodola and Levernier 1993; Castiglia 1996).

derfull providence of God" that intervened to prolong the war as God's judgment for the colonies. Ultimately, Rowlandson's narrative attributes the reasons for the victorious outcome of the war to the spiritual regeneration of the colonies and a renewal of their trust in God's providential interposition. While the narrative has been read as a variant of the Puritan jeremiad or as an elaborate spiritual autobiography charting Rowlandson's spiritual affliction and quest for conversion, the captivity narrative also functions as a providential reading of the war. It also suggests a parallelism between her own rescue from captivity and Rowlandson's spiritual regeneration, on the one hand, and the victorious outcome for the colony of the military conflagration, on the other hand.

Different from the histories of Winthrop, Bradford, and Johnson, however, the parallelism between Rowlandson's account of her personal afflictions and the Lord's chastisement of His chosen people in the war exhibit the permeability of the distinction between the spiritual and secular dimensions of historical processes. Historical events like the inability of the Puritan forces to cross a river to continue the pursuit of the Native Americans are interpreted as the expression of God's corrective love for the Puritan saints (cf. *KC*, 144). Thus the narrative attests to the belief that despite the current crisis New England has not been abandoned by God and is still part of His providential plan. Although the narrative has been noted for its subversive aspects, especially in its description of Rowlandson's relationship with her Native American captors, it remains questionable whether the narrative abandons a providential world view, in which everything that comes to pass is conceivable as part of God's pre-ordained plan whose details and outcome might be mysterious but whose alleged existence implied a continual transcendent meaning for earthly sufferings and hardships.

The precariousness of distinguishing secular from salvation history in Increase Mather's and Rowlandson's providential readings of King Philip's War resonates in Cotton Mather's copious *Magnalia Christi Americana; or, The Ecclesiastical History of New England, from Its First Planting in the Year 1620, unto the Year of Our Lord, 1698*, whose subtitle announces the writer's intention to provide not a secular but a church history of the colonies in New England from their separatist beginnings to the turn of the seventeenth century. In the Christian tradition of church history, the church was presented as the prime agent under the guidance of the Holy Spirit effecting the redemption of the elect from eternal damnation. Returning to this genre in his history of New England, Mather proudly allocates the New England churches an important role in the history of redemption and compares the successful establishment of new churches in New England with the achievement of the Reformation in Europe. Mather's valorization of ecclesiastical history resonates with Augustine's dualistic conception. Both privilege the Christian church as the prime agent of God's salvation and as the connection between redemptive and profane history. While Mather locates the ultimate meaning of all profane history beyond this world and thus establishes the transcendent significance of all historical processes, he attributes a special role to the Puritans as "the *People*, whom the *Son* of God hath *Redeemed* and *Purified* unto himself" and who constitute a *"Peculiar People"* under the special guidance and the *"Supernatural Operations"* of "the *Spirit* of God" (*KC*, 150).[30] Mather's frequent references to God's benevolent providence and to recurring divine interventions through "amazing Judgments and Mercies" defend a theory of history that conceived of God as the supreme ruler of the universe, whose benevolent or judgmental interventions in the material world were primarily directed at His chosen people. Analogous to Calvin's definition of a "most special providence," Mather turns to the "Dispensations of his *wondrous Providence* toward this people" in order to invest "their Calamities, their Deliverances, the Dispositions, [...] the considerable *Persons* and *Actions*" with an anchor in human history's providential design (*KC*, 150). Thus, Mather's history continues the tradition of providential histories that chronicle the dispensation of God's special favors and judgments through "special providences" and revalidates the cosmological world view of early modern providentialism within the genre of ecclesiastical history.

While Cotton Mather maintains the supremacy of church history as the principle genre for narrating history, the "General Introduction" integrates diverse historiographical traditions within the providential framework of the *Magnalia Christi Americana*. Mather's introduction invokes God's special care toward his *"Peculiar People"* upon whom God bestows his special favors and "dispensations" (*KC*, 150).[31] Mather's reference to the *"Peculiar People"* is not explicitly commensurate with American Puritanism, but rather with the community of Reformed Protestant churches. At the same time, Mather establishes "special providences" as a privileged and exclusive resource of knowledge, suggesting that their readability depends on the perspective of the properly trained theologian and historian taking up the pen to relate "Matters of *Admiration* and *Admonition*, above what any other Story can pretend unto" (*KC*, 150). Thus, Mather is not only able to capture the precariousness of New England's past, present, and

---

[30] Whereas earlier scholarship has assumed that the *Magnalia Christi Americana* presented American Puritans as God's chosen people due to a liberal use of a typological hermeneutics that presented New England as the antitype of Israel in the Old Testament, a closer examination of Mather's understanding of typology has raised the question of whether Mather consistently used typological explanations in extra-biblical contexts (cf. Engler 2006). In a similar way, scholars have pointed out the inconsistencies in earlier interpretations that have assumed that Mather's millenarianism conceived of New England as the place of the New Jerusalem whose coming was prophesied in the Book of Revelation (cf. Smolinski 1990). The conflation of sacred and secular history in Cotton Mather's historical thinking can thus not be summarily attributed to Mather's typological or millenarian mode of narrating "American" history but is founded on his providential application of church history to the Puritan experiment in New England.

[31] The initial pages of the *Magnalia Christi Americana* also echo the opening of Bradford's "Of Plymouth Plantation" (1629-1646) by renewing the plea for a purification of the church and a return to the primitive roots of Christianity. Mather anchors his account of the Puritan experiment in the New World in the context of the Reformation by stressing the contemporaneity of these events.

future history, but he also salvages the authority of the historian who becomes the interpreter of God's providential signs revealed in history.

As the "General Introduction" to the *Magnalia Christi Americana* explains, the historian's authority derives from the primacy of ecclesiastical history as the paramount historiographical genre. Although the "General Introduction" introduces the voice of the historian, his modest "I," at the beginning of the narrative, this 'humble' introduction also asserts the historian's authority as the truthful recorder of the Lord's great deeds in the New World. The self-characterization of Cotton Mather as historian also indicates the larger framework for his history as the quasi-prophetic record of "the *Wonderful Displays* of His Infinite Power, Wisdom, Goodness, and Faithfulness" that attest to the workings of "His Divine Providence" (*KC*, 147). In contrast to previous histories, notably Edward Johnson's *Wonder-Working Providence* (1654), however, Cotton Mather conceives of his role as a historian who can only intuit God's plan from a limited human point of view (cf. Arch 1994, 146-7). For Mather, the historian generally remains inside the providential order of time and history and can only praise the exterior "*Wonderful Displays*" of divine providence. The *Magnalia Christi Americana* thus exhibits a residue of Calvinistic skepticism about the proper and feasible interpretation of the "wonders" of history. Despite these qualifications and the repeatedly articulated doubts about the ultimate meaning and success of the Puritan experiment, Mather seeks to valorize the voice and authority of the historian to counter the erosion of the magistrates' traditional authority in New England (cf. Arch 1994, 187).[32]

Within the larger shifts in Puritan historical consciousness, the establishment of analogical and typological parallelisms between individual saints and the Puritan community in Cotton Mather's *Magnalia Christi Americana* remained an important ingredient in ascertaining New England's location in God's providential plan of history and in vindicating the founding generation's role. The biographical narratives of such exemplary figures as John Eliot, John Winthrop, and governor Sir William Phips reveal that Cotton Mather not only relied on the creation of typological allusions in his characterizations, but also freely compared his subjects with eminent persons from classical antiquity. As Cotton Mather's reference to the parallel biographies of Plutarch, who had written a history consisting of pairs of Greek and Roman biographies, attests, this analogical model amounted to a "jumbling of pagan mythology and the Old and New Testament" with the history of the Puritan experiment in the New World (Bercovitch 1976, 231). Although he was aware of the far-reaching changes in the conceptualization of historiography during the seventeenth century, Cotton Mather also retained the customary parallelisms between Israel as God's chosen people in the Old Testament and its antitype in the Reformed church of early modern Protes-

---

[32] In accordance with the tradition of earlier compendious providential histories, Mather's history creates a "universal historiographic intertext" and establishes a parallelism between biblical history and the known history of the world (Stievermann 2004, 269-70).

tantism. Based on a rather artificial distinction between "figural" and "secular" providences, Bercovitch has argued that Mather's sketch of Winthrop conflates spiritual biography and secular history and thus creates a new synthesis of providential history that blends secular history with the workings of divine grace. A close reading of Mather's biographical sketch of Winthrop, however, reveals that the typological references are muted in favor of the more secular strategy of Plutarch's parallel biographies. Although Mather constantly compares Winthrop to biblical figures such as Moses, Jacob, Joseph, and David, he uses these parallelisms to emphasize the exemplary character of Winthrop as colonial magistrate and the epitome of Christian virtue.[33] Trumpeting the imitable Christian conduct of Winthrop in various domestic and political instances, Mather insists on treating Winthrop primarily in his role as governor in which he compares him to Nehemiah and presents him as the ruler of an "American Jerusalem." Mather explicitly refers to this analogy as a *"Parallel"* (*KC*, 125) and not as the antitypical fulfillment of an ancient prophecy. The sketch also lacks the explicit homiletics of spiritual biographies, as Mather neither dwells on the spiritual state of his subject nor on the question of whether Winthrop had received God's saving grace.[34]

Providing a plethora of filiopietistic biographies of eminent Puritan churchmen and magistrates, Mather effectually blends ancient models of historical biography with a hagiographical tradition within the Puritan historical imagination that extends at least back to Foxe's narratives of the Protestant martyrs during Queen Mary's reign. As it remains questionable whether Cotton Mather generally conflated the realms of sacred and secular history in his biographical sketches, his historical vision clearly exhibits the notion that the supernatural and the natural are intertwined, especially in the historiographical genre of ecclesiastical history that focuses on the church as God's agent in the history of redemption. Whereas Mather's millennial expectations were less exclusively centered on New England than has often been maintained, the most characteristic features of the *Magnalia Christi Americana*, its biographical appraisals of first- and second-

---

[33] Mather's epitomes fall into three basic categories. Whereas the magistrates are presented as Puritan communities' "shields" against external enemies, the English-trained ministers are stylized as the protectors of Puritan piety, and the American ministers augment the number of saintly church members in the New World (cf. Arch 1994, 155).

[34] The only indirect venue for establishing Winthrop as a Puritan saint lies in Mather's narration of the several afflictions that Winthrop suffered throughout his life. While these afflictions could assume the function of "special providences" that should test or confirm Winthrop's piety, Mather recalls the fact that these "afflictions" were read by contemporaries as judgmental interventions for an allegedly sinful character, a view that Mather "would not have mentioned, but that the Instances may fortifie the Expectations of my *best Readers* for such Afflictions" (1977, 226-7). Although Bercovitch captures the intricate and complex relationship between salvational and profane history in the Puritan doctrines of divine providences, these intricacies are not explicitly reflected in the biographical sketch on Winthrop, who is not presented as an antitype of biblical figures (cf. Engler 2006, 191-4).

generation Puritans and its conceptualization of history in terms of divine interventions, remained indebted to an early modern providential world view.

The problematic aspects that derive from the assumption of an intimate connection between the supernatural and the natural sphere in Mather's conceptualization of history is evinced by the biographical sketch of Sir William Phips, the first governor of Massachusetts who was appointed after the revocation of the old charter and the Glorious Revolution in Great Britain (doc. 73). Stylizing Phips's achievements as governor according to the model of the Puritan magistrate as defender of the Congregational theocracy and an "Instrument of easing the Distresses of the Land" (*KC*, 156), Mather praises Phips for his intervention in the Salem witchcraft craze, especially his banning the admittance of specter evidence in witchcraft trials (cf. Ruttenburg 1998, 31-82; Winship 1996).[35]

The witchcraft crisis at Salem exhibited inherent contradictions and instabilities in the Puritan fusion of the early modern providential world view and their basically Calvinistic theology. Providentialism recognized worldly events as the effects of supernatural causes, and even the machinations of the devil were usually subsumed to God's sovereignty. The exertion of the devil's power, not necessarily but also through the use of witches and witchcraft, was considered to depend on "*Divine permission*" and to be restrained by God's overruling providence (*KC*, 152). As Increase and Cotton Mather lament, however, this tenet of Calvinistic providentialism was overturned during the Salem witchcraft crisis. During the trials, suspects accused of consorting with the devil began to incriminate other members of the Puritan community by alleging that spectral representations of their bodies inflicted bodily and mental harm on them. The court reacted to these charges by a line of reasoning that allowed for the conviction of those accused of sending out their specters to inflict injuries on their victims. Both Increase and Cotton Mather rejected this line of argument and derided it as "specter evidence." Cotton Mather successfully argued that God's providence precludes that the devil would be allowed to use the ghostly representation of an innocent and saintly member of the church to vex his victims. He concluded "[t]hat the *Providence* of God would not permit an *Innocent Person* to come under such a *Spectral Representation*" (*KC*, 157). The court ultimately followed this argument.

The allegations of spectral representations undermined the Puritan zeal for the maintenance of a pure church. In early Puritanism, believers were granted full membership rights only after their spiritual character had been revealed to

---

[35] For a contextualization of the Salem witch hunt in conflicting conceptualizations of sin, witchcraft, and magic in popular religion and ministerial theology, see Godbeer (1992). The events at Salem have also been examined from the perspective of social historians (cf. Boyer and Nissenbaum 1974), as well as from the perspective of women's history (cf. Norton 2003). Mary Beth Norton's account also provides an insightful interpretation that locates the crisis at Salem in the conflicts of the English settlers with the indigenous population of New England.

the congregation through the public profession and a genuine conversion that indicated their receptive response to God's saving grace. Thus striving for the maintenance of a purified church consisting of visible saints, allegations of spectral apparitions subverted, however, the principle of visible sainthood as the orthodox prerequisite for determining full church membership. Instead, afflicted accusers assumed the authority to decide and attest to the spiritual state of the alleged perpetrators as followers of Satan and enemies of the church (cf. Ruttenburg 1998, 63). This also challenged the ministry's authority to define the conceptual boundaries between the visible and the invisible. As Nancy Ruttenburg has argued, those allegedly afflicted by specters claimed access to an occult sphere of knowledge located at the borderline between the earthly and the spiritual, the visible and invisible world (cf. 1998, 63).

In the context of the late seventeenth century, Puritan theocracy attempted to affirm the existence of supernatural causes. Simultaneously, the ministry aimed at regulating popular and occult interpretations of events either as supernatural or natural signs. In doing so, the Puritan clergy defended their definitions of providentialism against explanations by lay men and women. This attempt is illustrated by the documents included in the anthology. While the Mathers generally refrained from any scathing critique of the conduct of ministerial and magisterial authorities during the trial, they challenged the basis of specter evidence by returning to a more conservative interpretation of providentialist doctrine. Maintaining the doctrine of *gubernatio*, God's unlimited sovereignty and rule over the universe through his providence, Cotton Mather inferred it to be a "*notorious Thing, that a* Daemon *may, by God's Permission, appear even to ill purposes in the shape of an* Innocent, *yea, and a* Virtuous Man" (KC, 158). In his influential treatise *Case of Conscience Concerning Evil Spirits Personating Men* (doc. 72), which argued against the use of specter evidence in legal proceedings, Increase Mather answered in the affirmative to the question "*whether Satan may not appear in the Shape of an Innocent and Pious, as well as of a Nocent and Wicked Person to Afflict such as suffer by Diabolical Molestations?*" (KC, 153). Although the theological argumentation of the Mathers questioned the validity of the legal proceedings at Salem, they did not question the fundamental belief in the existence of witches and witchcraft, nor did they eschew popular beliefs about the operations of the devil and possible contacts between the supernatural and the natural. This structural homology between popular providential beliefs and the theology of divine providence indicates the problematic underside of early modern providentialism. It also leaves room for the conceptualization of the supernatural in Manichaean terms, as the eternal clash between the forces of evil and the salutary efficacy of divine providence. The documents about the Salem witch trials as well as the recording of "illustrious providences," especially in the *Magnalia Christi Americana*, demonstrate the dependence of the Puritan vision of history on early modern providentialism and on the early modern culture of wonders. In the world of early modern Puritanism, God frequently intervenes in the natural order of the universe through his "special providences," thereby enabling the divine will, guiding individual believers or communities according to a cosmic plan, and bringing down God's judgment on the reprobate individual as well as the unregenerate community.

Instructional Strategies and Classroom Issues

I. Key Concepts and Major Themes

1. Providentialism (docs. 67-8, 73)
   According to the doctrine of divine providence, God effects his will in the temporal world through His power of continual creation and the works of special or particular providences. Providence thus realizes the divine will either through secondary or natural causes, or through supernatural or primary causes. Extremely popular throughout the seventeenth century, providentialism often provided the ground for conflicting interpretations of everyday occurrences between political and sectarian opponents as well as between the Puritan clergy and lay men and women professing more popular accounts of the doctrine.

2. Jeremiad (docs. 66, 69)
   The jeremiad is a sermon that laments the spiritual decline of the Puritan experiment and that became a prominent element in Puritan sermonic literature during the second half of the seventeenth century. Amounting to a collective ritual, jeremiads were intended to admonish the Puritan community to revert to the piety and purity of the first generation and to reassure the community of a glorious future. Arguably, the formula of the jeremiad was not limited to the occasion of the election day sermon, but its structure also influenced other literary genres, such as life writing and historical narrative.

3. Typology (doc. 64)
   Originally, typology was an exegetical method to explain the meaning of sacred writings, especially the Old Testament. Typological readings of the Bible interpreted persons and events from the Old Testament as types that anticipate and foreshadow anti-types in the New Testament and the Book of Revelation. Presenting Old Testament types as prophecies to be fulfilled in the New Testament, typology turned the Bible into a complex self-elucidating language system to be expanded into a system of divination that enabled an observer to interpret current events as foreshadowed by biblical accounts.

4. Filiopietism (docs. 60-1)
   The term filiopietism generally refers to the veneration and spiritualization of ancestors in American Puritanism. First-generation settlers in New England in particular were presented to second- and third-generation Pu-

ritans as exemplars of Christian virtues. The tradition of justifying social norms through reference to the legacy of exemplary ancestral figures remained a central tenet of the Puritan myth of New England.

II. Comparison – Contrasts – Connections

Example: Docs. 4, 57, 67-8, 70

A good starting point for readers unfamiliar with the ideas of a providential world view is the frontispiece of Walter Raleigh's *History of the World* (doc. 57). As the title page illustrates, Raleigh aims at reconciling the contingency of historical developments with a sense of security derived from a providential foundation of history. The emblematic character of the title page combines an architectural design with the representation of allegorical figures characteristic of Renaissance print culture. The emblematic engravings further include Ben Jonson's sonnet "The Minde of the Front" that serves as an explication of the allegorical character of the frontispiece (*KC*, 108). The sonnet takes up the identification of the central allegorical figure as *magistra vitae* to which the poet refers as "The Mistresse of Mans Life." Addressing "Historia" as "Times witnesse, Herald of Antiquitie, The light of Truth, and life of Memorie," the poem re-articulates the title page's reference to the Ciceronian definition of history inscribed on the four Corinthian columns as *testis temporum, nuncia vetustatis, lux veritatis, vita nemoriae*. The title page thus emphasizes historiography's didactic function and represents Cicero's popular dictum, which Raleigh also cites in the preface of his history. Cicero's epithet remained popular throughout the seventeenth century and is also referred to by Cotton Mather who praises it as a conceptualization of history "whereto all Mankind subscribe" (*KC*, 151).

The educational function of historiography as a repository of knowledge about former times is allegorized by the books added to the column on the left. The rendition of Egyptian hieroglyphs as an enigmatic sign system attests to the Renaissance fascination with the origins of classical learning in Egypt. The beams of light and the laurels decorating the columns to the right emphasize the function of history as the messenger of truth and the judge of historical fame. The title page further includes allegorical figures in the architectural setting, for instance a personification of Experientia, which is equipped with a chastising rod and a leadline to sound the hidden depths of history. The figure Veritas appears as the messenger of the light of truth. The combination of the crown of laurels and the light of truth that appears in the nimbus of *magistra vitae* emphasizes that the "Mistresse of Mans life" (cf. *KC*, 108) overcomes death and oblivion, which are allegorically represented at the feet of Historia.

The eternalizing function of history is displayed as concerning the whole world, which is represented in the form of a globe modeled on the *Theatrum Orbis Terrarum* by Abraham Ortelius (cf. *KC*, 7; Scheiding in this vol., 6-8).

Historia connects human affairs to transhistorical truth and endeavors the vindication of the world in the light of eternity. The preservative function of history is further emphasized by the eye of Providentia which dominates the scene and represents an allegory of God's foreknowledge and overruling power over history. Beneath, the allegorical figures of Fama Bona and Fama Mala personify the good and bad destiny that providence has in store for the world. As the agent of divine providence, Fama Bona is attributed with the light of truth and a crown of laurels while her wings are speckled with ears, eyes, and tongues. In stark contrast to this figure of light, Fama Mala stands in front of a dark host of clouds and is spotted with black dots. Both figures hold trumpets that announce the constant vigilance and the intervention of providence in human affairs (cf. Corbett and Lightbown, 135). This notion is also emphasized in Jonson's sonnet, in which the reader is assured of the interventionist character of providential justice:

> High Providence would so: that nor the good
> Might be defrauded, nor the Great secur'd,
> But both might know their ways are understood,
> And the reward, and punishment assur'd. (*KC*, 108)

The idea of an uncontrollable fate is mitigated by a trust in providence as an impartial judge of human affairs. The allusion to Christian themes and salvation history is toned down in Raleigh's frontispiece. Nevertheless, minute references to the Fall – a representation of the tree of knowledge flanked by Adam and Eve is included in the globe north of the Black Sea – signal Raleigh's attempt to combine secular and Christian notions of history.

The frontispiece of Raleigh's history underlines the proximity between secular adoptions of providential beliefs and the inclusion of the doctrine of providence into the Puritan historical imagination. Increase Mather's *The Doctrine of Divine Providence Opened and Applied* (doc. 68) provides an insight in the practical application of theological doctrine to historical thought and illustrates how the history of New England is inserted into the context of secular and salvation history (*KC*, 140-1). As Increase Mather and other theologians are not as explicit as Raleigh about the punitive aspects of God's providence, his fellow ministers emphasize the doctrine of *gubernatio* to provide a sense of order and stability in what amounts to inexplicable historical events. The cornerstone of the Puritans' theocentric world view is summarily articulated in Urian Oakes's and Increase Mather's adoption of the doctrine of *gubernatio* and their conviction that "God is the Lord of Time, and Orderer, and Governor of all Contingencies" (*KC*, 138). Puritan ministers and historiographers established God as the supreme governor of the natural order of the cosmos as well as master of the unfolding of history through time.

Following their Calvinistic antecedents in ascribing "all Successes, or Frustrations" to the workings of a divine power (*KC*, 138), Oakes and Mather retain Calvin's insistence on the occult character of God's "Ancient, Eternal, Unchangeable decree of Heaven" (*KC*, 140). Although God is believed to intervene in one's life according to a preconceived plan, its provisions, according to Oakes, are referred to as the "secret Counsel" of God (*KC*, 138) and remain "deep and incomprehensible" according to Increase Mather (*KC*, 140).

In their attempts to systematize the epistemological quandary raised by the supernatural origin of divine providence, Oakes returns to the philosophical distinction between primary (supernatural) and secondary (natural) causes, while Mather's conceptualization emphasizes the enigmatic and mysterious character of God's providence. Drawing from the prophetic imagery of a "wheel-within-a-wheel" from the Old Testament, Mather thus emblematizes providence's impenetrable aspect and its seemingly contradictory character (cf. Bercovitch 1975, 48). In a Calvinistic line of reasoning, however, this epistemological dilemma is redressed by finding solace in the overruling sovereignty of a fundamentally benevolent though vigilant God, who may castigate and afflict those under His special care. Urian Oakes even exhorts his readers that the experience of present adversities and hardships might be attributable to an "Infinite Wisdom" that guides the individual Christian toward "the prosperity of your soul" and might be extricable from an arcane preordained plan (*KC*, 139). The insecurity about this impenetrable plan is assuaged by a belief in God's adherence to the covenant of grace and his intention to lead the Puritan churches of New England on the way to salvation. Increase Mather shares Oakes's fundamentally optimistic but disconcerting outlook, and for him the trust in an underlying divine care provides the ground for the conviction that divine afflictions "will not destroy us" (*KC*, 141). Despite the skepticism inherent in the doctrine, both writers embrace history as a source of consolation and to convince their audience that a benevolent divine power guides those under his special care.

III. Reading and Discussion Questions

1. Compare Bradford's account of the separatist Pilgrims' decision to migrate to the New World (doc. 58) with John Winthrop's vision of the Puritan community (doc. 62). How do these texts highlight the differences between separatist and non-separatist conceptualizations of American history? How can their view of historical processes be described as being influenced by early modern providentialism?

2. Read and analyze the poems by Michael Wigglesworth and William Bradford (docs. 61-2, 65). Which fundamental shifts in Puritan historical consciousness do these poems address? Discuss the various ideas that Puritans used to conceptualize their relationship to the past in the second half of the seventeenth century.

3. Read the "General Introduction" to Cotton Mather's *Magnalia Christi Americana* (doc. 70) and compare it to the biographical sketches of various

Puritan dignitaries (docs. 34, 64, 73). How does Mather conceive of himself in the role of the historian of Puritan New England? Which models of history does he draw from? What is his intention in providing his reader with biographical sketches of selected historic figures?

4. Outline the different aspects of the theological conceptualization of providentialism as it is developed in Increase Mather's treatise (doc. 68). Discuss the various aspects of the Puritan conceptualization of special providences.

5. Research the Salem witch hunt trials. How do the occurrences at Salem challenge Puritan authorities and how are Increase and Cotton Mather involved in the crisis? Read Cotton Mather's biographical account of Sir William Phips (doc. 73) and discuss how providentialism contributed to the rise of the witch hunt craze.

IV. Resources

a. Recommended Reading

Stephen Carl Arch. *Authorizing the Past*: *The Rhetoric of History in Seventeenth-Century New England*. DeKalb: Northern Illinois University Press, 1994. Arch's book builds on Peter Gay's classic study of colonial American historiography and argues that the historical narratives of eminent Puritans assumed a foundational cultural function that resembled the role of Puritan sermonic literature in the seventeenth century. Arch's book is especially valuable for his insightful interpretations of individual Puritan voices that shaped Puritan historical thought from John Winthrop to Cotton Mather.

Ursula Brumm. *Die religiöse Typologie im amerikanischen Denken*: *Ihre Bedeutung für die amerikanische Literatur- und Geistesgeschichte*. Leiden: Brill, 1963. [*American Thought and Religious Typology*. Transl. John Hoaglund. New Brunswick: Rutgers University Press, 1970.] Brumm's study claims that the symbolic mode of literary production discernible in the literary works of Edward Taylor, Nathanial Hawthorne, and Herman Melville emerged from the hermeneutic system of Puritan typology. According to Brumm, American Puritanism is characterized, on the one hand, by an allegorical understanding of history which related the world to a divine will through the idea of providence, and, on the other hand, by a typological strategy of investing history with a transcendent meaning. Through typology, Puritans were able to connect the history of their community with the larger framework of Christian salvation history. Brumm's argument for the centrality of typology as an explanatory framework for the conceptualization of American history and for processes of symbolization in American literary history still reverberates in current debates about typology in Puritan Studies.

David D. Hall. *Worlds of Wonder, Days of Judgment: Popular Religious Belief in Early New England*. New York: Knopf, 1989. In this classic study of popular religion in New England, David D. Hall extends the traditional understanding of religion in colonial American studies. Examining the contentious relationship between the Puritan clergy and articulations of popular religion, Hall uncovers the pervasive transformations of religion and society in the New England colonies by concentrating on the role of literate and opinionated lay men and women and their responses to orthodox Puritan doctrines.

Perry Miller. *The New England Mind: The Seventeenth Century*. Cambridge: Harvard University Press, 1954. Although his interpretation of American Puritanism has often been criticized and revised, Miller's study, together with his numerous other monographs and essays, remains a foundational treatment of central ideas and ideologies in Puritan cultural and intellectual history. Miller's interpretations of Puritan piety and logic, its notions of human nature, and such central doctrines as providence and the covenant have not only established the field of colonial American studies but continue to provide students and scholars with an intriguing starting point for any examination of American Puritanism.

Michael P. Winship. *Seers of God: Puritan Providentialism in the Restoration and Early Enlightenment*. Baltimore: Johns Hopkins University Press, 1996. Winship's book is the most comprehensive and detailed account of providentialism and its impact on American Puritanism. Although Winship's study focuses on the Mathers and their intellectual legacy, the study contextualizes their writings in the debates and conflicts that surrounded the engagement of providential notions by American Puritans.

b. Works Cited and Reading Suggestions

Anderson, Douglas (2003). *William Bradford's Books: Of Plimmoth Plantation and the Printed Word*. Baltimore: Johns Hopkins University Press.
Arch, Stephen Carl (1994). *Authorizing the Past: The Rhetoric of History in Seventeenth-Century New England*. DeKalb: Northern Illinois University Press.
Bercovitch, Sacvan (1968). "The Historiography of Johnson's *Wonder-Working Providence*." *Essex Institute Historical Collections* 54, 138-161.
– (1972). *Typology and Early American Literature*. Amherst: University of Massachusetts Press.
– (1975). *The Puritan Origins of the American Self*. New Haven: Yale University Press.
– (1978). *The American Jeremiad*. Madison: University of Wisconsin Press.
– (2000). "Puritan Origins Revisited: The 'City Upon a Hill' as a Model of Tradition and Innovation." *Early America Re-Explored: New Readings in Colonial, Early National, and Antebellum Culture*. Ed. Klaus H. Schmidt and Fritz Fleischman. New York: Lang, 31-48.

Boyer, Paul, and Stephen Nissenbaum (1974). *Salem Possessed: The Social Origins of Witchcraft*. Cambridge: Harvard University Press.

Bozeman, Theodore D. (1988). *To Live Ancient Lives: The Primitivist Dimension in Puritanism*. Chapel Hill: University of North Carolina Press.

Breitwieser, Mitchell Robert (1990). *American Puritanism and the Defense of Mourning: Religion, Grief, and Ethnology in Mary White Rowlandson's Captivity Narrative*. Madison: University of Wisconsin Press.

Brumm, Ursula (1963). *Die religiöse Typologie im amerikanischen Denken: Ihre Bedeutung für die amerikanische Literatur- und Geistesgeschichte*. Leiden: Brill.

Burnham, Michelle (1993). "The Journey Between: Liminality and Dialogism in Mary White Rowlandson's Captivity Narrative." *Early American Literature* 28.1, 60-75.

Calvin, Jean (1960). *Institutes of the Christian Religion*. Vol. 1. Ed. John T. McNeill. Philadelphia: The Westminster Press.

Castiglia, Christopher (1996). *Bound and Determined: Captivity, Culture-Crossing, and White Womanhood from Mary Rowlandson to Patty Hearst*. Chicago: University of Chicago Press.

Cohen, Lester H. (1980). *The Revolutionary Histories: Contemporary Narratives of the American Revolution*. Ithaca: Cornell University Press.

Collingwood, Robin G. (1961). *The Idea of History*. London: Oxford University Press.

Conkin, Paul Keith (1976). *Puritans and Pragmatists*. Bloomington: Indiana University Press.

Corbett, Margery, and Ronald Lightbown (1979). *The Comely Frontispiece: The Emblematic Title-Page in England 1550-1660*. London: Routledge and Kegan.

Daly, Robert (1973). "William Bradford's Vision of History." *American Literature* 44.4, 557-569.

Davis, Margaret H. (1992). "Mary White Rowlandson's Self-Fashioning as Puritan Goodwife." *Early American Literature* 27.1, 49-60.

Derounian, Kathryn Zabelle (1988). "The Publication, Promotion, and Distribution of Mary Rowlandson's Indian Captivity Narrative in the Seventeenth Century." *Early American Literature* 23.3, 239-261.

Derounian-Stodola, Kathryn Zabelle, and James Arthur Levernier (1993). *The Indian Captivity Narrative, 1550-1900*. New York: Twayne.

Dunn, Richard S. (1984). "John Winthrop Writes His Journal." *The William and Mary Quarterly* 41.2, 185-212.

Elliott, Emory. (1994). "New England Puritan Literature." *The Cambridge History of American Literature*. Vol. 1: *1590-1820*. Ed. Sacvan Bercovitch. Cambridge: Cambridge University Press, 169-306.

Engler, Bernd, and Oliver Scheiding (1998). "Re-Visioning the Past: The Historical Imagination in American Historiography and Short Fiction." *Re-Visioning the Past: Historical Self-Reflexivity in American Short Fiction*. Ed. Bernd Engler and Oliver Scheiding. Trier: Wissenschaftlicher Verlag Trier, 11-37.

Engler, Bernd (2006). "Typologische Präfiguration und apokalyptisch-millennialistische Prophetie in Cotton Mather's *Magnalia Christi Americana.*" *Literaturwissenschaftliches Jahrbuch* 47, 181-204.
Fitzpatrick, Tara (1991). "The Figure of Captivity: The Cultural Work of the Puritan Captivity Narrative." *American Literary History* 3.1, 1-26.
Fussner, F. Smith (1976). *The Historical Revolution: English Historical Writing and Thought, 1580-1640.* Westport: Greenwood.
Gallagher, Edward J. (1970). "An Overview of Edward Johnson's *Wonder-Working Providence.*" *Early American Literature* 5.3, 30-49.
– (1975). "The *Wonder-Working Providence* as Spiritual Biography." *Early American Literature* 10.1, 75-87.
Gay, Peter (1968). *A Loss of Mastery: Puritan Historians in Colonial America.* New York: Vintage.
Godbeer, Richard (1992). *The Devil's Dominion: Magic and Religion in Early New England.* Cambridge: Cambridge University Press.
Gura, Philip F. (1984). *A Glimpse of Sion's Glory: Puritan Radicalism in New England, 1620-1660.* Middletown: Wesleyan University Press.
Hall, David D. (1989). *Worlds of Wonder, Days of Judgment: Popular Religious Belief in Early New England.* New York: Knopf.
– (1996). *Cultures of Print: Essays in the History of the Book.* Amherst: University of Massachusetts Press.
Hartman, James D. (1999). *Providence Tales and the Birth of American Literature.* Baltimore: Johns Hopkins University Press.
Hill, Christopher (1980). *Intellectual Origins of the English Revolution.* Oxford: Clarendon Press.
Holifield, Elmer Brooks (1989). *Era of Persuasion: American Thought and Culture, 1521-1680.* Boston: Twayne.
– (2003). *Theology in America: Christian Thought from the Age of the Puritans to the Civil War.* New Haven: Yale University Press.
Johnson, Edward (1974). *Wonder-Working Providence of Sions Saviour in New-England.* 1654. Ed. Edward J. Gallagher. Delmar: Scholars' Facsimiles and Reproductions.
Kemp, Anthony (1991). *The Estrangement of the Past: A Study in the Origins of Modern Historical Consciousness.* New York: Oxford University Press.
Langford, Michael J. (1981). *Providence.* London: SCM Press.
Levin, David (1972). "William Bradford: The Value of Puritan Historiography." *Major Writers of Early American Literature.* Ed. Everett Emerson. Madison: University of Wisconsin Press, 11-31.
– (1976). "Forms of Uncertainty: Representation of Doubt in American Histories." *New Literary History* 8.1, 59-74.
Lowance, Mason I. (1980). *The Language of Canaan: Metaphor and Symbol in New England from the Puritans to the Transcendentalists.* Cambridge: Harvard University Press.

Mather, Cotton (1977). *Magnalia Christi Americana*. Ed. Kenneth B. Murdock. Cambridge: Harvard University Press.

McGrath, Alister E. (1988). *Reformation Thought: An Introduction*. Oxford: Blackwell.

Miller, Perry (1954). *The New England Mind: The Seventeenth Century*. Cambridge: Harvard University Press.

Morton, Nathaniel (1979). *New Englands Memoriall*. 1669. Ed. Howard J. Hall. New York: Scholars' Facsimiles and Reprints.

Moseley, James G. (1992). *John Winthrop's World: History as a Story, the Story as History*. Madison: University of Wisconsin Press.

Murdock, Kenneth B. (1955). "Clio in the Wilderness: History and Biography in Puritan New England." *Church History* 24, 221-238.

Nelsen, Anne Kusener (1970). "King Philip's War and the Hubbard-Mather Rivalry." *The William and Mary Quarterly* 27.4, 615-629.

Norton, Mary Beth (2002). *In the Devil's Snare: The Salem Witchcraft Crisis of 1692*. New York: Knopf.

Oakes, Urian (1673). *New-England Pleaded With and Pressed to Consider the Things Which Concern Her Peace, at Least in This Her Day, or, a Seasonable and Serious Word of Faithful Advice to the Churches and People of God (Primarily Those) in the Massachusets Colony, Musingly to Ponder and Bethink Themselves, What Is the Tendency, and Will Certainly Be the Sad Issue, of Sundry Unchristian and Crooked Wayes Which Too Many Have Been Turning Aside Unto, If Persisted and Gone on In: Delivered in a Sermon Preached at Boston in New-England, May 7. 1673, Being the Day of Election There*. Cambridge: Samuel Green.

Perry, Dennis R. (1994). "'Novelties and Stile Which All Out-Do': William Hubbard's Historiography Reconsidered." *Early American Literature* 29.2, 166-182.

Read, David (2005). *New World, Known World: Shaping Knowledge in Early Anglo-American Writing*. Columbia: University of Missouri Press.

Rosenmeier, Jesper (1974). "'With My Owne Eyes': William Bradford's *Of Plymouth Plantation*." *The American Puritan Imagination: Essays in Revaluation*. Ed. Sacvan Bercovitch. New York: Cambridge University Press, 77-106.

– (1991). "'They Shall No Longer Grieve': The Song of Songs and Edward Johnson's *Wonder-Working Providence*." *Early American Literature* 26.1, 1-20.

Rumsey, Peter Lockwood (1986). *Acts of God and the People, 1620-1730*. Ann Arbor: UMI Research Press.

Ruttenburg, Nancy (1998). *Democratic Personality: Popular Voice and the Trial of American Authorship*. Stanford: Stanford University Press.

Sargent, Mark L. (1992). "William Bradford's 'Dialogue' with History." *New England Quarterly* 65.3, 389-421.

Scobey, David M. (1984). "Revising the Errand: New England's Ways and the Puritan Sense of the Past." *The William and Mary Quarterly* 41.1, 3-31.

Slotkin, Richard (1978). *So Dreadfull a Judgment: Puritan Responses to King Philip's War, 1676-1677*. Middletown: Wesleyan University Press.
Smolinski, Reiner (1990). "Israel Redivivus: The Eschatological Limits of Puritan Typology in New England." *New England Quarterly* 63.3, 357-395.
Stein, Stephen J. (1978/79). "Providence and Apocalypse in the Early Writings of Jonathan Edwards." *Early American Literature* 13.3, 250-267.
Stievermann, Jan (2004). "Writing 'To Conquer All Things': Cotton Mather's *Magnalia Christi Americana* and the Quandary of *Copia*." *Early American Literature* 39.2, 263-297.
Thomas, Keith (1980). *Religion and the Decline of Magic: Studies in Popular Beliefs in Sixteenth- and Seventeenth-Century England*. Harmondsworth: Penguin.
Thompson, James Westfall (1942). *A History of Historical Writing*. Vol. 1: *From the Earliest Times to the End of the Seventeenth Century*. New York: Macmillan.
Vander Molen, Ronald J. (1978). "Providence as Mystery, Providence as Revelation: Puritan and Anglican Modifications of John Calvin's Doctrine of Providence." *Church History* 47.1, 27-47.
Walsham, Alexandra (2003). *Providence in Early Modern England*. Oxford: Oxford University Press.
Wendel, François (1968). *Calvin: Ursprung und Entwicklung seiner Theologie*. Trans. Walter Kickel. Neukirchen-Vluyn: Neukirchener Verlag des Erziehungsvereins.
Wenska, Walter P. (1978). "Bradford's Two Histories: Pattern and Paradigm in *Of Plymouth Plantation*." *Early American Literature* 13.2, 151-164.
Winship, Michael P. (1996). *Seers of God: Puritan Providentialism in the Restoration and Early Enlightenment*. Baltimore: Johns Hopkins University Press.
Winthrop, John (1931). "A Modell of Christian Charity." *Winthrop Papers*. Vol. 2: *1623-1630*. Boston: Massachusetts Historical Society, 282-295.
Zakai, Avihu (1987). "Reformation, History, and Eschatology in English Protestantism." *History and Theory* 26.3, 300-318.
– (1992). *Exile and Kingdom: History and Apocalypse in the Puritan Migration to America*. Cambridge: Cambridge University Press.

JAN STIEVERMANN

Interpreting the Role of America in New England Millennialism, 1640 to 1800

I. Themes and Arguments

Millennialism or chiliasm in the early history of English-speaking North America is a very broad and rich field of scholarly investigation that has been examined very productively from a variety of perspectives,[1] some of which I have touched upon in my short introduction to the respective segment in the anthology.[2] In this companion-piece I want to focus on what seems to me the most pertinent

---

[1] Like most scholars I use the Latin-derived term 'millennialism' (from Latin *mille*, 'a thousand,' and *annus*, 'a year') and the Greek-derived term 'chiliasm' (from *khilioi*, 'a thousand') interchangeably. Unlike some scholars, however, I do not employ the distinction between millennialism/millennialist and millenarianism/millenarian. Particularly in some of the older studies, 'millennialism' is used to refer to those who believed in a gradual progress towards redemption, while 'millenarianism' signifies the expectancy of the world's (imminent) destruction before its apocalyptic regeneration. In my view, this binarism is not helpful in dealing with the theological complexities one encounters, especially in the apocalyptic literature before 1800.

[2] The scholarship on New England millennialism, even of the pre-nineteenth century period, is extensive, so all I can give here are a few general hints. The first and foremost perspective is that of the religious historian who examines in close detail the development of 'local' theological debates over the biblical prophecy of Christ's thousand-year reign. An excellent and very reliable survey of New England millennialist theology from this perspective is offered by Smolinski's article (2003), which will also introduce students to more specialized studies. Another rewarding take on the subject was defined by myth-studies, which highlight the cultural function of millennialist rhetoric, the ways in which it addresses certain fundamental existential anxieties or needs of believers. The most prominent studies of early American millennialism from this perspective are Davidson (1977) and O'Leary (1994). Thirdly, millennialism has been investigated as a discourse of community-building and identity-formation which exerted considerable power in American history, especially in conjunction with other discourses such as anti-Catholicism, the Puritan jeremiad, or, later on, revolutionary republicanism, nationalism and the manifest-destiny discourse. This is the predominant perspective on millennialism in the classical studies by Miller (1956), Heimert (1966), Tuveson (1968), and Bercovitch (1975, 1978). For the revolutionary period in particular, see Hatch (1977) and Bloch (1985); for the use of millennialist discourse as a symbolic reservoir for the creation of enemy-images, see Fuller (1995). A broad cultural studies-approach with a focus on identity-issues is also taken by many of the essays collected in Engler, Fichte, and Scheiding (2002).

and, at the same time, the most perplexing question raised by the millennialist texts that have been excerpted for the anthology. As you will notice, all of the selected documents were written in New England, and all of them, in one way or the other, seem to have a regional dimension in the sense that they reflect on the place this region, and later the United States at large, might occupy in the last age prophesied by the Scriptures.[3] What specific role then, I will ask throughout my readings of the documents, did the successive generations of New England divines assign to their own colonies and America during the millennium?

Considering that America had been unknown to biblical authors and earlier Christian exegetes alike, I will begin my inquiry by looking at the ways in which Puritan theologians attempted to place the newly found continent and their colonies within the existing "*Christianography*" (*KC*, 182-3) of the Last Times.[4] Were they indeed, as it has often been claimed, hoping to give an eschatological centrality to a region whose political institutions and churches occupied no more than a peripheral position in the factual geography of worldly power and spiritual influence at the time? Was the faith and identity of seventeenth-century Puritan emigrants really predicated on the assumption that the New England churches would play a leading part in Christ's thousand-year reign? As we move into the second half of the eighteenth century in section IV of the essay, my guiding question will then lead us to explore the complex intersections of traditional New England millennialism with Enlightenment philosophy, the revolutionary ideology, and the discourse of nationalism that is reflected in the last documents in the section.

In pursuing this line of inquiry I hope to demonstrate that, contrary to a very dominant model of interpretation, there was no high road from the purported Puritan belief in a millennial errand into the wilderness to the establishment of a

---

[3] The fact that all the respective texts in the anthology are of New England origin should not mislead students into the assumption that millennialism did not play a significant role in the cultural history of colonial America outside the British settlements on the northeastern seaboard. On the contrary, scholars have long found millennialism to have been an important factor in the discovery, early exploration and colonization of the New World by the Spanish and Portuguese. Christopher Columbus's writings from and about the New World, for instance, clearly show the impact of Franciscan and Joachimite millennialism (cf. Milhou 2003 and Schilson 1995). Similarly, the subsequent Franciscan missions in New Spain (cf. Philan 1970) and those of the French Jesuits in New France were informed by chiliastic expectations. Also, the earliest British colonization efforts in Virginia were by no means purely commercially motivated. At least some people connected to the Virginia Company, such as Samuel Purchas, saw the English colonization of the New World as part of the latter day events leading to the millennium. And later on, Britain's southern colonies were also swept along by the revivals of the Great Awakening, which, like in New England, had a strong millennialist dimension. Moreover, many of the German-speaking Pietist sectarians settling in Britain's mid-Atlantic colonies during the eighteenth century believed that the last age was at hand (cf. Roeber 1995).

[4] The term was used by Cotton Mather to refer to the geography of salvation as defined by Christ's redemptive work (cf. doc. 81).

post-revolutionary ideology of American exceptionalism and messianism.[5] Even though, as my readings will show, Puritan millennialism was indeed later appropriated by patriotic discourse and, once divested of its original context, did become an important component of America's national identity, the latter was not a direct outgrowth of the former. Instead, American nationalism, like Enlightenment progressivism, should be regarded as a distinct discourse which originally even contradicted many of the convictions central to traditional millennialism. It was only in the second half of the eighteenth century that millennialism entered a complex relationship with these other discourses, resulting in the nineteenth century beliefs in America's manifest destiny and role as a world redeemer.[6]

---

[5] Students should be aware that the thesis of a direct causal connection between Puritan millennialism and the American nationalism of the nineteenth century has formed the foundation of one of the master-narratives of American studies. According to some of the founding fathers of the discipline, among them Perry Miller, Alan Heimert, and Ernest Tuveson, the first Puritan emigrants already conceived of themselves as God's new chosen people predestined to establish an ideal church polity that would take a leading role in the unfolding of the millennium. Some Puritan divines are even said to have propagated the vision of New England as the seat of the New Jerusalem itself, which would stand at the center of Christ's earthly kingdom. Following this master-narrative, the 'apocalyptic exceptionalism' of the Puritans then underwent a nationalization process during the second half of the eighteenth century, at the end of which it became one of the main ideological driving forces behind the Revolution. In the nineteenth century, the Puritan belief in their Errand into the Wilderness and the promise of its fruition in an American New Jerusalem is understood to have finally transformed into the belief "that the United States has been called to be a chief means of worldwide redemption, and that as a chosen people it was assigned a new promised land" (Tuveson 1968, 91). With his famous studies *The Puritan Origin of the American Self* (1975) and *The American Jeremiad* (1978) Sacvan Bercovitch, who is probably the most renowned Americanist of his generation, gave a new sophistication to this time-honored model and guaranteed its continuing impact on the scholarly community. Although much more critical of Americas exceptionalist identity than his scholarly predecessors, Bercovitch affirmed their interpretation that the millennialism of the Puritans already contained the "protonationalistic tendencies" (Bercovitch 1978, 105) which were simply drawn out by their eighteenth and nineteenth centuries' successors.

[6] Information was drawn from the revisionist critique of the 'From Puritan Millennialism to Manifest Destiny' master-narrative propagated by traditional American Studies. During the last two decades, scholars such as Theodore Dwight Bozeman (1988) and Reiner Smolinski (1990, 1995) started to challenge this narrative, which they regard to be in many respects a backward projection of a nation-centered (no matter how critical) historiography in search of an origin of a distinct American identity. While these scholars do not deny that millennialism did play a significant role in the theology as well as the popular imagination of American Puritanism, they no longer see millenarian ideology as the decisive reason for the first wave of emigration between 1620 and 1640. Also, the revisionists emphasize that the undeniable concern of late seventeenth-century Puritan exegetes with placing America on the millennial map must not be interpreted (or rather overinterpreted) as an attempt to associate the prophecies of Christ's glorious reign on earth exclusively with New England history and territory. In short, the Puritan exodus from England was not conceived of as a mission to reform the world and inaugurate the millennium. Nor did any traditional New England theologian ever proclaim Boston as the future site of the New Jerusalem. Consequently, Puritan eschatology

II. The Origins of Puritan Millennialism and the Eschatological Self-Definition of the Early New England Churches

As so many discussions about millennialism (especially in the classroom) are hampered by false presuppositions and definitional problems, I want to begin this section with a short reminder of what the term actually means, or is supposed to mean, when employed in a theological context or used to talk about traditional Scripture-centered forms of Christianity such as New England Puritanism. Here, one has to stay clear of modern practices using the term as a fit-all metaphor for any kind of ideology invested in notions of historical progress, or as an expression referring to the vague hopes and anxieties associated with the calendar event of the millennium. Instead, one should only talk about millennialism to denote the religious belief in a quasi-paradisiacal interval of a thousand (actual or figurative) years in the cosmic battle between good and evil over the redemption of mankind, which is how the Bible describes all of history. According to Christian millennialists, this interval will be brought about by Christ's Second Coming, whether abruptly in the body or gradually in the spirit, and the bliss and glory that is promised to the true believers (also called saints) for this period will be the effect of his reign on earth, during which Satan will not be allowed to further persecute mankind. One must be careful, however, to distinguish this hope for a millennial reign on earth from the hope of a paradisiacal afterlife or "a new heaven and a new earth" which will occur only after Judgment Day and hence after the end of history, but, much to the confusion of the modern reader, is sometimes also called the (eternal) millennium.

Millennialism or chiliasm, in the strict sense, thus designates the belief, to quote Tuveson's succinct definition,

> that, before the final judgment of all mankind, Christ [either in the body or as a spiritual ruler] will return to the earth and, together with resurrected saints, will reign over a glorious kingdom which will last a thousand years. The authority for this belief is Revelation 20:1-5, which relates how the cosmic battles between the divine and the Satanic powers will in part end with the fall of the latter's stronghold, 'Babylon.' An angel will come down from heaven and imprison the 'dragon' for a thousand years [...]. After this millennium Satan is to be loosed once more. He will gather the nations of the earth for one grand last stand at 'Armageddon,' but he will be defeated. Then he will be thrown into the 'lake of fire' and the universal judgment will occur, followed by the establishment of the eternal heavenly state. (Tuveson 1973, 223)

While they always integrated many other parts of the Old and New Testament into their readings, Christian exegetes, as suggested by Tuveson, mainly derive this vision of the latter days from St. John's Book of Revelation, particularly

---

cannot be said to be the main root from which the later ideology of American exceptionalism and messianism grew. Rather, the existing millennialist tradition of Puritan theology was appropriated and radically re-interpreted by the new nationalist discourse.

chapter 20.[7] Needless to say, they differed widely in their interpretations of the prophetic events described there. Yet it is the basic assumption that these events, in one way or the other, referred to a historical reality that constitutes the core of traditional Christian millennialism.

It should be emphasized, however, that millennialism was by no means embraced by all traditional, Scripture-centered forms of Christianity. In my introduction to the anthology (*KC*, 159-62), I have already suggested that it was rather a very controversial aspect of Christian eschatology; i.e., those parts of Christian thinking and teaching which concerned the 'last things.' Among early Christian communities of the first centuries AD, expectations of Christ's immanent return (*parousia*) and the advent of his thousand-year reign were rampant. Speculations about the literal fulfillment of John's prophecies surrounding the millennium can also be found in the writings of some of the major early Christian theologians, like Lactantius, Tertullian, and Irenaeus. But after the institutionalization of Christianity as a state religion, the spokespersons for the church usually maintained a distance, or were openly opposed, to any kind of chiliastic enthusiasm. Most of the church fathers also worked towards a theological "'taming' of apocalyptic thinking in order to integrate it into a larger picture of a Christian world order" (Daley 2003, 223). This Christian world order, as it was now conceived most prominently by Augustine of Hippo in his *De civitate Dei* (413-26), rested on a fundamental distinction between those actions and events which directly concerned God's relationship to mankind and were recorded or prophesied by the Bible (*historia sacra*) and the vain affairs of the world (*historia profana*). With Creation, the original Fall, the incarnation of Christ, his crucifixion, and his resurrection all in the past, the *historia sacra* would "no longer contain decisive turning-points" (Markus 1970, 20-1) until the Second Coming and the Last Judgment. Until then the slow and gradual progress in the relationship of man and his heavenly father, which had been made possible by the intervention of the Son, would occur only inside and through

---

[7] Students who wish to study the development of American millennialist theology in more detail should familiarize themselves with the most important scriptural passages on which the exegetical debates were focused. Obviously the starting point has to be the Book of Revelation, especially chapter 20. Of central importance among the Old Testament texts is the Book of Daniel with its famous visions of the compound image (Dan. 2.31-45), the four beasts and the ten horns, as well as of the advent of the Son of man (Dan. 7). Moreover, the vision of the 2,300 prophetic days, of the seventy prophetic weeks and of the duration of the end times in the Book of Daniel (8.14; 9.24-7; 12.1-13), were often connected with the 1,260 days prophesied by the two witnesses in Rev. 11.3 in the ongoing speculative computations of the advent of the millennium. These computations were usually based on the biblical equation of thousand years with a day before the Lord (Ps. 90.4), which was combined with Gen. 2.2 into an overall understanding of earthly history as comprising a 6,000 year time-span before the millennial Sabbath of the world. Also significant is the 'small apocalypse' in Isa. 24-7 and 65.17-25. Among Jesus' own prophetic teachings millennialist theologians drew in particular on Matt. 24-5. The most relevant passages from the letters are the following: 1 Cor. 15.20-8, 1 Thess. 4.13-8 and 2 Thess. 2.1-12. With regard to the belief in a future conflagration of the earth, 2 Pet. 3.10-4 is essential.

the *civitas dei* or 'invisible church' of true Christians. By way of contrast, the affairs of the profane world and its political institutions (*civitas terrena*), even though superficially they changed constantly, were deemed to lack any inherent potential for significant change.[8]

Befitting such a cosmology, in which worldly history was without any real meaning, the church quite early on adopted an allegorical and spiritual reading of the biblical prophecies concerning Christ's millennial reign on earth. According to this reading, the millennium and the eschatological events surrounding it merely signified the last stage in the history of redemption, which had begun with Christ's first appearance on earth and would be brought to a close when he returned on Doomsday. In other words, the allegorical reading put forth by Augustine and others placed the beginning of the millennium in the past (interpreting it in a 'preterite' fashion), and viewed the thousand years not as calendar years, but as symbolic of 'a long time.' The proponents of such an allegorizing approach to the prophetic events also rejected the literalist belief that there would occur a physical binding of Satan, a military defeat of the Antichrist and his legions, or a corporeal first resurrection of the saints who would reign over an earthly dominion under King Jesus. They rather claimed that Christ's spiritual reign would come to be exercised gradually by and through the church as it became ever more pure and powerful through the grace of God, who, in His infinite mercy, had sent His son to restrict Satan's power of deceiving men. Having already begun with Christ's redemptive sacrifice on the cross, the millennium, then, had to be understood as the progressive convergence of the *civitas dei* with the institutional church and the outward spreading of true Christianity.[9]

Generally speaking, this Augustinian 'solution' of interpreting the millennium in an allegorical and preterite fashion became the orthodox position in the medieval church. Still, the literalist and futurite strand of early Christian millennialism never completely vanished and was regularly taken up by church re-

---

[8] In such an eschatology, there was relatively little room for a belief in man's meaningful historical agency, let alone in historical progress or human self-perfection through advancements in moral civilization and the sciences. If the orthodox position, following Augustine, assumed that the millennium had already begun and Christ's kingdom was growing in and through the members of his church, this notion of their spiritual betterment or *profectus* through the grace of God was not historical in the sense that the passing of time itself was understood as a meaningful continuity leading towards the desired regeneration of the world. Nor did it imply the idea of human capacity for meaningful innovation or real self-improvement inside worldly history. Medieval theology did not conceive of a history of redemption in the sense that human history was understood as a causal continuum in which the progress of time itself could assume a redemptive function because it would have marked a progress in man's moral nature and salvific knowledge. Such an integrated concept of redemption history came into being only as the combined result of previous radical changes within Christian, particularly Protestant theology, and the philosophy of the Enlightenment since the seventeenth century.

[9] According to such an allegorical reading, the apocalyptic tribulations of which the Scriptures spoke were to be decoded as the painful rebirth from spiritual death to be undergone by members of the 'invisible church.'

formers or radical sectarians, such as Joachim of Fiore and his followers, the Fraticelli, Girolamo Savonarola in Florence, the Lollards in England, or the Hussites and the Taborites in Bohemia.[10] Then, around the turn of the sixteenth century, a general revival of chiliastic beliefs occurred. This revival grew from and simultaneously fed into the various ecclesiastical movements and social upheavals we now call the Reformation, which swept across Europe under the wide-spread expectation that the latter days were at hand. Virtually all the reformers who challenged the authority of Rome associated the Pope and the established ecclesiastical system with the forces of Satan. More specifically, they identified them with the Antichristian "deceivers" of 1 John, the "Beast" described in Rev. 13, and the "Man of Sin" of 2 Thess. 2. Concomitantly, they interpreted their revolt as signifying the pending overthrow of the Antichrist and the downfall of Satan as foretold in the prophetic Scriptures. Whether or not the downfall of Satan would be followed by a millennial period of earthly bliss before Doomsday, however, remained a hotly contested issue. Luther, Zwingli, and Calvin had been careful to curb any enthusiastic expectations of a terrestrial kingdom of Christ in the future.[11] But a number of their own followers and several of the popular movements, which historians associate with the term 'the radical Reformation' (such as Anabaptists groups), did embrace a futurite, sometimes even a literalist type of millennialism.

In the late sixteenth century, the hope for a future, if not earthly then at least a spiritual, millennium, was also adopted by some of Calvin's heirs, including those churchmen who would define English reformed theology, which, during the reign of Elizabeth, was eventually institutionalized by the Anglican Church. Indeed, English reformed theologians such as John Bale, Thomas Brightman, and most importantly Joseph Mede as well as popular religious authors like John Foxe in his famous *Actes and Monuments* (1563), did much to foster a conviction among their followers that English Protestantism had been preordained to serve as God's vanguard in the battle against Antichristian Rome. If England would faithfully perform its role, people were told by countless tracts, books, and sermons, it could expect to play a central role in the advancement of Christ's kingdom and to share proportionally in its glory.[12] Thus, at the beginning of the seventeenth century, as historian Barry Coward notes, the belief in the imminent defeat of Satan, and the advent of Christ's reign on earth, "far from being the creed of a few

---

[10] For an excellent survey of chiliastic movements during the Middle Ages and late Middle Ages, see McGinn (2003) and Potestà (2003). The classical study on the subject is Cohn (1957).

[11] On Luther's apocalyptic (but not millennialist) worldview, see Oberman (1989). Orthodox Lutheranism emphasized the imminence of universal judgment and deliverance, but rejected chiliastic expectations. Article XVII of the Augsburg confession of 1530 denounced "certain Jewish opinions which are even now making their appearance and which teach that, before the resurrection of the dead, saints and godly men will possess a worldly kingdom and annihilate all the godless." For a similar denouncement, see Article XI of the *Confessio Helvetica*.

[12] On English apocalypticism and millennialism during the sixteenth and seventeenth centuries, see Lamont (1969), Bauckham (1978), and Firth (1979).

cranks, was part of the mainstream of English intellectual life [...] and was widely diffused throughout society at all levels" (1994, 239). Among members of the Puritan movement, which pressed for further reforms within the Anglican Church (cf. Spahr in this vol., 56-9), such chiliastic believes were particularly pronounced and occasionally took a turn towards radical literalism. This is particularly true for the period of the English Civil War and the Interregnum (c. 1642-1660) which produced such anarchic communitarians as the Diggers or the Fifth Monarchy Men (to which Oliver Cromwell was connected), who saw themselves as laying the groundwork for Christ's terrestrial kingdom through the erection of an English republican theocracy based on Old Testament laws.[13]

To be sure, the majority of English Protestants, including those associated with the Puritan cause, refrained from such hyperliteralist excesses, and interpreted the coming millennium as a spiritual transformation in the hearts of its individual followers and the *civitas dei* at large, in which they hoped a purified Anglican Church would play a central part. Nevertheless, English millennialists across the board viewed the political conflicts and tumults of their time through the lens of Scriptures as being part of the latter day tribulations leading towards spiritual regeneration. Especially among the Puritans, there was a tendency to blur the old line between *historia sacra* and *historia profana* into an integrated concept of history as a providentially controlled continuum of events leading towards redemption (cf. Obenland in this vol., 89-95). After all, to conceive of their own fight for ecclesiastical and parliamentary reforms in apocalyptic terms ultimately meant ascribing higher meaning to worldly events, and, at least potentially, to their own revolutionary actions and the changes wrought thereby. In other words, the period's acute sense of an ending went along with an altered sense of history, its sacred significance, and man's role in history.

This new historical consciousness was most forcefully expressed in the extensive commentaries written by English theologians on the prophetic Scriptures, particularly the Book of Revelation. In their works, Bale, Brightman, and Mede all continued a general trend in Protestant hermeneutics and historiography which, partly as an attempt to justify their revolutionary break from the Church of Rome and also to establish a central role for the Reformation in ecclesiastical history, had already begun to move away from Augustine's interpretation of salvation history.

> Instead of Augustine's dissociation of salvation and history, Protestant historians developed a new mode of historical consciousness based upon the utmost association between prophecy and history, providence and historical occurrences, grounded in an apocalyptic interpretation of history. [... E]schatology and apocalypse – and hence the millennium – were again brought within history. Divine providence works within history, and in fact, determines the whole process, in order to advance God's redemptive plan for fallen humanity. Salvation is inseparable from and intrinsic to the historical process, and vice versa. (Zakai 2003, 179)

---

[13] For these movements and groups see Hill (1971, 1972) and Capp (1972).

It is hard to overemphasize the importance of this theological revolution in historical consciousness, at the heart of which was an understanding of the Book of Revelation as a symbolic abridgment of history from Christ's time to the world's end. All history since Christ's departure, therefore, was viewed as having sacred or, more specifically, eschatological meaning, as Protestant interpreters causally linked all ages through a chain of prophetic events symbolized by the cycles of visions (seals, trumpets, vials, and woes) described in the Apocalypse. Inversely, the parallelization of historical occurrences and figures with the visions of the prophetic Scriptures was seen as the key to unlocking the mysteries of St. John.

Numerous English exegetes followed the general trend among Protestant theologians of the sixteenth and seventeenth centuries to decode the Book of Revelation and thereby to identify their own (temporal) position in the history of salvation. They all subjected the book's vision-cycles to a form of historical exegesis, in which they attempted to connect the specific prophecies with specific events in the past and present. In this way, they sought to identify those prophetic events which had yet to occur, and thereby obtain clues as to when the millennium would begin. Among the substantial number of such commentaries on Revelation, Mede's *Clavis Apocalyptica* (1627) in particular deserves further analysis here, if only because it would have such a lasting impact on Puritan millennialism in New England.

Translated into English as *Key of the Apocalypse* in 1650, Mede's commentary went to great lengths to demonstrate the inner order of the Book of Revelation by systematically synchronizing the different visionary cycles and their symbolic elements. Mede understood these to refer simultaneously to events in secular and church history, which he believed to be increasingly converging since the Reformation as the Protestant countries (presumably with England as a spearhead) developed into a holy polity that would reach its utmost purity during Christ's thousand-year reign. More importantly, however, Mede was the first renowned academic theologian in England to break with the preterite tradition of Augustine in his reading of Rev. 20.[14] Like many exegetes in Old and New England after him, Mede based his millennium mathematics on the basic assumption that the prophetic forty-two months, or 1,260 days of Rev. 11.2-3, each of which he interpreted as years, circumscribed the historical period of the rise and fall of the Antichrist in Western (church-)history. In order to know when the Antichrist would fall and the millennium begin, the decisive question to answer, therefore, was when to date the first rising of the Antichrist. Mede thought this

---

[14] In many respects, Mede's futurite interpretation followed the ideas of the German Reformed theologian Johann Heinrich Alsted (1588-1638) from the college of Herborn, whose tract *Diatribe de Mille Annis Apocalypticis* (1627), according to recent historians, has to be seen as a watershed in the development of radical Calvinist millennialism. Alsted's commentary on Rev. 20 used complex mathematical computations to predict the final realization of saintly rule in 1694.

had happened during Genseric's sack of Rome in 455 AD or with the dethroning of Rome's last emperor in 476 AD.

With this fulcrum in place he calculated that, except for the seventh vial, all of John's visions already lay in the past, and thus assumed that, following the fall of the Antichrist, the onset of millennial reign would occur sometime in the early eighteenth century. In placing the beginning of the millennium 'back into the future,' and a not-too-distant future to boot, Mede set an example that most New England exegetes would follow. Although succeeding generations of Puritan theologians in the British colonies differed considerably from Mede (as they did from each other) in the details of their calculations and had to push back the dates for the expected advent of Christ's glorious reign as the decades and centuries elapsed, they all followed Mede's basic example of a futurite interpretation situating their own times on the verge of the latter days.

Yet Mede also left an extremely problematic and long-lasting theological legacy to American Puritans. Contrary to many other exegetes of the time who had sought to fit the New World into their millenarian cosmologies, Mede claimed in an appendix (doc. 75) to the enlarged English edition of his *Key to the Revelation* (1650) that the "blessed kingdome" would only encompass the territory of Daniel's four empires, Babylon, Medo-Persia, Greece, and Rome (Dan. 2.31-45), making the Old World sole "partaker of the promised instauration." Whereas earlier Portuguese, Spanish, and English theologians had frequently interpreted the colonization of the Americas as the final stage in God's plan of redeeming the world and had seen it as a prerequisite to Christ's *parousia* (cf. Scheiding in this vol., 3-5), Mede emphatically insisted that "the inhabitants of the land of *America*, both Northern and Southern" could never join the "camp of the Saints" (*KC*, 165-6). On the contrary, he identified the inhabitants of the Americas as the apocalyptic people of Gog and Magog (cf. Rev. 20.8-9), writing that at the end of the millennium Satan's "army shall come from those nations, which live in the Hemisp[h]ere opposite to us" (*KC*, 164) to fight the armies of the saints in the battle of Armageddon. For at least four generations, Puritan theologians in the colonies would struggle in their commentaries on the Apocalypse to refute Mede's influential arguments for consigning not only the Native Americans, but also the European settlers in the New World to the outer darkness beyond the saving influence of Christ (cf. Smolinski, 1990).

For the first Puritans who would make their way across the Atlantic in the Great Migration (1620-1640), the notion that they might be leaving the future boundaries of the kingdom of Christ was not yet a serious concern, since Mede's view would only gain prominence in the last third of the seventeenth century. Neither were they driven, however, by the idea that they had been called by God to the howling wilderness of the New World to erect a new millennial Zion there while the corrupt Old World went down in flames. To be sure, like virtually all their English fellow-believers, the emigrants were convinced that the fall of the Antichrist, the binding of Satan, and the advent of the thousand-year reign were at hand. But like the majority of Puritans who stayed home, their goals were largely restorationist in nature (cf. Bozeman 1988). They were driven by the conviction that the church had to be restored to the original purity of the first Christian churches in Asia Minor. The Puritans believed that only by following this path could English Protestants fulfill their special role in the completion of the Reformation and escape God's wrath during the imminent apocalyptic tribulations. To achieve this desired purity, the Anglican Church had to be purged of all accretions since the Apostolic age, including the episcopal structure, as well as certain liturgical forms which had been established in the medieval church all over Europe and had survived the Reformation in England.

From the Puritan point of view, these remnants of Roman Catholicism tied the Church of England to the forces of the Antichrist. Hence, the leading Puritan theologians regularly couched their critique of the Anglican Church and its episcopal system in apocalyptic terms, as did John Cotton's *An Exposition upon the Thirteenth Chapter of the Revelation* (doc. 76). Here, "[t]*he visible Catholicke Roman Church*" (*KC*, 166) is shown to be the Beast of Rev. 13.1-2, whose monstrosity (a monster is literally an unnatural being composed of heterogeneous elements) is defined by its unlawful intermixing of spiritual and temporal power held by the English monarch, who, after all, was head of the church, and the bishops.[15]

Most of the Puritans who left England, then, did so during the reign of Charles I, who was widely perceived as having Catholic leanings, since they increasingly despaired over the present feasibility of their great goal of creating a church free from the monstrosities of intermixed power in England. Under the rule of Archbishop William Laud (1633-1640), things went from bad to worse, as the Puritans were now persecuted more actively and were increasingly less free to worship as they saw fit even within their own circles. On the far-away shores of North America they thus hoped to escape the pending wrath of God and continue their project of purifying English Protestantism of all postapostolic pollutions. Indeed, John Winthrop's famous sermon "A Model of Christian Charity" (doc. 62) testifies to the dream of setting up an exemplary model of a primitive Christian commonwealth that might eventually be adopted back home. John Cotton's 1642 *The Churches Resurrection* (doc. 74) illustrates how, and to what extent this project of mainstream Puritanism was tied into a millennialist framework. The text was written at a time when a first wave of chiliastic fervor hit the Massachusetts Bay Colony, which happened, however, only a full decade after the first groups of settlers had arrived. The main cause was the news of the

---

[15] Only the most radical of the Puritans, the so-called separatists, who founded Plymouth Colony in 1620 and later settled in Rhode Island, thought that the Anglican Church was irremediably Antichristian in nature, and that England would inevitably be dragged into the general downfall of the Antichrist. Hence, they no longer worked towards a further reformation of the Church of England and called rather for a complete separation of the New England churches from the mother country so that they could, in the words of William Bradford, "reverte to their anciente puritie, and recover their primative order, libertie, and bewtie" (*KC*, 109).

burgeoning Civil War at home, which would continue to stir up apocalyptic expectations in the Puritan community on both sides of the Atlantic for the next two decades, actually inspiring many New Englanders to return home (cf. Holifield 2003, 48-53).

Following Mede's synchronization approach to the Book of Revelation, Cotton came to the conclusion that the Antichrist's fall, Satan's binding, and the dawning of the millennium would occur even earlier than his colleague had conjectured, probably sometime around 1655. While insisting on an at least partially literalist interpretation of the millennial reign as such – which he subdivided into a celestial city in the heavens, where Jesus would rule with his martyrs, and an earthly, inchoate Christian dominion comprised of the regenerate among the saved nations – Cotton retained the Augustinian tradition of reading the saints' first resurrection (Rev. 20.4-6) in an allegorical fashion. For him, the resurrection therefore signified a spiritual rebirth, a "Resurrection [...] of mens soules and bodies dead in sinne" (*KC*, 163). More precisely, Cotton thought that following Christ's spiritual coming would be a rebirth of "particular persons" and also of specific churches within the Christian nations, "as they are recovered againe from their Apostatical and dead estate in [Roman Catholic] Idolatry and Superstition" (*KC*, 163). The gradual binding of Satan thus symbolized the increasing purification of the regenerated *civitas dei* which, however, would never include the world's entire nominal Christendom, and would not be completed before the end of the millennium when Christ would return in person for Judgment Day (cf. Smolinski 2002; Fichte 2002).

Since Cotton and his New England colleagues saw a demonstrable conversion experience as a prerequisite to the redemption of individuals and held that only the bodies of such reborn Christians could form truly regenerated churches, the Puritan concern over restricting church membership to converted persons was therefore directly linked to their millennialist theology. Puritan leaders like Cotton urged their fellow colonists not to relent in the great outward renovation of their churches in terms of church government, doctrines, ordinances, and liturgy, and, most importantly, to ensure by means of official tests that they would consist mostly of 'visible saints' because they thought the time was nigh when God would separate his sheep from the goats that would be slaughtered. To be sure, they took pride in the idea that, by setting up a Congregationalist system (cf. Spahr in this vol., 62-7), they had already taken their churches to a higher degree of primitive purity than could be found anywhere in contemporary Europe. Contrary to what many Americanists have claimed in the past, however, their church reforms were not motivated by any hopes of establishing a literal New Jerusalem on American shores, nor did they claim that they alone were God's new chosen people.[16] Rather, the first generation of Puritan di-

---

[16] Hence, when Cotton related the beginning emigration of the English Puritans to the 'colonization' of the promised land by the ancient Israelites in his famous 1630 sermon *Gods Promise to His Plantation* (doc. 16), he did so in terms of an analogy, and not to suggest that God's

vines, represented by John Cotton, Richard Mather and John Davenport wanted to ensure that their New England congregations would escape the brunt of cataclysmic catastrophes preceding the fall of the Antichrist, and would have a part in Christ's millennial church on earth. Their understanding of this future church therefore remained strictly universalist, i.e., they thought that it would be comprised of the reborn saints from all nations and would not be restricted to specific localities or peoples. And as most of them opted for an allegorical reading of Rev. 20, they also believed that this inchoate millennial church could do no more than anticipate the heavenly New Jerusalem that was to be established only after Christ's bodily return at the end of the thousand years in 2655.

With its figurative reading of the first resurrection and its emphasis on the remaining imperfection of the millennial church on earth, Cotton's *The Churches Resurrection* (doc. 74) marks the starting point of one of the two main developmental lines in New England millennialism. Influenced by a tendency to allegorize and hence spiritualize the millennium and the prophetic events surrounding it, this first tradition would later come to be associated with the term 'postmillennialism' because many of its representatives emphasized the fact that Christ would only return in the body for Judgment Day after the end of the inchoate millennium. The other main line of development, by way of contrast, can be distinguished by its penchant for literalist interpretations, and would come to be subsumed under the umbrella term 'premillennialism.' Like postmillennialism, the label premillennialism is somewhat reductionist because the expectation of Christ's corporeal *parousia* at the onset of his terrestrial reign of glory is only one of the convictions held by some, but not all, representatives of the literalist tradition. Indeed, this literalist tradition produced a great variety of beliefs (such as the bodily resurrection and the rapture of the saints), which are all characterized by a heightened supernaturalism.[17]

During the closing decades of the seventeenth century, the literalist tradition, which later on was pushed outside the boundaries of mainstream Protestantism to the evangelical fringes, temporarily came to dominate the eschatology of American Puritanism. By this time the earlier chiliastic fervor, expressed in John Cotton's writings, had long cooled down in the aftermath of the Stuart Restoration (1660-1688), which had dashed the high hopes of the Puritan community on both sides of the Atlantic. When millennialism now returned as a major cultural force to New England, it was more the symptom of a widespread anxiety about the colonies' future. From a religious point of view, Puritan orthodoxy was on the defense and many Congregationalist ministers perceived

---

covenant with the New England churches would be the typological fulfillment of the broken covenant with Old Israel. For the difference between analogical and typological readings, see the next section of this essay.

[17] The difference between the allegoric or figurative, and the literalist tradition in New England millennialism is well explained in the excerpt from Samuel Hopkins' *Treatise on the Millennium* (doc. 86), a postmillennialist tract written in 1793.

a general decline in doctrinal purity and popular piety. From a political point of view, the colonies had to face forceful integration into the administrative system of the British Empire, a process which considerably curtailed their rights of self-government and re-defined their former identity as a mostly independent religious commonwealth.

III. In Defense of America's Place in Christ's Glorious Kingdom: Second and Third Generation Puritan Millennialism

It has been argued by prominent Americanists that, in this critical situation, the conservative Congregationalist clergy utilized millennial discourse as a means of controlling and counteracting the fearful changes it was confronting. As the established Puritan theocracy threatened to disintegrate under the Second Charter of 1691, these divines are said to have revitalized popular expectations of an imminent apocalypse and whipped their parishioners back into line by telling them that New England stood in danger of losing God's special favor at the very moment that He was about to unleash His wrath upon the unregenerate world. Overcompensating for the perceived religious backsliding and the political marginalization of the New England colonies, the second and third generations of Puritan theologians aggressively pushed ahead with an Americanization of the millennial promise that had allegedly been started by their predecessors. According to Bercovitch and others, its leading representatives, such as Increase and Cotton Mather, claimed in their reading of the Scriptures that God had finally left the Old World to its ruin in the coming apocalyptic tribulations and had assembled His new chosen people in the wilderness of the New World. They purportedly told their congregations that if they only stayed true to the faith of their fathers and continued on their millennial errand, it would soon come to its fulfillment in the form of an American New Jerusalem.[18]

Scholars have suggested that key to this arrogation of the role of God's chosen people were the ways in which Puritans expanded their typological readings of Old Testament prophecies beyond their traditional scriptural limits by identifying themselves as the antitype of Old Israel.[19] In other words, they saw them-

---

[18] Bercovitch mainly based his thesis on textual evidence drawn from sermons belonging to the so-called jeremiad genre. The jeremiad was a very popular type of exhortative sermon loosely modelled on the rhetorical patterns of the prophet Jeremiah, who had chastised the people of Israel for their backsliding while simultaneously reminding them of their role as God's chosen people and the original promise connected with this role. For Bercovitch's understanding of the millennialist ideology at work in the Puritan jeremiad, see his *The American Jeremiad*, 75-83.

[19] Typology is a method of scriptural exegesis which had already been developed by the church fathers who drew on St. Paul's definition of Christ's role as savior in relation to persons and occurrences described in the Jewish Scriptures (most importantly Adam, and the original Fall). Originally, then, typology was a way of reading events, personages, ceremonies and objects of the Old Testament as having foreshadowed Christ's redemptive work, in which they

selves as the New Israel literally assuming the place and the prerogatives of the ancient Jews. This arrogation, or so the argument goes, allowed exegetes to connect the biblical revelations about the Last Times with the new continent and the historical development of the New England churches, which they believed to have entered the new covenant with God when the old one had been forfeited by the Jewish people. More specifically, they viewed the scriptural prophecies concerning Israel's restoration before the advent of the millennium – as predicted in Rom. 11.26 "And so all Israel shall be saved" – in typological terms as referring to their own election and purification.

Today, some leading experts on Puritan theology disagree with this interpretation.[20] As they see it, the New England Puritans of the second and third generations, in the tradition of their forebears and English Protestantism in general, continued to understand the eschatological meaning of Old Testament types as referring to Christ's true church, which was conceived as a transnational community of the saints and was never identified with a specific secular society, such as a colony or nation. In other words, they never thought of themselves as exclusive heirs to the old covenant of ancient Israel because the new covenant would encompass the whole community of the elect, who would be saved in Christ. It was only in a much more limited, analogous sense that the Puritans assumed to have entered, like other Christian churches of the time and before them, into a special 'national covenant' with God, which was described as similar to the national covenant with Israel. As such a covenanted people, they saw themselves under special obligations to carry out God's will, but also expected, when obedient, to have their share in the millennial glory that would be bestowed upon all the members of Christ's new covenant during the latter days. This "covenantal framework" of Puritan theology, as David Hall has written, "allowed them to

---

were also fulfilled. Or, to quote from the definition given by the Puritan divine Samuel Mather in his *The Figures or Types of the Old Testament* (doc. 46): "*A Type is some outward or sensible thing ordained by God under the Old Testament, to represent and hold forth something of Christ in the New*" (KC, 88). The two parts of the Bible were thus seen as corresponding to each other in terms of 'type' and 'anti-type,' thereby forming a larger unit, which, as David Hall put it, "thematically and structurally [organized] around the fulfilling of prophecy: Christ's coming is anticipated in the Old Testament and completed in the New" (2004, 327). For reformed theology, typology, especially in combination with the idea of the covenant, was of central importance. In accordance with the general trend of Protestant exegesis to correlate scriptural prophecy and history, Calvinist divines extended the ancient method of reading Scripture to the historical development of the Christian church. In this way, the Reformation could be seen as a prophetic event leading towards the establishment of Christ's true church of the saints, which would constitute the typological fulfillment of God's old covenant with Israel.

[20] Undoubtedly, the Protestant trend towards typological readings of church history was continued by New England theologians. But, "[d]espite what has been said by some modern historians, most English Protestants and the colonists limited the meaning of type to the church (the saints, or the elect) and did not extend it to encompass society (nation) as a whole" (Hall 2004, 327-8).

speak *as though* the colonies were a new Israel and to assume that events and situations in their own days were replays of previous episodes in Christian history" (2004, 328). Yet, these historical comparisons, should "be characterized as 'examples' as distinct from 'types,' the major difference being that examples did not directly recapitulate salvation history" (2004, 328; emphasis mine).[21]

These fine, but very important theological distinctions, which are implicit in all of the late seventeenth century millennialist texts collected in the anthology, are explicated by Nicholas Noyes' 1698 *New England's Duty and Interest* (doc. 80), which comments upon Jeremiah's vision of a future restoration of Israel. Firstly, Noyes reads Jer. 31.23 typologically as foreshadowing the 'new covenant,' or the reconciliation of God and His fallen creation through Christ's redemptive work, by which the elect members of "the Catholick Church" (here in the sense of the true church) will be saved. Secondly, the Old Testament passage is read "by way of *Analogy*" to refer "to Kingdoms, Countries & Places, Nations professing the Christian Religion" (*KC*, 178). In this manner, Noyes argues, "the New Testament teacheth us to interpret, accommodate and apply to our selves [i.e., in New England], Texts of the Old Testament" (*KC*, 178). Hence, Puritan divines of the late seventeenth century, such as Noyes, looked for God's guidance by comparing events and situations in contemporary New England with those recorded in the Bible, or the succeeding history of Christianity. Despite their very frequent references to the national covenant of the Jewish people for purposes of admonition, none of the leading second- or third-generation exegetes, "assumed that New England was the antitype of ancient Israel" (Holifield 2003, 77), but they maintained the view of the first New England theologians: Israel's eschatological antitype was still the true church of the elect among all nations. As a matter of fact, they would not even grant a privileged position to New England within the true church come the millennium, but were rather seeking to establish, in the words of Noyes "*Grounds of Hope, that America in General, & New-England in Particular, May Have a Part therein*" (*KC*, 178). For literalist exegetes such as Noyes or the Mathers, the leading role in the latter day events was still reserved for the Israelites, whom they expected to convert before the advent of Christ's glorious reign.[22]

---

[21] For the crucial difference between typological and exemplary or analogical readings of Scriptures, see also Morrisey (2000). The Puritan clergy, as Holifield puts it, "drew a clear distinction between typical and exemplary readings. Types were outward signs of future spiritual realities; examples were not. Types pointed beyond themselves; examples bore their meaning on the surface. The visible types were abolished when they found fulfillment in their Christian antitypes; examples endured as perpetual models. Yet almost everyone agreed that some types could be partially exemplary and some examples partially typical" (2003, 30).

[22] Or, as Smolinski succinctly put the revisionist argument: "The special role that modern critics attribute to American Puritans and their New English Jerusalem in Boston, Puritan millennialists bestowed upon the Jewish nation in Judea" (1990, 381-2). These millennialist expectations were the reason for a pronounced attitude of philosemitism among the Puri-

In his 1669 tract *The Mystery of Israel's Salvation Opened* (doc. 77), Increase Mather explained in great detail the dominant view on the connection between the coming of the millennial age and the national restoration of Israel. When he wrote that "surely the day will not be long before the Lord appear in glory to build up *Sion*" (*KC*, 169), he did not mean this as a version of New England's future. What he asked his fellow Puritans to pray for was the speedy conversion of the diasporic Jews to the faith of the savior they had once rejected and their return to Judea before the Second Coming. New England's relation to Israel is understood in analogous terms (the Puritans also being "in an exiled condition in this wilderness"), and the hope expressed is to be among "the Elect amongst *all Nations*" when Christ would return (*KC*, 168).

Taking their cues from the providential "signs of the times," such as earthquakes, comets, ominous deaths of religious leaders, both Mathers, like many Puritan ministers at the time, assumed that these events were not far off, expecting to witness during their own lifetime the onset of the fearful catastrophes during the apocalyptic "day of trouble" that would precede the millennial dispensation. "We are in expectation of glorious times," Increase Mather told his congregation in two sermons published in 1673 under the same title (doc. 78), "wherein Peace and Prosperity shall run down like a River [...]; but immediately before those dayes, there will be such horrible Combustions and Confusions, as the like never was" (*KC*, 171). In his scheme for synchronizing the prophetic events of the Scriptures with the course of history AD, Mather linked the present age with the pouring out of the fifth of the seven apocalyptic vials, which would entail the destruction of Rome. The sixth vial, for him, signified the imminent conversion and national restoration of Jews, which would then be followed by the first resurrection leading to the millennium.

As representatives of a new kind of hyperliteralism, which marked a decisive departure from the allegorical readings of John Cotton, Increase Mather was certain that not only would there be a literal restoration of Israel in the future,[23] but also that the apocalyptic tribulations would entail very real calamities of cataclysmic proportion, which would climax in the conflagration of the globe predicted in 2 Pet. (for a later representation of the conflagration see doc. 90). He equally foresaw a corporeal first resurrection of the saints, who would then rule the world from a divine metropolis during Christ's thousand-year reign in which, in contrast to the inchoate millennium of the allegorists,

---

tan clergy, which, of course, was always connected with efforts for converting Jews in America and elsewhere.

[23] Only towards the end of his career did Cotton Mather part ways with his father and the majority of his theological colleagues in New England by arguing against a literalist and futurite reading of Israel's national conversion. This is evident in his final millennialist tract *Triparadisus* (ed. Smolinski 1995). Here, he also developed a radical new interpretation of the globe's apocalyptic conflagration and the saints' escape from this holocaust by means of their 'rapture' (cf. Smolinski 1995, 295-318, and 2003, 452-3).

evil, sin, death, or even religious imperfection would have been banished from the earth, renewed by the supernatural power of God's grace.[24]

As is the case with most millennialist writings of the literalist tradition, Increase Mather could mean several different things (often at once) when speaking of the New Jerusalem. He equally used the term to refer to the "'church triumphant' in the highest heaven, the 'metropolis' of the new millennial world, and the 'state of the church on earth' during the millennium" (Holifield 2003, 76; cf. Smolinski 1990). With regard to second meanings, Increase Mather, unlike his son Cotton, who unequivocally pointed towards Judea, never specified the location of Christ's millennial throne. But one thing is certain: He did not situate it in Boston. In *The Day of Trouble Is Near*, he emphasized the analogical meaning of his words in writing about New England that God had "as it were" caused "*New Jerusalem* to come down from Heaven" (*KC*, 173) by entering a covenant with the colonists and allowing them to establish their exemplary church system. Half a century after their forebears had crossed the Atlantic, Mather, like many of his colleagues at the time, was worried that New England was not fulfilling its part of the covenant since he felt an increasing worldliness and "great decay as to the power of godliness amongst us" (*KC*, 172). With "the troubles of the last times" (*KC*, 171) looming in the near future, Mather and his fellow ministers feared the consequences could be dire. The question that concerned them most was how hard America would be hit if things continued to deteriorate. In the typical fashion of the Puritan jeremiad, Mather, simultaneously raises the specter of annihilation and asserts the original promise of the covenant in order to turn his wayward flock back to the godly way. He assures them that, though they certainly would be punished for their backslidings, there is still hope. If they reformed, God would not let them perish, but allow them to participate in the glory of the *civitas dei* during the last age.

But the perceived waning of "the old *New-England Spirit*" (*KC*, 174) was only one reason for the anxious and defensive tone in many of the millennialist writings of the second and third generations. The other reason was, as has been suggested above, the mounting weight that Joseph Mede's condemnation of America carried in the international circles of millennialist theologians. Consequently, New England divines felt extra pressure to assert the possibility that their home region would be included in the millennial boundaries of Christ's saving in-

---

[24] Increase Mather described "the first resurrection as an event in which the bodies of the departed righteous would rise to be reunited in a celestial form with their souls, which had ascended to heaven. The risen righteous and the living saints would then, in accord with 1 Thess. 4.17 be caught up in the air in a divine rapture while God destroyed the wicked through fire in which the returning Christ appeared from heaven. Then the New Jerusalem would descend to the earth for a 'dispensation' of at least a thousand years, during which the saints in heaven would return to this lower world, the church would flourish, and pain and death would cease. Mather expressed doubts that Christ would reign personally, but he thought that the saints of the New Jerusalem would rule the world" (Holifield 2003, 76).

fluence. As Noyes did before him (*KC*, 180), Cotton Mather in the opening chapter of his ecclesiastical history of New England *Magnalia Christi Americana* (1702), as well as in a number of other publications, would go to great lengths to show that Native Americans also belonged to the posterity of Noah (cf. Scheiding in this vol., 15-6). The purpose of this argument, was to refute the assumptions of Mede, who "conjectures that the *American Hemisphere* [...] will not have a share in the Blessedness which the *Renovated World* shall enjoy [...a]nd that the Inhabitants of these Regions [...] will be the *Gog* and *Magog* whom the *Devil* will seduce to Invade the *New-Jerusalem*" (*KC*, 183). As far as a special role for New England was concerned, however, Cotton Mather, like his father, would not go beyond mentioning "*some feeble Attempts* made in the *American Hemisphere* to anticipate the State of *New-Jerusalem*, as far as the unavoidable *Vanity* of *Humane Affairs*, and *Influence* of *Satan* upon them would allow of it" (*KC*, 183).

If Puritan divines of the late seventeenth and early eighteenth centuries were, generally speaking, not inclined to challenge the centrality of Judea in the last age, Mather's friend, the judge Samuel Sewall, is one notable exception to this rule. First written in 1697 and revised in 1727, his *Phænomena quædam Apocalyptica* (doc. 79), did indeed go beyond a mere rebuttal of Mede by propounding "*the New World* [...] *as being so far from deserving the Nick names of* Gog *and* Magog [...] *stands fair for being made the Seat of the Divine Metropolis*" (*KC*, 175). What Sewall had in mind, however, was not the Atlantic seaboard of the Northeast, but the Mexican American Hemisphere of "*New-Spain.*" Sewall, President of the Society for the Propagation of the Gospel to the Indians, was convinced that the "aboriginal Natives of *America* are of *Jacob's* Posterity, part of the long since captivated Ten Tribes" (*KC*, 176), who upon the general restoration of the dispersed Jewish nation would be joined by their converted brethren from around the world and supply New Jerusalem with its citizens. Although Sewall agreed with most of his colleagues in insisting on the centrality of a literal restoration of the Israelites, he nevertheless ascribes a special role "to New English *Planters*" in the advent of the millennium (*KC*, 175). He felt entitled to this because they introduced the genuine gospel into the American hemisphere, thereby breaking the hold of Antichristian Spain on the New World and making possible the conversion of America's 'Indian Jews' to the true faith. This is why he associates them with the scriptural "*Morning Star, giving certain Intelligence that the Sun of Righteousness will quickly rise* [...] *upon this despised Hemisphere*" (*KC*, 175).[25]

---

[25] Yet, as his millennialist poem of 1701, *A Little before Break-a-Day at Boston of the Massachusets* (doc. 20) makes clear, Sewall's vision of the millennial church remains staunchly universalist. After all, he envisions that "*Asia* and *Africa,* / *Europa*, with *America*; / *All* Four, in Consort join'd shall Sing / *New* Songs of Praise to CHRIST our KING" (*KC*, 31). Sewall's theory that the indigenous peoples of the New World were the descendants of the ten lost tribes of Israel was widely held in the sixteenth and seventeenth centuries. The notion had first achieved prominence through José de Acosta in his *Historia Natural y Moral de las Indias* (1590) and later was further popularized by Menasseh ben Israel's *The Hope of Israel* (1652).

IV. New Light Eschatology and the Rise of Civil Millennialism

Tellingly enough, Mede's arguments continued to reverberate even in the eschatological writings of Jonathan Edwards, the great renovator of American Puritanism, who provided the theological basis for a new Evangelical kind of Calvinist theology (also called New Light Calvinism) during the second half of the eighteenth century and beyond. In his posthumous *A History of the Work of Redemption* (preached in 1739, publ. in 1774), Edwards still felt the need to disprove the eschatological exclusion of America as the home of Gog and Magog (cf. Edwards 1989, 9:434-5). It is in the context of an ongoing defensive debate that we should view his 1742 *Some Thoughts Concerning the Present Revival of Religion in New-England* (doc. 82). Therein Edwards – swept up by the enthusiasm of the massive revivals that had started to flare up since 1739 along the Connecticut valley (cf. Kelleter in this vol., 171-7) – expressed his hope to the world that the regenerated churches in the British colonies of North America would do "some great Thing to make Way for the Introduction of the Churches Latter-Day Glory, that is to have its first Seat in, and is to take its Rise from the new World" (*KC*, 185). Until quite recently, these speculations were regarded by many scholars as a milestone in the nationalization and democratization of the millennial promise in North America.[26] Today, most scholars agree, however, that *Some Thoughts* is an exceptional work for Edwards and that he quickly came to regret his rashness. Especially in his later works he did not ascribe a special role to America in the events of the last days. When envisioning the millennial reign itself, Edwards certainly did not think in (proto-)nationalist terms. Rather he predicted that during Christ's reign all people and nations of the earth would be, as he put it in his *Notes on the Apocalypse*, united in "sweet harmony," as the saints from across the globe would gather around a renovated Judea which, after the conversion of the Israelites, would be "at the center of the kingdom of Christ, communicating influences to all other parts" (Edwards 1977, 5:134).

While Edwards's eschatology is certainly not the most original aspect of his theology, the importance of his thoughts on the 'last things' lies in the fact that,

---

For a detailed reading and contextualization of Sewall's *Phaenomena*, see Scheiding 2002. In the *Magnalia Christi Americana*, Cotton Mather throws a skeptical light on the 'Indians as ten lost tribes'-theory (doc. 34) so emphatically embraced by his friend Sewall and many of his Puritan forebears, including the 'Indian apostle' John Eliot.

[26] Jonathan Edwards's millennial conjectures seemed to fit perfectly in their construction of the Great Awakening as a key event in American religious history because of the emphasis it put on equality in mass conversions, its purported social perfectionism, and its alleged focus on America's role in the latter day events. Edwards, therefore, was seen as a central figure who connected the Puritan idea of a holy errand with the republican spirit of egalitarian freedom, provided an ideological groundwork for the American Revolution, and powerfully contributed to the later national identity as a redeemer nation. For Edwards's role in American culture and his function in the foundational narrative of the nascent American Studies movement, see Conforti 1995.

due to his strong influence, it greatly helped to rejuvenate and re-popularize the allegorical strand in the American millennialist tradition. Drawing heavily on earlier works of English exegetes such as Joseph Mede, Daniel Whitby, and particularly Moses Lowman's *Paraphrase and Notes upon the Revelation* (1737), Edwards argued for a figurative as well as a gradualist understanding of the millennium and the prophetic events leading up to it. Spiritualizing the fall of the Antichrist, the binding of Satan, and the first resurrection allowed him and his disciples, including Joseph Bellamy and Samuel Hopkins, to keep God's supernaturalist interventions into earthly affairs to a minimum and thereby to reconcile, in certain respects, their apocalyptic outlook with the progressive view of history propagated by the new Enlightenment philosophy. But instead of primarily defining historical progress through the unfolding of human rationality, as many Enlightenment philosophers did, the gradual spiritual progress which the Edwardians read into the course of history had its beginning in the workings of God's grace. More precisely, Edwards's so-called postmillennialism was predicated on the notion that "the whole course and progress of history are based on the effusion of the [Holy] Spirit as manifested in periods of decisive revivals" (Zakai 2007, 91).

Adopting "an afflictive model of progress" common among eighteenth-century postmillennialists (Davidson 1977, 260), Edwards and his disciples viewed human history since the days of Christ as a seesaw of revivals and declensions which would continue in slow ascension until the great regeneration of Christianity which was figuratively foretold in the Book of Revelation by the first resurrection. After the collapse of Roman Catholicism, symbolized by the downfall of the Antichrist, the actual millennium would begin, marked not by an interruption of history or a complete overthrow of the historical order, but by an intensification of spiritual progress. The onset of the millennium, which Edwards and his followers expected around the year 2000,[27] was understood as the beginning of Christ's spiritual reign on earth which would continue to grow and improve unperturbed over the course of the thousand years of Satan's figurative binding. As it had been for the seventeenth-century allegorists, however, "Edwards' millennium remains inchoate, a mixture of the saints in heaven ruling through their spiritual successors over their mortal and sinful counterparts in the earth" (Smolinski 1998, xxix). This natural, if much improved, state of affairs would continue until the closing of the millennial era at the end of history in the description where Edwards shifted to a literalist reading of the prophecies.[28] Sig-

---

[27] Edwards calculated that the 1,260 prophetic days of Revelation had started in 606 AD when the Pope became universal bishop, and that the year 1866 would bring the downfall of the papacy which would pave the way for the commencement of the millennium that would occur around the year 2000.

[28] In these readings, he indulged in a supernaturalism worthy of the Mathers: Satan would be released from bondage to harass the world once more with a vengeance, and Christ would come down from heaven as the dead rose to be reunited with their souls (an event signified by the scriptural second resurrection) for the Last Judgment which would bring the literal

nificantly for many later millennialist texts, Edwards also applied a double interpretation, one figurative, the other literalist, to Rev. 21.1-2, which he read as simultaneously referring to the New Jerusalem of the inchoate millennium and to the saints' heavenly abode that would be located in a literal "new heaven and new earth" at the end of history.

Its remaining imperfections and the continuing blight of death notwithstanding, the millennial reign, according to Edwards, would be a time not only of unprecedented piety and perfection of the Christian church across the globe, but also of great temporal prosperity for all its people. In his 1793 *A Treatise on the Millennium* (doc. 86), Samuel Hopkins undertook the task of describing these earthly improvements in great detail. Conjecturing about continuous betterments in the areas of physical health and ease, material wealth, as well as spectacular advances in the arts and sciences, Hopkins' text in many ways betrays the influence of the utopian projections of the Enlightenment. Yet the gradualist or developmental postmillennialism propagated by him and other New Light Calvinists should not be misread as smoothly blending into an ideology of secular progressivism, let alone one that was nation-centred. In stark contrast to the Enlightenment prophets of man's perfectibility, Edwards and his pupils consistently emphasized how limited the redemptive possibilities of human behavior actually were, due to man's natural depravity. Concerted praying was usually advertised as the adequate means to prepare for the advent of the millennium. History did not appear to them as an open field of possibilities for human self-realization stretching into an indefinite future, but was understood as the manifesttation of God's glorious work of redemption in the course of history. This course, however, would by necessity be brought to an end by the Second Coming.[29] By the same token, secular forms of progress, such as the accumulation of knowledge or social reforms, were always presented as a byproduct of and as sec-

---

conflagration of the globe. Then the wicked would be cast into hell for eternal punishment, while the saints would enter the celestial city descending upon a supernaturally transformed and relocated 'new earth' to live there happily forever in the presence of God (cf. Smolinski 2003, 458).

[29] Thus, despite all the points of intersection and mutual influence, there are at least two irreconcilable discrepancies between the new secular progressivism and the spiritual progressivism of a gradualist postmillennialism. The first is a fundamentally different understanding of historical agency. Calvinist eschatology, whether old or New Light, held the triune God to be the sole and sovereign ruler of history, by whose free grace the elect would ultimately be allowed to redeem themselves from history. Enlightenment philosophy, in contrast, was characterized by a belief in man's reason and capacity for self-redemption in history, and hence emphasized his moral freedom and ability to control as well as to improve his own fortune. In his polemical remarks on "Predestination" (doc. 99), Thomas Paine highlights this first discrepancy in very aggressive form. Secondly, Enlightenment secular progressivism tends to represent history as an indefinite continuum stretching into an open future. In contrast to this, a traditional, Scripture-based millennialism (both post- and pre-) was characterized by an acute sense of the finiteness of history, the end of which was already determined and foretold by the Book of Revelation.

ondary to an increase in true Christian faith.[30] And how little conservative theologians such as Edwards or Hopkins had to do with the nineteenth-century advocates of America's millennial destiny as the republican empire of liberty, is perhaps best illustrated by the fact that *The Treatise on the Millennium* does not even once mention the American Revolution or the future of the newly founded United States.

As a general tendency, "[u]ntil about midcentury Protestant theology and republican discourse remained mostly distinct" (Noll 2002, 78). Only in the second half of the eighteenth century, after the final collapse of Puritanism as an integrated worldview and a comprehensive life system,[31] a close alliance between evangelical Protestantism (with its millennialist eschatology) and civic republicanism came into being. Mixed with notions of Enlightenment progressivism this hybrid ideology would then provide a new comprehensive framework for America's future national identity. This hybridization was effected not so much by the elaborate scriptural commentaries of academic theologians who are famous today, such as Edwards, Bellamy, or Hopkins, but the cultural work of a host of lesser known clergymen, mostly New England Congregationalists and Presbyterians. In the aftermath of the French and Indian War (a conflict which had re-ignited millennialist expectations all over New England), these men increasingly employed republican arguments in the religious contexts of their preaching, especially when addressing the political controversies created by the widely detested fiscal measures passed by the British parliament. Often apocalyptic in outlook, their sermons were thus characterized by an unprecedented

---

[30] In his *A History of the Work of Redemption*, Edwards would thus argue with regard to man's gradual improvement in history before and during the millennium: "God will improve this great increase of learning as an handmaid to religion, a means of a glorious advancement of the kingdom of the Son, when human learning shall be subservient to understanding the Scriptures and a clear explaining and glorious defending the doctrine of Christianity" (1989, 9:441). This stands in stark contrast to the largely utilitarian concept of knowledge and self-improvement as well as the predominantly technological understanding of progress put forth by someone like Benjamin Franklin (cf. doc. 104).

[31] In his insightful study *America's God*, Noll argues that the specifically American synthesis between evangelical Protestant religion, political republicanism, and Enlightenment philosophy, which would come to characterize the cultural life of the new nation at least until the Civil War, only began to emerge as the existing Puritan canopy collapsed around the middle of the eighteenth century. In the following century, this amalgamated Christian republicanism, according to Noll, replaced the Puritan covenant-theology as the "long-lived and explicitly biblical construct for linking together God, self, church and society. In its place came a mixed set of modern alternatives that used social or political, but not primarily theological, categories to unify existence" (Noll 2002, 32). Following Noll, the New Light theology of Jonathan Edwards and his academic disciples must not be misinterpreted as the cause for the disintegration of traditional Puritanism and the new alliance of Pietism and republicanism. Even though Edwardian evangelicalism in the long run probably helped along this alliance against its own intentions, it did aim at restoring the covenantal theology of Puritanism in its original purity. For an older, but still useful study of the convergence of Protestant theology and republican patriotism in America, see Berens (1978).

priority of civil issues which clearly sets them apart from traditional eschatology of New England Puritanism. Simultaneously, between the mid-1760s and the mid-1780s historians have discovered a more and more "ready use of traditional religion by the political leaders of the Revolution" (Noll 2002, 78), who, even where skeptical of traditional religion, did not shy away from fostering latter-day anxieties and hopes as the conflict escalated. Finally, we can say that the (pre-)revolutionary period established a new form of discourse informed by powerful popular amalgam of religious and political ideas, which has been labeled by cultural historians "apocalyptical Whiggism" (Tuveson 1968, 24) or "civil millennialism" (Hatch 1977, 23).[32] While the exact importance of chiliastic beliefs relative to other ideological sources remains an object of debate, most historians of the period today agree in seeing a politically refashioned millennialism as an important "structure of meaning through which contemporary events were linked to an exalted image of an ideal world" and that was thereby "basic to the formation of American Revolutionary ideology in the late eighteenth-century" (Bloch 1985, xiii).[33]

Samuel Sherwood's 1776 *The Church's Flight into the Wilderness* (doc. 85) is a striking example of the ways in which the vocabularies of millennialism and eighteenth-century Whig ideology were drawn together in the pulpit rhetoric of the period. Moreover, the text illustrates the high degree of theological license which revolutionary clergymen like Sherwood assumed for themselves in creating this potent mixture of enthusiastic end-time expectations and political propaganda, which so galvanized the colonists in their rebellion.[34] In contrast to many later propagators of America's millennial destiny, Sherwood is very self-conscious. He allows a perhaps unduly "large, extensive sense and latitude" in his interpre-

---

[32] Basic to the ideological formation as well as to the rhetorical power of Christian republicanism in late eighteenth century America is a synthesis of the ideas of religious and political liberty. "The terms of the synthesis," as Moorhead puts it, "were simple: Civil liberty created conditions favorable to the flourishing of the gospel, and the gospel in turn secured the voluntary order without which society – religious or secular – could not endure" (1984, 532-3). A striking historical exemplification of this synthesis is Ezra Stiles Connecticut election sermon, where the president of Yale college argues that "true RELIGION" is necessary to perfect "our system of dominion and CIVIL POLITY," while "the diffusion of virtue" provided the "greatest secular happiness of the people" (1783, 7; cf. *KC* web site).

[33] Whereas Hatch and Bloch see millennialist or apocalyptic ideas as absolutely central to the American Revolution, Endy, for instance, de-emphasizes their role for the majority of colonists, arguing that "only a small minority [...] came close to seeing the colonies as a crusading theocracy like ancient Israel" (1985, 12).

[34] Although most leaders of the Revolution leaned towards a highly rationalized form of Protestantism or deism that had moved far away from the Puritan tradition, they did not hesitate to utilize the rhetoric of millennialism. In many of their speeches and writings, they defined the Revolution and the new American nation in "a grand apocalyptic interpretation of universal history, the only conceptual framework acceptable to a people still rooted in the providential assumptions of the English Reformation" (McLear 1971, 183); see, for instance, Thomas Paine's vaguely millennialist rhetoric in his 1776 *Common Sense* (doc. 130).

tation of the apocalyptic Scriptures by assuming "that many of them have reference to the state of Christ's church in this American quarter of the globe; and will sooner or later, have their fulfillment and accomplishment among us" (*KC*, 191). But even though in theory he still claims to observe the traditional distinction between typological and analogical readings, he effectively collapses that difference in his rhetorical practice.[35] For all intents and purposes, he identifies the "United Colonies" as the eschatological fulfillment of the true church symbolized by the women in the wilderness (Rev. 12.14-7), while interpreting the British crown as the latter day antitype of the persecuting dragon.

To a degree inconceivable in the writings of his Puritan forebears, Sherwood extends his apocalyptic reading of history beyond the realm of the church, freely blending politics and religion. According to his interpretation, "the dragon, sometimes called the beast, and the serpent, satan, and the devil" does no longer exclusively signify Roman Catholicism with its ecclesiastical corruptions (*KC*, 194). It also stands for all political manifestations of "the design of the dragon […] to erect a scheme of absolute despotism and tyranny on the earth, and involve all mankind in slavery and bondage" (*KC*, 194). Inversely, the cause of the true church, persecuted by the dragon throughout history, is understood by Sherwood to be the realization of "that liberty and freedom which the Son of God came from heaven to procure for, and bestow on them" (*KC*, 194).[36] This kind of view, of course, enabled revolutionary clergymen like Sherwood to demonize doubly the king, parliament and British politics: The alleged attempts of the Church of England (which, especially after the Quebec Act of 1774 was perceived as increasingly Popish) to forcibly 'Anglicize' the colonies, and the curtailment of civil liberties in form of the coercive acts passed during the 1760s by the British government are interpreted as parts of one big Antichristian conspiracy against America. At the same time, America is presented as the divinely preordained city of refuge for the true church, where she was to enjoy "her liberties and privileges, civil and religious, that no power on earth can have any right to invade" (*KC*, 193).

In this manner, as Sherwood's formulations demonstrate, the revolutionary clergy worked effectively towards endowing a local conflict in the British Empire

---

[35] Sherwood's wavering between a traditional exegetical method (demanding differentiation between type and example) and a rhetorical purpose that demands ignoring the fine points of theology can be seen most clearly in doc. 85 (*KC*, 192).

[36] Sherwood's sermon is also an early example of the way in which the revolutionary generation, for the purpose of legitimization, began to construct a new historical narrative about the colonial past, according to which their Puritan forebears had emigrated to "this then howling wilderness" because "the cruel hand of oppression, tyranny and persecution drove them out of their pleasant seats and habitations […] and that the purest principles of religion and liberty, led them to make the bold adventure across the wide Atlantic ocean" (*KC*, 193). Guided by divine providence, they then, like Old Israel in "the land of Canaan," turned "an uncultivated wilderness" into a "pleasant field or garden" of plenty (*KC*, 192). For a further discussion of this construction of a Puritan Errand into the Wilderness, see section II of this essay, 124-34.

with cosmic significance. In their sermons and tracts, they represented the civil war following the Declaration of Independence as the last act in the apocalyptic battle between good and evil, which would be followed by a millennial reign of earthly bliss. They also managed to establish an intimate connection in the minds of their audiences between an American civic republican ideology and Christian virtues opposed to British tyranny, which they effectively associated with sin and the forces of Satan. In so doing, men like Sherwood helped to create the synthetic ideology of a Christian republicanism which, during the nineteenth century, would be instrumental in integrating an extremely heterogeneous American people under the canopy of a new national self-definition and would endow the nation with a strong sense of historical purpose.

Of central importance in this respect was the millennial promise that North America would "make a great and flourishing empire" (*KC*, 191), where Christian piety would thrive with civil liberty and would grow in worldly power beyond anything recorded in history. Already shortly before and during the war, this promise of America as the millennial "abode for unadulterated christianity, liberty and peace" (*KC*, 193) was routinely evoked in the pulpit oratory of ministers such as Sherwood and became a stock motif of contemporary political speeches and literature (cf. docs. 143, 152-3). In the field of literature, the elaboration of this promise even developed into a distinct lyrical genre, the so-called vision poems; an umbrella term under which all of the remaining documents (docs. 83-4, 87-9) can be subsumed. Usually, these poems were publicly declaimed at academic or political occasions (such as graduation or commencement ceremonies of universities, or political celebrations like the Fourth of July) and consisted of detailed visions of the rising glories of America.

The excerpts from Timothy Dwight's very popular poem *America* (doc. 84) contain in condensed form all the structural and thematic elements that are typical of most vision poems, including those by Freneau, Richards, and Humphreys. Published in 1780, Dwight's patriotic poem is dedicated "[T]o *the Friends of Freedom, and their Country,*" and addresses the still struggling colonies but soon-to-be nation as

> O Land supremely blest! to thee tis given
> To taste the choicest joys of bounteous heaven;
> Thy rising Glory shall expand its rays,
> And lands and times unknown rehearse thine endless praise. [...]
> "Hail Land of light and joy! thy power shall grow
> Far as the seas, which round thy regions flow;
> Through earth's wide realms thy glory shall extend,
> And savage nations at thy scepter bend [...]
> Round thy broad fields more glorious ROMES arise,
> With pomp and splendour brigh'ning all the skies;
> EUROPE and ASIA with surprise behold
> Thy temples starr'd with gems and roof'd with gold. (*KC*, 190)

Firstly what makes Dwight's poem exemplary is its apostrophe of America as a "Land supremely blest" in which "more glorious ROMES [will] arise" and outdo the civilizations of "EUROPE and ASIA." This calls upon the traditional notions of a providentially prescribed westward movement of the true church as well as a *translatio imperii, religionis et studii* from east to west.[37] Secondly, the poet and later president of Yale college invokes the United States' divinely preordained role to expand and rule over the entire (North) American continent, an idea that would later be associated with the term manifest destiny. Thirdly, and most importantly for our concerns, Dwight not only envisions a gloriously exalted American nation as playing an essential part in bringing about the millennium, because it will bring civilization and the gospel to "savage nations." Without mentioning any specifics, such as the location of the New Jerusalem, he also predicts the last great empire of America to hold a central position in the "heavenly kingdom" that "shall descend" upon the world (*KC*, 190), if only in the spiritual sense, sometime around the year 2000.[38] While it is certainly true to say, then, that earlier vision poems such as Dwight's *America* began to nationalize millennial discourse in the sense that they ascribed a special role to the US in the last age, they by no means argue that the millennium would be confined to their national borders, or principally exclude the peoples of the Old World. In other words, the American empire of liberty and Christian righteousness, which supposedly would take shape in the near future, was imagined only as a part, albeit a central one, of a general reign of bliss on earth.

Also, one must not overlook the careful eschatological distinctions and qualifications which at least a traditionalist Calvinist theologian like Dwight still thought important to make. True to the postmillennialist tradition of Edwards, Dwight continued to differentiate between an inchoate spiritual millennium and the literal new heaven and earth to be established after the Second Coming and Judgment Day, when "the last trump" will announce the corporeal resurrection of "the slumbering dead" (*KC*, 191). Following the conflagration of

---

[37] The *translatio*-motif has a long history going back to Renaissance culture and beyond. After George Herbert's "The Church Militant" (1633), its most famous expression in English is probably George Berkeley's 1752 "On the Prospect of Planting Arts and Learning in America" (doc. 21). For a variation of the *translatio*-motif, see also George Richards's "Anniversary Ode on American Independence, for the Fourth of July, 1788" (doc. 87). Here the voice from the heavenly throne addresses his angels with the following lines: "To the WEST your cares be transferr'd. / That *Vine* which from Egypt to Canaan I brought, / With an outstretche'd, omnipotent arm, / In AMERICA's soil, from Britannia's bleak isle, / Shall flourish – and brave ev'ry storm" (*KC*, 199-200). In a way, then, these visions of a rising American empire combine a secular model of the cyclical rise and fall of great nations with a Christian postmillennialism that sees a gradual spiritual progress at work in history.

[38] In his millennium mathematics, as in most other aspects of his eschatology, Dwight leaned on his grandfather Jonathan Edwards. Hence, Dwight envisioned that the rising American empire of piety and liberty would blend into the progressive realization of a spiritual, inchoate millennium during which the true church would triumph across the globe until Christ would finally return in person.

the earth upon Jesus's descent in a "flaming cloud," "GOD's happy children" will be allowed to ascend to the actual New Jerusalem to "[d]rink streams of purest joy and taste immortal love" (*KC*, 191). At least for Dwight, nations and nationality would no longer matter at this stage.

On the Rising Glory of America (doc. 83), which the young Philip Freneau wrote together with his fellow Princeton student Hugh Henry Brackenridge as a university commencement poem in 1771, is equally careful to describe the glorious future of the American empire before and during the inchoate millennium only as a "blissful prelude to Emanuel's [personal] reign" (*KC*, 189). Hence, in contrast to Freneau's later deistic poems and many nineteenth century evocations of an indeterminate process of human perfectibility, the co-authored poem envisions a millennial reign of progress. It is circumscribed by the apocalyptic termination of history which they expected to occur in a not-too-distant future. Only after history's "rolling years are past":

> A new Jerusalem sent down from heav'n
> Shall grace our happy earth, perhaps this land,
> Whose virgin bosom shall then receive, tho' late,
> Myriads of saints with their almighty king,
> To live and reign on earth a thousand years
> Thence call'd Millennium. Paradise a new
> Shall flourish, by no second Adam lost. (*KC*, 189)

What Freneau and Brackenridge (herein following Edwards's double application of Rev. 21.1-2) call the "Millennium" in this potentially misleading passage designates the actual celestial city after its descent to earth, in which there will be no more death or sin, and Jesus will personally reign together with "Myriads" of resurrected saints until the end of time itself. For the most part, then, *On the Rising Glory of America* puts into verse a fairly conventional Edwardsian theology. What is truly remarkable and, certainly for its time, quite exceptional about the poem, however, are its speculations about America as a possible seat of Christ's millennial throne on the supernaturally transformed new earth.

By their truly daring suggestion that "perhaps this land" might be at the very center of the new earth, Freneau and Brackenridge anticipate by several years a significant shift in American millennialism that would occur, as I already suggested above, during and after the revolutionary period. In this shift towards a millennialist nationalism, the formerly important fine points of eschatology, such as the Edwardsian double application or the basic distinction between typological and analogical sense, were increasingly neglected, at least outside the confines of academic theology. If the postmillennialism of the Edwardsian school had paved the way for a predominantly figurative readings of Revelation, many later writers of popular religious literature indeed took this allegorizing tendency one decisive step further. Instead of engaging in any methodical interpretations of the Scriptures, they increasingly drew on the vocabulary of traditional millennialism as a kind of metaphorical reservoir for their patriotic and progressivist rhetorics. This is especially true for authors who leaned toward deism or very liberal forms of Protestantism, such as Universalism or Unitarianism, which self-consciously rejected the biblicism (reliance on the Bible as the literal and ultimate revelation of truth) and Christocentrism (emphasis on Christ's redemptive work as the heart of true religion) of the evangelical majority. Looking at such works, it becomes indeed questionable whether their largely metaphorical and free-wheeling references to biblical prophecies should still be called millennialism at all, or whether this does not constitute a new cultural practice which is informed by philosophical assumptions and ideological goals that are clearly distinct from the scriptural beliefs outlined in the previous section of this essay.[39]

For example, the imagery of an imminent future in which "the bright golden-age shall triumphant return," and "Millennium's new paradise bloom" (*KC*, 200), with which the Universalist pastor George Richards concludes his "Anniversary Ode on American Independence, for the Fourth of July, 1788" (doc. 87) is employed rather casually. The poet no longer feels the necessity to distinguish between a first inchoate millennium of earthly progress and a second millennium of the new earth. Ultimately, Richards seems to make the same use of Christian millennium as he does of the Greco-Roman myth of a golden age: as tropes expressive of his belief in humanity's progress and America's rise to the status of the world's leading power. Free from exegetical restraints, writers such as Richards or Humphreys thus pushed forward with the nationalization of the erstwhile universal promise of millennialism which for centuries had extended to the invisible church comprised of all the peoples of the earth. Where the Puritans had always thought in transatlantic terms and hoped to be part of the international community of true saints who would share in the glory of Christ's kingdom, their

---

[39] One decisive difference between the traditional millennialism of Puritanism (both of the post- and pre-kind) and this new metaphoricized postmillennialism thus seems to be that the latter is no longer based on a closed biblical worldview. In other words, it no longer unquestionably assumes that the Bible accurately foretells and literally contains the whole course of history which was predetermined from the moment of the world's creation. Instead, metaphoricized millennialism tries to integrate an important and very powerful concept of an existing religion into a new worldview defined by Enlightenment philosophy and the modern sciences which claimed that history is an open, ever-evolving field. In its 'poetical' approach to the Book of Revelation, this new kind of millennialism follows the general trend of liberal Protestantism and especially of deism to view the prophetic Scriptures as ancient cultural documents which have to be subjected to rational criticism and whose potential truth-value lies in expressing ethical wisdom as well as spiritual insights about nature or history in highly figurative language. McLear convincingly argues that the most important factor in this metaphoricization of postmillennial eschatology may have been the work of the new biblical critics leading to an increasing historicization of the concept after 1800: "Doctrinal historicization of the millennium combined with revivalistic yearning for its realization to foster confidence in man's ability to reach the glorious historical state. Gospel preaching, mass conversions, and prayers for the millennium passed quickly into the reform crusades designed to achieve the ultimate perfection of men and institutions" (1971, 191).

descendants imagined a new, national community which had been collectively chosen to become the world's most glorious empire.

Significantly, there is also not much in Richards's poem to remind the reader of the cataclysmic catastrophes which used to be such an integral part of millennialist eschatology. Only the last two lines vaguely nod to the traditional notion of history's end. Reflecting the predominant optimism of the period, progress appears as a seamless continuum, and no expectations of any imminent apocalyptic afflictions disturb the "confidence in the future felicity and glory of [… our] country," to quote from the introduction to David Humphreys's 1804 *"A Poem on the Future Glory of the United States of America"* (doc. 89). As with Richards and the older, deistically inclined Freneau of "On the Emigration to America and Peopling the Western Country" (doc. 88), Humphreys's reference to "heav'n's millennial year!" has little to do with the Scripture-based hopes in Christ's glorious kingdom harboured by the Puritans, but simply signifies a "better æra" of advancement and prosperity for the United States (*KC*, 203-4). This era, moreover, is given an indefinite duration since Humphreys calls his millennium "heav'n's perennial year" (*KC*, 204), so that the ultimate closing of the drama of history, which the poem does at least mention in passing, is deferred indefinitely.

In the writings of many liberal Protestants and deists, who no longer subscribed to a traditional biblical worldview, the civil millennialism of the Early Republic thus ultimately merged with Enlightenment discourse about human perfectibility and continuous historical betterment brought about by man's own efforts. What better illustration for this than the fact that Humphreys, in the full version of the text, supports his poetic prophecy about the future greatness of the American people with statistical tables documenting the feats that have already been achieved in the areas of land improvement, growth of the population, economic expansion, and military strength. Both the belief in the efficacy of human agency and the belief in history as an uninterrupted, indefinite continuum of progress, which inform the metaphoricized postmillennialism of these later vision poems, mark a significant departure from, if not an actual break with, the Puritan tradition.

Yet even during the revolutionary era and even more strongly after 1800, hyperliteralism, which had shaped the apocalyptic vision of many second- and third-generation Puritan divines, would return in the beliefs held by many Protestant sects outside the mainstream. These included Shakers (United Society of Believers in Christ's Second Coming), Mormons (the Church of Jesus Christ of Latter-day Saints), Millerites, and later Seventh-Day Adventists (cf. Stein 2003). For the nineteenth century, one can thus speak of a basic bifurcation in American millennialism: On the one hand, we find the strict scripturalism and hyperliteralism of the so-called premillennialists groups. Generally speaking, they expected the more or less imminent Second Coming of Christ, who would return in the body to establish his millennial reign, the corporeal resurrection and/or rapture of the saints as well as the literal fulfillment of many other scriptural events. These expectations are, of course, still characteristic of many so-called Fundamentalist churches in the US today.[40] On the other hand, we find a gradualist type of postmillennialism in which belief in the historical truthfulness of the scriptural prophecies was increasingly supplanted by a loosely metaphorical approach to Revelation, and that easily glided into an essentially secular progressivism. Initially, the postmillennialism of the Edwardsian school had been an attempt to strike a balance between a new progressive view of history and the traditional apocalyptic outlook. Already during the period of the Early Republic, however, postmillennialism increasingly turned into "an understanding of history as gradual improvement according to rational laws that human beings could learn and use. It was becoming a faith in an orderly ascent of history into the golden age" (Moorhead 2003, 73). In the course of the nineteenth century, the original conviction that historical progress would ultimately come to a close at the end of the millennial age frequently lost its hold on mainstream Protestants as "the progressive elements of the older postmillennial vision displaced its apocalyptic features. What remained was the notion of an immanent, this-worldly kingdom of God from which the sense of a definitive end had been removed" (Moorhead 2003, 86). With this sense of an ending lost, the vocabulary of traditional millennialism had at last become purely metaphorical and freely interchangeable with the ideas and terms form neighboring discourses. This shading away of millennialism into the discourses of Manifest Destiny and American world redeemership is powerfully exhibited in John L. O' Sullivan's famous 1839 "The Great Nation of Futurity" (doc. 169), which invokes the vision of an ever-improving "boundless future," in which America "is destined to manifest to mankind the excellence of divine principles; to establish on earth the noblest temple ever dedicated to the worship of the Most High – the Sacred and the True" (*KC*, 387).

Instructional Strategies and Classroom Issues

I. Key Concepts and Major Themes

1. The 'futurite turn' in seventeenth century English millennialism (docs. 74, 76)
   The Reformation era saw a general revival of chiliasm, which had long been marginalized by the church. In the theology and popular culture of English Protestantism, beliefs in a future reign of Christ on earth became widespread. They were especially important for the Puritans, who confronted the king in the English Civil War, or who, like John Cotton, propagated emigration to the New World.

---

[40] The millennialist theology of the Shakers is discussed at length in Stein (1992); the best general introduction to the Millerites and their cultural context are the essays edited by Numbers and Butler (1987). For Seventh-Day Adventism and the Mormons, see Gaustad (1974) and Underwood (1993) respectively. The classical study on millennialism in contemporary evangelical churches is Boyer (1992); see also Hochgeschwender (2007).

2. Reassessing the millennial impulse behind the Puritan migration and church reforms (docs. 74, 76, 80-1)
Contrary to what many scholars have claimed, New England Puritans did not think of themselves as God's New Israel sent into the western wilderness to erect a millennial New Jerusalem. Their exodus from England was never conceived of as a mission to reform the world and inaugurate Christ's reign in America, but rather intended as an escape from the perceived corruption and increasing restrictiveness of the Anglican Church. Seeking to restore church and society in their primitive purity, i.e., in accordance with the ordinances of biblical times, the Puritans hoped to share in the glory that would be bestowed on all true followers of Christ during the millennium.

3. The Puritan argument against America's exclusion from the millennium (docs. 75, 78-9, 81-2)
The undeniable concern of seventeenth-century Puritan exegetes with placing America on the millennial map must not be interpreted as an attempt to associate exclusively the prophecies of Christ's glorious reign on earth with New England history. Instead, this concern should be understood as expressive of an anxiety and resistance against the eschatological marginalization of America in the millennialist discourse of contemporary English theologians such as Joseph Mede.

4. The partial intersections as well as major differences between eighteenth-century postmillennialism and the new Enlightenment philosophy of history (docs. 83-4, 86, 88)
During the second half of the eighteenth century, a new type of millennialism becomes dominant in British North America which holds that human history AD has been a gradual spiritual progress which will finally lead towards Christ's millennial reign. This so-called postmillennialism is partly influenced by new secular views of historical progress, but also contradicts them in many respects.

5. The amalgamation of republican ideology and millennialist beliefs in popular religious literature and sermons of the revolutionary period (docs. 83, 85)
Between the 1760s and 1780s, many clergymen and popular writers hybridized in their rhetoric idea(l)s of republican liberty, patriotic resistance, and religious expectations about apocalyptic struggles, and a subsequent reign of earthly bliss. This so-called civil millennialism provided an important motive and interpretative framework for the American Revolution.

6. The convergence of millennialism and nationalism in the formation of American nationalist ideology (docs. 83-5, 87-9)
Following a shift from theological, Scripture-based millennialism to a popular, metaphoricized millennialism, this vague religious belief in an ongoing progress of humanity towards a new earthly paradise freely blends into a re-

ligiously charged American nationalist ideology. This ideology propagates the notion of the US as the torchbearer of progress destined to enlighten the American continent in the process of national expansion and, ultimately, to redeem the entire world.

II. Comparison – Contrasts – Connections

Examples: Docs. 87-8, 169-70, 174, 176, 178

One of the central aims of the first part of this article was to caution the reader against the traditional master narrative that constructs a direct causal or developmental continuity between seventeenth-century Puritan eschatology and modern nationalist ideology. Having gained a heightened appreciation of the often subtle, but very significant, differences that separate traditional Scripture-centered millennialism from its later cultural derivatives, students can then be encouraged to explore on their own the much more obvious continuities between the civil millennialism of the (post-)revolutionary period and the religiously charged American nationalism of the nineteenth century.

Students may begin this study unit by comparing Philip Freneau's 1795 poem "On the Emigration to America and Peopling the Western Country" (doc. 88) to three selected documents from the section on "Expansionism" (169, 174, 176). Similarities and lines of influence should become readily apparent between the metaphoricized millennialism of Freneau and the nationalist discourse propagated by John L. O'Sullivan and William Gilpin with its key notions of Manifest Destiny and American world redeemership. On the road to this national messianism of the nineteenth century, Freneau's text represents a significant intersection between a residual Calvinist eschatology, new Enlightenment philosophy, republicanism, and early American patriotism. In the poem, one can also see how the traditional *translatio imperii, religionis et studii*-motif was being extended at this time into a larger concept of man's progressive (self-)redemption in history, and how the role of humanity's vanguard was being ascribed to the United States. According to the concept of historical progress suggested by Freneau, mankind had always advanced in a westward direction and would reach its final destination with the establishment of an American civil millennium in which the principles of reason and freedom reign, and the arts, sciences, as well as commerce would flourish.

In the later documents, this embryonic 'national religion' has developed into the full-fledged form of an aggressively self-assertive American exceptionalism and messianic imperialism that we commonly associate with the concept of Manifest Destiny. O'Sullivan and Gilpin not only assert the United States' claim to 'civilize' the continent, but openly tout the belief in American civilization as the ultimate fulfillment of humanity's entire history. In their texts, the United States are simultaneously represented as being destined to bring to completion humanity's past accomplishments and to forever transcend all its historical encumbrances. Drawing on proto-Darwinian notions about the destiny of races, the American people are thus hailed as "the great nation of futurity" (*KC*, 386), the redeemer nation providentially chosen to deliver mankind from its benighted state and lead it into a future golden age. In the words of William Gilpin, the United States are to become the last of the world's great empires that is providentially preordained

> to establish a new order in human affairs – to set free the enslaved – to regenerate superannuated nations – to change darkness into light – to stir up the sleep of a hundred centuries – to teach old nations a new civilization – to confirm the destiny of the human race – to carry the career of mankind to its culminating point – [...] to perfect science – to emblazon history with the conquest of peace – [...] to unite the world in one social family – to dissolve the spell of tyranny and exalt charity – to absolve the curse that weighs down humanity, and to shed blessings round the world! (*KC*, 396)

Where Freneau had taken a decisive step in nationalizing earlier millennialist beliefs in the sense of ascribing a special place to the new republic in the final age of the world, the United States have now become the primary agent of redemptive history. The Puritan hope to be part of Christ's true church during the millennium has ultimately metamorphosed into the vision of an American millennial empire.

Obviously, this ideology of Manifest Destiny and world redeemership serves to give higher meaning and historical legitimacy not only to the expansion of the United States all the way to the Pacific coast, but also to the ruthless means employed in the process, including the displacement of Native American tribes of the west. Even war and military annexations appear justified "by the right of our manifest destiny to overspread and to possess the whole of the continent which Providence has given us for the development of the great experiment of liberty" (*KC*, 397). In this respect, Freneau also appears as a forerunner. After all, he invites his audience in 1795 to imagine the newly opened territories east of the Ohio as part of the national domain that would soon be peopled by armies of European immigrants. Moreover, in its imaginary territorial expansion, his poem describes a necessary cultivation of the hitherto idle or unused western wilderness, which will inevitably entail the retreat of the "unsocial Indian" (*KC*, 201). Thus, the millennialist vision poem already rehearses the same basic rhetorical strategies which would be used with even greater force by the later advocates of Manifest Destiny: It interprets the geography of the American continent through a framework of providentialism and thereby represents its gradual inclusion into the national territory as a predestined, necessary event in the progressive history of mankind that, as a matter of course, will be accompanied by the disappearance of 'lesser races' blocking the Euro-American advance, be they Mexicans or Indians.

In the second half of this study unit, students will read George Richards "Anniversary Ode" (doc. 87) side by side with Robert Charles Winthrop's "Address" (doc. 170) and the anonymous "The Destiny of the Country" (doc. 178). Looking at the mid-nineteenth-century documents first, they will learn how the idea of America's Manifest Destiny, for all its ostentatious orientation towards the future, was simultaneously being projected onto the past. Evoking a providential model of national history, myriad writers and orators like Winthrop celebrated "this wonderful rise and progress of our Country, from the merely nominal and embryo existence which it had acquired at the dawn of the seventeenth Century, to the mature growth, the substantial prosperity, the independent greatness and National grandeur in which it is now beheld" (*KC*, 387). More specifically, they often engaged in (mis-)construing the providential narrative of the Puritan Errand into the Wilderness. In this narrative, the Pilgrim Fathers appeared as direct precursors of the revolutionary Founding Fathers of the nation, as they were said to have been driven from the mother country "by the love of religious liberty and political freedom" alike (*KC*, 402).[41] Indeed, the Puritans were imagined as having settled in the new world inspired by their self-definition as the new chosen people, who were being led by God into the promised land to establish a reign of freedom and piety that would pave the way for and stand at the center of Christ's coming millennial kingdom. From the perspective of the nineteenth-century ideologues, the purported Puritan sense of a millennial mission to erect a New Jerusalem in the American wilderness was thus seen as having been fulfilled by the founding of the American nation state and its ongoing rise to power. Unimpaired by the strict scripturalism of their forebears, which had insisted on a distinction between analogy and typology, the American people were now hailed without any reserve as the New Israel and the United States as "a new heavens and a new earth wherein dwelleth righteousness" (*KC*, 401).

Working their way back in time to Richards's ode, students will then be able to see that the civil millennialism of the late eighteenth-century vision poems is one important root from which this popular, nationalistic historiography of the nineteenth century grew. Freely appropriating his imagery from Ps. 80, Richards identifies the first Puritan colonists as the new Israelites, who were guided by God's providential rule to escape the persecutions in England associated with Egyptian bondage, and to conquer their New World Canaan, where their children would build a new reign of liberty. Only five years after the Peace of Paris (1783), the poet already engages in a historical revisionism that interprets the American Revolution and its final victory over the old "tyrant" (*KC*, 200) as the quasi-typological fulfillment of the Puritans' millennial Errand into the Wilderness.

III. Reading and Discussion Questions

1. Read Freneau's and Brackenridge's *On the Rising Glory of America* (doc. 83) and the poem "Columbia, the Pride of the World" (doc. 157), which was written half a century later by Samuel Woodworth during the era of expansionism.

---

[41] For earlier examples of texts engaged in the construction of the 'Puritan Errand,' see documents 85 and 149.

Discuss continuities, but also radical changes both in terms of the underlying beliefs and the rhetorical strategies that are employed.

2. Compare Samuel Hopkins's non-nationalist speculations about the millennium in his *A Treatise* (doc. 86) with later, more secularized visions of the millennium that represent America as the spearhead of progress and as the land of plenty (docs. 155, 158).

3. Discuss the fundamental differences between a traditional apocalyptic worldview, as illustrated in Increase Mather's *The Day of Trouble Is Near* (doc. 78), and the kind of historical consciousness exhibited in nineteenth-century texts such as John L. O'Sullivan's "The Great Nation of Futurity" (doc. 169).

4. Discuss the different roles ascribed to Native Americans by Puritan millennialists (docs. 34, 79) and later representatives of a secularized civil millennialism (docs. 88, 177).

IV. Resources

a. Recommended Reading

Sacvan Bercovitch. *The Puritan Origins of the American Self*. New Haven: Yale University Press, 1975. While very critical of modern US nationalism, this influential work, together with Bercovitch's *The American Jeremiad* (1978), gave new argumentative strength to the time-honored narrative that conceives of Puritan millennialism as directly leading towards the nineteenth-century ideology of American exceptionalism and world redeemership.

Ruth H. Bloch. *Visionary Republic: Millennial Themes in American Thought, 1756-1800*. Cambridge: Cambridge University Press, 1985. The most extensive study of millennialism during the second half of the eighteenth century. While emphasizing the general importance of millennialist thinking for the American Revolution, it simultaneously demonstrates the great diversity of theological standpoints and highlights their often conflicting political implications as well as their different relations vis-à-vis Enlightenment thinking, republican ideology, and nationalism.

Theodore Dwight Bozeman. *To Live Ancient Lives: The Primitivist Dimension in Puritanism*. Chapel Hill: University of North Carolina Press, 1988. A far-reaching critique of established views on the Puritan emigration as being primarily driven by millennialist hopes for the future. Instead, it argues that the intentions of the colonists are best understood as a specific form of Christian primitivism reclaiming the authority of the New Testament and seeking a return to the 'first times' of the Apostles in America.

John J. Collins, Bernard McGinn, and Stephen J. Stein, eds. *The Continuum History of Apocalypticism*. New York: Continuum, 2003. A selection of essays from the three-volume *Encyclopedia of Apocalypticism* (1999), which provides a comprehensive guide to the history of apocalyptic thought in all world religions, and, more specifically, to Christian millennialism. The high-profile essays in the one-volume edition provide students with an expert account of apocalypticism and millennialism from the days of early Christianity to the present time and give easy access to scholarly literature and debates. Especially pertinent for our concerns are the essays "Apocalypticism in Colonial North America" (Smolinski, 441-467), "Apocalypticism in Mainstream Protestantism, 1800 to the Present" (Moorhead, 467-492), and "Apocalypticism Outside the Mainstream in the United States" (Stein, 493-515).

Bernd Engler, Joerg O. Fichte, and Oliver Scheiding, eds. *Millennial Thought in America: Historical and Intellectual Contexts, 1630-1860*. Trier: Wissenschaftlicher Verlag Trier, 2002. An important collection of essays examining the transformations of millennial thought in America from the 1630s to the 1840s. Most of the essays take a cultural studies-approach to their subject and focus on the complex interaction of millennialism with other discourses, such as reform ideologies, evangelicalism or nationalism, in defining the collective identities of colonists and, later on, US citizens.

E. Brooks Holifield. *Theology in America: Christian Thought from the Age of the Puritans to the Civil War*. New Haven: Yale University Press, 2003. A magisterial contemporary survey of the history of theology in British North America that is also very helpful for students who want to study the development of American millennialism in a larger religious framework.

Perry Miller. *Errand into the Wilderness*. Cambridge: Harvard University Press, 1956. Probably the single most influential work among a number of related studies from the post World War II-era that transformed the existing cultural myth about the Puritans' belief in their millennial errand into a scholarly master narrative that argues for the Puritan origin of modern American nationalism.

Reiner Smolinski. "Israel Redivivus: The Eschatological Limits of Puritan Typology in New England." *New England Quarterly* 63.3 (1990), 357-395. A pathbreaking revisionist essay that convincingly challenges the widely-accepted idea that the Puritan settlers hoped to establish a millennial New Jerusalem in America.

b. Works Cited and Reading Suggestions

Bauckham, Richard, ed. (1978). *Tudor Apocalypse: Sixteenth-Century Apocalypticism, Millenarianism and the English Reformation*. Appleford: Courtenay.
Bercovitch, Sacvan (1975). *The Puritan Origins of the American Self*. New Haven: Yale University Press.
– (1978). *The American Jeremiad*. Madison: University of Wisconsin Press.
Berens, John F. (1978). *Providence and Patriotism in Early America, 1640-1815*. Charlottesville: University of Virginia Press.

Bloch, Ruth H. (1985). *Visionary Republic: Millennial Themes in American Thought, 1756-1800*. Cambridge: Cambridge University Press.

Boyer, Paul (1992). *When Time Shall Be No More: Prophecy Belief in Modern American Culture*. Cambridge: Harvard University Press.

Bozeman, Theodore Dwight (1988). *To Live Ancient Lives: The Primitivist Dimension in Puritanism*. Chapel Hill: University of North Carolina Press.

Capp, Bernard (1972). *The Fifth Monarchy Men: A Study in Seventeenth-Century English Millenarianism*. Totowa: Rowman and Littlefield.

Cohn, Norman (1957). *The Pursuit of the Millennium: Revolutionary Messianism in Medieval and Reformation Europe*. New York: Harper.

Collins, John J., Bernard McGinn, and Stephen J. Stein, eds. (2003). *The Continuum History of Apocalypticism*. New York: Continuum.

Conforti, Joseph A. (1995). *Jonathan Edwards, Religious Tradition & American Culture*. Chapel Hill: University of North Carolina Press.

Coward, Barry (1994). *The Stuart Age: England 1603-1714*. 2nd ed. London: Longman.

Daley, Brian E. (2003). "Apocalypticism in Early Christian Theology." *The Continuum History of Apocalypticism*. Ed. Bernard McGinn, John J. Collins, and Stephen J. Stein. New York: Continuum, 221-254.

Davidson, James West (1977). *The Logic of Millennial Thought: Eighteenth-Century New England*. New Haven: Yale University Press.

De Jong, J. A. (1970). *As the Waters Cover the Sea: Millennial Expectations in the Rise of Anglo-American Missions, 1640-1810*. Kampen: J. H. Kok.

Edwards, Jonathan (1957-2006). *The Works of Jonathan Edwards*. Gen. ed. Perry Miller, John E. Smith, and Harry S. Stout. New Haven: Yale University Press.

– (1977). *The Works of Jonathan Edwards*. Vol. 5: *Apocalyptic Writings*. Ed. Stephen J. Stein. New Haven: Yale University Press.

– (1989). *The Works of Jonathan Edwards*. Vol. 9: *A History of the Work of Redemption*. Ed. John F. Wilson. New Haven: Yale University Press.

Endy, Melvin B., Jr. (1985). "Just War, Holy War, and Millennialism in Revolutionary America." *The William and Mary Quarterly* 42, 3-25.

Engler, Bernd, Joerg O. Fichte, and Oliver Scheiding, eds. (2002). *Millennial Thought in America: Historical and Intellectual Contexts, 1630-1860*. Trier: Wissenschaftlicher Verlag Trier.

Fichte, Joerg O. (2002). "The Negotiation of Power in John Cotton's Commentaries on Revelation." *Millennial Thought in America: Historical and Intellectual Contexts, 1630-1860*. Ed. Bernd Engler, Joerg O. Fichte, and Oliver Scheiding. Trier: Wissenschaftlicher Verlag Trier, 39-61.

Firth, Catherine (1979). *The Apocalyptic Tradition in Reformation Britain 1530-1645*. Oxford: Oxford University Press.

Fuller, Robert C. (1995). *Naming the Antichrist: The History of an American Obsession*. New York: Oxford University Press.

Gaustad, Edwin S., ed. (1974). *The Rise of Adventism*: *Religion and Society in Mid-Nineteenth-Century America*. New York: Harper and Row.

Hall, David, ed. (2004). *Puritans in the New World*: *A Critical Anthology*. Princeton: Princeton University Press.

Hatch, Nathan O. (1977). *The Sacred Cause of Liberty*: *Republican Thought and the Millennium in Revolutionary New England*. New Haven: Yale University Press.

Heimert, Alan (1966). *Religion and the American Mind*: *From the Great Awakening to the Revolution*. Cambridge: Harvard University Press.

Hill, Christopher (1971). *Antichrist in Seventeenth-Century England*. London: Oxford University Press.

– (1972). *The World Turned Upside Down*: *Radical Ideas During the English Revolution*. London: Temple Smith.

Hochgeschwender, Michael (2007). *Amerikanische Religion*: *Evangelikalismus, Pfingstlertum und Fundamentalismus*. Frankfurt/M.: Verlag der Weltreligionen.

Holifield, E. Brooks (2003). *Theology in America*: *Christian Thought from the Age of the Puritans to the Civil War*. New Haven: Yale University Press.

MacLear, J. F. (1971). "The Republic and the Millennium." *The Religion of the Republic*. Ed. Elwyn A. Smith. Philadelphia: Fortress Press.

Markus, R. A. (1970). *Saeculum*: *History and Society in the Theology of St. Augustine*. Cambridge: Cambridge University Press.

McGinn, Bernard (2003). "Apocalypticism and Church Reform, 1100-1500." *The Continuum History of Apocalypticism*. Ed. Bernard McGinn, John J. Collins, and Stephen J. Stein. New York: Continuum, 273-299.

Miller, Perry (1956). *Errand into the Wilderness*. Cambridge: Harvard University Press.

Moorhead, James H. (1984). "Between Progress and Apocalypse: A Reassessment of Millennialism in American Religious Thought, 1800-1880." *The Journal of American History* 71, 524-542.

– (2003). "Apocalypticism in Mainstream Protestantism, 1800 to the Present." *The Continuum History of Apocalypticism*. Ed. Bernard McGinn, John J. Collins, and Stephen J. Stein. New York: Continuum, 467-492.

Morrisey, Mary (2000). "Elect Nations and Prophetic Preaching: Types and Examples in the Paul's Cross Jeremiad." *The English Sermon Revised*: *Religion, Literature and History, 1600-1750*. Ed. Lori Anne Ferrell and Peter McCullough. Manchester: Manchester University Press, 43-48.

Milhou, Alain (2003). "Apocalypticism in Central and South American Colonialism." *The Continuum History of Apocalypticism*. Ed. Bernard McGinn, John J. Collins, and Stephen J. Stein. New York: Continuum, 417-440.

Noll, Mark (2002). *America's God*: *From Jonathan Edwards to Abraham Lincoln*. Oxford: Oxford University Press.

Numbers, Ronald L., and Jonathan M. Butler, eds. (1987). *The Disappointed*: *Millerism and Millenarianism in the Nineteenth Century*. Bloomington: Indiana University Press.

Oberman, Heiko (1989). *Luther: Man Between God and the Devil*. New Haven: Yale University Press.
O'Leary, Stephen D. (1994). *Arguing the Apocalypse: A Theory of Millennial Rhetoric*. New York: Oxford University Press.
Patrides, C. A., and Joseph Wittreich, eds. (1984). *The Apocalypse in English Renaissance Thought and Literature*. Ithaca: Cornell University Press.
Phelan, John Leddy (1970). *The Millennial Kingdom of the Franciscans in the New World*. Berkeley: University of California Press.
Potestà, Gian Luca (2003). "Radical Apocalyptic Movements in the Late Middle Ages." *The Continuum History of Apocalypticism*. Ed. Bernard McGinn, John J. Collins, and Stephen J. Stein. New York: Continuum, 299-323.
Roeber, A. Gregg (1995). "Der Pietismus in Nordamerika im 18. Jahrhundert." *Die Geschichte des Pietismus*. Vol. 2. Ed. Martin Brecht. Berlin: Vandenhoeck and Ruprecht, 668-701.
Scheiding, Oliver (2002). "Samuel Sewall and the Americanization of the Millennium." *Millennial Thought in America: Historical and Intellectual Contexts, 1630-1860*. Ed. Bernd Engler, Joerg O. Fichte, and Oliver Scheiding. Trier: Wissenschaftlicher Verlag Trier, 165-185.
Schilson, Arno (1995). "Die Entdeckung des Kolumbus in religionsgeschichtlicher Sicht: Ein neuer Blick auf Bekanntes und Unbekanntes." *Amerika: Entdeckung, Eroberung, Erfindung*. Ed. Winfried Herget. Trier: Wissenschaftlicher Verlag Trier, 33-48.
Smolinski, Reiner (1990). "Israel Redivivus: The Eschatological Limits of Puritan Typology in New England." *New England Quarterly* 63.3, 357-395.
– , ed. (1995). *The Threefold Paradise of Cotton Mather: An Edition of Triparadisus*. Athens: University of Georgia Press.
– (1998). "General Introduction." *The Kingdom, The Power, & The Glory: The Millennial Impulse in Early American Literature*. Ed. Reiner Smolinski. Dubuque: Kendall/Hunt, viii-xlvi.
– (2002). "'The Way to Lost Zion': The Cotton-Williams Debate on the Separation of Church and State in Millenarian Perspective." *Millennial Thought in America: Historical and Intellectual Contexts, 1630-1860*. Ed. Bernd Engler, Joerg O. Fichte, and Oliver Scheiding. Trier: Wissenschaftlicher Verlag Trier, 61-97.
– (2003). "Apocalypticism in Colonial North America." *The Continuum History of Apocalypticism*. Ed. Bernard McGinn, John J. Collins, and Stephen J. Stein. New York: Continuum, 441-467.
Stein, Stephen J. (1992). *The Shaker Experience in America: A History of the United Society of Believers*. New Haven: Yale University Press.
– (2003). "Apocalypticism Outside the Mainstream in the United States." *The Continuum History of Apocalypticism*. Ed. Bernard McGinn, John J. Collins, and Stephen J. Stein. New York: Continuum, 493-515.

Stiles, Ezra (1783). *The United States Elevated to Glory and Honor*. New Haven: Thomas and Samuel Green. <http://digitalcommons.unl.edu/etas/41/> (March 8, 2008).

Tuveson, Ernest Lee (1968). *Redeemer Nation: The Idea of America's Millennial Role*. Chicago: University of Chicago Press.

– (1973). "Millenarianism." *Dictionary of the History of Ideas: Studies of Selected Pivotal Ideas*. Vol. 3: *Law, Concept of*, to *Protest Movements*. Ed. Philip P. Wiener. New York: Scribner, 223-226.

Underwood, Grant (1993). *The Millenarian World of Early Mormonism*. Urbana: University of Illinois Press.

Zakai, Avihu (1992). *Exile and Kingdom: History and Apocalypse in the Puritan Migration to America*. Cambridge: Cambridge University Press.

– (2003). *Jonathan Edward's Philosophy of History: The Reenchantment of the World in the Age of Enlightenment*. Princeton: Princeton University Press.

– (2007). "The Age of Enlightenment." *The Cambridge Companion to Jonathan Edwards*. Ed. Stephen J. Stein. Cambridge: Cambridge University Press, 80-103.

FRANK KELLETER

The Great Awakening and the Enlightenment

I. Themes and Arguments

Four decades before the Revolution of 1776, recurring waves of religious revivalism began to sweep the British colonies in North America.[1] In their cumulated effect they constituted the so-called Great Awakening of the late 1730s and early 1740s. While the social and intellectual causes of this mass movement were manifold and complex – most of them having to do with the decline of established religious institutions and the rapid economic modernization of American colonial societies in the late seventeenth century – the ignition of the Great Awakening was largely the work of one man, George Whitefield (pronounced *Whit*field), a British Methodist who traveled repeatedly through Scotland, Ireland, Wales, and the British colonies in North America to preach to large crowds of people and make converts.

In so doing, Whitefield and other British Methodists, such as John and George Wesley, practiced a new style of Calvinist Protestantism that changed the course of religious history, especially in America. Their evangelism aimed at bringing forth a spiritual rebirth in the believer: a deep and inwardly felt conviction of God's grace that would fundamentally regenerate the life of the convert. At first glance, this doctrine had much in common with more orthodox forms of Protestant belief, especially the Congregational faith of the Puritans in New England. The Puritan Congregationalists, too, believed that the workings of God's grace culminated in a radically new sense of selfhood. However, for orthodox Puritans the reception of God's grace was a complicated process, in which the believer had to be assisted by his or her minister and pastor, who provided guidance for biblical study and spiritual self-scrutiny (cf. Spahr in this vol., 60-7). In the words of Thomas Hooker (cf. doc. 44), there was a work of "preparation" to be done, and this preparation required life-long dedication without final certainty. Hence, the believer could never be sure whether he or she was saved or not. This "Puritan ordeal" (Delbanco 1989) helps to explain why pious New Englanders were constantly looking for signs concerning the state of their

---

[1] I wish to thank Christy Hosefelder, Daniel Stein, and Alexander Starre for assistance and critique.

salvation. In order not to give in to wild interpretations on their search for divine providence, and not to fall victim to either excessive spiritual pride or self-destructive despair, they felt that they had to be controlled and moderated by people specifically trained in such typological reading: professional and learned ministers (cf. Stievermann in this vol., 134-5).

By contrast, the evangelists held that converts are touched by God in one momentous, supremely individual instant. George Whitefield had little patience with the orthodox insistence on guided self-inspections and communal intellectual reckonings. According to him and other itinerant preachers, the prime task of a Christian minister was not to teach, explain, or interpret Scripture for the sake of a self-governing and locally circumscribed congregation (because faith was a matter of the 'heart,' not of rational social organization), but rather to provoke a situation of spiritual crisis which made people receptive to the claims of the Holy Ghost. Often this was achieved by shattering the audience's sense of emotional security. The chief intention of many an evangelical sermon was to violently wake up its audience with graphic descriptions of impending punishment. Out of this crisis, a new sensibility for divine communication was supposed to emerge – and frequently did in the 1740s, as the massive success of "fire and brimstone" sermons such as Jonathan Edwards's *Sinners in the Hands of an Angry God* (doc. 92) illustrates.

The new evangelical rhetoric was a far cry from the rational, doctrinally controlled, and logically structured oratory of orthodox Puritan sermons (cf. doc. 16). Whitefield and other evangelists insisted that the reception of God's grace was an *immediate* affair, both in the sense of 'sudden,' and 'unmediated.' Thus, conversion happened in an *instant*, and it required *no mediators*: no clergy, no church, no professional scriptural exegesis. From the perspective of orthodox ministers, these features of evangelical conversions – their suddenness and their relinquishment of intellectual and institutional mediation – were clear signs of enthusiasm and antinomianism, two key heresies in the Protestant faith.[2]

The man who took these evangelical dispositions to their logical extreme in eighteenth-century America was James Davenport, an itinerant preacher from Massachusetts. He claimed that the established and stationary ministers of New England were not inwardly converted but preached a formalist religion – a religion not of 'the spirit,' but of 'the letter.' Therefore, Davenport demanded that true believers should boycott these ministers. The New England clergy felt reminded of an earlier affair: the banishment in 1636 of radical Puritan Anne Hutchinson from Massachusetts Bay on charges of enthusiasm and antinomianism. This time, however, a century later, the Congregational establishment was no longer confronted with one woman and a small circle of dissenting believers, but a mass movement that transcended local communities. Thus, when the most

---

[2] 'Enthusiasm' describes the presumptuous belief in direct, personal communication with God; 'antinomianism' holds that true converts are no longer subject to the written laws or established practices of their community because they are authorized by an infinitely higher law and power.

radical propagandist of the Great Awakening, James Davenport, was finally censured, the colonial orthodoxy may have scored a victory, but their war against a modernized religion could no longer be won. Dynamic forms of religious communication such as itinerancy and camp meetings (cf. doc. 96) had already undermined the authority of traditional religious institutions, and they had done so more fundamentally than even evangelical doctrines.

When the revivals finally subsided, American religion and culture were no longer the same. The Great Awakening drew many people from the lower classes and from marginalized groups into Protestant sects and churches, producing a dramatically diversified religious landscape in the colonies. "The Spiritual Travels of Nathan Cole" (doc. 95) describes the attraction of Whitefield's evangelism on a farmer from Kensington, Connecticut. Like many converts, Cole followed the itinerant preacher from place to place – another instance of the spatial and social mobilization of American Protestant faiths during the 1730s and 1740s. For the first time, many women, African Americans, and Native Americans (such as Samson Occom) were granted recognition and a voice in religious matters, being authorized through a covenant of grace that bypassed social decorum or the laws of the state. In this context, it is no coincidence that almost all eighteenth-century slave narratives, including the popular *Interesting Narrative of Olaudah Equiano, the African, Written by Himself* (1789), contain a scene in which the black narrator tells his readers where and how he first heard George Whitefield preach.

As a result of the Great Awakening, the number of churches and sects in North America proliferated tremendously. About 150 new denominations came into existence because of the revivals. In consequence, the religious and cultural influence of the established denominations – Anglicanism in the South, Quakerism in Pennsylvania, and Congregationalism in New England – weakened, while Presbyterians, Baptists, and Methodists became dominant forces in American Protestantism. This new diversity prepared the way for the specifically American ideal of (trans-)denominationalism, which soon regarded all (Christian) churches as legitimate expressions of faith, deserving of equal esteem and independence, as long as they stayed within their own sphere and did not interfere in public affairs (cf. Leypoldt in this vol., 292). Again, this was a far cry from the religious vision of the Plymouth settlers in 1620, the so-called Pilgrim Fathers, but also from the non-separatist outlook of the Puritans who founded Massachusetts Bay in 1629-30.

The Great Awakening modernized colonial religion and society in other ways as well. In order to provide education and training for their own people – and to counter their critics, who held powerful positions at institutions such as Harvard College – the revivalists founded new colleges and universities, some of which became leading institutions in the country, not always, however, maintaining to the evangelical beliefs of their founders. The most important schools founded in this vein during or after the Great Awakening include Princeton, Columbia, Brown, Rutgers, and Dartmouth. Possibly even more important in terms of cultural history was the influence of revivalist enthusiasm on the sentimental reform literatures of the nineteenth century, particularly on the abolitionist movement. *Uncle Tom's Cabin* (1851-1852) by Harriet Beecher Stowe – daughter of the charismatic Presbyterian preacher and temperance leader Lyman Beecher – owes a great deal to the evangelical idea of a religion that is felt in the 'heart,' and not in the rational mind of the believer. Holding that emotions are a better guide to moral action than the laws of the country, abolitionists such as Stowe and William Lloyd Garrison translated the enthusiasm and antinomianism of the Great Awakening into a principled opposition to slavery and other legally sanctioned ills (such as alcohol, prostitution, and child labor). Garrison, whose rhetoric of alarm had much in common with the evangelical immediacy of sermons such as *Sinners in the Hands of an Angry God*, explicitly stressed the antinomianism of his position when he publicly burned the American Constitution in 1854, claiming that his attacks on the institution of slavery were authorized by a 'higher law' (cf. docs. 256, 266-7, 269).

Many historians have argued that the Great Awakening provided the mental and cultural foundations for the colonial revolt against British imperial rule three decades later. Ideologically, both events had little in common. However, in terms of its socio-cultural reverberations, the Great Awakening did prepare in numerous ways for the Revolution of 1776. At a time when British North America was divided by internal rivalries and conflicts of interest, the tours of George Whitefield and the attendant revivals, transcending geographical borders as well as social boundaries, produced the rare instance of a common experience shared by all thirteen colonies. Most evangelists were shrewd in exploiting the possibilities of new media, foremost newspapers, to advertise their spatially transgressive movement. They also developed innovative modes of promotion, such as the utilization of controversy for the sake of publicity, serial sermon tours (predecessors of the nineteenth-century "lecture circuit"), book signing events, and camp meetings. With measures such as these, the Great Awakening created something like a trans-colonial public sphere in North America, which the secular elites would use to political advantage thirty years later during the American Revolution (cf. Hurm in this vol., 192-7).

According to Jürgen Habermas (1990), the eighteenth-century emergence of a bourgeois public sphere marks one of the crucial origins of Western modernity. Significantly, in North America this transformation first occurred in connection with a spiritual event. It was not initiated by secular elites who argued against the feudal order but by religious extremists who practiced a Protestant faith both radically individualized and radically reproducible, centered on the masses. The secular revolutionaries arrived on the scene later. In North America, then, modernization – particularly the modernization of public communication – was initially accompanied and motivated by changes in religious discourse and practice. This helps to account for North America's divergent paths into modernity.

II. Heartfelt Religion, Sublime Nature: Jonathan Edwards's "Account of His Conversion"

It is unfortunate that the Great Awakening is known to modern readers chiefly through the example of Jonathan Edwards, and Jonathan Edwards chiefly through the example of his most frequently anthologized sermon, *Sinners in the Hands of an Angry God*. Although he acted as an apologist for the movement, Edwards, who was also a staunch Congregationalist, had a nuanced and critical attitude toward the revivals' antinomianism and enthusiasm. He was particularly interested in the linguistic foundations of evangelical rhetoric and in the natural conditions of conversion (cf. doc. 93). Both interests reveal his early readings in British empiricism and other modern philosophies, particularly the moral sense-school of the Scottish Enlightenment (cf. Stievermann in this vol., 140-3).

Edwards's dual allegiance to the Puritan faith and to modern British thought is clearly visible in "An Account of His Conversion" (doc. 94). "I made seeking my Salvation the main Business of my Life," Edwards declares (*KC*, 218), sounding a note familiar from orthodox conversion narratives such as Thomas Shepard's "The Autobiography" (doc. 42) or Anne Bradstreet's letter to her children (doc. 43). Thus, unlike other eighteenth-century autobiographers such as Jean-Jacques Rousseau, Giacomo Casanova, or Benjamin Franklin (cf. doc. 104), Edwards confronts his readers with a completely heteronomous self: a self that is literally nothing without God's grace, non-existent and devoid of reliable self-knowledge in an unconverted state. And yet, on closer inspection Edwards's "Account" reveals itself as a surprisingly modern text. Shepard's *ordo salutis*, for instance – the ordered, ministerially guided succession of alternating conversional stages of doubt and certainty – no longer applies. True, Edwards is troubled by suspicions and backslidings; like Shepard, he continually wavers between assurance and doubt (whereas Franklin, starting his autobiography thirty years later, tells a relatively straightforward success story). But it is revealing to see what Edwards's doubts are primarily about: "From my Childhood up, my Mind had been wont to be full of Objections against the Doctrine of GOD'S Sovereignty, in choosing whom he would to eternal Life, and rejecting whom he pleased; leaving them eternally to perish, and be everlastingly tormented in Hell. It used to appear like a horrible Doctrine to me" (*KC*, 218).

Like Edwards, seventeenth-century Puritans regularly admitted to their religious doubts, struggling for example (as Anne Bradstreet did most poignantly) with the mysterious providential meaning of death and disaster in this world. But their theological misgivings hardly ever centered so explicitly and predominantly on the doctrine of God's sovereignty, that eschatological cornerstone of the Puritan faith. Edwards, by contrast, lived and wrote in an age that had begun to believe in humankind's almost unlimited capacity for self-improvement and self-creation. Since Edwards was well acquainted with John Locke's theory that every human being is born a *tabula rasa*, a blank space of future possibilities, the old Puritan doctrine of sovereignty, with its assumption of human helplessness and passivity in matters of salvation, presented an inevitable stumbling block to his eighteenth-century mind. The protagonist of Edwards's autobiography finally manages to overcome this enlightened doubt. Again, it is illuminating to see exactly how he does so: not by choosing an established faith over modern thought, but by modernizing his religion, i.e., by reconciling his need for orthodox salvation with the demands of Lockean empiricism. In fact, his skepticism about religious dogma prompts Edwards to do something that will later become a habit among American intellectuals when they lose faith in scripture or church – he turns to nature:

> [And I] found, from Time to Time, an inward Sweetness, that used, as it were, to carry me away in my Contemplations; in what I know not how to express otherwise, than by a calm, sweet Abstraction of Soul from all the Concerns o[f] this World; and a kind of Vision, or fix'd Ideas and Imaginations, of being alone in the Mountains, or some solitary Wilderness, far from all Mankind, sweetly conversing with Christ, and wrapt and swallowed up in GOD. The Sense I had of divine Things, would often of a sudden as it were, kindle up a sweet burning in my Heart; an ardor of my Soul, that I know not how to express. (*KC*, 219)

Thus, the protagonist of Edwards's conversion narrative overcomes his doubts about scriptural doctrine not only by studying the Bible even harder or asking the assistance of his minister (as an orthodox seventeenth-century Puritan would have done) but also and principally by closing the book and heading outdoors. The nature he finds there strikingly resembles John Locke's nature: It is a realm of sensuous experience and empirical knowledge. The great paradigm shift set in motion by Locke's *Essay Concerning Human Understanding* (1689/1700) revolved around the idea that knowledge is dependent on man's natural senses rather than on libraries or the sayings of wise and learned men. This paradigm shift is visibly reflected in the vocabulary of Edwards's spiritual literature. Again and again, Edwards insists on having a "sense" of divine things; he speaks of conversion as a sensual experience – of seeing, hearing, smelling, and tasting grace. Thus, in his most sophisticated sermon, *A Divine and Supernatural Light* (1733), Edwards distinguishes between a sensuous-empirical and an intellectual-doctrinal knowledge of God:

> There is a twofold knowledge of good of which God had made the mind of man capable. The first, that which is merely notional; as when a person only speculatively judges that anything is, which by the agreement of mankind, is called good or excellent [...]. And the other, that which consists in the sense of the heart; as when the heart is sensible of pleasure and delight in the presence of the idea of it. [...] Thus there is a difference between having an opinion, that God is holy and gracious, and having a sense of the loveliness and beauty of that holiness and grace. There is a difference between having a rational judgment that honey is sweet, and having a sense of its sweetness. A man may have the former, that knows not how honey tastes; but a man cannot have the latter unless he has an idea of the taste of honey in his mind. (Edwards 1995, 122)

According to Edwards, only the second kind of judgment, the one based on empirical experience, yields true knowledge. As a result, Edwards's conversion narrative abounds in sensual terminology whenever it speaks of God's grace. This textual feature seemingly conflicts with another, equally pronounced one: Throughout his narrative, Edwards describes his religious feelings as inexpressible. In the passage from "An Account" quoted above, he does so twice. He speaks of being carried away "*in what I know not how to express otherwise*, than by a calm, sweet Abstraction of Soul," and at the end of the passage he mentions "a sweet burning in my Heart; an ardor of my Soul, *that I know not how to express*" (emphasis mine). There are numerous other passages in which the narrator of "An Account" indicates that something cannot be communicated properly or that words fail him.

Why should this be so? Precisely because the experience he is recounting is not an intellectual one. As a true evangelical, Edwards in these passages refers to sensual, not doctrinal, knowledge. According to his epistemology, anyone who ever tasted honey knows this taste, yet is unable to describe or explain it to people who have never tasted it. These people may be perfectly able to use the word *honey* in conversation or to lecture competently about honey, but, strictly speaking, they do not know what they are talking about. Thus, there are no words or metaphors that could tell or teach a person the taste of honey if that person does not have a "sense" of it. According to Edwards, the same is true for the experience of God's grace. To read the Bible and to believe in what is written there is one thing, but real knowledge of God's sovereignty is like tasting honey: It is an empirical and sensual experience, and therefore inexpressible to those who have never had it.

This emphasis on an inward knowledge of God, on a religion of the heart rather than the mind, has always been a central part of the Protestant faith. Already the basic Protestant doctrine of *iustificatio sola fide* contained an inevitable appreciation of the affections. Significantly, however, it was only in the age of Enlightenment that these sensual tendencies came fully to the fore and managed to revolutionize the religious landscape of modernity. The colonial Great Awakening, too, while not being an 'enlightened' movement, participated in an intellectual climate that valued sensual evidence as the chief road to knowledge. As in Locke's more secular version of the same disposition, this entailed a patent threat to established doctrinal authorities. Suddenly, religious competency – particularly the right to spiritual instruction – no longer depended on education, social background, or institutional standing.

On the one hand, then, colonial religion, especially in its Puritan shape, was altered in fundamental ways by incorporating Lockean conceptions of knowledge. On the other hand, however, eighteenth-century evangelism also formulated a new and timely critique of secular, enlightened knowledge – a critique far advanced from the chiefly doctrinal arguments of traditional Christian positions. Consider Edwards's "Vision [...] of being alone in the Mountains, or some solitary Wilderness, far from all Mankind, sweetly conversing with GOD": Edwards's insistence on *isolation* ("far from all Mankind") points to an epistemological situation that in the hands of Ralph Waldo Emerson and Henry David Thoreau would later serve as a starting point for a trenchant criticism of Lockean empiricism (cf. docs. 196, 198-201). In a striking dialectics, then, the evangelical absorption of enlightened thought in the eighteenth century prepared for various Romantic attacks on the Enlightenment in the nineteenth century.

Nowhere is Edwards's proto-Romantic understanding of nature more evident than in his surprising usage of the term 'wilderness.' When he describes his vision of being alone in a "Wilderness," Edwards obviously employs one of the key terms of American Puritanism. But seventeenth-century Puritans used this term in a manner that was markedly different. For them, to describe America as a wilderness, as an uncultivated, possibly vacant land, suggested that their natural environment was a divine ordeal. Doing God's work in the New World consisted in *overcoming* the wilderness; God's grace would arrive only after the wilderness had been transformed into a garden. For Edwards, the term 'wilderness' still refers to uncultivated lands but no longer indicates the absence or an anticipation of grace. Rather, and biblically more accurate, the untouched and untouchable wilderness is now the very place where divine grace can be received directly. William Bradford still needed to domesticate and civilize America's nature to please his God (cf. doc. 32), but for Edwards the situation is reversed: Here the believer needs to flee civilization – the cultivated gardens of social order – to find his God.

Edwards's reinterpretation of the term 'wilderness' introduced a type of nature in American literature that in due time became a Romantic topos. This was the topos of *sublime* nature, one of the most successful concepts to record the meaning of material existence in the Western intellectual tradition. Edmund Burke, the preeminent eighteenth-century theoretician of the sublime in English, argued against the Lockean Enlightenment that there is a specific type of nature that cannot be grasped empirically. Mountains and oceans, for instance, because of their sheer size and grandeur, arouse a feeling of sweet terror according to Burke (1992), completely overwhelming the observer, leaving no room for "human understanding." Since it is impossible to measure the ocean and to make empirical sense of it, all an observer can do when confronted with this massive proof of his or her limitations is to feel the strangely contradictory emotions of awe and fear: sweet terror. The sublime, in this fashion, acts as a last bastion of supernatural power in an otherwise disenchanted natural environment.

There are various examples of this kind of natural sublimity in Edwards's "An Account." Here is one of them:

> [S]carce anything, among all the works of nature, was so sweet to me as thunder and lightning. Formerly, nothing had been so terrible to me. I used to be a person uncommonly terrified with thunder: and it used to strike me with terror, when I saw a thunderstorm rising. But now, on the contrary, it rejoiced me. I felt God at the first appearance of a thunderstorm. And used to take the opportunity at such times, to fix myself to view the clouds, and see the lightnings play, and hear the majestic and awful voice of God's thunder: which often times was exceeding entertaining, leading me to sweet contemplations of my great and glorious God. And while I viewed, used to

spend my time, as it always seemed natural to me, to sing or chant forth my meditations; to speak my thoughts in soliloquies, and speak with a singing voice. (Edwards 1998, 794)

The narrator of Edwards's conversion narrative is fond of life-threatening thunderstorms because he feels that here at last is a phenomenon beyond the grasp of modern thought. Sublime nature illustrates for Edwards, as it will for the Romantics, an inevitable human dependency on higher forces, an insurmountable helplessness in the face of a power that can kill on a whim. This terror is "sweet" precisely because it attests to the existence of something larger than the autonomous, supposedly enlightened self. By giving himself up to this greater being, and by feeling both powerless and ecstatic in its presence, Edwards ultimately manages to make room for old Puritan doctrines in an eighteenth-century mind. The feeling of sublime self-loss allows him to experience by natural means a phenomenon that actually lies outside and above the realm of both natural understanding and enlightened language, and hence can only be spoken in a singing voice. Here, Edwards believes, is the empirical proof of *super*natural sovereignty – until Benjamin Franklin steps out into American thunderstorms with a different purpose in mind and with different technological and discursive equipment in his hands.

III. Liberal Religion and Modern Mass Psychology: Charles Chauncy's *Enthusiasm Described and Cautioned Against*

To understand the range of discursive possibilities within the field of competing positions that is eighteenth-century American culture, it is useful to discuss the Great Awakening in the context of two writers who, each in his own way, can be read as antipodes of Jonathan Edwards: Benjamin Franklin, who created – or at least popularized – the utilitarian version of American selfhood, and Charles Chauncy, who was Edwards's most outspoken critic within the Congregational establishment. Whereas Edwards's transformation of orthodox Puritanism looked forward to Romantic discourse, both Franklin and Chauncy modernized colonial notions of spirituality and selfhood in the context of discourses and practices usually described as bourgeois.

If Chauncy, minister of the First Church of Boston, is something of a forgotten figure in American cultural history, this is because modern anthologies tend to put a premium on dissident and heterodox voices, often at the cost of misrepresenting the cultural forces that provoked such dissidence and heterodoxy in the first place. Modern anthologies also tend to select their material according to the tastes and interests of a contemporary readership – and Jonathan Edwards's proto-Romantic sensibilities seem much closer to the spiritual views of a modern academic milieu than Chauncy's bourgeois re-orientation of orthodox Puritanism. But Chauncy was by no means the conservative disciplinarian that he is portrayed as in much of the secondary literature on the Great Awakening. Like Edwards, he was an avid reader of Isaac Newton, John Locke, and the moral philosophers of the Scottish Enlightenment. Like Edwards, too, he deployed these sources to create a decidedly modern, if counter-evangelical, version of colonial religion. In this sense, Charles Chauncy was a key figure in the transformation of seventeenth-century Congregationalism to a more liberal theology that would finally culminate in William Ellery Channing's Unitarianism (cf. doc. 193), a theology that did away with the traditional Puritan doctrines of original sin and unconditional election.

Chauncy's sermon *Enthusiasm Described and Cautioned Against* (doc. 98) was delivered in 1742, at the height of the debate between "New Lights" and "Old Lights," the advocates and critics of the revival in New England. Remarkably, Chauncy's argument is as empirical as it is doctrinal. In the rhetorical shape of an orthodox sermon, Chauncy presents a well-nigh clinical description of what he thinks is happening in the country at the time, diagnosing in effect a socio-psychological mass hysteria. He begins by defining enthusiasm, quite conventionally, as the false belief in direct personal communication with God. It is "an *imaginary*, not a *real* inspiration: according to which sense, the *Enthusiast* is one, who has a conceit of himself as a person favoured with the extraordinary presence of the *Deity*" (*KC*, 229). This false belief in divine presence, Chauncy explains, is usually accompanied by rantings and ravings, convulsions of the body, a wild countenance, and speaking in tongues. It is, in short, a supremely physical state which to an external observer looks like madness. To the enthusiast, however, it is the ecstatic abandonment that attends his or her sensual confrontation with a sublime and sovereign God.

Chauncy is insistent on this last point. As a Puritan, he believes that to receive God's grace is an inwardly moving and even life-shattering experience; it transforms the believer into a "new creature" (Chauncy 1741a). Also, Chauncy believes that the revivalists really think they are being converted. They truly feel that they have been awakened by a direct and personal revelation from God. For Chauncy, then, the Great Awakening is not a fraud. Other orthodox ministers surmised that the revivals were actually impostures; the colonial press suspected George Whitefield in particular of embezzling donations intended for his orphanage in Georgia.[3] By contrast, Chauncy in *Enthusiasm* maintained that the Great Awakening is based on self-delusion rather than on a deliberate attempt to deceive. But why are good Christians suddenly convinced that they have heard the voice of God and stand above the law? What is the cause of enthusiasm?

---

[3] In his *Letter to the Reverend Mr. George Whitefield* (1745), Chauncy refrained from making such charges but held that "your Travelling about as an Itinerant Preacher was not to your Disadvantage, on temporal Accounts" (16). As a result of such allegations, some colonial churches allowed Whitefield to preach only on the condition that he did not collect money and did not comment on the conversional state of local ministers: cf. the invitation of the Eastern Consociation in Fairfield County, Connecticut, from October 1740, reprinted in Bushman (1989, 25); on the colonial debate about Whitefield's fund-raising, see Lambert (1994, 176-82, 195).

Chauncy's answer to this question is remarkable: "The cause of this *enthusiasm* is a bad temperament of the blood and spirits; 'tis properly a disease, a sort of madness: and there are few; perhaps, none at all, but are subject to it" (*KC*, 229). With this answer, Chauncy effectively 'naturalizes' the supposedly supernatural revivals, comparing them to a contagious virus whose irresistibility is distinct from the irresistibility of grace. There were pressing political interests behind this interpretation. Unlike John Winthrop a hundred years earlier, who, backed by a civil court, banished Anne Hutchinson from Massachusetts Bay because her evangelism endangered the social cohesion of the community, Charles Chauncy is acutely aware that banishment on charges of heresy is no realistic option in a modernized society. The people thus banished from the congregation might just choose to reorganize around charismatic leaders and establish a plethora of competing sects – which is exactly what happened in the Great Awakening. Chauncy thus understood that the major threat of the Great Awakening was diversification: a threat to the homogeneity of the religious and social establishment in New England. Thus, Chauncy had a vested interest in describing the theological-institutional crisis of the 1740s as only a temporary aberration: Enthusiasm was not to be regarded as an unpardonable transgression (as colonial governor Winthrop still saw it), but as a natural disease that occurred without responsibility on the part of those who suffered from it and that, most importantly, could be cured. Rather than court trials and ostracism, Chauncy recommended leniency and care as proper treatment for enthusiasts:

> And much to be pitied are the persons who are seized with [enthusiasm]. Our compassion commonly works towards those, who, while under distraction, fondly imagine themselves to be Kings and Emperors: And the like pity is really due to those, who, under the power of *enthusiasm*, fancy themselves to be *prophets*; *inspired of GOD*, and *immediately called* and *commissioned by him to deliver his messages to the world*: And tho' they should run into disorders, and act in a manner that cannot be but condemned, they should notwithstanding be treated with tenderness and lenity; and the rather, because they don't commonly act so much under the influence of a *bad mind*, as a *deluded imagination*. (*KC*, 230)

Unfortunately, Chauncy admits, it is not easy to reason with enthusiasts in a gentle and understanding manner, because their very condition is defined by hostility to reasoned argument, especially if put forth by institutional authorities.[4] Like all participants in the public debate on the revival, Chauncy thus faced a problem of (Lockean) linguistics: If empirical knowledge is dependent on sensual experience rather than correct semantic identifications, how can one even tell if other people have truly had the experience they claim? There is nothing *in their words* that could demonstrate whether they really tasted honey or only talk about it – whether they had really received God's grace or only used, and possibly believed

---

[4] Chauncy knew what he was talking about, having been told to his face by James Davenport that he was an unconverted minister and bound for hell.

in, words. Worse still, enthusiasts themselves have no way of telling whether their innermost feelings are true or not.

The relationship between inward emotions and their external signs, such as words, gestures, and facial expressions, was one of the major intellectual problems of the eighteenth century, and it bothered defenders and critics of evangelical religion alike.[5] Jonathan Edwards wrote a long and subtle study, *Religious Affections* (1746), to show how genuine spiritual feelings could be distinguished from delusions. Charles Chauncy also believed that there were ways to tell authentic religious affections from inauthentic ones, despite the inherent inexpressibility of sensual grace. Significantly, however, Chauncy's solution to the problem of individual sign-usage reestablished the importance of communal control and moderation through learned and professional, i.e., institutionalized, interpretations. Since a private language of faith was impossible, the semantic content of a revelation must be publicly recordable.

The entire second part of Chauncy's sermon attempts to establish an "infallible rule of tryal" (*KC*, 231) by which people can judge their feelings of sublime revelation. The first of these rules is as simple as it is orthodox: If a revelation is not consistent with Scripture, Chauncy holds, then it must be wrong. In theological terms, this means that whereas the supporters of the Great Awakening valued the "spirit" of their faith higher than its 'letter,' Chauncy asked believers to constantly check the sensual manifestations of their faith against the revealed letter. So while Edwards's "Account" advised the God-seeking subject to go out alone into nature, and there to abandon oneself to God's sublimity (i.e., to live the Bible, more than to study it), Chauncy's sermon claimed the exact opposite: not to isolate oneself from all community but to consult the book and to seek the advice of competent and legitimate readers, such as parents or ministers, in order to situate one's emotions within a larger social and doctrinal framework. Thus, Chauncy argued, if a believer is told by God to kill himself in order to arrive earlier in grace (as happened in at least one instance in Edwards's hometown of Northampton, Massachusetts), or if a believer is asked by God to prove his faith by slaughtering his family (a scenario memorably described by Charles Brockden Brown in his 1798 novel *Wieland; or the Transformation*), then these commandments cannot have been spoken by the voice of God, because the Bible does not condone suicide or the sacrificial killing of loved ones.

This neo-orthodox confidence in the legibility of Scripture is based on a complex, thoroughly anti-Romantic psychology. Chauncy refuses to take for granted the transparency of individual emotions; strength of feeling and strength of inner conviction are not accepted as self-evident signs of truth. At the core of this skepticism, there is an altogether enlightened awareness of the artificiality – the mediated character – of even the most immediate and intimate feelings. Thus, Chauncy's writings on the Great Awakening, especially his longer and

---

[5] For a more detailed version of the following argument, see Kelleter (2002, 242-310).

more systematic publications such as *Seasonable Thoughts on the State of Religion in New-England* (1743), offer some of the most refined contributions to the wide-ranging eighteenth-century debate on emotional manipulation and (self-) delusion. Other colonial ministers added to the socio-psychological sophistication of the debate, most notably William Rand in *The Late Religious Commotions in New-England Considered; An Answer to Jonathan Edwards "Distinguishing Marks"* (1743) and John Caldwell in his remarkable sermon *The Nature, Folly, and Evil of Rash and Uncharitable Judging* (1742). In all these cases, the critics of the Great Awakening, frequently denounced by modern scholars as "conservatives," insisted on the empirical agency of natural and social causes. Like a social constructivist *avant la lettre*, Chauncy asked in *Seasonable Thoughts* if the surprising mass conversions were not public rather than subjective events. To assess what happened within a convert's soul, Chauncy believed it was important to ask "how the Word was preached, either as to Matter, or Manner" (1743, 87). Thus agreeing with Shaftesbury that religious enthusiasm is "social and communicative," Chauncy pointed to "the natural Influence of awful Words and frightful Gestures" (Shaftesbury 1732, 1:16; Chauncy 1743, 80). Many an evangelist, he noted, coerced onto his audience heartfelt reactions whose appearance then proved the evangelist's own charismatic authority. Chauncy regarded this dramatic constitution of a public sphere (and the entire repertory of its communicative practices, from direct emotional addresses to comprehensive trans-local press coverage) as the proper object of a religious mass psychology:

> [I]n order to give the People a plain Intimation of what he wanted, [a] Preacher sometimes told them of the *wonderful Effects* wrought by the Sermon, he was then preaching; how in *such* a Congregation, they were all melted and dissolved, and in another so over-poured, that they could not help *screaming out*, or falling down, as though they had been *struck dead* [...]. And what is it more than might be expected, to see People so affrightned as to fall into *Shrieks* and *Fits*, under such Methods as these? Especially, when they have first been possest of the Notion, that the Persons who make Use of them, are *Men of GOD* in an *extraordinary Sense*; as being sent immediately, as it were, to deliver his Messages to them. The Mind is now prepared to receive almost any Impression from this Kind of Persons [...], 'till the Noise of such *extraordinary* Effects, as *Arguments* of an *immediate divine Power*, in one Place and another, had alarmed the People, and made many of them think, it was necessary they also should be in like Circumstances. (1743, 94-100)[6]

This answer to the question of enthusiastic motivation is remarkable for what it does not say. Unlike Edwards, who was also troubled by the possibilities of manipulation and self-delusion (cf. doc. 93), Chauncy refused to trace back false inspirations to evil – i.e., supernatural – causation. A satanic interpretation would

---

[6] Similarly, in his sermon *An Unbridled Tongue a Sure Evidence, that Our Religion Is Hypocritical and Vain* (1741b), Chauncy suggested that sudden conversions can occur because the converts hope for social distinction, i.e., "the commendation and applause of others," or for political advantage, i.e., "the better to compass their worldly designs" (8-9).

have been the most plausible answer for an older generation of Puritans and it was, in fact, the strongest answer provided by Jonathan Edwards and George Whitefield for the widely discussed cases of revivalism gone wrong (e.g., serial suicides): If inspiration is felt but does not come from the true spirit, then it must be a stratagem of the devil to undermine a congregation's cohesiveness or to endanger an ongoing revival. Chauncy was not impressed by the logic of this argument. Conceding the reality of supernatural evil, he found it unnecessary to explain enthusiasm in this fashion. In his *Letter to the Reverend Mr. George Whitefield*, he declared: "I never tho't there was the Hand of Satan in this Matter. A *disturbed* or *over-heated Fancy* will sufficiently account for it, without any Help from him" (Chauncy 1745, 37).

Chauncy's insistence on explanatory *sufficiency* recalls David Hume's famous maxim on supernatural phenomena: "[N]o testimony is sufficient to establish a miracle, unless the testimony be of such kind, that its falsehood would be more miraculous, than the fact, which it endeavours to establish" (1975, 115). Following this axiom, Chauncy's *Enthusiasm* explicitly situates itself in a post-Satanic age: Anomalous occurrences in the natural world are no longer traced back to supernatural causation but are explained within the limits of the enlightened concept of nature itself. At the same time, however, Chauncy was deeply troubled by the consequences of this thought. Thus, it would be wrong to read Chauncy's sermon merely as a Lockean critique of evangelical religion. Like Edwards but with different results, Chauncy in *Enthusiasm* attempted to uphold the epistemological priority of religious discourse over purely empirical or scientific reason:

> 'Tis true, you must not go about to set up your own *reason* in *opposition* to *revelation*: nor may you entertain a thought of making *reason* your *rule* instead of *Scripture*. The Bible, as I said before, is the *great rule* of religion, the grand test in matters of salvation: but then you must use your reason in order to understand the *Bible*: nor is there any other possible way, in which, as a reasonable creature, you should come to an understanding of it. (1742, 18)[7]

This is a nuanced, if desperate, position. Rejecting evangelical anti-intellectualism and the proto-Romantic cult of sublime affections, Chauncy wished to contain enlightened thought within a differently modernized religion: a 'reasonable' Christianity. This was a dangerous gamble, because the Christian religion, as David Hume observed, "is founded on *Faith*, not on reason; and it is a sure method of exposing it to put it to such a trial as it is, by no means, fitted to endure" (1975, 130). Thus, the very reason Chauncy wished to instill in Christian practice was capable of undoing it; taken to its logical conclusion, empirical reason led to deism, i.e., to natural religion.

---

[7] Compare Chauncy's sermon *Ministers Exhorted and Encouraged to Take Heed of Themselves, and to Their Doctrine* (1744): "[Ministers] must take heed to it, that [their Doctrine] be Christian, in Opposition to that which is the Result of meer Reason [...]. His preaching should not be in Words of Man's Wisdom, but the Truth as it is in Jesus" (16-7).

Like the revivalists of the pre-revolutionary era, deists insisted on the epistemological priority of the human senses. Their conclusions, however, were diametrically opposed to the evangelical doctrine of immediate grace – and to stress this point, they liked to quote the same passage from Locke's *Essay Concerning Human Understanding* that was quoted by Chauncy in *Enthusiasm*. Deists or freethinkers held that God created the universe as a perfect and fully rational mechanism. Hence, they claimed, the creator-God no longer has to intervene in his creation. He is, quite literally, above miracles and spectacular communications, such as Christ's sacrifice. Instead of relying on such supernatural measures, he communicates with humankind exclusively through the regular laws of his creation. With this thought, enlightened reason, which had always tried to establish itself within or alongside Christian mythology, at last dismissed the Christian narrative of God's active and constant care for a fallen world. Deism replaced this narrative of divine incarnation with a narrative of scientific progress, claiming that the only way to know and worship God was to study his creation, i.e., to study the empirical laws of nature. In this vein, Thomas Paine and others held that the legitimate source of human knowledge was no longer the Bible, nor the scholastic wisdom of dead philosophers who merely 'thought' about the world and erected complex rational systems in their books, but nature in its enlightened definition as a realm of physical cause-and-effect relations. The natural sciences thus attained the status of true religion.

In his major writings of the 1740s, including *Enthusiasm*, Charles Chauncy tried to have it both ways: His desire was to establish a religion that would live up to the demands of enlightened reason without being transformed into a natural religion. He thus envisaged a religion that would stand its ground against the most radical consequences of Lockean empiricism and yet stay clear of the Romantic mass-delusions of modern evangelism. It was a strenuous two-front war, and it resulted in the conception of a scrupulously liberal and humane Puritanism, well adapted to the social and spiritual needs of Chauncy's Boston clientele. Chauncy's mature "Universalism" (systematized in books such as *The Benevolence of the Deity* and *The Mystery Hid from Ages and Generations*, both published in 1784) had little in common with the eschatological anxiety of William Bradford and John Winthrop. It left its mark on the American Revolution, which Chauncy supported, and proved to be a lasting influence on New England cultural history, paving the road for Unitarianism. In sum, it was a thoroughly bourgeois faith, crucially concerned with the conflicting claims of science and Christianity. Another – partly compatible, partly competing – attempt to come to terms with America's postcolonial demand for a modern theology can be found in the writings of Benjamin Franklin.

IV. From Utilitarianism to Trans-Denominationalism: Benjamin Franklin's *Autobiography*

Most American revolutionaries toyed with the deist faith in the 1770s. Many experienced its intellectual radicalism as a liberating force, among them Benjamin Franklin, who admitted in *The Autobiography* to a youthful infatuation with natural religion. Even *The Declaration of Independence* (doc. 131) flaunted deist vocabulary, in Jefferson's talk of the "Creator" (rather than "God") who endowed all men with inalienable – i.e., natural – rights, as well as in Jefferson's reference to "the laws of nature and of nature's God" (*KC*, 303). But deism was never a dominant strain within the American Enlightenment. The continued cultural authority of Protestant Christianity, together with the sobering influence of the republican-agrarian tradition, did much to tone down the more radical varieties of enlightened thought after the American Revolution. Throughout the 1790s, then, when the French Revolution sent its shock waves through the United States, the specter of deism produced numerous paranoid scenarios and manifold fears of conspiracy. Thomas Paine, whose pamphlet *Common Sense* (doc. 130) had introduced a new and thoroughly modern tone into the previously accommodating rhetoric of the American rebels in 1776, now bore the brunt of the political changes of the 1790s. Much maligned as a radical atheist after the publication of his deist manifesto *The Age of Reason* (1794), he spent the last years of his life as a *persona non grata* in America and died almost forgotten in 1809.

While deism failed to establish itself as the new creed of a secular nation, revolutionary America produced other, stunningly original and successful syntheses of enlightened thought and the Christian faith. Benjamin Franklin's *The Autobiography* provided a model narrative for many of these attempts at reconciliation. In the first part of his memoirs, written in 1771 with a British readership and the prospect of an imperial career in mind, Franklin gave a short survey of his religious development:

> My Parents had early given me religious Impressions, and brought me through my Childhood piously in the dissenting Way [Congregational, later Presbyterian]. But I was scarce 15 when, after doubting by turns of several Points as I found them disputed in the different Books I read, I began to doubt of Revelation itself. Some Books against Deism fell into my Hands [...]. It happened that they wrought an Effect on me quite contrary to what was intended by them: For the Arguments of the Deists which were quoted to be refuted, appeared to me much Stronger than the Refutations. In short I soon became a thorough Deist. My Arguments perverted some others, particularly Collins and Ralph: but each of them having afterwards wrong'd me greatly without the least Compunction, and recollecting Keith's Conduct towards me, (who was another Freethinker) and my own towards Vernon and Miss Read which at Times gave me great trouble, I began to suspect that this Doctrine tho' it might be true, was not very useful. (1986, 45-6)

Thus, the narrator of Franklin's *The Autobiography* asserts the intellectual superiority of natural religion but complains about the practical (social and moral) results of his enlightened creed. Franklin's reminder that all deists he knew were immoral men – and that he himself, while a deist, wronged other people – reflects a common opinion about freethinkers in the eighteenth century: Since they no longer believe in an active and involved God, they neither believe in divine reward nor punishment. Hence, their 'freethinking' is not only an intellectual but also an ethical disposition: They act without bothering about the consequences of their actions. In the popular imagination of the eighteenth century, then, the words *freethinker* and *libertine* became almost interchangeable.

But despite his realization that freethinking was morally deficient, Franklin refused to re-convert to any of the socially more useful forms of Protestant Christianity. After his contact with deism he could not bring himself to regain faith in traditional creeds. So even though he abandoned natural religion, this did not return him to revealed religion:

> Revelation had indeed no weight with me as such; but I entertain'd an Opinion, that tho' certain Actions might not be bad *because* they were forbidden by it, or good *because* it commanded them; yet probably those Actions might be forbidden *because* they were bad for us, or commanded *because* they were beneficial to us, in their own Natures, all the Circumstances of things considered. (*KC*, 244)

In other words, although biblical revelation might not be divine communication, its application is extremely useful in social life. The conclusion that Franklin drew from this observation was spectacular: If the primary truth of revelation is its appeal to morality, whereas the idea of revelation itself is irrational, why not have this truth without its irrational counterpart? Thus, in the third part of his autobiography, written in 1788, one year before the ratification of the American Constitution, Franklin designed an entirely new, synthetic theology, which he thought would do justice to both his critical and social-utilitarian interests:

> I put down from time to time on Pieces of Paper such Thoughts as occur'd to me respecting [this subject]. Most of these are lost; but I find one purporting to be the Substance of an intended Creed, containing as I thought the Essentials of every known Religion, and being free of everything that might shock the Professors of any religion. It is express'd in these Words, viz.,
>
> "That there is one God who made all things.
>
> "That he governs the World by his Providence.
>
> "That he ought to be worshiped by Adoration, Prayer and Thanksgiving.
>
> "But that the most acceptable Service of God is doing Good to Man.
>
> "That the Soul is immortal.
>
> "And that God will certainly reward Virtue and punish Vice either here or hereafter."
> (1986, 77-8)

Competing varieties of revealed religions are thus translated into one common ethical system without any reference to revelation itself. The privileged status of particular holy books or documents, which Chauncy still insisted upon, is replaced by the principle of social utility: The "Service of God" is to do good to man. That

Franklin did not want to have this ingeniously secular faith confused with either evangelical or neo-orthodox forms of worship and charity is evident in the name he proposed for his new religion: "the Society of the *Free and Easy*" (1986, 78). Thus, Franklin's basic version of human belief was supposed to be an organized and integrative creed rather than a private religion, in the Romantic sense of the term, or an elaborate theological system bent on orthodoxy. This "Free and Easy" creed – which to good Christians must have sounded as bad as "freethinking" – was ultimately closer to deism than to traditional forms of Protestantism, including Cotton Mather's orthodox apology of "good works" (doc. 105).

On the whole, what Franklin presented was a natural religion with the additional assumption that God created human beings not only as rational but also as moral beings. Similar to earlier enlightened notions of a non-institutionalized, popular ur-form of Christianity, such as in John Locke's *The Reasonableness of Christianity* (1695), Franklin's universal religion was a self-evident one and claimed to be comprehensible to all people without specialized training or authoritative exegesis. More importantly, it was a democratic faith, not only because people at large could believe in it, but because its anti-schismatic character made possible the close cohabitation of widely different kinds of people. In this sense, Franklin's enlightened theology aimed not at establishing an unrivaled dogmatic truth but at organizing a peacefully inhabitable social environment in the face of religious diversity.

It is no coincidence that this idea took center stage in the writings of an American colonial and revolutionary. Like most American founders, Franklin was deeply concerned with the problems posed and the solutions suggested by a cultural environment unlike any in eighteenth-century Europe. To say that a certain idea might be true but not very useful takes on a special meaning and urgency in a heterogeneous frontier and settlement culture. Franklin – and with him the entire American Enlightenment – explicitly searched for religious and political institutions that were suitable and necessary for the highly improbable formation of a post-classical, post-European republic in faraway provinces.[8]

Franklin's surprising solution to this problem prepared the way for a spiritual paradigm that determined the course of American religious history from the 1780s until at least the 1980s. It was the rather un-European idea that no single church, creed, or holy document had a monopoly on truth, and that therefore none of them should have a privileged say in the political affairs of the nation, *but* – and this was the revolutionary point, frequently misunderstood in Europe – that *all* of them, in their very diversity, fulfilled an indispensable social function by providing moral guidance and communal cohesion to the citizens of a paradoxically large and heterogeneous republic. This is what President Eisenhower meant in the 1950s, when he claimed: "Our government makes no sense unless it is founded in a deeply felt religious faith – and I don't care what it is" (quoted in Bellah 1967, 3).

---

[8] For a more detailed discussion of these issues, see Kelleter (2008).

Franklin anticipated this thought when he justified his list of religious principles, saying that "these I esteem'd the Essentials of every Religion, and being to be found in all the Religions we had in our Country I respected them all, tho' with different degrees of Respect as I found them more or less mix'd with other Articles which without Tendency to inspire, promote or confirm Morality, serv'd principally to divide us & make us unfriendly to one another" (*KC*, 247).

That such (trans)denominationalism fulfilled a civic service was clear to all delegates who, in 1787, drafted the American Constitution together with Benjamin Franklin. Avoiding both the fervor of evangelism and the skepticism of the radical Enlightenment without abandoning either, the drafters of the Constitution opted for a maximum extension and diversification of the religious landscape, hoping that the existence of an abundant number of local sects and churches would prevent any one of them from establishing a monopoly, while each single creed would instill in its members that sense of civic commitment necessary for a pluralistic republic to flourish. It was a small step from this functional understanding of faith to some of the more contemporary forms of American civil religion.

Instructional Strategies and Classroom Issues

I. Key Concepts and Major Themes

1. Enthusiasm and Antinomianism (docs. 93-4, 98, 256, 265)
   Enthusiasm is, in the Protestant terminology, the false belief in direct, personal communication with God. It is frequently accompanied by antinomianism, i.e., the conviction that true converts are no longer subject to the written laws or established practices of their community because they are authorized by the Holy Ghost. The American antinomian tradition was secularized in the abolitionist movement by William Lloyd Garrison and in the late phase of New England transcendentalism (cf. Henry David Thoreau's concept of "civil disobedience"; cf. Leypoldt in this vol., 278).

2. Deism, Natural Religion (docs. 99-102)
   According to deism, God created the universe as a fully rational mechanism, comparable to clockwork. Hence, God can safely withdraw from his perfect creation and no longer intervenes in it. The only way to know God is to study the laws of his creation, i.e., the empirical laws of nature. The natural sciences are thus identified as the only legitimate form of religious worship.

3. Denominationalism (docs. 101, 104)
   The idea of denominationalism argues that all (Christian) churches are legitimate expressions of faith, deserving of equal esteem and independence, as long as they stay within their own sphere and do not interfere in public

affairs. Religious diversity is thought to prevent monopolies and thus to make possible the establishment of a federal republic.

4. Evangelism (docs. 82, 91, 93, 95-6)
   This modern and modernizing variety of Protestantism is both radically individualistic and reproducible, i.e., mass-based. Evangelists believe that to receive God's grace is a sensual and *immediate* affair, both in the sense of 'sudden' and 'unmediated.' Thus, evangelical conversion happens in an instant and requires no mediators (clergy, church, or professional scriptural exegesis). Evangelism is usually innovative in its usage of modern media technologies. It is frequently close to, but not identical with, biblical fundamentalism. Ideologically, evangelism and fundamentalism are highly flexible; in American history, they have at different times occurred in conjunction with progressive reform and civil rights movements or in conjunction with conservative and reactionary movements.

5. Modernization (docs. 95-6, 98, 104)
   This term denotes the increasing diversification of life-worlds, ideologies, and religions, accompanied by spatially and socially ever more pervasive technologies of communication. Modernization is not a teleological or uniform process, but it produces competing and contradictory discourses and practices, e.g. sensual empiricism (Edwards) versus social empiricism (Chauncy), Romantic notions of selfhood versus utilitarian notions of selfhood, etc. Hence, reconciliation is one of the primary intellectual and institutional tasks in modern societies.

II. Comparison – Contrasts – Connections

Example: Docs. 32-3, 42-3, 94, 104, 115, 119-20, 130, 200

More than other disciplines, American Studies suffers from the (omni)presence of popular and academic stereotypes concerning its object of study. Students entering the discipline frequently hope to make sense of the massive influence of US culture on their lives by reducing 'America' to simple and simplified master concepts such as the American Dream, the American way of life, America as redeemer nation, Puritanical America, etc. While these concepts hold a good deal of explanatory power in terms of anecdotal and everyday knowledge, their utility in terms of academic knowledge is less impressive. In fact, their usage in educational contexts (handbooks, anthologies, classrooms, etc.) is often counterproductive, as it tends to strengthen rather than question popular stereotypes, while giving them an air of scholarly expertise. Thus, it is often helpful to encourage students to question and unlearn the knowledge of America they already possess and to replace it with more reflective and self-critical forms of knowledge, i.e., with diversified, problematical, and rigidly historicized reconstructions and contextualizations of American culture.

A good starting point for this task is Benjamin Franklin's *The Autobiography*. Students will quickly be able to identify familiar concepts such as the self-made man and American nationalism in this text. This conventional reading can be enhanced by a more nuanced look at the autobiography's internal structure. The canonized title *The Autobiography* with its direct article glosses over the fact that this is not a unified text, either in terms of literary structure (authorial persona, narrator, addressee, etc.) or in terms of ideology (political allegiance, theory of social organization, religious conviction, etc.). To address these issues, students can be asked to identify the addressee of each part. Thus, they will recognize that the long first part is written with a British readership in mind and that it reproduces not genuinely "American" but British and imperial topoi, as well as some of the most basic conventions of early modern life-writing, such as humility topos, familial didactic focus, etc.

Next, students can compare these dispositions to the later, more 'American' parts, asking how this Americanization is achieved by semantic, discursive, and literary means. At the level of semantics, students will probably notice that many values and concepts we usually identify as 'typically American' originate within a larger transatlantic framework, but are then successfully appropriated into an emerging, though controversial, national discourse. At the same time, there are a number of values and concepts that are abandoned or dramatically redefined in the course of Franklin's serial autobiography, such as that of 'humility.' Students might want to explore the literary reverberations of this semantic trajectory. To do so, they can discuss Franklin's clever way of invoking, while at the same time undermining, the traditional autobiographical humility topos by opening the second part of his text with quotations from letters by Abel James and Benjamin Vaughan (rather than in his own voice). Between parts 1, 2, and 3, there are obvious shifts in the narrator's voice – and hence in the implied author's position – that counteract Franklin's attempt to give the impression of a smooth chronological narrative.

This reading of Franklin's *The Autobiography* can be followed by a discussion of Gordon Wood's statement that the historic Franklin "was never quite as self-made as he sometimes implied or as the nineteenth century made him out to be" (2004, 27). According to Wood, Franklin was even the most reluctant of revolutionaries. But then, comparing Franklin's autobiography with equally conflicted documents of the American Revolution (cf. docs. 115, 119-20) and further sources (especially from the republican rather than Lockean end of the revolutionary spectrum), students might want to ask if the American Revolution was not a reluctant revolution to begin with. Wood also calls Franklin "the least American and the most European of the nation's early leaders" (2004, 9). Here, too, students may want to critically examine the statement: To what extent were the early revolutionaries, and not only Franklin, forced to fulfill their desires for a post-European identity against the background of a European, specifically British heritage? Significantly, the most radical political position in the second half of the 1770s was carved out by Thomas Paine (cf. doc. 130), who was not a native-born American but arrived only shortly before the revolution in the New World. In any case, Gordon Wood's reminder that Benjamin Franklin was not *born* a paragon of American patriotism but had to be *made* one will probably prevent students from an overtly homogenizing reading of *The Autobiography*.

Another possible comparison is with earlier and later modes of life-writing. A comparison between Franklin's *The Autobiography* and earlier texts such as William Bradford's "Of Plymouth Plantation" (doc. 32), Mary Rowlandson's *The Soveraignty & Goodness of God* (doc. 33), Thomas Shepard's "The Autobiography" (doc. 42), or Anne Bradstreet's "To My Dear Children" (doc. 43) reveals stark contrasts between orthodox Puritan and enlightened views of selfhood, but also within the various genres of Puritan life-writing itself. Even more revealing are the contrasts with evangelical autobiographies, such as Jonathan Edwards's "An Account of His Conversion" (doc. 94), and transcendentalist autobiographies, such as Henry David Thoreau's *Walden* (doc. 200); possible themes and issues for this comparison are suggested in the essay above.

III. Reading and Discussion Questions

1. Discuss and evaluate Jonathan Edwards's description of his "sinfulness" in "An Account of His Conversion."

2. To what extent does the Puritan doctrine of "regeneracy" contribute to the practice of evangelical preaching, e.g. in Jonathan Edwards's *Sinners in the Hands of an Angry God*?

3. Compare the structure of traditional Puritan sermons to Jonathan Ewards's *Sinners in the Hands of an Angry God*.

4. Compare Charles Chauncy's evaluation of the Great Awakening to Benjamin Franklin's evaluation of it. How can we account for Franklin's description of George Whitefield in *The Autobiography*?

5. How can we account for Franklin's references to Cotton Mather in *The Autobiography*?

6. In what sense can Benjamin Franklin's *The Autobiography* be described as a modern autobiography? Compare Franklin's text to earlier forms and genres of American life-writing.

7. Assess the utility of narratological approaches to autobiographical writing in the context of cultural studies.

8. What are the chief concerns of the Scottish Enlightenment? Why are they important for our understanding of eighteenth-century American cultural history?

IV. Resources

a. Recommended Reading

Ernst Cassirer. *Die Philosophie der Aufklärung*. Tübingen: Mohr, 1932. Cassirer's seminal study, though old, is still one of the best introductions to enlightened philosophy. While it is not concerned with the American Enlightenment in particular, it provides detailed analysis of the sensualist, anti-rationalist, and anti-Cartesian strains of enlightened thought, thus allowing for interesting comparisons with the colonial Great Awakening.

Michael J. Crawford. *Seasons of Grace: Colonial New England's Revival Tradition and Its British Context*. New York: Oxford University Press, 1991. Crawford's book provides an accessible survey of the Great Awakening in New England. This regional study of revivalism is then evaluated within a larger, transatlantic (though not trans-colonial) framework.

Robert A. Ferguson. "The American Enlightenment, 1750-1820." *The Cambridge History of American Literature*. Vol. 1: *1590-1820*. Ed. Sacvan Bercovitch. Cambridge: Cambridge University Press, 1994, 345-537. Ferguson's chapter examines the literary dimension of the American Enlightenment, providing a succinct and well-written overview of major works, genres, themes, and styles. This chapter is also available as a single-volume publication.

Norman Fiering. *Jonathan Edwards's Moral Thought and Its British Context*. Chapel Hill: University of North Carolina Press, 1972. Fiering's study is a landmark in Edwards scholarship. It systematically traces Edwards's engagement with the Scottish Enlightenment, arguing that his theology is best understood as a continued attempt to come to terms with the philosophical consequences of the moral sense school. Critics have modified many of Fiering's conclusions in recent decades to account for the specifically colonial status of Edwards's writing, but his book remains relevant and influential.

Frank Kelleter. *Amerikanische Aufklärung: Sprachen der Rationalität im Zeitalter der Revolution*. Paderborn: Schöningh, 2002. A comprehensive account and analysis of the American Enlightenment from the Great Awakening to Jefferson's presidency. It stresses the interaction and competition of enlightened discourses and practices in North America. Many of the issues discussed in my essay above are treated in detail in this book.

Frank Lambert. *"Pedlar in Divinity": George Whitefield and the Transatlantic Revivals, 1737-1770*. Princeton: Princeton University Press, 1994; *Inventing the Great Awakening*. Princeton: Princeton University Press, 1999. Lambert's two interconnected studies examine the commercial and modernizing aspects of colonial evangelism, the first focusing on George Whitefield, the second on the Great Awakening in general. Lambert is particularly good at reconstructing the innovative communicative practices of the evangelical public sphere in North America.

Henry F. May. *The Enlightenment in America*. New York: Oxford University Press, 1976. A pioneering study, differentiating between distinct varieties of enlightened thought in North America. While many of May's conclusions have been superseded by subsequent scholarship, the book remains an excellent introduction to the field.

Gordon Wood. *The Americanization of Benjamin Franklin*. New York: Penguin Press, 2004. An easily read biography with an important thesis. Although criticism of the topos of the self-made man may not be a new enterprise in Franklin scholarship, it has rarely been presented in such a popular (and indeed populist) manner as in Wood's Pulitzer Prize-winning book. Thus, while not as original as it claims to be, Wood's publication itself is an example of successful public enlightenment.

b. Works Cited and Reading Suggestions

Aldridge, A. Owen (1997). "Natural Religion and Deism in America before Ethan Allen and Thomas Paine." *The William and Mary Quarterly* 54.4, 835-848.
Baker, Frank (1976). *From Wesley to Asbury: Studies in Early American Methodism*. Durham: Duke University Press.
Bellah, Robert (1967). "Civil Religion in America." *Daedalus* 96.1, 1-21.
Bercovitch, Sacvan (1972). *Typology and Early American Literature*. Amherst: University of Massachusetts Press.
– (1978). *The American Jeremiad*. Madison: University of Wisconsin Press.
– (1993). *The Rites of Assent: Transformations in the Symbolic Construction of America*. New York: Routledge.
Berry, Christopher J. (1997). *Social Theory of the Scottish Enlightenment*. Edinburgh: Edinburgh University Press.
Brumm, Ursula (1963). *Die religiöse Typologie im amerikanischen Denken: Ihre Bedeutung für die amerikanische Literatur- und Geistesgeschichte*. Leiden: Brill.
Bumsted, John M., and John E. van de Wetering (1976). *What Must I Do to Be Saved? The Great Awakening in Colonial America*. Hinsdale: Dryden.
Burke, Edmund (1992). *A Philosophical Enquiry into the Origin of Our Ideas of the Sublime and the Beautiful*. 1756. Ed. Adam Phillips. Oxford: Oxford University Press.
Bushman, Richard L., ed. (1989). *The Great Awakening: Documents on the Revival of Religion, 1740-1745*. Chapel Hill: University of North Carolina Press.
Butler, Jon (1992). *Awash in a Sea of Faith: Christianizing the American People*. Cambridge: Harvard University Press.

Caldwell, Patricia (1983). *The Puritan Conversion Narrative*: *The Beginnings of American Expression*. Cambridge: Cambridge University Press.

Carwadine, Richard (1978). *Transatlantic Revivalism*: *Popular Evangelicalism in Britain and America, 1790-1865*. Westport: Greenwood.

Cassirer, Ernst (1932). *Die Philosophie der Aufklärung*. Tübingen: Mohr.

Chauncy, Charles (1741a). *The New Creature*. Boston: Rogers for Edwards and Eliot.

– (1741b). *An Unbridled Tongue a Sure Evidence, that Our Religion Is Hypocritical and Vain*. Boston: Rogers and Fowle.

– (1742). *Enthusiasm Described and Caution'd Against*. Boston: Draper for Eliot and Blanchard.

– (1743). *Seasonable Thoughts on the State of Religion in New-England*. Boston: Rogers and Fowle for Eliot.

– (1744). *Ministers Exhorted and Encouraged to Take Heed of Themselves, and to Their Doctrine*. Boston: Rogers and Fowle for Eliot.

– (1745). *Letter to the Reverend Mr. George Whitefield*. Boston: Rogers and Fowle for Eliot.

Coalter, Milton J. (1986). *Gilbert Tennent, Son of Thunder*: *A Case Study of Continental Pietism's Impact on the First Great Awakening in the Middle Colonies*. Westport: Greenwood.

Crawford, Michael J. (1991). *Seasons of Grace*: *Colonial New England's Revival Tradition and Its British Context*. New York: Oxford University Press.

Davidson, Edward H., and William J. Scheick (1994). *Paine, Scripture, and Authority*: *The Age of Reason as Religious and Political Idea*. Bethlehem: Lehigh University Press.

Delbanco, Andrew (1989). *The Puritan Ordeal*. Cambridge: Harvard University Press.

Edwards, Jonathan (1957-2006). *The Works of Jonathan Edwards*. Gen. ed. Perry Miller, John E. Smith, and Harry S. Stout. New Haven: Yale University Press.

– (1995). *A Jonathan Edwards Reader*. Ed. John E. Smith, Harry S. Stout, and Kenneth P. Minkema. New Haven: Yale University Press.

– (1998). *The Works of Jonathan Edwards*. Vol. 16: *Letters and Personal Writings*. Ed. George S. Claghorn. New Haven: Yale University Press.

Ferguson, Robert A. (1994). "The American Enlightenment, 1750-1820." *The Cambridge History of American Literature*. Vol. 1: *1590-1820*. Ed. Sacvan Bercovitch. Cambridge: Cambridge University Press, 345-537.

Fiering, Norman (1972). *Jonathan Edwards's Moral Thought and Its British Context*. Chapel Hill: University of North Carolina Press.

Franklin, Benjamin (1986). *The Autobiography*. Ed. J. A. Leo Lemay and P. M. Zall. New York: Norton.

Gaustad, Edwin Scott (1957). *The Great Awakening in New England*. New York: Harper and Brothers.

Gay, Peter (1995-96). *The Enlightenment*. 2 vols. 1966-69. New York: Norton.

Goen, C. C. (1962). *Revivalism and Separatism in New England, 1740-1800.* New Haven: Yale University Press.

Griffin, Edward M. (1980). *Old Brick*: *Charles Chauncy of Boston, 1705-1787.* Minneapolis: University of Minnesota Press.

Habermas, Jürgen (1990). *Strukturwandel der Öffentlichkeit*: *Untersuchungen zu einer Kategorie der bürgerlichen Gesellschaft.* 1962. Frankfurt/M.: Suhrkamp.

Hall, David D., ed. (1968). *The Antinomian Controversy, 1636-1638*: *A Documentary History.* Middletown: Wesleyan University Press.

– (1989). *Worlds of Wonder, Days of Judgment*: *Popular Religious Belief in Early New England.* 1983. New York: Knopf.

Hatch, Nathan O. (1989). *The Democratization of American Christianity.* New Haven: Yale University Press.

Heimert, Alan (1966). *Religion and the American Mind from the Great Awakening to the Revolution.* Cambridge: Harvard University Press.

Herget, Winfried (1998). "A Culture of the Word: Puritanism and the Construction of Identity in Colonial New England." *(Trans)Formations of Cultural Identity in the English-Speaking World.* Ed. Jochen Achilles and Carmen Birkle. Heidelberg: Winter, 15-25.

Hume, David (1975). *Enquiries Concerning Human Understanding and Concerning the Principles of Morals.* 1748, 1777. Ed. P. H. Nidditch. Oxford: Clarendon.

Jones, James W. (1973). *The Shattered Synthesis*: *New England Puritanism before the Great Awakening.* New Haven: Yale University Press.

Kelleter, Frank (2002). *Amerikanische Aufklärung*: *Sprachen der Rationalität im Zeitalter der Revolution.* Paderborn: Schöningh.

– (2008). "Benjamin Franklin and the Enlightenment." *The Cambridge Companion to Benjamin Franklin.* Ed. Carla Mulford. Cambridge: Cambridge University Press, 77-90.

Lambert, Frank (1994). *"Pedlar in Divinity"*: *George Whitefield and the Transatlantic Revivals, 1737-1770.* Princeton: Princeton University Press.

– (2003). *The Founding Fathers and the Place of Religion in America.* Princeton: Princeton University Press.

Lesser, M. X. (1988). *Jonathan Edwards.* Boston: Twayne.

Lovejoy, David S. (1985). *Religious Enthusiasm in the New World*: *Heresy to Revolution.* Cambridge: Harvard University Press.

May, Henry F. (1976). *The Enlightenment in America.* New York: Oxford University Press.

Miller, Perry (1949). *Jonathan Edwards.* New York: W. Sloane.

Morais, Herbert (1960). *Deism in Eighteenth-Century America.* 1934. New York: Russell and Russell.

Morgan, Edmund S. (1963). *Visible Saints*: *The History of a Puritan Idea.* Ithaca: Cornell University Press.

– (1965). *Puritan Political Ideas, 1588-1784.* Indianapolis: Bobbs-Merrill.

Morgan, Edmund S. (1967). Rev. of *Religion and the American Mind from the Great Awakening to the Revolution* by Alan Heimert. *The William and Mary Quarterly* 24.3, 454-459.

Oberg, Barbara B., and Harry S. Stout, eds. (1993). *Benjamin Franklin, Jonathan Edwards, and the Representation of American Culture*. New York: Oxford University Press, 13-26.

Pettit, Norman (1966). *The Heart Prepared: Grace and Conversion in Puritan Spiritual Life*. New Haven: Yale University Press.

Ruttenberg, Nancy (1993). "George Whitefield, Spectacular Conversion, and the Rise of Democratic Personality." *American Literary History* 5.3, 429-458.

Scheick, William J. (1975). *The Writings of Jonathan Edwards: Theme, Motif, and Style*. College Station: Texas A&M University Press.

Shaftesbury, Anthony Earl of. (1732). *Characteristicks of Men, Manners, Opinions, Times*. London: John Darby.

Stout, Harry S. (1994). *The Divine Dramatist: George Whitefield and the Rise of Modern Evangelicalism*. Grand Rapids: William B. Eerdmans.

Walters, Kerry S. (1992). *The American Deists: Voices of Reason and Dissent in the Early Republic*. Lawrence: University Press of Kansas.

Weber, Donald (1988). *Rhetoric and History in Revolutionary New England*. New York: Oxford University Press.

Wood, Gordon (2004). *The Americanization of Benjamin Franklin*. New York: Penguin.

GERD HURM

Founding Dissent: Revolutionary Discourse and the Declaration of Independence

> This was the object of the Declaration of Independence. Not to find out new principles, or new arguments, never before thought of, not merely to say things which had been said before; but to place before mankind the common sense of the subject; in terms so plain and firm as to command their assent, and to justify ourselves in the independent stand we are compelled to take. [...] All its authority rests then on the harmonizing sentiments of the day, whether expressed in conversation, in letters, printed essays, or in the elementary books of public right, as Aristotle, Cicero, Locke, Sidney, &c.
>
> Thomas Jefferson, Letter to Henry Lee, 1825
> (in Ginsberg 1967, 32-3)

I. Themes and Arguments

The revolutionary period in American history is a definitive discursive moment which generates and modifies a host of cultural key concepts.[1] The agitated exchanges and debates over the rights of taxation and representation paved the way for independence from Britain and helped establish the American republic. More importantly, these debates negotiate, frame, and delimit the discursive field so that the revolutionary rupture is interpreted predominantly as an affirmative commitment to tradition, continuity, and order. The introductory quote by Thomas Jefferson indicates that the "harmonizing sentiments of the day" often cast the new and revolutionary as a version of the old and known. His contemporary James Madison was even more pronounced in asserting the containment

---

[1] Alan P. Grimes explains the larger significance of revolutionary founding moments as follows: "It is a common characteristic of modern political systems that their legitimatizing myths are derived from the rhetoric of their founding revolutions. Nations born out of revolutions turn back to their revolutions for their statement of political principles, as though the revolutions themselves had placed the stamp of a national imprimatur upon their political ideology. In the United States to return to the principles of the Revolution is to return to the principles of the Declaration of Independence" (1976, 1).

of change, arguing that the American Revolution was "a gentle revolution to end all revolutions" (in Kammen 1978, 212).² Founded in dissent, the revolutionary period defines the parameters of its political legacy in such ways as to channel, marginalize, or silence dissent in the young nation. An investigation of this decision's discursive results is the subject of subsequent sections in this chapter. The present chapter focuses on the confluence of competing discourses that led to the revolutionary rupture and discusses the problematic foundations established at this crucial historical juncture.

As the period's preeminent document, the Declaration of Independence is central to a better understanding of revolutionary key concepts. A crucial text in its own right, it derives additional meaning and significance from its dual political function. It serves as the period's discursive conclusion and climax in focusing and uniting dominant impulses and ideas. But it also marks the beginning of a new era, sanctifying key concepts like "equality" and "liberty" (*KC*, 303) as central points of orientation for the emerging nation. The great impact of the Declaration in the nineteenth and twentieth centuries, which secured its status as "the most sacred of all American political scriptures" (Brogan 1944, 135), may in part be attributed to its success in merging discourses to "accommodate different interpretations" (Goetsch 1992, 21).³ Yet the very rhetorical strategy of generating the greatest appeal possible by incorporating disparate discursive elements also founded dissent within the political legacy of the Revolution in periods to come.

The present essay will first set the Declaration in the context of ideas and arguments from John Locke in 1689 to Thomas Paine in 1776. Next, the underlying similarities and differences in justifying rebellion and unifying protest in the prominent discourses of the day – liberalism, republicanism, English constitutionalism, Protestantism and Enlightenment philosophy – will be assessed in detail. Finally, the dissent inherent in these foundational discourses will be closely examined and assessed.

II. The Centrality of the Declaration of Independence

The Revolutionary War from 1775 to 1783 represents the culmination of tensions and conflicts that persisted and multiplied in the British Empire in the second half of the eighteenth century. The texts in the anthology reflect the various stages in this development and document responses to some of the major events in the British American colony. The writings by John Locke, Jonathan

---

[2] Sacvan Bercovitch notes such a trend in the general representation of the American Revolution: "It is not too much to say that representing revolution was the chief strategy of ideological consolidation for the propertied middle classes that controlled the country's growth from independence through civil war. Having inspired the majority of colonists by re-presenting [sic] national self-determination as revolution, they pre-empted the option of revolt by naturalizing American revolution as the 'organic development' of the culture" (1988, 31).

[3] On the early reception of the Declaration, see Detweiler (1972).

Mayhew, and James Otis (docs. 108-11), for instance, examine the problematic relationship between power and liberty, the submission to public laws and the duty of disobedience to unjust usurpations of authority. The arguments in these documents disclose that the controversy over the necessity to retain "the consent of the governed" (*KC*, 303) does not begin with the taxation questions in the aftermath of the Seven Years' War (1756-1763), but that these conflicts hark back to seventeenth-century disputes and the known historical crises in the British system of checks and balances apparent in the beheading of Charles I. in 1649 and the Glorious Revolution of 1688. After the Seven Years' War, however, attempts to reorganize the British Empire intensified the debates about political representation in the colonies. The Sugar and Currency, and above all the Stamp (doc. 114) and Quartering Acts led to open forms of rebellion against economic and legal measures which were seen as undermining the constitutional rights and liberties of British American colonists.[4] Riots that broke out in Boston and other places in the late 1760s opposed taxation without representation and indicated a new quality in colonial resistance. Formerly submerged social tensions and conflicts now rose to the surface. In Boston, in particular, the stationing of British forces severely aggravated the political situation. In early March of 1770, after weeks of agitation and brawls, serious street fighting broke out between soldiers and civilians when a Boston ropemaker insulted a British soldier by offering him a job cleaning his outdoor toilet. On March 5, these hostilities escalated when intimidated and panicked customhouse sentries responded to verbal and physical threats by opening fire on a crowd of protesters. Five civilians were killed and several more wounded in the so-called Boston Massacre (cf. docs. 121-2). The question of who was responsible for the brawl and for the lethal shots could not be settled conclusively, neither by the jury which acquitted the soldiers, nor by subsequent historians.[5]

Some colonial leaders, however, left no doubt in the public imagination about who bore the political responsibility. The fact that the jury found the soldiers acted in self-defense and thus rightfully acquitted them did not deter patriots from turning the day into a symbolic event that showcased the evil intentions of British imperial policy. John Hancock's 1774 Boston oration (doc. 122) was an important speech in a series of commemorative orations that used the Boston Massacre to advance the notion that British rule had taken on despotic traits (cf.

---

[4] Franklin's image of the rattlesnake highlights the new sense of unity and identity in the colonies. Ironically, the closing of ranks in the war against France now served the country's purpose. The sense of common purpose in the colonies had been established and was now nourished by imperial policies that affected economic and political life in the colonies (docs. 110, 117-8).

[5] John Adams defended the British soldiers and had only derogatory terms for Hancock's heroes: "We have been entertained with a great variety of names to avoid calling the persons who gathered at the custom-house a mob. Some have called them shavers, some call them geniuses. The plain English is, gentlemen, a motley rabble of saucy boys, negroes and molattoes, Irish teagues and outlandish jack tars. And why should we scruple to call such a set of people a mob?" (in Hurm 1992, 61).

Hurm 1992, 57-84). Increased agitation against imperial policy added to the readiness for open rebellion. The outbreak of hostilities in Lexington and Concord – Ralph Waldo Emerson's famous "shot heard round the world" (1904, 139) – called for further rhetorical interventions on behalf of the British American colonists. Even though the tensions between the British Empire and colonial Americans were pervasive, the colonists still were far from unanimous in their stance towards independence in 1775. It was the immense impact of Thomas Paine's aptly titled pamphlet *Common Sense* (doc. 130), published in early 1776, that convinced many hesitant colonists that the dissolution of political bonds was the inevitable step to be taken. Still, even then it was estimated that only one third of the populace was in favor of independence, that another third opposed independence, and that the remaining third was undecided. *The Declaration of Independence* (doc. 131) thus acquired the double function of providing an irrefutably clear justification for rebellion and of presenting Americans as a unified entity in their rejection of British rule.[6]

The Declaration manages to harmonize the conflicting discourses of the time and merges them into a persuasive whole.[7] The famous introduction sets the tone and strategy for the document in establishing an "aura of objectivity" (Lucas 1989, 75):

> When, in the course of human events, it becomes necessary for one people to dissolve the political bands which have connected them with another, and to assume among the powers of the earth the separate and equal station to which the laws of nature and of nature's God entitle them, a decent respect to the opinions of mankind requires that they should declare the causes which impel them to the separation. (*KC*, 303)

The emphasis in the opening passage is on reason and fair judgment. It casts the separation in universal terms as the general effect of the historical "course of human events" and its underlying "laws of nature." The rhetoric mimics the detached and objective language of a scientific tract, creating the impression that the purpose of the document is to "declare" facts to "a candid world." At the same time, the seemingly neutral language, which was soon heralded as a paradigm of eighteenth-century Enlightenment prose, obscures its partisan perspective and propagandistic slant. British loyalists, for one, could not accept the rhetorical construct of "one people" (*KC*, 303) as an objective "fact." To them, it was a "false hypothesis": Americans were Britons in "manners, habits, and ideas" (Lucas 1989, 77), and not a distinct people.

---

[6] It is certainly telling in this respect that the attribute "unanimous" could only be added at a later stage to the title of "the Declaration of the Thirteen United States of America." Initially, not all representatives in the Second Continental Congress were authorized to back a drive for independence (cf. Lucas 1989, 74).

[7] The Declaration is based on a draft by Thomas Jefferson. With slight revisions it was adopted by the Second Continental Congress. For detailed accounts of the textual genesis, see Wills (1979), Fliegelman (1993), and Maier (1997).

The preamble resumes the detached stance of Enlightenment prose, but also demonstrates its indebtedness to the disparate discourses of liberalism, republicanism, Protestantism, and English constitutional law:

> We hold these truths to be self evident: that all men are created equal; that they are endowed by their creator with certain inalienable rights; that among these are life, liberty, and the pursuit of happiness; that to secure these rights, governments are instituted among men, deriving their just powers from the consent of the governed; that whenever any form of government bec[o]mes destructive of these ends, it is the right of the people to alter or to abolish it, and to institute new government, laying its foundation on such principles, and organizing its powers in such form, as to them shall seem most likely to effect their safety and happiness. Prudence, indeed, will dictate that governments long established should not be changed for light and transient causes; and accordingly all experience hath shown that mankind are more disposed to suffer while evils are sufferable, than to right themselves by abolishing the forms to which they are accustomed. But when a long train of abuses and usurpations, pursuing invariably the same object, evinces a design to reduce them under absolute despotism, it is their right, it is their duty to throw off such government, and to provide new guards for their future security. (*KC*, 303)

The "timeless principles" (Lucas 1989, 68) of "equality," "liberty," and "the pursuit of happiness" refer to dominant discourses of the day and have divergent definitions and connotations in different contexts. Lockean liberalism, for instance, shows in the reference to "inalienable" natural rights, ideas from French Enlightenment hedonism influence the formulation of the "pursuit of happiness" (which replaced the term "property" of the original Lockean triad), republican ideas appear in the steadfast opposition of modest, prudent, and "patient" colonials to tyrannous "injuries and usurpations," the concept of "evils" highlights the objection to despotism based on Christian grounds,[8] and the "consent of the governed" refers to an important principle from English common law.

The mixed stance and fusion of disparate secular and religious elements in the two opening sections is not an anomaly. This stance reflects Jefferson's conviction that an appeal to the intellect needs to be accompanied by and fused with an appeal to the emotions: that the "heart," in the revolutionary struggle, was no less important than the "head" (Lucas 1989, 107). Logic and rationality are generally stressed, however, because they best advance the ultimate goal of the Declaration: The document is intended to end debate, not to trigger new discussions. Consequently, a syllogistic triad is chosen to imply a definitive and fair solution to the questions raised. The Declaration's deductive syllogism can be

---

[8] The document's unifying narrative gestures towards a religious reading by evoking parallels between the fate of the colonials and the biblical "slave narrative" of the Exodus. British dissenters are turned into a chosen people that is freed from enslavement and granted new leadership that guarantees its "safety and happiness." For a detailed discussion of the relationship with slave narratives, see Gittleman (1974).

expressed in the terms of Thomas Jefferson's well-known personal motto: "Rebellion to tyrants is obedience to God."⁹ Its logical steps are as follows:

> Major premise: Rebellion to tyrants is obedience to God.
> Minor premise: George III is a tyrant.
> Conclusion: Rebellion to George III is obedience to God.

The obvious problem posed by the syllogism was that the Declaration needed to prove George III a tyrant. But this proposition was far from "self-evident." Scholarship has characterized the reign of George III and the validity of the grievances as follows:

> The reality, of course, as modern revisionist historians have shown, is that George III was not the would-be tyrant of tradition but an earnest, if not very clever, politician, working hard at the job which the British constitution of the time assigned to him. But in the Declaration 'HE' bears complete responsibility for deliberately contriving 'Evils' under which the colonies believed they were suffering. 'HE' is less the third George, King of Great Britain, than a personification of the political-social-economic circumstances, domestic as well as foreign, frustrating American ambitions in the New World, produced in large measure but not exclusively by the archaic system of British colonialism which no longer functioned effectively. (Gittleman 1974, 252)

The middle section of the Declaration thus bears the rhetorical burden of turning the British monarch into the tyrant which the syllogism demands. Its extensive list of accusations has to prove George III to be the ultimate source of evil. Assessed critically, the long list of grievances, however, consists mostly of "exaggerations of facts" and "one-sided summaries of complex situations" (Goetsch 1992, 23). The fourth grievance, for instance, holds that the malicious despot has called together colonial legislative bodies at distant, unusual, and uncomfortable places "for the sole purpose of fatiguing them into compliance with his measures" (Jefferson in Goetsch 1992, 260). In his excellent analysis of the document, Stephen E. Lucas presents the real background to this and other self-evident "truths":

> In fact, moving colonial assemblies from their normal meeting places occurred only in three colonies (Massachusetts, Virginia, and South Carolina) and happened more than once only in Massachusetts, where the legislature was convened at Cambridge, four miles outside Boston, from 1769 to 1772. Although this became a simmering dispute between the legislature and the governor, it came about initially because the legislature had refused to conduct business as long as British troops stood guard over the Court House in Boston. As for meeting in Cambridge, the legislature had voluntarily moved there in 1721 to escape the threat of smallpox in Boston, and again in 1747 following a fire in the Boston Town House. (1989, 98)

In its strategy to show the split colonists unified against their 'evil' ruler, the emotional appeal is further strengthened in the Declaration's last section by introducing metaphors of family and kinship. George III is assigned the part of an

---

⁹ Jefferson borrowed the phrase originally from Benjamin Franklin (cf. Hall 2003, 8).

unjust, tyrannical patriarch who privileges some family members over others. In contrast, Americans have not been "wanting in attention to their brethren" (Jefferson in Goetsch 1992, 260). Evoking notions of universalism and scientific objectivity at the beginning, the Declaration invokes unity through subjectivity and familial emotions in its conclusion. The rebels finally affectively pledge to each other their "sacred honor."

The unifying appeal of the Declaration is based on its fusion of intellectually and emotionally highly charged disparate discourses. The texts assembled in the anthology document Jefferson's reliance on these diverse modes of thought. The Declaration blends phrases, ideas, and discursive patterns from Lockean liberalism, Enlightenment thinking, dissenting Protestantism, classical republicanism, and English constitutional law to produce a successful 'harmonizing' whole (Jefferson in Ginsberg 1967, 32). In the following sections, each one of the above discursive fields will be related to prominent examples from the anthology, highlighting the similarities and differences in their interpretation of revolutionary key concepts like liberty, equality, public good, or virtue.

III. The Declaration of Independence and Discursive Diversity

Lockean liberalism exerted a great influence on the conception of liberty and other key terms in the Declaration. John Locke's 1689 treatise "An Essay Concerning the True Original, Extent, and End of Civil Government" (doc. 108) developed and explained the chief paradigm for the success of liberalism in the revolutionary period and later in the young American republic. Locke sees rights like liberty, equality, and property based on laws that can be deduced from an original, pre-social "state of nature" (*KC*, 262). Individuals are born free and equal in Lockean nature. In order to guarantee the exercise of liberty, all individuals agree on a contract in which their rights are transferred to a governing body. This contract will become void, however, if the installed legislative body assumes powers that violate the egalitarian rights of the individual. According to Locke, tyrants who unjustly appropriate these powers declare war on their people: "[W]henever the *Legislators endeavour to take away, and destroy the Property of the People*, or to reduce them to Slavery under Arbitrary Power, they put themselves into a state of War with the People, who are thereupon absolved from any farther Obedience" (*KC*, 264).

Versions of Lockean liberalism inform arguments in a variety of texts (docs. 111, 115, 119, 125). Samuel Adams, for example, deduces his opposition to English measures in his 1772 publication "The Rights of the Colonists" in exemplary fashion as follows:

> Among the Natural Rights of the Colonists are these First. A Right to *Life*; Secondly to *Liberty*; thirdly to *Property*; together with the Right to support and defend them in the best manner they can. [...]

> All Men have a Right to remain in a State of Nature as long as they please: And in case of into[l]erable Oppression, Civil or Religious, to leave the Society they belong to, and enter into another. –
>
> When Men enter into Society, it is by voluntary consent; and they have a right to demand and insist upon the performance of such conditions, And previous limitations as form an equitable *original compact*. (*KC*, 279)

Rights are not derived from a royal privilege granted to the settlers but are assumed to be granted by the "state of nature" (*KC*, 262). As Adams makes clear, individuals who perceive a violation of common interest may dissolve the existing contract. In his *Summary View of the Rights of British America*, Thomas Jefferson expands such liberal ideas and suggests that the dissenting forefathers' emigration actually established the right to the present drive for independence. By discarding their British bonds, the early dissenters reclaimed their original civil liberties:

> To remind him that our ancestors, before their emigration to America, were the free inhabitants of the British dominions in Europe, and possessed a right which nature has given to all men, of departing from the country in which chance, not choice, has placed them, of going in quest of new habitations, and of there establishing new societies, under such laws and regulations as to them shall seem most likely to promote public happiness. [...] America was conquered, and her settlements made, and firmly established, at the expence of individuals, and not of the British public. (*KC*, 289)[10]

Lockean liberalism thus established the individual as the sovereign source of power and as the sole owner of rights. In Locke's own words, all men might be considered "Kings" (*KC*, 263).

The prominence given to "laws of nature" (*KC*, 303) in the Declaration also refers beyond Lockean liberalism to Enlightenment thinking in general. Enlightenment discourse stresses the importance of logic and reasoning in discovering and defining natural laws. It further emphasizes the importance of science, technology, and progress in liberating mankind from bondage to irrational, mythic modes of existence and expression. Thomas Paine is one of the chief proponents of this emancipatory political project. In the opening lines of *Common Sense*, Paine appeals forcefully to his readers' capacity for critical reasoning (*KC*, 298). He repeatedly applies and invokes the power of logical deduction to dispel false modes of thinking and even includes quasi-scientific evidence from natural history to argue for his point of view. According to Paine, it goes against the physical laws of nature that a small island should rule a large continent:

> Small islands not capable of protecting themselves, are the proper objects for government to take under their care; but there is something very absurd, in supposing a Continent to be perpetually governed by an island. In no instance hath nature made the satellite larger than its primary planet, and as England and America with respect to

---

[10] See also similar arguments by Dickinson (doc. 115).

each other reverses the common order of nature, it is evident they belong to different systems. England to Europe: America to itself. (*KC*, 301)

The superiority of rational modes of thinking is also seen as justifying a general rejection of feudal forms of government. For James Otis, monarchy is an antiquated, irrational form of rule. The claim that kings possess divine rights cannot withstand the critical scrutiny of enlightened reason:

> It is evidently contrary to the first principles of reason, that supreme *unlimited* power should be in the hands of *one* man. It is the greatest "*idolatry*, begotten by *flattery*, on the body of *pride*," that could induce one to think that a *single mortal* should be able to hold so great a power, if ever so well inclined. Hence the origin of *deifying* princes: It was from the trick of gulling the vulgar into a belief that their tyrants were *omniscient*; and that it was therefore right, that they should be considered as *omnipotent*. [...] Thus deities of all kinds were multiplied and increased in *abundance*; for every devil incarnate, who could enslave a people, acquired a title to *divinity*. (*KC*, 269)

Other writers, too, use Enlightenment principles to argue for the superiority of a republican mode of government. Repeatedly, a civic republic is associated with historical progress. For David Ramsay, Americans thus become "the first people in the world" who have it in "their power to choose their own form of government" (*KC*, 307). In a related argument, the progress which occurs in the American colony is turned into a symbol of universal progress. Americans fight for "the *Liberties of Mankind*" (*KC*, 291) and represent "the cause of Human Nature" (*KC*, 308). Thomas Paine also envisions the new republic as a haven for the uninhibited rule of liberty and rationality. In *Common Sense*, he suggests the following utopian reading of America's future role in the world:

> O ye that love mankind! Ye that dare oppose not only the tyranny, but the tyrant, stand forth! Every spot of the old world is over-run with oppression. Freedom hath been hunted round the Globe. Asia and Africa have long expelled her. – Europe regards her like a stranger, and England hath given her warning to depart. O! Receive the fugitive, and prepare in time an asylum for mankind. (*KC*, 302)

Thomas Paine's approach in *Common Sense* is also a good reminder that the use of one set of ideas, i.e., a radical commitment to Enlightenment ideas, does not necessarily preclude the presence of competing and conflicting modes of argumentation. As many critics have pointed out, the powerful effects of *Common Sense* are not just related to its pronounced championing of reason, but also to its electrifying use of religious imagery. Thomas Paine's Quaker upbringing provided him with an intimate knowledge of biblical rhetoric, the strong language of Old Testament prophets that constituted the main discourse familiar to the common people in the revolutionary period.

Protestant rhetoric in general is another central source for voicing and defending pleas for independence. An important early text that justifies political protest from an explictly religious standpoint is "A Discourse Concerning Unlimited Submission and Non-Resistance to the Higher Powers" by the Boston liberal minister Jonathan Mayhew (doc. 109). In his sermon on St. Paul's doctrine in 1750, Mayhew approaches from an explicitly biblical perspective the question of the "consent of the governed" and the duty to resist tyranny. Civil society is based on Christian values, Mayhew argues, so that any magistracy that undermines them needs to be challenged: "It is blasphemy to call tyrants and oppressors, *God's ministers*. They are more properly *the messengers of satan to buffet us*" (*KC*, 266). Mayhew argues that it is important to learn to be both free and loyal, stressing in particular the need for obedience to legitimate leadership. In the context of his overall argument, this may imply the duty to actively resist restrictions on rights in defending the public good:

> For a nation thus abused to arise unanimously, and to resist their prince, even to the dethroning him, is not criminal; but a reasonable way of vindicating their liberties and just rights; it is making use of the means, and the only means, which God has put into their power, for mutual and self-defense. And it would be highly criminal in them, not to make use of this means. It would be stupid tameness, and unaccountable folly, for whole nations to suffer *one* unreasonable, ambitious and cruel man, to wanton and riot in their misery. And in such a case it would, of the two, be more rational to suppose, that they did NOT *resist*, than that they who did, would *receive to themselves damnation*. (*KC*, 267)

Religious texts time and again highlight that rights are based ultimately on divine authority, on "nature's God" (*KC*, 303) – the formulation Jefferson had selected in the Declaration to accompany the explicitly liberal "laws of nature." From a religious perspective, it is not "natural liberty" or licentiousness, however, that is to be defended in the conflict with the British Empire, but the superior "moral liberty" (Foner 1998, 4). Hence, in criticizing the rise of vice and corruption in the colonies, several texts use religious discourse to associate British rule with the reign of the "prince of darkness" (*KC*, 277). John Hancock's Boston oration appropriates such rhetoric in describing in detail the forms of degeneracy which the colonists had to face.

Finally, religious discourse is implemented to channel protest and to make citizens return to a more pious path. Independence jeremiads frequently stress the necessity to merge public revolution with personal reform. Samuel Williams, for instance, exhorts his listeners to return to the root of Christian morals (cf. doc. 126):

> The surest way we can take to promote the good of our county, is to attend to this. It should lead us to repent of all the vice, wickedness, and moral evils that are among us. It is our interest to renounce whatever is contrary to the rules of religion, to purity of morals, and the prosperity of the state. It is our duty to reform every kind of extravagance, superfluity, and unnecessary expence. It would be our wisdom to put on the most strict frugality, œconomy, and self-denial, in all unnecessary articles of food, raiment, convenience and pleasure. – Such virtue will naturally tend to promote the

good of our country. And this is what the united councils and voice of America now call us to. (*KC*, 292)[11]

The characterization of the rebels in the Declaration as "virtuous and long-suffering colonists" (Becker 1922, 207) need not solely be contextualized by Christian concepts of humility and submission. The rhetoric of piety and austerity is also present and argued over in the revolutionary period in republican discourses on civic humanism and civil engagement. The "Proclamation by the Great and General Court of the Colony of Massachusetts Bay" (doc. 129), for instance, fuses religious and republican rhetoric to ensure that public peace can be guaranteed in times of strife and warfare:

> That piety and virtue, which alone can secure the freedom of any people, may be encouraged, and vice and immorality suppressed, the Great and General Court have thought fit to issue this proclamation, commanding and enjoining it upon the good people of this colony, that they lead sober, religious, and peaceable lives, avoiding all blasphemies, contempt of the Holy Scriptures, and of the Lord's Day, and all other crimes and misdemeanors, all debauchery, profaneness, corruption, venality, all riotous and tumultuous proceedings, and all immoralities whatsoever; and that they decently and reverently attend the public worship of God, at all times acknowledging with gratitude His merciful interposition in their behalf, devoutly confiding in Him, as the God of armies, by whose favor and protection alone they may hope for success in their present conflict. (*KC*, 298)

As many scholars in the field have pointed out, republicanism grew into a most effective discourse in the revolutionary period. Its proponents derived republican values and principles directly from classical antiquity and the Renaissance, but also from English appropriations and transformations (cf. Pocock 1975). At the core of republicanism is the concept of the independent citizen whose virtuous engagement is for the *res publica*, the common good. In contradistinction to liberalism, which held that liberty was an individual, pre-social right that needed protection from political institutions, republicanism believed that liberty needed to be lived and cultivated through participation in the political realm. Virtuous citizens put the commonweal above destructive, corrupting self-interest. Benjamin Rush, one of the signers of the Declaration, even held that "every man in a republic is public property" (in Wood 1969, 61).

Various texts in the anthology reflect the republican "obsession with corruption and disorder" (Wood in Appleby 1992, 161). British American colonists and, later, patriotic rebels were seen in clear opposition to the luxury and degeneracy of a moneyed aristocratic British elite. Philo Patriæ (doc. 113) develops at

---

[11] Jacob Duché likewise links sin and slavery: "Go on, ye chosen band of Christian Patriots! Testify to the world, by your example as well as by your counsels, that ye are equally the foes of VICE and of SLAVERY – Banish the Syren LUXURY, with all her train of fascinating pleasures, idle dissipation, and expensive amusements from our borders. Call upon honest industry, sober frugality, simplicity of manners, plain hospitality and christian benevolence to throw down the usurpers, and take possession of their seats" (*KC*, 296).

length the argument that British oppression is responsible for violence and moral decay in the American colonies:

> The terrible effects of those popular tumults, are likely to startle men who have been accustomed to venerate and obey lawful authority, and who delight in peace and order; and to make them doubt the justice of the cause attended with such direful consequences. But the guilt of all these violences is most justly chargeable upon the authors and abettors of the Stamp Act. They who endeavour to destroy the foundations of the English constitution, and break thro' the fence of the laws, in order to let in a torrent of tyranny and oppression upon their fellow-subjects, ought not to be surprized if they are overwhelmed in it themselves. (*KC*, 272)

Moreover, the rhetoric of slavery is used to argue historical precedents in which the corruption of civic government led to degeneracy in all fields of public life:

> The inhabitants of Greece, Rome, and Constantinople, were once free and happy, and the liberal arts and sciences flourished among them; but slavery has spread ignorance, barbarism and misery over those once delightful regions, where the people are sunk into a stupid insensibility of their condition, and the spirit of liberty, after being depressed above a thousand years, seems now to be lost irrecoverably. It is better to die in defence of our rights, than to leave such a state as this to the generations that succeed us. (*KC*, 272)

Time and again, revolutionary period documents make appeals to protect and enhance civic virtue. In his oration, John Hancock celebrates adherence to "righteous government" (*KC*, 284), and in *A Summary View of the Rights of British America* (doc. 125), Thomas Jefferson emphasizes that the "whole art of government consists in the art of being honest" (*KC*, 290). Winning the revolutionary conflict is conquering baser, corrupting instincts: The virtuous male citizen devotes himself fully to the observation of the law and the strengthening of the public good. Samuel Williams, for instance, explains:

> But while we see every thing in a state of disorder and confusion around us, it is of the last importance that we keep up a steady regard to the rules of righteousness, of personal and social virtue. Now is the time, my brethren, when our enemies expect that we shall run wild and mad, for want of something to guide us. The extremes of power, and the wanton abuse of liberty, you may assure yourselves will always end alike, in absolute tyranny at last. (*KC*, 292)

The last important discursive tradition to be discussed is British constitutional law, which profoundly shapes the arguments for order and continuity in the Declaration.[12] The rights of liberty and property, as deduced in the so-called Ancient Constitution, derive from the British tribal past. Opposing and fighting the Norman yoke, Englishmen permanently secured their rights to liberty and property. The statutory and common law guaranteed them among others the right to trial by jury, representative government, and *habeas corpus*. In contrast to liberal-

---

[12] In *American Scripture* (1997), Pauline Maier argues that the Declaration in form and content closely follows the *English Declaration of Rights* of 1689.

ism, the rights of British common law were not deduced from a *tabula rasa* "state of nature" but founded on a unique home-grown tradition in which liberty was a privilege granted historically by the crown to its sovereign subjects. This tradition, best represented by the *Magna Carta* of 1215, encompassed a mutual respect for both feudal and republican ideals.

The implied reference to common traditions and the open appeal to "British brethren" in the Declaration reflect this strand of justification. Several texts in the anthology address this revered institution explicitly. The article in the 1765 *Constitutional Courant* by Philoleutherus (doc. 112) stresses respect for British parliamentary procedures and therefore claims these rights as a colonial privilege:

> We cherish the most unfeigned loyalty to our rightful sovereign; we have a high veneration for the British parliament; we consider them as the most august assembly on earth; but the wisest of kings may be misled; [...] Parliaments also are liable to mistakes, yea, sometimes fall into capital errors, and frame laws the most oppressive to the subject, yea, sometimes take such steps, which, if persisted in, would soon unhinge the whole constitution. Our histories bear innumerable attestations to the truth of this. It cannot be treason to point out such mistakes and the consequences of them, yea to set them in the most glaring light, to alarm the subject. By acting on this principle, our ancestors have transmitted to us our privileges inviolated; let us therefore prosecute the same glorious plan. (*KC*, 271)

Philo Patriæ similarly emphasizes veneration for time-honored British traditions. In insisting on their Saxon descent, on their "birth-right and inheritance" (*KC*, 273), the dissenters resume ancient constitutional prerogatives. To call their acts rebellion is a misrepresentation of their rights and their duty. Should the crown succeed in violating these rights, the severance of ties would have to follow:

> We consider ourselves as one people with them, and glory in the relation between us; and we desire our connection may forever continue, as it is our best security against foreign invaders, and as we may reciprocally promote the welfare and strength of each other. Such are our sentiments and affections towards our mother country. But, at the same time, we cannot yield up to her, or to any power on earth, our inherent and most valuable rights and privileges. If she would strip us of all the advantages derived to us from the English constitution, why should we desire to continue our connection? We might as well belong to France, or any other power; none could offer a greater injury to our rights and liberties than is offered by the Stamp Act. (*KC*, 273)

In this line of argument, Americans become the true inheritors of British tradition. They simply ask that their rights now be similarly respected by the crown.

IV. Conclusion: A Legacy of Competing and Conflicting Discourses

The existence of disparate political discourses mirrors the presence of conflicting interests in the revolutionary period. The tidy separation of five major discourses in the preceding analysis is only valid for heuristic purposes. In the life and minds of British American colonists, the discourses overlapped and existed in mixed forms. Moreover, as various critics have pointed out, key oppositional terms like liberalism or republicanism are founded on "vague premises" (Shalhope 1990, 46) so that a precise distinction at times becomes impossible.[13]

In some of the texts, the confluence and coexistence of contradictory discourses show directly. As noted, Thomas Paine blended Enlightenment ideas with Protestant discourse in *Common Sense*. Inconsistent in various other respects, Paine suggests that the historical moment when America was discovered might be related to divine design: "The Reformation was preceded by the discovery of America; As if the Almighty graciously meant to open a sanctuary to the persecuted in future years, when home should afford neither friendship nor safety" (*KC*, 298).[14] The fusion of contrary discourses, of Enlightenment deism and providential Calvinism, in thinking about the American cause is not an exceptional flaw of Paine's *Common Sense*. In the words of one critic, the coexistence of seemingly compatible, yet ultimately conflicting, discourses can be seen as one of the sources of "tremendous interpretative disagreement" about the revolutionary period (Shalhope 1990, xi).

In other instances, the fusion of conflicting discourses is more difficult to spot. At times it becomes almost imperceptible because of the ways in which these merged discourses blur distinctions. Republican rhetoric, in particular, provided specific terms of negotiation which concealed conflicting economic and social interests at work in the nation. This can be best seen when key terms like the "public good" or "virtue" are compared in their liberal and republican usage. In Locke's liberalism, the "publick good" is primarily associated with the preservation and protection of individual "property" (*KC*, 262). In republican theory, however, the "public good" is identified with the rejection of individual self-interest. Yet the rules of the rapidly changing eighteenth-century marketplace demanded that both republican and liberal colonists follow the laws of self-interest in economic matters.[15]

The concept of virtue is essential in turning this problematic pursuit of self-interest into a republican service to the community. In liberal and republican dis-

---

[13] It is only in the hands of scholars that they become powerful terms to argue one way or the other. Ultimately, they in themselves fail to provide precise analyses of the complexities of social reality. Mitchell, for instance, criticizes the usefulness of the dichotomy: "As already observed, and as recently a number of writers have demonstrated, current historiographical debate continues to be hampered by the maintenance of a dichotomized view of the liberal and republican traditions. Republicanism does not have a monopoly on the language of virtue, nor liberalism on the language of rights. Equally, the two traditions do not represent a choice between, on the one hand, engagement with the public sphere and, on the other, political or social apathy" (2004, 601).

[14] Various critics have pointed out that Paine hardly follows any discourse consistently. Pocock held that it is difficult to fit Paine "into any kind of category" (1985, 276).

[15] Various studies have emphasized the discrepancy between the dominant republican rhetoric and the new nation's successes at modernization, driven by self-interest economics (cf. Appleby 1992, 161-87).

course, virtue functions as a broad common denominator by incorporating shared civic values like honesty, ingenuity, frugality, and industry. Whether a member of the community can be seen as virtuous in these terms will inevitably show in his economic performance. Ideally, wealth signals the existence and exercise of virtue in liberal and republican understanding. Empowering individuals to pursue selfish desires, the formula of the "publick good" thus conceals the causes for the severe disregard for communal interests.[16] The rhetoric of the commonweal and of civic virtue blurs the fact that, theoretically, liberal and republican positions remain incompatible.[17] Republican discourse fears self-interest as the foremost source of corruption, whereas liberal discourse praises it as the ultimate right of free individuals. Robert Shalhope concludes:

> Most Americans clung to a harmonious, corporate view of themselves and their society even while behaving in a materialistic, utilitarian manner in their daily lives. Thus, while rapidly transforming their society in an open, competitive, modern direction, Americans idealized communal harmony and a virtuous social order. Republicanism condemned the values of a burgeoning capitalistic economy and placed a premium upon an ordered, disciplined personal liberty restricted by the civic obligations dictated by public virtue. In this sense, republicanism formalized or ritualized a mode of thought that ran counter to the flow of history; it idealized the traditional values of a world rapidly fading rather than the market conditions and liberal capitalistic mentality swiftly emerging in the late eighteenth century. (in Greene 2000, 671)

In this context, a congenial chain of images assumes special importance. Metaphors of family and kinship help to negotiate and regulate competing claims between possessive individualism and republican communalism. Family metaphors provide a unifying basis in that they conceive the public sphere in domestic terms. The discourse about the "tender parent" (*KC*, 291), the "mother country" (*KC*, 294), or the "genuine sons of liberty" (*KC*, 271) offers a mode of thinking that helps bridge the gap between private and public selves, between self-interest and the commonweal. In addition, metaphors of family and kinship evoke the notion of an organic model of community and politics. The "body politick" (*KC*, 280) consists of members that are connected not only by mutual interest, but also by affection and "consanguinity" (Jefferson in Goetsch 1992, 262). Finally, kinship imagery suggests the simultaneous cultivation of virtue in the family and in the community. All in all, virtue, public good, and family imagery help blend incompatible liberal and republican ideas into a powerful discursive field.

The selection of texts and authors in the anthology clearly documents that the discourses analyzed here only represent a minority of colonial society and

---

[16] Appleby states that "[n]ot through the cultivation of virtue or wisdom did one fulfill self-interest, but, rather, through ambition, desire, and a rising standard of living achieved by individual application of industry, ingenuity, and effort" (1992, 172).

[17] Shalhope also notes: "Rather than instilling a regard for moderation, communal good order, and deference to natural authority, republicanism seemed to be breeding a utilitarian, materialistic individualism" (1990, xiii).

thus cannot really claim to speak for "mankind" or for the "laws of nature." The chosen texts mostly reflect the viewpoints and interests of the powerful group of economically independent white males. Women, Native Americans, African Americans, indentured servants, working-class members, and several other groups are virtually barred at this point in history from direct participation in defining the public good. But this exclusion in the eighteenth century does not imply that the analysis of the prevailing modes of writing and thinking is therefore necessarily one-sided, biased, and ineffective. On the contrary, the examination of the governing modes of thought is essential since it assesses the very discourses available for the excluded groups to voice their dissent. As much as it is important to point out the limitations of the eighteenth-century republican and liberal conception of society and politics, it is as important to analyze critically the parameters in which remedies to the conflicts would be devised. Ultimately, Howard Zinn's astute assessment of political exclusion still holds true:

> To say that the *Declaration of Independence*, even by its own language, was limited to life, liberty, and happiness for white males is not to denounce the makers and signers of the *Declaration* for holding the ideas expected of privileged males of the eighteenth century. Reformers and radicals, looking discontentedly at history, are often accused of expecting too much from a past political epoch – and sometimes they do. But the point of noting those outside the arc of human rights in the *Declaration* is not, centuries late and pointlessly, to lay impossible moral burdens on that time. It is to try to understand the way in which the *Declaration* functioned to mobilize certain groups of Americans, ignoring others. Surely, inspirational language to create a secure consensus is still used, in our time, to cover up serious conflicts of interest in that consensus, and to cover up, also, the omission of large parts of the human race. (1980, 73)

The history of social movements in the eighteenth and nineteenth centuries, analyzed and discussed in detail in other essays in this volume, demonstrates that some of the affirmative revolutionary period discourses which produced the Declaration would eventually provide empowerment for underprivileged groups to voice opposition and protest. The abolition movement and Abraham Lincoln, for instance, would refer to the Declaration as a radical text that guaranteed equality to all. Lincoln saw the intention of the dissenting Founding Fathers as follows:

> They meant to set up a standard maxim for free society, which should be familiar to all, and revered by all; constantly looked to, constantly labored for, and even though never perfectly attained, constantly approximated, and thereby constantly spreading and deepening its influence and augmenting the happiness and value of life to all people of all colors everywhere. The assertion that 'all men are created equal' was of no practical use in effecting our separation from Great Britain; and it was placed in the Declaration not for that, but for future use. Its authors meant it to be – as, thank God, it is now proving itself – a stumbling-block to all those who in after times might seek to turn a few people back into the hateful paths of despotism. (in Grimes 1976, 6)

The Declaration has been effectively used by many political groups who dissented from the American majority over the years. The dissenters in the women's rights movement at Seneca Falls in 1848 also explicitly linked their cause to the Declaration (cf. Klaiber in this vol., 319-21). Various minority and countercultural authors, from Frederick Douglass to Henry David Thoreau, frequently used its radical potential for their purposes (cf. docs. 200, 268; Lanzendörfer in this vol., 413-6).

In contrast to such disruptive appropriations of the American Revolution, which radically changed the face of the nation, republican and liberal leaders of the founding era mostly emphasized order, unity, and continuity. Still, dissent was also ubiquitous in the revolutionary period, foreshadowing the ruptures to come. The constant negotiations of continuity and discord in the period left traces in all fields and on all levels. When John Trumbull was commissioned to paint "The Declaration of Independence" for the rotunda of the Capitol in 1817, he made the revolutionary figures appear as paragons of unity and order. While Trumbull painted the individual characters from life, the design of the meeting was a perfect historical fiction: no such meeting with all the delegates present had ever occurred (cf. McCullough 2001, 627). Trumbull thus generated an icon of harmony that was placed in the center of power in the Capitol and later used as a popular representation of American revolutionary legacy on the bicentennial two-dollar bill in 1976. However, by placing the political opponents Thomas Jefferson and John Adams in the middle of its aesthetic harmony, Trumbull's rotunda painting also allowed for projections of submerged rifts among the Founding Fathers. An optical illusion had many viewers assume that Jefferson steps on Adams's foot and has thus given rise to the popular belief that Trumbull placed a hidden trace of discord in the painting (cf. McCullough, 2007).[18] Even on the anecdotal level of a misplaced foot, it may be said that those who look for signs of founding dissent in connection with the Declaration may find it amidst the dominant trends of order, unity, and harmony. In a larger sense, the writings and key concepts of the revolutionary period remain open for dissenting inspection, interpretation, and revision.

---

[18] As many commentators have noted, the misplaced foot is surprisingly absent on the two-dollar bill. This puzzling omission on the bill is best explained by the existence of three different versions of Trumbull's painting. The illusion of Jefferson stepping on Adams's foot is strongest in the rotunda version but is not as prominent in the two others. In all versions, however, Trumbull's foot choreography reflects his representation of Jefferson and Adams's vying for political predominance. For detailed information on the various paintings, see the monograph by Jaffe (1976); for a version of the popular belief cf. "John Trumbull's Declaration of Independence" (1995) <http://www.ushistory.org/declaration/trumbull.htm> (April 28, 2007).

Instructional Strategies and Classroom Issues

I. Key Concepts and Major Themes

1. Equality (docs. 108, 130-1, 133)
   Equality is a key principle in American political thought, seen by many as even more fundamental than the principle of liberty. It implies the possession of the same inalienable, natural rights by all individuals. Precise definitions of equality, however, vary according to legal, political, economic, and religious contexts. Equality in the revolutionary period may imply, for instance, the equal possession of legal rights, of natural freedom, or of an innate moral sense, but also the Christian notion of the equality of men in depravity.

2. Jeremiad (docs. 109, 116, 126, 128, 132)
   The jeremiad, America's "first distinctive literary genre" (Bercovitch 1978, 162), is based on the secular appropriation of prophetic Old Testament discourse. To avoid impending disaster and destruction, the jeremiad speaker/critic admonishes his audience to correct wrongdoings, and to return to the right path. American jeremiads, in contrast to European versions which stress apocalyptic aspects, tend to emphasize a regenerative, optimistic dimension.

3. Liberalism (docs. 108, 111, 114, 119, 125, 131)
   This prevalent eighteenth-century political theory is closely related to John Locke's writings. Central to its tenets is the notion that independent individuals exist in a pre-social "state of nature" (*KC*, 262). These individuals then sign a mutual contract in order to protect their natural rights. Society is seen primarily as a means to preserve these individual liberties. Liberalism develops into an influential discourse that nourishes various historical versions of American possessive individualism.

4. Liberty (docs. 108-9, 113, 119, 130-2)
   Part of the Lockean triad of "life, liberty, and property" (*KC*, 268), liberty was a central, but also highly embattled, concept in the revolutionary period. It was interpreted to mean both personal freedom (liberalism) and collective liberty (republicanism). Depending on the interpretation, the emphasis could be placed more on the protection of individual rights (negative definition of liberty in liberalism) or on an active civic engagement for the public good (positive definition of liberty in republicanism).

5. Pursuit of Happiness (docs. 108, 125-6, 131, 133)
   This term covers ideas related to Enlightenment hedonism (worldly enjoyment of a virtuous life) and Puritan morality (happiness lying in the pursuit of the path preordained by Providence). Later readings redefine the term to imply a general promise of material well-being.

6. Republicanism (docs. 113, 126-8, 133)
The major political discourse of republicanism is based on traditions from classical antiquity, the Renaissance, and English constitutionalism. In the revolutionary period, it was as powerful as it was vague in its tenets. Basic to its conception is a commonwealth governed by the people, with political leadership generated by an elective system. The protection of liberty is seen as best achieved by the cultivation of public virtue through the civic engagement of its citizens.

7. Virtue (docs. 122, 126-8, 133-4)
Virtue generally refers to the outstanding moral character of a person. Virtuous citizens possess qualities like courage, honesty, austerity, and industriousness, which are seen as essential for establishing and upholding a harmonious republican community. The definition of virtue changes substantially within different political and historical contexts (such as classical political theory, Christian ethics, or gender theory).

II. Comparison – Contrasts – Connections

Example: Docs. 122, 133

Scholarly opinions on the precise definition of virtue in the revolutionary period vary greatly. Most critics agree with Robert Shalhope that virtue was immensely important: "The republican concern with virtue pervaded the revolutionary movement and extended a shaping influence over American culture" (1990, 45). However, many critics also voice doubts about the precision of claims made for the concept, and, as Kloppenberg notes, as "[a]n all-purpose term of approbation, virtue had different, and occasionally incompatible, meanings in different contexts" (in Greene 2000, 696). The goal of this study unit is to examine and compare three texts that focus their arguments with reference to specific facets of virtue (John Hancock, doc. 122; David Ramsay, doc. 133; Jonathan Loring Austin, *KC* web site). The texts selected offer themselves for analysis because they belong to the same rhetorical genre: Hancock's 1774 Boston oration as well as Ramsay's 1778 and Austin's 1786 Fourth of July speeches follow closely the rules of the epideictic oratory.

The first task for students in this unit is to research definitions of the various types of oratory (with a special focus on the epideictic and its relationship with virtue). The insight into formal rules and restrictions will guarantee a better appreciation of the speeches' rhetorical strategies. First, the specific relation between speaker and audience should be at the center of class discussion. Next, the issue of virtue should be assessed in the context of the speaker's self-image and the attributions of value to the audience. Finally, the speeches should be examined for their uses of virtue in defining the public good and then compared as to their differing overall interpretations of virtue.

The discussion of the speeches may be focused on the core passages cited below. Each quote highlights a central aspect of virtue for the respective speech.

1. John Hancock, *An Oration*:

> But this was not all: As though they thought it not enough to violate our civil Rights, they endeavoured to deprive us of the enjoyment of our religious privileges, to vitiate our morals, and thereby render us deserving of destruction. Hence the rude din of arms which broke in upon your solemn devotions in your temples, on that day hallowed by Heaven, and set apart by God himself for his peculiar worship. Hence, impious oaths and blasphemies so often tortur'd your unaccustomed ear. Hence, all the arts which idleness and luxury could invent, were used, to betray our youth of one sex into extravagance and effeminacy, and of the other to infamy and ruin; and did they not succeed but too well? Did not a reverence for religion sensibly decay? Did not our infants almost learn to lisp out curses before they knew their horrid import? Did not our youth forget they were Americans, and regardless of the admonitions of the wise and aged, servilely copy from their tyrants those vices which finally must overthrow the empire of Great-Britain? And must I be compelled to acknowledge, that even the noblest, fairest part of all the lower creation did not entirely escape the cursed snare? (*KC*, 285)

Hancock's oration suggests that a Manichaean struggle between the forces of good and evil underlies the political conflict. The importance of virtue shows in its temporary suppression and absence: The actions of the devilish oppressors are demeaning and spread corruption and degeneracy among the virtuous colonists.

Questions for class discussion:

- Explain the ways in which Hancock instrumentalizes virtue to serve the politics of separation.
- Discuss the implicit relation between Machiavellian *virtù* and Christian notions of virtue in the speech.
- Discuss the causes and effects of American corruption and degeneracy from a British perspective.

2. David Ramsay, "On the Advantages of American Independence":

> Our present form of government is every way preferable to the royal one we have lately renounced. It is much more favourable to purity of morals, and better calculated to promote all our important interests. Honesty, plain-dealing, and simple manners, were never made the patterns of courtly behaviour. Artificial manners always prevail in kingly governments; and royal courts are reservoirs, from whence insincerity, hypocrisy, dissimulation, pride, luxury, and extravagance, deluge and overwhelm the body of the people. On the other hand, republics are favourable to truth, sincerity, frugality, industry, and simplicity of manners. Equality, the life and soul of Commonwealths, cuts off all pretensions to preferment, but those which arise from extraordinary merit: Whereas in royal governments, he that can best please his superiors, by the low arts of fawning and adulation, is most likely to obtain favour. (*KC*, 306)

Ramsay sets virtue in a providential context and sees it related to the westward march of progress. He predicts a great future for the American model republic and thinks it will attract "thousands and millions of [...] virtuous peasants" (*KC*, 307).

Questions for class discussion:

- Assess the function of virtue in the debate between monarchical and republican forms of governance.
- Discuss the connection between progress and tradition in the speech with regards to virtue.
- Explain the role of nature in the production of virtue.

3. Jonathan Loring Austin "An Oration Delivered July 4, 1786" (*KC* web site):

> The American history has become a chart, wherein at one view, we can behold the transaction of different ages and nations, men and manners – do we revere the stern virtues of the SPARTAN? – do we respect the polite and learned ATHENIAN? – are we animated with the heroism, and honor of the ROMAN? – virtues like these have shone conspicuous in America, and *patriotism* the most rigid has been frequently displayed. – The steady uniform measures of an AMERICAN CONGRESS, when surrounded with dangers, evince, not only the greatest fortitude, but superior wisdom and address. – The persevering virtues, the polite manners, the valor and bravery of the AMERICAN ARMY, demand our loudest approbation and applause. In our illustrious GENERAL, we behold – here language fails me to do justice to his merit! – He is – WASHINGTON – To excite our emulation to generous and humane actions, let us trace these virtues in the conduct of our ILLUSTRIOUS ALLIES.[19]

The speech proposes with Benjamin Franklin that "only a virtuous people are capable of freedom" (in Greene 2000, 609). Austin wants to retain the high standard of virtue that he sees in the revolutionary generation. Their behavior should be a model for the new nation in meeting its present and future fiscal and political responsibilities.

Questions for class discussion:

- Discuss the role of submission and the return to first principles in Austin's definition of virtue.
- Assess the function of virtue in the above comparison of different ages and cultures.
- Relate the concept of virtue to Austin's discussion of freedom.

The overall goal of the study unit is for students to obtain an enhanced insight into the reasons why the concept of virtue achieved such a prominent role in revolutionary discourse. This includes an assessment of the divergent definitions of the term (e.g. similarities and differences in Christian, classical, republican,

---

[19] For a comprehensive discussion of the speech, see Hurm (1992, 57-85; cf. Goetsch 1992, 273).

and liberal usage). But it also implies a critical discussion of the potential instrumentalization of virtue as an 'all-purpose term.'

The discussion of virtue can be extended to related issues in subsequent sections of the volume, particularly to debates in the Early Republic, to negotiations in transcendentalist writings, and to gendered redefinitions within the context of nineteenth-century conceptions of domesticity.

III. Reading and Discussion Questions

1. Research and discuss the different associations eighteenth-century British American colonists would bring to Benjamin Franklin's snake imagery (docs. 110, 118). Discuss the snake's changing interpretations within the distinct historical and political contexts of 1754 and 1774. Relate the snake imagery to organicist notions of the human body and the "body politick" (*KC*, 280) in Franklin's 1767 representation of "Magna Britannia: Her Colonies Reduc'd" (doc. 117). What is the significance of the globe, the shield, the tree, and the brooms?

2. Relate issues and motifs in John Dickinson's poem to other texts in this section (cf. docs. 110-1, 113, 130). What is implied by emphasizing the courage of the forefathers? What types of slavery are invoked in the poem? Relate the concept of enslavement to other texts in the revolutionary period and to documents in the section on slavery.

3. Discuss the effects of Benjamin Franklin's extensive use of irony (doc. 120). What does Franklin gain from depicting the conflict through the *topos* of the 'world upside-down' as opposed to presenting his arguments in straightforward fashion? Explain the reasons why Franklin opens the essay with a reference to the sage Themistocles. Clarify its relation to other allusions to classical myths and personae in the section. Finally, discuss Franklin's text together with the engraving by Philip Dawe (doc. 123) and its depiction of chaos in the British colony.

4. Use one of the annotated key publications to research the actual events in Boston on March 5, 1770. With the research results discuss the rendition of the conflict in Paul Revere's engraving (doc. 121). How are the two opposing groups presented? What is the effect of the accompanying poem? How does it negotiate and extend the visual representation? Research the significance of Crispus Attucks in the context of the Boston Massacre. How do representations of Attucks change with nineteenth-century abolitionism? Compare the representation of Attucks in Revere's print with that in John Bufford's 1856 chromolithograph (cf. *KC* web site).

5. Relate the iconography of the 1782 illustration "America Triumphant and Britannia in Distress" (doc. 134) to congenial passages in the anthology

texts. Discuss the changes in the representation of the two nations by comparing the 1782 print by Weatherwise with two examples from 1770 and 1775 (cf. *KC* web site).

IV. Resources

a. Recommended Reading

Joyce O. Appleby. *Liberalism and Republicanism in the Historical Imagination*. Cambridge: Harvard University Press, 1992. Important monograph, based on a series of previously published essays. Appleby explains the success of American liberalism as a result of its challenge to and transformation of pre-modern republican discourses.

Bernard Bailyn. *The Ideological Origins of the American Revolution*. Cambridge: Harvard University Press, 1967. Influential study of the discursive backgrounds of the revolutionary period, introducing the shift away from Lockean liberalism toward republicanism as a key explanatory force.

Carl Lotus Becker. *The Declaration of Independence*: *A Study in the History of Political Ideas*. New York: Knopf, 1922. The classic study of the Declaration. It established the centrality of Lockean philosophy for Jefferson's argumentation.

Robert Ginsberg, ed. *A Casebook on the Declaration of Independence*. New York: Crowell, 1967. Important collection of contemporary responses and early scholarly work. It is a good starting point for discussions about the Declaration.

Paul Goetsch and Gerd Hurm, eds. *The Fourth of July*: *Political Oratory and Literary Reactions, 1776-1876*. Tübingen: Narr, 1992. A volume of essays, which looks at Fourth of July rhetoric and political oratory in the revolutionary period and discusses the functions and uses of the Declaration in eighteenth- and nineteenth-century literary and popular discourses.

Jack P. Greene and J. R. Pole, eds. *A Companion to the American Revolution*. Malden: Blackwell, 2000. Extremely useful encyclopedic volume with entries on central events, topics, and concepts in the revolutionary period. Excellent starting point for research on major issues.

Stephen E. Lucas. "Justifying America: The Declaration of Independence as a Rhetorical Document." *American Rhetoric*: *Context and Criticism*. Ed. Thomas W. Benson. Carbondale: Southern Illinois University Press, 1989. 67-130. One of the best compact discussions of the discursive and stylistic backgrounds to the Declaration. The essay covers vast ground in a short space and manages to analyze the relation of rhetoric and politics in illuminating ways.

Pauline Maier. *American Scripture: Making the Declaration of Independence*. New York: Knopf, 1997. This thoroughly researched and carefully crafted volume is one of the best recent accounts of the drafting of the Declaration.

Gary B. Nash. *The Urban Crucible: Social Change, Political Consciousness, and the Origins of the American Revolution*. Cambridge: Harvard University Press, 1979. A monumental work that looks at the revolutionary period from the perspective of domestic urban protest and unrest. It adds an important social and economic dimension to the debate about the influence of liberal and republican discourses in bringing about American independence.

John G. A. Pocock. *The Machiavellian Moment: Florentine Political Thought and the Atlantic Republican Tradition*. Princeton: Princeton University Press, 1975. Central study of transatlantic influences on revolutionary rhetoric and writing. Pocock argues that Machiavellian thought (via British appropriations) had a great impact on American republican discourse.

Gordon S. Wood. *The Creation of the American Republic, 1776-1787*. Chapel Hill: University of North Carolina Press, 1969. One of the most important books written about the American Revolution, it cemented the centrality of republican discourse in discussions of the period. It claims that Americans did not revolt against English constitutional tradition but on behalf of it.

b. Works Cited and Reading Suggestions

Albanese, Catherine L. (1976). *Sons of the Fathers: The Civil Religion of the American Revolution*. Philadelphia: Temple University Press.
Appleby, Joyce O. (1992). *Liberalism and Republicanism in the Historical Imagination*. Cambridge: Harvard University Press.
Austin, Jonathan Loring (1992). "An Oration Delivered July 4, 1786, at the Request of the Inhabitants of the Town of Boston." 1786. *The Fourth of July: Political Oratory and Literary Reactions, 1776-1876*. Ed. Paul Goetsch and Gerd Hurm. Tübingen: Narr, 264-274.
Bailyn, Bernard (1967). *The Ideological Origins of the American Revolution*. Cambridge: Harvard University Press.
Bailyn, Bernard, and Jane N. Garrett, eds. (1974). *Pamphlets of the American Revolution, 1750-1776*. Cambridge: Harvard University Press.
Becker, Carl Lotus (1922). *The Declaration of Independence: A Study in the History of Political Ideas*. New York: Knopf.
Bercovitch, Sacvan (1978). *The American Jeremiad*. Madison: University of Wisconsin Press.
– (1988). "Representing Revolution: The Example of Hester Prynne." *The Early Republic: The Making of a Nation – The Making of a Culture*. Ed. Steve Ickringill. Amsterdam: Free University Press, 29-51.

Boyd, Julian P. (1999). *The Declaration of Independence: The Evolution of the Text*. Washington: Library of Congress.
Brogan, Denis William (1944). *The American Problem*. London: Hamish Hamilton.
Brown, Richard D., ed. (1992). *Major Problems in the Era of the American Revolution 1760-1791*. Lexington: Heath.
– (1996). *The Strength of a People: The Idea of an Informed Citizenry in America, 1650-1870*. Chapel Hill: University of North Carolina Press.
Bush, Harold K., Jr. (1999). *American Declarations: Rebellion and Repentance in American Cultural History*. Urbana: University of Illinois Press.
Countryman, Edward (1985). *The American Revolution*. New York: Hill and Wang.
Derrida, Jacques (1986). "Declarations of Independence." *New Political Science* 15, 7-15.
Detweiler, Philip F. (1972). "The Changing Reputation of the Declaration of Independence: The First Fifty Years." *The William and Mary Quarterly* 19, 557-574.
Diggins, John P. (1986). *The Lost Soul of American Politics: Virtue, Self-interest, and the Foundations of Liberalism*. Chicago: University of Chicago Press.
Dworetz, Steven M. (1990). *The Unvarnished Doctrine: Locke, Liberalism and the American Revolution*. Durham: Duke University Press.
Eicholz, Hans L. (2001). *Harmonizing Sentiments: The Declaration of Independence and the Jeffersonian Idea of Self-Government*. New York: Lang.
Emerson, Ralph Waldo (1904). "Concord Hymn." 1837. *The Complete Works of Ralph Waldo Emerson*. Vol. 9: *Poems*. Ed. E. W. Emerson. New York: Sully and Kleinteich, 139.
Fliegelman, Jay (1982). *Prodigals and Pilgrims: The American Revolution Against Patriarchal Authority, 1750-1800*. Cambridge: Cambridge University Press.
– (1993). *Declaring Independence: Jefferson, Natural Language, and the Culture of Performance*. Stanford: Stanford University Press.
Foner, Eric (1976). *Tom Paine and Revolutionary America*. New York: Oxford University Press.
– (1998). *The Story of American Freedom*. New York: Norton.
Ginsberg, Robert, ed. (1967). *A Casebook on the Declaration of Independence*. New York: Crowell.
Gittleman, Edwin (1974). "Jefferson's 'Slave Narrative': The Declaration of Independence as a Literary Text." *Early American Literature* 8, 239-256.
Goetsch, Paul (1992). "The Declaration of Independence." *The Fourth of July: Political Oratory and Literary Reactions, 1776-1876*. Ed. Paul Goetsch and Gerd Hurm. Tübingen: Narr, 11-31.
Greene, Jack P., ed. (1987). *The American Revolution: Its Character and Limits*. New York: New York University Press.
Greene, Jack P., and J. R. Pole, eds. (1994). *The Blackwell Encyclopedia of the American Revolution*. Malden: Blackwell.
– , ed. (2000). *A Companion to the American Revolution*. Malden: Blackwell.

Grimes, Alan P. (1976). "Conservative Revolution and Liberal Rhetoric: The Declaration of Independence." *The Journal of Politics* 38, 1-19.

Hall, David W. (2003). *The Genevan Reformation and the American Founding*. Lexington: Lexington Books.

Hartnett, Stephen John (2002). *Democratic Dissent & the Cultural Fictions of Antebellum America*. Urbana: University of Illinois Press.

Hurm, Gerd (1992). "The Rhetoric of Continuity in Early Boston Orations." *The Fourth of July: Political Oratory and Literary Reactions, 1776-1876*. Ed. Paul Goetsch and Gerd Hurm. Tübingen: Narr, 57-85.

Jaffe, Irma B. (1976). *Trumbull: The Declaration of Independence*. New York: Viking Press.

Jensen, Merrill (1968). *The Founding of a Nation: A History of the American Revolution, 1763-1776*. New York: Oxford University Press.

Kammen, Michael (1978). *A Season of Youth: The American Revolution and the Historical Imagination*. New York: Knopf.

Kramnick, Isaac (1990). *Republicanism and Bourgeois Radicalism: Political Ideology in Late Eighteenth-Century England and America*. Ithaca: Cornell University Press.

Lucas, Stephen E. (1976). *Portents of Rebellion: Rhetoric and Revolution in Philadelphia, 1765-76*. Philadelphia: Temple University Press.

– (1989). "Justifying America: The Declaration of Independence as a Rhetorical Document." *American Rhetoric: Context and Criticism*. Ed. Thomas W. Benson. Carbondale: Southern Illinois University Press, 67-130.

Maier, Pauline (1972). *From Resistance to Revolution: Colonial Radicals and the Development of American Opposition to Britain, 1765-1776*. New York: Random House.

– (1997). *American Scripture: Making the Declaration of Independence*. New York: Knopf.

Matson, Cathy D., and Peter S. Onuf (1990). *A Union of Interests: Political and Economic Thought in Revolutionary America. American Political Thought*. Lawrence: University Press of Kansas.

McCullough, David (2001). *John Adams*. New York: Simon and Schuster.

– (2007). "An Icon's Secret: How John Trumbull's Revered Depiction of July 4, 1776, Mixes Fiction and Fact." *The Wall Street Journal*, June 30, P1.

Middlekauff, Robert (1982). *The Oxford History of the United States. Vol. 2: The Glorious Cause: The American Revolution, 1763-1789*. New York: Oxford University Press.

Mitchell, Annie (2004). "A Liberal Republican 'Cato.'" *American Journal of Political Science* 48, 588-603.

Morgan, Edmund S. (1956). *The Birth of the Republic, 1763-89*. Chicago: University of Chicago Press.

Nash, Gary B. (1979). *The Urban Crucible: Social Change, Political Consciousness, and the Origins of the American Revolution*. Cambridge: Harvard University Press.

Nash, Gary B. (2005). *The Unknown American Revolution: The Unruly Birth of Democracy and the Struggle to Create America*. New York: Viking.
Norton, Mary Beth (1980). *Liberty's Daughters: The Revolutionary Experience of American Women, 1750-1800*. Boston: Little Brown.
Pangle, Thomas (1988). *The Spirit of Modern Republicanism: The Moral Vision of the American Founders and the Philosophy of Locke*. Chicago: University of Chicago Press.
Pocock, John G. A. (1975). *The Machiavellian Moment: Florentine Political Thought and the Atlantic Republican Tradition*. Princeton: Princeton University Press.
– (1985). *Virtue, Commerce, and History: Essays on Political Thought and History, Chiefly in the Eighteenth Century*. Cambridge: Cambridge University Press.
Rahe, Paul A. (1992). *Republics Ancient and Modern: Classical Republicanism and the American Revolution*. Chapel Hill: University of North Carolina Press.
Raphael, Ray (2001). *A People's History of the American Revolution: How Common People Shaped the Fight for Independence*. New York: New Press.
Shalhope, Robert E. (1990). *The Roots of Democracy: American Thought and Culture, 1760-1800*. Boston: Twayne.
Silverman, Kenneth (1976). *A Cultural History of the American Revolution: Painting, Music, Literature, and the Theatre in the Colonies and the United States from the Treaty of Paris to the Inauguration of George Washington, 1763-1789*. New York: Crowell.
Trees, Andrew S. (2003). *The Founding Fathers and the Politics of Character*. Princeton: Princeton University Press.
Tyler, Moses Coit (1957). *The Literary History of the American Revolution. 1763-1863*. New York: Ungar.
Vincent, Bernard (2005). *The Transatlantic Republican: Thomas Paine and the Age of Revolutions*. Amsterdam: Rodopi.
Wallach, Glenn (1997). *Obedient Sons: The Discourse of Youth and Generations in American Culture, 1630-1860*. Amherst: University of Massachusetts Press.
White, Morton (1978). *The Philosophy of the American Revolution*. New York: Oxford University Press.
Wills, Garry (1979). *Inventing America: Jefferson's Declaration of Independence*. Garden City: Doubleday.
Wood, Gordon S. (1969). *The Creation of the American Republic, 1776-1787*. Chapel Hill: University of North Carolina Press.
– (1992). *The Radicalism of the American Revolution*. New York: Knopf.
Young, Alfred F., ed. (1976). *The American Revolution: Explorations in the History of American Radicalism*. DeKalb: Northern Illinois University Press.
Zinn, Howard (1980). *A People's History of the United States*. London: Longman.
Zobel, Hiller B. (1970). *The Boston Massacre*. New York: Norton.

DENNIS HANNEMANN / ULRICH ESCHBORN

The Early Republic and the Rites of Memory

I. Themes and Arguments

The Early Republic has been investigated from an impressive variety of critical perspectives. It is safe to say, though, that the most visible of these remains the 'biographical perspective,' an approach highlighting the few figures that shaped the early stages of the American nation politically. As Gordon Wood once conceded in an attempt to reassess the historical significance of the Early Republic, the decades following the struggle for independence had marked, of all periods in US history, a "period of 'great men'" in the historical imagination (1988, 3). Indeed, the era which arguably stretches from the Treaty of Paris in 1783 to Andrew Jackson's rise to the presidency in 1829 saw the political careers of such eminent men as George Washington, Thomas Jefferson, Alexander Hamilton, and James Madison, who have been ascribed central functions in the formation of America's cultural memory. Nevertheless, countless cultural historians in different fields have, for the last two decades or so, made considerable efforts to revise the well-established and yet reductive image of the Early Republic, according to which there was something of an aristocracy of politicians who ruled over an anonymous community. Instead, we have now become aware of the intricate and complex social and cultural dynamics that characterized America's post-revolutionary years. Although the political careers and writings of the Founding Fathers continue to be fascinating grounds for historical and literary inquiry, a more recent critical approach has directed our view to the popular dimension of the political, cultural, and economic transformations that occurred in the first four decades of US history.[1]

The following chapter focuses on the problem of national identity formation in the Early Republic. Its argument is based on a critical reading of the documents collected in the section "Early Republic" of the anthology. Mainly examples of occasional literature as well as political prints, these documents allow the student of early American culture to trace the strategies and concepts that were employed primarily by intellectuals in their attempts to sketch and negotiate an American national identity around the beginning of the nineteenth century. It

---

[1] This change of perspective is documented in an exemplary fashion in a collection of essays tellingly entitled *Beyond the Founders* (Pasley et al. 2004; cf. Johnson 2007).

must be noted, however, that the occasional literature of the Early Republic does not constitute an autonomous realm of intellectual discourse. Rather, commemorative orations, political sermons, and Fourth of July odes should be read as testimony of a nationwide festive culture in which Americans of various social, ethnic, and religious backgrounds participated and by which they constructed a communal identity on a strongly symbolic level (cf. Waldstreicher 1997; Travers 1997; Newman 2000). As a formative part of a highly ritualized festive culture, such texts display a specific ideological tension within which intellectuals of the Early Republic sought to provide a frame of reference which would allow the inhabitants of the United States to define themselves as members of one nation. The ideological tension characterizing the Early Republic is the result of a continuous emphasis on America's singularity on the one hand and the necessity to position the United States in the progressive movement of universal civil history on the other.

The following chapter revolves around four documents which enable the reader to pinpoint some of the ideologies and concepts that were crucial in providing a basis for collective identification during the Early Republic. The documents selected will simultaneously be placed in a referential context with other texts and images across the range of different sections of the anthology. Thus, the cultural significance and force of these ideologies and concepts will be revealed. Aspasio's "Anniversary Ode, for July 4th, 1789" (doc. 136) is ideologically driven by the conviction that the present marks the starting point of a blissful and ever-lasting era of republicanism in North America. Moreover, it mirrors the iconic function attributed to George Washington after his inauguration as the United States' first president. In an Independence Day "Ode" written for the year 1798 (doc. 141), Thomas Green Fessenden gives voice to a 'Francophobia' that many Federalists shared around the turn of the century. As a strategy of cultural homogenization, Fessenden evokes a distinctly American legacy of liberty that he deduces from the heroic achievements of the Revolutionary War. John Quincy Adams in his *Oration Delivered at Plymouth, December 22, 1802. At the Anniversary Commemoration of the First Landing of Our Ancestors at That Place* (doc. 149) reads the landing of the Pilgrims as a genuine foundational myth of the United States. By emphasizing the providential quality of America's early settlement, Adams justifies, among other issues, the conquest of regions claimed by Native Americans. Hugh Swinton Legaré's *Oration, Delivered on the Fourth of July, 1823* (doc. 151) reveals that by the 1820s Americans had developed a strong sense of national identity that could be derived from the nation's own revolutionary legacy. In his enthusiastic speculations about the ever-expanding republic, Legaré relies on the concept of American exceptionalism, which is re-employed by the orator with a strong emphasis on America's secular achievements.

II. Allegorizing America

The four decades following the American Revolution witnessed a good deal of political turmoil and instability. Nonetheless, the majority of occasional literature published during the Early Republic is marked by its all-encompassing optimism. In hindsight, such optimism must be read as a highly efficient strategy of placation and self-assurance. When an independent nation of the United States was politically implemented in 1783, many Americans felt themselves in the midst of a daring, if not risky, experiment. Declaring a number of culturally diverse colonies politically independent and autonomous, albeit on a continent far removed from the civilized world of Europe, was historically unprecedented. Hence, Americans lacked models that would guide them through the first steps of running their 'new' nation. Moreover, republican states in particular were notorious for their fragility and short duration. According to Enlightenment historiography, political bodies resembled biological organisms; that is, they were subject to an incessant movement of growth and decay.[2] Alluding to the Greek historian Polybios, John Warren in his *Oration, Delivered July 4th, 1783* notes "that every State must decline more or less rapidly, in proportion as she recedes from the principles on which she was founded" (*KC*, 318). And virtue, which was by common consent taken to be the ethical principle of republican states, was considered extremely prone to corruption. It is of little surprise, then, that in a climate of political instability and disorientation patriotic Americans craved symbols that could function as warrants for future national accomplishments.

The Fourth of July ode by the pseudonymous Aspasio written in 1789, serves as a telling example of how the optimism of the young American nation concerning its future progress found literary expression. The author employs three strategies: the poetic device of allegory, the concept of *translatio imperii*, and the vision of a thriving modern republic. Aspasio takes a first step in elevating the United States to a subject matter worthy of public praise by reverting to the form of the ode, which is by genre tradition noted for its high poetic register, complex metrical structures, and celebratory tone. As in any Fourth of July ode or oration of the Early Republic, the overriding theme of the text is, by means of metonymy, the United States in its history, present situation, and future outlook. Aspasio frames his ode by inducing the allegorical figure of Liberty. Personifying the very principle which constituted the driving impulse of the American Revolution, the poet not only reminds his readers of the successful struggle for independence, but also sanctions America as a land partaking in the republican tradition. The "blest goddess" Freedom establishes an ideological link to the Roman

---

[2] This concept of politics and history was articulated most succinctly by Lord Bolingbroke, who wrote in *The Idea of a Patriot King*: "The best instituted governments, like the best constituted animal bodies, carry in them the seeds of their destruction: and, though they grow and improve for a time, they will soon tend visibly to their dissolution" (1997, 252; cf. Scheiding 2003, 50-3).

goddess Libertas, which functioned as an important emblem for the republican resistance in imperial Rome (cf. Silverman 1987, 85-7). In addition to this historical allusion, Aspasio increases the rhetorical force of allegory by blending it with the concept of *translatio imperii*:

> While Freedom, blest goddess, expell'd from their shores,
> Their stupor and blindness, and folly deplores.
> Thus, exil'd those regions, the seraph has flown
> And left the dull myriads in shackles to groan;
> While Europe invites her, she skims o'er the main,
> And in this new empire commences her reign. (*KC*, 315)

Here, *translatio imperii* undergoes a poetic variation typical of the Early Republic's occasional literature. Earlier applications of the trope to America, as in Edward Hayes's and Christopher Carleill's "Discourse Concerning a Voyage Intended for the Planting of Chrystyan Religion and People in the North West Regions of America" (1592; doc. 12), or as in Philip Freneau's poem *On the Rising Glory of America* (1772; doc. 83), put major emphasis on the individual geographical stages through which civil power passes in its westward progression. Thus, these applications make the biblical origins of the trope as rendered in the Book of Daniel visible. Aspasio, on the other hand, shifts perspective and moves the political principle of liberty to the center of his application. By doing so, the author advances the secularization of the trope. Built around an allegorized figure of Liberty, *translatio imperii* is re-articulated here as *translatio libertatis*. In his *Oration, Pronounced at Hanover, New Hampshire, the 4th Day of July, 1800*, Daniel Webster also resorts to the idea of liberty transferred when warning his audience of the 'French danger' in the context of the federalist-republican controversy: "Our ancestors bravely snatched expiring liberty from the grasp of Britain, whose touch is *poison*; shall we now consign it to France, whose embrace is *death*?" (*KC*, 331).[3]

Aspasio employs Columbia as a second personification in his "Anniversary Ode," an allegorical representation of America prominent not only in the visual arts but also in the commemorative literature of the period. In such texts, Columbia is used as a poetic synonym for America in a strongly standardized fashion. Not only by applying this well-established allegory, but also by repeatedly presenting it in an apostrophe, Aspasio heightens the celebratory quality of his ode: "'Twas thou, O Columbia! [...] / Awake fair Columbia, thou child of the skies; / [...] / Thou fountain of goodness! Columbia combine" (*KC*, 315-6). If

---

[3] Other political authors of the Early Republic devote even longer sections to the image of *translatio libertatis*. Henry Alexander Dearborn, for example, evokes it in a retrospective glance at the American Revolution. By also referring to classical antiquity, the author at the same time constructs a narrative of universal civil history: "The Genius of Freedom, banished from the ancient Republics of Greece and Rome, wandered a neglected exile round the globe [...], until hailed by the hardy sons of Columbia, as a protectress and guardian angel of their natural and indefeasible rights" (1806, 6).

one takes a look at other commemorative odes sung and published in post-revolutionary America, one will realize that the majority of them contains, in one way or another, such invocations to Columbia.[4] Thus, the poets did justice to the genre convention of addressing the deity to which the ode was dedicated. That the revolutionary struggle for liberty as well as its ongoing cultivation is closely linked to the figure of Columbia becomes evident both in the Early Republic's festive poetry and in its visual arts. Thomas Green Fessenden, for example, opens his 1798 "Ode" with the following address typical of Fourth of July poetry: "Ye sons of Columbia, unite in the cause / Of liberty, justice, religion, and laws" (*KC*, 328). In the *Apotheosis of Washington* (1802; doc. 137), a commemorative engraving by John James Barralet, the female allegory America-Columbia sits beneath Washington's tomb, her body in a sorrowful gesture, while the late president, illuminated by a cone of light and spreading his arms majestically, is about to be lifted up to the heavens by angelic figures. Bemoaning the loss of the father of her country, America-Columbia leans against a scepter on top of which sits the liberty cap. Although the artist himself proposes to read this arrangement as "emblematical of his [Washington's] mild administration" (*KC*, 317), the highly symbolic liberty cap also points to the colonial resistance against British rule and thus evokes Washington's instrumental part in the Revolutionary War.[5]

Aspasio in his "Anniversary Ode" attributes a prominent role to George Washington, too, mentioning him as the only historical figure in a poem otherwise grounded in ideas and concepts:

> 'Twas thou, O Columbia! thy CHIEFTAIN arouse,
> Who, aided by Heaven, defeated our foes;
> Caus'd the tumults and horrors of combat to cease,
> And raised us to freedom, to glory and peace. (*KC*, 315)

As in countless other texts, Washington is figured here as the savior of the American nation, an honorary title the Virginian owed to having successfully commanded the Continental Army in their struggle against the British. The section quoted forms part of a process of iconization whose impact can be felt in the United States' 'symbolic vocabulary' up to the present. Already in the late 1770s orators, poets, and painters began to conceptualize Washington as a heroic persona which allowed inscriptions of primarily republican values and norms. In

---

[4] Such invocations or apostrophes to Columbia can also be found in George Richards, "Anniversary Ode on American Independence, for the Fourth of July, 1788" (doc. 87), Thomas Green Fessenden, "An Ode" (doc. 141), and John Howard Payne, "Ode: For the Thirty-First Anniversary of American Independence" (doc. 148).

[5] The liberty cap was one of several symbols patriots appropriated during the American Revolution. On many town squares, liberty poles were erected. Thus, the patriots visibly communicated their defiance against British rule. After hanging British officials in effigy from a Boston Common tree during the Stamp Act crisis, patriots named the very tree 'Liberty Tree'; see also the engraving *The Bostonians Paying the Excise-man* (doc. 123).

the Early Republic, a highly efficient strategy of this process of iconization consisted in linking Washington typologically to exemplary figures from the Bible and classical antiquity. In this way, authors and artists furthered the process of national identity formation significantly, for they implicitly ascribed the United States a legitimate role both in God's providential plan and in the progress of civil history. An example of this cultural practice is offered in George Richards's "Anniversary Ode on American Independence, for the Fourth of July, 1788," in which Washington appears as a 'second Joshua,' the biblical commander of the ancient Israelites:

> T' accomplish my pleasure, a HERO I'll raise,
>   Unrivall'd in counsel and might,
> Like the PROPHET of old, wise, patient, and bold,
>   Resistless as JOSHUA in fight. (*KC*, 200)

The second half of Aspasio's festive poem is devoted to visualizing America as a thriving republic. The author finally casts his view, as is characteristic of the Fourth of July rhetoric of the period, to a 'field of futurity' and thus seeks to spread confidence among his audience as to the future course of America's national project. Aspasio's vision of America's future unfolds in three steps, beginning in the third stanza with an elaboration on the practical implications of republicanism. On the one hand, he stresses that the cultivation of knowledge needs to be a major concern in any republic: "The fountains of science and wisdom explore" (*KC*, 316), reads one of the tasks Columbia is asked to complete. On the other hand, Americans should advance their republic economically: "See rich agriculture exult o'er the land, / And new manufactures, fast rising, expand" (*KC*, 316). By the mention of "manufactures," the poet implicitly takes a Hamiltonian stance in the controversy over the economic make-up of the American republic, a controversy that would continue well into the first decade of the nineteenth century. Other than Jeffersonian Republicans, who sought to rest the American economy primarily on agriculture, Federalists, whose traditional stronghold were the Northern states, supported national industries and manufactures and thus hoped to see the United States less dependent on international trade. By referring to manufactures and commerce, Aspasio, it must be noted, advertises a progressive and fairly modern view of republicanism. In the same period, conservative authors like Benjamin Rush (cf. doc. 139) still favored a more Spartan model of republicanism, putting major emphasis on military virtue and warning Americans of the seemingly harmful effects of effeminate luxury.

In the fourth stanza, the lyrical I changes perspective once more and, as a second step of Aspasio's republican vision, creates an image of America's fertile lands, sketching it as a country of natural abundance and magnitude. The lines "See verdant savannas and landscapes display, / Where steeds, herds and lambkins promiscuously stray" (*KC*, 316) remind the reader of Arcadia, the idealized land of bucolic harmony, and thus allude to a future golden age of prosperity and peace. In two concluding lines, however, the poet returns to the economic foundations of the American republic and thus, at least partially, demystifies the vision of Arcadia: "Hence gladness and plenty exults o'er the plain, / And commerce triumphant glides over the main" (*KC*, 316). The third and last step of the poem's visionary outlook is presented in the form of a prayer, with apostrophes to both God ("Essence divine") and 'civil deities' such as Columbia and Liberty. Aspasio completes his visionary outlook into the American future by delimiting the United States both in spatial and in temporal terms: "'Extend with the main and dissolve with skies.' / [...] / And liberty bless us till time be no more" (*KC*, 316). By concluding with this gesture toward the eternal and the boundless – which marks another genre convention of the Early Republic's festive odes and orations –, the poet hyperbolically confirms his optimism concerning America's national project.[6]

III. Demonizing France

When John Adams was elected president after George Washington's resignation in 1796, American interior politics had already come under the spell of a gradually emerging partisan conflict between Federalists and Republicans (cf. Smelser 1958; Sharp 1995; Ferguson 2006). One of the questions that set Federalists and Republicans apart from one another in the first place was the controversy on how to assess the French Revolution and its political aftermath. While the majority of Americans welcomed the early stages of the French Revolution rather enthusiastically, many felt estranged and even appalled by the events of 1793, when the French beheaded their former king Louis XVI and the Jacobin Reign of Terror broke out. Nevertheless, the Republicans, who began to form loosely as an opposition group to Federalist politics, considered the American and the French cause as ideologically linked to one another and continued to celebrate the French Revolution as the harbinger of a transatlantic democratic order. The ruling circles of the Federalists, on the other hand, identified the French turmoil as nothing less than a 'mobocracy,' i.e., the uncontrolled rule of the many, and feared that its subversive potential could gain ground in America, too. As a consequence of the Federalists' skeptical stance, the political relations between the United States and its former revolutionary ally began to deteriorate rapidly around the middle of the decade. After the Federalists had implemented the Jay Treaty in 1796, which regulated trade relations between the United States and France's number one enemy Great Britain, the provocation of the French foreign minister Talleyrand in the so-called 'XYZ Affair' caused a rather severe diplomatic

---

[6] See the similar endings in George Richards, "Anniversary Ode on American Independence, for the Fourth of July, 1788" (doc. 87), Daniel Webster, *An Oration, Pronounced at Hanover, New Hampshire, the 4th Day of July, 1800* (doc. 142), and Thomas Green Fessenden, "Almighty Power: An Ode" (doc. 147). For the conventions of Fourth of July rhetoric, see Lubbers (1994).

crisis between the two nations. This crisis culminated in an undeclared 'Quasi-War' fought out between French and American vessels, an armed conflict stretching from July 1798 to October 1800.

The Federalists' 'Francophobia' became visible not only in their governmental policy, but also on a symbolic level. Demonizing France was an omnipresent strategy in the Federalist rhetoric of the day, be it in partisan propaganda against Republicans in general and their leading figure, 'Francophile' Thomas Jefferson, in particular (cf. doc. 145), or as a strategy to put Americans on the alert against forces supposedly subverting the republican order enshrined in the United States Constitution. For the latter, Thomas Green Fessenden's "An Ode" (doc. 141) is a case in point. Set to music and performed in Rutland, Vermont, on the Fourth of July, 1798, the poem mirrors the then common Federalist practice of using France as a counter-image in the process of national identity formation. For an understanding of the ode's strikingly provocative and militaristic tone, the political circumstances of its composition need to be taken into account. The ode was written around the start of the French-American Quasi-War, which, as is documented in an authorial footnote to the 1806 publication of the ode, fomented fears in Federalist circles of a French invasion of the United States. "At that time," the footnote reads, "the warship which afterwards sailed to Egypt under Bonaparte lay at Toulon: its destination was not known in America, but many supposed it was intended to waft the blessings of *French liberty* to the United States" (*KC*, 328). As is indicated in italics, this comment reflects one of the key motifs of Fessenden's festive poem: the conviction that the French revolutionaries had deceptively misused the concept of civil liberty to legitimize their arbitrary usurpation of political power.

The main objective of Fessenden's "Ode" can be described as ideologically mobilizing Americans to actively defend their territory against any intrusive foreign power. This objective is echoed in the concluding couplet of each of the six stanzas and thus structurally emphasized. With only slight alterations in each stanza, the couplet reads: "For foes to our freedom we'll ever defy, / Till the continent sinks, and the ocean is dry!" (*KC*, 329). The author brackets his ode by a double invocation to God at the beginning and at the end of the poem and thus sanctions the American community as being particularly favored by divine providence: "Should foes then invade us, to battle we'll hie, / For the GOD OF OUR FATHERS will be our ally!" (*KC*, 328) and "Let those rights be yours, / While Nature endures, / For OMNIPOTENCE gave you the charter!" (*KC*, 330). On the whole, the poem shows a dual structure. While the first part (stanzas one to three) mainly deals with the present 'aggressor' France, the second half (stanzas four to six) seeks to assure the readers of the United States' defensive strength in any upcoming political conflict. The ode derives its persuasive potential from two complementary rhetorical strategies, each of which is prominent in one respective part of the poem. On the one hand, Fessenden demonizes France and thus constructs alterity, while on the other hand the author recollects the achievements of the American struggle for liberty and thus evokes a narrative of national history allowing for collective identification. From the outset, France is stigmatized as a foreign power whose chief interest seems to lie in subjugating the United States. Fessenden sketches a counter-image by employing an imperialistic vocabulary whenever referring to France. The author has France "advance" and design America's "conquest" and "plunder" (*KC*, 328). As the poem runs on, the French government is referred to as Napoleon Bonaparte's "sans culotte band" (*KC*, 328) and is thus rhetorically thwarted and degraded to the rank of a criminal conspiracy. The ideological dimension of this stigmatizing rhetoric is retained, however, when the author ironically speaks of "a new sort of freedom we don't understand" and of "*Frenchified* Freedom" (*KC*, 328-9). In doing so, Fessenden castigates the French government as ultimately despotic and anti-republican, while at the same time advocating the United States, albeit implicitly, as the very nation that alone has conserved a valid concept of republican liberty.

As soon as the author casts his view on the United States, the poetic register changes significantly. Instead of polemic driven by partisan interests and distinctly Federalist fears, the poem now displays the celebratory and laudatory quality appropriate to the form of the ode. The language Fessenden uses here is not merely an expression of the dominant classicist poetics of the day, but it also reflects a repertoire of tropes and figures that are characteristic of the Early Republic's occasional literature. Among them, we find the allegorical personification of political concepts, as in: "We're anxious that Peace may continue her reign, / We cherish the virtues which sport in her train" (*KC*, 329), or "At Liberty's call, / Unite one and all" (*KC*, 329). Furthermore, the poet adds an affective dimension to the ode by including two overtly sentimentalist lines: "Our hearts ever melt, when the fatherless sigh, / And we shiver at Horror's funeral cry!" (*KC*, 329). In turn, the political message of the following lines is emphasized, when Fessenden offers a contemporary American reading of republican virtue, according to which republican citizens were considered free, but at the same time had to be disinterested and self-sacrificing:

> But still, though we prize
> That child of the skies,
> We'll never like slaves be accosted.
> In a war of defence
> Our means are immense,
> And we'll fight till our *all* is exhausted. (*KC*, 329)

The author's attempt at highlighting an American legacy of liberty and establishing a sense of nationhood culminates in the apotheosis of two late revolutionary figures, Joseph Warren and Hugh Mercer. Fessenden introduces them as 'heavenly' messengers of freedom who take up the formerly uttered plea for defensive awareness once more:

> The flood-gates of glory are open on high,
> And Warren and Mercer descend from the sky! [...]

"Americans, seek no occasion for war;
"The rude deeds of rapine still ever abhor:
"But if in defence of your rights you should arm,
"Let toils ne'er discourage, nor dangers alarm. (*KC*, 328-9)

The author undertakes a significant step in terms of national identity formation here, insofar as he constructs a catalogue of national heroes on which future generations of Americans would be able to draw when recollecting the origins of their national history. By introducing Warren and Mercer as heroic personas, Fessenden suggestively reads the United States as a 'historical nation,' as a political community whose members can, despite the factual 'youth' of the nation, relate to a symbolic repertoire representing a collective past. This strategy of historicization, which must be read as a peculiarly Early Republican form of American ancestral veneration, can also be traced in a number of other documents of occasional literature.[7] Apart from offering a set of symbols allowing contemporary Americans to experience a sense of community, the strategy of historicization as applied by Fessenden and other Early Republican authors also provided what would constitute key components – i.e., individual personalities, locations, and battles – for future historiographies of the American Revolution.

IV. Rereading the Pilgrim Fathers

As Homi Bhabha famously argued in an essay on the narrative structure of the nation, "[n]ations, like narratives, lose their origins in the myths of time and only fully realize their horizon in the mind's eye" (1990, 1). Projecting the origin of one's community into a past that has, due to its quasi-mythical remoteness, become subject to an ongoing process of interest-driven inscriptions, is a crucial characteristic not only of the modern nation state, but, quite obviously, of any political community seeking stability and temporal continuity. Although most Americans had been quick to accept the Declaration of Independence as the foundational moment of the United States – a moment annually commemorated in Fourth of July festivals across the nation – they also craved more distant myths of communal origin. To meet this need, some referred to the landing of the Pilgrims on the coast of Massachusetts in 1620 and read it as a foundational myth for the entire American community.[8] During the host of annual festivals of

---

[7] In the Early Republic, orators and poets began to include numerous revolutionary leaders in their Fourth of July rhetoric. This constituted an instrumental step in fostering the idea of the United States being a republican community that would not limit its panegyrics to Washington alone, thus turning him into a quasi-monarchical leader. Early examples of extended catalogues of revolutionary figures include Baldwin (1788, 7) and Porter (1791, 12); see also Legaré (doc. 151).

[8] The emigration of the Puritan English dissenters to Massachusetts via Holland is famously documented in William Bradford's account "Of Plymouth Plantation" (1629-1646), sections of which are reprinted in doc. 58; cf. Obenland in this vol., 95-8.

commemoration, the town of Plymouth, together with its legendary rock, was transformed into what the French scholar Pierre Nora once called a "lieu de mémoire," a location in which memory is actualized as collective experience and at the same time inscribed in space (1989).[9] Although regional in character at least up to the bicentenary in 1820, early Forefathers' Day commemorations, as they were commonly nick-named, functioned as platforms for articulating the indispensability of a set of values and ideas shared by the entire American nation. At the same time, a day like December 22, the legendary day the Pilgrims were supposed to have landed on the American continent, could be appropriated from a partisan angle in times of political conflict. The latter certainly holds true for the Forefathers' Day celebration at Plymouth in 1802, which New England Federalists used in order to display and propagate their political opposition to Thomas Jefferson's recent victory in the presidential election (cf. Hebel 1999). Notwithstanding its partisan overtones, John Quincy Adams's festive address entitled *An Oration Delivered at Plymouth, December 22, 1802* (doc. 149) brings up a number of concepts that were instrumental not only in Early Republican occasional literature but also in shaping American cultural history throughout the eighteenth and nineteenth centuries. These concepts include ancestral veneration, providentialism, expansionism, and *translatio imperii*.

The idea of paying tribute to one's ancestors runs through John Quincy Adams's Plymouth address of 1802. Adams, who at that time was in the early stages of a political career that would culminate in his serving as the sixth US president from 1825 to 1829 (cf. doc. 152), advocates the veneration of the community's ancestors both as civic duty and as an act of filial piety. The author points out the significance of ancestral veneration by first commending it in general, even humanistic, terms. Together with "love for our posterity," "veneration for our forefathers" is considered a praiseworthy endeavor, for it "excites in the breast of man, interest in their history, attachment to their characters, concern for their errors, involuntary pride in their virtues" (*KC*, 345). However, Adams then postulates that ancestral veneration be enacted publicly and made a civic duty, as exemplified in the annual Plymouth celebrations:

> These sentiments are wise – they are honorable – they are virtuous – their cultivation is not merely innocent pleasure, it is incumbent duty. Obedient to their dictates, you my fellow-citizens have instituted and paid frequent observance to this annual solemnity. (*KC*, 346)

After this plea for ancestral veneration as civic practice and duty, the author gives an account of the Pilgrim Fathers themselves. His interest now focuses on "the characters of those men who gave the first impulse to a new series of events in the history of the world" (*KC*, 346). As the allusion to the Virgilian motto

---

[9] On the legend of Plymouth Rock, the very rock on which the Pilgrims are said to have landed upon reaching the coast of Cape Cod, as well as on the Rock as a memorial site, see Seelye (1998) and Hurm (2001).

line of the Great Seal (*Novus ordo seclorum* – "A new series of the ages") indicates,[10] the Pilgrims are, as the legitimate founders of the American commonwealth, ascribed a prominent role not only in the American consciousness, but even in the successive unfolding of universal history. Hence, it is of little surprise that Adams reads the Pilgrims as exemplary figures in political and moral terms, as well as role models for contemporary Americans. The religious motivations of the Pilgrims' first settlement are particularly underlined:

> In many instances the convictions of religious obligation formed one and a powerful inducement of the adventurers; but in none, excepting the settlement at Plymouth, did they constitute the sole and exclusive actuating cause. Worldly interests and commercial speculation entered largely into the views of other settlers: but the commands of conscience were the only stimulus to the emigrants from Leyden. (*KC*, 346)

The exceptionality and singularity attributed to the Pilgrims' religiosity in this account implicitly transfers to the United States as a whole; for there is, as Adams points out earlier in his oration, "no previous example of a nation, shooting up to maturity and expanding into greatness with the rapidity which has characterized the growth of the American people" (*KC*, 345).

Adams intensifies his laudatory rhetoric to the point of addressing the Pilgrims in the second person. "Venerated shades of our forefathers! No! ye were indeed not ordinary men!" (*KC*, 346) reads the opening apostrophe to a sentimentalist section that is devoted to the hardships the first settlers had to endure. Although Adams does not integrate the Pilgrim Fathers into a biblical scheme of history here, he nonetheless adds a providential quality to his narrative of America's origins in emphasizing the Pilgrims' exceptional Christian piety and the sustaining success of their new world endeavors. "Conscious of the purity," Adams addresses them in an enthusiastic voice, "and convinced of the importance of your motives, you put your trust in the protecting shield of Providence, and smiled defiance at the combining terror of human malice and of elemental strife" (*KC*, 346-7). At the end of his speech, Adams returns to the civic dimension of ancestral veneration by drawing a significant historical parallel:

> Yet, as the original founder of the Roman State is said once to have lifted upon his shoulders the fame and fortunes of all his posterity, so let us never forget that the glory and greatness of all our descendants is in our hands. Preserve in all their purity, refine if possible from all their alloy, those virtues which we this day commemorate as the ornament of our forefathers. (*KC*, 348-9)

Here, Adams references the myth of Aeneas, who rescued his father Anchises, his son Ascanius, and the Palladium from the flames of conquered Troy before setting out to Italy in order to found a new commonwealth. By implicitly linking the Pilgrim Fathers with Rome's mythical origins, the author inscribes the Unit-

---

[10] On the adaption of Virgil's prophecy in the Early Republic's occasional literature, see the following section on "Secularizing American Exceptionalism," 233-7.

ed States in a progressive tradition of secular history, a tradition originating in classical antiquity and culminating, as it were, in the American republic of the present and the future (cf. Shields 2001, xx-xlv). For, as Adams optimistically puts it in the final paragraph of his address: "The destinies of this empire, as they appear in prospect before us, disdain the powers of human calculation" (*KC*, 348).

A fairly extensive section of Adams's anniversary address is devoted to the early settlers' acquisition of land from Native Americans. Adams's focus on a rather marginal constituent of the Pilgrim Fathers' foundational myth indicates that in occasional literature the structure of texts is not necessarily guided by intrinsic reasons. Rather, occasional addresses and poems are often appropriated as a medium for immersing in current political debates. In Adams's case, the speech is doubtless informed by the recent governmental politics of territorial expansion. It is fairly probable that this lengthy excursus on the rightful acquisition of land by European settlers was to some extent influenced by the diplomatic prelude to the Louisiana Purchase, the largest acquisition of land in US history which came into effect in March 1803. Although there is no explicit mention of President Jefferson's negotiations with France concerning the huge territory that unclosed west of the Mississippi River, the contemporary audience of the speech is likely to have associated Adams's more general remarks on territorial possession with the government's intentions of significantly expanding the United States' territory to the west.

In his depiction of the Pilgrims' territorial politics, Adams follows a double strategy of justification. On the one hand, the author transfigures the forefathers into role models of Christian benevolence and diplomatic sincerity. On the other hand, the deduction of territory from indigenous Americans is read as the cogent result of a progress of civilization that has come to unfold across the American continent. Progress of civilization is itself sanctioned as the imminent product of divine providence and hence functions as a historical imperative. Once again, the forefathers' righteousness, in the author's view, defies comparison: "No European settlement ever formed upon this," the excursus opens, "has been more distinguished for undeviating kindness and equity towards the savages" (*KC*, 347). The piece of land on which the Pilgrims put up their settlement figures as a waste land in Adams's representation of the myth, the former property of a tribe of Natives "totally extirpated by that devouring pestilence which had swept the country" (*KC*, 347). Nonetheless, the Pilgrims, endowed with a royal charter to found a colony, purchased the land from the neighboring tribes. Hence, their territorial politics shines, according to Adams, "in the whiteness of innocence" and they will be remembered by posterity, the author predicts, for having performed acts of "kindness and benevolence" towards Native Americans (*KC*, 348).

What turns Adams's Plymouth address into a rather blunt propagandistic document of American expansionism, then, derives from a series of rhetorical questions in which Adams sketches a scenario of a modern, industrial, and progressive

American republic. Throughout Adams's account, Native Americans figure as an inferior race due to their exclusion from transatlantic civil history. Their right to possess and inhabit the American soil is compared to "the right of the huntsman to the forest of a thousand miles over which he has accidentally ranged in quest for prey" (*KC*, 347) and thus virtually nullified. In turn, the expulsion of native peoples appears as the inherent consequence of a progress of civilization:

> Shall the liberal bounties of Providence to the race of man be monopolized by one of ten thousand for whom they were created? Shall the exuberant bosom of the common mother, amply adequate to the nourishment of millions, be claimed exclusively by a few hundreds of her offspring? Shall the lordly savage not only disdain the virtues and enjoyments of civilization himself, but shall he controul the civilization of a world? [...] Shall he forbid the oaks of the forest to fall before the axe of industry, and rise again, transformed into the habitations of ease and elegance? [...] Shall the fields and the vallies, which a beneficent God has formed to teem with the life of innumerable multitudes, be condemned to everlasting barrenness? (*KC*, 347)

Quite evidently, Gen. 1.28-9 functions as a subtext to this section. In the biblical account, the seminal thought of *dominium terrae* is established, according to which man is entitled by God to exert power over nature (cf. Scheiding in this vol., 11-3). Although the European settlers are not explicitly mentioned by Adams in the above quote, it is obvious that they constitute the tacit subjects of the American *dominium terrae*. The latter is envisioned here as a process of civilization and industrialization gradually taking shape across the American continent. In both ideological and rhetorical terms, however, the most cunning step Adams undertakes in this apologetic piece of propaganda consists in taking this very process as an integral part of God's plan, as is indicated by the references to "God" and "Providence" in the section quoted above. By drawing on the concept of providentialism, Adams authorizes the Pilgrim Fathers and their heirs, i.e., the political nation of the United States, as the legitimate executives of a 'divine' mechanism of civilization and territorial expansion. In this divine mechanism, Native Americans, who are identified by the collective singular "the lordly savage," function as the antagonists to God's providential design. Adams's Plymouth address, then, incorporates not only an early plea for the United States' westward expansion but also an argumentative pattern for justifying the subjugation and the expulsion of Native American tribes.

What adds to the impression that Adams does advocate westward expansion is the integration of *translatio imperii* as another key concept of early American cultural history. The conclusive paragraph of the address, in which the author ponders the prospective "destinies of this [i. e. the American] empire," includes a slightly altered quote from the famous visionary verse by George Berkeley: "Westward the Star of empire takes its way" (*KC*, 349).[11] In earlier texts, Ameri-

---

[11] Berkeley's original verse reads "Westward the Course of Empire takes its Way" (*KC*, 32). American authors continued quoting this line far into the nineteenth century. It came to

can authors made reference to *translatio imperii* with the primary intention of ascribing to New World residents the prospective role of a culturally and politically powerful community that would advance the ancient and European heritage of culture and civilization. Adams, however, suggests a new, alternative reading of the trope in the current political debate of the impending Louisiana Purchase. The notion of a westward movement of cultural hegemony is re-employed as an all-American ideological concept in the sense that its geographical scope, which used to comprise the Mediterranean and later the transatlantic world, may now exclusively refer to the American continent. Thus, *translatio imperii* undergoes a substantial shift in semantics. For Adams and other optimistic Early Republican authors, empire has already been successfully transplanted to the United States. Nonetheless, the Berkeleyan prophecy is believed, as Adams phrases it, to "continue unfolding into history" (*KC*, 349). Hence, the westward movement of the original trope can now be construed as the settlers' incessant advancement of the American frontier. The westward course of empire is here identified with the United States' systematic westward expansion of territory. Adams's reference to Berkeley's famous poem, then, indicates another secular transformation of the biblical trope of *translatio imperii*. The trope has been adjusted, as it were, to the ongoing debate of America's territorial expansion and thus allows it to be re-employed as justification in political practice. Against this background of re-articulating *translatio imperii*, one realizes on an ideological level the emergence of a notion that will, until the end of the nineteenth century, function as a new master concept in American cultural history: expansionism.

V. Secularizing American Exceptionalism

Having survived its first international military conflict, the War of 1812 against the former motherland Great Britain (1812-1815), the United States experienced some ten years of political calm and economic growth. Historians have sometimes resorted to the label 'Era of Good Feelings' when analyzing the years of and around the presidency of James Monroe (1817-1825). Although the descriptive adequacy of such a label may be disputed, one can pinpoint a number of political developments that do indicate a first phase of stability and tranquility in American history. When fighting against Great Britain in the War of 1812 – a "forgotten conflict" (Hickey 1989) terminating in a *status quo ante bellum* – the United States realized that it could, despite a number of drawbacks, confront one of the most dominant military powers of the day as their equal. While the Federalist Party had still played a major part in criticizing and even sabotaging the war policy of Republican President Madison, they once and for all dissolved as political opposition soon after the war had ended. As a consequence, Presi-

---

function as a well-established formula epitomizing America's westward expansion; see also Henry David Thoreau, "Walking" (doc. 160).

dent Monroe, who was elected to office in 1816 and re-elected in 1820, saw times of almost unanimous political support from the US Congress. The United States' recent growth in international self-confidence gained formal expression in the so-called 'Monroe Doctrine' of 1823. At its core, the doctrine proclaimed that the United States would no longer tolerate European interferences or attempts at re-colonization on the North American continent. At the same time, the American frontier was incessantly moving ahead, both to the west and to the south. By 1819, the Union consisted of 22 member states. In addition, territorial expansion was furthered when the United States, by terms of the Adams-Onís-Treaty, received the territory of Florida from Spain in the same year.

Hugh Swinton Legaré's *Oration, Delivered on the Fourth of July, 1823* (doc. 151) captures both the optimism and the heightened sense of national identity that seem to have been prevalent in the public consciousness of the late 1810s and early 1820s. In fact, Legaré's speech is a telling document indicating that the United States, some fifty years after its foundation, has finally come of age as a political nation. Even if Legaré largely employs tropes and argumentative patterns that can also be traced in countless earlier festive orations, one notes a striking difference in two respects: first, the author insists on America's superiority and singularity in light of historical comparisons; second, the American Revolution figures as a historically remote and distanced subject matter that has been incorporated in collective memory.

The latter is certainly due to the fact that in the 1820s a new generation of Americans rose to political, economic, and cultural leadership. Members of this new generation were either children or not even born when the Revolution occurred. An author like Hugh Swinton Legaré, who belonged to the intellectual circles of Charleston, South Carolina, could relate to the Fourth of July only in the sense of a 'site' of collective memory. Hence, the challenge for Legaré and other commemorative orators of his age was to do justice to a date that had been used as one of the most prominent symbols of the nation since its inception. Intending not to imitate the laudatory rhetoric of their forebears, such authors sought new forms of praising the achievements of the revolutionary generation:

> It has been usual on this occasion [...] to expatiate upon the events of the revolutionary contest, and to honour in a suitable strain of panegyric, such of the founders of the republic as were supposed to have rendered it the most important services, at a crisis so full of peril and glory. But as these topics [...] are become so trite that it would be difficult by any art of composition, to bestow upon them the graces of novelty, I have chosen rather to exhibit some of the *general features* – the great *leading characteristics* – by which, I conceive that memorable event to be distinguished from all others of a similar kind, that are recorded in the annals of empire. (*KC*, 352)

This passage documents the transitory moment a young American intellectual like Legaré found himself in at that time. On the one hand, celebratory orators were expected to live up to a well-established tradition of ritualizing the Fourth of July; on the other hand, they felt the necessity of emancipating themselves from this very tradition in order to come to terms with the revolutionary legacy and its significance for the present. Legaré's attempt to renegotiate the American Revolution consists in transcending retrospective hero worship and in emphasizing the United States' unique position in world history.

The difficulties of this endeavor can be seen in the historical parallel the author draws at the beginning of his oration. Using Cicero's praise of the Roman general Pompeius as a frame of reference, Legaré relies on the generic convention of enumerating America's revolutionary heroes in order to evoke a communal past:

> What were the victories of Pompey – to the united ach[ie]vements of our Washingtons and Montgomeries and Greenes – our Franklins and Jeffersons and Adams' and La[ur]ens' – of the Senate of Sages, whose wisdom conducted – of the band of warriors, whose valour accomplished – of the "noble army of martyrs" whose blood, sealed and consecrated, the Revolution of '76? (*KC*, 351)

While the author still displays the rhetoric of earlier occasional texts in both listing revolutionary figures and likening America to classical antiquity, one notes, however, that the historical reference is literally eclipsed by the brilliance attributed to the American Founding Fathers. The fact that historical referencing itself has been reduced to a mere rhetorical gesture indicates that by the 1820s many Americans had developed a clear notion of what it meant to be an American, i.e., they had constructed an autonomous collective self-image that was no longer dependent on historical models or predecessors.

The dominant concept of Legaré's festive oration is American exceptionalism which can be identified in numerous sections of the text. American exceptionalism provides the ideological basis for the author's praising of the revolutionary heritage and for his casting a compellingly optimistic outlook into the immediate future of the United States. Scholars often locate the roots of American exceptionalism in Puritan New England. Essentially a specific reading of history, the concept originally embraces the notion that the early Puritan settlers have been chosen by God to form a community of piety and righteousness that would function as a model for the rest of reformed Christianity (cf. Bozeman 1988). In its Puritan cast, exceptionalism often merges with providentialism and millennialism; moreover, it bears a missionary impulse. The earliest articulation of exceptionalism is found in John Winthrop's treatise "A Model of Christian Charity" (1630), in which the Puritan clergyman famously identifies his future New World parish with the "City upon a Hill" of the Gospel of Matthew, adding that "the eies of all people are uppon us" (*KC*, 121). To orators commemorating Independence Day in the late stages of the Early Republic, however, exceptionalism materializes rather in America's secular achievements. Such secular achievements can be located, as these authors contend, both in the young history of the nation and in its prosperous present.

In Legaré's account, America figures as the very country whose politics and culture are informed by Enlightenment notions in most consistent terms: "*Our* triumphs are the triumphs of *reason* – of happiness – of human nature"

(*KC*, 352). In order to support his conviction that America is by far the most progressive of all nations, the author applies the rhetorical device of hyperbole:

> It is the singular fortune [...] that in the race of moral improvement, which society has been every where running for some centuries past, we have outstript every competitor and have carried our institutions in the sober certainty of waking bliss, to a higher pitch of perfection than ever warmed the dreams of enthusiasm or the speculations of the theorist. (*KC*, 352)

Legaré employs a distinctly exceptionalist rhetoric in passages containing religious expressions and notions. America figures as the home of "the pursuit of happiness upon rational principles," it embodies both "modern science" and "political liberty," and by virtue of its being a separate continent, it is 'detached' from the corrupt world of Europe, "as if it were holy ground" (*KC*, 352). Furthermore, the fact that America was discovered late in the history of mankind appears to be "special providence," for it occurred at a time when "the elect of the earth" had a chance to move across the Atlantic and settle in the New World (*KC*, 353).

To Legaré, America's exceptional status in civil history becomes most visible once the nation's economic and territorial growth is taken into consideration. "Behold how the pomœrium [*sic*] of the republic advances in the wilderness of the West," Legaré proclaims enthusiastically (*KC*, 352). Again, the author adds a religious component to the American experience in renaming the frontier as the *pomerium* of the republic, which used to signify the sacred boundary of the city of Rome in ancient times. Moreover, the author praises "the peaceful triumphs of industry" and "the growth of populous cities" that spread across the American continent (*KC*, 353). Legaré's firm belief in America's progressive potential culminates in his speculative outlook into the near future when the westward movement of civilization will be accomplished and "the language of MILTON shall be spoken from shore to shore" (*KC*, 353).

On a more allusive level, American exceptionalism also functions as the driving ideological force behind Legaré's inclusion of Virgil's famous *Fourth Eclogue*. It must be noted, however, that quoting the line "Novus ab integro sœclorum nascitur ordo" (*KC*, 353; "A new series of the ages begins again") – a free adaptation of the Virgilian verse – is far from innovative in the 1820s. In its shortened form (*Novus ordo seclorum*), the line had been familiar to Americans as an imprint on the reverse of the Great Seal since 1782. Moreover, the Virgilian prophecy appeared as a motto line to a Fourth of July oration as early as 1778.[12] Legaré uses the line in casting a retrospective glance at the revolutionary age. To him, the United States' present prosperity and its striking similarity to a golden age of civilization – the notion of the latter is implied in the Virgilian statement – testify that the 'prophecy' of 1776 has indeed been fulfilled.

---

[12] See Ramsay (1778). The title page of Ramsay's oration contains two well-known prophecies from Virgil's poems. Sections of the oration are reprinted in doc. 133.

Finally, Legaré's Fourth of July oration also takes up the missionary impulse that originally went along with the idea of American exceptionalism. One is reminded of Winthrop's treatise when Legaré praises the "heroes and sages of '76" and speaks of "the example they set to the world" (*KC*, 353). Furthermore, the notion of the United States performing the role of a secular 'redeemer nation' is anticipated when the orator contends: "Many ages of glory and freedom are before us – many nations shall learn, from our example, how to be free and great" (*KC*, 353). In conclusion, then, one has to assert that Legaré's 1823 oration – even if it is silent on the most precarious of all American issues to come, i.e., slavery – already looks ahead to concepts and ideologies that will not gain full momentum before the middle and the end of the nineteenth century: Manifest Destiny and American imperialism (cf. Hietala 2003). Both concepts are continuations and re-articulations of American exceptionalism.

Instructional Strategies and Classroom Issues

I. Key Concepts and Major Themes

1. *Translatio imperii*, *translatio libertatis* (docs. 136, 149, 151-2)
   Translatio imperii derives from biblical history. It explains the course of world history in terms of a rise and fall of the great empires that progress from east to west. In texts written before the Early Republic, *translatio imperii* gave New World settlers the prospective role of a powerful community that would advance the ancient and European heritage of culture and civilization. Political authors of the Early Republic saw the commercial and territorial expansion of the United States as evidence for the actual completion of the westward course of the Old World empires on America's soil. In post-revolutionary America, *translatio imperii* was sometimes modified into *translatio libertatis* recasting America as the home of liberty. By means of allegorizing liberty and thus alluding to the central Roman emblem of republican Libertas, the legacy of classical antiquity in American political thought was emphasized. While former religious meanings of *translatio imperii* gradually faded, secular ideas moved to the center and liberty turned out to be the major theme in the Early Republic's occasional literature.

2. Progress (docs. 149, 155)
   Given the steady territorial growth and the increasing number of the young nation's population, authors of the Early Republic celebrated America's success. First conceived of in rather universal terms as a force of Western civilization, progress is now declared to be an inevitable law conditioning America's particular role in the course of world history. Writers and orators of the Early Republic begin to invent historical genealogies with secularizing impact. By showing that the young republic

stands in line with the great nations of the past, writers draw parallels between the Founding Fathers and the origins of the Roman Republic. They thus make the United States appear to be the leading agent in progressive history that starts with classical antiquity and culminates in the American republic. The idea of progress also serves to interpret the acquisition of Native American land as the result of an inevitable progress of civilization. Many writers portray this process as part of God's providential plan in which the Puritans and their American heirs are to carry out a mission of civilization and territorial expansion.

3. Virtue (docs. 136, 138-9, 141, 149)
To numerous writers of the Early Republic, virtue is a central value or ideal which they regard as the prerequisite for freedom and therefore as vital to the existence of the state. Virtue and freedom are believed to distinguish a republic from other forms of governments, most notably monarchy. In this context, virtue does not refer to private actions but to the citizens' patriotic public responsibility for the republic as a whole. According to Benjamin Rush, this responsibility is rooted in religion and should be acquired by students during their school education (doc. 139). A virtuous citizen is expected to place the public good above his own well-being and thus to be ready to sacrifice his property if a threat to the country makes it necessary. Such a citizen should emulate the exemplary virtue of the Founding Fathers.

4. Exceptionalism (docs. 149, 151)
Exceptionalism has been a key component of America's self-image since the arrival of Puritan settlers in the seventeenth century. Based on a firm belief in America's singularity, exceptionalism implies the conviction that America functions as a model community for other nations around the world. Exceptionalists contrast the advantages and achievements of the United States with the corruption of the older civilizations of Europe.

5. Federalism versus Republicanism (docs. 141-6)
The embittered partisan political conflict between Federalists and Republicans gradually emerged after the ratification of the Federal Constitution in 1788. The two parties were deeply divided upon the question of America's relationship with revolutionary France. Whereas Federalists regarded the aftermath of the French Revolution as a tyranny of the mob which might be transferred to America, the Republicans saw an ideological link between the American cause and the French Revolution and celebrated the latter as a step towards transatlantic democratic order. The Federalists sought to demonize France as well as the Republicans and their leader, 'Francophile' Thomas Jefferson. For Federalists, France functioned as a counter-image to the development of a republican American nation. In 1798, the Federalist-dominated Congress responded to the alleged French

threat by passing four laws known as the Alien and Sedition Acts which made it more difficult for foreigners, especially the Irish, to become American citizens. The Alien and Sedition Acts gave Federalists the power to interpret criticism of the president or the government as sedition. After being elected president in 1800, Jefferson called for a reconciliation of the two parties in his "Inauguration Address" (doc. 144): "We are all republicans – we are federalists" (*KC*, 339). Federalist opposition dissolved after the War of 1812 against Great Britain.

6. Commemoration (docs. 135-153)

   Forging a collective national identity was central to the Early Republic. Confronted with countless coexisting regional, ethnic, political, and religious identities, post-revolutionary authors saw the need to stress national coherence to prevent American society from disintegrating. During that period, political orations and festive poetry represented the commemorative genres which addressed a wide audience in the form of pamphlets, printed speeches, broadsides, and newspapers. Cartoons, engravings, and illustrations were also used to promote a collective iconography. They were specifically designed to re-dedicate the audience to the norms and values of the nation's ancestors. Originating in earlier forms of Puritan filiopietism and the jeremiad, commemoration has been transformed into a general culture practice of national celebrations and annual fetes that are linked to either particular events of the nation's history (Forefather's Day, the Declaration of Independence) or eminent figures such as George Washington.

II. Comparison – Contrasts – Connections

Example: Docs. 136, 138, 140-3, 147-9, 151, 171, 174

A major concern of the Early Republic was the formation of a collective national identity. The documents in the anthology's section "Early Republic," deal with the great merits of the forefathers in the past, the threats and the opportunities of the young republic in the present, and the predicted glorious development of America in the future. While the Founding Fathers conjured up the vision of a strong national union in spite of the former colonies' regional differences, an embittered political conflict between Federalists and Republicans arose after the ratification of the Constitution in 1788.[13]

---

[13] None of the authors of the Early Republic presented in the anthology addresses the issue which, a few decades later, divided the nation even more deeply, namely the institution of slavery (cf. chapter on "Slavery"; *KC*, 553-618). These authors celebrated liberty as a central characteristic of the United States and regarded the Declaration of Independence – which was written by the slaveholder Thomas Jefferson – as the founding document of the nation, but they ignored that the nation denied most African Americans freedom. In his Fourth of July address (doc. 268), the former slave Frederick Douglass demanded that the United

The occasional literature of a nation-wide festive culture, including commemorative orations, political sermons, and Fourth of July odes and speeches, contributed to the formation of an American national identity. On the one hand, authors warned their audiences of the present difficulties and dangers threatening the young republic. Evoking Roman and Greek models, virtue, which included the citizens' willingness to place the common good above private welfare, was portrayed as a core value necessary to preserve the nation. On the other hand, intellectuals of the Early Republic glorified the merits of the forefathers (cf. docs. 143-9, 151) and expressed great optimism about the future growth and strength of America (cf. docs. 136, 138, 140-1).

The veneration of the forefathers, a concept which is central to the formation of any collective identity, helped create foundational myths for the United States which were either based upon the Founding Fathers or, reaching further back in history, upon the Pilgrim Fathers. Both ancestral groups were described as models whose exemplary virtue citizens of the Early Republic should emulate to serve the republic. Among the Founding Fathers, George Washington is the key figure who has been venerated as an icon, a savior of the country, since the 1770s. The fate of the Puritans allowed intellectuals to fulfill the need to construct an older myth of origin reaching back beyond the relatively recent Declaration of Independence. In his Plymouth oration (doc. 149) celebrating the landing of the Puritans, John Quincy Adams attributed the Pilgrims a leading role not only in the course of American history but also in the course of world history. Although Adams underlined the singularity of the Puritans who, he claimed, came to America solely for religious reasons, he placed them in the context of secular world history by drawing a parallel to Rome and its legendary founders. Students should therefore examine the differences and correspondences between the representation of the Pilgrim Fathers and the Founding Fathers and the ways in which authors made use of religious and secular elements in order to commemorate the past.

Adams's emphasis on the Pilgrims' singularity implies that these qualities are also characteristics of their heirs, and, taken in a larger sense, of the United States as a whole. It also reveals another key concept which has been prominent in American political rhetoric since the Early Republic: American exceptionalism (docs. 142-3, 149, 151). American exceptionalism relates to and transforms ideas of divine providence (cf. Obenland in this vol., 100-1), *translatio imperii*, and American imperialism (cf. doc. 319; Mackenthun in this vol., 262-7).

Students can trace these concepts in several texts. In their odes, Thomas Green Fessenden (doc. 147) and John Howard Payne (doc. 148), for instance, intertwine religious and secular images. In doing so, they stress America's singular role by calling special attention to the new nation as being both a future "miniature of

---

States finally live up to the founding principles of the nation by abolishing slavery (cf. Fritsch in this volume, 350-2).

Heaven" (*KC*, 344) and an "Eden of the World" (*KC*, 345). Divine providence has been regarded as America's guide leading the country through difficult times such as the early settlement among 'savages' and the Revolutionary War; it secures the country's future growth as well as its greatness as a future world power. Numerous texts present the history of their young country as a steady and inevitable political, economic, and cultural advancement and predict an increasing population and territorial expansion (cf. doc. 89, 202-3). Others, embracing the notion of *translatio imperii*, believe that the empire has already been transplanted to America due to its westward course or will be so soon, finally turning the country into the "Great Nation of Futurity" (*KC*, 386).

III. Reading and Discussion Questions

1. Which dangers and difficulties threatening the young republic are mentioned in the anthologized documents? Which problems had to be solved? What were the propagated values and ideals which citizens ought to acquire to protect and preserve the state? (cf. docs. 138-43, 149)

2. How did the veneration of the forefathers contribute to the formation of a collective national identity? How did texts and images (e.g. doc. 137) succeed in linking secular and religious traditions?

3. How did John Quincy Adams (doc. 149) and other authors such as John Warren (doc. 138), Thomas Green Fessenden (doc. 147), and John Howard Payne (doc. 148) characterize Native Americans? How did Adams deny the Native Americans' right to the land and justify American territorial expansion? To what extent did his justification of the American expansion into Native American land foreshadow the concept of Manifest Destiny (docs. 171, 174)?

4. The festive oratory of the Early Republic ignores slavery. Compare Hugh Swinton Legaré's "Oration, Delivered on the Fourth of July, 1823" (doc. 151) – or other Fourth of July odes or speeches– with Frederick Douglass's *What to the Slave Is the Fourth of July?* (doc. 268).

5. Explain the conflict between Federalists and Republicans and Thomas Jefferson's role in this confrontation (cf. docs. 141-2, 144, 147, 152). Also refer to the satirical pictures directed against Jefferson (docs. 145-6). How did Jefferson convey and defend his belief in the strength of the government (cf. doc. 144)?

6. In the Early Republic, the concept of American exceptionalism was often promoted by contrasting America as a shining model of peaceful democracy with a corrupt Europe, especially with Britain and France. Show how different authors described that contrast and made use of it (cf. docs. 136, 138, 141-3).

IV. Resources

a. Recommended Reading

Robert A. Ferguson. *Reading the Early Republic*. Cambridge: Harvard University Press, 2006. Drawing on a wide range of works, Ferguson's study offers readings of several different kinds of sources, including novels, pamphlets, journals, legal records, and slave narratives. The book focuses attention on the forgotten dynamism of rebellion, slavery, and treason in the founding era.

Paul E. Johnson. *The Early American Republic, 1789-1829*. New York: Oxford University Press, 2007. Focusing on the politics and process of nation-making, the book illustrates the formative years of American nationhood, democracy, and free-market capitalism. The book explores such topics as family life, religion, the construction and reconstruction of gender systems, the rise of popular print and other forms of communication, and evolving attitudes toward slavery and race. It also covers the social history of market society, territorial expansion, and the growth of slavery.

Jeffrey L. Pasley, Andrew W. Robertson, and David Waldstreicher, eds. *Beyond the Founders: New Approaches to the Political History of the Early American Republic*. Chapel Hill: University of North Carolina Press, 2004. The collection of essays proposes new directions for the study of the political history of the American republic before 1830. The volume is very much inspired by new cultural and social histories. It argues that the early history of the United States was not just the product of a few Founding Fathers, but was also marked by widespread popular involvement, political conflicts and influences that crossed lines of race, gender, and class.

Dietmar Schloss. *Die tugendhafte Republik: Politische Ideologie und Literatur in der amerikanischen Gründerzeit*. Heidelberg: Winter, 2003. The book's central thesis is that the Early Republic is not primarily characterized by a certain structure of institutions, but by a moral disposition, namely, virtue. It is an indispensable study for all students interested in the relationship between literature and Early Republican civic culture.

David Waldstreicher. *In the Midst of Perpetual Fetes: The Making of American Nationalism, 1776-1820*. Chapel Hill: University of North Carolina Press, 1997. This innovative study investigates the importance of political festivals in the Early Republic. Drawing on newspapers, broadsides, diaries, and letters, Waldstreicher shows how Americans in the Early Republic worked out their political differences by creating patriotic celebrations, and, in so doing, helped connect local politics to national identity. Examining these celebrations, the study explores the interplay of region, race, class, and gender in the development of a national identity.

Gordon Wood. *The Radicalism of the American Revolution*. New York: Knopf, 1992. This compelling study surveys the formative years of the United States. It traces the transformation of disparate and quarreling colonies into the Early Republic. Wood puts major emphasis on the social forces that changed American society in the years between 1760 and 1820. The book demonstrates how a monarchical and ordered society became a liberal and commercial one, in which the concept of equality, democracy, and private interest caused the democratization of the American mind.

b. Works Cited and Reading Suggestions

Baldwin, Simeon (1788). *An Oration Pronounced Before the Citizens of New-Haven, July 4th, 1788*. New Haven: J. Meigs.
Bhabha, Homi K., ed. (1990). *Nation and Narration*. London: Routledge.
Bolingbroke, Henry St. John (1997). *The Idea of a Patriot King*. 1738. *Political Writings*. Ed. David Armitage. Cambridge: Cambridge University Press, 217-294.
Bozeman, Theodore Dwight (1988). *To Live Ancient Lives: The Primitivist Dimension in Puritanism*. Chapel Hill: University of North Carolina Press.
Dearborn, Henry Alexander S. (1806). *An Oration, Delivered at Salem, on the Fourth of July, 1806*. Salem: Register Office.
Ferguson, Robert A. (2006). *Reading the Early Republic*. Cambridge: Harvard University Press.
Hannemann, Dennis (2008). *Klassische Antike und amerikanische Identitätskonstruktion: Untersuchungen zu Festreden der Revolutionszeit und der frühen Republik, 1770-1815*. Paderborn: Schöningh.
Hebel, Udo J. (1999). "The Forefathers' Day Celebrations of 1802 and the Enactment of Federalist Constructions of the American Republic." *The Construction and Contestation of American Cultures and Identities in the Early National Period*. Ed. Udo J. Hebel. Heidelberg: Winter, 303-330.
Hickey, Donald R. (1989). *The War of 1812: A Forgotten Conflict*. Urbana: University of Illinois Press.
Hietala, Thomas R. (2003). *Manifest Design: American Exceptionalism and Empire*. Rev. ed. Ithaca: Cornell University Press.
Horn, James P. P., Jan Ellen Lewis, and Peter S. Onuf, eds. (2002). *The Revolution of 1800: Democracy, Race, and the New Republic*. Charlottesville: University of Virginia Press.
Hurm, Gerd (2001). "Nationales Urgestein: *Plymouth Rock*, die Pilger und der amerikanische Bürgerkrieg." *Geschichtsbilder und Gründungsmythen*. Ed. Hans-Joachim Gehrke. Würzburg: Ergon, 229-244.
Johnson, Paul E. (2007). *The Early American Republic, 1789-1829*. New York: Oxford University Press.
Lubbers, Klaus (1994). "Modelle nationaler Identität in amerikanischer Literatur und Kunst, 1776-1893." *Nationales Bewußtsein und kollektive Identität: Stu-

dien zur Entwicklung des kollektiven Bewußtseins in der Neuzeit. Ed. Helmut Berding. Frankfurt/M.: Suhrkamp, 82-111.

Newman, Simon P. (2000). *Parades and the Politics of the Street: Festive Culture in the Early American Republic*. Philadelphia: University of Pennsylvania Press.

Nora, Pierre (1989). "Between Memory and History: Les Lieux de Mémoire." *Representations* 26, 7-24.

Pasley, Jeffrey L., Andrew W. Robertson, and David Waldstreicher, eds. (2004). *Beyond the Founders: New Approaches to the Political History of the Early American Republic*. Chapel Hill: University of North Carolina Press.

Porter, Robert (1791). *An Oration, To Commemorate the Independence of the United States of North-America*. Philadelphia: T. Dobson.

Ramsay, David, (1778). *An Oration on the Advantages of American Independence*, Charleston: John Wells jun.

Scheiding, Oliver (2003). *Geschichte und Fiktion: Zum Funktionswandel des frühen amerikanischen Romans*. Paderborn: Schöningh.

Schloss, Dietmar (2003). *Die tugendhafte Republik: Politische Ideologie und Literatur in der amerikanischen Gründerzeit*. Heidelberg: Winter.

Seelye, John (1998). *Memory's Nation: The Place of Plymouth Rock*. Chapel Hill: University of North Carolina Press.

Sharp, James Roger. (1995). *American Politics in the Early Republic: The New Nation in Crisis*. New Haven: Yale University Press.

Shields, John C. (2001). *The American Aeneas: Classical Origins of the American Self*. Knoxville: University of Tennessee Press.

Silverman, Kenneth (1987). *A Cultural History of the American Revolution*. 1976. New York: Columbia University Press.

Smelser, Marshall (1958). "The Federalist Period as an Age of Passion." *American Quarterly* 10, 391-419.

Travers, Len (1997). *Celebrating the Fourth: Independence Day and the Rites of Nationalism in the Early Republic*. Amherst: University of Massachusetts Press.

Waldstreicher, David (1997). *In the Midst of Perpetual Fetes: The Making of American Nationalism, 1776-1820*. Chapel Hill: University of North Carolina Press.

Wood, Gordon S. (1988). "The Significance of the Early Republic." *Journal of the Early Republic* 8, 1-20.

– (1992). *The Radicalism of the American Revolution*. New York: Knopf.

GESA MACKENTHUN

Expansionism

> We talk of accomplishing our destiny. So did the late conqueror of Europe; and destiny consigned him to a lonely rock in the ocean, the prey of an ambition which destroyed no peace but his own.
> William E. Channing, "A Letter to the Hon. Henry Clay" (*KC*, 385)

> The white man made us many promises, but he kept only one. He promised to take our land and he took it.
> Mahpiya Luta, Lakota (in Churchill 1993, 113)

> Will it not go on, this epic of civilization, this destiny of the races, until at last and at the ultimate end of all, we who now arrogantly boast ourselves as Americans, supreme in conquest, whether of battle-ship or of bridge-building, may realize that the true patriotism is the brotherhood of man and know the whole world is our nation and simple humanity our countrymen?
> Frank Norris, "The Frontier Gone at Last" (*KC*, 422)

I. Themes and Arguments

The term "expansionism" conjures up different critical narratives: first, a description of the process of the territorial expansion of the United States in the nineteenth century; secondly, a wider description of American imperial attitudes from its inception as a nation until today; and thirdly, a description of the *ideology* that accompanies either of these processes. The present essay will engage all three of these narratives, with an emphasis on the last one. As the section on expansionism in the anthology is limited to documents written between 1789 and 1914, I will make only passing reference to the long prehistory of the concept of westward expansion (cf. Hannemann, Scheiding, Stievermann in this vol.) and concentrate on the nineteenth century and the documents testifying to continental expansion in North America. However, my account of the particular arguments generated in that period, whether in favor or critical of expansion, will necessarily pay tribute to the significance of expansionism as an ideology that both precedes and survives the specific period covered here – a period whose beginning may be identified with the Louisiana Purchase of 1803 and which is usually thought to have terminated with the "closing" of the frontier in the 1890s. In foregrounding the ideological nature of expansionism, this essay will occasionally make reference to a wider geographical area than the continent of North America, to which some historians still limit the process of expansion.

An investigation of expansionism as an ideology reveals the difficulty of limiting it both temporally and geographically. It also suggests a conceptual affinity between "expansionism" and "imperialism" on the one hand and between "expansionism" and "internal colonialism" on the other. While Hartmut Keil distinguishes between the former two by referring to American expansionism as an "anticipated imperialism" (1991, 69), many scholars of American expansionism agree that the field of investigation should not remain limited to the continent and the process of western settlement but that, as the same ideology was deployed in the hemispheric and transoceanic schemes of the United States, those areas (like Mesoamerica, the Caribbean, and the Pacific) should also be included in a study of expansionism (cf. van Alstyne 1960, 100; Keil 1991, 82-4; Sundquist 2006). The distinction between "expansionism" and "internal colonialism" is more difficult: It may best be discussed in the context of America's acquisition of the Louisiana territory and the definition of its legal relationship to the indigenous inhabitants of the land to be settled.

As a process, the westward expansion of the United States beyond the geographical boundary line of the Mississippi River began with the Louisiana Purchase of 1803. Through this contract with France, the United States acquired for the sum of 15,000,000 US dollars a huge area of almost 900,000 square miles, extending from today's Montana to Louisiana and from Colorado to Minnesota. Practically overnight the territory of the United States increased by 140 percent. Most of this gigantic area was unsettled by Europeans, and much of it was uncharted, with the important exception of New Orleans: Jefferson originally sought only the acquisition of New Orleans because of its strategic location between the internal trade route of continental North America and the Gulf of Mexico, but Napoleon surprised him by offering the whole of Louisiana to the United States. Originally claimed by France, Louisiana had changed owners when it was ceded to Spain in a secret treaty in 1762; it had only recently been retroceded to France by Spain in 1802.[1] Though it was legally purchased by the United

---

[1] Louisiana had originally been claimed for France by the explorer Sieur de La Salle in 1682 and declared a crown colony in 1731. In 1762, France ceded the area to Spain in exchange for the Duchy of Parma after having lost the Seven Years War. Louisiana remained Spanish until 1801 when it was returned to France. Meanwhile, Napoleon had lost interest in the American possessions, especially because of the painful defeat of French troops in trying to suppress the Haitian Revolution. Ironically, the first successful rebellion against colonial

States from Napoleonic France, the property rights to Louisiana may seem dubious if considered from a non-European perspective. Neither Spain nor France had undertaken any systematic settlement of the vast territory, with the exception of New Orleans and a few other trade stations alongside the Mississippi River. Though claimed, ceded, and sold between three different European countries, the largest part of Louisiana was effectively inhabited and controlled by various Native tribes who, of course, had neither known of nor agreed to the transactions. According to the law of nations, Louisiana "belonged" to France by the right of discovery, but this only meant that it was claimed vis-à-vis other European powers. It had not been properly taken into possession according to contemporary European standards – by being subjected to human labor, husbandry, and cultivation (cf. Scheiding in this vol., 12-3).

This difference between laying claim to a tract of land under the doctrine of discovery and taking possession of it was pointed out in 1823 by Chief Justice Marshall in *Johnson v. McIntosh*, the first of a series of US Supreme Court rulings seeking to regulate and legitimate the removal of Native American tribes to the Indian Territory west of the Mississippi. Here Marshall writes that the discovery of territory in the New World entitled European nations to "an exclusive right to extinguish the Indian title of occupancy, either by purchase or by conquest" and that "discovery gave title to the government by whose subjects, or by whose authority, it was made, against all other European governments, *which title might be consummated by possession*" (in Williams 1990, 313; emphasis mine). The semblance of legality established by multiple transactions between various European powers – a legality that was never questioned either by those powers or by most historians – perfectly illustrates the monological character of colonial discourse. As Albert Weinberg correctly points out, the United States was left with the problem of dealing with the "native" inhabitants of Louisiana – but ironically and symptomatically, he only refers to the French Creole population of New Orleans (1963, 33-5). American historiography of western settlement and expansion up to the present blatantly ignores the fact that the Louisiana Territory was, in terms of international legal principles shared by the US Supreme Court, only to be gradually brought into American possession either by voluntary cession or by conquest – that is, either by contracts of purchase or by waging a "defensive" war against the indigenous inhabitants of the American West.[2]

In a second Supreme Court ruling, Chief Justice Marshall further defined the relationship between the United States government and the native inhabitants. In *Cherokee Nation v. Georgia* (1831), he explores the paradox between regarding the Indian tribes as "foreign nations" according to international legal stan-

---

slavery paved the way for the expansion of slavery in North America and the rise of the United States as an imperial nation.

[2] For discussions of the legal background of American colonization and settlement, see Hanke (1965) and Pagden (1995).

dards on the one hand and the title claims made by the United States to their lands on the other. He writes:

> Though the Indians are acknowledged to have an unquestionable, and, heretofore, unquestioned, right to the lands they occupy, until that right shall be extinguished by a voluntary cession to our government; yet it may well be doubted, whether those tribes which reside within the acknowledged boundaries of the United States can, with accuracy, be denominated foreign nations. They may, more correctly, perhaps, be denominated domestic dependent nations. They occupy a territory to which we assert a title independent of their will, which must take effect in point of possession, when their right of possession ceases. Meanwhile they are in a state of pupilage. Their relation to the United States resembles that of a ward to his guardian. (*KC*, 378)

The secret resides in the term "meanwhile," which seeks to rhetorically bridge the chasm between Marshall's assertion of Indian sovereignty and the claims of the United States to their lands. Of course, the Five Civilized Tribes whose rights were being debated here were not ready to part with their lands and move west "voluntarily." The "state of pupilage" was accordingly established rhetorically rather than legally. Ever since the times of Andrew Jackson, the discourse of Indian-white relations was dominated by the trope of paternalistic care, expressed in the childish description of the American president as the Indians' "Great White Father" (cf. Rogin 1975). This act of rhetorical domestication and infantilization is condensed in the legal term which Marshall coined for defining the status of indigenous tribes within the borders of the United States: He refers to them as "domestic dependent nations" – an oxymoron, as domestic dependency is incommensurate with national sovereignty.

The occasion for Marshall's definition was a suit brought to the Supreme Court by the Cherokee Nation in their attempt to avoid the removal from their lands that had been decreed by the Indian Removal Act in 1830. The denomination of Indians as "domestic dependent nations" thus derives from a conflict between one of the Five Civilized Tribes and the State of Georgia within whose borders it resided. Yet the definition would continue to be used for all Indian tribes west of the Mississippi as well. Marshall, who strongly antagonized Jackson's ruthless expansionism, was apparently aware of the inconsistency between American Indian policy and international legal standards, but in *Cherokee Nation v. Georgia* he denied the responsibility of the US Supreme Court to decide the case: "If it be true, that the Cherokee nation have rights, this is not the tribunal in which those rights are to be asserted. If it be true, that wrongs have been inflicted, and that still greater are to be apprehended, *this is not the tribunal which can redress the past or prevent the future*" (*KC*, 378; emphasis mine).[3]

---

[3] A similar historical determinism was already expressed in his ruling *Johnson v. McIntosh* (1823), where Marshall writes: "However extravagant the pretension of converting the discovery of an inhabited country into conquest may appear; if the principle has been asserted in the first instance, and afterwards sustained, if a country has been acquired and held under it; if

Although the ruling of 1831 was followed in 1833 by a third one, *Worcester v. Georgia*, in which Marshall departed from the logic of domesticity and historical determinism and even granted Indian nations the status of "extraterritoriality" to state law (Wilkinson 1987, 30), the definition of Indian tribes as "domestic dependent nations" has determined the legal status of Native Americans ever since. The "Marshall trilogy" is symptomatic of the moral dilemma to which the humanistically inspired intelligentsia of the United States was subject. President Jackson, who was more of a sentimentalist than a humanist (cf. doc. 162), ignored such moral and legalistic quibbles and enforced the Cherokee Removal in 1838, which entered history books as the "Trail of Tears" because thousands of people lost their lives during this mass exodus.

Any discussion of the territorial expansion of the United States since 1803 in terms of "internal colonialism" thus misses the fact that the territory to be traversed and settled west of the Mississippi was – according to the very definition of property by which European colonial discourse denied a right of property to America's indigenous inhabitants – not "internal" to the United States at all (cf. Rowe 2000, 5-6). To speak of the process of western expansion as an act of "internal colonialism" consequently amounts to accepting the symbolic rituals of possession by cession, retrocession, and purchase enacted between various European and Euro-American colonial powers.[4] It accepts the logic of domestication initiated in the Jacksonian era. Perhaps the most convincing evidence for the recognition that the vast territory of Louisiana was considered *external* to the United States is the fact that more than a hundred treaties for the cession of property were entered between the United States and western Indian tribes. A government would hardly feel pressed to form treaties with its own "wards."

The physical process of western expansion by the United States was inaugurated directly after the Louisiana Purchase by the expedition of Lewis and Clark (1804-1805) who were sent by Jefferson to find a land route to the Pacific. Their westward journey ended on the mouth of the Columbia River where the German immigrant John Jacob Astor established a trade station, Astoria, in 1811. Envisioned by Astor and Jefferson as an *entrepôt* between the continental land route and the transpacific route to Asia, Astoria was destroyed by the British one year later (cf. Ronda 1990). All governmental schemes at western exploration since Jefferson's presidency were primarily aimed at opening a trade route to Asia.[5]

---

the property of the great mass of the community originates in it, it becomes the law of the land and cannot be questioned" (in Williams 1990, 316).

[4] On narratives and rituals of (dis)possession in early colonial discourse about America, see Hulme (1986), Seed (1995), and Mackenthun (1997).

[5] As early as 1783, Jefferson had encouraged the American adventurer John Ledyard to try to find an overland route to the Pacific Northwest. Unable to raise the funds for such a venture, Ledyard instead crossed Europe on foot all the way to Siberia in 1787/1788, where he was imprisoned as a spy. While subsequently embarking on a trip to Central Africa under the auspices of the Royal Society of London, he died in Cairo (cf. Johnson 1966, 466; Ledyard 2005).

After the withdrawal of France from continental America, the defeat of the British in the War of 1812 removed the only other major contender for territorial expansion south of the Canadian border. In quick succession, the United States now acquired extensive territories by purchase, annexation, violent dispossession, and war: Florida was ceded by Spain in the Adams-Onís Treaty of 1819, and the area east of the Mississippi was cleared of most of its indigenous inhabitants by 1838. The Indian Removal, justified by Andrew Jackson in the language of sentimentalism (*KC*, 374-6) and defended against heavy criticism both in the United States and Europe by Lewis Cass (*KC*, 370-4), was followed by the annexation of Texas under the presidency of James Polk in 1845 (*KC*, 389-94), the almost simultaneous reception of the Oregon territory from Britain by contract in 1846 (*KC*, 379-81), and the acquisition of the vast tract of land that fell to the United States as a result of the Mexican War of 1846 to 1848 (today's California, Arizona, New Mexico, Utah, and Nevada). Thus, by 1860 the United States had brought itself into the possession of the northern continent (with the exception of Canada and Mexico), and by the end of the nineteenth century, its present territorial extent was accomplished. The process was completed by the purchase of Alaska from Russia in 1867, the annexation of Hawaii in 1898, and of Puerto Rico and the Philippines as a result of the Spanish-American War of 1898.

To actually *possess* the land thus acquired on paper, United States troops began to wage a long and bloody war against the indigenous peoples of North America. They were aided in this scheme by vast numbers of settlers who began a massive movement across the continent, both to establish farms under the Homestead Act of 1862 and to move on to California, where gold had been discovered in 1848. One by one, the great Indian tribes of the western plains and the southwest were defeated during this military offensive, which had started during the Civil War and increased after 1865. The tactics ranged from benevolent paternalistic rhetoric and promises of a better life as farmers on the mostly infertile reservations to blatant violations of international codes of justice and rules of war. Of the many massacres committed, Sand Creek (1862) and Wounded Knee (1890) stand out as the most brutal. In 1884, after most tribes had been driven onto reservations where they continued to be decimated by starvation, disease, and broken hearts, the Lakota chief Mahpiya Luta (Red Cloud) summarized the attitude of the United States by saying: "The white man made us many promises, but he kept only one. He promised to take our land and he took it" (in Churchill 1993, 113).

The settlement of the West and the war against the Indians were aided by the completion of the transcontinental railway in 1869, whose global significance as an international trade route Walt Whitman aptly celebrated in his poem "Passage to India" by comparing it with the completion of the Suez Canal in the same year (doc. 181). Whitman's poem reminds us in heroic rhythms that ever since the times of Jefferson and even Columbus, the ultimate aim of expansion was to find a navigable route to the markets of Asia:

> Passage to India!
> Lo, soul, seest thou not God's purpose from the first?
> The earth to be spann'd, connected by network,
> The races, neighbors, to marry and be given in marriage,
> The oceans to be cross'd, the distant brought near,
> The lands to be welded together.
>
> A worship new I sing,
> You captains, voyagers, explorers, yours,
> You engineers, you architects, machinists, yours,
> You, not for trade or transportation only,
> But in God's name, and for thy sake O soul.
> 			(Whitman 1978, 128-9)

Continental expansion, then, must be viewed within a larger context of transoceanic commercial expansion. The dominant historical narrative, which was first molded by the Monroe Doctrine and later reiterated by the mythology of the West propagated by Frederick Jackson Turner, and which views the United States as a continental nation with its western border limited by the Pacific, has recently undergone some revision. Another, less isolationist view has gained ascendancy, and scholars now foreground American designs and military activities in the Caribbean and Mesoamerica (attempts of so-called filibusters to gain control of Cuba, the isthmus at Nicaragua, and later Panama) and contradict the long-held thesis that the United States had not been an imperial nation until the late 1890s, when American troops backed the annexation of Hawaii and conquered the Philippines (cf. Kaplan and Pease 1993; Sundquist 2006).

The most powerful propagator of a continentalist narrative of American expansion is Frederick Jackson Turner. In a famous speech delivered at the World's Columbian Exposition in Chicago in 1893 and later published as "The Significance of the Frontier in American History" (doc. 185), Turner declared the frontier as "closed" while at the same time emphasizing its great mythical power in the forging of an American character and of American values such as democracy, individualism, inquisitiveness, inventiveness, materialism, and nervous restlessness, together with an inborn capacity to regenerate these character traits out of a continuous contest with the primitive forces of the wilderness. Surrounded by the neoclassicist plaster buildings of the White City – itself a symbolic mixture of Roman antiquity and the Puritans' long-sought "City upon a Hill" – Turner claims that America has continually reasserted the most advanced stages of civilization through its "continuous touch with the simplicity of primitive society" (*KC*, 415). Through this perennial battle against savagery, the "land which has no history reveals luminously the course of universal history":

> The United States lies like a huge page in the history of society. Line by line as we read this continental page from West to East we find the record of social evolution. It begins with the Indian and hunter; it goes on to tell of the disintegration of savagery by the entrance of the trader, the path-finder of civilization; we read the annals of the

pastoral stage in ranch life; the exploitation of the soil by the raising of unrotated crops [...]; the intensive culture of the denser farm settlements; and finally the manufacturing organization with city and factory system. (Turner 1995, 63)

Turner here projects a stadialist account of the development of human culture on a map of North America – from the primitive stage through pastoralism and agriculturalism to the manufacturing and industrial stages, suggesting that the American settlers have been forced again and again to race through those various stages at lightning speed.[6] It is through this constant clash of vastly different cultural levels, Turner claims, that America has forged its very peculiar character as a nation at once savage and highly civilized. Richard Slotkin would later refer to the same process as a "regeneration through violence" (1973), while Richard Drinnon follows suit and speaks of a "metaphysics of empire building and Indian hating" (1980). We may remark, in accordance with Gregory Nobles, the conspicuous absence in Turner's account of any reference to the recent "closing" of the frontier which culminated in the final defeat of the last free Indian bands – Geronimo's surrender in 1886 and the massacre of Big Foot's Minneconjou band at Wounded Knee just after Christmas, 1890. By this time, as Turner could read in the very population census which he used for his speech, the Indian population in the United States had reached its lowest point. Another instrument in sealing the "closing" of the frontier was the General Allotment or Dawes Act of 1887, which split up reservation lands into small private allotments or family homesteads of 160 acres a piece and thus paved the way for white settlers who bought up the lands and disrupted the tribal land base (cf. Nobles 1997, 241-2). As Turner's map-and-book metaphor reveals, his view of history tended to regard such discrete historical events within the context of a grander design – what he calls the "universal course of history," or what Whitman calls "God's purpose."

II. The Providential Narrative of Empire

After this account of the major events of the process of continental expansion, the second part of the essay will trace some of the ideological narratives, or ideologemes, deployed in rationalizing and legitimating that process. Albert Weinberg correctly speaks of a "motley body of justificatory doctrines" which frequently come into logical conflict with each other (1963, 2). Like all legitimating strategies, those used in the context of American expansion tend to contradict each other, especially as they become more numerous. In attempting to steer a straight course through this ideological thicket, the following analysis will limit itself to four major strategies: first, the providential narrative of the westward course of empire; second, the argument of legitimate action by the law of "nature";

---

[6] For a superb aestheticization of the stadialist theory of empire, see the cycle *The Course of Empire* by Thomas Cole (1833-1836), discussed below (cf. section "Comparison – Contrasts – Connections," 269-72, and *KC* web site).

third, the argument of geography and archaeology – or what Weinberg (1963, chap. 2) calls "geographical predestination"; and fourth, the argument of biological determinism and racial superiority.

"It is well known that empire has been travelling from east to west," Jedidiah Morse was able to assert in 1789 (*KC*, 362). Indeed, the notion of the westward course of empire had, by the nineteenth century, become a stock item of expansionist rhetoric. We can find it, for instance, in the excerpt from Henry David Thoreau's *Walden*. "And that way the nation is moving, and I may say that mankind progresses from east to west," he writes (*KC*, 369), and later he directly adapts from George Berkeley's poem "On the Prospect of Planting Arts and Learning in America" (1752) the famous line, "Westward the star of empire takes its way" (cf. *KC*, 32, 370; footnote 11, 232). We find the same line in John Quincy Adams's oration of 1802 (*KC*, 349), as well as in John Fiske's essay on "Manifest Destiny" of 1885, this time with a racial inflection: "The race thus spread over both hemispheres [...] from the rising to the setting sun" (*KC*, 413). More examples could be quoted. Berkeley's prediction was that, after the passing of the first four "acts" of human history, the fifth act "shall close the Drama with the Day; / Time's noblest Offspring is the last" (*KC*, 32). As Peter Freese, Anthony Pagden, and many others have shown, the trope of the westward course of empire derives from a specifically Judaeo-Christian philosophy of world history according to which the arts and sciences, together with the "light" of Christianity, move from east to west. The historical roots of this ideologeme of "ex oriente lux" are difficult to determine; most likely it has various origins, both secular and ecclesiastical. An early key text establishing this powerful mythology is the *Fourth Eclogue* of Virgil (c. 42-39 BC), with its promise of a future new golden age. Freese and Pagden trace the notion of *translatio imperii* back to the Book of Daniel (cf. Stievermann in this vol., 125), where Daniel, after describing the four empires of antiquity, prophesies a fifth and final empire "which shall never be destroyed: and the kingdom shall not be left to other people, *but* it shall break in pieces and consume all these kingdoms, and it shall stand for ever" (Dan. 2.44; original emphasis, in Carroll and Brickett 1995, 971; cf. Pagden 1995, 42)

Frances Yates shows the transformation of that trope as the master narrative of Western empire since the time of the unification of the Roman empire with a Christian eschatological worldview during the reign of Constantine the Great (c. 280-337), the first Roman emperor to convert to Christianity (1975, 34-5). As Yates shows in a stunning analysis of imperial iconography and the writings of the early modern European national epics by Ariost and Spenser, the trope was used by the Spanish emperor Charles the Great before it migrated to Elizabethan England (cf. Scheiding in this vol., 8-9). In America, the myth forms a fusion between its secular branch and its decidedly theological branch introduced to

America by the Puritans, who viewed themselves as God's chosen people.[7] The Puritan sense of divine electedness, which is the germ of American intellectual exceptionalism, is derived from their typological interpretation of history as a repetition of biblical events: the Puritan errand into the wilderness was viewed as a repetition of Israel's migration to the "promised land" of Canaan (cf. Obenland in this vol., 101-10; Stievermann, 134-5). Read allegorically, the errand became the dominant trope for a metaphysical struggle between the powers of light and darkness – a legacy of Calvinistic dualism that has permeated American political rhetoric ever since. At the same time, the notion of the errand became a powerful political allegory for expansion. As Albert Weinberg argues in what is still the best analysis of the concept of Manifest Destiny, the Puritan sense of special mission was inherited by the Founding Fathers and quickly developed into a "dogma of special delegation" (1963, 39). The notion of Americans as God's chosen people was particularly promoted by Thomas Jefferson, who had originally proposed that the national seal of the United States should represent the people of Israel led into the promised land by a pillar of light. Many American political leaders felt justified in their view of their nation's "destiny" by several earthly signs of success – independence from Britain, the successful establishment of a democratic republic (many of whose key items were later adopted by France and other republics) – and they tended to read these accomplishments as divine or providential signs or dispensations (cf. Weinberg 1963, 39). By the time Melville expressed this idea through the voice of White Jacket in his novel of the same title (1850), those divine signs had become only too manifest: He regards the process of expansion by purchase, war, and annexation itself as a "dispensation" that

> we Americans are the peculiar, chosen people – the Israel of our time; we bear the ark of the liberties of the world. Seventy years ago we escaped from thrall; and, besides our first birth-right – embracing one continent of earth – God has given to us, for a future inheritance, the broad domains of the political pagans. [...] The rest of the nations must soon be in our rear. We are the pioneers of the world; the advance-guard, sent on through the wilderness of untried things, to break a new path in the New World that is ours. (*KC*, 404-5)

The quotation fuses the providential thinking inherited from Puritanism with the aggressive jingoism of the period after Mexico's defeat. The quote then reinscribes the expansionist project into the biblical narrative of St. John's Revelation when White Jacket refers to Americans as the "political Messiah" (405). It is difficult to tell how much Melville himself identified with this position – he had

---

[7] The Puritans had been preceded by Christopher Columbus who, late in his life, plowed the Bible for announcements of his discovery and assembled all "prophetic" references to his deed in his *Libro de las Profecías* (written 1502-1504). The secular branch of the myth was evoked by the early national poets of the United States Joel Barlow, Philip Freneau, and Timothy Dwight, and later by Walt Whitman in his poem "Passage to India," which emphasizes the myth's civilizational aspect, i.e., the perfection in the arts, in scientific exploration, and engineering.

severely criticized both European and American imperialism before in *Typee* and would do so again in *Moby-Dick* (cf. my Introduction to the section "Expansionism" in *KC*, 359-61). White Jacket's words reiterate the tone of John L. O'Sullivan, editor of the *Democratic Review*, who in 1845 coined the term "manifest destiny" in an essay propagating the annexation of Texas (doc. 171). Like many of his contemporaries, he argues that Texas must be "saved" from being taken by rival nations whose intention it was to limit and check "the fulfillment of our manifest destiny to overspread the continent allotted by Providence for the free development of our yearly multiplying millions" (*KC*, 389). Thus was born the powerful expansionist slogan, according to which the incorporation into the United States of all adjacent lands was legitimate since it was the fulfillment of a historical destiny devised long ago by providence itself (cf. Weinberg 1963, 1-2).

O'Sullivan and the other promoters of annexation argued on more grounds than simply God's will. The short quotation above contains the argument of security: Texas was to be annexed to prevent European imperial contenders from doing so and thereby endangering American democratic values with their monarchic presence. Another argument O'Sullivan uses is that of population growth: America has to expand because the ever-growing tide of immigrants cannot be stilled or crowded into the existing territory. Both arguments belong to the larger complex of legitimating expansion on the grounds of "nature" – the natural layout of the land or natural phenomena like population growth.

From 1845, the concept of "manifest destiny" began its triumphal march through the political writings of American expansionists. It reflects a providential theory of history, inherited from earlier Puritanical discourse (cf. Obenland in this vol., 89-95), which is surprisingly incompatible with other key American concepts – that of individual liberty, free will, and self-government. "Destiny" apparently leaves little room for individuals to shape the course of history; the individual is rather the pawn and instrument of an inscrutable metaphysical will. While the ideology of Manifest Destiny denies agency to the individual, it is readily invoked by ambitious individuals against the voice of morality and reason. Thus, William Channing refers to the plan to annex Texas and expand the territory of the United States into an area presently held by Mexico as a "crime" and to the ideology of Manifest Destiny as a justification for rapaciousness (*KC*, 385), and he sarcastically adds: "We talk of accomplishing our destiny. So did the late conqueror of Europe; and destiny consigned him to a lonely rock in the ocean, the prey of an ambition which destroyed no peace but his own." Channing's pessimistic vision of possible catastrophic results of American expansion was translated to the canvas by Thomas Cole in his painting cycle "The Course of Empire" (1833-1836).

III. The Expansionist Law of Nature

O'Sullivan's reference to the forces of nature evoke a second narrative used for the justification of continental expansion, perhaps best articulated by John

Quincy Adams in his oration delivered at Plymouth in 1802 (just one year before the Louisiana Purchase; cf. Hannemann in this vol., 229-33). "The Indian right of possession," Adams contends, stands "upon a questionable foundation":

> Their cultivated fields; their constructed habitations; a space of ample sufficiency for their subsistence, and whatever they had annexed to themselves by personal labor, was undoubtedly by the laws of nature theirs. But what is the right of a huntsman to the forest of a thousand miles over which he has accidentally ranged in quest of prey? Shall the liberal bounties of Providence to the race of man be monopolized by one of ten thousand for whom they were created? Shall the exuberant bosom of the common mother, amply adequate to the nourishment of millions, be claimed exclusively by a few hundreds of her offspring? [...] Shall he doom an immense region of the globe to perpetual desolation [...]? Shall the fields and the vallies, which a beneficent God has formed to teem with the life of innumerable multitudes, be condemned to everlasting barrenness? [...] No, generous philanthropists! Heaven has not been thus inconsistent in the works of its hands! Heaven has not thus placed at irreconcileable strife, its moral laws with its physical creation. (*KC*, 347)

Adams goes on to refer to the particularly fortunate situation of the Puritans in New England, who occupied lands that had previously been vacated by the native tribes because of the ravages of terrible epidemics the colonizers introduced to America. While Adams is at first aware that Indians too practice agriculture, he then argues that the native inhabitants were predominantly hunters whose lifestyle would render the land "barren" and "desolate" while egotistically depriving millions of immigrants of their deserved subsistence. Adams resorts to the well-known civilizational narrative organized around the dualistic construct of culture versus nature (teeming valleys versus everlasting desolation), in which an economy based on hunting is subsumed under the rubric of 'nature.' In a commentary on the debate over the doctrine of discovery, Supreme Court Judge Joseph Story would use the same idea in asserting that all Indians were hunters and savages. "The title of the Indians," he writes,

> was not treated [in European legal discourse] as a right of property and dominion, but as a mere right of occupancy. As infidels, heathens, and savages, they were not allowed to possess the prerogatives belonging to absolute, sovereign, and independent nations. The territory over which they wandered, and which they used for this temporary and fugitive purpose, was, in respect to Christians, deemed as if it were inhabited only by brute animals. (in Williams 1990, 316)

This comment evokes the justificatory arguments used by an earlier generation of colonizers, rooted in the Lockean notion of possessive individualism. "In the beginning," writes Locke in his *The Second Treatise of Government* (1993, 285), "all the world was America." The "Americans" (i.e., Indians), "for want of improving [the land] by labour," lack the conveniences of civilized nations. Although they live in a "fruitful territory," they are "clad worse than a day-labourer in England" (281). While anticipating Adams in arguing that the savage lifestyle was extremely wasteful, Locke also defined the principle of rightful ownership.

By using the labor of his hands and his body to remove out of the state of nature a piece of land, a man establishes himself as the true proprietor of that land: "As much land as a man tills, plants, improves, cultivates, and can use the product of, so much is his property. He by his labour does, as it were, enclose it from the common" (276). Locke finds authority for this rule in both God and reason. Six decades before, John Cotton had already spelled out the same principle in his sermon *God's Promise to His Plantation* (doc. 16), where he writes: "[It is] a principle in Nature, That in a vacant soyle hee that taketh possession of it, and bestoweth culture and husbandry upon it, his Right it is" (*KC*, 26). In his tract "Reasons to be Considered," John Winthrop follows suit in arguing: "The natives in New England, they inclose no land neither have any settled habitation nor any tame cattle to improve the land by, and so have no other but a natural right to those countries." Winthrop distinguishes between this natural right, by which he means the common use of land, and a "civil" right which belonged to those who engaged in "enclosing" the land with a "particular manurance" (1985, 73).

Winthrop's argument was shared by Samuel Purchas in "Virginia's Verger" (1625) and by a long list of other early promoters of English settlement who legitimated English possession by referring to the "vagrant" lifestyle of the native inhabitants. They, it was claimed, "range rather than inhabit" the land, "live and lie up and downe in troupes like heards of Deare in a Forest," "live not in great numbers together, but dispersed and in small companies," "wander up and down like beasts," "live but like deer in heards," and they "range up and down little otherwise than the wild beasts" of the "vast and unpeopled countries."[8] This dualistic notion of a culturally homogenized "Indian" as a hunter and wanderer extended its influence to international legal discourse; it returns, for example, in the writings of Emmerich de Vattel's *Droit de Gens* of 1758 (cf. Weinberg 1963, 78). Given its prominence, it is not surprising to discover the same trope in Andrew Jackson's "Second Annual Message" of 1830 (doc. 162) in which he expresses "melancholy reflections" about the Indians' unavoidable westward migration:

> Philanthropy could not wish to see this continent restored to the condition in which it was found by our forefathers. What good man would prefer a country covered with forests and ranged by a few thousand savages to our extensive Republic, studded with cities, towns, and prosperous farms [...]? (*KC*, 375)

He is seconded by Lewis Cass, his later Secretary of War, who claims that "[t]he new race of men, who landed upon these shores, found that their predecessors had affixed few distinctive marks of property in the forests where they roamed"

---

[8] This potpourri of early modern quotations is taken from writings by Samuel Purchas, Robert Johnson, Edward Waterhouse, Robert Gray, William Symonds, and William Bradford (in Mackenthun 1997, 267-8). Of course the Puritans also had the argument of God's Providence up their sleeves, but their use of the Lockean definition of property would remain the stronger argument in the long run, as international legal discourse was gradually purged of religious elements.

and that "[l]ike the bear, and deer, and buffalo of his own forests, an Indian lives as his father lived, and dies as his father died. [...] His life passes away in a succession of listless indolence" (*KC*, 372-3). Therefore, both agree, the Indian "is perhaps destined to disappear with the forests" (Cass, *KC*, 373). The ubiquitous identification of the lifestyle of Native Americans as hunters was of course nourished by the cultural discourses of the time – above all by the frontier romances of James Fenimore Cooper and others. Contrary evidence, such as the agricultural lifestyle of the Five Civilized Tribes whose fate was decided at that time, was powerless against the seductiveness of long-accustomed fictions and images (cf. Peterfy in this vol., 28-33). The frequently used collective singular ("the Indian") testifies to the inability of the writers to register the vast differences that existed between the subsistence modes of different Native American groups. What is perhaps most striking in these quotations is the ambiguous attitude toward the concept of "nature." While Americans found their own legal identity in the "laws of nature and of nature's God" (*KC*, 303), the rights of Indians were denied on the ground that they were not willing to improve nature, as Adams makes most clear in the above quote. We are obviously dealing with two different concepts of nature, one derived from the natural rights discourse of the Enlightenment in which nature was invoked as an authority above the rights of existing clerical and worldly powers, and another derived from the Protestant discourse of territorial property being held by those who submitted the wilderness to cultivation and agriculture. While the concept of nature in the first discourse was strongly inflected by the Romantic aesthetic of the time (nature as unpolluted and sublime), that of the second is a mere economic fact to be overcome by the labor of cultivation. We find both concepts in conflict with each other in contemporary documents. This is evident, for example, in Thoreau's *Walden*, where he invokes the trope of *translatio imperii* and human progress from east to west but then associates the west with "the Wild" and locates "the preservation of the world" in that "Wildness" (*KC*, 370). This is a far cry from Adams's desolate regions and barren fields. Thoreau's nature would not need the touch of the "axe of industry" to be able to "blossom like a rose" (Adams, *KC*, 347). For him, nature ought to be preserved in its pristine state.

The nature argument was used in another narrative for legitimating American expansion, which Gilbert Chinard calls "protective imperialism" (in Weinberg 1963, 29). The essential question for many students of American imperial history is why the United States should define itself as an "empire for liberty" in the first place – why, in other words, it was thought necessary to protect the newly-won liberties and republican values by *extending the territorial area* of the United States.[9] Enlightenment philosophers such as Thomas Paine and Emmerich de Vattel (one of the leading contemporary experts in international law) strictly opposed this nexus between republicanism and imperialism; they strictly ruled

---

[9] This famous phrase by Thomas Jefferson was included in an 1809 letter to James Madison (Smith 1995, 3: 1586).

out the legitimacy of aggressive expansion, arguing that it was contrary to the laws of nature, i.e., the philosophical foundation of sovereign nations (cf. Weinberg 1963, 14). The simple reason for this was that the expansion of one nation would tend to inhibit the freedom and equal rights to territorial sovereignty of another. The phrase "empire for liberty" may initially not have referred to a desire for physical expansion; the Founding Fathers, most of whom were ardent cosmopolitans, believed rather that democratic forms of government would increase on a worldwide scale if the American experiment proved successful (cf. Weinberg 1963, 102). The slogan only assumed its contemporary meaning – as the necessity to secure the democratic system of the United States by shunning any direct contact with European nations on the North American continent – in 1843, when Andrew Jackson translated it into the phrase "extending the area of freedom" (in Weinberg 1963, 109). The historical context was the debate over the annexation of Texas and growing apprehensions about British interests in the region. In other words, Jacksonian expansionists argued that the principle of the Monroe Doctrine of 1823, which demanded that European powers keep out of the western hemisphere, was endangered by British encroachments in Texas. The proponents of annexation, led by public figures like John L. O'Sullivan and slavery advocates dreaming of "expanding" the American empire to include Cuba, argued that the geographical vicinity of a monarchical power would endanger the survival of the United States as a democratic republic. Expansion was seen as the only means of avoiding such a contaminating presence. Whether the fear was real or invented is hard to decide. In any case, as Weinberg writes, "European encroachment must […] be thanked for making manifest the destiny of continental dominion" (112). He notes that

> [t]he alchemy which transmuted natural right from a doctrine of democratic nationalism into a doctrine of imperialism was thus the very idea of manifest destiny which the doctrine of natural right created. But manifest destiny was such a creature as Frankenstein fashioned. Gaining control over the doctrine of natural right, it in effect changed the impartial law of nature into the unique code favorable to the rights of one nation. In the end natural right was not a right universal, moderate, and innocuous, but a right special, exorbitant, and potentially aggressive. To be sure, the transmutation was so largely unconscious that from the viewpoint of formal definition the doctrine of natural right continued to bear its original features. But from the viewpoint of application it had the change of bulk which comes with elephantiasis. (1963, 41)

Evidently, the argument of "protective" – or, more recently, "preemptive" – imperial action has remained one of the foremost justifications of American foreign interventions ever since.[10]

---

[10] In section V of the *National Security Strategy* of September, 2002, the White House asserts its right to "preemptive action" in the case of an "imminent threat" to national security: "The United States has long maintained the option of preemptive action to counter a sufficient threat to our national security. The greater the threat, the greater is the risk of inaction – and the more compelling the case for taking anticipatory action to defend ourselves, even if uncer-

IV. Geographical and Archaeological Arguments of Imperial Expansion

As we saw in the previous section, geography was a decisive factor in discourses promoting and justifying American expansion. It was argued that the United States would have to bring itself into full possession of the continent for safety reasons. Voices like that of William Channing, who demanded that expansion be curbed in the name of morality (to "stop in the career of acquisition and conquest," *KC*, 384) and expediency (the United States would not be able to govern a country of such size), went largely unheard. As early as 1789, the American geographer Jedidiah Morse argued that, for reasons of the continent's geographical layout alone, the Mississippi would not remain the western boundary of the "American Empire" (*KC*, 362). While Morse was still referring to America's geographical distance from Europe as a reason for establishing an independent nation in the western hemisphere, later writers used the configuration of the geography of the land as legitimation for expansion across the North American continent and sometimes beyond. This line of reasoning brought two areas into the orbit of possible expansion: Canada in the north and Mexico and Central America in the south. While designs on Canada were particularly strong during the War of 1812, the 1830s and 1840s increased American activities in Mesoamerica. The discovery and exploration of ancient monuments in Mexico and Guatemala by adventurer-diplomats like John Lloyd Stephens and George E. Squier and their comparison with ancient structures unearthed along the Mississippi and in Ohio introduced the idea that North and Central America were culturally united by the prehistoric migrations of an indigenous "high" culture. The scientific interpretation was that the high cultures of the Aztecs and Maya were derivations of the ancient indigenous culture within US territory. The historian Albert Gallatin, for example, in *On the Ancient Semi-Civilization of New Mexico and the Great Colorado of the West* (1845), compared the remains of Cahokia in the Mississippi Valley with the great pyramid of Cholula (cf. Kennedy 1994, 37-8). Moreover, as early as 1820, Caleb Atwater announced in his "Description of the Antiquities Discovered in the State of Ohio and other Western States" that

> [a]n observing eye can easily mark, in these works, the progress of their authors, from the lakes to the valley of the Mississippi, thence to the Gulph of Mexico, and round it, through Texas, into New Mexico, and into South America; their increased numbers, as they proceeded, are evident; while the articles found in and near these works, show also the progressive improvement of the arts among those who erected them. (Atwater 1820, 189)

---

tainty remains as to the time and place of the enemy's attack. To forestall or prevent such hostile acts by our adversaries, the United States will, if necessary, act preemptively" (White House 2002, 15). In the subsequent section the text clarifies its definition of "freedom": "Global Economic Growth Through Free Markets and Free Trade" (17).

Further on, Atwater writes: "*Our* ancient works continue all the way into Mexico, increasing indeed in size, number, and grandeur, but preserving the same forms, and appear to have been put to the same uses" (244; emphasis mine). Atwater's perception of "a line of ancient works" reaching from the Great Lakes "quite into Mexico" and erected "by the same people" (248) may invite expansionist fantasies. John Lloyd Stephens, traveling through Central America in 1839 in search of both monuments and a legitimate Central American government (his official mission as an envoy of the van Buren government), was surprised by the Mesoamericans' apprehensions of further US invasions after the gradual invasion of Texas: "We [the US] were considered as bent upon the conquest of Mexico; and, of course, Guatimala would come next" (Stephens 1969, 1:311). On the other hand, he shared Atwater's migration theory and even sought to buy up whole Maya sites (Copán for 50 US dollars) in order to display them in a "national museum of American antiquities" in New York City, as part of the cultural heritage of the United States (Stephens 1969, 1:115). Stephens's generous disregard of national boundaries in the name of a common culture effectively staged the expansionist dreams of his contemporaries – and effectively shocked his Mexican hosts.

Others uttered their expansionist interests in a less culturalist way: As early as 1804, there were calls for extending American power to the isthmus of Panama on the grounds that the territory north of this "natural" divide formed a homogeneous unity (cf. Weinberg 1963, 56). Jefferson "broached" the idea of leaving the mainland behind and extending American national control to the Gulf Stream (Weinberg 1963, 54). That America's destiny was not only "rooted in the earth" (61) but occasionally also anchored in the sea is further demonstrated by John Quincy Adams and others who predicted the acquisition of Cuba and other Caribbean islands on the grounds of their being "appendages to the North American continent" (65). Similar arguments could be found later in the nineteenth century in favor of the annexation of Hawaii, which was "naturally" destined to be controlled by that republic closest to it, and of the Philippines because of their vicinity to Hawaii (Weinberg 1963, 67-8; cf. Lanzendörfer in this vol., 404-5). The latter views remained unrepresentative, and their absurdity shows that the geographical argument had its "natural" limits. Furthermore, from the middle of the nineteenth century onwards, another powerful discourse arose which rendered an overstretching of the geographical imagination obsolete.

V. Biological Determinism and Imperial Discourse

In a letter to James Monroe in 1801, Jefferson wrote:

> However our present interests may restrain us within our own limits, it is impossible not to look forward to distant times when our rapid multiplication will expand itself beyond those limits, and cover the whole northern, if not the southern continent, with a people speaking the same language, governed in similar forms, and by

similar laws; nor can we contemplate with satisfaction either blot or mixture on that surface. (in Merk 1995, 9)

This passage, which often serves as evidence of Jefferson's designs on Latin America, exemplifies a fundamental contradiction in the American expansionist discourse. Clearly the father of African colonization (by which freed blacks were "repatriated" in the infertile swamps of Liberia to prevent cohabitation with the races in America) could not envision admitting a colored population to the "nest" of the union. Many politicians agreed that a mixture of the Anglo-Saxon stock of the United States with colored Creole populations in Central America or the Caribbean should by all means be avoided. Even the French and Spanish Creoles of New Orleans and Florida were regarded by many with distaste. The receptivity to republican values of this "Gallo-Hispanic-Indian *omnium gatherum* of savages and adventurers," opponents of racial mixture argued, was as great as that of the "otters of the wilderness" (Ames in Merk 1995, 11). Frederick Merk interprets these racialist misgivings as proof of the lack of a will to expand, but they may perhaps more aptly be judged as evidence of a crucial contradiction within early republican political discourse: While expansion was applauded, the "mongrelization" of the American population which it produced was seen as a threat. The Indian Removal and the annexation of Texas are cases in point. While the reasons for expelling the Five Civilized Tribes were rooted both in economic envy and racist prejudice, the annexation of Texas was applauded because the Mexican territory had been taken over by US settlers; the cry for annexation was preceded by a gradual encroachment by Anglo-Saxon settlers. During the Mexican War of 1846-48, occasional calls for annexing even more territory were stifled not primarily on moral or legal grounds but rather on racial grounds. Mexicans were regarded as a mongrel race, indolent, irrational, and Catholic. The admission of such a population, it was believed, might endanger the principles of democracy just as it would threaten the racial integrity of the United States. Thus the fear of racial hybridization – the loss of Anglo-Saxon features due to racial degeneration – inflected the desire for territorial expansion. Ironically, the major ideologemes of American imperial expansion, racial supremacy and a quasi-religious civilizational mission, tended to impair each other out of a fear of racial amalgamation.

But the problematic proximity of mongrel races could also be twisted into a more favorable direction by a theory that predicted the impending demise of 'inferior' races. In his *Legends of Mexico* (1847), the Gothic novelist George Lippard appeals to the racial superiority of Anglo-Americans:

> To this hardy People – this people created from the pilgrims and wanderers of all nations – this People nursed into full vigor, by long and bloody Indian wars and hardened into iron, by the longest and bloodiest war of all, the Revolution, to his People of Northern America, God Almighty has given the destiny of the entire American Continent. [...] As the Aztec people crumbled before the Spaniard, so will the mon-

grel race, molded of Indian and Spanish blood, melt into, and be ruled by, the Iron Race of the North. (in Sundquist 2006, 50)

Certainly Lippard's early version of the melting pot thesis was not shared by all his contemporaries, many of whom feared the dilution of pure Anglo-Saxon stock. The theory of Anglo-Saxon racial superiority gained enormous mileage out of the theories of Darwin; in translating Darwin's findings about processes of natural selection in the animal world to contemporary human affairs, they predicted the extirpation of inferior races. The fate of American Indians, who had visibly disappeared from the eastern part of the United States and whose numbers were further reduced by starvation and genocidal warfare in the west, was sometimes referred to as ample proof of this pseudo-Darwinistic thesis.

As Horsman remarks, racial Anglo-Saxonism gained ascendancy in American political discourse during the time of the Mexican War, and it reached its height by the end of the nineteenth century (1981, 1). The semantics of the term "Anglo-Saxon" was far from precise: In the version used by Jefferson in his "Summary View of the Rights of British America" (doc. 125), it referred to the inhabitants of England who were subjected by the Norman conquest. Jefferson here establishes an analogy between the American colonists, whom he compares to the ancient Anglo-Saxons, and the British mother country, which he identifies with the Norman conquerors. Although Jefferson argues less on racial than on political grounds – the Anglo-Saxons had always been regarded as especially gifted in the arts of government – later writers would, under the influence of early anthropologists and ethnologists like Johann Friedrich Blumenbach, Samuel George Morton, George Gliddon, and Josiah Nott, trace the social superiority of Anglo-Saxons to their superior racial characteristics. Racial genealogy would later be extended to include the Caucasian or Teutonic race, which was believed to have evolved from the ancient Aryans (cf. Horsman 1981, 5). It was believed to be the destiny of these successors of pure Aryan stock to spread civilization not only from east to west, but also from north to south.

The popular mid-century theory of racial hierarchy is articulated by Senator Thomas Hart Benton (doc. 177), who, commenting on the necessity of extending American rule to Oregon, predicted the arrival of the "Celtic-Anglo-Saxon" race on the banks of Asia (*KC*, 398). While the "Ethiopian, or Black" race inhabits the bottom of this hierarchy and the "Malay, or Brown" race and the "American Indian, or Red" race are hardly more advanced, the only race to vaguely approach the superior level of the "Caucasian race" is the "Mongolian, or Yellow race" which had once spread itself all through Europe. But the "divine command, to subdue and replenish the earth" was only heeded by the "White race," which is why Caucasians now occupied such a privileged position (*KC*, 398-9). Benton's racial typology – which is nearly identical with that of Blumenbach, as well as Josiah Nott and George Gliddon's scientific study *Types of Mankind* (1854) – then merges into the well-known narrative of the westward course of empire. Less inspired with ideas of divine providence than Benton, an anonymous writer in *The American Review* (doc. 178) envisions a powerful "new race" consisting of a blend of the best racial elements of Europe, which would "insensibly ooz[e]" into the territories of Mexico with the effect of "changing her customs, and out-living, out-trading, exterminating her weaker blood" (*KC*, 401, 404). This he regards with "as much certainty, as we do the final extinction of the Indian races, to which the mass of the Mexican population seem very little superior." Thus before long, "South America will speak the English tongue and submit to the civilization, laws and religion of the Anglo-Saxon race" (*KC*, 404). By the end of the century, in the writings of the historian John Fiske and the Reverend Josiah Strong, this largely non-biological definition of "race" would be fully integrated into the language of natural selection. In his 1885 essay "Manifest Destiny" (doc. 184), Fiske fuses the *translatio imperii*-motif with scientifically grounded theories of racial superiority:

> [The] work which the English race began when it colonized North America is destined to go on until every land on the earth's surface that is not already the seat of an old civilization shall become English in its language, in its religion, in its political habits and traditions, and to a predominant extent in the blood of its people. The day is at hand when four-fifths of the human race will trace its pedigree to English forefathers. (*KC*, 413)

Fiske's contemporary Josiah Strong follows suit in his influential tract *Our Country* (doc. 318) by predicting the expansion of the "Anglo-Saxon race" to "Mexico, down upon Central and South America, out upon the islands of the sea, over upon Africa and beyond." With the Anglo-Saxon race thus "populating themselves [...] into the possession of all countries and climes," there is no doubt in his mind that the result of this "competition of races will be the 'survival of the fittest'" (*KC*, 709). Strong's language, even more keenly than that of Fiske joins the recent discourse of social Darwinism, or more correctly Spencerianism (contained in the phrase "survival of the fittest"), with the millennial narrative of Christianity: "The time is coming when [...] the world [will] enter upon a new stage of its history – *the final competition of races, for which the Anglo-Saxon is being schooled*" (*KC*, 709).

Written at the end of the continental phase, Fiske's biological conquest and Strong's racial Armageddon extend the area of influence even beyond Asia to incorporate the whole world. The powerful evocation of the apocalyptic narrative, even at a time in which Christianity underwent an authority crisis due to recent scientific findings, demonstrates the superiority of the Christian narrative over all others. The God of Fiske's and Strong's theories was, as Richard Drinnon ironically remarks, "a Darwinian deity who spoke English with a slight Teutonic accent" (1980, 239). Until this very day, the narrative of world mission has been able to incorporate numerous justifications for empire from a diversity of religious, political, and scientific discourses, some of which were presented in this chapter.

I want to end this section with a short reference to the literary mythology that was developed in America in response to, but perhaps also in preparation for, a politics of westward expansion. As numerous documents testify, expansionists were convinced of the impending extinction of the "Indian races" (*KC*, 404).

Andrew Jackson was driven to "melancholy reflections" by envisioning the sad fate of the Native American and expecting to "follow to the tomb the last of his race and to tread on the graves of extinct nations" (*KC*, 375). The trope of the vanishing or dying Indian effectively translated the ideology of Manifest Destiny into aesthetic language. The rise of the science of ethnology in America can be partly explained by the need to collect the last remains and artifacts of a vanishing race. Early ethnologists like Henry Rowe Schoolcraft or painters like George Catlin ventured forth to the western tribes to collect their tales and mythologies and fix their cultures on canvas. Writers like James Fenimore Cooper and Henry Wadsworth Longfellow eternalized the image of the dying Indian in the figure of *The Last of the Mohicans* or in the popular epic *Hiawatha*, which ends with the protagonist's retreat into the wilderness and the arrival of the first white missionaries bringing the Bible and a deadly disease (cf. detailed treatments of this trope in Fiedler 1968; Slotkin 1973; also Sundquist 2006).

When Huckleberry Finn, at the end of Twain's novel of the same name, "light[s] out for the Territory ahead of the rest" (1985, 369), he parodically repeats the action of Cooper's Natty Bumppo, whom we see, at the end of *The Pioneers*, disappear into the setting sun: "the foremost in that band of pioneers who are opening the way for the march of the nation across the continent" (1964, 350). While Cooper is engaged in "romancing" western settlement in full keeping with the language and iconography of the trope of the westward course of empire, Twain's vision is at once more modest and more subtle. Rather than carrying the torch of civilization across the continent, Huckleberry Finn goes west to escape a "sivilization" full of social strife and racial violence. Two decades later, Twain would directly express his critique of American imperial politics in his essay "To the Person Sitting in Darkness":

> Shall we? That is, shall we go on conferring our Civilization upon the peoples that sit in darkness, or shall we give those poor things a rest? Shall we bang right ahead in our old-time, loud, pious way, and commit the new century to the game; or shall we sober up and sit down and think it over first? Would it not be prudent to get our Civilization tools together and see how much stock is left on hand in the way of Glass Beads and Theology, and Maxim Guns and Hymn Books, and Trade Gin and Torches of Progress and Enlightenment (patent adjustable ones, good to fire villages with, upon occasion), and balance the books and arrive at the profit and loss, so that we may intelligently decide whether to continue the business or sell out the property and start a new Civilization Scheme on the proceeds? (1978, 253)

Instructional Strategies and Classroom Issues

I. Key Concepts and Major Themes

1. Westward Course of Empire / God's Providence (docs. 154-5, 181-2)
   The historical roots of the master narrative of European, and later American, westward expansion may be found in the classical trope of *translatio*

imperii et studi (the translation of empire and knowledge), which in the first century AD united with the Christian apocalyptic narrative of world mission. Its main tenet is that the settlement of the west and the conversion of the pagans to Christianity and civilization was the work of God's chosen people. The biblical model for God's Providence is His promise to the people of Israel to settle in Canaan.

2. Manifest Destiny (docs. 162, 167, 171, 174, 184)
   Coined by the journalist John L. O'Sullivan in 1845, Manifest Destiny is a further development, and adaptation to secular purposes, of the concept of God's Providence. It was seen as America's manifest destiny that it act as a haven for the oppressed of Europe and bring the light of civilization and democracy to the "pagans" of the American West, the western hemisphere, or the whole world. The ideology of Manifest Destiny is the major legitimation of American expansion, while its critics (doc. 167) accused it of immorality and hypocrisy.

3. The Law of Nature and Security (docs. 149, 160-1)
   Derived from the justification of American independence from the colonial mother country on the grounds of the "laws of nature and of nature's God" (*KC*, 303), the argument of nature was joined by the Protestant labor-based definition of property in legitimations of westward expansion. The right to take possession of Indian land was derived from the colonizers' act of improving the wilderness. The annexation of adjacent territories (like Texas) was likewise legitimated by the law of nature, or the natural right to ascertain a nation's security against foreign aggression.

4. Geographical Predestination (doc. 154)
   The choice of physical boundaries shifted according to the stages of expansion. While at first the Mississippi was regarded as the geographical limit to expansion, it was soon followed by the view that the whole northern continent (excluding Canada and Mexico) should be united as the national territory of the United States. In the mid-nineteenth century the imagined territory of the United States was further extended to include the area north of the isthmus in Central America, as well as geographically 'adjacent' islands (especially Cuba).

5. Domestic Dependent Nations (doc. 163)
   Coined by Supreme Court Justice John Marshall in 1831, this term described the legal status of America's indigenous population with regard to the United States government. It represents the paradox of the American Indian policy of regarding the territory inhabited by Indian tribes as part of the United States while forming treaties of land cession with these very tribes and thus acknowledging their status as foreign political entities.

6. Racial Determinism / Anglo-Saxonism (docs. 177, 184, 318)
   The ideologeme of Anglo-Saxon superiority began to join narratives of God's Providence and Manifest Destiny in the middle of the nineteenth century. Based on the racial typologies of Blumenbach, Morton, Gliddon, Nott, and others, the legitimacy of expansion was asserted on the grounds of white American racial superiority (identified as Anglo-Saxon or Caucasian). The providential determinism of Manifest Destiny was enriched by the biological determinism developed in light of – and against the original meaning of – Darwin's theory of natural selection.

7. Frontier (doc. 185, 187)
   Popularized by Frederick Jackson Turner in 1893, the concept of the frontier unites many aspects of previous narratives and ideologemes. Turner defined the frontier as the physical and metaphysical site at which Americans perpetually reasserted the essential American values of individualism, democracy, inquisitiveness, inventiveness, materialism, and nervous restlessness in constant contest with the forces of savagery. Its closure in the 1890s would necessitate the search for new challenges at new frontiers.

II. Comparison – Contrasts – Connections

Example: Doc. 182; Thomas Cole, "The Course of Empire" (cf. *KC* web site)

The unit opens with a reading of John L. O'Sullivan's definition of Manifest Destiny (doc. 171) and of Thoreau's description of his instinctual impulse to move west. In his famous statement that it is the "manifest destiny" of Americans "to overspread the continent allotted by Providence for the free development of our yearly multiplying millions" (*KC*, 389), O'Sullivan condenses various tropes used for legitimating westward expansion: the trope of God's Providence, the argument of democracy, and the argument of population growth. After tracing the genealogy of these tropes, we continue by applying them to our reading of the lithograph "American Progress" by John Gast (doc. 182). The dominant theme of this painting is the movement of various groups of people (Indians, settlers, stage coach travelers) and symbols of civilizational progress (railway, telegraph) from east to west. His use of a panoramic and elevated perspective, clearly inspired by the dioramas and panoramas of cities and landscapes exhibited in major American cities, invites a comparison with Turner's use of the map-and-book metaphor. Our reading requires additional investigations into the theme of the westward course of empire, which leads us to documents from earlier sections, such as George Berkeley's poem "On the Prospect of Planting Arts and Learning in America" (doc. 21), or the poems of the early national poets (Freneau, Dwight, Humphreys, Barlow) who likewise appeal to the symbolism of "ex oriente lux" (docs. 83-4, 89, 107). Students compare the representation of nature in Gast's painting to Thoreau's notion of nature in the excerpt from *Walden* (doc. 160), where Thoreau associates the east with bondage and the west with freedom, where he refers to the Atlantic as a "Lethean stream," and where he remarks on the natural "pull" and beauty of the western landscape, referring to the sunset as the "Great Western Pioneer whom the nations follow" and the "Wildness" as the "preservation of the world" (*KC*, 369-70). To what extent does Thoreau's vision agree with the light and color imagery of the painting by Gast, and where do they deviate from one another? Another point of discussion may be Thoreau's replacement of Berkeley's "course of empire" with "star of empire": what is the symbolism of a "star" in American political discourse?

The guiding element in Gast's painting is of course the gigantic female figure at the center, with flowing hair, white dress that barely conceals her nudity, with a star on her forehead, a schoolbook under her right arm, and unfolding a telegraph wire with her left hand. The figure – the American national allegory "Lady Columbia" – alludes to other allegorical feminizations of nations and empires, such as Joan of Arc, but at the same time evokes early modern allegorizations of America as a naked female (docs. 28-31). What are the differences between these early modern representations and the one by John Gast?

In a second step, the study unit compares Gast's patriotic representation of American progress with Thomas Cole's famous painting cycle "The Course of Empire" (1833-1836). The cycle consists of five canvases entitled "The Savage State," "The Pastoral or Arcadian State," "The Consummation of Empire," "Destruction," and "Desolation." Thomas Cole, one of the foremost Romantic painters of the United States, executed these paintings during Andrew Jackson's presidency (1829-1837), when American political rhetoric began to be dominated by the discourse of expansionism. Cole, who was a (born) Englishman, felt ambivalent about American expansionism. Although the painting cycle was probably not primarily meant as an allegory of the United States, it is noteworthy that Cole was one of the leading landscape painters of the American wilderness and one of the most articulate proponents of the aesthetic of the sublime. Clearly his representations of the savage and pastoral state bear the imprint of American landscapes.

In discussing, the paintings special attention may be given to the way they symbolize a stadialist theory of history – history as consisting of various stages which all cultures would undergo on their way to the highest stage: urban, technological, and commercial civilization. It may be noted that Cole's civilization reaches the urban state, but without the practical attainments of civilization emphasized in Gasts's image: The painting "Consummation of Empire," clearly influenced by the pictures of the French Baroque artist Claude Lorrain, shows a civilization reminiscent of the Roman empire. The painting also shows a certain material saturatedness, as the city is teeming with buildings, people, and ships. Compare this to O'Sullivan's and John Adams's references to population growth as a reason for expansion. Perhaps the error of Cole's empire is that it did not expand far enough? The fact that conquests were made is evident from the triumphal march in the center foreground. There is no reference to Christianity; the culture seems to be pagan. Is this perhaps another reason for its impending destruction?

A further avenue may be taken by discussing the iconology of savagery and pastoralism in the first two canvases. While some items in "State of Savagery" refer to America (the canoes, the teepees), others contradict this interpretation (the hunter looks Greek rather than Native American). In "Pastoral or Arcadian State" there is a shift of geographical emphasis – as the geographical site portrayed remains the same (indicated by the unchanging cliff rock in the distance), we may assume that the cycle refers to no specific culture but makes a statement about universal civilization. A comparison with the representation of the relevant states of human development in Gast's painting may sharpen the view of what is present and absent in Gast and Cole. For example, at the center of Cole's canvas is a representation of Stonehenge (as a site of religious worship), framed by images of agriculture and shepherding. What about religion and pastoralism in Gast? A comparison of the representation of vegetation in these three paintings also offers itself; where can we find traces of Thoreau's idealized wilderness?

In a comment on the canvas "Consumption," Cole writes that we can already see the causes of decline: the "ostentatious display of riches has succeeded to the efforts of virtuous industry, and the study of nature and truth (symbolized by the pensive old man in the left foreground in 'Pastoral' and the right foreground in 'Consummation'). We see that man has attained power without the knowledge of its true use and has already abused it" (in Wilton and Barringer 2002, 104). The fourth canvas, "Destruction," fully exploits the aesthetics of the sublime. The scene of violent battle is dominated by the gigantic figure of a headless warrior, which may symbolize the dissociation of power from intellect that Cole refers to above. The female figure at the center of the scene, who jumps to her death to escape a worse fate, may be compared with the "Lady Columbia" figure in "American Progress." Which relationship do both paintings suggest between femininity/virginity (both women are clad in white) and empire?

The canvas which concludes the cycle, "Desolation," reveals no sign of human presence. Nature is reclaiming the scene, and after the pomp and violence of the previous two canvases, this one communicates a mood of tranquility. A guiding question in comparing Cole's cycle with Gast's painting may refer to the respective theories of history underlying their works: the teleological and optimistic plot of Enlightenment and progress in Gast, versus the catastrophic and apocalyptic plot of Cole, which is inspired by the Romantic critique of the arrogance of power, as well as its emphasis on the transience and mutability of power. How can Cole's cycle be brought into dialogue with the concept of Manifest Destiny or the argument of "nature" – both in its role as legitimating democratic government and as a "desolate wilderness" to be tamed?

III. Reading and Discussion Questions

1. In discussing the trope of the Westward Course of Empire, try to distinguish religious from non-religious elements. Consider the trope's adjustments to changing historical situations (docs. 179, 181, 318).

2. Discuss the romantic image of the Vanishing Indian. Compare the language and the reasoning of John Marshall with that of Andrew Jackson (docs. 163, 162).

3. Discuss the various meanings of "nature" in American republican, expansionist, and Romantic discourse (docs. 131, 149, 160).

4. Compare the iconography of John Gast's "American Progress" (doc. 182) and Thomas Cole's "Course of Empire" (cf. *KC* web site). Discuss the implicit theory of history embedded in these paintings in terms of Enlightenment and Romantic historical thinking. Name writers from the section whose view of history may likewise be characterized as "Romantic."

IV. Resources

a. Recommended Reading

Richard Drinnon. *Facing West: The Metaphysics of Indian Hating and Empire Building*. New York: Schocken Books, 1980. A classic which traces the rhetoric of expansion and empire throughout American history, from the New England Puritans to the discourse about the Philippines and Vietnam. Drinnon draws multiple cross-connections between different stages of American history.

Reginald Horsman. *Race and Manifest Destiny: The Origins of American Racial Anglo-Saxonism*. Cambridge: Harvard University Press, 1981. The most representative and systematic account of the fusion of expansionist providentialism with racial Anglo-Saxonism in the mid-nineteenth century. Situates discussions about expansion and slavery within debates about racial characteristics.

Amy Kaplan and Donald Pease, eds. *Cultures of United States Imperialism*. Durham: Duke University Press, 1993. A collection of essays by leading scholars of American literature and culture who reassess the historiography of American expansion, race relations, and slavery from a transnational, non-exceptionalist perspective. Essays reinterpret American history as a special form of imperialism, including a section on the "imperial spectacles" of Hollywood.

Anders Stephanson. *Manifest Destiny: American Expansion and the Empire of Right*. New York: Hill and Wang, 1995. A short but magisterial and sophisticated analysis of American expansionist ideology, starting with the British settlements and ending with the political rhetoric of the Reagan administration. Puts particular emphasis on the religious component.

Eric J. Sundquist. *Empire and Slavery in American Literature, 1820-1865*. Jackson: University Press of Mississippi, 2006. Largely identical with Sundquist's contribution to volume 2 of the *Cambridge History of American Literature*, edited by Sacvan Bercovitch (1995). Includes probably the fullest account of the major themes of literature in relation to expansion, with particular emphasis on lesser known and non-literary texts and on texts transcending the national and continental borders of the United States. The book suffers from a complete lack of documentation.

Albert K. Weinberg. *Manifest Destiny: A Study of Nationalist Expansionism in American History*. Chicago: Quadrangle Books, 1963. Originally published in 1935, this is one of the best critical histories of the "red decade." It traces expansionist rhetoric both chronologically and thematically. All later studies relied on this classic. The main source for the essay in this section because it is still considered the best.

b. Works Cited and Reading Suggestions

Atwater, Caleb (1820). "Description of the Antiquities Discovered in the State of Ohio and other Western States." *Transactions of the American Antiquarian Society* 1, 105-313.

Brown, Dee (1970). *Bury My Heart at Wounded Knee: An Indian History of the American West*. New York: Bantam.

Carroll, Robert, and Stephen Brickett (1995). *The Bible: Authorized King James Version*. Oxford: Oxford University Press.

Churchill, Ward (1993). *Struggle for the Land: Indigenous Resistance to Genocide, Ecocide, and Expropriation in Contemporary North America*. Monroe: Common Courage Press.

Cooper, James Fenimore (1964). *The Pioneers*. 1823. New York: Airmont.

Drinnon, Richard (1980). *Facing West: The Metaphysics of Indian Hating and Empire Building*. New York: Schocken Books.

Fiedler, Leslie (1968). *The Return of the Vanishing American*. New York: Stein and Day.

Freese, Peter (1996). "'Westward the Course of Empire Takes Its Way': The *translatio*-Concept in Popular American Writing and Painting." *Amerikastudien/American Studies* 42.2, 265-295.

Hanke, Lewis (1965). *The Spanish Struggle for Justice in the Conquest of America*. 1949. Boston: Little Brown.

Hietala, Thomas R. (1985) *Manifest Destiny: Anxious Aggrandizement in Late Jacksonian America*. Ithaca: Cornell University Press.

Horsman, Reginald (1981). *Race and Manifest Destiny: The Origins of American Racial Anglo-Saxonism*. Cambridge: Harvard University Press.

Hulme, Peter (1986). *Colonial Encounters: Europe and the Native Caribbean, 1492-1797.* London: Methuen.
Johnson, Thomas H. (1966). *The Oxford Companion to American History.* New York: Oxford University Press.
Kaplan, Amy, and Donald Pease, eds. (1993). *Cultures of United States Imperialism.* Durham: Duke University Press.
Keil, Hartmut (1991). "Die Vereinigten Staaten von Amerika zwischen kontinentaler Expansion und Imperialismus." *Imperialistische Kontinuität und nationale Ungeduld im 19. Jahrhundert.* Ed. Wolfgang Reinhard. Frankfurt/M.: Fischer, 68-86.
Kennedy, Roger G. (1994). *Hidden Cities: The Discovery and Loss of Ancient North American Civilization.* London: Penguin.
Ledyard, John (2005). *The Last Voyage of Captain Cook: The Collected Writings of John Ledyard.* Ed. James Zug. Washington: National Geographic Books.
Locke, John (1993). *The Second Treatise of Government: An Essay Concerning the True Original, Extent and End of Civil Government.* 1689. *John Locke: Political Writings.* Ed. David Wotton. Harmondsworth: Penguin, 261-348.
Mackenthun, Gesa (1997). *Metaphors of Dispossession: American Beginnings and the Translation of Empire, 1492-1637.* Norman: University of Oklahoma Press, 1997.
May, Robert E. (2002). *The Southern Dream of a Caribbean Empire, 1854-1861.* 1973. Gainsville: University Press of Florida.
Merk, Frederick (1995). *Manifest Destiny and Mission in American History.* 1963. Cambridge: Harvard University Press.
Nobles, Gregory (1997). *American Frontiers: Cultural Encounters and Continental Conquest.* New York: Hill and Wang.
Pagden, Anthony (1995). *Lords of all the World: Ideologies of Empire in Spain, Britain, and France, c.1500-c.1800.* New Haven: Yale University Press.
Rogin, Michael Paul (1975). *Fathers and Children: Andrew Jackson and the Subjugation of the American Indian.* New York: Vintage.
Ronda, James P. (1990). *Astoria & Empire.* Lincoln: University of Nebraska Press.
Rowe, John Carlos (2000). *Literary Culture and U.S. Imperialism: From the Revolution to World War II.* New York: Oxford University Press.
Seed, Patricia (1995). *Ceremonies of Possession in Europe's Conquest of the New World, 1492-1640.* New York: Cambridge University Press.
Slotkin, Richard (1973). *Regeneration Through Violence: The Mythology of the American Frontier, 1600-1860.* Middletown: Wesleyan University Press.
Smith, James Morton, ed. (1995). *The Republic of Letters: The Correspondence between Thomas Jefferson and James Madison, 1776-1826.* Vol. 3: *1804-1836.* New York: Norton.
Stephanson, Anders (1995). *Manifest Destiny: American Expansion and the Empire of Right.* New York: Hill and Wang.
Stephens, John Lloyd (1969). *Incidents of Travel in Central America, Chiapas and Yucatan.* 2 vols. 1841. New York: Dover.

Sundquist, Eric J. (2006). *Empire and Slavery in American Literature, 1820-1865*. Jackson: University Press of Mississippi.
Turner, Frederick Jackson (1995). "The Significance of the Frontier in American History." 1893. *A Cultural Studies Reader: History, Theory, Practice*. Ed. Jessica Munns and Gita Rajan. London: Longman, 58-78.
Twain, Mark (1985). *The Adventures of Huckleberry Finn*. 1884. Harmondsworth: Penguin.
– (1978). "To the Person Sitting in Darkness." 1901. *America in Literature*. Vol. 2. Ed. Alan Trachtenberg and Benjamin De Mott. New York: John Wiley, 249-262.
van Alstyne, R. W. (1960). *The Rising American Empire*. New York: Oxford University Press.
Weinberg, Albert K. (1963). *Manifest Destiny: A Study of Nationalist Expansionism in American History*. 1935. Chicago: Quadrangle Books.
White House, The (2002). *The National Security Strategy of the United States of America*. September 2002.
Whitman, Walt (1978). "Passage to India." 1871. *America in Literature*. Vol. 2. Ed. Alan Trachtenberg and Benjamin De Mott. New York: John Wiley, 128-129.
Wilkinson, Charles F. (1987). *American Indians, Time, and the Law*. New Haven: Yale University Press.
Williams, Robert A., Jr. (1990). *The American Indian in Western Legal Thought: The Discourses of Conquest*. New York: Oxford University Press.
Williams, William Appleman (1969). *The Roots of the Modern American Empire: A Study of the Growth and Shaping of Social Consciousness in a Marketplace Society*. New York: Vintage.
Wilton, Andrew, and Tim Barringer (2002). *American Sublime: Landscape Painting in the United States, 1820-1880*. London: Tyte Publishing.
Winthrop, John (1985). "Reasons to be Considered." 1629. *The Puritans in America*. Ed. Alan Heimert and Andrew Delbanco. Cambridge: Harvard University Press, 71-74.
Yates, Frances A. (1975). *Astraea: The Imperial Theme in the Sixteenth Century*. London: Ark.

GÜNTER LEYPOLDT

The Transcendental Turn in Nineteenth-Century New England

I. Themes and Arguments

American transcendentalism emerged in the 1830s with the literary, religious, philosophical, and socio-political activities of loosely connected groups of New England intellectuals based in greater Boston. By far the most influential representative is the essayist and poet Ralph Waldo Emerson, whose extensive work is generally considered transcendentalism's thematic and stylistic center. Emerson's shaping influence on New England literary culture begins with his treatise on *Nature* (1836) – a foundational formulation of the late-romantic nature religion emerging in the Transcendental Club – and two important Harvard speeches: the so-called "American Scholar" oration (1837), which has become canonical as America's "intellectual Declaration of Independence" (Holmes 1892, 11: 88), and the notorious "Divinity School Address" (1838), an implicit rejection of traditional Christianity that made Emerson a controversial figure among the New England elites.[1]

Emerson's two collections of essays further broaden and develop the transcendentalist vision.[2] His best essays are remarkable for their compositional complexity, turning the essayistic genre into a highly literary exercise in contrapuntal style whose evasion of clear moral stances or truth-claims contrasts sharply with much contemporary expositional writing (cf. Poirier 1987). Among Emerson's later and less canonical books, three can be singled out as notable introductions to the range of transcendentalist thought: *Representative Men* (1850) is a meditation on the cultural centrality and historical "representativeness" of individual minds; *English*

---

[1] For a critique of the "nationalizing" of Emerson's oration, see Buell (2003, 43-58).
[2] See *Essays: First Series* (1841) and *Essays: Second Series* (1844). The first collection contains the essay "Self-Reliance," which can be said to be Emerson's most trenchant statement of his non-conformist concept of self-culture as a quest for spiritual presence. The second series contains among others, the influential essays "The Poet" and "Experience." "The Poet" invokes the image of the artist as prophetic genius who, inspired by a transcendent presence beyond rational understanding, transforms the dazzling "poem" America into national literature. "Experience" has a more meditative and skeptical voice that influenced the generation of Nietzsche and William James and continues to resonate with today's epistemological uncertainties.

Traits (1856) combines Emerson's recollections of transatlantic travel with a critique of British culture and society; *The Conduct of Life* (1860) is a collection of later essays whose best-known piece "Fate" deepens Emerson's self-reliance theme with regard to social and natural constraints on individual freedom.

Henry David Thoreau has been portrayed as the Transcendental Club's nature buff, an eccentric who, in contrast to Emerson's interests in high theory and speculative abstraction, liked to "saunter" through New England forests with an eye for the concreteness and real presence (rather than mere spiritual significance) of natural objects. This caricature is borne out by Thoreau's recent elevation to the status of a prescient pioneer in today's ecocritical campaign against anthropocentric nature concepts (cf. Buell 1995).

Thoreau's most famous work, *Walden; or, Life in the Woods* (1854; cf. doc. 200), is a fictionalized account of his sojourn in a log cabin on a piece of Emerson's woodland, not far from Concord, Massachusetts. Thoreau stayed there between 1845 and 1847, in a state of imagined rather than real isolation, since during that time he entertained visitors, kept contact with his family, lectured in the Concord Lyceum, spent one night in jail for not paying his poll taxes, and interrupted his stay with a trip to the Maine forests. His extensive journals indicate that the time spent at Walden combined periods of meditation, practical gardening, and subsistence farming with regular literary pursuits, including the completion of his first book, *A Week on the Concord and Merrimack Rivers*, and the first version of *Walden*. Thoreau spent seven years revising this first draft, which indicates the extent to which *Walden* is a literary endeavor that embeds Thoreau's autobiographical recollections within a carefully constructed and highly symbolic pastoral space, based on the speculative and allegorical concepts of nature characteristic of transcendentalist thought. Thoreau's detailed description of the Walden landscape turns the wilderness into a metaphor for moral harmony, serving as a foil for a proto-Marxist critique of Western consumerism and materialism. As a remedy for the acute cultural alienation of modern civilization, the book suggests a program of spiritual rejuvenation based on free-thinking individualism, active living ("to suck out all the marrow of life," *KC*, 448), Spartan primitivism, economic agrarianism and, most importantly, empathetic immersion in wild nature.

Walden already develops the socioreligious leanings and countercultural attitude characteristic of Thoreau's radical political statements. Good examples of this are "A Plea for Captain John Brown" (1859), in which he passionately defends Brown's abolitionist raid on Harper's Ferry and refers to him as an "Angel of Light" (Thoreau 1973, 137), and his influential essay on "Civil Disobedience" (1849). The latter speaks of one's duty to resist the official government if its actions clash with one's conscience; it was prompted by Thoreau's disgust with Southern slavery and the War on Mexico, and became an important influence on twentieth-century ideas of peaceful resistance such as those of Gandhi and Martin Luther King. In the 1850s, Thoreau became more interested in natural history, and an "amateur field biologist of considerable skill" (Buell 1995, 130), producing less allegorical (hence less Emersonian) nature writing that has only recently attracted critical interest.³ This lesser known side of Thoreau is represented in a variety of late essays (such as "Autumnal Tints" and "Wild Apples"), but also in his remarkable and substantial journals (sixteen of the twenty volumes of the 1906 edition of his works; cf. Thoreau 1906). Thoreau's posthumously published essay on "Walking" provides the most succinct formulation of his view of the untouched wilderness and the open road as important tonics for modern disorders.⁴

Emerson and Thoreau remain the most popular representatives of the transcendentalist movement – in fact the only mid-century intellectuals that twentieth-century critics deemed important enough to consider key members of the so-called American Renaissance (cf. F. O. Matthiessen), the nineteenth-century flowering of American literature associated with the fiction of Nathaniel Hawthorne and Herman Melville, and the poetry of Walt Whitman. Emerson and Thoreau might well have been flattered by this honor, but they had comparatively little interest in narrative fiction, which in the mid-1800s was still considered of lower rank than poetry. They felt more closely connected to the vibrant network of now lesser-known intellectuals and poets with whom they were in close collaboration, most of them emerging, like Emerson, from the New England Unitarian clergy. The most prominent among them were the socialist visionary and activist Orestes Brownson, the educators Amos Bronson Alcott and Elizabeth Peabody, the theologians and Unitarian ministers Theodore Parker and Frederic Henry Hedge, the Fourierist reformers George and Sophia Ripley (cf. Klaiber in this vol., 323-6), the politician-historian George Bancroft, and the "minor" poets Jones Very, Christopher Pearse Cranch, and W. E. Channing.

Even more important to Emerson was Margaret Fuller, who collaborated with him on the transcendentalist journal *The Dial* (which she edited between 1840 and 1842). Fuller contributed to the movement's most influential aesthetic and social criticism. She was also considered an erudite conversationalist, and organized educational conversation classes for women on literary and philosophical topics. Today she is best known for her feminist treatise on *Woman in the Nineteenth Century* (doc. 235) and a lyrical account of Midwest prairie life, *Summer on the Lakes, in 1843* (doc. 201).

---

3   Allegorical or symbolic representations of nature mainly treat natural objects as symbols or signs for spiritual facts. The idea of a correspondence between natural phenomena and divine meanings goes back to the Christian topos of the Book of Nature, and underlies the work of the Swedish mystic Emanuel Swedenborg, which both Emerson and Thoreau knew well. Emerson is known as the great allegorizer of the natural landscape because he theorized this problem extensively (cf. his chapters on "language" in *Nature* and "Swedenborg" in *Representative Men*; cf. Thoreau 1906, vols. 1, 4). But Thoreau's *Walden* also bristles with moral interpretations of natural facts (cf. Thoreau's meditation on the thawing sandbanks; *KC*, 451). For the Swedenborgian idea of natural connection and symbolism, see Cranch's "Correspondences" (doc. 191) and Sampson Reed's *Observations on the Growth of Mind* (doc. 192).
4   "Walking" also shows Thoreau's complicity with manifest destiny, as the excerpts in the *KC* section on expansionism show (doc. 160); see Mackenthun in this vol., 255-7.

The movement reached its critical mass in the 1830s, when it centered around a number of discussion groups of shifting membership. In 1836, Emerson, Ripley, and Hedge founded the Transcendental Club out of a frustration with what they considered the shallowness of the intellectual scene at Harvard. The club functioned as a forum for entertaining new ideas in informal and open-ended discussion sessions that often revolved around a single topic.[5] From the mid-1830s to the 1840s, the transcendentalists engaged in joint publication projects, translating and reprinting selections from contemporary literature and philosophy.[6] They participated in the rich review culture hosted by Unitarian journals, beginning with *The Christian Examiner*, which had connections to the Harvard Divinity School and became, under the influence of Henry Hedge, a forum for liberal ideas and a mouthpiece for transcendentalist intellectuals. After the éclat over Emerson's "Divinity School Address" more or less closed the *Examiner* to transcendentalist thought, alternative publication organs were the Ohio-based *Western Messenger* (which took Emerson's side until it folded in 1841), and the *Boston Quarterly Review* (under Brownson's editorship until 1844). The short-lived *Dial*, which was edited by Fuller and Emerson from 1840 to 1844, lacked broad support in the New England scene but published some of the most lasting transcendentalist writings.

By the 1850s, the Transcendental Club had lost its cohesion and force, as its middle-aged members became settled in their ministries or drifted towards differ-

---

[5] For a glimpse of the driving interests behind the transcendentalist scene, see Richardson's selection of topics for the club meetings: "On October 3, 1836, at Alcott's in Boston the topic was 'American Genius – the causes which hinder its growth, and give us no first rate productions.' On October 18, 1836, at Brownson's house in Boston it was 'Education of Humanity.' On May 29, 1836, at Ripley's in Boston it was 'What is the essence of Religion as distinct from morality?' In the summer of 1837 at Emerson's house, 'Does the species advance beyond the individual?' On May 20, 1838, at Stetson's house in Medford, 'Is Mysticism an element of Christianity?' In June of 1838 at Bartol's house in Boston, 'On the character and genius of Goethe'; in December of 1838 at the same place, 'Pantheism.' On May 13, 1840, at Emerson's, 'the Inspiration of the Prophet and Bard, the nature of Poetry, and the causes of sterility of poetic Inspiration in our Age and country'" (Richardson 1995, 246; cf. Myerson 1972).

[6] For example, George Ripley's series *Specimens of Foreign Standard Literature* (1838-1842) amounted to fourteen volumes of translated works from the French and German. The first two volumes reprinted Ripley's translations of "philosophical miscellanies" from the speculative philosophy and historiography of Victor Cousin, Benjamin Constant, and Theodore Simon Jouffroy. It was followed by translations of Schiller's and Goethe's poetry (vol. 3, translated by John Sullivan Dwight with the assistance of Longfellow), Eckermann's *Conversations with Goethe* (vol. 4, translated by Margaret Fuller), Jouffroy's *Introduction to Ethics* (vols. 5 and 6, translated by William Ellery Channing), Wolfgang Menzel's 1836 treatise on *German Literature* (vols. 7-9), Wilhelm Martin Leberecht de Wette's 1828 theological romance *Theodore, or the Skeptic's Conversion* (vols. 10 and 11) and his treatise on *Human Life, Or Practical Ethics* (vols. 13 and 14), and finally (vol. 14) a selection of songs and ballads from German lyric poets (Uhland, Körner, Bürger, and others). Another important anthology was Hedge's *Prose Writers of Germany* (1848).

ent worlds and views.⁷ When Emerson published *Representative Men*, he had acquired international standing and mingled with the Boston elite,⁸ becoming less interested in the countercultural attitude and religious debate of the 1830s. Meanwhile Thoreau was stacking his own library with the unsold four-fifths of his *Week on the Concord and Merrimack Rivers* (1849).⁹ His reputation as a central voice in the movement emerged only later in the century.

II. Locations, Periodizations

Strictly speaking, transcendentalists must be considered late romantics, although the generic categories of European literary history do not match well with American developments. Transcendentalists participated in the religious, political, and aesthetic discourse associated with European romanticism: Fuller translated Goethe, Emerson was fascinated by the poetry of Wordsworth and Mme de Staël's *De l'Allemagne*, and he developed a close relationship with Carlyle, whose own transcendentalism was influenced by Coleridge and the Jena romantics. The founding of the Transcendental Club was motivated by Henry Hedge's interest in Coleridge's philosophical sources (or more precisely, Hedge's exasperation with the lack of a similar interest at Harvard).

At the same time, the most productive phase of Emersonian transcendentalism (roughly between the 1830s and 1860s) covers the post-romantic period that cultural historians generally associate with the rise of positive science, biological evolutionism, and, in Europe, literary realism – Flaubert's *Madame Bovary* appeared in 1857, the same decade that saw the publication of Thoreau's *Walden* (1854), Whitman's *Leaves of Grass* (1855), Hawthorne's *Scarlet Letter* (1850) and Melville's *Moby Dick* (1851). For all of their fascination with European romantic idealism, New England intellectuals were open to the materialist, technological, and scientific obsessions of mid- to late-century Victorianism. Consequently, combined their romantic models of culture as a *bildungsroman* of "spirit" with emerging theories on the social and material determinants of spiritual realities that revolved around notions of climatic influence, embodied sexuality, and racial identity. Whitman, for example, liked to portray the body with electromagnetic metaphors and was a follower of the pseudo-science of phrenology, which

---

[7] Fuller emigrated to Italy but soon died after Ripley took over the regular book review department of Horace Greeley's New York *Tribune*; Alcott became Superintendent of the Concord school system; Parker took an active part in the abolitionist movement; Bancroft was elected into political office; and Brownson converted to Catholicism and, renaming his journal *Brownson Quarterly Review*, became a religious and social activist.

[8] In 1855, he became a member of the Saturday Club, an influential network that comprised Harvard professors and scientists as well as leading Boston publishers and intellectuals.

[9] As Thoreau put it with heroic stoicism, in a diary entry from October 28, 1853: "I have now a library of nearly nine hundred volumes, over seven hundred of which I wrote myself. Is it not well that the author should behold the fruits of his labor?" (1906, 11: 459).

assumed that mental propensities can be measured by feeling the shape of a person's skull. Thoreau was fascinated by the idea that America's spatial configuration would influence the future emergence of an American philosophy (big canyons, big ideas, as he implies in "Walking"). In the Saturday Club, Emerson conversed with a positivistic scientific community that theorized about the connections between dry climates and American 'restiveness' and, like the Harvard geologist Louis Agassiz, speculated about the separate origin of black and white races. The lateness of the transcendentalist brand of romanticism can also be seen in the tendency towards what Leo Marx has called "the rhetoric of the technological sublime" (Marx 1964, 195), the construction of American symbolic landscapes in terms that extend Wordsworthian visions of awe-inspiring natural sublimity to include the wonders of man-made technology.

Another factor complicating the periodization of American transcendentalism is the continued (if partial) cultural authority of pre-romantic discourse in mid-century Boston. Some of the most influential New England writers at the time, and especially the members of the so-called "genteel" generation of poets whom Emerson regularly met at the Saturday Club,[10] remained open to the neoclassical aesthetic sensibilities that preceded the European romantic generation, and the rhetorical views of literary production generic to the eighteenth-century textbooks that continued to be read and taught in American colleges. Also, given the cultural "lag" inherent in Boston's distance from the more dynamic European centers of knowledge production, the US print market was defined by a simultaneity of the non-simultaneous. Mid-nineteenth-century transcendentalist writers accordingly faced a literary public that read two generations of European romantics (from Goethe to Keats) together with the great Victorians (from Carlyle to Dickens) and such neoclassical fixtures as Swift, Pope, and Dr. Johnson.

The transformations of authorship in the Early Republic provided another source of inconsistency. Transcendentalist intellectuals felt the transatlantic effects of the late-eighteenth-century print market revolution – the widening of readership resulting from rising standards of education and literacy, and the accompanying extension of print capitalism, as well as the commodification of the book – which led to a differentiation of literary culture that gradually enabled authors to support themselves in the field of *belles lettres* and prompted an array of literary professions competing for status and recognition, such as journalists,

---

[10] This circle includes the Fireside Poets Henry Wadsworth Longfellow, one of the best-known nineteenth-century American writers, who had just retired from a Harvard professorship of modern languages; Oliver Wendell Holmes, poet, novelist, and Harvard professor of anatomy; and James Russell Lowell, poet, essayist, and critic, who in 1855 took over the Harvard professorship from which Longfellow had just retired, and in 1857 became founding editor of the important high-brow journal *Atlantic Monthly* (which published works by Emerson, and, posthumously, a number of Thoreau's essays). The Fireside Poets, and especially Longfellow, were perceived as America's most representative intellectuals before they were dropped from the literary canon around 1900.

magazine editors, religious or political pamphleteers, university professors, pedagogues, and commercial novelists. In New England, this process of differentiation proceeded in fits and starts, producing sites of heightened professionalism that co-existed with less dynamic areas dominated by older models of intellectual authority – such as the holistic concepts of the Jeffersonian gentleman scholar equally at home in the fields of politics, scientific inquiry, moral reasoning, aesthetic perception, and polite feeling. In its more vibrant locations, the New England intellectual field produced self-reliant men of letters (Emerson and Thoreau, and to a lesser extent, the younger Brownson and Bancroft), who considered themselves engaged in the serious business of visionary world-making and cultural healing, and like the so-called Victorian "sages" in England, Thomas Carlyle, Matthew Arnold, and John Ruskin, wanted to see their projects justified by peer recognition rather than economic success (cf. Leypoldt 2007). Like the modernist avant-garde, these men of letters defined themselves against what they considered the downside of modern publishing, the commercially more successful sensationalist, sentimental, and domestic works by popular novelists and intellectuals who, in Carlyle's terminology, were engaged in mere literature as opposed to the prophetic powers of poetic "Song" (1984, 392).

III. The Transcendental Turn

The Emersonian creed defies concise summary, yet no single defining feature brings American transcendentalism as close to the previous generation of European romantics as its creative appropriation of the critical and speculative philosophies indicated in the movement's label. The late-eighteenth-century transcendental turn begins with Immanuel Kant's *Critique of Pure Reason* (1781), which can be summarized as the attempt to base the theories of knowledge (epistemology) and practical reason (morality and ethics) on principles internal to the human mind, severing them from their traditional foundations (in empirical reality, human sentiment, or utility). This implies that the most direct route to moral truth lies in the pure judgments of innate reason, purged of the fickle impulses of senses and feelings and the calculation of consequences.

Surely the romantic success story of Kantianism is overdetermined. But it is worth considering, for a moment, how transcendentalist moves negotiate modern political and economic conditions – the social anxieties, for instance, that accompanied the displacement of hereditary governmental hierarchies by democratic change, as well as the economic instabilities of the growing capitalist markets. In earlier periods, culture and commerce were largely regarded as mutually reinforcing agents of progress – according to the French political theorist Montesquieu, commerce cures prejudices, produces human sympathy, and brings Europeans closer together in a culture of gentle politeness (cf. 1989, 337-53). But with the economic acceleration towards the end of the century, "culture" was increasingly considered antithetical to commerce – it became a space of refuge *against* the economic cycles of consumption and commodity exhaustion. This is connected to the origin of the modern "reversal of the economic world" in the cultural domain (Bourdieu 1996, 114), which assures that the highest prestige (the most symbolic capital) is conferred to cultural artifacts with the smallest commercial value (i.e., the avant-garde). It seems that as modern consumerism accelerates the commercial circulation of things, it also produces spaces of extraterritoriality where objects receive a sacred aura by being removed from the cycle of commodities and consumption (cf. Böhme 2006, chap. 3). The reversal of the economic world turns cultural fields into sites of transcendence as well as social distinction. Inasmuch as the Kantian notion of human moral autonomy describes human reason as a faculty *within* – inaccessible to sensual perception and conceptual knowledge – it makes moral deliberation extraterritorial to the market, withdrawing moral truths from the indignities of economic cycles of consumption.[11]

Within the context of eighteenth-century debates, the transcendental turn solved a number of conceptual problems that troubled the romantic reception of classic sensualist identity models. For empiricists like John Locke, personal identity had been hardly problematic: Individuals were born as blank pages, then formed by experiential sense impressions. Personal identity simply emerged from whatever educational experience inscribed itself on an individual's mental receptors. But David Hume's *Treatise of Human Nature* (1739) shows how later empiricists complicated the sensualist paradigm. Hume famously described the individual as a "bundle [...] of different perceptions, which succeed each other with an inconceivable rapidity, and are in a perpetual flux and movement" (1978, 252). Hume implied, in other words, that we would all be changing our identity with every new sense perception, if it were not for the faculty of memory that helps us to impose the "fiction" of a coherent self. With another famous analogy, Hume compared the "soul" to the unstable conditions of democratic consensus: Identity arises out of the uncoordinated circulation of sense impressions in the same way that "a republic or commonwealth" is tossed about in "incessant changes of its parts," its people and laws determined by the vicissitudes of democratic process (261). To be tossed around by sensual influence is precisely how romantic intellectuals experienced the scandal of commodified culture, and the specters of political, economic, and aesthetic mob rule. Kant participates in a discursive shift that addresses this scandal when he rejects the sensual model, arguing that the mind is not blank, but hardwired with universal categories that assure a coherent sense of selfhood by imposing a transcendental unity of apperception on the experiential data.

---

[11] The same economy of the sacred holds for the concept of aesthetic autonomy, implied in Kant's *Critique of Judgment* (1790): To define beauty as pure (non-conceptual) form is a way of 'reauratizing' art by making it extraterritorial to moral or cognitive uses.

IV. Post-Kantian Intuitionism: Reason as an "Inner Light"

Kant's transcendentalism provides new ways of solving the empiricist conundrum of personal identity, but it also leads the romantic vocabulary of inwardness to a distinctly unromantic punch line: It holds that because experience is based on mere appearances, the reality *behind* appearances ("the thing in itself") cannot be known. We can investigate the mental filters (*a priori* categories) with which the human mind fashions the spatial, temporal, and causal parameters of experience and synthesizes them into ideas about coherent existence, such as "God," "World," or "Soul." But we will have to surrender the hope that these ideas can ever be grounded in actual reality. One could simplify the complex reception history of Kant's ideas by saying that romantic thinkers admired his turn to interiority but resisted his radical skepticism. In the creative misreadings of romantic idealists, the concept of "pure reason" changes from a subjective mode of structuring experience to an innate organ for intuiting spiritual knowledge (analogous to the Quaker metaphor of an "Inner Light"). This change begins with the speculative idealism of the Schlegel brothers and Schelling's *Naturphilosophie*, and it arrives in Boston with a distinctly religious spin through the mediation of, among others, James Marsh's 1829 edition of Coleridge's *Aids to Reflection* and two notable reviews in the *Christian Examiner*: Hedge's explication of Coleridge's philosophical sources (1833), and Brownson's discussion of Victor Cousin's Hegelian lectures on the history of philosophy (doc. 194). In the course of this conceptual reconfiguration, Kant's dichotomy of pure reason versus understanding (*Vernunft* versus *Verstand*) was reinterpreted in terms of a neoplatonic natural theology that posited a mystical correspondence between material nature and the realm of spiritual existence (cf. docs. 188-92, 195-6, 199-201). Transcendental reason was considered an organic faculty through which sensitive artists who immersed themselves in the primal beauties of natural environments could reach levels of introspection that revealed mystical, i.e., pre-conceptual, experiences of capital-N Nature (variously labeled "the Infinite," "the Absolute," "Oversoul," "World Spirit," etc.). The faculty of understanding was downgraded to the level of a mechanical perception and cold conceptual analysis of the world's tangible surfaces, which made it the preferred mental faculty of dry dogmatists, empirical scientists, neoclassical poets, and aristocratic despots.[12]

---

[12] Consider, for instance, Emerson's own explanation of the transcendental turn, in a lecture of 1842: "It is well known to most of my audience, that the Idealism of the present day acquired the name of Transcendental, from the use of that term by Immanuel Kant, of Königsberg, who replied to the skeptical philosophy of Locke, which insisted that there was nothing in the intellect which was not previously in the experience of the senses, by showing that there was a very important class of ideas, or imperative forms, which did not come by experience, but through which experience was acquired; that these were intuitions of the mind itself; and he denominated them *Transcendental* forms. The extraordinary profoundness and precision of that man's thinking have given vogue to his nomenclature, in Europe and America, to that extent, that whatever belongs to the class of intuitive thought, is popularly called at the present

V. Transcendentalist Models of Culture and Authenticity

The romantic revision of the Kantian *Critiques* provided intellectuals around 1800 with powerful rhetorical tools to cope with (or make sense of) the perceived alienation caused by modern levels of social differentiation and literary commercialization. The post-Kantian vocabulary of transcendental intuition as an inner light cohered well with emerging historicist culture models based on what I would like to call "dissociation of sensibility" narratives.[13] Such narratives conceptualize the effects of social differentiation – the specialization and professionalism of social activities – in classic terms of alienation, imagined as the unhealthy dispersal of society's experiential center into fragmented extremes of sensualist hedonism on the one hand, and a dessicated and detached rationalism on the other. Modernist variants of the dissociation narratives express contemporary fears of social alienation at least partly in terms of economic critique – for instance, Van Wyck Brooks' famous late-nineteenth-century claim that American culture had broken up into low-brow frontier capitalism and detached high-brow culture (or, in Santayana's terminology, into the bland masculinity of the skyscraper versus the effeminate unreality of genteel poetry) resonates with a Marxist despair about the accelerated print market without which the division of culture into high and low domains would not be possible (cf. Brooks 1934, 19; Santayana 1968, 37). Romantic narratives of dissociation, by contrast, tend to displace economic and social anxieties into specters of psychological deficiency, attributed, for instance, to a cultural lapse into the mechanical empiricism preceding the Kantian turn. In *Letters of Aesthetic Education* (1793), Schiller portrays society as having broken up into debilitated masses of cannibalistic sensuality (the "hordes" of the French Revolution) and a detached and despotic elite (absolute monarchs, dry rationalists). This dystopia corresponds with a dispersal of cultural energies into cold rationality (driven by analytical understanding)

---

day *Transcendental*" (1903-1904, 1: 339-40). Emerson's account transforms Kant's theory into an intuitionist model suited to romantic religiosity, while it transfers the epithet "skeptical" to Locke. Precisely because conservative New England Unitarians associated skeptical "infidelity" with Kant rather than Locke, the transcendentalists had an interest in presenting the transcendental turn in terms of a religious awakening. This intention seems even more obvious in Bancroft's *A History of the United States* (1834-1875), whose second volume presents Kantian philosophy as a restatement of the Quaker doctrine of a divinely inspired "Inner Light." By deriving "philosophy from the voice of the soul" (1841, 355), Bancroft argues, Kant resembles the Quaker leaders George Fox, Robert Barclay, and William Penn. Thus the term "transcendental" is adapted to the purposes of New England thinkers to legitimate their cultural work (in a similar way, perhaps, that today such epithets as "deconstructive" or "discursive" are often appropriated to theoretical uses only remotely connected to their Derridean and Foucauldian origins).

[13] In his essay on "The Metaphysical Poets," Eliot diagnosed a "dissociation of sensibility" as a general tendency in Western culture after 1700 to think and feel in fits (1975, 64). His model draws from a long romantic tradition of presenting modernity as depriving cultures of their holistic middle.

and animalistic feeling (driven by the senses). In romantic theory, eighteenth-century concepts of psychological equilibrium are rephrased in terms of an early nineteenth-century psychology of interiority. While Schiller's dissociation anxieties still tend to revolve around metaphors of lopsided bodily energies, the transcendentalist narratives understand the "mechanical" condition of alienation as the result of a disconnection from an interior presence.[14]

The redefinition of alienation in these terms can be seen in the romantic preoccupation with the difference between "mechanical" and "organic" experience. According to A. W. Schlegel, form becomes mechanical if it follows from an "external force" that suppresses an object's "innate" quality. By contrast, "organic" form "unfolds itself from within" (1846, 340).[15] Another way of putting this point is to say that mechanical actions are accidental and arbitrary, while organic ones are authentic, since they follow from an inner necessity. New England transcendentalists adapt these terms by redescribing received tradition and canonical knowledge as arbitrary facts distracting individuals from the true learning that can only be acquired by tapping the rich resources deep within the individual's mind. Emerson likes to phrases this transcendentalist chestnut in postcolonial terms: The "courtly muses of Europe" (*KC*, 445) may be beautiful enough, but they are "sepulchres of the fathers" (*KC*, 440), external to the lived experience of the New England present. Emerson also extends the exteriority/interiority distinction to political and philosophical systems, arguing that the "politics of monarchy" is related to the mechanical because "all hangs on the accidents of life and temper of a single person," while in democracy "the power proceeds organically from the people and is responsible to them" (1903-1904, 12: 304). If this view of the democratic process as an inward necessity (cf. doc. 202) seems almost to go without saying today, it is useful to recall that many leading nineteenth-century intellectuals in Europe arrived at the opposite conclusion. William Hazlitt and Thomas Carlyle, for instance, considered democratic rule as an arbitrary imposition of anarchy as opposed to the more authentic political action by a natural aristocracy of great men.[16]

---

[14] On the romantic shift towards interiority, the emergence of a concept of the self as having inner depth, see Taylor (1989) and Cronin (2000).

[15] Schlegel made this influential point in 1809, in his Vienna lectures, with reference to Shakespeare. His definition reappears almost verbatim in Coleridge's influential lectures on Shakespeare of 1812-1813, which were published in 1836, in his *Literary Remains* (cf. Coleridge 1992, 128). By this time the argument had become a commonplace of romantic criticism. It plays a prominent role in Carlyle's 1829 *Edinburgh Review* essay on the "mechanical" state of modern society which was well received by Boston transcendentalists (cf. Carlyle 1984, 34-5).

[16] The "Great Man Theory of History," crucial to nineteenth-century culture models, first emerged when romantic idealists became fascinated by the idea that the "spirit of the age" or the "nation" may find its truest and most beautiful expression in the work or deeds of a few brilliant minds, who thus become "representative" of their age (common candidates were Napoleon and Shakespeare). Representationality plays a role in Hegel's *Philosophy of History*

Emerson's rejection of British institutions does not amount to a rejection of English culture. The conceptualization of America as a distinct cultural whole (as a spatialized "other" to the culture of England) is a twentieth-century view that the founders of the American Studies movement after 1900 reprojected on Emerson's "American Scholar" oration.[17] For the most part, New England transcendentalists consider American history as part of the history of Anglo-Saxon civilization. They merely emplot this history in terms of a temporal dissociation narrative, marked by a cyclical swerve towards and away from authentic presence (understood as an "emanating" source of authenticity, which transcendentalists like to figure in tropes of depth and light).[18] The most influential transcendentalist cultural historiographies (for instance, Emerson's *English Traits*, or Bancroft's *History of the United States*) interpret the Elizabethan Age with its great cultural achievements as an age of authenticity, followed by a post-Elizabethan disconnection from spiritual presence that accounts for the shallowness (or darkness) of seventeenth and eighteenth-century rationalism, materialism, pragmatism, and empiricism. Transcendentalist intellectuals thus see themselves as participating in a contemporary effort to free the blocked spiritual channels of modern culture, reinstituting an organic hol-

---

(1822-1830), and, more relevant to the Transcendental Club, Victor Cousin's *History of Modern Philosophy* (1828-1829). The best known transcendentalist versions are Carlyle's *On Heroes, Hero-Worship, and the Heroic in History* (1840) and Emerson's *Representative Men* (1850). After the demise of "Great Man" theories, the idea of representationality survives in the guise of spatial metaphors of cultural depth. In 1853, for instance – three years after Emerson's *Representative Men* – Hippolyte Taine asserts that "the deeper [a poet] penetrates into his art, the more he has penetrated into the genius of his age and race" (1861, 343, my translation). A decade later, in his Paris lectures on the *Philosophie de l'Art* (1865-1869), Taine offers a "spiritual geology" that locates representationality on an ascending scale of cultural penetration, where lesser authors represent mere fashions, better ones might capture the essence of a school or whole generation, and the greatest artists will embody a historical period or even the essence of a race (Taine 1985; my translation). To be sure, Taine uses a nineteenth-century concept of race that still includes both biological and cultural traits (hence he can speak of a contrast between the "French" and the "Anglo-Saxon" races).

[17] The emergence of the spatial concepts underlying today's cultural pluralism (or multiculturalism) is complex and open to critical debate (for a good introduction, cf. Hegeman 1999). Most critics agree that nineteenth-century concepts of culture were used in the singular, and based on temporal frameworks that conceived the difference between modern and "primitive" cultures (such as the Greeks, or colonial natives) in terms of the difference between parents and children. The coexistence of different cultures (in the plural) is an invention of twentieth-century anthropological relativism (in America, the work of Franz Boas, Edward Sapir, and Ruth Benedict). What complicates this development, however, is the relatively early invention of spatial concepts of nationhood (for instance, in the work of Herder) that anticipate, to an extent, modern concepts of cultural plurality. At any rate, New England transcendentalism, despite the popularity of Herder's works, remained squarely within the temporal concepts of nationality that cohered with the open concepts of culture or civilization (in the singular) that characterized Matthew Arnold's *Culture and Anarchy* (1867) and Edward Tylor's *Primitive Culture* (1871).

[18] "Emanation" is a term from Greek neoplatonism crucial to the transcendentalist nature religion, according to which a spiritual force radiates outward from a divine core within.

ism that will not overcome but rejuvenate their Anglo-Saxon heritage, purging it of such "mechanical" symptoms as neoclassical verse, utilitarian thought, sensualist philosophy, and aristocratic politics. Emerson's "American Scholar" oration diagnoses the division of US society into spiritually impoverished practical men and an inactive, detached, and feminized clergy. His essay on "Art" (1841) bemoans a division of lived experience into impoverished sequences of work and play ("weary chores" alternating with "voluptuous reveries") that a thoroughly transcendentalist culture should overcome ("Beauty must come back to the useful arts, and the distinction between the fine and the useful arts forgotten," he says; 1903-1904, 2: 367).[19] In 1836, Orestes Brownson phrases this demand in the socio-religious language of the early Transcendental Club, when he announces the millennial hope that soon America's intellectual and practical social domains will be reunited, so that "our whole population will be philosophers, and all our philosophers will be practical men" (in Miller 1950, 122).

VI. Transcendental Religiosity

The impact of Neoplatonism and idealism on New England intellectuals must be viewed in the context of their deep religious preoccupations (most transcendentalists were, or had been at one point in their lives, practicing clergy). The gradual disintegration of Calvinism during the Early Republic coincided with a shift towards liberalism, individualism, and inwardness in religious theory and practice. The so-called Second Great Awakening destabilized traditional church hierarchies with a burst of religious enthusiasm that 'burned over' rural New England, while the theological centers in Yale, Harvard, and Princeton challenged the Calvinist dualism of an angry God and a fallen humanity (cf. Kelleter in this vol., 171-7). By the early 1800s, the Boston area was under the influence of the Unitarian belief in man's intrinsic divinity (his 'Likeness to God'). Unitarianism was an upper-class creed whose proponents disapproved of the emotionalism of lower-class revivalisms and attempted to combine religion with the premises of eighteenth-century science. But it also had a Rousseauist impulse that encouraged its more liberal theologians, such as William Ellery Channing, to locate the divine in nature rather than in formal dogma, and spiritual revelation in imaginative insight rather than in theological speculation (cf. doc. 193). Most transcendentalist intellectuals of Emerson's generation began as liberal Unitarians attempting to convince their more conservative peers of Channing's teachings (cf. doc. 197) – until during the 1830s these attempts propelled them beyond Unitarianism altogether. The tran-

---

[19] This appears to anticipate Matthew Arnold's hugely influential thesis (in *Culture and Anarchy*, 1869) that the cultural deficits of English civilization – the division of social unity into lower class barbarism, middle class philistinism and upper class ignorance – result from a failure to balance the forces of Hebraism and Hellenism, the propensities for practical morality Arnold associated with Christianity, versus the tolerance of truth and free mental play he located in ancient Greece (cf. 1978, 223-7).

scendentalists' dissent was mainly directed at the Unitarian belief in miracles and adherence to empiricist or sensualist science. They accused their teachers of being too half-hearted to dispense with Calvinist supernaturalism and too cold-hearted to appreciate the importance of intuitive religious feeling compared with intellectual rationalization. The transcendentalist positions mediate contemporary theology with the romantic vocabularies of inwardness, expressive individualism, and poetic inspiration. Emersonianism accords with Friedrich Schleiermacher's conceptualization of religion as a form of consciousness – being religious, Schleiermacher said in his treatise *Über die Religion*, means to have a "sense and taste for the Infinite" (1821, 66; my translation).

The transcendentalist argument with established religion draws from the fascination with which an earlier generation of New England Unitarians had already debated the "higher criticism" by eighteenth-century liberal theologians seeking to solve scriptural conundrums through a hermeneutics of biblical authorship. Higher criticism treats the Bible as a literary artifact whose divine referent is refracted by the perspectives of man-made historical sources. By the 1830s, even conservatives like the important Unitarian leader Andrews Norton, who is now mainly known as transcendentalism's raging opponent, accepted the thesis of historical authorship and the resulting importance of informed biblical criticism to sort out corrupt and authentic passages. But they drew the line at questioning the authenticity of the recorded events. The impending theological rift became most apparent when Emerson argued, in his controversial 1838 "Divinity School Address" (doc. 199), that the historical Jesus was a great poet-prophet who had seen the mysteries of soul (rather than the Son of God who had worked miracles). The implication was that Christ's teachings were to be understood, not as eternal truths, but as poetic renditions of divine nature that should not be ossified into dogmatic beliefs and institutionalized rites but extended and injected with fresh visions by inspired poets of present-day America. The uproar over Emerson's address was fueled by his outspoken stand on an issue around which the theological difference between liberals and conservatives had crystallized: Two years earlier, Ripley had prompted the so-called "miracle controversy" by suggesting in the *Christian Examiner* that regardless of whether accounts of Jesus's miraculous deeds are authentic or not, they cannot be regarded as proper touchstones of the dignity of the Christian faith. Emerson went a step further when he dismissed biblical accounts of miracles as false literalizations of spiritual symbolisms.

Emerson's argument can be related to Herder's *On the Spirit of Hebrew Poetry* (1782-1783), which James Marsh translated in 1833. Herder proceeded from the eighteenth-century belief that primitive cultures conversed in a vivid metaphorical language, in contrast to the analytic forms of literal representation generic to modern ages. Thus Herder read the Old Testament as a remnant of an ancient Hebrew civilization that expressed its intuitive grasp of spiritual truths in poetic figures and mythical symbols, which cannot be mistaken for literal truths. Emerson makes a similar point when he portrays Jesus as a true prophet who "saw [...] the mystery of the soul," but expressed what he saw in his own poetic terms: "He spoke of miracles" metaphorically because "he felt that man's life was a miracle." The Christian tradition has misread Jesus's living "idioms" and "figures" by viewing them through the mechanical faculty of the "understanding" rather than the poetic intuition of reason. As a result, "the word Miracle, as pronounced by Christian churches, gives a false impression" and becomes a "Monster" (Emerson 1903-1904, 1: 129).[20]

Emerson's assertion that "Christianity became a Mythus" (1903-1904, 1: 129) points toward the radical dismantling of biblical truth-claims by David Friedrich Strauß, whose *Life of Jesus* of 1835 attributes most of the events narrated in the gospel to human myth. New England transcendentalists did not generally go quite that far: Theodore Parker's 1840 review of *Life of Jesus* for the *Christian Examiner* shows how difficult it was even for radical theologians to accept Strauß' conclusions. But the most influential statements of transcendentalist religiosity had less to do with the intricacies of these theological debates. What is now known as the Emersonian nature religion appeals to the sublime landscapes of the US as privileged sites for the gaining of personal self-reliance and national identity (cf. docs. 198, 201, 203).

Emerson's most famous (and perhaps most parodied) religious statement, in the first chapter of *Nature* (doc. 196), shows well how transcendentalism combines the tropes of mystical experience with the rhetoric of the sublime. It describes how Emerson, as he crosses a "bare common" "at "twilight," is suddenly struck by a feeling of deep presence of nature that fills him with a mixture of terror and delight ("I am glad to the brink of fear")[21] and a sense of merging with the divine ("the currents of the Universal Being circulate through me; I am part or particle of God," *KC*, 441). The experiential flow of deep nature seems to tap directly into his transcendental intuitions, short-cutting his understanding in a way that makes him feel like a "transparent eye-ball" (*KC*, 441), a free-floating organ of vision through which pure perception circulates without filters of rational reflection. His identity seems to disappear ("all mean egotism vanishes"), along with his memories ("[t]he name of the nearest friends sounds then foreign or accidental," *KC*, 441). This view of felt religiosity figures importantly in Emerson's dialectic concept of self-reliance: Overcoming the received habits that sedimented tradition imposes from without is only a first step. It needs to be followed by a second step, when the "mean egotism" of personal identity is overcome through spiritual connection with a larger Self ("the currents of the Universal Being"), which can only be accessed by an inward turn. If this Emersonian creed has a nationalist inflection at

---

[20] The excerpt in doc. 199 provides most of the argument. For the full text, see the digital edition of the *Complete Works of Ralph Waldo Emerson*, Centenary Edition: <http://quod.lib.umich.edu/e/emerson> (August 24, 2008).

[21] This quote is from the revised edition (Emerson 1903-1904, 1: 9). The simultaneity of terror and fear is a stock motif of mystical experience, and of the seventeenth- and eighteenth-century concept of the sublime; see also Margaret Fuller's description of Niagara (doc. 201).

all, it lies in the pastoralist assumption that America's stupendous natural resources provide the happiest setting for the act of spiritual connection ("In the woods we return to reason and faith," as Emerson puts it; *KC*, 441).

We can better understand the historical location of transcendentalist spirituality if we consider how it relates to the transformation of religious beliefs and practices that Charles Taylor has attributed to a modern process of subjectivization and individualization of religious experience that already begins with sixteenth-century varieties of denominationalism.[22] In contrast to earlier periods represented by medieval Catholicism, where church membership was largely "co-extensive with society," Protestant forms of denominationalism connected worshippers "to a broader, more elusive 'church'" in which membership was increasingly considered a matter of choice and authenticity, and characterized by a sense, in Taylor's words, that the religion I join "must speak to me" (2002, 93-4). At the beginning of the nineteenth century, New England Unitarians and many of the new revivalist creeds originating in the Second Great Awakening[23] were torn between the communitarian ideal of religious unity, however loosely defined, and an emergent belief that the core of religion has to do with "[d]eeply felt personal insight." In the romantic view of religiosity around 1800, it was considered "more crucial" to explore the "powerful feeling of dependence on something greater" (the infinite, the absolute, the universal soul, etc.) than knowing the right theological "formula" (Taylor 2002, 93-4). Thus, Emersonianism participates in a general romantic rejection of institutionalized forms of worship in favor of a more private search for technologies of introversion that enable the individual to succeed in a private quest for deep spiritual resources (cf. Spahr in this vol., 60-2).

This romantic religious sensibility was an elite phenomenon, restricted mainly to well-educated groups of artists and intellectuals, while the larger part of the population followed traditional patterns of church attendance and affiliation (controversial as Emerson's "Divinity School Address" was among the elites, it would have been incomprehensible to lower social circles). As Taylor points out, this changed in the twentieth century, when romantic identity models "penetrated in some general form deep into our culture," so that, after World War II, it became a mainstream assumption that "adhering to a spirituality that does not present itself as your path, the one that moves and inspires you," seems "absurd" (2002, 100).[24]

---

[22] The term derives from Latin "de nomina" ("of names"), which implies that doctrinal differences can be regarded as superficial to the core of Christian belief. Thus, it is common to view Eastern Orthodox, Catholic, and Protestant churches as denominations within a common Christian framework. In the United States, the policy of religious tolerance (guaranteed by the First Amendment to the US Constitution) led to a plurality of largely Protestant denominations (for instance, Baptists, Anabaptists, Congregationalists, Episcopalians, Lutherans, Methodists, Presbyterians, Quakers, and many more).
[23] See Williams (1998) for an overview of the new religious movements emerging from the culture of antebellum evangelicalism, such as Mormonism.
[24] Taylor's analysis of the modern process of subjectivization is meant to suggest that the privatization of religiosity that seems natural today (though to a lesser extent, perhaps, in

The present interest in Emersonian forms of spirituality thus accords with a post-1950s transition in Western religious sensibilities (especially in the US) that Robert Wuthnow has defined as a shift towards "a new spirituality of seeking," where relatively unaffiliated believers now search for "fleeting glimpses of the sacred" and "partial knowledge and practical wisdom," in marked contrast to a more traditional "spirituality of inhabiting sacred places" based on regular church membership and attendance, and a fairly coherent "metaphysic" of belief (1998, 3). If therefore the transcendentalist rhetoric of the sublime seems so familiar today, it is partly because the Emersonian creed anticipates the radically privatized late twentieth-century forms of religiosity represented by the anti-clerical attitudes of "seeker churches" or the anti-establishment attitudes of popular forms of esotericism (cf. Roof and Caron 2006). Moreover, the transcendentalist connection of spiritual self-reliance with a disciplined effort of introvertive self-culture inclines towards the utilitarian logic of the contemporary religious self-help manual, combining as it does questions of religious authenticity (such as "how do I best connect with my deep spiritual sources?") with pragmatic queries about the uses of specific beliefs (e.g., "what can a religion do for me?"). Protestantism has always tended to link spiritual and material success in a symbolic relationship of mutual reinforcement (as in Max Weber's reading of the Protestant work ethic).[25] But modern "seeker" religions have a way of foregrounding the use value of spiritual pursuits as technologies of self-perfection to the extent that the object of worship may become less important, as long as it works – in Peter Sloterdijk's caricature, this entails a view of the divine as "an inner Texas" whose "deep energies" can be "mined" for "fuel" to power our "life-motors," which means that religious practices are looked upon as tools to be tried out and discarded if they fail to produce suitable results (1997, 28-30, my translation). Emersonian transcendentalists would have rejected such a strong pragmatism,[26] but Sloterdijk's metaphor of the spiritual oil field captures well (even in parody) the transcendentalist conviction that spiritual connection and rejuvenation may effect both social progress and economic prosperity.

countries such as Poland or Ireland) is not as self-evident as it seems. It has an intellectual, institutional, and economic history that is worth considering, especially to get a better understanding of the communitarian aspects of religious practice that run against the grain of today's liberal individualism (23-4). Whether or not one agrees with Taylor's view on religion, his historical analysis of the connection between romantic identity models and religious privatization is trenchant, and has been fleshed out recently in *A Secular Age* (2007).

[25] Weber's thesis is, roughly, that the Protestant work ethic is connected to the Calvinist belief that material success can be considered evidence of one's personal salvation.

[26] Both Sloterdijk's and Taylor's analyses of modern religion proceed from William James's *Varieties of Religious Experience* (1902), which exemplifies well how romantic spirituality is already half-way to twentieth-century pragmatism. As many commentators have pointed out, James seems to be undecided whether the religious impulse he analyses in such depth should be taken as evidence for a spiritual presence "out there" (which brings him close to Emerson's romantic sublime) or whether religious insights are simply "good to believe," regardless of whether or not they are true (which points towards postmodern notions of a religiosity without foundations).

VII. Social Perfectionism, Transcendental Utopias

The idea that America might be a natural setting for social improvement and spiritual rejuvenation ties in with another important aspect of transcendentalist literary culture, its affinities to the "perfectionist" millennialism in contemporary American religious discourse (cf. Stievermann in this vol., 150-1). Based on the belief that the Second Coming of Christ (and hence the salvation of the world) would be preceded by a thousand-year period of earthly harmony and peace, millennialism stimulated American visions of a utopian Christian society in which religious inspiration encourages social and educational reform (cf. doc. 205) and economic and political advancement, as preconditions of the approaching rule of Christ on Earth.[27] Most transcendentalist intellectuals did not literally expect the Lord to return in person, but their conviction that spiritual regeneration requires a major reorganization of social structure carries a millennialist signature. This socioreligious approach to human perfectibility led them to propose communitarian visions of democratic progress (cf. doc. 202), and it may partly explain the openness with which the deeply religious transcendentalist visionaries treated not only the Christian socialism of Henri de Saint-Simon, but also the radically secular utopias of European social materialists such as Frances Wright, Robert Owen (cf. doc. 206), and Charles Fourier. The influence of this tradition can be seen in Brownson's "The Laboring Classes" (doc. 204), which proceeds from Carlyle's critique of British laissez faire capitalism to a proto-Marxist indictment of the property-holding American merchant class.

The more practical effects of social utopianism can be seen in the series of short-lived community experiments in the US modeled on Owenite and Fourierist examples. Owen was as notorious for his declared atheism as he was famous for the successful welfare programs with which his community project New Lanark in Great Britain had fought industrial pauperism (although his attempt to repeat his success in 1825 in New Harmony, Indiana, was a financial failure). Fourier developed an influential model of "phalanxes," autonomous communities in which precisely 1620 souls would live and work under natural conditions, independent of government interference, sustained by an economically self-sufficient arts-and-crafts agrarianism. Fourier's vision arrived in the US under the label "associationism," and its promise to overcome the alienating effects of industrial specialization inspired a number of Fourierist experiments, most of them of moderate scale and limited duration. The best known transcendentalist venture (and indeed, apart from Alcott's "Fruitlands" debacle in 1844, virtually the only one) is the Brook Farm community founded by George Ripley in 1841, and continued by Albert Brisbane as a small-scale Fourierist phalanx until 1847 (cf. docs. 207-9). All leading transcendentalists were interested in the outcome of this project, but

---

[27] This literal approach to the apocalyptic texts differs in kind from Augustine's reading of Christ's return as a spiritual development beyond history and the temporal realm.

many doubted the use of communitarian attempts for spiritual regeneration. Thoreau's famous retreat at Walden Pond can be considered symbolic of the pervasive belief among Emersonian intellectuals that the route to social utopia led through the solitary effort of individualist self-culture.

Instructional Strategies and Classroom Issues

I. Key Concepts and Major Themes

1. Post-Romantic Identity (docs. 192, 194-6)
   The idea of a self with inner depth; concept of authenticity as being true to one's inner self; discourse of individualism; transcendentalism as intuitionist and reminiscent of the "Inner Light" concept of the Quakers; rejection of eighteenth-century sensualism.

2. Nature Religion (docs. 188-92, 196, 199, 200-1)
   Celebration of American landscape as a site of spiritual presence; transformation of the Book-of-Nature-idea that considers natural objects as spiritual symbols.

3. Concept of the Genius (docs. 189-90, 198-9, 205)
   Romantic concept of inspiration: the artist functions as medium for divinely inspired universal insights.

4. Cultural Alienation (docs. 194, 196, 198-9, 200-1, 204)
   Anxieties of cultural dissociation, critiques of social differentiation and economic exploitation.

5. Democracy, Social Reform (docs. 200, 201-9, 273)
   Defense of democracy at a time when it was still regarded as an unrealistic experiment; critique of capitalist division of labor; experiments with agrarian communes based on utopian ideals of social perfectionism and progress; abolitionist sympathies.

6. Romantic Spirituality (docs. 189-200)
   Unitarian roots of the belief in the divinity of the individual; rejection of institutionalized religion and scriptural dogma; religion as a form of consciousness based on technologies of introversion that lead to mystic experiences of unity and presence.

7. American Sublime (docs. 188-9, 196, 200-1)
   Terror and bliss of mystic experience; sublimity of the American wilderness.

8. America's Manifest Destiny (docs. 160, 198, 201-3)
   America as a country of cultural youth (as against the ossified systems of Europe). The American "virgin land" as a site of future social utopia.

9. Ecocriticism (docs. 189, 200)
   Early environmentalism; appreciation of nature on its own terms, not merely as a spiritual symbol.

10. Postcolonialism (docs. 196, 198, 201, 203, 273)
    Anxieties of provinciality and belatedness; rejection of cultural dependence on European centers; ideal of America as a culture of apocalyptic novelty ("American Adam"); repression or displacement of transatlantic and transcultural networks. Interior colonization (construction of Native Americans as "savages").

11. Self-Reliance (docs. 198-9, 200, 203)
    Rejection of religious and cultural traditions; disdain for ecclesiastic and governmental institutions; quest for ethico-political objectivity based on introspective discovery of a universal Self.

II. Comparison – Contrasts – Connections

Example: Docs. 65, 181-2, 185-6, 201-3

We can begin exploring the cultural framework of American transcendentalism by looking at John Gast's famous allegory "American Progress" (doc. 182). The painting figures US expansionism in providential terms that can be traced back to the *translatio imperii* motif and the Puritan and millennialist concepts collected in the sections "Early Conceptualizations of America," "Providential Readings of American History," and "Expansionism" (cf. Scheiding, Obenland, Mackenthun in this vol.). Gast's lithograph is an extended metaphor of America's role within the progress of civilization. The personification of American progress ("a beautiful and charming female [...] floating westward through the air"; *KC*, 410) represents imperial expansion as a process of cultural enlightenment. Gast plays upon the light and darkness imagery of Puritan tracts (cf. Michael Wigglesworth, doc. 65), but he omits generic Puritan references to a covenant with a monotheistic God and instead focuses on the idea of Enlightenment as technical progress. The most significant symbols of technical progress are the locomotives moving from east to west and the telegraph cable that "American progress" carries along with her. In fact, Gast's painting appeared just after the Union Pacific and Central Pacific railroads had met in Utah, connecting the eastern and western coasts. As we can gather from Whitman's "Passage to India" of 1871 (doc. 181), the US establishment of western communication and transport lines was considered symbolic of America's unifying role within an impending world brotherhood. Whitman's poem celebrates the completion of the "mighty railroad" as a part of a divine human "network" (*KC*, 408) that brings nations closer together through the opening of the Suez Canal (1869) and the laying of the transatlantic cable (1866).[28] For Whitman, therefore, the westward movement offers a metaphorical "passage to India," towards a utopian spiritual democracy that is both a homecoming (India as the cradle of mankind) and historical progress (India as the endpoint of spiritual evolution). Earlier transcendentalist texts were rarely that explicit, but the providential framework looms large in George Bancroft's "On the Progress of Civilization" (doc. 202) and Emerson's "The Young American" (doc. 203). The latter text, a lecture held before the Mercantile Library Organization in Boston, shows how Emersonian nature religion locates itself within agrarian ideas about the providential role of America's massive territories that lend themselves well to expansionist ideologies. In Emerson's view, the virgin land is "the appointed remedy for whatever is false and fantastic in our culture," so that "the gravity of nature" in America will "infuse itself into the code" of US "laws and institutions" (*KC*, 461).[29] The idea that American culture is a product of the sublime landscape, to be excavated by multitudes of small homesteaders, points towards the so-called Turner thesis (docs. 185-6; cf. Mackenthun in this vol., 253-4) about the democratizing influence of the frontier. It is visualized in Gast's image of farmers tilling the soil in a westward direction, while the Indian nomads are pushed into the dark plains along with wild beasts. Indeed nineteenth-century ethnography often deems the waning of "Indian civilization" as a natural consequence of the natives' "primitive" stage, which renders them incapable of bringing forth the land's intrinsic potential. Thus Native Americans were allocated to the realm of the wilderness outside the pastoral "middle landscape" that, according to Leo Marx, defined the most influential nineteenth-century constructions of American place (cf. 1986, 36-69).[30] The ambivalence of this construction can be seen in Margaret Fuller's *Summer on the Lakes* (doc. 201). On the one hand, like most romantic intellectuals, Fuller regrets the waning of Indian culture – which she deems a culture of beauty, authenticity, and dignity – in the face of ugly and destructive onslaught of a "Gothic" settler culture insensitive to the beauties of nature (*KC*, 454). On the other hand, Fuller also participates in the nineteenth-century concept of primitive culture as representing the night side of nature: In a famous passage, she recalls how the "wonder" of seeing Niagara inspired her with "an undefined dread" that made her constantly turn around expecting "naked savages stealing behind me with uplifted tomahawks." This experience made her comprehend,

---

[28] For an earlier providential reading of telegraphic communication, see Emerson's poem "The Adirondacs," which recalls a hiking trip in 1858, where Emerson and some of his Boston acquaintances react with awe to newspaper reports about the completion of an earlier transatlantic cable (which did not work for long). Emerson describes the cable as "pulsating / With ductile fire" and views it as a "glad miracle" that will bring cultural improvement (1903-1904, 9: 191; for a full text version see *KC* web site).

[29] For a similar view of the wilderness as cultural remedy, see Thoreau (1862).

[30] The middle landscape is an imagined place equidistant from both corrupt cities and the inhospitable wilderness. It is perhaps most famously represented by Thoreau's description of Walden Pond.

she said, the common primeval ground of Niagara's sublimity and the primeval savagery of the native cultures ("I realized the identity of the mood of nature in which these waters were poured down with such absorbing force, with that in which the Indian was shaped on the same soil"; *KC*, 453).

III. Reading and Discussion Questions

1. Read Emerson's "Two Rivers" (doc. 190) and discuss how, in his description, natural phenomena become symbolic of spiritual presence (doc. 191). How does Emerson's poem relate to Cranch's "Correspondences"?

2. Compare Channing's "Likeness to God" (doc. 193) with Emerson's "Divinity School Address" (doc. 199) and Ripley's *Discourses on the Philosophy of Religion* (doc. 195). Discuss the shift from Unitarianism to the transcendentalist nature religion. Think about the function of the nature description at the beginning of the "Divinity School Address." Why begin a theological tract with a poetic invocation of natural beauty?

3. Read Emerson's *Nature* (doc. 196) and his "American Scholar" oration (doc. 198) and discuss his view of modern social alienation (the "divided" state). What, according to Emerson, is America's function in overcoming alienation?

4. Compare Thoreau's individualist project of self-discovery in *Walden* (doc. 200) with the communitarian aspects of social utopianism represented by the Brook Farm experiment (docs. 207-9).

IV. Resources

a. Recommended Reading

1. Anthologies

Lawrence Buell, ed. *The American Transcendentalists*: *Essential Writings*. New York: Modern Library, 2006.

Perry Miller, ed. *The Transcendentalists*: *An Anthology*. Cambridge: Harvard University Press, 1950.

Joel Myerson, ed. *Transcendentalism*: *A Reader*. New York: Oxford University Press, 2000.

Miller's classic and wide ranging selection with exhaustive introductory headnotes is still very useful today. It reflects Miller's interest in theological issues. Myerson's anthology offers additional material; Buell's smaller and cheaper volume is an affordable compromise.

2. Biographies

Lawrence Buell. *Emerson*. Cambridge: Harvard University Press, 2003. An up-to-date and very readable summary of Emerson's work and his significance, it contains a lucid overview of critical trends.

Robert D. Richardson. *Emerson: The Mind on Fire. A Biography*. Berkeley: University of California Press, 1995; and *Henry Thoreau: A Life of the Mind*. Berkeley: University of California Press, 1988. Informative and accessible biographies that situate Emerson and Thoreau within the intellectual currents of their times.

3. Introductions

Lawrence Buell. *New England Literary Culture: From Revolution through Renaissance*. Cambridge: Cambridge University Press, 1989; and Dieter Schulz. *Amerikanischer Transzendentalismus: Ralph Waldo Emerson, Henry David Thoreau, Margaret Fuller*. Darmstadt: Wissenschaftliche Buchgesellschaft, 1997. Concise and scholarly introductions to the movement's major figures and main stylistic traits.

Philip F. Gura. *American Transcendentalism: A History*. New York: Hill and Wang, 2007. Introductory history of the transcendentalist movement, which includes lesser known representatives as well.

Joel Myerson, ed. *A Historical Guide to Ralph Waldo Emerson*. New York: Oxford University Press, 2000; and William E. Cain, ed. *A Historical Guide to Henry David Thoreau*. New York: Oxford University Press, 2000. Collections of concise introductory essays on Emerson's and Thoreau's lives and works intended for student readers.

Joel Porte and Saundra Morris, eds. *The Cambridge Companion to Ralph Waldo Emerson*. Cambridge: Cambridge University Press, 1999; and Joel Myerson, ed. *The Cambridge Companion to Henry David Thoreau*. Cambridge: Cambridge University Press, 1995. Collections of introductory essays for both students and scholars on the most important issues of Emerson's and Thoreau's lives and letters, with useful bibliographies for further study.

4. Secondary Literature

Lawrence Buell. *The Environmental Imagination: Thoreau, Nature Writing, and the Formation of American Culture*. Cambridge: Harvard University Press, 1995. Foundational discussion of Thoreau's role in the romantic emergence of nature writing, and his significance to contemporary ecocriticism.

Leon Chai. *The Romantic Foundations of the American Renaissance*. Ithaca: Cornell University Press, 1987. Good introduction to the (French, German, and English) romantic ideas and writings that New England transcendentalists appropriated for their late romantic purposes.

Kris Fresonke. *West of Emerson*: *The Design of Manifest Destiny*. Berkeley: University of California Press, 2002. Discusses Emerson and Thoreau with regard to contemporary exploration narratives, situating New England transcendentalism within the rhetoric of Manifest Destiny.

Michael Gilmore. *American Romanticism and the Marketplace*. Chicago: University of Chicago Press, 1985. Considers Emersonian transcendentalism with regard to the print market revolution.

Len Gougeon. *Virtue's Hero*: *Emerson, Anti-Slavery, and Reform*. Athens: University of Georgia Press, 1990. Deals with the issue of transcendentalism's social engagement.

Patrick J. Keane. *Emerson, Romanticism, and Intuitive Reason*: *The Transatlantic "Light of All Our Day."* Columbia: University of Missouri Press, 2005. A comparative study looking at the transatlantic emergence of Emersonian notions of inwardness and intuition.

Jan Stievermann. *Der Sündenfall der Nachahmung*: *Zum Problem der Mittelbarkeit im Werk Ralph Waldo Emersons*. Paderborn: Schöningh, 2007. Discusses Emerson's romantic preoccupation with the idea of originality and mediation. Offers detailed analyses of the philosophical and theological contexts underlying Emerson's thought.

b. Works Cited and Reading Suggestions

Arnold, Matthew (1978). *Selected Poems and Prose*. Ed. Miriam Allot. London: Everyman's Library.
Bancroft, George (1841). *A History of the United States, from the Discovery of the American Continent*. Vol. 2: *History of the Colonization of the United States*. 8th ed. Boston: Little and Brown.
Böhme, Hartmut (2006). *Fetischismus und Kultur*. Hamburg: Rowohlt.
Bourdieu, Pierre (1996). *The Rules of Art*: *Genesis and Structure of the Literary Field*. Stanford: Stanford University Press.
Brooks, Van Wyck (1934). "America's Coming of Age." *Three Essays on America*. New York: Dutton, 13-112.
Buell, Lawrence (1989). *New England Literary Culture*: *From Revolution through Renaissance*. Cambridge: Cambridge University Press.
– (1995). *The Environmental Imagination*: *Thoreau, Nature Writing, and the Formation of American Culture*. Cambridge: Harvard University Press.
– (2003). *Emerson*. Cambridge: Harvard University Press.
– , ed. (2006). *The American Transcendentalists*: *Essential Writings*. New York: Modern Library.
Cain, William E., ed. (2000). *A Historical Guide to Henry David Thoreau*. New York: Oxford University Press.

Carlyle, Thomas (1984). "Signs of the Times." *A Carlyle Reader*: *Selections from the Writings of Thomas Carlyle*. Ed. G. B. Tennyson. Cambridge: Cambridge University Press, 31-54.

Chai, Leon (1987). *The Romantic Foundations of the American Renaissance*. Ithaca: Cornell University Press.

Coleridge, Samuel Taylor (1992). "Shakespeare's Judgment Equal to His Genius." 1812-1813. *The Romantics on Shakespeare*. Ed. Jonathan Bate. Harmondsworth: Penguin, 128-129.

Cronin, Richard (2000). *The Politics of Romantic Theory*. New York: St. Martin's.

Eliot, T. S. (1975). "The Metaphysical Poets." 1921. *Selected Prose*. Ed. Frank Kermode. London: Faber, 59-67.

Emerson, Ralph Waldo (1903-1904). *The Complete Works of Ralph Waldo Emerson*. Centenary Edition. 12 vols. Boston: Houghton Mifflin. <http://quod.lib.umich.edu/e/emerson> (August 23, 2008)

Fresonke, Kris (2002). *West of Emerson*: *The Design of Manifest Destiny*. Berkeley: University of California Press.

Gilmore, Michael (1985). *American Romanticism and the Marketplace*. Chicago: University of Chicago Press.

Gougeon, Len (1990). *Virtue's Hero*: *Emerson, Anti-Slavery, and Reform*. Athens: University of Georgia Press.

Gura, Philip F. (2007). *American Transcendentalism*: *A History*. New York: Hill and Wang.

Hegemann, Susan (1999). *Patterns for America*: *Modernism and the Concept of Culture*. Princeton: Princeton University Press.

Holmes, Oliver W. (1892). *Works*. Standard Library Edition. 13 vols. Boston: Houghton Mifflin.

Hume, David (1978). *A Treatise of Human Nature*. 1739. Ed. L. A. Selby-Bigge. Oxford: Clarendon.

Kant, Immanuel (1987). *Critique of Judgment*. 1790. Trans. with an introd. Werner S. Pluhar. Indianapolis: Hackett.

– (2005). *Critique of Pure Reason*. 1787. Trans. Norman Kemp Smith. Introd. Howard Caygill. Rev. 2nd ed. Basingstoke: Palgrave Macmillan.

Keane, Patrick J. (2005). *Emerson, Romanticism, and Intuitive Reason*: *The Transatlantic "Light of All Our Day."* Columbia: University of Missouri Press.

Leypoldt, Günter (2007). "Aesthetic Specialists and Public Intellectuals: Ruskin, Emerson, and Contemporary Professionalism." *Modern Language Quarterly* 68.3, 417-34.

Marx, Leo (1964). *The Machine in the Garden*: *Technology and the Pastoral Ideal in America*. Oxford: Oxford University Press.

– (1986). "Pastoralism in America." *Ideology and Classic American Literature*. Ed. Sacvan Bercovitch and Myra Jehlen. Cambridge: Cambridge University Press, 36-69.

Matthiessen, F. O. (1941). *American Renaissance*: *Art and Expression in the Age of Emerson and Whitman*. London: Oxford University Press.
Miller, Perry, ed. (1950). *The Transcendentalists*: *An Anthology*. Cambridge: Harvard University Press.
Montesquieu, Charles Louis de Secondat de (1989). *The Spirit of the Law*. 1748. Cambridge: Cambridge University Press.
Myerson, Joel (1972). "Calendar of Transcendental Club Meetings," *American Literature* 44.2, 197-207.
– (1995). *The Cambridge Companion to Henry David Thoreau*. Cambridge: Cambridge University Press.
– , ed. (2000a). *A Historical Guide to Ralph Waldo Emerson*. New York: Oxford University Press.
– , ed. (2000b). *Transcendentalism*: *A Reader*. New York: Oxford University Press.
Poirier, Richard (1987). *The Renewal of Literature*: *Emersonian Reflections*. New Haven: Yale University Press.
Porte, Joel, and Saundra Morris, eds. (1999). *The Cambridge Companion to Ralph Waldo Emerson*. Cambridge: Cambridge University Press.
Richardson, Robert D. (1988). *Henry Thoreau*: *A Life of the Mind*. Berkeley: University of California Press,
– (1995). *Emerson*: *The Mind on Fire. A Biography*. Berkeley: University of California Press.
Roof, Wade Clark, and Nathalie Caron (2006). "Shifting Boundaries: Religion and the United States: 1960s to the Present," *The Cambridge Companion to Modern American Culture*. Ed. Christopher Bigley. Cambridge: Cambridge University Press, 113-34.
Santayana, George (1968). *Santayana on America*: *Essays, Notes, and Letters on American Life, Literature, and Philosophy*. New York: Harcourt, Brace, and World.
Schlegel, August W. von (1846). *Lectures on Dramatic Art and Literature*. 1815. Trans. John Black. London: Bohn.
Schleiermacher, Friedrich (1821). *Über die Religion*: *Reden an die Gebildeten unter ihren Verächtern*. Berlin: Reimer.
Schulz, Dieter. *Amerikanischer Transzendentalismus*: *Ralph Waldo Emerson, Henry David Thoreau, Margaret Fuller*. Darmstadt: Wissenschaftliche Buchgesellschaft, 1997.
Sloterdijk, Peter (1997). "Chancen im Ungeheuren: Notiz zum Gestaltwandel des Religiösen in der modernen Welt." *Vielfalt religiöser Erfahrung*. By William James. Frankfurt/M.: Insel, 11-34.
Stievermann, Jan (2007). *Der Sündenfall der Nachahmung*: *Zum Problem der Mittelbarkeit im Werk Ralph Waldo Emersons*. Paderborn: Schöningh.
Taine, Hippolyte (1861). *La Fontaine et ses fables*. Paris: L. Hachette.
– (1985). *Philosophie de l'Art*. 1865-1869. Paris: Fayard.

Taylor, Charles (1989). *Sources of the Self*. Cambridge: Harvard University Press.
- (2002). *Varieties of Religion Today: William James Revisited*. Cambridge: Harvard University Press.
- (2007). *A Secular Age*. Cambridge: Harvard University Press.

Thoreau, Henry David (1862). "Walking." *Atlantic Monthly* 9.56, 657-674.
- (1906). *The Writings of Henry David Thoreau*. Walden Edition. 20 vols. Boston: Houghton Mifflin.
- (1973). "A Plea for Captain John Brown." 1859. *Reform Papers*. Princeton: Princeton University Press, 111-138.

Williams, Peter (1998). *America's Religions: Traditions and Cultures*. Urbana: University of Illinois Press.

Wuthnow, Robert (1998). *After Heaven: Spirituality in America since the 1950s* Berkeley: University of California Press.

ISABELL KLAIBER

Women's Roles in American Society: Difference, Separateness, and Equality

I. Themes and Arguments

Almost all debates about gender roles from the seventeenth to the end of the nineteenth centuries were based on the assumption of men's and women's different natures and/or different purposes in life. Consequently, men and women filled different roles in society and moved in 'separate spheres,' which were the 'feminine' private sphere of the home and the family versus the 'masculine' public sphere of politics and the marketplace.[1] Established female gender roles were always highly contested by alternative ideas of women's personal independence in the private and especially in the public realm. Both conventionalized and alternative conceptualizations of women's roles were the products of an ongoing controversial discussion of intersecting issues such as woman's moral power, her education, and her role both in society and as wife and mother. In the following, the intersections of these discursive issues will be discussed with regard to a few sample texts from that section of the anthology and further reference to other texts of the anthology. Thus, this chapter will trace the respective lines of argumentation in the various transformations of the concept of woman as Goodwife to the Republican Mother then as the True Woman to, eventually, the New Woman.

Although it has been questioned again and again for more than a decade (cf. Harris 1978; Elbert 2000; Davidson and Hatcher 2002), the concept of separate spheres for the two sexes, as well as the female gender roles resulting from it, can still be considered the normative standard. The concepts of femininity mentioned above were in their respective times thought to be universal, although they were deeply rooted in white middle-class culture and, in fact, only viable for rather well-to-do white middle- and upper-class women.[2] To look at gender is-

---

[1] Men's roles were not as prominent in the public debate as women's; thus, it can be argued that due to the predominant idea of men's and women's 'separate spheres' (and roles) in society, the various conventionalized concepts of femininity determined the respective concepts of masculinity indirectly, i.e., ex negativo.

[2] As Jean V. Matthews points out, the ideology of 'separate spheres' was not only embraced by the middle class in spite of its restricted viability, but "the same insistence on role separation

sues in isolation, as is done here, is a rather dangerous endeavor, as they were closely related to other aspects of American culture and history, such as class and race. In fact, women concerned with the so-called "woman's question" often connected their own struggle for cultural and/or political equality with the issues of class and race. Nevertheless, white middle-class women were the most visible social spokespersons of their sex in the nineteenth century, and their experiences, values, and aims were broadly considered the desirable cultural standard, even for women who were not members of that class.[3]

While some of the selected documents give an insight into a set of established, rather conservative gender concepts, others contain feminist arguments.[4] However, the texts presented here do not exemplify a history of the feminist movement,[5] but rather reflect the gender discourse, i.e., women's images and self-images, from early colonial times through the late nineteenth century. Although women's disadvantages resulting from heterosexual gender ideology may today be considered well known,[6] it is not a matter of the simple, one-dimensional repression of women by men, for "the [gender] ideology's tenacity owed as much to women's motives as to the imposition of men's or society's wishes" (Cott 1977, 197).[7] In fact, by the mid-nineteenth century, women's roles were more often than not depicted as highly privileged in comparison to men's, especially in moral terms. Paradoxically, this made it rather attractive for women to identify with these roles, no matter how restrictive they actually were. Thus, many women (unintentionally) supported and perpetuated the cultural power structures which restricted them to the domestic sphere, kept them in financial dependency, and denied them access to political power, higher education, or 'male' professions.

[could] be found among the skilled artisan class," too (1997, 7). For further research on the situation of women belonging to other classes and ethnicities than the white Anglo-Saxon middle class, see for example DuBois and Ruiz (1990).

[3] This is probably due to the fact that most spokeswomen who were not of the white middle class did not have an audience as broad and as capable as their well-to-do Anglo-Saxon sisters; their deviating experiences were not discussed as part of the 'universal' state of affairs in middle-class publications.

[4] Although the terms 'feminism' and 'feminist' were not used until the early twentieth century, these terms are used here for reasons of convenience for present-day readers, referring to the idea of legal, social, and cultural equality between the sexes.

[5] For this purpose, see other anthologies of historical documents such as Kraditor (1968) and Cott (1972).

[6] Eighteenth- and nineteenth-century American gender ideology was entirely heterosexual. Although relationships among women or among men may well have had a homoerotic quality, they were not thought of or talked about in sexual terms but only in terms of asexual friendship (cf. Smith-Rosenberg, 1985a).

[7] For a critical evaluation of the repression hypothesis, see Michel Foucault, who defines gender discourse of a given time as "the set of effects produced in bodies, behaviors, and social relations by a certain deployment deriving from a complex political technology" rather than a one-dimensional relation between oppressor and oppressed (1978, 127).

Before the rhetorical and political strategies used to support this line of argumentation are illustrated by a few selected examples, the predominant concepts of femininity will be introduced. This will be followed by a critical discussion of the strategies employed to modify those concepts according to different interests. The effect(s) which the transformation of these concepts had on the various aspects of female life will be of special interest here. The concepts of marriage, motherhood, a woman's religious and moral qualities, her particular contribution to society, as well as her education were greatly affected by that transformation. While these issues have been broadly discussed with special regard to their psychological, social, cultural, or their political dimensions, this article will highlight the continuities and discontinuities across discursive fields in a number of sample texts.[8]

II. Female Gender Concepts

All the female gender concepts discussed here are more or less determined by woman's reproductive and nurturing function in the home, i.e., giving birth and supporting her husband and children. An overwhelming majority of Americans used to subscribe to the belief that men and women were essentially different in physiology, intellectual ability, moral character, and interests; these characteristics were declared to be part of a God-given order of things. Men and women's different functions in society, including their different spheres, were therefore broadly thought to be only the logical consequence of their fundamental differences.

This assumption led to the subordinate position of women in American society, which legally excluded them from political, economic, and public social life. Until the late nineteenth century, married women remained under coverture, i.e., 'dead in law,' as most state legislations did not entitle them to own property, keep their wages, or sign contracts without the consent of their husbands; and it was not until 1920 that federal law gave them the right to vote (cf.

---

[8] Selected issues can be correlated with other segments of the anthology. The interference of women in political affairs on the eve of the American Revolution can be contextualized with documents from the section on the "Revolutionary Period" (docs. 108-34) and the "Early Republic" (docs. 135-53); women's efforts to end slavery can be connected with documents in the "Slavery" section (docs. 248-73); and the idea of women's self-reliance may be correlated with texts from the segment on "Transcendentalism" (docs. 188-209). For a discussion of the psychological, social, cultural, and political dimensions of the topic see, from an empirical point of view, Parker (1972). For general studies of women's traditional role in the home in the nineteenth century consult Cott (1977), Okin (1982), and Matthews (1987). Cogan (1989) pays special attention to everyday life. For a focus on the family, see Degler (1980). The history of sexuality is discussed in Rosenberg (1973), Smith-Rosenberg (1985b-d), Smart (1992), and Battan (1992). Smith-Rosenberg (1985a) deals with the psychological function of women's mutual support within the domestic sphere. A comprehensive study of feminizing American culture is provided by Douglas (1977). Ryan (1975) and Cott (2000) survey the social history of women.

Hannam 2000).[9] Practically speaking, the state of early colonial American women, including their restriction to the domestic sphere and their personal dependence on men in everyday life, was not all that different from that of their descendants in the nineteenth century. The explanations and concepts of femininity which justified women's underprivileged position, however, varied considerably and ranged from the Goodwife in colonial times and the Republican Mother as the guardian angel of the young American republic, to the more private, apolitical True Woman during most of the Victorian Age, who was finally rivaled by the professional New Woman in the progressive era. The following paragraphs will briefly introduce these different concepts of femininity.

In a pre-industrial farming economy like early colonial America, the family as the functioning unit relied on a female work force in domestic crafts as a complement to men's share in their common struggle for subsistence: The colonial Goodwife acted mainly as her husband's helpmeet (cf. doc. 210).[10] In practice, this gave women a comparatively important position in the family, although not as individuals in society. For instance, women might have acted as 'deputy husbands' and shouldered male responsibilities in the family and the community, but only a few women took on non-domestic roles (printers, attorneys, merchants) that belonged to an all-male province. In seventeenth-century Puritan New England (cf. *KC*, 63-101), women were defined in contradictory terms: On the one hand, their souls were considered to be as precious and immortal as those of men, but on the other hand, they were subject to men according to biblical (esp. Pauline) dictate (cf. Ulrich 1991, 8). Going back to Eve's lapse in Paradise, women were considered inherently dangerous, i.e., potentially evil, shrewish, treacherous, or witchlike (cf. Cott 1972, 7). As the 'weaker sex,' women always ran the risk of going astray and leaving the path of morality, reason, and propriety. This can be easily illustrated by the verdict of John Winthrop (doc. 212), who, as the governor of the Massachusetts Bay Colony, was famous for his imperious treatment of dissenters. Declaring a woman who pursued an education and who gave "herself wholly to reading and writing" a lunatic (*KC*, 480), he proposed a social discipline based on religious doctrine:

> [I]f she had attended her household affairs, and such things as belong to women, and not gone out of her way and calling to meddle in such things as are proper for men, whose minds are stronger, etc., she had kept her wits, and might have improved them usefully and honorably in the place God had set her. (*KC*, 480)

---

[9] Until the end of the Civil War, enslaved women found themselves in an even worse situation as they were not recognized as legal persons to any degree.

[10] As Ulrich argues, the colonial Goodwife did not live in an enchanted and sealed sphere but was rather defined by a set of roles and tasks interrelated with each other (cf. 1991, 239-40). Woman's sphere had, however, become more and more sealed by the time the concept of the Republican Mother emerged.

Not only does Winthrop argue that this particular woman has left her God-given place in society, but he also implies that women's mental capacities are by nature weaker than men's, and thus he insists on an essential difference between, and a hierarchy of, the sexes (cf. Spahr in this vol., 67-71).[11]

In the course of the eighteenth century, the range of lifestyles diversified as different regions reached different stages of settlement, economic progress, urbanization, and cultural refinement. Along with the general secularization of life came more secular definitions of woman's nature and capacities, especially in those parts of American society that did not participate in farm and frontier life: Her primary functions were seen as decorative and supportive, which she fulfilled best by "preserving [...] a respectable piety" and "a cultivated gentility," "reflect[ing] credibility to her father or husband," and by thus "making her company and her home a place of refreshment and harmony." For these purposes, ladies could rely on their "taste," "delicacy," and "sentiment" (Cott 1972, 10). This fundamental change in woman's role, however, did not do away with presumably essential differences between the two sexes. Instead, the new gender concept rather highlighted them in two ways: first, in terms of woman's mental inferiority and, second, in terms of moral purity. Woman was particularly idealized and declared superior to man in terms of her supposedly innate moral sense and 'natural' piety. In fact, her moral sovereignty not only put her on a pedestal but also functioned as the most crucial determinant of a woman's role in society for more than a century. It was assumed that her moral superiority could only be maintained by staying in the private realm, in order to be protected against the temptations and corruptions of the outside world. Furthermore, she could make best use of her moral privilege in her role as mother and wife.

Thomas R. Dew's "Dissertation: On the Characteristic Differences between the Sexes" (doc. 224) illustrates how women's moral sovereignty was integrated into a catalogue of supposedly natural and essential 'masculine' and 'feminine' features which were considered common sense in American culture from the late eighteenth until the turn of the twentieth century. Here, man is depicted as having "greater physical strength [...], courage and boldness." He is always active and "plunges into the turmoil and bustle of an active, selfish world" in which "he has to encounter innumerable difficulties, hardships and labors" (*KC*, 505). Woman, by contrast, is passive and functions as the 'angel in the house' because she is morally more refined than man; in "timidity and modesty," she stays in the safe haven of the home, exercising "[g]race [...] and loveliness," which are "emblematical of that of divinity" (*KC*, 506). Although she seems weak, it is "out of

---

[11] However, this essentialist gender dichotomy did not remain unchallenged. In "The Prologue" to her poetry collection *The Tenth Muse* (1650), Anne Bradstreet questions the essentiality of these differences with sarcastic irony and exposes the double standard which the essentialist gender concepts are based on as a social practice that discriminates against women: "For such despight they cast on female wits: / If what I doe prove well, it wo'nt advance, / They'l say its stolne, or else, it was by chance" (*KC*, 479).

that very weakness and dependence" that "an irresistible [moral] power" springs (*KC*, 506). These sets of gender-specific characteristics were considered to display the essential nature of men and women.

This gender dichotomy prevailed until the end of the nineteenth century and was integrated into a number of different female gender roles. During the Early Republic, the concept of the Republican Mother provided women's lack of full citizenship with an ideological justification, claiming that women's role as the safeguards of the nation's welfare was really a more desirable position within the national project than full citizenship.[12] As it was explained in an anonymous essay of 1795 (doc. 220), by means of their "female influence" within their immediate family circle, women could teach their sons the republican virtues of future citizens, and their daughters how to become virtuous Republican Mothers themselves. The mother's influence was meant to "conduct [the son] invariably in the paths of undisguised honour, of truth, of virtue and religion [… and turn him into the] support of his aged parents, the boast of his country, and the glory of humanity" (*KC*, 497). In the education of her daughters, a mother "not only diffuse[d] more widely her benign influence over the present generation, but also to the future ages" by instructing the future mothers (*KC*, 497). Thus, women paved the ground for "the rising glory of confederated America" and ensured the survival of the perilous American experiment of a republican government: "[T]he solidity and stability of the liberties of your country rest with you [i.e., the women]" (*KC*, 498). By highlighting the mother's moral influence as a crucial factor in the whole nation's welfare – "[w]hile you thus keep our country virtuous, you maintain its independence and ensure its prosperity" (*KC*, 497) – the concept of the Republican Mother elevated woman from being a simple Goodwife to the powerful, almost omnipotent position of the moral arbiter of her nation's fate: "In what an exalted rank in the scale of existence has the God of nature placed the lovely sex? [...] Yes, ye fair, the reformation of the world is in your power. [...] The solidity and stability of the liberties of your country rest with you" (*KC*, 498). This female influence could only be considered so very powerful because of the wide prevalence of Lockean thought. The anonymous essay writer, in accordance with Locke, presumes that children's "characters are not yet formed [… and their] minds are in some measure a blank," so that it is the upbringing through the mother that "must effectually tend to humanize, purify, and ennoble the mind[s]" of both children and men, thus "ordain[ing] them to be honourable and useful members of society." In this responsibility, woman as mother "is regarded as a conducting angel" (*KC*, 496).

However, the national scope of woman's power was, in fact, considered to be no more than a side effect of her primary purpose, which was her family:

---

[12] With the exception of New Jersey, where women were briefly entitled to vote, they were denied suffrage as well as most civil rights (cf. Matthews 1992, 57). For further information on the concept of the Republican Mother, see Norton (1980), Kerber (1980; 1999), and Matthews (1992, 52-71).

"The cares, the studies, the desires of a virtuous woman are all undoubtedly concentered in her husband, and her attention pre-eminently engaged by her family affairs" (496). As a wife, woman refined her husband's moral being in a 'femininely' passive way:

> By the sympathetic effusions of a feeling heart, by the sweet accents flowing from a persuasive tongue, she restrains his imperious passions, and obliterates every gloomy, doleful impression. It rests with her, not only to confirm those virtuous habits which he has already acquired, but also to excite his perseverance in the paths of rectitude. By continually attracting him towards home, she prevents man of the greatest evils that befall mankind. [...] This domestic propensity will serve as a never-failing antidote against the most dangerous temptations to vice. (*KC*, 496)

It was widely claimed, however, that woman could only maintain her moral omnipotence as long as she did not strive for more tangible rights. Paradoxically, her political powerlessness was the source of her supposedly enormous moral power through 'influence.' In fact, her moral power was envisioned as a much greater one than the practical power any political or legal right could grant her – thus, any political ambitions of hers were checked.

Once the "republican form of government ha[d] been *tried* and [was] *settled* in the United States" by the 1830s (*KC*, 511), the political dimension of female influence faded into the background of interest, and its purely moral quality came into focus.[13] Thus a slightly changed ideal of femininity evolved and began to replace the former concept of the Republican Mother by that of the True Woman, which not only put an even stronger emphasis on her piety, moral purity, and the private sphere, but also highlighted her willing and happy self-sacrifice for her family's needs: "Her great mission is self-denial," as Catherine E. Beecher and her sister Harriet Beecher Stowe pointed out in 1869 (*KC*, 540). Accordingly, in her seminal essay "The Cult of True Womanhood" (1966), Barbara Welter defined the True Woman by her four cardinal virtues: piety, purity, domesticity, and submissiveness.[14] Her morally refining influence on her husband and children would still ensure the moral health of American society in general, but less in a political than a Christian sense, since she now functioned as the stronghold against the corruptions and temptations of the emerging capitalist middle class. Her feminine example of disinterested love and ready self-sacrifice for others was to amend and counterbalance the materialistic egotism of capitalism, which characterized the male world of business: "[h]er love [... to be] unselfish, ever known / To seek our interest, not her own" (*KC*, 513) – thus Lewis Jacob Cist praised the True Woman in his poem "Woman's Sphere." Under her hand, "home" becomes a sanctified and semi-magical place, the center of all goodness, purity, piety, love,

---

[13] This becomes evident in docs. 229 and 230, in which woman's morally refining or spoiling influence on her immediate family, and through that, on American society as such, is evoked again as being the special privilege and "power possessed and wielded by women [...] to be used or abused for the good or evil of mankind" (*KC*, 513).

[14] For contemporary revisions of Welter's "Cult of True Womanhood," see Rupp (2002, 149-73).

and peace: "There hers it is a power to wield, [...] / The god-like gift to save and bless! / [...] To bless – in every stage of life, / AS MOTHER – DAUGHTER – SISTER – WIFE!" (*KC*, 512). While her submission and her services to others were, in fact, duties, they were depicted as her privileges and sacred 'rights': "The right to labor and to pray, / The right to watch while others sleep, / The right o'er others' woes to weep" (*KC*, 531).[15]

The concept of the True Woman did not go without criticism. Barbara Welter identified two strategies of resistance to this ideal during the second half of the nineteenth century: "[S]ome challenged the standard, some tried to keep the virtues and enlarge the scope of womanhood. Somehow through this mixture of challenge and acceptance, or change and continuity, the True Woman evolved into the New Woman" (1966, 174). However, this was a rather slow process which emerged only tentatively after the Civil War and culminated in the 1890s, "a time of wild agitation concerning the portion of power that belong[ed] to woman, as well as of wild conjecture concerning the limits of the sphere within which her power [was] to be exerted," as the conservative Rebecca L. Leeke observed in 1896 (*KC*, 547). The New Woman (cf. Forrey 1974; Dowling 1979; Smith-Rosenberg 1985d; Köhler 2004) primarily rebeled against men's presumed superiority, the doctrine of 'feminine' submissiveness, her being restricted to the home, as well as her being denied access to higher education and all-male professions. New Women such as Sarah Grand (doc. 242) contemptuously depicted the True Woman as a "cow-kind of woman" put to man's service "as his domestic cattle" (*KC*, 541). Furthermore, she openly attacked both men for determining women's lives and women for granting them this very liberty: "[W]e have allowed him to exact all things of us" (*KC*, 541). This practice had a chilling effect on women's opportunities: "Man deprived us of all proper education, [...] narrowed our outlook on life [... and] he set himself up as a sort of a god and required us to worship him" (*KC*, 542).

It is hardly surprising that these boldly ambitious New Women met with bitter resistance from their contemporaries. What both male and female critics feared most was the breakdown of the order of the separate spheres (cf. doc. 240). In fact, 'strong-minded' New Women threatened to turn the tables and take the lead themselves, offering their "strong hand" to the "child-man" for guidance (*KC*, 542). According to established gender ideology, the New Woman "would [... thus] step out of the natural modesty of her sex and strive to become man's equal in his special and peculiar province, his rival in [his own] struggle," as John P. MacCarrie feared (*KC*, 548). Whether or not she tried to enter a profession or the

---

[15] The concept of True Womanhood, like all female gender roles discussed here, was only valid for white middle-class women. Enslaved African-American women, for instance, were conceptualized in quite different stereotypes, i.e., as either a highly emotional Mammy who in complete dedication to the white family did the cooking and nursed and raised the white children, or a Jezebel, i.e., a morally loose seductress of white men who was obsessed with sexual desire (cf. White 1985, 27-61).

realm of politics by demanding the right to vote, conservative men like Max O'Rell looked at the New Woman with abhorrence: "I LOATHE the domination of woman" (*KC*, 545). Publicly active women had to face the old accusation that they were "unsexing" themselves: "The new woman wants to retain all the privileges of her sex and secure, besides, all those of man. She wants to be a man and to remain a woman. She will fail to become a man, but she may succeed in ceasing to be a woman," O'Rell warned (*KC*, 546).

In fact, first-generation New Women claimed and enjoyed independence, higher education, a profession to make a living, etc., up to the point when they married – then, they more often than not returned almost entirely to the domestic sphere of the True Woman. As can be seen from the selected texts, the concept of the True Woman remained the predominant and often solely acceptable idea for the majority of the middle class and was therefore never entirely replaced by the more progressive New Woman during the nineteenth century. This process of constant rivalry would continue until the beginning of the twentieth century when childcare – most women's primary reason to stay at home – began to be professionalized in the form of nursery schools and kindergartens; only then did the concept of the New Woman become an equally respected alternative to the prevailing ideal of the True Woman.

III. Strategies of Modification

In their respective periods of time, these various womens' roles – the Goodwife, the Republican Mother, and the True Woman – represented well-established standards in white middle-class American culture and were affirmed and consolidated by cultural authorities such as the clergy (cf. doc. 230). As a matter of fact, with the exception of the New Woman, all these female gender roles eventually affirmed the ideologies of essentialism and separate spheres, as well as the traditionally 'feminine' virtues in women, while at the same time they allowed for an expansion of the scope of women's influence beyond the domestic realm. How may such apparently contradictory effects be explained? The answer can be found in the ways in which the competing ideas of a difference between the sexes versus their 'natural' equality, or the notion of their separate realms in society, were evaluated by different groups of interest at different times. For those who considered the assumption of a fundamental borderline between the sexes a 'given truth,' the question remained what was to be concluded from this: Was woman different and inferior or different but equal to man? Did the difference lie in men and women's abilities or in their social roles? Was a woman 'unsexing' herself once she stepped outside her 'proper' sphere, or were there arguments to justify such trespassing?

At least three fundamentally different strategies of how to deal with the doctrine of separate spheres can be identified in texts from the revolutionary era to the end of the nineteenth century: These are, firstly, the affirmation of an essential difference between the sexes; secondly, the claim to equality by natural right, questioning essentialist concepts while retaining the idea of somewhat separate spheres; and thirdly, open attacks on the ideology of separate spheres as a natural order of things. Together with their sub-variants, these standpoints mustered a wide range of different strategies and arguments to resolve how the two sexes were related to each other.

1. Affirming the Gender Hierarchy

Presumably the most conservative strategy was to affirm the differences between the sexes and thus to consolidate the idea of separate, implicitly hierarchical spheres. According to the assumption of a fundamental and natural difference between the two sexes regarding physical and moral ability, men possessed a more powerful body as well as mind; with regard to their innate moral and emotional power, however, they were clearly surpassed by women. While man was to act as the intellectual leader for both, these gender-specific characteristics seemed to particularly qualify him for the public realm and woman for the private realm.

This affirmation of an essential difference between the sexes allowed for various interpretations: The emphasis on women's moral superiority was used by some to strengthen their role *within* the domestic realm as it was presumed to work best when women were protected by and restricted to the home. In direct contrast to this, other advocates of women's moral superiority argued that her moral influence reached *beyond* the private sphere into the public realm; thus, her little 'empire' of moral influence and power was extended to those in the public sphere who were in need of her sympathy and moral guidance. Neither of these approaches challenged the legal exclusion of women from political power because not only was it assumed that nature had not endowed them with the intellectual capacities needed for leading and governing a nation with a growing economy, but women would also lose their particular moral power once they exposed themselves to the corrupt world of business and politics.

The first of these two lines of argument was employed for the legitimization of the ideals of the Republican Mother and the True Woman. Both claimed the privilege of higher virtue and moral purity for woman which could only be maintained while she stayed in the safety of the domestic sphere. However, the scope of woman's influence was not restricted to the private sphere, but presumably shaped the destiny of the entire nation. While the Republican Mother, through the education of future citizens, acted as the moral safeguard of the political experiment of the republic, the True Woman of the mid-nineteenth century used her moral influence on man to protect a quickly growing capitalist society against the corrupting temptations of a materialistic marketplace. During the Early Republic, its male spokespersons in particular repeatedly evoked the argument of woman's supposedly great power through her "female influence" in order to practically confine women to their homes and, at the same time, pacify politically ambitious women in the face of their actual lack of civil rights (cf. doc. 220).

This strategy seemed to work, for the focus of many (male and female) commentators of the earlier concept quickly shifted from tangible political rights to other issues that seemed more relevant to the ideal of the Republican Mother, such as women's access to higher education (cf. docs. 214, 217-9): A well-educated mother was much better qualified for the education of America's future citizens than an ignorant one. This argument found not only many supporters among women, but among men, too. The anonymous author of the essay "Female Influence" (doc. 220) cheerfully trusted that "if their [i.e., women's] minds be duly cultivated, the consequences [would] be highly beneficial to society" (*KC*, 494), and in 1787, Benjamin Rush, one of the signers of the Declaration of Independence, made a case for the well-educated Republican Mother: "[O]ur ladies should be qualified to a certain degree, by a peculiar and suitable education, to concur in instructing their sons in the principles of liberty and government" (*KC*, 484).[16] For the True Woman, the argumentation went along very similar lines, as her morally refining influence on her husband and children was to counteract the materialistic and egoistic tendencies of middle-class business and industrial production and thus ensure the moral health of nineteenth-century American society. The concepts of the Republican Mother and the True Woman thus brought great practical empowerment to women through education, but also functioned as substitutes for tangible civil rights for women.

It is almost impossible to decide in retrospect whether most women were really satisfied with their indirect pseudo-political role in the young republic or whether politically and socially ambitious women just pragmatically changed the site of battle from political rights to education because a victory there seemed more likely, without, however, abandoning their former goals, i.e., women's social, legal, and financial autonomy. No matter what women's real motivation in demanding higher education for themselves, men could easily subscribe to this demand, as female education aimed at improving women's morally refining influence on society and did not seem to threaten the social division of separate spheres – all the more because female education remained far from equal to men's and did not serve the same purpose, i.e., the preparation for a profession outside the home. These arguments made it easy for many to support the improvement of women's education while still denying them greater privileges, such as the vote.

A different and more empowering interpretation of the doctrine of separate spheres was chosen some decades later by a considerable number of middle-class women, who since the 1830s had actively participated in various reform move-

---

[16] Benjamin Rush (1787) argued that institutionalized female education plays a vital role in a democratic system. According to Rush, it defines the young American republic as "very different from [...] Great Britain" (*KC*, 482) and thus prevents America from assimilating to the mother country's vices.

ments to help the poor, the intemperate, and orphans and prostitutes. How could moral and social reform movements, joined and actively supported by women, emerge within the restrictive ideology of separate spheres? After all, for their 'acts of benevolence,' women had to leave their domestic sphere; furthermore, they endeavored to relieve the poor and, thus, to eventually change society and social politics. Was this, strictly speaking, not a usurpation of and interference with men's political power?

In fact, many middle-class supporters of moral and social reform did subscribe to the cult of True Womanhood without questioning its core ideas, as they argued along the line of woman's moral superiority.[17] Their strategy for opening up the path to an active role in the public realm was to expand the field of application of woman's highest virtue, i.e., Christian self-denial and altruistic love, by drawing a parallel between the children in her family and the needy in society. Woman with her supposedly innate piety qualified for the role of the unsophisticated but effective minister and role model within the family. Her obedience to Christ's commandment to love one's neighbor was considered an essential part of her femininity in dedicating her whole life, love, and abilities to the service of her family.[18] According to the sisters Catharine E. Beecher and Harriet Beecher Stowe, the extension of the scope of woman's self-sacrificial love from her family to the weak, the needy, and the fallen in American society arose naturally from the same Christian commandment (doc. 241). Furthermore, since the True Woman functioned as a stronghold against materialistic gain and selfishness, she could counteract men's egotistical rush for worldly treasures in business by storing up treasures in heaven[19] – she could possibly not only redeem herself but also the male-dominated business world entangled in materialist endeavors:

> The family state then, is the aptest earthly illustration of the heavenly kingdom, and in it woman is its chief minister. Her great mission is self-denial, in training its members to self-sacrificing labors for the ignorant and weak: if not her own children, then the neglected children of her Father in heaven. She is to rear all under her care to lay up treasures, not on earth, but in heaven. All the pleasures of this life end here; but those who train immortal minds are to reap the fruit of their labor through eternal ages. (*KC*, 540)

---

[17] Ginzberg investigates this very "conflation of femininity and morality" and emphasizes that the diversity of "the ideology of female benevolence [which] was used differently by women of different social groups in different settings" (1990, 8).

[18] This was, in part, Christ's answer when the Pharisees asked him about the greatest commandment in the Law. His full answer was: "'Love the Lord your God with all your heart and with all your soul and with all your mind.' This is the first and greatest commandment. And the second is like it: 'Love your neighbor as yourself.' All the Law and the Prophets hang on these two commandments'" (Matt. 22.37-40).

[19] The idea that the True Woman's self-sacrifice was to be rewarded in the afterlife goes back to Christ's words on worldly and heavenly treasures: "Do not store up for yourselves treasures on earth, where moth and rust destroy, and where thieves break in and steal. But store up for yourselves treasures in heaven […]. For where your treasure is, there your heart will be also" (Matt. 6.19-21).

Thus, the benevolent woman's trespassing on man's cultural territory was justified by incorporating certain societal issues and segments of the public realm, such as the orphaned, the poor, the fallen, and the intemperate who supposedly needed her moral guidance and refinement as much as her immediate family, into her own domestic sphere: "[T]he world [was] only a large home," for which reason the female reformer could "act *in* the world in order to protect the home and to preserve its morality" (Degler 1980, 298; emphasis mine). Such "religious activities opened up new horizons without calling into question [women's] domestic duties or outlook" (302). With the support of popular mass culture and the churches as well as moral reform organizations, society's poorhouse was incorporated into woman's sphere.[20] While some nineteenth-century reform movements can be traced back to male, intellectual origins such as the social and socialist variant of transcendentalist philosophy (cf. *KC*, 423-73; cf. Leypoldt in this vol., 279-81), most of these movements were supported by women who considered their reformist concerns and aims, such as charity, temperance, sexual purity, etc., to be genuinely 'feminine.'

It must be kept in mind, however, that these arguments, which were based on nineteenth-century gender ideology, were often used to camouflage more tangible factors in the various causes of social reform. Apart from moralistic reasons, women joined the temperance movement, for instance, for the very practical reason that married women were not entitled to hold their own property in most states of the US until the late nineteenth century; thus, women and their children depended financially entirely on their husbands' bringing home their wages and not spending them in the barroom – temperance was thus not only a moral vice but represented an existential threat to married women and their dependent children.

As the benevolent woman did not leave her home for her own sake but only for that of others, her presence in the public realm at first did not seem to pose any threat to man's dominance in society and politics. However, after years of petitions to Congress and the elected representatives of single states calling for laws against intemperance, child-labor, over-long working hours, etc., it became evident that, under the disguise of their 'feminine duty,' women had, in fact, entered the political arena.

2. Different but Equal

According to a second approach, men and women were by nature equal in their abilities and rights, which did not imply a hierarchical relationship. However, due to their different roles in life and the practical necessity of a division of labor, different skills were required by and fostered in the two sexes. Thus, the difference in men's and women's mental capacities was considered the result of

---

[20] According to Douglas (1977), this led to a feminization of religion and of American middle-class culture in the nineteenth century.

their different social functions: While man's education served as his professional qualification, woman's education was solely meant to improve her in her functions as a mother and first educator of her children, as a sensible companion to her husband, and as a useful housewife.

This was, in fact, the core argument in favor of higher education for the Republican Mother: The anonymous author of the essay "Female Influence" (doc. 220) promised that "if their [i.e., women's, especially mothers'] minds be duly cultivated, the consequences will be highly beneficial to society" (*KC*, 494). To an anonymous author of 1794 (doc. 219), education qualified woman for being a better companion to society in general and her husband in particular, as he would "feel a certain pleasure in her company" (*KC*, 493). In 1819, Emma Willard (doc. 221), a women's rights advocate and founder of the first women's school of higher education (Middlebury Female Seminary, founded in 1814) called for institutionalized higher education for women guaranteed by law (cf. *KC*, 499). Taking the ideal of Republican Motherhood as a starting point, Willard's concept of education aimed at, among other things, scientific instruction in housewifery "[which] could be raised to a regular art, and taught upon philosophical principles" (*KC*, 501; cf. doc. 223). The improvement of women's education she declared a "patriotic" and "noble [...] object" (*KC*, 502).

These advocates of women's higher education presupposed that women's intellectual powers were naturally in accordance with their specifically feminine needs – they thus affirmed the idea of women's own purpose in life and role in society as being different from, but not inferior to, men's. The fundamental difference between the sexes was, therefore, not questioned, as explained by Jonathan F. Stearns in 1837: "The truth is, there is a natural *difference*, in the mental as well as physical constitution of the two classes – a difference which implies not *inferiority* on the one part, but only *adaptation* to a *different sphere*" (*KC*, 507). According to this concept, men and women were "different but equal,"[21] a doctrine that made it possible to serve both masters at the same time, the Enlightenment idea of the natural equality of all human beings and the gender-specific ideology of separate spheres.

The idea of the sexes being different but equal was prevalent until the late nineteenth century. No matter how progressive the advocates of this idea were, they would not give up the idea of woman's genuine, innate piety, purity, delicacy, and moral power which culminated in her 'sacred' role of mother. 'Feminine' virtues such as submissiveness and domesticity, however, increasingly gave way to other values such as equal education, civil rights, or personal and financial independence for women.

---

[21] It is not an accident that the phrase "different but equal," which was not an accepted expression at the time, resembles the "separate but equal" doctrine of the Supreme Court decision in *Plessy v. Ferguson*, 1896. In fact, the consequences were very similar – just as segregation produced anything but equality between the races, different educational systems and different spheres in life cemented deeply-rooted hierarchical gender structures.

This becomes evident in the case of Theodore Parker's plea for women's civil rights in which, however, he did not abandon the idea of an essential difference between men and women (cf. doc. 238). Parker, a transcendentalist, Unitarian minister and prominent advocate of women's rights, argued along the lines of both natural rights and women's 'feminine' qualities when he highlighted the benefit for the moral state of American politics and society that was to be gained from women's participation in the public realm. He trusted that, through their moral superiority and fundamentally Christian outlook on life, women would counteract materialistic selfishness in American society and morally refine it because "God ha[d] treasured up a reserved power in *the nature of woman* to correct many of those evils which are Christendom's disgrace to-day" (*KC*, 536; emphasis mine). Parker saw the remedy for those evils in granting woman "her natural rights as the equal of man, and [allowing her to take] her natural place in regulating the affairs of the family, the community, the church and the state" (*KC*, 536). Although Parker ascribed the development of different intellectual and emotional powers in men and women to "circumstance," he also subscribed to the idea of biological determinism, citing man's "bigger brain" and woman's "better heart [and] truer intuition of the right, the lovely, the holy" (*KC*, 536). Therefore, his goal was to have "the masculine and feminine element coöperating and conjoined" in mutual, complementary influence: "Woman is to correct man's taste, mend his morals, [... while m]an is to quicken her intellect, to help her will" (*KC*, 537). Although Parker demanded equal political rights for women, he still held on to the notion of difference in equality and conceived the two sexes as complementary opposites.

Parker's semi-radical stance represented the middle ground between a more conservative, subtly hierarchical gender concept based on the assumption of an essential, complementary difference between men and women on the one hand, and their essential equality on the other. While Parker argued against a hierarchy of the sexes and propagated suffrage for women, which would open up the public realm to them, he still retained the idea of different social roles for women. Very subtly, the notion of separate spheres lingered beneath the surface of the equal rights debate, in that the notion of men's and women's gender-specific talents and their different tasks in society survived even in radical proposals such as Parker's.

3. Questioning the Ideology of Separate Spheres

Other advocates of women's natural rights launched an open attack on the ideology of separate spheres. According to this third approach, the idea of natural, inalienable rights suggested that anything preventing one half of the population from exercising their natural rights should not exist.[22]

---

[22] A few proponents of this approach demanded much more than equal political rights and women's access to traditionally male professions when they argued for the practice of free love.

Most critics of the ideology of separate spheres aimed at gaining the right to vote and other civil rights for women, which would allow them access to the public realm of political power. The strongest argument in women's political struggle for civil rights was based on the idea of inalienable natural rights and the essential equality of the members of the two sexes – which meant that all discernable differences were seen as being derived only from custom, circumstances, and different opportunities. This idea could be traced back to the revolutionary era and its ideas of Enlightenment and republicanism as well as its concept of the (male) individual being endowed with natural rights, reason, and moral responsibility for himself (cf. *KC*, 311-57). Some eighteenth-century women readily adopted these ideas and supported the cause of the American Revolution along with men. Consequently, politically self-conscious women such as Abigail Adams hoped for the men in power to apply their own ideals of natural rights to the female population of colonial America, too. In 1776, in her famous letter to her husband John Adams (doc. 215), then a member of the Continental Congress, she demands equal rights for women and thus the legal restriction of the "unlimited power [in] the hands of the husbands" (*KC*, 483). She goes as far as to warn her husband of women such as herself who "are determined to foment a rebellion, and will not hold [them]selves bound by any laws in which [they] have no voice or representation" (*KC* 483), thus appropriating and redirecting the revolutionary argument against British despotism against men as tyrants – without any success.[23]

Some fourteen years later, the feminist essayist, playwright, and poet Judith Sargent Murray (cf. doc. 217) went further by not 'only' demanding equal civil rights for women, but also claiming women's equality in intellectual capacity on the basis of their inalienable natural rights and equality with all other human beings. Murray therefore ascribed women's seeming inferiority in intellectual ability

---

However, they were abhorred for that by the respectable middle-class branch of the women's rights movement. A prominent advocate of such aims was the scandalous Victoria Woodhull (cf. Frisken 2004; Schrupp 2002). Not only did she, together with her sister Tennessee Claflin, open the first women's brokers' office on Wall Street in 1870, but she also propagated free love, the acknowledgement of prostitution as a regular profession, and the abolition of marriage laws. In the *New York Herald* in April 1870, Woodhull went so far as to announce her candidacy for the presidential elections in November 1872; in May 1872, she co-founded the Equal Rights Party covering such heterogeneous reform issues as women's rights, free love, temperance, spiritualism, socialism, and abolitionism; the same party nominated her for the presidency. These actions, however, were more symbolical than practical (cf. Schrupp 2002, 167) – apart from African American men, hardly anybody who potentially supported these reform issues held the right to vote. In fact, the established women's rights movement under the leadership of Elizabeth Cady Stanton and Susan Anthony soon distanced itself both from Woodhull's immoral aims as well as her unpromising Equal Rights Party, such as hers which would absorb the votes of the few male supporters of their own cause and thus render them lost to political power.

[23] It is important to note that Abigail Adams did not address her request to a public audience but asked her husband in a private letter to use his political influence on other male politicians on the behalf of women's legal status.

to one-sided customs, i.e., that a gender-specific upbringing that did not offer girls the same opportunities as boys: "what partiality! how is the one exalted, and the other depressed, by the contrary modes of education which are adopted! the one is taught to aspire, and the other is early confined and limitted" (*KC*, 491). Thus, Murray exposed the constructedness of women's inferiority which was disguised as nature: "Grant that their minds are by nature equal, yet who shall wonder at the *apparent* superiority [of men], if indeed custom becomes *second nature*" (*KC*, 491).[24] The differences between the sexes were thus, firstly, blamed upon society and convention which created a lack of opportunity for women. Secondly, Murray held women's own lack of courage, self-confidence, and ambition responsible for their lagging-behind in intellectual progress (cf. doc. 217). By calling for women's adoption of 'masculine' qualities such as courage, self-confidence, and ambition, which were generally thought to be 'naturally' shunned by 'delicate' ladies, she enhanced the established gender concept of femininity. The only natural difference between the sexes acknowledged by Murray was "bodily strength," due to which "nature formed [men] for [women's] protectors" (*KC*, 492). However, this difference in physical shape was not considered to be essential to the soul or intellect, as Murray promised that "if [women were] allowed an equality of acquirement, [...] they would] bid [their] souls to arise to equal strength" (*KC*, 492).[25]

Long dormant since the revolutionary period, the argument for women's natural equality was picked up again in all its radicalism at the Seneca Falls Convention in 1848 and turned into one of the core arguments of the women's rights movement. The *Declaration of Sentiments* of 1848 (doc. 237), in which Elizabeth Cady Stanton revised the Declaration of Independence, based its claim to the equality of the sexes on the idea of natural, inalienable rights (cf. Hurm in this vol., 192-7). In close imitation of the original document, Stanton first listed the numerous practical discriminations and legal disadvantages women suffered from in all compartments of life, ranging from their exclusion from the elective franchise and their denial of higher education to their lacking the right to hold property when

---

[24] Murray's idea of women's supposed inferiority as being socially constructed could be considered an early anticipation of the differentiation between the categories of sex and gender.

[25] Another instance of reversed gender roles can be found in Milcah M. H. Moore's poem "Female Patriots" (doc. 213). When, in the run-up to the American Revolution women measured men's behavior against revolutionary ideals, women poets like Moore were bitterly disappointed by men's political passivity, which rendered men effeminate in their eyes, as she makes clear in her poem "The Female Patriots, Address'd to the Daughters of Liberty in America" (*KC*, 481). Along with the poem she sent a letter to the editors of the *Pennsylvania Chronicle* with the hope that "it may contribute any thing to the [...] reformation of your male readers" (in Lauter 1994, 683) – thus she self-confidently usurped the position of a teacher to the other sex by "point[ing] out their Duty to Men" (*KC*, 481). In the poem, she both has men "blush" for their being 'slaves' to Britain and praises women's patriotism when she suggests that the cowardly male politicians should be replaced by the more capable and courageous – and, by implication, more 'manly' and patriotic – women in America: "If the Sons (so degenerate) the Blessing [of Freedom] despise, / Let the Daughters of Liberty, nobly arise, / [...] tho' we've no Voice, but a negative here" (*KC*, 481).

married (cf. *KC*, 534-5). Based on the pursuit of happiness as a universal "law of Nature" (*KC*, 533) which could not be overruled by any man-made law, Stanton demanded the revision of US laws to establish women's legal equality with men. The equality of men and women's human rights resulted from their equal capabilities and responsibilities – the allocation of separate spheres by man was denounced as his usurpation of the "prerogative of Jehovah" (*KC*, 532). The final aim of the signers of the *Declaration of Sentiments* was to "secure [...] to woman an equal participation with men in the various trades, professions and commerce" (*KC*, 534). This, in fact, meant the collapse of the idea of separate spheres.

Other women's rights activists chose different battlefields than the strictly political one for their struggle for equality – religion, for example. Women's inferior position was traditionally justified as a God-given truth, authenticated by the Bible: "The appropriate duties [...] of woman are clearly stated in the New Testament. [... These] God has given her" (*KC*, 517-8). In their letters to the supporters of woman's subordination to man, especially to Catherine E. Beecher and to the General Association of Massachusetts, the Grimké sisters (doc. 232) conjoined the assertion of women's natural equality in the more secular Lockean sense with the theological claim that Scripture puts women as Christians on an equal footing with male believers who were "giv[en] the same directions [as] women" (*KC*, 517): "Men and women were CREATED EQUAL: they are both moral and accountable beings, and whatever is right for man to do, is right for woman to do," Sarah Moore Grimké insisted (*KC*, 518).[26] Due to their exclusion from the study and profession of theology, women who wanted to contradict this argument were clearly disadvantaged because they could only speak as laypersons in the face of the centurylong authority of male-centered theology. However, Grimké did not shy away from an assault on this monopoly of men when she

> protest[ed] against the false translations of some passages by the MEN who did that work, and against the perverted interpretation by the MEN who undertook to write commentaries thereon. I am inclined to think, when we are admitted to the honor of studying Greek and Hebrew, we shall produce some various readings of the Bible, a little different from those we now have. (*KC*, 517)[27]

By claiming the essential equality of men and women in the eyes of God, and by trespassing onto the masculine cultural territory of science and theology, Grimké clearly crossed the borderline between the separate spheres. Further-

---

[26] Already in the Declaration of Independence religion and nature are closely related since nature is seen as God's creation; therefore, "[men] are endowed *by their creator* with certain inalienable rights" (*KC*, 303; emphasis mine).

[27] Such critique of the misogynic implications of the established and authorized translations of the Bible eventually culminated in the *Woman's Bible* of 1895, a revisionist commentary on the Scripture in English, undertaken by Elizabeth Cady Stanton and a "Revising Committee." Their intent was to evaluate the Judeo-Christian legacy from a feminist point of view, to highlight those passages of the Bible that focused on women, and to offer an interpretation of the biblical text which was less biased against women.

more, as Southerners, the Grimké sisters also employed their unorthodox readings of the Bible in order to combat slavery; to this end, they connected their critiques of gender relations and women's underprivileged legal status to their critiques of slavery (cf. doc. 259; Fritsch in this vol., 333-7).

Others, such as Margaret Fuller (cf. doc. 235), added the transcendentalist concept of self-reliance to this religious argument by applying it to women in the nineteenth century: Fuller claimed that women, too, partook of the divine spirit inherent in all human beings because the two sexes were "twin exponents of a divine thought" (*KC*, 526).[28] Woman, therefore, could best develop her full potential as a human being by relying on herself rather than on man. Fuller did not only compare women's inferior legal status to that of children and slaves (cf. *KC*, 527), but also demanded "inward and outward freedom for Woman as much as for Man [...] as a right, not [...] as a concession" (*KC*, 528). Thus, she wanted to give woman a chance to develop her full identity as an independent human being. Furthermore, Fuller questioned the clear division of the sexes: Although she did not deny the existence of feminine and masculine qualities in a human being – "[m]ale and female represent the two sides of the great radical dualism" – they were, she claimed, not clearly distributed between men and women, "[b]ut, in fact, they are perpetually passing into one another. [...] There is no wholly masculine man, no purely feminine woman" (*KC*, 529). Thus, she argued for the fundamentally androgynous nature of all humans, which belied the concept of separate spheres.

During the 1870s and 1880s, the concept of the New Woman gradually emerged, which explicitly declared that all "was wrong with Home-is-the-Woman's-Sphere" (*KC*, 541) and that woman "want[ed] to be admitted into public life" (544). This was generally interpreted as a reversal of roles, i.e., as "the domination of woman" (*KC*, 545): "The new woman wants to retain all the privileges of her sex and secure, besides, all those of man. She wants to be a man" (*KC*, 546). These complaints typically culminated in the "contention that [the New Women] were all unsexing [them]selves," as Sarah Grand wrote in 1894 (*KC*, 541). This evoked the fear that the borderlines between the sexes would become so blurred they would vanish entirely – thus overturning not only women's clear and reliable gender identity, but men's, too. Gender identities therefore threatened to get out of control.

From colonial times to the end of the nineteenth century, the concept of separate spheres was at the center of any consideration of women's roles. This required the various pressure groups to take a firm stand – be it by interpreting the concept in terms of difference and/or equality or by questioning it altogether.

---

[28] For documents following this philosophy, see the section on transcendentalism in the anthology (docs. 188-209; cf. Leypoldt in this vol., 275-96).

Instructional Strategies and Classroom Issues

I. Key Concepts and Major Themes

1. Goodwife (doc. 210)
   This was the predominant concept in colonial America until the emergence of Enlightenment ideas and the American Revolution. The notion of woman as Goodwife or her husband's helpmeet goes back to the Bible, which describes woman as subordinate to man, and was particularly fostered by New England Puritans.

2. Republican Mother (docs. 216, 219, 220-1)
   This concept emerged during the Early Republic and prevailed until the 1810s. The mother and wife as the moral stronghold passed republican virtues on to her sons, the future citizens, and thus ensured the survival of the young American republic. Women themselves, however, were denied full citizenship.

3. True Woman (docs. 224-30, 241)
   This concept was predominant from the late 1820s to the 1860s, then was gradually relativized by the concept of the New Woman. The True Woman was characterized by the four cardinal virtues of piety, purity, domesticity, and submissiveness (cf. Welter 1966), which all culminated in her joyful self-sacrifice for her family's benefit. As a representative of Christian benevolence, she counterbalanced the materialistic and egoistic forces of 'masculine' capitalism.

4. New Woman (docs. 242-7)
   Gradually emerging from the 1870s through the 1890s, the concept of the New Woman coexisted side by side with that of the True Woman for several decades. The New Woman obtained higher education and entered into professional life. However, her independence usually terminated with marriage or the birth of the first child.

5. Separate Spheres (docs. 224, 228, 230-46)
   The concept of separate spheres was based on the assumption that men and women were fit for different tasks in life which necessitated separate social realms: Men acted in the world of business and politics and were often rewarded by material success and fame while women unobtrusively lived for their family at home, for which they were promised rewards in heaven. The two spheres were characterized by different moral qualities, as the public world was full of temptations which constantly threatened to corrupt and morally debase man, while the home functioned as a safe haven in which woman, with her innate piety and purity, reigned supreme. In spite of the doctrine of separate spheres, man as the sole breadwinner in the family had considerable power in the domestic sphere, too, as he

earned the money with which his wife provided a comfortable home for him; woman, however, was legally as well as practically excluded from the outside world. Thus, the doctrine of separate spheres de facto only held for white middle-class women, not for men.

6. Female Influence (docs. 220, 225-6, 229)
   In spite of women's actual political powerlessness until 1920, female influence promised women an enormous amount of power which reached well into the world of politics and society at large. Woman's morally uplifting influence was exercised indirectly through the men in her family, who would take her morally virtuous behavior at home as an example for their own behavior and values when dealing with business and politics. Presumably, women thus ensured the moral and political welfare of the entire nation – their political and legal powerlessness was thus camouflaged as female 'privilege.' While female influence mainly implied political power for the Republican Mother, by the mid-nineteenth century the concept's focus had shifted towards the idea of the True Woman as a counteracting moral force against increasing materialism.

7. Female Education and Its Purposes (docs. 214, 216-21, 223, 227, 246)
   The demand for higher education for women is one of the oldest aspects in the controversy about women's roles, and was often interwoven with other issues of the "Woman's Question." Some put women's education in the service of established female gender roles: While, in the Early Republic women demanded higher education as a qualification for being Republican Mothers, later their education was to qualify them as better housekeepers and providers of a comfortable home. Others made higher education for women part of their struggle for equal civil rights (cf. doc. 237) or a fulfilled life as full human beings (cf. doc. 234-5). Traditionally, the education of young children and girls was the mother's primary field of influence.

II. Comparison – Contrasts – Connections

Example: Docs. 230, 234-5

The article "Woman" (doc. 234) published anonymously by Sophia Ripley in 1841, appeared at the intersection of various contemporary discourses, all contributing to the controversial public debate about women's 'proper sphere'; this involved, among many others, women's demands for higher education and equal legal status, the transcendentalist concepts of self-reliant individualism and self-culture, as well as the complaints and warnings of conservative religious moralizers in New England.

Sophia Willard Dana Ripley, the wife of George Ripley, was a feminist as well as a transcendentalist in the style of her friend Margaret Fuller. Sophia Ripley was among the few regular women guests of the Transcendental Club in the 1830s, and her essay "Woman" was published in the transcendentalist magazine *The Dial*. As a co-founder of the communal experiment Brook Farm in the 1840s, she also became an active practitioner of her reformist and feminist ideas. Her statements in "Woman" can be easily related to documents from other sections of the anthology, especially "Transcendentalism" (cf. Leypoldt in this vol., 294-6), as well as further documents within the section on women's roles, e.g. documents 230 and 235.

Ripley subscribed to the idea of men's and women's fundamental natural equality as human beings and individuals. For her as a transcendentalist, this assumption was based on the idea that "[t]he currents of the Universal Being circulate through [the individual, who] is part or particle of God" (*KC*, 441), for which reason the individual feels "animate[d] to create [his/her] own world" (*KC*, 442). Margaret Fuller, both in her series of conversations (1839-1844) and her major written work *Woman in the Nineteenth Century* of 1844 (doc. 235), extends and applies this concept of an innate divine power in every 'Man' to women and thus justifies their right to self-culture and self-development in order to find "a standard in herself" (*KC*, 527): "By Man I mean both man and woman; these are the two halves of one thought" (*KC*, 526), as "[t]here is but one law for souls" (*KC*, 528).

In her essay "Woman," Ripley argues from the basis of transcendentalist thought when she attacks men in general and the clergy in particular for their misconception of the whole 'class' of women as man's inferior, being good only for the private realm. Woman's restriction to the domestic sphere is frequently enforced by the clergy, as the "Pastoral Letter of the Massachusetts Congregationalist Clergy" of 1837 attests (doc. 230).[29] Ripley goes so far as to expose the religiously justified gender hierarchy as a mere flattery to women, on the one hand, and an abuse of religious authority, on the other:

> [E]ven the clergy have frequently flattered 'the feebler sex,' by proclaiming to them from the pulpit what lovely things they may become, if they will only be good, quiet, and gentle, attend exclusively to their domestic duties, and the cultivation of religious feelings. (*KC*, 523)

By means of irony, she ridicules man's pride in his "very kindly relinquish[ing to woman]" the 'privilege' of acting as the guardian of piety and morality. In Ripley's opinion, this gender-specific interpretation of religion is a gross misconception by man because "religion belongs to [humans] as beings, not as male and female." Thus, she exposes the religiously propagated image of woman as "only the spiritualized image [...] he loves the best, – one whom no true woman could or would become" (*KC*, 523) and which only serves to sustain man's privileged position. In-

---

[29] There, it is claimed that the "appropriate duties and influence of women are clearly stated in the New Testament. Those duties and that influence are unobtrusive and private" just as women's character is "mild" and "dependent" (*KC*, 516).

stead of being considered a concession to women by men, Margaret Fuller points out, "inward and outward freedom [... ought to] be acknowledged as a *right*" (*KC*, 528). Furthermore, as a transcendentalist, Ripley strongly criticizes the restriction and reduction of women to a simplistic type, i.e., that of 'Woman,' instead of conceptualizing women as individual beings in their own right: "All adjusting of the whole sex to a sphere is vain, for not two persons naturally have the same. Character, intellect creates the sphere of each. What is individual and peculiar to each determines it" (*KC*, 523).

Therefore, Ripley refuses to accept the idea of "different qualities of head and heart" in men and women merely on the basis of the "variety of [their] positions" in society (*KC*, 523), i.e., their allocation to separate spheres. Instead, she deems the concept of a fundamental gender-dichotomy inessential. In comparison to men's and women's primary identities as individual human beings, their sexual identities are merely secondary. All regulations emanating from outside the human being, such as the doctrine of separate spheres, impose restrictions onto a person's natural growth as an individual, which, according to the transcendentalist philosophy of both Emerson and Fuller, need to be fought against like any form of dependence (cf. doc. 198). In contrast to Emerson, Fuller has women's self-reliance in particular on her mind when she proclaims that she "would have every arbitrary barrier thrown down [... and] every path laid open to Woman as freely as to Man" (*KC*, 528).

This gender-indifferent and all-inclusive concept of human beings was further supported by a realistic description of woman's role in the home: In stark contrast to the strongly idealizing cult of True Womanhood, Ripley claims that any real woman did not "make peace and warmth there [...] by her sweet religious sensibility, her gentle benevolence, [and] her balmy tenderness," but rather by supposedly 'unfeminine' traits such as "strength and energy as great and untiring as leads man to battle" as well as by "sturd[y] qualities" (*KC*, 523). As woman's strength proved, she was not a dependent and weak creature in constant need of man's protection, but rather united 'feminine' and 'masculine' features within her all-human self. Due to misogynic nineteenth-century middle-class culture which denied True Women such 'masculine' qualities, "[w]oman [was] educated with the tacit understanding, that she is only half a being, and an appendage [to man ...]. Thus she loses her individuality" as well as her vitality (*KC*, 524). According to Ripley, women's immaturity was not only caused by their inferior legal status as men's property and a lack of useful and equal education for women, but it was also self-inflicted due to a lack of self-confidence (cf. *KC*, 522-5). Consistent with transcendentalist philosophy, the potential to become a complete human being lay hidden within each individual's soul and could be retrieved by self-reliance without looking for support in others: "Union is only possible to those who are units. To be fit for relations in time, souls, whether of Man or Woman, must be able to do without them in the spirit," as Fuller pointed out (*KC*, 530). From this, Ripley concluded that "[woman's] own individuality should be as precious to her as his love" (*KC*, 525). She thus proposed a new concept of matrimonial partnership based on mutuality and equality rather than hierarchy, rendering the wife a "watchful friend" to her husband since her mental and emotional powers equaled his (*KC*, 525).

According to conservative gender standards, this call for women's self-esteem, self-affirmation and, most of all, independence from others came close to outright blasphemy, or at least woman's "unsexing" herself, since one of the most crucial 'feminine' virtues had hitherto been her pious self-abnegation in service to others, most of all to her husband and her children. Fuller's and Ripley's demand for female or rather all-human self-reliance equaled a frontal attack on the gender hierarchy implied in the concept of an essential, natural and God-given difference between the sexes, of the doctrine of separate spheres, and the gender-specific division of labor in the American middle class.

In contrast to Fuller, Ripley never explicitly referred to the peculiarly transcendentalist concept of the divine Oversoul pervading everything and everybody as the source of the essential equality of all human beings, but only included it by implication in her essay. Instead, she gave other approaches the opportunity to connect the idea of all-human equality with, for instance, the republican concept of natural rights as proposed by John Locke (cf. doc. 108) and the advocates of the Declaration of Independence of the American colonies in 1776 (cf. doc. 131). Furthermore, she established the ground for connecting the idea of self-culture with the humanistic concept of man's perfectibility (cf. doc. 104). This compatibility of Ripley's essay with other ideas made it accessible and acceptable for different groups supportive of gender equality at the time.

III. Reading and Discussion Questions

1. Discuss how the roles of colonial Goodwives were reflected and evaluated by their contemporaries (docs. 210-3).

2. Discuss how and for what purpose(s) the concept of "female influence" was instrumentalized by different authors (docs. 210, 220, 225-6, 229).

3. Discuss how and for what purpose(s) the demand for higher education for women was justified at different times in history (docs. 214; 216-21, 223, 227, 246).

4. The concept of separate spheres (docs. 224; 228; 230-46):

    a) Discuss the arguments employed in these texts to justify the concept of separate spheres.

    b) Discuss the argumentative strategies used in attempts to broaden women's restricted sphere in the home without overturning the concept of separate spheres. Why would advocates of this last stance not attack the idea of separate spheres as such?

c) How did the concept of the New Woman affect the concept of separate spheres?

5. Discuss whether or not the transformations of female gender roles from the seventeenth to the late nineteenth centuries may be considered a continuous process of emancipation (cf. the entire section "Women's Roles in American Society").

6. Discuss how the concept of Republican Motherhood is related to some core ideas of the revolutionary period and Early Republic (docs. 213, 215-6, 219, 220-1).

7. Relate Sophia Ripley's and Margaret Fuller's arguments to the philosophy of transcendentalism (docs. 234-5 and the section "Transcendentalism").

8. Discuss why free women often saw themselves as slaves to men. How did Angelina Grimké relate women's struggle for legal rights to her plea for the abolition of slavery? (docs. 232, 235, 259)

IV. Resources

a. Recommended Reading

Nancy F. Cott. *No Small Courage*: *A History of Women in the United States*. Oxford: Oxford University Press, 2000. This book gives a valuable and very readable chronological introduction to the history of women and their living conditions in America from around 1600 to the present. Although white middle-class women are extensively discussed, Cott pays some attention to the different experiences of women of various ethnic minorities.

Linda K. Kerber. "Separate Spheres, Female Worlds, Woman's Place: The Rhetoric of Women's History." *Toward an Intellectual History of Women*: *Essays by Linda K. Kerber*. Chapel Hill: University of North Carolina Press, 1997, 200-223. Kerber offers a lucidly argued analysis of the concepts of femininity and their transformation with regard to ideological implications and rhetorical strategies.

Angelika Köhler. *Ambivalent Desires*: *The New Woman between Social Modernization and Modern Writing*. Heidelberg: Winter, 2004. In the first three chapters, Köhler gives a thorough analysis of the concept of the New Woman and its transgressions of cultural boundaries, while in the following chapters, she investigates the image of the New Woman in magazines and literature.

Laurel Thatcher Ulrich. *Good Wives*: *Image and Reality in the Lives of Women in Northern New England, 1650-1750*. 1980. New York: Vintage, 1991. Ulrich provides a vivid historical account of women's everyday life, their chores and cares in colonial America.

Barbara Welter. "The Cult of True Womanhood." *American Quarterly* 18.2 (1966), 151-174. This seminal essay defines the concept of True Womanhood by its four cardinal virtues of piety, purity, domesticity, and submissiveness. In connection with Welter's essay, the reading of Mary Louise Roberts's brief "True Womanhood Revisited" (*Journal of Women's History* 14.1, 2002, 150-155) is particularly recommended, as Roberts identifies both the strong and the weak points in Welter's conceptualization of the stereotype of the True Woman.

b. Works Cited and Reading Suggestions

Armstrong, Nancy, and Leonard Tennenhouse, eds. (1987). *The Rise of the Domestic Woman*. New York: Methuen.
Battan, Jesse (1992). "'The Word Made Flesh': Language, Authority, and Sexual Desire in Late Nineteenth-Century America." *Journal of the History of Sexuality* 3.2, 223-244.
Cogan, Frances B. (1989). *All-American Girl: The Ideal of Real Womanhood in Mid-Nineteenth-Century America*. Athens: University of Georgia Press.
Cott, Nancy F. (1972), ed. *Roots of Bitterness: Documents of the Social History of American Women*. New York: Dutton.
– (1977). *The Bonds of Womanhood: "Woman's Sphere" in New England, 1780-1835*. New Haven: Yale University Press.
– (2000) *No Small Courage: A History of Women in the United States*. Oxford: Oxford University Press.
Davidson, Cathy N., ed. (1998). *No More Separate Spheres!* Special Issue. *American Literature* 70.3.
– , and Jessamyn Hatcher, eds. (2002).*No More Separate Spheres! A Next Wave American Studies Reader*. Durham: Duke University Press.
Degler, Carl N. (1980). *At Odds: Women and the Family in America from the Revolution to the Present*. New York: Oxford University Press.
Douglas, Ann (1977). *The Feminization of American Culture*. New York: Knopf.
Dowling, Linda (1979). "The Decadent and the New Woman in the 1890s." *Nineteenth-Century Fiction* 33.4, 434-454.
DuBois, Ellen Carol, and Vicki L. Ruiz, eds. (1990). *Unequal Sisters: A Multicultural Reader in U.S. Women's History*. New York: Routledge.
Elbert, Monica M., ed. (2000). *Separate Spheres No More: Gender Convergence in American Literature, 1830-1930*. Tuscaloosa: University of Alabama Press.
Forrey, Carolyn (1974). "The New Woman Revisited." *Women's Studies* 2, 37-56.
Foucault, Michel (1978). *The History of Sexuality*. Vol. 1: *The Will to Knowledge*. Trans. Robert Hurley. London: Penguin.

Frisken, Amanda (2004). *Victoria Woodhull's Sexual Revolution*: *Political Theater and the Popular Press in Nineteenth-Century America*. Philadelphia: University of Pennsylvania Press.

Ginzberg, Lori D. (1900). *Women and the Work of Benevolence*: *Morality, Politics, and Class in the Nineteenth-Century United States*. New Haven: Yale University Press.

Hannam, June, Mitzi Auchterlonie, and Katherine Holden (2000). *International Encyclopedia of Women's Suffrage*. Santa Barbara: ABC-CLIO.

Harris, Barbara J. (1978). *Beyond Her Sphere*: *Women in the Professions in American History*. Westport: Greenwood.

Kerber, Linda K. (1980). *Women of the Republic*: *Intellect and Ideology in Revolutionary America*. Chapel Hill: University of North Carolina Press.

– (1997). "Separate Spheres, Female Worlds, Woman's Place: The Rhetoric of Women's History." 1988. *Toward an Intellectual History of Women*: *Essays by Linda K. Kerber*. Chapel Hill: University of North Carolina Press, 200-223.

– (1999). "The Republican Mother: Women and the Enlightenment – An American Perspective." 1966. *Locating American Studies*: *The Evolution of a Discipline*. Ed. Lucy Maddox. Baltimore: Johns Hopkins University Press, 143-165.

Köhler, Angelika (2004). *Ambivalent Desires*: *The New Woman between Social Modernization and Modern Writing*. Heidelberg: Winter.

Kraditor, Aileen, ed. (1968). *Up from the Pedestal*: *Selected Writings in the History of American Feminism*. New York: HarperCollins.

Lauter, Paul, ed. (1994). *Heath Anthology of American Literature*. 2nd ed. Vol. 1. Lexington: Heath.

Matthews, Jean V. (1987). *"Just a Housewife:" The Rise and Fall of Domesticity in America*. New York: Oxford University Press.

– (1997). *Women's Struggle for Equality*: *The First Phase, 1828-1876*. Chicago: Dee.

Norton, Mary Beth (1980). *Liberty's Daughters*: *The Revolutionary Experience of American Women, 1750-1800*. Boston: Little Brown.

Okin, Susan (1982). "Women and the Making of the Sentimental Family." *Philosophy and Public Affairs* 11.1 (1982), 65-88.

Parker, Gail, ed. (1972). *The Oven Birds*: *American Women on Womanhood, 1820-1920*. Garden City: Anchor.

Roberts, Mary Louise (2002). "True Womanhood Revisited." *Journal of Women's History* 14.1, 150-155.

Rosenberg, Charles E. (1973). "Sexuality, Class and Role in Nineteenth-Century America." *American Quarterly* 25.2, 131-153.

Rupp, Leila J. (2002). "Women's History in the New Millennium: A Retrospective Analysis of Barbara Welter's 'The Cult of True Womanhood, 1820-1860.'" *Journal of Women's History* 14.1, 149-173.

Ryan, Mary P. (1975). *Womanhood in America from Colonial Times to the Present*. New York: New Viewpoints.

Schrupp, Antje (2002). *Das Aufsehen erregende Leben der Victoria Woodhull*. Königstein/Taunus: Helmer.
Smart, Carol, ed. (1992). *Regulating Womanhood*: *Historical Essays on Marriage, Motherhood and Sexuality*. London: Routledge.
Smith-Rosenberg, Carroll (1985a). "The Female World of Love and Ritual: Relations between Women in Nineteenth-Century America." 1975. *Disorderly Conduct*: *Visions of Gender in Victorian America*. New York: Oxford University Press, 43-76.
– (1985b). "Bourgeois Discourse and the Age of Jackson: An Introduction." 1975. *Disorderly Conduct*: *Visions of Gender in Victorian America*. New York: Oxford University Press, 79-89.
– (1985c). "The Hysterical Woman: Sex Roles and Role Conflict in Nineteenth-Century America." 1972. *Disorderly Conduct*: *Visions of Gender in Victorian America*. New York: Oxford University Press, 197-216.
– (1985d). "The New Woman as Androgyne: Social Disorder and Gender Crisis, 1870-1936." *Disorderly Conduct*: *Visions of Gender in Victorian America*. New York: Oxford University Press, 245-296.
Ulrich, Laurel Thatcher (1991). *Good Wives*: *Image and Reality in the Lives of Women in Northern New England, 1650-1750*. 1980. New York: Vintage.
Welter, Barbara (1966). "The Cult of True Womanhood, 1820-1860." *American Quarterly* 18.2, 151-174.
White, Deborah Grey (1985). *Ar'n't I a Woman*: *Female Slaves in the Plantation South*. New York: Norton.

MELANIE FRITSCH

Slavery and Racial Thought in American Cultural History

> I John Brown am now quite *certain* that the crimes of this *guilty land: will* never be purged *away*; but with Blood.
> John Brown on the day of his execution
> (in Trodd and Stauffer 2004, 159)

I. Themes and Arguments

American debates about slavery during the antebellum period mark a pervasive point of reference for contestations and affirmations of national and ethnic identities throughout United States history. Nineteenth-century discussions about the future of slavery shaped the political, economic, intellectual, social, religious, and cultural life of Americans, since they were conducted in view of contested notions of racial difference. As the documents in the section on slavery in the anthology reveal, American slavery's peculiarity lies in the inseparable link that was established early on between slavery and notions of race. The beginnings of slavery as a system of forced labor can be traced to the colonial period when slavery replaced indentured servitude, a temporary working arrangement, in the last decades of the seventeenth century. As chattel, i.e., the movable property of another person, the slave was fully subject to his owner's control. Over the course of only a few decades, Africans were relegated to a position of permanent unfreedom and inferiority on account of race, which served as an essential marker of ethnic difference. Covering the period from the late eighteenth century through the 1850s, the documents in the chapter on slavery demonstrate that the meaning of race changed perpetually and that race neither carries an essential identity nor a transhistorical significance. Instead, as a "product of history," race was "continually redefined" over the course of time and introduced a social hierarchy between different groups in colonial America (Berlin 1998, 1-14, 358-65; cf. Berlin 2006). Whereas today the constructed character of race is widely acknowledged, race was perceived as a scientific category well into the twentieth century.

The interdependency between the American discourse on race and the institution of slavery became conspicuously visible in debates about the future of slave labor, which began on a larger scale after the American Revolution and intensified in the final three antebellum decades. As defenders of slavery and antislavery activists argued over the meaning of the inalienable rights codified in the Declaration of Independence, Northern states set in motion the gradual abolition of slavery while Southern states reinforced their commitment to the institution in light of the augmented demand for unpaid labor after the invention of the cotton gin.

The debate about slavery figures prominently in some of the major literary texts by nineteenth-century American and African American writers, and slavery continues to be a source of inspiration for authors to this day.[1] Even beyond the literary, slavery never ceases to raise questions of national identity and values not only among intellectuals, but also in American popular culture. As the documents in the anthology show, slavery remained a national concern even after its termination in one part of the country. The antislavery movement in the North developed an effective institutional network that united black and white, male and female opponents of slavery and thrived owing to the concerted commitment of philanthropists, publishers, lecturers, and ministers. Reliance on the invocation of America's founding principles was widespread in black and white radical abolitionist rhetoric. Although abolitionism was not a unified movement, the members of the different factions shared the demand for the immediate end of slavery and the integration of African Americans into American society. As the sectional discord about the extension of slavery into new territories intensified in the middle of the nineteenth century, both sides of the divide underwent a period of rapid radicalization. At the end of the fierce struggle for or against the 'peculiar institution' stood national disunion, the eruption of the Civil War (1861-1865), and finally the ratifications of the Thirteenth Amendment (1865), pronouncing the official end of slavery, as well as the Fourteenth Amendment (1868), conferring citizenship on the freedmen.

The defeat of the South in the Civil War did not eclipse the ideological formations on which the 'peculiar institution' had been erected. In debates about the legacy of slavery, stereotypical views of racial difference persist to this day. The current invocation of 'race' as an underlying notion in the debates about identity politics has been challenged on the grounds that it reifies a superseded mode of speaking about ethnic identity. The historical documents assembled in the anthology demonstrate, however, that the connection between slavery and notions of race lies at the heart of one of the most profound debates in nineteenth-century America.

---

[1] For studies looking at the intersection of slavery and literature, see McDowell and Rampersad (1989), LaCapra (1991), Sundquist (1993), Castronovo (1995), Lee (2005), Riss (2006).

II. The Origins of Slavery and Racial Thought

The question of the origins of slavery in North America has always interested historians, but data and evidence have not been complete and conclusive enough to settle the issue satisfactorily yet. At mid-twentieth century, a pronounced scholarly debate, the so-called origins debate, emerged among American historians, who were intrigued by the question of whether racial slavery preceded racism or whether prejudice was incipient and thus expedited the institutionalization of slavery (cf. Young 2005, 143-4).[2] But even beyond the confines of the origins debate, historians and philosophers began to explore the intertwined character of slavery and race in the revolutionary and antebellum periods.[3]

By the 1660s, slavery had become institutionalized in the colonies through legislation that defined the status of slaves and free blacks (cf. Kolchin 2003, 17). However, the condition of African laborers and free blacks in the years between 1640 and 1660 and, even more so, in the two decades following the arrival of the first Africans in Jamestown in 1619 has remained a matter of controversy (cf. Jordan 1968, 44). Oscar and Mary F. Handlin, whose groundbreaking essay initiated the origins debate in 1950, argued that the status of African servants in colonial Virginia was at first comparable to that of white servants and that economic reasons contributed to a heightened deterioration of the condition of black laborers as compared to white laborers. This development, according to the Handlins, resulted in racial slavery and finally brought forth racial prejudice (cf. Handlin and Handlin 1950). Their scholarship was rebutted by Carl N. Degler, who showed that black servants met severer treatment from the beginning. The debasement of black servants did not temporally correspond with the growing economic needs of the colony and the preference for white labor; rather, prejudice served as the basis on which to enslave Africans (cf. Degler 1959). In the tracing of racial prejudice, Winthrop D. Jordan substantiated Degler's position by showing that English prejudices against Africans preexisted and stemmed primarily from what came to be perceived as their racial difference, i.e., their

---

[2] Young provides a concise overview of the origins debate, putting in perspective all the major studies and developments important to the dispute from the 1960s through the 1990s (cf. Vaughan 1995; Wood 1997; Young 2005; Baptist 2006, 1-18). For a compendious synthesis of the first two hundred years of American slavery and the role of race and class in that development, see Berlin (1998).

[3] The findings of scholars of American slavery and race raised issues that continue to engage historians to this day. The sizeable interest in the beginnings of slavery was accompanied by a problematization of the category 'race' (cf. Anderson 2005). A plethora of critical studies on race and racism has since appeared. The most important voices in this ongoing discussion are: Takaki (1979), Horsman (1981), Fields (1982; 1990), Gates (1986), Fredrickson (1987; 1988; 1997; 2002), Appiah (1989; 1992), Goldberg (1990), Hannaford (1996), Gossett (1997), Mills (1997), Jacobson (1998), Smedley (1999), Dain (2002).

blackness, their heathenism, and their savagery (cf. Jordan 1968, 3-28).[4] None of these isolated factors, however, is still considered the decisive root cause in the development toward African slavery (cf. Kolchin 2003, 15). Jordan suggested attributing the enslavement of Africans to an "unthinking decision" and concluded that "[r]ather than slavery causing 'prejudice,' or vice versa, they seem rather to have generated each other [… and] may have been equally cause and effect, continuously reacting upon each other, dynamically joining hands to hustle the Negro down the road to complete degradation" (1968, 80; cf. Morgan 1975, 315). In an attempt to move the focus of the discussion away from any monolithic array of explanations, historian Peter Kolchin points out that "the most appropriate question is not whether slavery caused prejudice or prejudice caused slavery […] but rather how slavery and prejudice interacted to create the particular set of social relationships that existed in the English mainland colonies" (2003, 14). One possible conclusion in this debate suggests that a combination of Africans' racial difference and the specific economic factors in colonial America ostensibly led to a favoring of African slavery.

Although some historians doubt that race is an appropriate analytical category for the colonial period (cf. Fields 1990), colonial Americans created an exclusionary terminology to describe the difference between free Anglo-Americans and enslaved Africans. As the primacy of either factor – slavery and race – remained contested, Americans implemented a nomenclature that allowed the classification of the colonial population along lines of difference. At the beginning, English colonists referred to themselves as 'Christians' more frequently than as 'English' when they distinguished themselves from Africans and Native Americans, whose difference derived from a combination of complexion, heathenism, and savagery. However, as soon as Christian conversion became more common among these groups, the dichotomous use of 'Christian' and 'heathen' as a marker of difference became obsolete – not least because conversion did not entail freedom. The colonists began to exchange the term 'Christian' with 'English' and 'free' at the middle of the seventeenth century, and finally the term 'white' emerged (after 1680), identifying white males with full citizenship rights (cf. Jordan 1968, 91-8). Thus, a terminological shift concerning Englishmen's self-appellation as 'white' was necessary to introduce a system of racial classification that would henceforth codify the inferiority of blacks.

Discrimination of blacks on account of color persisted through the Revolution, and the Constitution did not explicitly mention slavery, but talked instead about slaves as "those bound to service for a term of years" (in Boyer et al. 2004, A-7). However, the revolutionary period also, and for the first time, generated a sense of suspicion against slavery among the revolutionaries. Their own oppression at the hands of the mother country necessarily raised questions about slavery. But the

---

[4] For studies of Englishmen's prejudices against Africans, see Jordan (1968, 3-43), and more recently, Wheeler (2000).

egalitarian atmosphere provoked a far-reaching rethinking only in the North. Prompted by the principle that "all men are created equal" in the Declaration of Independence, all states north of Delaware passed some form of emancipation legislation between 1777 and 1804. Some states abolished slavery immediately, but most preferred gradual emancipation. Slaves in the rest of the country remained the property of others for an indefinite time frame. The founders, in pursuing their egalitarian project, at the same time reinforced racial prejudices against blacks by denying them the natural rights available to the white population.[5]

Enlightenment documents proposing the inferiority of blacks scarcely exist – with the notable exception of the writings of Thomas Jefferson (cf. Fredrickson 1987, 1), who has received wide attention from scholars of the American Revolution, slavery, and race. Jefferson's discussion of racial differences and the natural inferiority of blacks in his 1788 *Notes on the State of Virginia* (doc. 251) is one of the earliest publicized statements accounting for racial slavery on a scientific basis; it is also one of the most controversially debated documents among scholars, who disagree on the founder's definite position on slavery. On the one hand, Jefferson crafted the Declaration of Independence with its egalitarian and libertarian credo and contemplated the emancipation of slaves in his *Notes*; on the other hand, he kept a large slave estate and advocated the colonization of emancipated slaves. Above all, Jefferson's expressions of his thoughts on race in *Notes* reveal that he shared with his fellow Enlightenment thinkers the view that racial features explain differences between Anglo-Americans and African Americans, who remain "inferior to the whites in the endowments both of body and mind" (*KC*, 560), according to Jefferson.

Jefferson's discussion of race in Query XIV of his *Notes* is informed by political deliberations about slavery dominant at the time. The Virginian lawmakers considered a gradual emancipation scheme, yet not without pondering the question of whether to "retain and incorporate the blacks into the state" (*KC*, 558). Jefferson does not confine himself to articulating political objections to blacks' incorporation, but rather aims to also include the physical and moral arguments against the integration of blacks. His catalog of black people's physical differences – ranging from color to a transpiration allowing them to bear greater heat – essentially serves to "prov[e] a difference of race" (*KC*, 558) in an Enlightenment discourse. Even though black people's color entails an "eternal monotony,

---

[5] The landmark study of slavery in the revolutionary period and its aftermath is Davis (1975). Matthew Mason's more recent book on slavery's political relevance for the founding of America and the Early Republic works from the assumption that "[t]he political history of slavery in North America began in earnest with the American Revolution" (2006, 9). For a comprehensive study of slavery in the American Constitution, see Finkelman (1996, 1-33, 80-104). Finkelman shows how slavery was protected by the Constitution and debunks the Founding Fathers' hypocrisy in crafting a proslavery Constitution. Finkelman's overall project, like Mason's, is to unfold the centrality of slavery in the process of the founding of the American republic (cf. Finkelman 1996, ix).

which reigns in the countenances, that immovable veil of black" which, Jefferson explains, conceals their emotions, they are driven "more [by] sensation than reflection" (*KC*, 558-9). Jefferson's perception of an imbalance between intellectual and emotional aspects of the African American psyche discloses that he is informed by a Lockean faculty psychology; accordingly, his comparison of black and white people regarding the "faculties of memory, reason, and imagination" reveals that "in memory [black people] are equal to the whites; in reason much inferior [...]; and that in imagination they are dull, tasteless, and anomalous" (*KC*, 559).⁶ Finally, Jefferson places himself explicitly among the natural historians of his day, ruminating about blacks' classification in the taxonomies which circulated at the time:

> I advance it therefore as a suspicion only, that the blacks, whether originally a distinct race, or made distinct by time and circumstances, are inferior to the whites in the endowments both of body and mind. It is not against experience to suppose, that different species of the same genus, or varieties of the same species, may possess different qualifications. Will not a lover of natural history then, one who views the gradations in all the races of animals with the eye of philosophy, excuse an effort to keep those in the department of man as distinct as nature has formed them? (*KC*, 560)

Jefferson decides that the physical and mental differences (and supposed deficiencies) of blacks preclude their emancipation – or would at least require their removal in order to prevent miscegenation. He thus adopts the standard quasi-scientific position of the eighteenth century on questions of racial difference.⁷

Jefferson also articulates the unfavorable effects of slavery in Query XVIII of his tract. However, he is primarily concerned about the harm of slavery on white Americans. He refers specifically to the moral degeneration slavery causes among white people. Jefferson fears an adverse influence on the future generation of American citizens whose republican principles he sees in danger of being corrupted by living in a slave society. The prospect of slavery transforming re-

---

[6] The African American poet Phillis Wheatley illustrates this, Jefferson purports. Despite Wheatley's Christian upbringing, he claims, she was not able to write great poetry; in fact, he deems her poems "below the dignity of criticism" (KC, 559). Concerning the faculties of reason and imagination, Native Americans surpass blacks, according to Jefferson's assessment: "The Indians, with no advantages of this kind, will often carve figures on their pipes not destitute of design and merit. They will crayon out an animal, a plant, or a country, so as to prove the existence of a germ in their minds which only wants cultivation. They astonish you with strokes of the most sublime oratory; such as prove their reason and sentiment strong, their imagination glowing and elevated" (KC, 559).

[7] For an elaboration on the context of natural history in which Jefferson's ideas of race in *Notes* must be viewed, see Dain (2002, 1-39). Dain's overall argument is concerned with showing that American scientific racism does not begin with *Notes on the State of Virginia*. Dain argues that Jefferson's ideas of "self, nature, and nation" differ from nineteenth-century scientific racism's biological conceptions based on "inner structures and substance" and that Jefferson's views are rather informed by convictions of natural history, e.g. the "idea of a natural harmony self-evident to the senses and, through the senses, to the mind" (2002, 3-4).

publican citizens into tyrannical despots is even aggravated by the vision of alienating Africans from an "amor patriæ" (*KC*, 561) toward the United States. The exploitation and alienation of the slave population, Jefferson argues, preclude African Americans from fulfilling their potentials as human beings, and this precarious situation conjures up the nightmare of a possible war between the races. His fear of race conflict results from his insecurity as to God's interference in such a conflict. Jefferson dreads "a revolution of the wheel of fortune, an exchange of situation [... in which t]he Almighty has no attribute which can take side with us in such a contest" (*KC*, 561). Both lines of thinking – the moral decline of the white population and the fear of black-white hostilities – are clear expressions of Jefferson's qualms about the detrimental effect of slavery on the United States. Here, Jefferson anticipates important arguments to be adopted in nineteenth-century antislavery discourse.

Scholars disagree on the antislavery record of Thomas Jefferson, especially because earlier biographers' and historians' hagiographic approach forestalled a balanced portrait. While present-day scholars note Jefferson's dislike of slavery and recall the historical context of Jefferson's actions, they also tackle the question of incongruence between his official record as a political leader and his private record as a slaveholder (cf. Finkelman 1996). Condemning the public statesman for the caution he exercised toward antislavery measures, Paul Finkelman concludes that "race presented an insurmountable barrier to emancipation for Jefferson" and that "[h]is deeds are those of a self-indulgent and negrophobic Virginia planter" (1996, 108, 135). To qualify the founder's antislavery disposition, historians point out that Jefferson did not consent to any emancipation plans that did not also involve the emancipated blacks' expatriation (cf. Finkelman 1996, 133-5, 150-1).[8] Thus, what most scholars agree upon in their discussions of Jefferson is his "introspective ambivalence" toward slavery (Kolchin 2003, 89), i.e., the irreconcilability of his egalitarian Enlightenment ideas with the historical, especially the economic, realities of the period.

III. Proslavery Thought and Racial Stereotypes

While Jefferson may count as an example of the eclectic ways of thinking about slavery in the revolutionary period, nineteenth-century Americans increasingly expressed decidedly unequivocal positions on the moral, political, and economic aspects of slavery. The rise of the Southern plantation economy, which was triggered by Eli Whitney's invention of the cotton gin in 1794, turned slavery into the defining socio-economic system in the American South and added new vigor to the debates about the future of slavery. Different antislavery efforts emerged

---

[8] Contextualizing Jefferson's views, David Brion Davis has criticized the founder's comments by explicating enlightened views that would qualify as blatantly racist from a contemporary perspective (2006, 74-5).

in the immediate aftermath of the Revolution. Not only did Northern states abolish slavery or pass gradual emancipation laws in the last quarter of the eighteenth century, but slavery was also banned from the Northwest Territory, and the international slave trade was outlawed by 1808.[9] In the face of these challenges, proslavery advocates produced increasingly elaborate political, economic, religious, and pseudo-scientific justifications for slavery. The growing conflict between pro- and antislavery forces also affected the politics of admitting new states to the Union.

In 1819, Missouri's intention to join the Union as a slave state constituted the first major political confrontation over the question of slavery. The Missouri Compromise of 1820 finally determined that Missouri could enter the Union as a slave state while Maine would simultaneously be admitted as a free state, a ruling that kept the balance between slave and slave-free states equal. Aware of the hostility towards expanding slavery into the western territories, two developments alarmed the South in the following decade: an increase in slave insurrections and a growing abolitionist movement in the North. Terrified by the thwarted slave uprising by Denmark Vesey in South Carolina and the violent 1831 Nat Turner slave revolt in Virginia, Southerners responded critically to the rise of abolitionism. As a response to these developments, and to leave no doubt that the South was determined to defend its interests and way of life, Southern intellectuals refined and publicized their defenses of slavery more widely. Scholars of proslavery thought recorded defenses of slavery as far back as colonial America and also discovered proslavery writing in the North. Nevertheless, Southern proslavery activity in the 1830s through the 1850s received the fullest attention (cf. Tise 1987; Faust 1981, 3-4). It was during these decades that a "more systematic and self-conscious" proslavery thought emerged and "took on the characteristics of a formal ideology with its resulting social movement" (Faust 1981, 4). Significantly, proslavery advocates never neglected the evils inherent in the system of slavery, but tended to pass over slavery's defects and praise its alleged strengths as the debate grew fiercer (cf. Faust 1981, 6). Some defenses were informed by a pronounced religious, scientific, political, or economic argumentation, whereas other proslavery documents aimed at a more comprehensive justification of slavery.

Religious defenses of the institution referred to both Testaments of the Bible, in order to refute antislavery declarations that slavery was not compatible with Christian principles. The Old Testament records the existence of slavery among the Israelites, God's chosen people, and provides the often-cited example of Noah's "curse of Ham" which is really a curse condemning Ham's son Canaan who was "to be the slave of slaves" and the servant of Ham's brothers, Shem and

---

[9] In her monograph on gradual emancipation in New England, Joanne Pope Melish debunks the "mythology of a historically white New England" (1998, 200), which is untarnished by the blemishes of slavery, and vindicates a history of the region that includes African Americans, slave and free.

Japheth (cf. Gen. 9.20-7). Southern apologists employed this passage to illustrate God's relegation of blacks (the sons of Ham) to an eternal slave status.[10] Likewise, defenders of slavery pointed out that the New Testament did not contain a condemnation of slavery, especially none by Jesus Christ himself; instead, the apostle Paul appears to have encouraged the continuation of slavery (cf. Faust 1981, 10-1; Kolchin 2003, 192).

Scientific racism also became a steady ingredient in proslavery thought, starting in the 1830s and developing in the 1840s and 1850s. To defend the institution, scientists of the emerging American School of Ethnology advanced the thesis of polygenesis, i.e., that blacks originated from a separate creation and hence belonged to a distinct species. Furthermore, scientists such as Samuel George Morton, George R. Gliddon, and Josiah C. Nott conducted phrenological and craniometrical research. They analyzed and measured human skulls to determine mental skills and dispositions and eagerly attempted to prove that blacks were physiologically different and mentally inferior. Although these theories were refuted by other scientists at the time, they provided proslavery activists with supposedly rational justifications for the enslavement of blacks. Although the polygenesis position posed a stark contrast to the common biblical view of a single creation, a popularized version of this thesis served as a convincing scientific justification for the perpetuation of the Southern system (cf. Fredrickson 1987, 71-90; Gossett 1997, 54-83).

Most proslavery arguments referred to the practical necessity of the institution, adopting either an economic or political reasoning in favor of black bondage. Economic justifications of slavery pointed out that Southern prosperity could only be maintained with the help of slaves in labor-intensive Southern agriculture. Politically informed defenses focused on the alleged impracticality of freeing all slaves and the supposedly negative consequences of emancipation for social stability (cf. Kolchin 2003, 190-1). John C. Calhoun's reasoning in favor of slavery also took into consideration the future of the American nation, which he saw jeopardized by the debate over the abolition of slavery. In Calhoun's famous 1837 speech before the United States Senate (doc. 260), the South Carolina Senator warns that "unless prompt and efficient measures [...] be adopted" to fight against the rise of abolitionism and its growing leadership in the churches, schools, and press, "we must become, finally, two people[s]" (*KC*, 586). He advances the view that maintaining the status quo in the South is crucial to the perpetuation of the Union and that the North and South must unite against abolitionism in order to avoid secession and disunion (cf. *KC*, 586-7). Even though opponents of slavery asserted the contrary, Calhoun affirms that "the relation now existing in the slave-holding States between the two [races], is,

---

[10] For a detailed history of how Noah's curse of Ham was interpreted and utilized by advocates of slavery, see Haynes (2002). Haynes shows that Southerners were able to relate to the biblical story of the curse of Ham so effectively because it presented honor as a central concept in human interaction (cf. 2002, 65-86).

instead of an evil, a good – a positive good" (*KC*, 586-7). Both the black and the white population in the South – and in the whole country – profit from slavery, Calhoun argues. blacks should count themselves lucky, as slavery has not only civilized and improved them "morally and intellectually," but also provides a paternalistic system of care for the sick and elderly unknown in labor economies (cf. *KC*, 586-7). White Americans benefit in equal measure from slavery because it "forms the most solid and durable foundation on which to rear free and stable political institutions" (*KC*, 587). Slavery, Calhoun thus suggests, is indispensable for the stability, union, and freedom of the whole country.

Similarly stressing the advantages of slavery for all involved, the sociologist and lawyer George Fitzhugh goes even further in his radical defense of slavery. Slavery is an institution that does not necessarily require racial differences between masters and slaves, Fitzhugh claims. In *Cannibals All! or Slaves without Masters* (1857), he advocates slavery as a beneficial system for both black and white laborers, thus offering slavery as a remedy for the grievances caused by free labor in the industrialized North (cf. Faust 1981, 18). His central idea is that, as chattel, black slaves enjoy better treatment by their owners than white Northern factory workers, who do not enjoy the benevolent, paternal protection that is common practice among the slaveholders in the South (cf. *KC*, 593). In *Sociology for the South, or the Failure of Free Society* (doc. 264), Fitzhugh reproduces the proslavery argumentation of his time when he contends that the relationship between slave and master essentially resembles that of a child and his parent/guardian and that, due to their inferiority, emancipated blacks "would be far outstripped or outwitted in the chase of free competition" (*KC*, 593). Fitzhugh echoes Calhoun and others when he emphasizes slavery's supposedly civilizing effect, for "slavery here relieves [the negro] from a far more cruel slavery in Africa, or from idolatry and cannibalism, and every brutal vice and crime that can disgrace humanity; and [...] it christianizes, protects, supports and civilizes him; [...] it governs him far better than free laborers at the North are governed" (*KC*, 593). Fitzhugh's views, especially his claim that white workers would also benefit from the system of slavery, were seen by his contemporaries as "incendiary and dangerous," "absurd," "odd, eccentric, extravagant, and disorderly" (in Faust 1981, 18)[11] – not least because most Southerners were "non-slaveholders who must inevitably wonder about their proper place in a society where slavery was based on criteria other than race" (Kolchin 2003, 196). Regardless of Fitzhugh's radicalism and singularity among proslavery advocates, his reasoning was permeated by the often-voiced fundamental belief in the preservation of a superior Southern way of life – of which slavery was a constitutive component.

---

[11] Drew Gilpin Faust details the contemporary interest in Fitzhugh as a proslavery theorist as well as today's scholarly attention to him – which she attributes to "his very unrepresentativeness" (1981, 18-20).

IV. The Antislavery Movement and Antebellum Reform

Even though their public avowals in favor of slavery were rife with racist rationales for its perpetuation, spokesmen like Fitzhugh touched upon a practical question that the foes of slavery avoided considering in public: What was to be done with black people once they were emancipated? Colonizationists tackled this urgent question without prevarication during the 1810s and 1820s. They advocated the relocation of blacks to places outside the United States, preferably Africa, and thus did not envision a future for emancipated African Americans on American soil. Combining the vision of a protracted process of ending slavery in the United States with exclusionary politics, the gradualist approach of the colonization movement provoked more radical activists to press for the immediate abolition of slavery and the inclusion of African Americans into American society.[12] Incipient in the late 1820s, the abolitionist movement responded not only to the evangelical fervor of the age but also coalesced with other prominent reform movements in the Jacksonian period (cf. Walters 1997). In contrast to other reform efforts such as the temperance movement and the early women's rights movement, immediate abolitionists constituted an increasingly radical segment of the antislavery faction. While they initially produced more pronounced moral arguments for the slaves' freedom than the colonizationists, the prolonged confrontation during the 1840s and 1850s between pro- and antislavery activists led many abolitionists to embrace extra-legal and violent measures.

Colonization and Gradualism

Colonization schemes evolved as a response to an increase in free black populations, especially in the North, where emancipation laws had terminated slavery in the three decades following the Declaration of Independence, but also in the South, where private manumissions occurred. In addition, the potential interference of Southern free blacks with slaves was considered a possible source of slave revolts and a hazard to the security of the white Southern population. As racist prejudice against free blacks was widespread among Northerners as well, it is no surprise that Northerners joined Southern colonizationists in founding the American Colonization Society in 1816. Northerners participated under the cloak of philanthropy, hoping that Southern slaveholders would gradually and voluntarily free all their slaves and that the relocated blacks would help Christianize Africa. But they also clearly saw the opportunity to get rid of free blacks and the problem

---

[12] Scholars often use the terms 'antislavery' and 'abolitionist' interchangeably. However, 'antislavery' is the broader term which refers to those people who opposed the institution of slavery for a variety of reasons in the period between the American Revolution and 1865. 'Abolitionism' denotes a specific (interracial) intellectual movement – starting at the beginning of the 1830s and ending with the ratification of the Thirteenth Amendment in 1865 – whose militant call for immediate emancipation of all slaves arose from evangelical religion and included egalitarian demands (cf. Lowance 2000, xv-xvii).

of defining their social role in American society (cf. Mason 2006, 112-3; Bay 2000, 22).[13] The reasoning of the movement's spokesmen was for the most part devoid of ideas of blacks' natural inferiority known from proslavery discourse. Rather than referring to innate factors, colonizationists pointed out that it was black people's cultural inferiority, resulting from their "degraded" condition, which made their assimilation impossible (cf. Fredrickson 1987, 12-6). Such an environmentalist argument, however, did not prevent colonization advocates from developing a "protoracist" view of black Americans by pointing out "an inevitable and legitimate white prejudice against a black skin" (Fredrickson 1987, 17-8).

Although proponents of colonization discussed the possibility of a settlement for free blacks on United States territory, e.g. in the west, a majority of white Americans preferred their colonization in Africa (cf. doc. 254). Not only was there "a peculiar, a moral fitness in restoring them to the land of their fathers," they argued, but blacks would also be able to spread "the arts, civilization and Christianity," while America would at the same time be able to "extinguish a great portion of that moral debt which she has contracted to that unfortunate continent" (*KC*, 570). However, free blacks, while not rejecting colonization schemes as such, voiced their displeasure about the prospect of being exiled. Consenting to settle even "in the most remote corner of the land of our nativity [i.e., the United States]," they entreated Congress to grant them such a place (*KC*, 572).[14] The American Colonization Society had, with the help of government funding, founded the colony of Liberia in 1822, but by 1831 only some 2,000 blacks had left the United States to settle in Africa, almost a negligible number in light of the 300,000 free blacks living in the United States (cf. Dumond 1961, 129).

Among the most radical black spokesmen against colonization was David Walker, a free black from North Carolina.[15] Drawing upon history as well as classical and biblical rhetoric in the preamble to his 1829 *Appeal to the Colored Citizens of the World* (doc. 255), Walker depicts slavery as a global phenomenon and American blacks as "the most degraded, wretched, and abject set of beings [...] that ever lived since the world began" (*KC*, 572). Walker attacks the institution of slavery as an exploitative system and problematizes the notion of black inferiority as it was introduced by Jefferson (cf. *KC*, 576). Rejecting biological conjectures about the alleged proximity between Africans and apes, Walker ponders the ques-

---

[13] Goodman offers a succinct depiction of the founding of the American Colonization Society and its entanglement with the political and religious elites (cf. 1998, 11-22).

[14] For a delineation of free black objections to the colonization schemes devised by the American Colonization Society and the ensuing debate over questions of race and identity, see Bay (2000, 22-6) and Goodman (1998, 23-35).

[15] The most comprehensive study of David Walker and the context and implications of his *Appeal* is Hinks (1997). Although most intellectual historians place Walker squarely in the radical nationalist tradition of antebellum black thought (cf. Stuckey 1987, 120-37), Hinks proposes to read Walker as a conciliatory integrationist whose "commitment to a racially integrated society in which racial distinctiveness would play little role has been relatively ignored" (1997, 249-50).

tion whether history has not indeed proved white people to be the morally inferior race. Since they "have always been an unjust, jealous, unmerciful, avaricious and blood-thirsty set of beings, always seeking after power and authority," Walker doubts "whether they are as good by nature as we are" (*KC*, 576-7; cf. Bay 2000, 35). Walker's rational accounts of the position of blacks in American society are counterbalanced by more emotional appeals; his delineation of the history of slavery and prejudice in Europe and America, for instance, serves "to awaken in the breasts of my afflicted, degraded and slumbering brethren, a spirit of enquiry and investigation respecting our miseries and wretchedness in this *Republican land of Liberty*!!!!!" (*KC*, 573). Walker criticizes the submissiveness of blacks and calls in his pamphlet for concerted violent resistance to the institution of slavery. Above all, he castigates the inertia of the clergy and the dishonesty of the colonizationists. In the fourth article of his *Appeal*, Walker refutes "the colonizing trick" and voices his incomprehension regarding those blacks who have left the country for Africa (2000, 70). For America, Walker argues, belongs even more to blacks who have "enriched it with our *blood and tears*" than to whites (71). Besides this black nationalist strain in his argument, Walker also applauds those white proponents of colonization who are truly dedicated to blacks' "redemption from wretchedness and miseries," and hopes for their support outside the parameters of the American Colonization Society (cf. 70-1).

Within the African American community, Walker's article sparked a controversy over whether or not to organize and fight alongside white activists. This very question was taken up by annual national black conventions starting in 1830. By the end of the 1820s, free blacks skeptical of emigration to Africa had won the assistance of white antislavery leaders. The participation of and exchange with white abolitionists in these African American conventions paved the way for the biracial abolitionist movement of the ensuing decades (cf. Goodman 1998, 32-5). Since the true motives for the colonizationists' engagement were at best dubious – "as much an act of self-interested patriotism as of humanity," as Matthew Mason puts it (2006, 113) – the more humanitarian opponents of slavery soon began to turn away from colonization and toward immediate abolitionism, most prominently William Lloyd Garrison. However, as the example of the Quakers, who embraced an antislavery agenda as early as 1750, shows, abolitionism and racial egalitarianism did not always go hand in hand (cf. Goodman 1998, 7-8). Not until the 1830s did abolitionists shift their focus to a repudiation of racial prejudice and the American Colonization Society's activities (cf. Goodman 1998, 35). Walker's *Appeal* can thus be credited with sparking the beginning of this biracial movement to abolish slavery in the name of racial equality.

Abolitionism and Immediate Emancipation

The anti-colonizationist stance propounded by Walker was echoed by a growing number of white antislavery activists. Among these, William Lloyd Garrison emerged as the most prominent figure in the following years. Garrison's shift away from colonizationism is exemplary of the transition from the gradualist to the immediatist phase in the American antislavery movement. The 'conversion' of Garrison was instigated by his experiences as a journalist and editor with African Americans in Baltimore (cf. Goodman 1998, 36-44). Although Garrison still formally adheres to gradualist doctrines in his 1829 Fourth of July address at Boston's Park Street Church, the speech already includes more radical views, such as the argument for the political equality of African Americans. Their birth on American soil, as Garrison argues, "entitled [them] to all the privileges of American citizens" (1995a, 64). He also broaches the question of racial prejudice. "Suppose that, by a miracle, the slaves should suddenly become white," reads Garrison's provocation, "[w]ould you shut your eyes upon their sufferings, and calmly talk of Constitutional limitations?" (1995a, 66-7). Criticizing the implicit proslavery tendencies in the Constitution, Garrison more specifically exposes Northern racial prejudices which "bristle, like so many bayonets, around the slaves" (1995a, 67) and which need to be tackled to advance the project of slave emancipation and ultimately of racial equality.[16] Finally, in the inaugural editorial to *The Liberator* on January 1, 1831, Garrison testifies in print to his change of heart. He has come to reject "the popular but pernicious doctrine of *gradual* abolition" and links his "full and unequivocal recantation," as he calls it, with the demand for the "immediate enfranchisement of our slave population" (1995b, 71). Garrison's tone bespeaks the urgency of his immediatist program:

> I am aware that many object to the severity of my language; but is there not cause for severity? I *will be* as harsh as truth, and as uncompromising as justice. On this subject, I do not wish to think, or speak, or write, with moderation. No! no! Tell a man whose house is on fire, to give a moderate alarm; tell him to moderately rescue his wife from the hands of the ravisher; tell the mother to gradually extricate her babe from the fire into which it has fallen; – but urge me not to use moderation in a cause like the present. I am in earnest – I will not equivocate – I will not excuse – I will not retreat a single inch – AND I WILL BE HEARD. The apathy of the people is enough to make every statue leap from its pedestal, and to hasten the resurrection of the dead. (1995b, 72)

Severity and persistence, not compromise and moderation, are Garrison's new tactics in combating the lethargy of the advocates of gradual emancipation and accomplishing the immediate abolition of all slaves.[17] The announcement that he

---

[16] Paul Goodman traces the beginnings of Garrison's 'conversion' to abolitionism to his 1829 Fourth of July address, arguing that "in setting forth a vision of a society based on racial equality, he was implicitly challenging the cardinal assumption of colonization" (1998, 41). Henry Mayer discusses the address in his seminal biography of Garrison, assessing it as an "epochal moment in the history of freedom" (1998, 64). Characterizing the speech as a rewritten Declaration of Independence which includes African Americans and aligning it with the jeremiads of the Puritan colonists, Mayer demands its "recognition [...] as a notable state paper" (67).

[17] In addition to his editorial work for *The Liberator*, Garrison further reiterated his position in an extended anticolonization treatise, *Thoughts on African Colonization* (1832), which con-

"will be heard" ushers in thirty-five years of weekly abolitionist writing in *The Liberator*. From 1831 to 1865, Garrison's newspaper offered a platform for white and black abolitionists, whose interracial alliance was further invigorated by the founding of the American Anti-Slavery Society in 1833.[18] The organization and its local chapters arranged speaking tours, distributed antislavery literature in both North and South, and flooded Congress with petitions, a measure that led to the implementation of the infamous gag rule in 1836. Participation in these abolitionist activities exposed the antislavery movement to charges of collaboration in and instigation of bloody slave rebellions such as Nat Turner's in Virginia. Therefore, during the foundational stage of the American Anti-Slavery Society, immediatists agreed upon subscribing explicitly to a nonviolent approach and refraining from directly addressing Southern slaves. Fears of antiabolitionist mob assaults were not unsubstantiated, as the martyrdom and murder of the abolitionist editor Elijah Lovejoy in 1837 demonstrated.

Disputes about the tactics of the American Anti-Slavery Society soon surfaced and led to its disintegration in 1840. Members disagreed on such integral issues as abolitionists' political involvement and women's rights.[19] The small circle around Garrison was committed to women's rights, ruled out any political involvement, reprimanded the churches for their hypocrisy in the slavery question, and condemned the American Constitution as a proslavery document. Garrisonians even promoted "disunion," i.e., the North's initiative to dissolve the Union. The church-based supporters of Lewis Tappan, on the other hand, did not share the Garrisonians' view on women's rights, and they were less skeptical about an active political involvement. The group left the American Anti-Slavery Society and established the American and Foreign Anti-Slavery Society which henceforth supported the Liberty Party, the first political group to target the abolition of slavery. In addition to these organizational rifts, one question increasingly dominated both white and black abolitionists' discussions of the suitable measures in the struggle to abolish slavery: Was the use of violence permissible, given the urgency of the matter? While abolitionists initially dismissed violence and close cooperation with the enslaved population in the South, activists came to realize that a closer orientation toward the slaves and the implementation of more aggressive tactics were necessary (cf. Harrold 2004, 2-4). Here, they followed in the footsteps of David Walker, whose demands in his *Appeal* included dauntless interven-

---

tributed to the demise of the colonization movement in favor of immediatism within the next years (cf. Goodman 1998, 56-7).

[18] Among the 62 founders were Quakers, orthodox evangelicals, three African Americans, and four women. A concise survey of the rise of immediatism and the course of its most important organizations and individuals is provided in Harrold (2001, 25-38).

[19] For a discussion of abolitionists' commitment to women's rights and its role in the schism within the American Anti-Slavery Society, see Sklar (2000, 1-76), who locates the beginnings of the women's movement in the immediatist activism of the 1830s and traces the interrelatedness of the two movements throughout the antebellum period; see also Sánchez-Eppler (1988), Yellin (1989), and Aptheker (1989, 77-93).

tion and a forcible overthrow of the institution. Two addresses to slaves published in 1843 attest to the changing strategies: Garrison's speech (doc. *267*) differs significantly from the radical positions of a black abolitionist spokesman, the Presbyterian minister Henry Highland Garnet (doc. 265). Garnet's address is much more outspoken, even passionate, in his embrace of the slaves' use of violence, whereas Garrison's speech only tentatively shows a change of mind. He neither forsakes nonviolence nor does he contemplate going south to help the slaves.[20]

Garrison's "Address to the Slaves of the United States" was held at the end of May 1843 on the occasion of a New England antislavery convention in Boston. Garrison assures his distant slave addressees of the sympathy and devotion of their abolitionist friends "who are laboring to effect your emancipation without delay, in a peaceable manner, without the shedding of blood," and confirms his progressive notion of them "as brethren and countrymen" (*KC*, 600):

> In the first place, then, you are men – created in the same divine image as all other men – as good, as noble, as free, by birth and destiny, as your masters – as much entitled to "life, liberty, and the pursuit of happiness," as those who cruelly enslave you – made but a little lower than the angels of heaven, and destined to an immortal state of existence – equal members of the great human family. These truths you must believe and understand, if you desire to have your chains broken, and your oppression come to a speedy end. (in Harrold 2004, 196)

Garrison not only invokes the Declaration of Independence to claim the same rights for African Americans that all other Americans enjoy; he also debunks the proslavery view of black inferiority, especially the erroneousness of the biblical defense of slavery, and the myth of the happy and contented slave (in Harrold 2004, 170-2). Quoting extensively from the beginning of the Declaration, Garrison explains to his absent slave audience that their masters, as the descendants of the revolutionaries, "[b]y precept and example [...] declare that it is both your right and your duty to wage war against them, and to wade through their blood, if necessary, to secure your own freedom." But Garrison also warns that "should *you* attempt to gain your freedom in the same manner [as other oppressed people around the globe], *you* would be branded as murderers and monsters, and slaughtered without mercy!" (in Harrold 2004, 172-3; emphasis mine). After having delivered this lecture on the world history of revolutions, Garrison stops and in an apostrophe bids his audience to "[t]ake courage! Be filled with hope and comfort! Your redemption draws nigh" (*KC*, 600). Despite the potentially incendiary first part of his "Address to the Slaves," Garrison does not encourage the slaves to rise up, but rather beseeches them to remain patient and wait passively for their emancipation.

---

[20] For a discussion of the 1843 addresses to the slaves by Garrison and Garnet, and an earlier lecture by the white philanthropist Gerrit Smith, see Harrold (2004). Harrold's study also provides the unabridged versions of the addresses in an appendix.

Garrison is unable to resolve the dilemma between his nonviolent credo and the possibility of rebelling against an oppressor, a right that is codified in the founding document of the nation. In the course of his address, Garrison vehemently reaffirms the original immediatist nonviolent strategies which do not include "bowie knives, pistols, swords, guns, or any other deadly implements," but rather "consist of appeals, warnings, rebukes, arguments and facts, addressed to the understandings, consciences and hearts of the people" (*KC*, 601) – in other words, moral suasion. But he is well aware of a shifting position among abolitionists concerning violence:

> Many of your friends believe that not even those who are oppressed, whether their skins are white or black, can shed the blood of their oppressors in accordance with the will of God; while many others believe that it is right for the oppressed to rise and take their liberty by violence, if they can secure it in no other manner. (*KC*, 601)

Garrison detects two abolitionist camps with contrasting views: those who see the irreconcilability of violent means with a Christian outlook and therefore reject the shedding of blood, and those who believe that the end justifies the means, i.e., that slaves have the right to rise against their oppressors to gain their freedom. Although Garrison here avoids an explicit statement regarding his own position on the question, it becomes clear that he does not depart from his former peaceable approach. Garrison invokes the revolutionary discourse of liberty (cf. Hurm in this vol., 192-7) but stops short of encouraging slaves to stage revolts. Instead, he calls upon slaves "peaceably to escape from the plantations" (*KC*, 601). He pleads the bondsmen to remain "patient, long-suffering, and submissive, yet awhile longer" until an incessantly growing number of Northern abolitionists will redeem them (*KC*, 601). Even though Garrison approached an acceptance of violent means in the "Address" (cf. Harrold 2004, 23), the vocabulary he uses does not differ much from the wording in his 1831 "Universal Emancipation" (doc. 266), a poem published more than a decade earlier in the first issue of *The Liberator*. In the poem – as in the later "Address" – Garrison's vision of slave uprisings with "kindling flames of hot, rebellious war" leads him to advise the slaves to "[b]ear meekly" their sufferings (*KC*, 599-600).

While Garrison goes no further than suggesting to the slaves that they should make their escape if the opportunity arises, Henry Highland Garnet's "Address to the Slaves" is rife with the language of violence and revolt. Garnet gave his speech at the black national convention in Buffalo, New York, in August 1843. Like Garrison, he addresses the slaves in the South, but his immediate audience is comprised of the free black delegates participating in the gathering. Whereas Garrison deems it morally wrong for slaves to rise up, Garnet calls it "sinful" to remain submissive and inactive (*KC*, 597). He argues that it is the "moral obligation" of slaves to follow the divine commandments, which it is impossible to do in slavery (*KC*, 597). Hence, Garnet explains, slaves need to act immediately to restore themselves to a virtuous life in the name of God. Unlike Garrison, Garnet utters a frank call for resistance:

> Brethren, the time has come when you must act for yourselves. It is an old and true saying that, "if hereditary bondmen would be free, they must themselves strike the blow." You can plead your own cause, and do the work of emancipation better than any others. (*KC*, 597)

Whereas Garrison admonishes the slaves to remain patient and wait for the aid of Northern abolitionists, the black advocate of freedom blames his brethren in the South exactly for their patience (cf. *KC*, 598).

Garnet places the initiative firmly within the slaves' hands, and he makes his position unmistakably clear when he discloses his belief that "[y]ou had far better all die – *die immediately*, than live slaves, and entail your wretchedness upon your posterity" (*KC*, 598). Almost frantically, Garnet reminds the slaves that "you are three millions" and urges them to adopt "RESISTANCE! RESISTANCE! RESISTANCE!" as their motto (*KC*, 599). In contrast to Garrison, Garnet aggressively asserts that "[n]o oppressed people have ever secured their liberty without resistance" (*KC*, 599). While Garrison advocates a peaceful running away to achieve liberty, Garnet appears to have warfare in mind. The black pastor, it seems, does not waver at the thought of violent assault as he believes "there is not much hope of Redemption without the shedding of blood" (*KC*, 598). However, Garnet's position is more ambiguous. On the one hand, he does not categorically exclude violence from his thought; on the other, he declines to encourage revolt explicitly. Indeed, Garnet declares that "[w]e do not advise you to attempt a revolution with the sword, because it would be INEXPEDIENT. Your numbers are too small, and moreover the rising spirit of the age, and the spirit of the gospel, are opposed to war and bloodshed" (*KC*, 598). Whereas in other parts of the speech Garnet encourages slaves to action on account of their great number, here he openly expresses his apprehension about the feasibility of a violent uprising, both in terms of numbers and moral righteousness.[21] In fact, Garnet recommends in this passage that slaves "cease to labor for tyrants who will not remunerate you" (*KC*, 598), a position more resembling Garrison's call to run off than being a signal for militant revolt.

Garnet's lecture did not immediately meet a majority vote at the convention due to what was perceived as his militancy (cf. Harrold 2004, 64-70). The leading black abolitionist Frederick Douglass used the same occasion to affirm his pacifism by speaking out against Garnet's address. In the end, a highly divided crowd of delegates decided against adopting Garnet's address by a vote of nineteen to eighteen (with twenty-one abstaining; cf. Harrold 2004, 69). Still, compared to

---

[21] Most readings of Garnet's "Address" overlook this passage, tending instead to make a case for Garnet's violent radicalism. As Stanley Harrold illustrates, it is possible that the passage containing the revocation of violent revolution on grounds of expediency was added to the speech later, when Garnet prepared it for publication, together with Walker's *Appeal*, in 1848 (cf. Harrold 2004, 33-4). The absent disclaimer would also explain the harsh response to Garnet's address at the convention, especially by Frederick Douglass, who vehemently opposed Garnet's forthright call to arms.

similar speeches of the time, Garnet's address "came closest to endorsing slave revolt," and the document – a "landmark in African-American history" – indicates the "emerging militancy among black abolitionists" (Harrold 2004, 70). Trying to make sense of Garnet's disparate record of propositions, one historian appraises the black minister's attempt to harmonize his belief in moral suasion with his belief in the use of violence, something David Walker had tried to accomplish before him (cf. Stuckey 1987, 158). Even though the "Address" reflects such an effort to unite opposing approaches to the abolition of slavery, Garnet by 1848 grew more and more convinced that Northern abolitionists would have to play "a potentially violent role [...] in the South" (Harrold 2004, 120).

Frederick Douglass, Garnet's fiercest adversary at the 1843 Buffalo convention, also evinces a change of heart about the use of violence long before the Fugitive Slave Act (1850) or the *Dred Scott* ruling (1857). As both measures further endangered the personal safety of African Americans, even in the North, Douglass and other black Garrisonians slowly surrendered their aversion to slave violence (cf. Harrold 2004, 121-3). According to Douglass himself, it was his first encounter with the white militant abolitionist John Brown in 1847 that prompted his loss of faith in moral suasion. Pondering Brown's plan to invade the South and carry out systematic raids aiming at the liberation of slaves, Douglass grew "less hopeful of [slavery's] peaceful abolition" (Douglass 1994, 719; cf. Stuckey 1987, 166). Douglass's growing rapprochement with abolitionists less skeptical about violent means roughly coincided with the decline of his relationship with his mentor Garrison. Garrison felt disgruntled with Douglass starting his own newspaper, the *North Star*, in 1847, and the final rift between the two abolitionists occurred in 1851, when Douglass rescinded his support for disunionism, the core of Garrisonian doctrine. Garrison rejected political compromises with slaveholders (cf. Garrison's *No Compromise with Slavery*, doc. 269) and began to view the Constitution as a proslavery document. Douglass's new emphasis on political action and the Constitution in the struggle for the abolition of slavery irrecoverably alienated the two companions (cf. Mayer 1998, 371-4, 428-30).[22]

Douglass began to launch antislavery interpretations of America's founding document in his own paper (cf. Cain 1995, 47). In 1852, he delivered his famous "Fifth of July" speech (doc. 268) in which he decries America's hypocrisy concerning slavery in light of the Declaration of Independence, and demands its full application to African Americans. Douglass was in fact invited to deliver the Fourth of July address at the Rochester Ladies' Anti-Slavery Society meeting, but he insisted on giving his speech one day after the customary festivities to expose the derision of Independence Day for the slave. Invoking the humility topos, the black ex-slave spoke to a racially mixed audience of six hundred "*Friends*

---

[22] See Colaiaco (2006, 73-107) for a detailed analysis of Douglass's process of "conversion to the United States Constitution" (83).

and Fellow Citizens." Douglass characterizes the Fourth of July as "the birthday of *your* National Independence, and of *your* political freedom" (*KC*, 602; emphasis mine). Disclosing what he perceives as the "inhuman mockery and sacrilegious irony" of inviting an escaped slave to deliver the Fourth of July address, Douglass challenges his audience by asking:

> What have I, or those I represent, to do with your national independence? Are the great principles of political freedom and of natural justice, embodied in that Declaration of Independence, extended to us? and am I, therefore, called upon to bring our humble offering to the national altar, and to confess the benefits and express devout gratitude for the blessings resulting from your independence to us? (*KC*, 605)

His questions remain rhetorical. Indeed, he considers himself "not included within the pale of this glorious anniversary," and "[t]he rich inheritance of justice, liberty, prosperity and independence, bequeathed by your fathers, is shared by you, not by me." And finally, Douglass states, "This Fourth [of] July is *yours*, not *mine*" (*KC*, 605). Douglass rhetorically surmounts the barrier between black and white by choosing to approach his topic from the slaves' perspective. He denounces the hypocrisy of a nation whose self-conception is based on such ideals as humanity, liberty, and justice, and resents America's violation of the founding document and desecration of the Bible (cf. 606-7). "The existence of slavery," Douglass argues, "brands your republicanism as a sham, your humanity as a base pretence, and your Christianity as a lie" (*KC*, 607). Operating in the tradition of the American jeremiad, Douglass sends out a warning to America that "a horrible reptile is coiled up in your nation's bosom" and that "the venomous creature is nursing at the tender breast of your youthful republic" (*KC*, 607).[23] But Douglass ends on a hopeful note, believing that "the glorious hour" of freedom will come and that the principles set forth in the Declaration will be applied to all Americans (cf. *KC*, 607-8).[24]

The significance of Douglass's address lies not only in its rhetorical mastery and sophistication, but above all in its controversial preoccupation with the question of America's legacy as a democratic nation. Should African Americans join the rest of the nation in celebrating revolutionary achievements such as freedom and equality when in fact America holds three million blacks in bondage? How should African Americans approach such documents as the Declaration of Independence and the American Constitution? Unlike his Garrisonian colleagues, Douglass encourages African Americans' participation in America's political sys-

---

[23] See Bell (1992) and Colaiaco (2006) for a detailed analysis of the rhetorical strategies that Douglass employs in his oration and of how Douglass adapts the jeremiad and "improvises on the triadic structure of promise, declension, and prophesied restoration" (Bell 1992, 148). Both situate *What to the Slave Is the Fourth of July?* in the tradition of the American and African American jeremiad.

[24] Although most critics view the Fourth of July address as an expression of Douglass's belief in the nation's egalitarian founding, Charles Mills (1999) is more skeptical about Douglass's source of optimism.

tem. Even though Douglass's belief in an antislavery Constitution did not attract many followers, it is thanks to his commitment to reclaiming the revolutionary legacy of the nation for African Americans that natural rights were perceived as incompatible with racial notions of difference in American debates about slavery.

Envisioning an egalitarian future society, Douglass became more militant in the 1850s and developed a decidedly millennialist perspective of America in which he himself figured as the prophet of a future age (cf. Stauffer 2002, 1-7; Stievermann in this vol., 150-1). Douglass sought to enter into an alliance with white abolitionists who "embraced an ethic of a black heart," that is, people who were able to "renounce their belief in skin color as a marker of aptitude and social status" (Stauffer 2002, 1). He found such a companion in the white militant abolitionist John Brown, whose "ability to blur racial categories" was complemented by pronounced perfectionist and millennialist visions and a readiness to use militant means to bring about this new society (Stauffer 2002, 6). The Unitarian minister Theodore Parker in his "Letter to Francis Jackson" (doc. 273) discusses the example of Brown who led an interracial group of men to raid the federal arsenal at Harpers Ferry in 1859. The attempt to arm the slaves in the area and lead them to a violent overthrow of slavery failed, and Brown was hanged in the aftermath of the foiled plot. Brown's violence, Parker argues, was inspired by his desire "to help his countrymen enjoy their natural right to life, liberty, and the pursuit of happiness" (*KC*, 617). Parker predicts more such actions by white abolitionists who consider it "their *natural duty* to their black countrymen" to help them gain their liberty (*KC*, 617). Although Parker believes that blacks are inferior "in general intellectual power, and also in that instinct for Liberty which is so strong in the Teutonic family" (*KC*, 617), he welcomes the prospect of violent slave uprisings in the future if nonviolent means fail to abolish slavery.

Parker's position on the differences between the races is characteristic of the antebellum period. Most white people in the North repudiated the thought that African Americans could become equal members of society. In fact, only a small number of white people were active participants in the antebellum abolitionist crusade, though, as a consequence of Harriet Beecher Stowe's popular novel *Uncle Tom's Cabin* (1852), most Northerners protested against the fugitive slave laws and acted sympathetically toward escaped slaves. The Northern response to John Brown's raid on Harpers Ferry and his subsequent execution was more diverse, however. While the newspapers' responses were mixed, Northern intellectuals united to sanctify Brown. The leading transcendentalists Henry David Thoreau and Ralph Waldo Emerson defended "the new saint awaiting his martyrdom [...] who [...] will make the gallows glorious like the cross" (Emerson 1903-1904, 7: 434; cf. Reynolds 2005, 343-69). Among the abolitionists, even Garrison, the guardian of nonviolence, in his eulogy for the martyred Brown lets himself get carried away with the observation that he sees "*four millions of living John Browns* needing our thoughts, our sympathies, our prayers, our noblest exertions to strike off their fetters" (Garrison 1995c, 157; cf. Mayer 1998, 502-4). The growing willingness on both sides to embrace radical means was accompanied by the violence employed in the quasi-civil war of "Bleeding Kansas" in 1856 and the raid on Harpers Ferry in 1859. The violence and militancy of the leading abolitionist activists, as well as the defenders of the "peculiar institution" within the panoply of pro- and antislavery approaches ultimately rendered disunion, secession, and even a civil war inevitable for many Americans.

Instructional Strategies and Classroom Issues

I. Key Concepts and Major Themes

1. Proslavery and Racial Discourse (docs. 251, 260-1, 264, 270-2)
   The development of pseudo-scientific explanations for social and biological differences between various ethnicities during the Enlightenment provided a fruitful basis for the defenders of slavery in antebellum America. Predominantly articulated by Southern intellectuals, but also voiced by their Northern counterparts, proslavery arguments exhibit a staple of racist stereotypes and maintain a rigid biological and/or cultural difference between the races. Used to justify the existence and the continuation of slavery, racial thought was not only expressed in pseudo-scientific treatises but also in religious and political contexts.

2. Colonizationism (docs. 251, 254)
   The most important forerunner of the abolitionist movement, colonization schemes favored the gradual emancipation of slaves and the subsequent expatriation of freedmen. The notion that ex-slaves should be settled in distinct colonies, either in Africa or in selected areas in the American West, appealed to Northerners as well as Southerners in the first three decades of the eighteenth century.

3. Abolitionism (docs. 251, 255, 262, 265-8, 273)
   The term 'abolitionism' connotes a biracial movement between 1830 and the Civil War demanding the immediate emancipation of slaves in all territories and states, as well as the political and social integration of African Americans. In contrast to earlier gradualist schemes, advocates of immediate abolition primarily argued on moral grounds and called for a prompt end to slavery without pecuniary compensation for the slave owners. Drawing from the same evangelical impulse as various other reform efforts, abolitionists sustained especially close ties with the early women's rights movement.

4. Unionism and Disunionism (docs. 260, 269)
   The controversy over slavery also affected Americans' considerations of the political coherence of the United States. Unionist advocates, such as

Calhoun, cherished the maintenance of the Union over the moral reservations raised by the institution of slavery. Disunionists in the North and their secessionist counterparts in the South were willing to sacrifice the unity of the country for the sake of a solution of the slavery question. Among the most fervent disunionists was William Lloyd Garrison who rejected any political involvement and compromise with slaveholders. His disunionist stance also induced him to reject the foundational documents of the United States.

5. Resistance and Violence (docs. 255, 265-7, 273)
The legitimacy of using violence was a central concern among abolitionists. The precariousness of this conundrum derived from Southern charges that abolitionist activism would instigate further violent slave revolts in the region. Whereas the nascent immediatist movement concentrated on the strategy of moral suasion, the inefficacy of this peaceful approach convinced a more radical group of abolitionists to seek an end to slavery through militant means. The approach appealed especially to African American abolitionists who deemed violence a viable solution, given the urgency of a speedy abolition.

II. Comparison – Contrasts – Connections

Example: Docs. 262, 270-2

The debate over slavery deeply affected nineteenth-century American cultural and intellectual history, especially as the sectional conflict about the extension of slavery into the new territories intensified after the Mexican War (1846-1848). Northern and Southern intellectuals publicized their views in the flowering print market. Pro- and antislavery messages were also expressed in poetry and fiction, as well as in visual representations of the period.

The iconic representation of a kneeling slave provided abolitionists with a symbol that was omnipresent in the publications and paraphernalia of the antislavery movement (cf. doc. 262). The image shows a black slave on his knees, chained at his hands and feet, and clad only in a white loincloth. Below the figure is a banner reading "Am I Not a Man and a Brother?"[25] The emblem of the kneeling slave was printed in abolitionist literature and reproduced on household objects such as pottery (cf. Savage 1996, 22-3). Variations of the image included a kneeling slave woman with the respective slogan "Am I Not a Woman and a Sister?" (cf. Fig. 11). While this modified version of the original symbol appealed

---

[25] The figure originated in the context of British abolitionism in the late eighteenth century and first appeared on jasper ware brooches manufactured by Josiah Wedgwood. A woodcut version was adopted by American abolitionists in the 1830s.

specifically to a female audience, it testifies, at the same time, to the growing role of women in the abolitionist movement (cf. Klaiber in this vol., 320-1).

Fig. 11: "Am I Not a Woman and a Sister?" Antislavery emblem originally attached to a print reproduction of a portrait of Lucrecia Mott. Friends Historical Library of Swarthmore College.

The posture of the slave is illustrative of nineteenth-century race relations in America, as the pleading slave appeals either to an invisible slavemaster, to white Northerners, or heavenward to God. Besides the common religious association of a kneeling and praying man, the slave's subservient and enchained position also represents the unequal power relation between master and slave, which is characterized by a loss of manhood alluded to in the caption. The gesture can also be read as the black man's general plea to be treated as a "brother" by his abolitionist friends in the North. Northerners frequently took a superior stance toward their black companions, their idea of equality often being only theoretical, as they rarely imagined blacks as full and equal citizens. The American Anti-Slavery Society broadside printed a poem by the English poet William Cowper along with the image of the kneeling slave. In "The Negroes Complaint" (doc. 262), Cowper argues for the fundamental humanity of all men. Commenting on slaves' role as commodities in an economic system, the speaker of this poem points out that the slaves' "[m]inds are never to be sold" (*KC*, 591). He maintains that black and white people do not differ beyond skin color; most importantly, all share a sense of affection. The poem's last two verses read like an alternative caption to the kneeling slave in the image above: "Prove that *ye* have human feelings, / Ere ye proudly question ours" (*KC*, 591).

While the antislavery movement publicized their views in an endless number of newspapers, magazines, and treatises, and developed a pronounced antislavery rhetoric and visual iconography, the proslavery network was less oriented toward reaching the broad public. Proslavery writing never reached the appeal of their antislavery counterparts, as most apologists penned complex scientific, economic, or religious justifications of slavery. Among the pieces with a more popular appeal, the 1841 set of lithographs entitled *Black and White Slaves* (docs. 270-1) by Edward Williams Clay, a Philadelphia-born artist and political cartoonist, is a good introduction to the common proslavery argumentation that slaves in the South are better off than white industrial workers in the North. The prints show racial slavery in the American South on one panel (*KC*, 613) and English wage slavery on the other (*KC*, 612). The idyllic picture of slavery in the South depicts an idealized slaveholding family consisting of the master, his wife, two children, their dog, and – a few steps back – a black nanny who carries another baby. By including the slaves in the representation of the master's family, the lithograph illustrates the myth of an extended family and appeals to the domestic sentiments of the viewer. To the left sits a slightly stooped aged slave with a cane, accompanied by an old black woman and a toddler at his feet. In the scene behind, two black couples are dancing to a black fiddler's music. The text at the top indicates the dutiful slaves' concerted gratitude for food, clothing, and the care administered to the aging slaves who are unable to continue to work. The respectable slaveholder understands it as "a sacred legacy from my ancestors […] to increase their comfort and happiness" (*KC*, 613). In this apologist portrayal of slavery, the myth of the contented and grateful slave dominates the scene; the fundamentally exploitative relationship between master and slave is glossed over for the sake of a highly idealized picture that survived as the Southern 'plantation legend' in literature and popular culture well into the twentieth century.

On the second plate, the scene shifts to a factory official's visit in a nearly unfurnished home of a destitute family. The depiction of a frail, sickly mother lying on the ground, and her husband in ragged clothes and children sitting close by, renders the desperation as a violation of the domestic ideals of the era. Another tired-looking woman looks in and opens the view on the high factory building with a huge chimney in the background, thus identifying the industrial context of the scene. The text indicates that the family is "starving for want of employment," and the well-clad gentleman can only recommend the poorhouse. The poor family cannot expect "relief from the purse of proud aristocracy" (*KC*, 612), for whom they have literally toiled themselves to death. Taken together, the two lithographs reiterate the well-established argument of apologists that racial slavery – with its long-established paternalistic care system – is preferable to wage slavery in Northern industries. Among Southern intellectuals, the sociologist George Fitzhugh was the most ardent advocate of this belief. He in fact campaigned for an extension of slavery into the Northern states (cf. doc. 264).

William J. Grayson's 1855 epic poem *The Hireling and the Slave* (doc. 272) can be read as a companion piece to the lithographs. In this excerpt from a two-part poem of over 1,500 verses, the poet from South Carolina argues that the hireling and the slave share essentially the same lot: Both must labor in order to receive "[f]ood, fire, a home and clothing" (*KC*, 614). The black slave's condition, however, is in many ways preferable to the white Northern industrial worker's, since he is not only "[g]uarded from want, from beggary secure" (*KC*, 614), but also receives an education that at the same time civilizes him and places him in a superior position over his fellow Africans. The slave owner not only teaches his slaves work skills such as industry and docility, but provides for their basic material needs until their death, whereas, for the aged hireling in the North – as for the destitute family in the lithograph – remains only "the poor-house door – / The last, vile, hated refuge of the poor" (*KC*, 614).

In his didactic poem, Grayson also problematizes the question of riots. The peaceful relationship between master and slaves, he makes the reader believe, leads to fewer riots and more security for all, whereas the situation can get out of hand more easily in the crowded Northern factories. Characterizing racial slavery as an arrangement that is fundamentally based on benevolence and peace and that generates a labor force much more content than in the industrial system, this poetic defense of slavery counters the abolitionist view of slavery as an inhumane, exploitative, and violent institution. Considering the poem's publication in 1855, it can also be read as a response to Harriet Beecher Stowe's depiction of slavery in her novel *Uncle Tom's Cabin* (1852).

III. Reading and Discussion Questions

1. Analyze the catalog of proslavery arguments provided by Matthew Estes in *A Defence of Negro Slavery as It Exists in the United States* (doc. 261). Identify the different strains of his defense of the institution of slavery and show how they relate to the positions of other leading proslavery advocates. Explain how notions of race contribute to their arguments.

2. Explain the significance of gradualist emancipation schemes for the antislavery movement. Discuss why black intellectuals like David Walker and white abolitionists like William Lloyd Garrison turned to an immediatist approach. How does Walker's *Appeal to the Colored Citizens of the World* (doc. 255) anticipate the radicalization of the abolitionist crusade in antebellum America?

3. Compare and contrast the two addresses to slaves by William Lloyd Garrison (doc. 267) and Henry Highland Garnet (doc. 265). Analyze the function of the multiple audiences in these speeches. Identify the different conceptualizations of the relations between the races in both texts and discuss the speakers' stance on the use of violence in the abolitionist struggle.

4. Analyze Frederick Douglass's oration *What to the Slave Is the Fourth of July?* (doc. 268). Which parallels are established between the antislavery cause and the revolutionary period? Consider the rhetorical strategies he employs in his speech to invoke the ideals of the Declaration of Independence. Discuss Douglass's position on the use of violent means for abolishing slavery.

IV. Resources

a. Recommended Reading

Ira Berlin. *Many Thousands Gone: The First Two Centuries of Slavery in North America*. Cambridge: Belknap Press, 1998. This study is a groundbreaking account of the rise of slavery as a political, economic, and social institution in the colonial period. Berlin discusses how racial thought informed the establishment of slavery and demonstrates the changes within the institution. Berlin particularly emphasizes the historical contingency of racial notions of difference and focuses on the hierarchization of the colonial population into dominant and subservient social classes.

David Brion Davis. *Inhuman Bondage: The Rise and Fall of Slavery in the New World*. Oxford: Oxford University Press, 2006. Together with his previous studies on slavery and the American Revolution as well as on the social, political, and cultural tensions arising from slavery throughout the western world, Davis's latest book is particularly valuable for its comparative scope. Davis considers slavery a transatlantic and hemispheric phenomenon, drawing careful comparisons between the situation in the United States and the slave economies of the Caribbean and Brazil. Especially noteworthy is his consideration of the different forms of abolitionism as well as slave revolutions throughout the Atlantic world.

George M. Fredrickson. *The Black Image in the White Mind: The Debate on Afro-American Character and Destiny, 1817-1914*. 1971. Hanover, NH: Wesleyan University Press, 1987. A standard volume of intellectual history, Fredrickson's interpretation of proslavery thought in the antebellum South concentrates on the idea of white supremacy over African American slaves. Fredrickson deems this notion central to the cultural identity of the Old South and unveils the ideological function of the traditionally hierarchical and paternalistic justifications of slave owners.

Thomas F. Gossett. *Race: The History of an Idea in America*. 1963. New York: Oxford University Press, 1997. Gossett's introductory account of the usage of race as a social construct in American intellectual history provides the best delineation of racial thought with regard to African Americans and the institution of slavery. Although Gossett does not include other minorities in his study, students will find this survey an invaluable resource.

Peter Kolchin. *American Slavery, 1619-1877*. 1993. Rev. ed. New York: Hill and Wang, 2003. This comprehensive overview of slavery in North America is a good starting point for anyone interested in the beginnings of slavery in colonial America. Kolchin carefully traces the emergence of an African American identity by examining the structure of slave families, the economic situation of Africans under slavery, and the African response to Christianization efforts. This synthesis also delineates the most important developments in the history of slavery up to the end of the Reconstruction period.

Joanne Pope Melish. *Disowning Slavery: Gradual Emancipation and "Race" in New England, 1780-1860*. Ithaca: Cornell University Press, 1998. In this study, Melish provides the definitive account of gradual emancipation schemes in New England. She establishes the importance of slavery for the economy of the North and successfully challenges the myth of the North as inherently white and traditionally hostile towards slavery.

James Brewer Stewart. *Holy Warriors: The Abolitionists and American Slavery*. 1976. Rev. ed. New York: Hill and Wang, 1996. Stewart's volume on the abolitionist movement remains a classic treatment of the thirty years between abolitionism's inception and the end of the Civil War. Although Stewart notes the persistent influence of abolitionist ideas in American culture even after 1865, he criticizes the movement for the failure of moral suasion as a suitable strategy to overcome slavery.

Larry E. Tise. *Proslavery: A History of the Defense of Slavery in America, 1701-1840*. Athens: University of Georgia Press, 1987. Deriving some of his most valuable insights on proslavery thought from an examination of the writings of American clergymen, Tise traces the origins of proslavery argumentation back to the turn of the eighteenth century. In addition, he not only shows that proslavery advocates operated within a transatlantic network of intellectuals, but also that proslavery thought had an important basis in the American North.

b. Works Cited and Reading Suggestions

Anderson, Jeffrey Elton (2005). "Ethnicity, Nationality, and Race in Colonial America." *A Companion to African American History*. Ed. Alton Hornsby. Malden: Blackwell, 89-104.

Appiah, Kwame Anthony (1989). "The Conservation of 'Race.'" *Black American Literature Forum* 23.1, 37-60.

– (1992). *In My Father's House: Africa in the Philosophy of Culture*. New York: Oxford University Press.

Aptheker, Herbert (1989). *Abolitionism: A Revolutionary Movement*. Boston: Twayne.

Baptist, Edward E., and Stephanie M. H. Camp (2006). *New Studies in the History of American Slavery*. Athens: University of Georgia Press.
Bay, Mia (2000). *The White Image in the Black Mind: African-American Ideas about White People, 1830-1925*. New York: Oxford University Press.
Bell, Bernard W. (1992). "The African-American Jeremiad and Frederick Douglass' Fourth of July 1852 Speech." *The Fourth of July: Political Oratory and Literary Reactions, 1776-1876*. Ed. Paul Goetsch and Gerd Hurm. Tübingen: Narr, 139-153.
Berlin, Ira (1998). *Many Thousands Gone: The First Two Centuries of Slavery in North America*. Cambridge: Belknap Press.
– (2006). "Coming to Terms with Slavery in Twenty-First-Century America." *Slavery and Public History: The Tough Stuff of American Memory*. Ed. James Oliver Horton and Lois E. Horton. New York: New Press, 1-17.
Boyer, Paul S., et al., eds. (2004). *The Enduring Vision: A History of the American People*. 5th ed. Boston: Houghton Mifflin.
Cain, William E., ed. (1995). *William Lloyd Garrison and the Fight against Slavery: Selections from* The Liberator. Boston: Bedford.
Castronovo, Russ (1995). *Fathering the Nation: American Genealogies of Slavery and Freedom*. Berkeley: University of California Press.
Colaiaco, James A. (2006). *Frederick Douglass and the Fourth of July*. New York: Palgrave Macmillan.
Dain, Bruce R. (2002). *A Hideous Monster of the Mind: American Race Theory in the Early Republic*. Cambridge: Harvard University Press.
Davis, David Brion (1975). *The Problem of Slavery in the Age of Revolution, 1770-1823*. Ithaca: Cornell University Press.
– (2000). "Looking at Slavery from a Broader Perspective." *American Historical Review* 105.2, 452-466.
– (2006). *Inhuman Bondage: The Rise and Fall of Slavery in the New World*. Oxford: Oxford University Press.
Degler, Carl N. (1959). "Slavery and the Genesis of American Race Prejudice." *Comparative Studies in Society and History* 2.1, 49-66.
Douglass, Frederick (1994). *Life and Times of Frederick Douglass*. 1892. *Autobiographies*. New York: Library of America, 453-1045.
Dumond, Dwight Lowell (1961). *Antislavery: The Crusade for Freedom in America*. Ann Arbor: University of Michigan Press.
Emerson, Ralph Waldo (1903-1904). "Notes on 'Courage.'" *The Complete Works of Ralph Waldo Emerson*. Centenary Edition. Vol. 7: *Society and Solitude*. Boston: Houghton Mifflin, 426-435.
Faust, Drew Gilpin, ed. (1981). *The Ideology of Slavery: Proslavery Thought in the Antebellum South, 1830-1860*. Baton Rouge: Louisiana State University Press.
Fields, Barbara J. (1982). "Ideology and Race in American History." *Region, Race, and Reconstruction: Essays in Honor of C. Vann Woodward*. Ed. J. Mor-

gan Kousser and James M. McPherson. New York: Oxford University Press, 142-177.

Fields, Barbara J. (1990). "Slavery, Race, and Ideology in the United States of America." *New Left Review* 181, 95-117.

Finkelman, Paul (1996). *Slavery and the Founders: Race and Liberty in the Age of Jefferson*. Armonk: M.E. Sharpe.

Fredrickson, George M. (1987). *The Black Image in the White Mind: The Debate on Afro-American Character and Destiny, 1817-1914*. 1971. Hanover: Wesleyan University Press.

– (1988). *The Arrogance of Race: Historical Perspectives on Slavery, Racism, and Social Inequality*. Middletown: Wesleyan University Press.

– (1997). "Understanding Racism: Reflections of a Comparative Historian." *The Comparative Imagination: On the History of Racism, Nationalism, and Social Movements*. Berkeley: University of California Press, 77-97.

– (2002). *Racism: A Short History*. Princeton: Princeton University Press.

Garrison, William Loyd (1995a). "Address to the American Colonization Society. July 4, 1829." *William Lloyd Garrison and the Fight against Slavery: Selections from* The Liberator. Ed. William E. Cain. Boston: Bedford, 61-70.

– (1995b). "To the Public. January 1, 1831." *William Lloyd Garrison and the Fight against Slavery: Selections from* The Liberator. Ed. William E. Cain. Boston: Bedford, 70-72.

– (1995c). "John Brown and the Principle of Nonresistance. December 16, 1859." *William Lloyd Garrison and the Fight against Slavery: Selections from* The Liberator. Ed. William E. Cain. Boston: Bedford, 156-159.

Gates, Henry Louis, Jr., ed. (1986). *"Race," Writing, and Difference*. Chicago: University of Chicago Press.

Goldberg, David Theo, ed. (1990). *Anatomy of Racism*. Minneapolis: University of Minnesota Press.

Goodman, Paul (1998). *Of One Blood: Abolitionism and the Origins of Racial Equality*. Berkeley: University of California Press.

Gossett, Thomas F. (1997). *Race: The History of an Idea in America*. 1963. New York: Oxford University Press.

Handlin, Oscar, and Mary F. Handlin (1950). "Origins of the Southern Labor System." *The William and Mary Quarterly* 7.2, 199-222.

Hannaford, Ivan (1996). *Race: The History of an Idea in the West*. Baltimore: Johns Hopkins University Press.

Harrold, Stanley (1995). *The Abolitionists and the South, 1831-1861*. Lexington: University Press of Kentucky.

– (2001). *American Abolitionists*. Harlow: Longman.

– (2004). *The Rise of Aggressive Abolitionism: Addresses to the Slaves*. Lexington: University Press of Kentucky.

Haynes, Stephen R. (2002). *Noah's Curse: The Biblical Justification of American Slavery*. Oxford: Oxford University Press.

Hinks, Peter P. (1997). *To Awaken My Afflicted Brethren*: *David Walker and the Problem of Antebellum Slave Resistance*. University Park: Pennsylvania State University Press.
Horsman, Reginald (1981). *Race and Manifest Destiny*: *The Origins of American Racial Anglo-Saxonism*. Cambridge: Harvard University Press.
Jacobson, Matthew Frye (1998). *Whiteness of a Different Color*: *European Immigrants and the Alchemy of Race*. Cambridge: Harvard University Press.
Jordan, Winthrop D. (1968). *White over Black*: *American Attitudes toward the Negro, 1550-1812*. Chapel Hill: University of North Carolina Press.
Kolchin, Peter (2003). *American Slavery, 1619-1877*. 1993. Rev. ed. New York: Hill and Wang.
LaCapra, Dominick, ed. (1991). *The Bounds of Race*: *Perspectives on Hegemony and Resistance*. Ithaca: Cornell University Press.
Lee, Maurice S. (2005). *Slavery, Philosophy, and American Literature, 1830-1860*. Cambridge: Cambridge University Press.
Lowance, Mason I., ed. (2000). *Against Slavery*: *An Abolitionist Reader*. New York: Penguin.
– , ed.(2003). *A House Divided*: *The Antebellum Slavery Debates in America, 1776-1865*. Princeton: Princeton University Press.
Mason, Matthew (2006). *Slavery and Politics in the Early American Republic*. Chapel Hill: University of North Carolina Press.
Mayer, Henry (1998). *All on Fire*: *William Lloyd Garrison and the Abolition of Slavery*. New York: St. Martin's.
McDowell, Deborah E., and Arnold Rampersad, eds. (1989). *Slavery and the Literary Imagination*. Baltimore: Johns Hopkins University Press.
Melish, Joanne Pope (1998). *Disowning Slavery*: *Gradual Emancipation and "Race" in New England, 1780-1860*. Ithaca: Cornell University Press.
Mills, Charles W. (1997). *The Racial Contract*. Ithaca: Cornell University Press.
– (1999). "Whose Fourth of July? Frederick Douglass and 'Original Intent.'" *Frederick Douglass*: *A Critical Reader*. Ed. Bill E. Lawson and Frank M. Kirkland. Malden: Blackwell, 100-142.
Morgan, Edmund S. (1975). *American Slavery, American Freedom*: *The Ordeal of Colonial Virginia*. New York: Norton.
Morton, Samuel George (1839). *Crania Americana, or, A Comparative View of the Skulls of Various Aboriginal Nations of North and South America*. Philadelphia: J. Dobson.
Reynolds, David S. (2005). *John Brown, Abolitionist*: *The Man Who Killed Slavery, Sparked the Civil War, and Seeded Civil Rights*. New York: Knopf.
Riss, Arthur (2006). *Race, Slavery, and Liberalism in Nineteenth-Century American Literature*. Cambridge: Cambridge University Press.
Sánchez-Eppler, Karen (1988). "Bodily Bonds: The Intersecting Rhetorics of Feminism and Abolition." *Representations* 24, 28-59.

Savage, Kirk (1997). *Standing Soldiers, Kneeling Slaves: Race, War, and Monument in Nineteenth-Century America*. Princeton: Princeton University Press.

Sklar, Kathryn Kish (2000). *Women's Rights Emerges within the Anti-Slavery Movement, 1830-1870: A Brief History with Documents*. Boston: Bedford/St. Martin's.

Smedley, Audrey (1999). *Race in North America: Origin and Evolution of a Worldview*. 2nd ed. Boulder: Westview.

Stauffer, John (2002). *The Black Hearts of Men: Radical Abolitionists and the Transformation of Race*. Cambridge: Harvard University Press.

Stewart, James Brewer (1996). *Holy Warriors: The Abolitionists and American Slavery*. 1976. Rev. ed. New York: Hill and Wang.

Stuckey, Sterling (1987). *Slave Culture: Nationalist Theory and the Foundations of Black America*. New York: Oxford University Press.

Sundquist, Eric J. (1993). *To Wake the Nations: Race in the Making of American Literature*. Cambridge: Belknap Press.

Takaki, Ronald T. (1979). *Iron Cages: Race and Culture in Nineteenth-Century America*. New York: Knopf.

Tise, Larry E. (1987). *Proslavery: A History of the Defense of Slavery in America, 1701-1840*. Athens: University of Georgia Press.

Trodd, Zoe, and John Stauffer, eds. (2004). *Meteor of War: The John Brown Story*. Maplecrest: Brandywine Press.

Vaughan, Alden T. (1995). *Roots of American Racism: Essays on the Colonial Experience*. New York: Oxford University Press.

Walker, David (2000). *David Walker's Appeal to the Coloured Citizens of the World*. Ed. Peter P. Hinks. University Park: Pennsylvania State University Press.

Walters, Ronald G. (1997). *American Reformers, 1815-1860*. 1978. Rev. ed. New York: Hill and Wang.

Wheeler, Roxann (2000). *The Complexion of Race: Categories of Difference in Eighteenth-Century British Culture*. Philadelphia: University of Pennsylvania Press.

Wood, Betty (1997). *The Origins of American Slavery: Freedom and Bondage in the English Colonies*. New York: Hill and Wang.

Yellin, Jean Fagan (1989). *Women and Sisters: The Antislavery Feminists in American Culture*. New Haven: Yale University Press.

Young, Jason R. (2005). "Origins and Institutionalization of American Slavery." *A Companion to African American History*. Ed. Alton Hornsby. Malden: Blackwell, 143-158.

WOLFGANG HOCHBRUCK

Civil War and Reconstruction

> What Americans need to remember about this great war of yesterday is not the battles, the marches, the conflicts, not the courage, the suffering, the blood, but only the causes that underlay the struggle and the results that followed from it.
>
> Albion W. Tourgée (1888, 32)

I. Themes and Arguments

The subtitle of Tony Horwitz's 1998 *Confederates in the Attic*, "Dispatches from the Unfinished Civil War," signals the ill ease with which this conflict and its outcome continues to be handled to this day. This holds true especially for the territory of the former Confederacy and those areas that have been 'southernized' since, i.e., states which in the Civil War had actually remained in the Union, but in which larger groups and percentages of the population were pro-secession: Kentucky, Maryland, and Missouri, or the former Indian Territory, now Oklahoma. In some areas, like Western Mississippi, as recently as ten years ago race relations signaled a condition that bore more signs of an uneasy truce than of a resolved and unselfconscious peace.[1]

This background already sets the scene for, and includes traces of, all of the main themes and arguments that surround the central issues of the most disastrous and costly, yet also the most thoroughly mythologized war the US has ever fought, the Civil War, and of the most botched period in American politics to date, the so-called Reconstruction. In the course of time, the American Civil War mutated from manslaughter on a grand scale during its actual duration to a set of myths, most of which had been established as common and binding by white America around 1890.[2] Among them is the myth of reunion, as exemplified

---

[1] The author of this article can attest to having been accosted, on the battlefield of Shiloh, on the occasion of the 135th anniversary of that Civil War battle (April 6-7, 1862), by two burly young men wearing t-shirts proclaiming "I've got a nigger in my family tree" and adorned with a rough-drawn sketch of a scene copying the message conveyed by The Dogwood Tree (doc. 290).

[2] McPherson reads the Civil War as an attempt at a conservative counterrevolution in the face of advancing industrialism, immigration, and societal change (cf. 1988, chap. 8). The first to

for instance by the cover of the June 1893 *Blue & Gray Magazine*, with its depiction of the Union (left) and the Confederate (right) soldier on an equal basis – note that the four iconic generals even cross the left-right scheme: Ulysses S. Grant (US) and Robert E. Lee (CS) in the top row are balanced by Thomas 'Stonewall' Jackson (CS) and William Tecumseh 'Uncle Billy' Sherman (US) in the bottom row.

Fig. 12: *Blue & Gray Magazine*. 1893.

The following unit will provide a critical analysis, literary and cultural background, and some guidelines on interpretation of the texts and images making up the section on "Civil War & Reconstruction" in the anthology. It will address the issues of how the parties involved started and ended the Civil War; the problematic reconciliation period; the increasing mythologization of the Civil War and of the 'South' in the war as a geographical region rather than as a political attempt at one-sided secession; and, finally, slavery and the post-war condition of the Africamerican[3] population in the re-united US – now grammatically singular.

---

see the secession in this light was Karl Marx, who called it an attempted counterrevolution in a letter to Abraham Lincoln in November 1864 (cf. Marx and Engels 1976, 223).

[3] The term "Africamerican" is used here in analogy to George Elliott Clarke's ethnoregional coinage "Africadian" for the people of mixed African, American, French, and Mi'kmaq descent in the Canadian Maritime Provinces.

II. Starting and Finishing the War of Secession

The issue of slavery had already been crucial in the eighty years preceding the Civil War, as the documents in the "Slavery" section (docs. 248-54; cf. Fritsch in this vol., 353-7) in the anthology show. The various compromises of the first half of the nineteenth century had been able to contain and alleviate the problem, but only temporarily. By 1860, four factors combined to make a conflict – if not necessarily a war – unavoidable. One, the westward movement and the political visions of a southward extension of the US demanded a decision on whether slavery was a receding or an expanding institution. Two, the success of Frederick Douglass's 1845 autobiography, as well as the increasing literary production of Africamericans contradicted the slaveholders' argumentation that people of African origin were not able to take care of their own affairs, and incapable of life on an advanced level, and that therefore chattel slavery was a necessary evil, or, in John C. Calhoun's words, even a "positive good" by gradually uplifting Africamericans (*KC*, 586). Three, the hysteria into which Southern and pro-slavery politicians had worked themselves during the year leading up to the presidential election, culminating in the threat that they would secede if an anti-slavery president were elected, made a quiet withdrawal from their extremist position impossible without severe loss of face. John Brown's suicidal raid in Virginia obviously had done nothing to alleviate the situation – there were fanatics on both sides of the smoldering crisis, ready to bring about a conflict that eventually claimed the lives of more than 600,000 soldiers and of uncounted civilians. Four, the existence of internally divided states like Maryland, Kentucky, Tennessee, Texas, and most notably Kansas and Missouri, practically guaranteed internal upheaval and bloodshed if and when these states attempted to pass an ordinance of secession. Armed groups on both sides were ready to wage war if they had not already done so in the clandestine low-intensity guerilla activities in "Bloody Kansas" since 1854 (cf. McPherson 1988, 152). The rebellion of politically powerful eastern states was a certain way to fan the violence in the west.

All four issues were enforced and simultaneously superseded by the secession of South Carolina and other Deep South states during the winter months of 1860-61, following a presidential election in which several pro-status quo and proslavery candidates had blocked each other for percentages of the votes, thus aiding Lincoln's victory. Whereas *The Address of the People of South Carolina* (doc. 275) and Jefferson Davis's "First Inaugural Address" (doc. 276) seem to imply that all that the slaveholding states of the Deep South ever desired was to be left in peace, the practical side of secession showed a different face. Neither South Carolina nor any of the other seceding states appealed to the Supreme Court for a decision on how, and under what conditions, a state might be allowed to leave the Union. The first round of attempts to get the conventions in Arkansas, Missouri, Tennessee, and Virginia to adopt secession failed in March of 1861, and only in a few states was the decision to secede eventually ratified by public acclaim. Instead, following the unilateral declarations of secession, Federal institutions and installations were seized or besieged until Federal employees and soldiers left. This was, obviously, political piracy.

The call for moderation and peace in Abraham Lincoln's "First Inaugural Address" of March 4, 1861 (doc. 277), seems to echo some of the sentiments already expressed by Jefferson Davis two weeks earlier. However, the two political leaders meant different things: Lincoln's speech, assuring slaveholders of the inviolate continuation of their rights to slave ownership (cf. *KC*, 628, 631), insisted on the inseparability of the Union, whereas Davis spoke of an "emergency" and called for preparations of armed conflict "to maintain [...] the position which we have assumed among the nations of the earth" (*KC*, 627). Lincoln's call for moderation weights even stronger if one considers that he spoke seven weeks *after* the first shots of war had been fired at a steamer trying to bring supplies to Federal Fort Sumter in South Carolina's Charleston harbor (cf. McPherson 1988, 266). President James Buchanan had apparently not deemed it necessary to react to this provocation, even though he had originally denied the right to secession in his message to congress on December 3, 1860 (cf. McPherson 1988, 246). He left to his successor a nation that he had allowed to fall apart.

By April, the new Confederacy had organized itself to the point that an open attack on a Federal institution seemed the next appropriate step, even though secession had suffered a set-back in North Carolina, and Virginia had not seceded yet either – only seven of the slave states had gathered in the Confederate quarter, as opposed to eight reluctant or hesitant cases: Beside North Carolina and Virginia, these were Arkansas, Tennessee, Kentucky, Missouri, Maryland, and Delaware. Fort Sumter, where a small garrison commanded by a major held out right in the middle of Charleston harbor, became a symbolic site when shelling by South Carolina state forces started on April 12, 1861. The fort being forced to surrender, and the Union flag taken down, Lincoln reacted by calling for 75,000 volunteers to form a *posse comitatus* accompanying US Federal marshals sent to the rebelling states to restore law and order.[4] This in turn provoked secession ordinances in Tennessee, Arkansas, North Carolina, and Virginia. The actual war, therefore, did not start over the issue of slavery, but over the question of whether a state might leave the Union by unilateral declaration and by force.

While the war led to the abolishment of slavery, it did not solve the problems of race relations in the USA and resulted in a continuation, and in some aspects even an aggravation, of the pre-war conditions. This, however, was probably unavoidable, considering that both sides went into the armed version of their ongoing conflict with no clear idea of how to end it. For the secessionists, the aim was clearly to avoid defeat – they did not necessarily have to win, but they would succeed as long as they managed to hold their own and win a war of attrition,

---

[4] A *posse comitatus* is a group of deputies, militia, or soldiers that supports Federal marshals in executing orders or pursuing criminals.

i.e., to convince the Unionists – and international powers like the British and French empires – that their return to the Union was out of the question and the secession a fait accompli.

As far as the Union side was concerned, its representatives were still facing the dilemma already exemplified by Daniel Webster's "The Constitution of the Union Speech" from 1850 (doc. 274). On the one hand, they had to actually win their case by military power once the war had started. On the other hand, for the better part of the war, the Lincoln administration dealt with the population in the seceded states leniently and tried to avoid unnecessary damage, already with a view on how to restore relations between the parties in a post-war environment (cf. Grimsley 1995). This situation determined the tone of Unionist literature and rhetoric throughout the war, anticipating the efforts at reconciliation that were to inform most of the post-war public culture.

The most visible and long-lasting effect of this politics of leniency was the fact that when the war finally ended, it was not finished properly. Lincoln's rhetoric of reconciliation as well as the immediate post-war policy of his successor Johnson, which argued that because secession had been illegal, it had not really happened, were not conducive to inspiring a sense of the new beginning which the end of the Civil War might have been.

The underlying message of the "Second Inaugural Address" is a spirit of re-union (cf. doc. 278), taking up the message that Lincoln had already conveyed sixteen months earlier in his famous "Gettysburg Address" (1863) through the use of myths and metaphors. This earlier text gives even clearer evidence of what might be called an envisioned new birth of freedom:

> Four score and seven years ago our fathers brought forth on this continent, a new nation, conceived in Liberty, and dedicated to the proposition that all men are created equal.
>
> Now we are engaged in a great civil war, testing whether that nation, or any nation so conceived and so dedicated, can long endure. We are met on a great battle-field of that war. We have come to dedicate a portion of that field, as a final resting place for those who here gave their lives that that nation might live. It is altogether fitting and proper that we should do this.
>
> But, in a larger sense, we cannot dedicate – we cannot consecrate – we cannot hallow – this ground. The brave men, living and dead, who struggled here, have consecrated it, far above our poor power to add or detract. The world will little note, nor long remember what we say here, but it can never forget what they did here. It is for us the living, rather, to be dedicated here to the unfinished work which they who fought here have thus far so nobly advanced. It is rather for us to be here dedicated to the great task remaining before us – that from these honoured dead we take increased devotion to that cause for which they gave the last full measure of devotion – that we here highly resolve that these dead shall not have died in vain – that this nation, under God, shall have a new birth of freedom – and that government of the people, by the people, for the people, shall not perish from the earth. (in Wills 1992, 263)

The classic speech of the Civil War, and one of its few literary texts of lasting importance, Lincoln's "Gettysburg Address" shows the main signs of the reconciliation spirit and of its key ingredient, a positive and future-oriented outlook that had also influenced Daniel Webster's 1850 "Union Speech" (doc. 274) and Lincoln's own "First Inaugural Address" (doc. 277).[5]

Lincoln's was not the main speech on November 19, 1863, at the dedication of the Gettysburg National Cemetery – that was given by Edward Everett, the defeated vice presidential candidate of 1860, and it lasted for two hours. Lincoln spoke for only three minutes, and few who heard it grasped the rhetorical brilliance of this address as well as did Everett, who congratulated Lincoln.

Note how the first person plural includes all listeners into the underlying construction of a renewed narrative of national creation. Starting as he did with the "new nation, conceived in liberty, and dedicated to the proposition that all men are created equal," Lincoln appealed to the memory of his audience and their knowledge of the Declaration of Independence and the preface to the Constitution of the United States (cf. Hurm in this vol., 197-203). This equality is upheld throughout in collective addresses of "us," and "they" – no one is singled out for praise, no leaders and generals are named. Thus, the battle, its participants and victims are linked inseparably in the promise of equality. This promise was also visible to Lincoln's audience: The National Cemetery at Gettysburg gave the same kind and size of marker to every soldier buried, regardless of state of origin, military rank, or background in civilian life.

The address then turns from the appeal to memory to an invocation of the present and an outlook on the future. The "great task remaining before us" is an envisaged "new birth of freedom," and this future result is supported by a whole series of images connected with procreation and birth. By employing these images and motifs in a cemetery, Lincoln's address upended all conventions of contemporary funereal customs. In its orientation towards the future, the text of the "Gettysburg Address," however, belongs to a whole system of political thought represented by Lincoln's two presidential inauguration addresses. The Union war effort aimed at reconciliation which found its most famous expression later in Lincoln's "Second Inaugural Address": "With malice toward none, with chastity for all" (*KC*, 635), combining Christian reconciliation and republican strategy in a rhetorical format.

The theme of spiritual rebirth makes the "Gettysburg Address" not a traditional retrospective eulogy, but a text imbued with a future-oriented mission, a mission encompassing not only the remembrance of the dead, but the historical task to investigate the question of whether a democratic government is really possible (cf. Goetsch 2001, 249).

Lincoln's address points beyond the moment and the occasion in another way: Brevity, precision, and rhetorical acumen make it a harbinger of the political rhetoric of modernity. It is a remarkably pragmatic text, an address com-

---

[5] Contrast this with the backwards-oriented vision of the Jefferson Davis inaugural and of South Carolina's secession ordinance (docs. 275-6).

posed for radio or television before either of those media existed. The main problem of the text's orientation towards the future, however, was that the war was far from over in November 1863, and that there were no usable concepts as to how to end it, or what to do exactly once it had ended.

Lincoln's death camouflaged this lack of a coherent concept for the post-war period, which resulted in the war's contradictory endings: The military victory of the Union forces as well as the consequent abolition of slavery and the enfranchisement of Africamericans saw a series of reversals in the following decade. By 1876, everything but chattel slavery was back in place – Africamericans were practically disenfranchised again, the old elites were back in power, and the more prominent and popular war heroes were Confederates.

The problem of the war's ending(s) has long been overshadowed in scholarship by the on-going debate over the causes of the war, and by the enormous number of military histories. Whereas the latter do not usually make an issue of the war's beginnings or endings but treat these as givens, the discourses on the causes of the war turn in on themselves when discussing slavery. That the early secession texts, *The Address of the People of South Carolina* (doc. 275) and Davis's "First Inaugural Address" (doc. 276), only obliquely refer to slavery at all was to be expected – a political rhetoric bluntly declaring that Southerners were breaking up the democratic federation because they were determined to keep their slaves would not have been advisable, not only with the white majorities in the slaveholding states, but with those foreign nations whose political recognition the secessionists were vying for, notably France, England, and Tsarist Russia. Instead, both texts refer back to the Constitution, and to the original Declaration of Independence, assuming that the relation between the secession states and the Union equals that between the rebelling colonies of 1775-76, and the British colonial power (cf. *KC*, 625, 627). The concentration on reinterpretations of past documents, together with the insistence on a slave-based, agrarian life-style and society (cf. *KC*, 626-7), however, signals a general tendency of the Confederates to look back to the past rather than forward to the future. It continued throughout the war and into the romantic view of the 'Lost Cause' after the military defeat (cf. Pollard 1994; Gallagher and Nolan 2000).

Most histories of the war, including the current study by James M. McPherson (1988), go into a lot of detail enumerating factors and events leading up to the conflict, but they usually end in late fall of 1865 at the latest, when the crew of the rebel raider CSS *Shenandoah* finally learned that the war had been over for months (cf. Schooler 2005, 1). This event corresponds with only the first ending of the Civil War, the military defeat of the rebellion. This first ending, the one still taught in schoolbooks, gave rise to the still prevalent culture of defeat in the South. There was, however, a second, less official, ending to the Civil War in 1876, resulting from badly planned and inconsequentially applied reconstruction measures, feeble attempts at implementing martial law, and the unwillingness of Union politicians, combined with post-Confederate recalcitrance.

In 1868, it had looked as if the politics of Reconstruction might prevail. The Freedmen's Bureau (officially the Bureau of Refugees, Freedmen and Abandoned Lands) was to provide services for those who until recently had been slaves, though it was much maligned in the media and by politicians, notably in the 1866 congressional elections (cf. doc. 283), as an institution that allegedly kept Africamericans from working.

Fig. 13: Alfred Waud. *Harper's Weekly*. 1868.

In a *Harper's Weekly* magazine cartoon by Alfred Waud (fig. 13), the Union officer now operating as an agent for the Freedmen's Bureau tries to keep white Southerners and Africamericans, some men on both sides recognizable as war veterans, from attacking each other. The responsibility for abandoned lands gave rise to the myth that the plantations were supposed to be divided up and that all Africamericans had been promised 40 acres and a mule. This did not happen. Still, by 1868, recalcitrance prevailed only in Texas, Mississippi, and Virginia, after the Reconstruction Act of March 1867 had made clear the conditions for official re-admittance to the Union. Among them were new constitutions for the former slave states, and the implementation of universal (male) suffrage. This was very much the war aim that Frederick Douglass had hoped and lobbied for in "What the Black Man Wants" (doc. 281).

Over the next eight years, one state after the other passed back from the Republican Reconstruction rule into Democratic hands. This was due partly to the kind of incompetence demonstrated by the former that an otherwise sympathetic Thomas Nast castigated in an 1874 cartoon (doc. 286), and partly to a mixture of the coercion of whites and Africamericans alike, pressure on Federal institutions and officials, instigated riots, and pure terror against Union sympathizers and Africamerican rights' activists as well as everyone who was perceived of as an "uppity nigger" not staying in their place. The result was the complete overthrow of the Republican Reconstruction rule by 1875/76, when the Tilden-Hayes compromise between Democrats and Republicans gave the presidency to former Union general Rutherford B. Hayes and the Republicans, but also terminated Reconstruction in the former Confederacy. Federal troops were withdrawn, leaving Southern Unionists and Africamerican war veterans at the mercy of the post-Confederates (cf. Zuczek 1996, 20; Murphy 1987, 143-5).

Firmly re-establishing white rule, and reversing the first ending in almost everything except the re-institution of chattel slavery, this second ending of the Civil War provided the basis for the third, the cultural ending. During the following so-called reconciliation period, the defeated Confederacy and notably its military leaders saw a rise in romantic fame unparalleled in the history of the cultural memory of wars. Already in the 1880s, former Union author and Freedmen's Bureau agent Albion Tourgée called this phenomenon a "literary Appomattox" which reversed the military surrender of Robert E. Lee's Army of northern Virginia in the spring of 1865. The diverse historical views on the war, and the heroic mythology favoring the Confederacy, can be seen as a result of a phenomenon pre-dating the war. The lofty rhetoric of 1861, relying on "the final arbitrament of the sword" (*KC*, 627), echoed a specifically Southern ideology of honor, and an anachronistic idea of what a war might look like (cf. Gispen 1990; Stevens 1940; Wyatt-Brown 1982). Ironically enough, the romantic view of the South as a cultural antidote, deflecting the problems and effects of industrialization, mass immigration, and social change, had already existed in the 1840s and 1850s and was largely manufactured in Northern printing presses and media. One could even claim that the Confederates believed the propaganda about themselves that had conflated auto- as well as heterostereotypes in the years before the war.

However, the war itself was conducted with more ferocity than anyone had imagined – the saying that the South stopped smiling after Shiloh, attributed to George Washington Cable, is a vivid commentary on a battle which, counting the casualties on both sides, allegedly killed and wounded more Americans than the War of Independence. The horrifying losses on both sides – more than 600,000 men died in the more than 2,000 battles and skirmishes, of diseases, cold, or starvation in prison camps – the ferocity of the warfare, especially on the western border, and the murders of US Colored Troops, and occasionally also of immigrant Federal soldiers, by Confederate regulars and irregulars shook the foundations of the images of friend and enemy alike (cf. Ailliot 1991; Hollandsworth 1994; Suderow 1997). From this point of view, it was an almost logical outcome to reestablish the Civil War as a mythological fiction.

This third ending guaranteed hegemonic dominance to a system of (post-)Confederate axioms: that the war had been a geographical conflict between North and South rather than a political contest, that it had not been about slavery, but about states' rights, that the greater nobility had been unilaterally on the Southern side whereas the Union employed its unfair advantage of sheer numbers and more advanced technologies, and, finally, that reconciliation was an issue resolved amongst the white, Anglo-Saxon men and women on either side. It also ensured that for more than a century, the cultural South would be able to continue and extend its Lost Cause-mythology (cf. Bailey 1991; Pollard 1994), which banked on a romantic concept and represented the Southerners as victims of the war, not only unjustly defeated, but denied victory, and unjustly deprived of rights and property.

Fig. 14: Henry Mosler. *The Lost Cause*. 1869. (Smith-Berry family collection, Alpharetta, GA)

Henry Mosler's painting *The Lost Cause* (fig. 14) is only one of a whole school of similar paintings which reinforced Southern beliefs in their own victimization – but note that the returned veteran is actually still carrying his rifle. This is as unusual for a defeated army as it is anticipatory of what was about to happen in the decade following 1865: The Lost Cause stayed lost only regarding its reproduction in memories, memoirs, and – increasingly – in the popular cultural industries.[6] A fourth ending can be hypothesized as a meta-ending evolving out of the first three; this ending, however, is productive almost exclusively in the works of scholar historians and cultural critics (cf. Pressly 1954; Hammett 1974).

III. Slavery and Reconciliation

The tendency to accept the issue of slavery as the cause of the American Civil War was very much a by-product of the Civil Rights Movement and of the parallel Civil War Centennial from 1961 to 1965. In its day, as documents 274 through 277 illustrate, the issue was treated with more circumspection than during the 1960s memorials, notably by Abraham Lincoln in his "First Inaugural

---

[6] This mythology provided the basis for cultural products from David W. Griffith's *The Birth of the Nation* (1915) via Margaret Mitchell's and David O. Selznick's *Gone with the Wind* as novel (1936) and film (1939) to the Civil War Centennial and even beyond, all glorifying the past 'South,' 'Southern values, and Confederate myths effectively subverting the traditional assertion that (cultural) history is written by the victors.

Address," which carefully avoided the confrontation that had been initiated by the secession of South Carolina in December of 1861.

Abolishing slavery had not initially been a war aim for the Lincoln administration, nor would many Unionists have fought for the freedom of slaves. The primary objective, much to the chagrin of Africamericans and the radical wing of Lincoln's own Republican Party, had been solely to restore the Union. The abolition of slavery became a war aim only in 1862 – until then, local commanders had in some cases, notably in the eastern theater of war, even returned slaves to their masters. A declaration precipitately freeing the slaves of secession supporters issued by General John Frémont in Missouri led to his replacement in November 1861. Moreover, Africamericans were not officially allowed to enlist until the fall of 1862, even though they already served in a number of units before that time, notably in the western theater of war.

There has been a long debate among scholars and critics as to whether the Lincoln government and the president himself were not as racist and prejudiced against the 'negro' as were their counterparts in secession states (cf. Fritsch in this vol., 339-40). As a matter of fact, the near ubiquity of anti-Africamerican predispositions can be attested on both sides of the Mason-Dixon Line, before, throughout, and after the war. Few groups were as determined to get rid of slavery as were Africamericans themselves, or the German Forty-eighters and their descendants, many of them organized in Turnvereinen, and volunteering for the Union in considerable numbers in 1861, and not even die-hard abolitionists were necessarily convinced that immediate equality and enfranchisement – what Frederick Douglass calls for in his speech "What the Black Man Wants" (doc. 281) – were naturally forthcoming after freedom had been gained. Even within the famous 54th Massachusetts Regiment of Volunteer Infantry, whose Boston Brahmin family Colonel Robert Gould Shaw had been buried "with his niggers" after the ill-fated attack on Fort Wagner, South Carolina, in July 1863, some of the white officers resigned their commissions when the first Africamerican lieutenants were appointed. Even the Africamericans themselves sometimes acted against their own interest: The "loyal darkey," so ubiquitous in Southern literature, was not a wholesale invention, and Africamerican slaves sometimes not only accompanied their masters – often enough their half-brothers – into the field, but even bore arms against Union forces.

In this situation, it is not surprising that Abraham Lincoln's policy concerning slavery could not afford to predicate itself on radical abolitionist positions. Responding to an editorial in Horace Greeley's influential *New York Tribune*, Lincoln insisted in a letter to the editor only months before the *Emancipation Proclamation* that his main aim was to save the Union and that if he could achieve this without liberating a single slave, he would do so. Consequently, there have been attempts to retrospectively enlist Lincoln as the "great heart" of the Confederate cause, starting with D. W. Griffith's insidious treatment of the Lincoln figure in *The Birth of a Nation* (1915). However, as historian James Oakes (2007) has shown, Lincoln said in the same letter that he would also save the Union if he could do it by freeing all the slaves or only part of them (cf. Lincoln 1953, 388).

Lincoln operated an oblique antislavery agenda throughout his presidential career, seeking to maintain a precarious balance between the radical wing of his Republican party, the Africamericans around Douglass, and the more moderate to anti-abolitionist Democrats. Lincoln's cautious approach ties in with a continuous line of political activities in his life that is pro-equality, regardless of race and class. James Oakes makes an enticing argument for all who want to see "Honest Abe" in the traditional role of the Great Emancipator.

The *Emancipation Proclamation* (doc. 278), announced by Lincoln in September 1862 and becoming effective on January 1, 1863, ironically did not, at first, free a single slave because it was designed to affect only the property of slave-owners in those areas still in armed rebellion against the United States. According to its wording, it was aimed at the liberation of all slaves in the Confederate-held territory, that is, exclusive of those areas in Louisiana and Tennessee already under Union control, and the four slaveholding states which had remained in the Union – Missouri, Kentucky, Maryland, Delaware, and the District of Columbia with the capital, Washington. Ultimately, however, it led many slaves – about one fifth of the total (cf. Barney 1980, 139) – to a vote for freedom with their feet; in effect robbing their masters of their property, and denying the Confederacy the man- and womanpower necessary to keep up the home front and to supply the fighting units in the field with provisions. The *Emancipation Proclamation* thus laid the ground for universal emancipation coming true with the end of armed hostilities in 1865. By 1868, Frederick Douglass's other war aim of Africamerican (male) suffrage had also been achieved through the Fourteenth and Fifteenth Amendments to the Constitution.

IV. The Undeclared War after the Civil War

A major problem which the emancipators had not foreseen was the post-war condition of former slave owners and newly freed slaves now living in close proximity to each other (cf. docs. 283-6). The continuing tension between fractions now divided along racial rather than class lines resulted in a century of undeclared interracial war, with most of the casualties on the Africamerican side. The second ending to the Civil War was thus only rectified again, at least in parts, in the Civil Rights Movement of the 1950s and 1960s.

In 1865, the situation was still a subject for satire: The white planter family in the illustration "The Great Labor Question from a Southern Point of View" (doc. 285), telling their former slave that now, after he has been taken care of for so long, he has to work, is clearly intended as comical, the object of humor being the 'idle rich' of the quasi-aristocratic Old South.

The dangers of the situation, however, should have been obvious. For the majority of slave owners, the abolition of slavery meant the enforced forfeiture of large sums of invested money. Able slaves – not just able-bodied field-hands, but skilled mechanics and craftsmen, even engineers – were worth a proverbial fortune. Once slavery was abolished, however, the investment was lost, and the formerly valued slave was now no longer an object of aspirations to slave-owning gentility and ascent into the 'planter' class, but a potential competitor for jobs and resources (cf. Fritsch in this vol., 355-6).

With many Africamericans moving out of the Confederate states and migrating north, job competition became a topic there, too. How popular "Negro suffrage" really was in states that had fought for the preservation of the Union, is visible from the racist binary opposition constructed by the 1866 gubernatorial election campaign poster from Pennsylvania (doc. 284). Given the culture of violence dominant in the South, interracial conditions deteriorated rapidly.

By the time of the second ending of the Civil War in 1876, the vision expressed in "The Promise of the Declaration of Independence Fulfilled" (doc. 279) must have looked like a fiendish satire. True, for a while the recalcitrance of post-Confederate governments to ratify and endorse the constitution amendments had been met with the establishment of military rule. The original Ku Klux Klan, founded in 1866 as a terrorist organization against Africamericans, Union sympathizers, and collaborators (so-called scalawags), had been officially disbanded after a wave of persecution, and many terrorists had been brought to justice in 1871/72.

However, all over the South new organizations sprang up to take its place. This time, they did not make the mistake of operating as secret organizations which might be persecuted by the law. The Red Shirts in South Carolina, the White Liners in Mississippi, the Knights of the White Camelia (Southerners had not lost their predilection for Walter Scott-ish romantic capers) and later the White League in Louisiana, as well as scores of similar organizations all over the former Confederacy, were male clubs and associations – good ol' boys, and mostly former comrades-in-arms. These groups and associations provided a paramilitary basis and support for the political efforts to turn the clock back.

Furthermore, most of the convicted terrorists either received lenient punishment or were pardoned. By 1875, all of them were at large again. Only larger massacres of Africamericans, including state militiamen, like the ones in Memphis and New Orleans in 1869, in Colfax, Louisiana, in 1873, and in Hamburg, South Carolina, in 1876, provoked more than half-hearted Federal reactions, but white supremacists continued their mixture of open and covert operations, threatening, coercing, and killing "uppity" Africamericans as well as "scalawags," and anybody suspected of being a Union sympathizer. This system of course was not abandoned with the restoration of white home rule in 1876, as E. Malcolm Argyle's "Report from Arkansas," Booker T. Washington's "Atlanta Exposition Address," and *The Dogwood Tree* (docs. 288-90) demonstrate. The culture of coercion and subjugation was always able to escalate into lynching and murder, of individuals as well as of whole families or groups – see the randomness of the murders reported from Arkansas in 1892 (doc. 288) and the five Africamericans lynched in Sabine County, Texas, in 1905, whose deaths were used in a white supremacist propaganda document, the poem *The Dogwood Tree* (doc. 290) that has even been copyrighted.[7]

In this situation of continuous undeclared race war, Booker T. Washington's famous "Cast down your bucket" speech at the Atlanta Exposition of 1895 must of necessity provoke a mixed response. On the one hand, it appears as a capitulation of sorts, a call for appeasement in hopes of a treatment more along the lines of that which good and faithful slaves received by their lenient and enlightened masters in the antebellum days. On the other hand, it has been argued by historians that his was the only possible stance and only reasonable way to go, given the conditions of race relations which evolved into legal segregation the next year. However, there was another, much less popularized, speech at the Atlanta Exposition which recalled the honors won by Africamericans during the Civil War in fighting for their own freedom, and urged them to build up self-esteem and confidence based on that experience. The speaker, Christian Fleetwood, then on the staff of the Washington Howard University and a Major in the Washington National Guard, was a recipient of the Congressional Medal of Honor for bravery in action as the Sergeant-Major of the 4th US Colored Regiment at Chapin's Farm in 1864. His address on "The Negro as a Soldier" (1895) targets the relegation of Africamerican bravery to the sidelines of history, after every conflict in which they had taken part in had given proof of their bravery and mettle. In its boldness, and given the place and time of its delivery, it can be seen as a continuation of Fleetwood's personal bravery in the Civil War.

Ironically, a similar message is conveyed by the monument to Colonel Shaw and his men of the 54th Massachusetts Regiment by the sculptor Augustus St. Gaudens, unveiled in 1897 on the Boston Commons. Unlike the generic monuments to white Union and Confederate soldiers, which were even cast in the same foundries, St. Gaudens individualized the features of every single one of the black soldiers on the monument. The individuation denied to them in public cultural history and especially in popular culture, was achieved here; the only Civil War monument to thus give credit to the bravery of the individual. Art was, as so often, far ahead of politics and society.

---

[7] This racist document actually closes the circle to the t-shirts of racist youths I encountered on the Shiloh battlefield in April 1997.

Fig. 15: Augustus St. Gaudens. *Shaw Memorial*. 1897. (Photo: Barbara Fischer / Florian Stocker)

Instructional Strategies and Classroom Issues

I. Key Concepts and Major Themes

1. The Coming of the War (docs. 274-6)
   The unsolved problem of slavery and the question of its continued existence under the conditions of westward (and possible southward) expansion divides the Union. The rhetoric of the period gives only a subdued impression of an increasingly hysterical situation. The election of Lincoln triggers a series of actions in the slaveholding states; conciliatory politics are of no use in a situation in which secession is attempted by force.

2. Emancipation (docs. 278-9, 281)
   To support the Unionist war effort, Lincoln issues the *Emancipation Proclamation*, effective January 1, 1863. Together with universal suffrage, at least for the male population, and the Thirteenth, Fourteenth, and Fifteenth Amendments to the Constitution, equality finally seems a reality.[8]

---

[8] For full texts of the Amendments, see "Primary Documents in American History": <http://www.loc.gov/rr/program/bib/ourdocs> (August 24, 2008); cf. Lanzendörfer in this vol., 395-401.

3. Racism as Propaganda (docs. 275, 282-6, 290)
   The assumed right of slaveholding states to break away from the Union is thwarted through the Unionist war effort, including more than 200,000 Africamerican soldiers. As a result, assumed racial supremacy turns into open racial hatred. Lack of political competence and acumen aggravate the situation.

4. Interracial Visions (docs. 279, 281, 284, 287)
   Note the interracial imagery in the vignettes as well as in the center of the 1870 *Frank Leslie's* drawing (doc. 279). However, Frederick Douglass's assumption that a new, hybrid race was already on its way to replace the black-white binary that ruled the country was thwarted less than ten years after his visionary speech by the Supreme Court's ruling on segregation, which established legal apartheid for more than half a century.

II. Comparison – Contrasts – Connections

Example: Docs. 262, 270-2, 282, 309

The pleading posture of a loin-clothed Africamerican slave in chains was very much a standard format by which abolitionists tried to support their claim to freedom for the slave – it was not, however, understood by all as a simultaneous claim to anything like equality (cf. Fritsch in this vol., 354). The posture of the slave returned in Civil War monuments; they show Lincoln redeeming the slave, but the Africamerican is still portrayed in a kneeling position. To show Africamericans as standing in their own right was still the exception rather than the rule – one of the exceptions being Thomas Nast's cartoon of October 1876 (doc. 282). In this image, Nast not only depicts unoffending Africamerican men, women, and children as murder victims, symbolically strewing them about a war-torn landscape of destroyed Africamerican homes and school houses. He also uses the tool of a public newspaper to bring to mind the propaganda of the then on-going political campaign of 1876. Among the texts shown in the illustration are what might still be called expressions of political opinion ("Evidently it needs a Democratic administration in the South to keep the Negro in his proper place"), but the range also includes blunt coercion ("We, the white people, are able and ready to protect all of your race who choose to vote for Democrats. We make no threats but we do claim that South Carolina belongs to her native sons, and by the eternal God we intend to have it," attributed to the former Confederate general Wade Hampton, from 1876 on governor of South Carolina) and direct threats of physical violence ("Gen. Gary said 'that he intended to carry the election, or he would fill every street in Edgefield with dead negroes'"). The texts also include open challenges and defiance of the Federal army (in the statement attributed to the *Reformed Solid South* platform at the Democratic Ratification Meeting in Columbia, South Carolina, on August 18: "Put out of the way the white Republicans first, then the mulattoes and then the negroes. – We do not fear the United States Army: We met it once without blenching and we are ready to do it again").

In the face of all this, Nast sends a double message. The half-naked Africamerican wielding a gun not only defends his freedom against murderous white "redeemers," "red shirts," hooded Ku Klux Klan-riders and the likes; he is also an image of danger, an armed giant on the loose. The image quotes not only the kneeling "man and brother" from whom the powerfully built Africamerican has evidently emancipated himself, it also makes reference to the "bloody shirt" that abolitionists used to wave to denounce slavery. Note, however, that the shirt is not being waved here. Instead, the giant – whose shirt it may be, given that he is undressed to his belt – steps on and over the shirt as he cocks his rifle. This three-band military issue rifle as well as the cartridge box hanging from his belt make another, somewhat oblique, reference to the 200,000 Africamericans who had served in the war to fight for their own freedom and who, Nast suggests, may be ready to fight again.

Historically, this was not the case. Having returned to their former homes in the South, many Africamerican veterans found that it was better not even to mention their service in the Union armies, even if this meant to vote Democrat and be a "loyal darkey" in public, while drawing a Federal pension:

> Lt. Hicks sent Charles Hicks home to central Georgia in the summer of 1864 [...]. In December 1864, Charles Hicks joined the 110th Colored Volunteer Infantry of the Union Army as Charles Page, government records show. He was discharged in February 1866 and he returned to Georgia to began [sic] life as a farmer under his real name. He applied for and received a pension as a Union veteran. But when he attended the 75th reunion of Gettysburg veterans in 1938, he registered as Confederate. (Anon. 1997, n. pag.)[9]

The other problem, that of wage slavery, which had been amply used by slave owners to defend their 'peculiar institution' before 1865, survived the war, too. It had been one of the main contentions of slave owners that theirs was a system of paternalistic care-taking rather than an economy based on exploitation (cf. Fritsch in this vol., 355).[10] The war over and the financial losses of emancipation written off, Southern plantation and factory owners found that the system of wage labor and of tenant farming actually held certain financial advantages compared to chattel slavery. In "Monopoly Is the Master," a musing Mary Elizabeth Lease marvels at what to her seemed inconsistencies:

> We fought England for our liberty and put chains on four millions of blacks. We wiped out slavery and by our tariff laws and national banks began a system of white

---

[9] Thanks to Sir Ian Campbell for sending this newspaper clipping to the author.
[10] D. W. Griffith's movie *The Birth of a Nation* (1915) adheres to this image, and is directly based on document 271 in configuration, tone, and even in the observance of dress codes of the figures.

wage slavery worse than the first. [...] The great common people of this country are slaves, and monopoly is the master. (*KC*, 696)

While part of this statement is correct, the rest is not: Slavery predated the War of Independence, and continued to exist afterwards. Slavery was not exactly wiped out, but in many places replaced by a system of tenant farming that bordered on peonage. And the overall domination of capital gain over ethical gain had been the predominant ruling force within the American economical system from the days of the Puritans. While the slaves were fighting for their freedom, and later for equality, early socialists in the post-war Gilded Age fought for a greater share of the spoils, and the anarchists for another abolition – that of the system itself. The response at the hands of a re-united white protestant America was the same throughout. Whatever and whoever the hegemonial system and its minions perceived of as "other" was met by coercion, oppression, violence, arson, and assassination, including judicial murder (cf. docs. 303, 306).

III. Reading and Discussion Questions

1. Discuss the development from political quarrels over issues of states' rights to open warfare.
2. Evaluate the roles of Abraham Lincoln and Frederick Douglass as apparent from their speeches and addresses in the anthology.
3. How could the interracial tensions and the century of undeclared war in the US have been avoided?

IV. Resources

a. Recommended Reading

David W. Blight. *Race and Reunion: The Civil War in American Memory*. Harvard: Belknap Press, 2001. Starts where McPherson leaves off, and provides the most comprehensive view of the aftermath of the Civil War. The focus on the question of race does block other important aspects on occasions, but the deconstruction of the mythology of reunion and the Lost Cause is thorough and encompassing.

Ken Burns and Geoffrey Ward. *The Civil War*. 10 videocassettes. PBS, 1990. Very popular in the 1990s, with regular re-runs in North America as well as in Germany. Technical basis is the skillful use of period photographs and stills, original documents, and scholars' opinions. Good to support study in the classroom, and to introduce issues, though the range of themes is limited, and issues are usually personalized.

Alice Fahs and Joan Waugh, eds. *The Memory of the Civil War in American Culture*. Chapel Hill: University of North Carolina Press, 2004. Excellent collection of papers focusing on various aspects of public and private cultural memories of the war, from the memoirs of Ulysses S. Grant, via children's literature, to the solid entrenchment of the Southern 'Cause' literature, from the works of war veterans to academic apologists of the South.

Shelby Foote. *The Civil War: A Narrative*. 3 vols. New York: Random House, 1958-74. This huge historical narrative is probably the most influential re-telling of the Civil War. With its focus on battles and leaders, and its tendency to personalize history, it is both a continuation of the traditional format of the 1880s *Century Magazine* series (later republished as *Battles and Leaders of the Civil War*) and anticipated Ken Burns's PBS series, in which Shelby Foote has numerous appearances as an expert.

James M. McPherson. *The Battle Cry of Freedom*. New York: Ballantine, 1988. This is the most accessible one-volume history of the war to date. The events leading up to it are given more room than in comparable publications, at the expense of the military history – a beneficial decision.

b. Works Cited and Reading Suggestions

Ailliot, Patrick (1991). "Une tache sur le drapeau: Le traitement des soldats noirs par les confédérés." *Le Courrier de la Guerre d'Amérique* 50, 25-38.

Anon. (1997). "Confederate Soldier to be Honored on Union Monument." *Atlanta Constitution*, n. p.

Bailey, Fred Arthur (1991). "The Textbooks of the 'Lost Cause': Censorship and the Creation of Southern State Histories." *Georgia Historical Quarterly* 75.3, 507-533.

Barney, William L. (1980). *Flawed Victory: A New Perspective on the Civil War*. Boston: University Press of America.

Blight, David W. (2001). *Race and Reunion: The Civil War in American Memory*. Harvard: Belknap Press.

Burns, Ken, and Geoffrey Ward (1990). *The Civil War*. 10 videocassettes. PBS.

Connelly, Thomas, and Barbara L. Bellows (1982). *God and General Longstreet: The Lost Cause and the Southern Mind*. Baton Rouge: Louisiana State University Press.

Fahs, Alice, and Joan Waugh, eds. (2004). *The Memory of the Civil War in American Culture*. Chapel Hill: University of North Carolina Press.

Fleetwood, Christian A. (1895). *The Negro as a Soldier: Written by Christian A. Fleetwood, Late Sergeant-major 4th U.S. Colored Troops, for the Negro Congress, at the Cotton States and International Exposition, Atlanta, Ga., November 11 to November 23, 1895*. Washington: Howard University Print. <http://www.medalofhonor.com/TheNegroAsASoldierFleetwood.htm> (6 March 2008).

Foote, Shelby (1958-1974). *The Civil War: A Narrative.* 3 vols. New York: Random House.
Gallagher, Gary W., and Alan T. Nolan., eds. (2000). *The Myth of the Lost Cause and Civil War History.* Bloomington: Indiana University Press.
Gispen, Kees, ed. (1990). *What Made the South Different?* Jackson: University Press of Mississippi.
Goetsch, Paul (2001). "Lincolns Gettysburg Address als 'Testament der nationalen Identität.'" *Geschichtsbilder und Gründungsmythen.* Ed. Joachim Gehrke. Würzburg: Ergon, 245-261.
Griffith, David W. (1991). *The Birth of a Nation or The Clansman.* Adapt. from the *Novels of Thomas Dixon.* 1915. Videocassette. Republic Pictures Home Video.
Grimsley, Mark (1995). *The Hard Hand of War: Union Military Policy Toward Southern Civilians, 1861-1865.* Cambridge: Cambridge University Press.
Hammett, Hugh B. (1974). "Reconstruction History Before Dunning: Hilary Herbert and the South's Victory of the Books." *Alabama Review* 27.3, 185-196.
Hollandsworth, James G. jr. (1994). "The Execution of White Officers From Black Units by Confederate Forces During the Civil War." *Louisiana History* 35, 475-489.
Horwitz, Tony (1998). *Confederates in the Attic: Dispatches from the Unfinished Civil War.* New York: Pantheon Books.
Lincoln, Abraham (1953). "To Horace Greeley." 22 August 1862. *The Collected Works of Abraham Lincoln.* Vol. 5: *1861-1862.* Ed. Roy P. Basler. New Brunswick: Rutgers University Press, 388-389.
Marx, Karl, and Friedrich Engels (1976). *Der Bürgerkrieg in den Vereinigten Staaten.* 1861. Ed. Günter Wisotzki and Manfred Tetzel. Berlin: Dietz.
McPherson, James M. (1988). *The Battle Cry of Freedom.* New York: Ballantine.
Murphy, Richard W. (1987). *The Nation Reunited: War's Aftermath.* The Civil War Series 20. Alexandria: Time-Life Books.
Oakes, James (2007). *The Radical and the Republican: Frederick Douglass, Abraham Lincoln, and the Triumph of Antislavery Politics.* New York: Norton.
Pollard, Edward A. (1994). *The Lost Cause.* 1866. Ed. Stefan Dziemianowicz. New York: Gramercy Books.
Pressly, Thomas J. (1954). *Americans Interpret Their Civil War.* Princeton: Princeton University Press.
Schooler, Lynn (2005). *The Last Shot: The Incredible Story of the CSS Shenandoah and the True Conclusion of the Civil War.* New York: HarperCollins.
Stevens, William O. (1940). *Pistols at Ten Paces: The Story of the Code of Honor in America.* Boston: Houghton Mifflin.
Suderow, Bryce A. (1997). "The Battle of the Crater: The Civil War's Worst Massacre." *Civil War History* 43.3, 219-224.
Tourgée, Albion W. (1888). *The Veteran and His Pipe.* Chicago: Belford Clarke.
Wills, Garry (1992). *Lincoln at Gettysburg: The Words That Remade America.* New York: Simon and Schuster.

Wilson, Charles Reagan (1974). "The Religion of the Lost Cause." *Myth and Southern History*. Vol. 1: *The Old South*. Ed. Patrick Gerster and Nicholas Cords. Chicago: Rand McNally, 169-189.

Wyatt-Brown, Bertram (1982). *Southern Honor: Ethics and Behavior in the Old South*. New York: Oxford University Press.

Zuczek, Richard (1996). "The Last Campaign of the Civil War: South Carolina and the Revolution of 1876." *Civil War History* 42.1, 18-31.

Tim Lanzendörfer

The Gilded Age:
The Emergence of Modern America

> This association of poverty with progress is the great enigma of our times. It is the central fact from which spring industrial, social, and political difficulties that perplex the world, and with which statesmanship and philanthropy and education grapple in vain. From it come the clouds that overhang the future of the most progressive and self-reliant nations. It is the riddle which the Sphinx of Fate puts to our civilization and which not to answer is to be destroyed. So long as all the increased wealth which modern progress brings goes to build up great fortunes, to increase luxury and make sharper the contrast between the House of Have and the House of Want, progress is not real and cannot be permanent.
>
> Henry George (1973, 10)

I. Themes and Arguments

In 1874, Mark Twain and Charles Dudley Warner published their novel *The Gilded Age: A Tale of Today*, a book that satirized American politics. It featured, among other things, corruption, greed, and industrialists who, under the guise of public welfare, worked the system to their benefit, and their benefit alone. In its description of the time, it seemed so apt that it later gave a period its name: the period between the end of Reconstruction in 1877 and the beginning of the progressive era, generally dated from the beginning of Theodore Roosevelt's presidency in 1901. Twain and Warner could not have foreseen how their term would be used to describe an age in which all outer indicators of national wealth, from population to industrial output and net wages, grew steadily, sometimes astoundingly, while, beneath the surface, popular discontent with topics as diverse as immigration, economic and political equality, and fears for the future prosperity of the nation became ever more powerful.

The varied concerns of the Gilded Age are the topic of the anthology's final section, and their very diversity can make it difficult to understand how American culture developed in those years. From the hopes of future prosperity that stood at the conclusion of the first century of American independence (cf. doc. 291), the selection of texts moves through the social problems of overcrowded cities with their increasing population of poor migrant workers (cf. docs. 294-8). Social Darwinist arguments and the socialist response to them are vital for the understanding of the increasingly violent relations between the social classes as the Gilded Age progressed, as are the influences of philanthropy (cf. docs. 299-310). Immigration, too, was seen from varied perspectives throughout the era, with opponents of further unlimited immigration becoming increasingly vocal and successful in their effort to curb specifically the influx from Asia (cf. docs. 312-6). The closing of the frontier and the growing trend towards expansion of American trade and territory into the Pacific rounds off the volume and brings it to the fringes of the progressive era (cf. docs. 317-22).

To understand the problems of the Gilded Age, it is necessary to tie in the historical developments, specifically the economic events, of the years 1873 to 1901 with the primary sources provided in the anthology. William M. Evarts's "Oration" (doc. 291) will provide a frame for the exploration of the different key concepts that this essay will attempt to illuminate. Evarts's Fourth of July oration of 1876 stands near the beginning of the Gilded Age. It is suffused with the cheerful message appropriate for such public commemorations and exemplifies the positive outlook prevalent in its time, at least among the upper classes. Evarts, "with a lover's enthusiasm for [his] country," sees the nation at the end of a "preparatory growth" and settled into "responsible development of character and the steady performance of duty" (*KC*, 654). Indeed, as Maureen Flanagan points out, "[f]or many Americans in 1876, their world seemed a wonderful place [...]. The future, it seemed, held nothing but promise of ongoing progress" (2007, 1). According to Evarts, therefore, the "spirit of the nation is at the highest, – its triumph over the inborn, inbred perils of the Constitution has chased away all fears [and] justified all hopes" (*KC*, 653), but, as events would show, the future did not hold in store what Evarts envisioned for the nation. This essay will look at the particulars of Evarts's oration to see why his own hopes and estimations were not justified, and how the Gilded Age was overshadowed by many unsolved problems at home and abroad.

II. Social Struggles: Industrialization, Wealth, and Socialism

William M. Evarts's Fourth of July oration of 1876 (three years into the first postwar depression) was pronouncedly hopeful where social issues were concerned: The last years had proven "the general congruity of our social and civil institutions with the happiness and prosperity of man" (*KC*, 653). As it turned out, both the almost non-existent social institutions as well as the civil institutions, the government and courts, would find it increasingly difficult to cope with the problems of Gilded Age society. Evarts's firm belief that "[e]ven the public discontents [...] ache with anxieties and throb with griefs which have no meaner scope than the honor and the safety of the nation" soon proved mistaken (*KC*, 653): the nation's honor and safety took a backseat to the more immediate, essential problems of finding work, homes, and a prosperous future in a rapidly changing society.

No other factor so profoundly altered the relationship between rich and poor, labor and capital, as the industrial revolution. America's industrial growth was a phenomenon of the years after the Civil War. Although industry had existed, mainly in the North, prior to and during the Civil War, and the number of factories had increased between 1860 and 1870 by 80 percent (cf. Raeithel 1988, 45), it was the boom that American industry experienced in the post-war decades that pushed it from a marginal industrial power to world leadership (cf. Cashman 1984, 12). A major factor for the rapid transformation of the American industrial landscape was the growth of the railroad system, for whose financiers the nickname "robber barons" was coined. Most of them were businessmen like Cornelius Vanderbilt, who had made their fortune in the Civil War and now strove to invest their money in the business that was most likely to render them the greatest possible profit. "The coming of the big business was the most disturbing side of the new American economy," Glenn Porter notes (2007, 18). In the beginning were the railroads, America's lifelines and the most visible symbols of national unity. "The railroads broke new ground in several respects. Not only did they represent and require unprecedentedly large pools of capital that called forth investment banking and the modern stock market" (Porter 2007, 20), they were also the first national corporations who found themselves in actual competition with one another – leading to the unsavory installation of various schemes for sharing markets such as pools, cooperative schemes that allowed railroads to work unimpeded in different markets, and later trusts and monopolies (cf. Porter 2007, 20-1). "Business monopolies were the inextinguishable flame of economic life in the Gilded Age," Sean Cashman writes (1984, 47). Indeed, they were both life force and incalculable risk to the economy, as well as a serious point of contention for those for whom the monopolies seemed like vampires on the people's throats (cf. the illustration "The Commercial Vampire," doc. 305). Larger monopolies and pools were increasingly prone to overproduction, a problem that was worsened by the low money supply due to the tying of the dollar to the Gold Standard (cf. Trachtenberg 1982, 19, 39-40; Cashman 1984, 221-3; Porter 2007, 24). With little money in circulation and the cost of running machinery and producing goods lower than the costs of shutting down plants, industrialists preferred to lower workers' wages – when they were not simply let go for the duration of the repeated depressions. The monopolies, vertically integrated as they were and spanning the whole gamut from raw material extraction through the sale of manufactured goods, simply could not afford to stand still, but through their overproduction and the consequent deflation of the already scarce money supply, they aggravated an already precarious situation. Big business frequently "found it both possible and profitable to control market conditions" (LaFeber et al. 1992, 35), and at the same time had unprecedented control over their workers and the conditions in which they worked. Businesses asserted their rights to contract with laborers under any conditions they wished, founding their legal claims on the interpretation of the Fourteenth Amendment that had originally sought to liberate black slaves in the South.[1] But with the growing influx of cheap immigrant labor, defending corporations' right to contract for whatever "wages, hours, and working conditions" (Flanagan 2007, 59) they offered became essentially a blank check for abuse. Businesses, in the vast labor market, could pick those workers willing to work for minimal wages and minimal standards of work safety. As Henry George notes, workers' liberty was liable to become "merely the liberty to compete for employment at starvation wages" (*KC*, 672).

In this situation, "[t]he fruits of American prosperity were harvested mostly by elites," and since workers could not "expect succor from their political leaders[,] humbler Americans created their own paths to power" (Weir 2000, 11-3) and their own alternatives to the system that increasingly seemed to oppress the lower strata of society. It was industrialization and the subsequent closing, to most people, of the hitherto permeable barrier between those who worked for wages and those who employed them that figured as the major cause of the social problems from the 1870s up to the closing years of the Gilded Age (cf. Trachtenberg 1982, 75). It was true, as Theodore Roosevelt writes, quoting Abraham Lincoln, that "[c]apital is only the fruit of labor" (*KC*, 718). But for most people, the fruits of their labor began to look pitiful compared to the financial gains that the people at the top of corporations made. "[L]ocked into a wage system which offered small hope of release from toil" (Trachtenberg 1982, 77), the workers in American industries would have found little to agree with in William Evarts's oration. "[T]he preponderance of public over private, of social over selfish, tendencies and purposes in the whole body of the people, and the persistent fidelity to the genius and spirit of popular institutions [...], of the great men of the country" (*KC*, 653) was nearly invisible to those for whom "the fact and the perception of a widening class rift" meant that they faced, powerlessly, "wage cuts, extended layoffs and irregular employment, and worsening conditions, even starvation" (Trachtenberg 1982, 79, 39). The old American dream of farm ownership died during the Gilded Age: As early as 1870, 67 percent of gainfully occupied people in the US worked for wages (cf. Arnesen 2007, 56). "Let a man become the owner of a home, and he is much less susceptible to socialistic propagandism," Josiah Strong claimed (*KC*, 665), but failed to see the problem: wage-earners, tied to the cities and their industries, could never earn enough to own a home; and this fact alone helped to push many of them towards socialism. The gilt of increased wages – wages in all sectors of industry doubled during the Gilded Age (cf. LaFeber 1998, 14) – obscured the hard facts underneath: "[S]killed craft workers, most often native-born white men or immigrants

---

[1] The Fourteenth Amendment's due process clause was interpreted as giving employers and employees almost unlimited freedom in the terms of the contracts they concluded, without much scope for government regulation or control.

from England or Germany, reaped a disproportionate share of the benefits" (Arnesen 2007, 56). More than that, the public believed that those at the very top of the social pile, the robber barons, had used "special privilege rather than personal virtue [...] to transform abundant natural resources into a profitable preserve. Behind every great fortune was a crime" (Cashman 1984, 51). The growing gap between the richest and the poorest of society provided a fertile ground for the growth of socialist, anarchist, communist, and other societies, parties, or groups that were completely repugnant to employers.

By 1873, the upswing that had marked the American economy's fortunes since the end of the Civil War was showing obvious signs of stress. In April, the stock market in Vienna crashed, and the New York stock market followed suit in September, triggering an international depression. It was the first episode of a thirty-year cycle of upswings and violent downturns that saw increasingly volatile relations between labor and capital, starting with a railroad strike in 1877,[2] which was "the first instance of machine smashing and class violence on a national scale" in America (Trachtenberg 1982, 39). Its immediate cause was an unexpected and unannounced 10 percent pay cut for the workers, meant to stabilize profits, and the unrest it created tapped reservoirs of anger at the railroad companies that, spreading along the main railway trunk lines, soon engulfed railroaders from Baltimore to San Francisco. This anger, of course, had its origins precisely in the behavior of the robber barons that were their employers. While the heads of companies stood to gain enormous amounts of money, their employees, especially the laborers, were often reduced to extreme conditions.

The strike of the railroad workers, finally beaten down with the aid of Federal troops, cost over one hundred lives and millions of dollars in property losses. The severe depression that had started in 1873 did not begin to ease until 1878. In late 1873, 500,000 men had no work; 5,000 businesses had gone under in only three months. By 1877, three million people were out of work (cf. Trachtenberg 1982, 40; Cashman 1984, 33; Weir 2000, 12). By late 1878, the US economy had been severely disrupted, and more importantly, the relationship between the government, whose troops had violently beaten down the railroad strike, the corporations, and their workers had sustained serious damage: "[T]he memory of 'the insurrection', which both the president and the New York Tribune called the strike, lingered on, serving as a wake-up call to politicians, economic elites, and workers alike" (Arnesen 2007, 54).

Recognizing the "elements of universality in the problems [they] faced" (Montgomery 1980, 203) and their individual inability to improve their status, workers saw themselves increasingly pushed into organizations that could lend their grievances and hopes more weight. One of the most important movements, the Knights of Labor, exemplified a desire for a "moral repudiation of the egotism

---

[2] Depending on the source and its estimation, as many as four "major depressions struck [in] 1873-74, 1877-78, 1884, and 1893-97" (Weir 2007, 12).

which that system spawned and acclaimed" (Montgomery 1980, 204): Through the "thorough unification of labor," the Knights wanted to "mak[e] knowledge a standpoint for action, and industrial and moral worth, not wealth, the true standard of individual and national greatness" (*KC*, 681). The Knights of Labor's 1878 *Constitution* (doc. 302) "submit[s] to the world" its object, much like the Declaration of Independence submitted its reasons for separation; and when contrasted with later labor manifestos, the whole program the Knights suggest is a remarkably constrained effort to make reasonable claims. It calls for assistance

> [t]o secure to the toilers a proper share of the wealth that they create; more of the leisure that rightfully belongs to them; more societal advantages; more of the benefits, privileges, and emoluments of the world; in a word, all those rights and privileges necessary to make them capable of enjoying, appreciating, defending, and perpetuating the blessings of good government. (*KC*, 681)

David Montgomery calls the Knights' stance and their claims a "moral universality amid the particularities of the workers' daily sectoral struggles" (1980, 203). The *Constitution* seeks to place "a check" upon the power of "aggregated wealth" and upon "unjust accumulation" (*KC*, 681), but it does not deny that there is such a thing as a just accumulation of wealth. Still, "[a]s 'reformist' as many of [the Knights of Labor's] goals sound today, they directly challenged the dominant business creed of the Gilded Age, which staunchly upheld laissez-faire economics" (Arnesen 2007, 62). Moreover, as the 1880s began, the humble demands of the Knights of Labor were increasingly superseded in the public perception by the more vigorous and extreme socialist and anarchist ideas that, at least in writing, seemed to threaten the very substance of the republic.

The early 1880s saw an increasingly violent approach to the labor question, in which more extreme statements became possible, such as "[t]he political institutions of our time are the agencies of the propertied class; their mission is the upholding of the privileges of their masters" (*KC*, 684). The 1883 call "To the Workingmen of America" (doc. 303) did away with the reformist approach that the Knights of Labor hoped to apply to the problem. Where the Knights had hoped to curb only the "unjust accumulation" of wealth and to reform the system by "prevailing upon governments" (*KC*, 682), the authors of "To the Workingmen" believed the capitalists were "plundering" the workers. The manifesto called for "[a]gitation for the purpose of organization; organization for the purpose of rebellion" (*KC*, 683). In due course, the Knights of Labor grew more radical themselves, their positions shifting from the reformist stance of the late 1870s to a revolutionary one in the mid-1880s. Eric Arnesen stresses that "[b]y the 1880s dependent workers were confronting increasingly powerful employers who seemed to exercise tremendous political influence[,] a state protective of private property, supportive of business interests, and hostile to labor's basic demands" (2007, 63). Combined with the memory of the government's use of force in suppressing the 1877 railroad strike, the situation seemed to question "the very meaning of America" in the minds of many (Arnesen 2007, 64).

The increased militancy of the labor movement, however, did not serve it well. Seemingly confirming the worst fears of such writers as William Graham Sumner, who feared the socialist ideals of some elements of the labor movement would "destroy civilization" (*KC*, 679), the authors of the pamphlet "To the Workingmen," with their open call for revolution and violence, were the obvious targets for retribution in the wake of the Haymarket events. In May 1886, while laborers demonstrated their support for a strike in favor of the eight-hour day, a bomb exploded in Chicago's Haymarket Square, killing and wounding bystanders and policemen. Without evidence, the police blamed the city's anarchist leaders (cf. Arnesen 2007, 64). Put on trial, August Spies, one of the authors of "To the Workingmen," put forward a spirited defense that linked socialism and anarchism (doc. 306). Denying the validity of the charges against him, Spies recapitulates the principles on which "To the Workingmen" had been based. He argues that "the ruling classes of today would no more listen to the voice of reason than their predecessors; that they would attempt by brute force to stay the wheels of progress" (*KC*, 689). That progress, however, will eventually lead to socialism, which "teaches that the machines, the means of transportation and communication are the result of the combined efforts of society [and therefore] rightfully the indivisible property of society." Spies's socialism as an economic system is paired with anarchism as a political one, in which "under economic equality and individual independence, the State will pass into barbaric antiquity. And we will be where all are free" (*KC*, 690). This envisioned anarchism was a serious threat to men like Andrew Carnegie, for whom the system as it stood was the best guarantee of prosperity, and it was a threat they were well aware of: "The Socialist and Anarchist who seeks to overturn present conditions is to be regarded as attacking the foundation upon which civilization itself rests" (*KC*, 693).

Both sides obviously feared the other's readiness to resort to violence, and indeed suspected each other of it. Spies's acknowledgment that "[i]f I had thrown that bomb [...,] I would not hesitate a moment to say so" is justified by yet another reference to the Declaration of Independence. Spies cites the passage "'[b]ut when a long train of abuses and usurpations [...] evinces a design to reduce the people under absolute despotism'" (*KC*, 691), to justify the anarchists' violent behavior by drawing a parallel to the revolutionary ideals of the Founding Fathers.

Many of the documents in the "Gilded Age" section of the anthology show the different reality to which especially the economic elites and workers awoke in the aftermath of the first depression and the first strikes, and how they interpreted their station and their prospects in a changing society. Under the conditions of widely fluctuating markets, insecure employment status for most unskilled and many skilled workers, with a growing social gap and, through immigration, an increase in the number of workers competing for jobs, it is not surprising that both sides, employers and laborers, found it necessary to publicize and explain their views on the issue. In their rhetorical strategies and arguments, they make use of historically effective topoi, especially Revolutionary War rhetoric (cf. Hurm in this vol., 192-7), as well as more current scientific and sociological concepts.

Some authors, like William Graham Sumner in "The Challenge of Facts" (doc. 299), sought to explain the stratification of society in terms of a then-new approach to sociology, social Darwinism, and to invalidate the theses of socialists. Applying the tenets of Charles Darwin's theory of evolution to the interplay between human societies and between individuals, social Darwinism sought to explain social success by "Darwinian concepts of struggle for existence, natural selection, and survival of the fittest" (Bannister 1979, 7) and "gave the patina of science and modernity to feelings that were unscientific and ahistorical" (LaFeber 1993, 44). Sumner's view of social struggle is a complex one. Man's life is first and foremost a "struggle against nature," whose gifts must be extracted by labor:

> Nature holds what is essential to him, but she offers nothing gratuitously. He may win for his use what she holds, if he can. Only the most meager and inadequate supply for human needs can be obtained directly from nature. There are trees which may be used for fuel and for dwellings, but labor is required to fit them for this use. There are ores in the ground, but labor is necessary to get out the metals and make tools or weapons. For any real satisfaction, labor is necessary to fit the products of nature for human use. In this struggle every individual is under the pressure of the necessities for food, clothing, shelter, fuel, and every individual brings with him more or less energy for the conflict necessary to supply his needs. The relation, therefore, between each man's needs and each man's energy, or "individualism," is that first fact of human life. [...]
>
> So far as I have yet spoken, we have before us the struggle of man with nature, but the social problems, strictly speaking, arise at the next step. Each man carries on the struggle to win his support for himself, but there are others by his side engaged in the same struggle. (*KC*, 675)

According to Sumner, socialism is a violation of natural order: "Competition, therefore, is a law of nature. [...] We can take the rewards from those who have done better and give them to those who have done worse [... but thereby w]e shall favor the survival of the unfittest." It is also a violation of republican liberties, the "guarantees of law that a man shall not be interfered with while using his own powers for his own welfare" (*KC*, 676).

Sumner becomes most interesting as a social theoretician when he undermines the basic creeds of American republicanism: "The notion of natural rights is destitute of sense, but it is captivating [...]. It lends itself to the most vicious kind of social dogmatism, for if a man has natural rights, then the reasoning is clear up to the finished socialistic doctrine that a man has a natural right to whatever he needs" (*KC*, 677). Sumner's rhetorical strategy here is to invalidate the claim that the labor movement's efforts at socialism are in a continuous line with revolutionary ideals. Lockean natural rights, which had so decisively informed the Declaration of Independence, no longer hold value for Sumner. He appeals to "the laws of nature," and suggests that it is the central failing of socialists not to have done so as well: "[T]hey assumed that they could organize society as they chose," instead of submitting to the natural laws that made "the social order [...] fixed [...] precisely analogous to those of the physical order" (*KC*, 678).

The theory of social Darwinism is taken up and discussed by two further texts in the anthology, Andrew Carnegie's "Wealth" (doc. 308) and Henry George's *Progress and Poverty* (doc. 298). Whereas George challenges the concept of social Darwinism as a whole, Carnegie's "Wealth" is an example of the responses that sought to provide answers to the nagging problems of the age without denying the validity of social Darwinism and of social stratification, even inequality. "It is well, nay, essential for the progress of the race," Carnegie argues, "that the houses of some should be homes for all that is highest and best in literature and the arts [...] rather than none should be so. Much better this great irregularity than universal squalor" (*KC*, 692). Carnegie agrees with Sumner that there is nothing to be done about the laws which govern human enterprise: "[W]hether the law be benign or not, we must say of it, as we say of the change in the conditions of men to which we have referred: It is here; we cannot evade it; [...] it is best for the race, because it insures the survival of the fittest in every department" (*KC*, 692). Competition inevitably leads to inequality, and competition is a law of nature. It is therefore inevitable that some men will end up with "more revenue" than others (*KC*, 693), and the problem of that additional revenue's use is the one that Andrew Carnegie tackles. This is already a significant departure from Sumner's stance, since Carnegie's concern for the "proper mode of administering wealth" (*KC*, 693) is a concern whose normative considerations are outside the scope of Sumner's individualist social Darwinism. After leaving wealth to either posterity or one's own offspring, Carnegie suggests that a man of "fortunes" (*KC*, 693) should "consider all surplus revenues which come to him simply as trust funds, which he is called upon to administer, and strictly bound as a matter of duty to administer in the manner which, in his judgment, is best calculated to produce the most beneficial results for the community" (*KC*, 694). Of course the wealthy man is himself best prepared to spend money for the benefit of the community, having, through his business acumen, acquired wealth in the first place and so proven his innate superiority, and Carnegie's charity is not a charity that gives to all in equal measure. Indeed, he asserts that "[i]t were better for mankind that the millions of the rich were thrown into the sea than so spent as to encourage the slothful, the drunken, the unworthy," so that in "bestowing charity, the main consideration should be to help those who will help themselves" (*KC*, 694-5). Aside from this almost blasphemous appropriation of biblical language, Carnegie believes that thus "is the problem of Rich and Poor to be solved [...]. Individualism will continue, but the millionaire will be but a trustee for the poor [...] administering it for the community far better than it could or would have done for itself" (*KC*, 695). Carnegie's stewardship over the well-being of society as a whole worked as his own personal philosophy, but it did not alleviate Gilded Age problems.

Those who were at the top of the social hierarchy almost naturally gravitated towards social Darwinism and were happy to justify their view of society by it, even if they found that they could not thereby justify social inaction. Those in the lower strata took an understandably dimmer view. In his *Progress and Poverty*, Henry George adapts the language of the Declaration of Independence to maintain that the rights to life, liberty, and the pursuit of happiness "are denied when the equal right to land [...] is denied" (*KC*, 672), and adopts a stance that is outdated at the time he writes. Land as the source of what had historically been known as a "competence," i.e., a sufficient income to live,[3] was no longer viable. George's belief that all men must "have liberty to avail themselves of the opportunities and means of life; they must stand on equal terms with reference to the bounty of nature" (*KC*, 673) seems to be close to Sumner's conception, but, in several respects, George is in opposition to Sumner. George believes social Darwinism to hold that "civilization is a development or evolution [...] by the operation of causes similar to those which are relied upon as explaining the genesis of species – viz., the survival of the fittest," while Sumner preferred to see it operating on the level of the individual. Consequently, when George claims that "[i]n allowing one man to own the land on which and from which other men must live, we have made them his bondsmen" (*KC*, 673), he sees true liberty denied. He thus believes the workings of social Darwinism disproved, as "liberty, when the equal right to land is denied, becomes [...] merely the liberty to compete for employment at starvation wages" (*KC*, 672). The removal of liberties previously granted would mean a regression into a previous state of civilization, an impossibility under the tenets of social Darwinism. Therefore, "nothing could be further from explaining the facts of universal history than this theory that civilization is the result of a course of natural selection which operates to improve and elevate the powers of man" (*KC*, 670).

Sumner's reply to this contention is that "[t]he more we break down privileges of class, or industry, and establish liberty, the greater will be the inequalities and the more exclusively will the vicious bear the penalties" (*KC*, 676). It is a striking denial of the call for liberty that the Declaration of Independence put forth, and a good example of why revolutionary rhetoric and its terms could so easily be adopted by both sides. The "liberty" Sumner denies here is manifestly George's liberty, not the "[l]iberty [which] means the security given to each man that, if he employs his energies to sustain the struggle on behalf of himself and those he cares for, he shall dispose of the product exclusively as he chooses" (*KC*, 675). Sumner's liberty is a liberty in opposition to socialism, whereas George's liberty, which Sumner picks up in his denial, is the citizen's liberty to "stand on equal terms with reference to the bounty of nature" (*KC*, 673). It is a liberty not of equal rights, but of equal substance. Taking recourse to the language and the content of the Declaration of Independence and its primary

---

[3] Carnegie himself still used the term in his "Wealth."

author Jefferson was a popular tactic for both sides of the conflict, because its sentiments were sufficiently vague and universal to be applied to almost any program. Thus, arguments as different as Sumner's social Darwinist defense of inequality, George's anti-social Darwinist call for equality, the Knights of Labor's progressivist and reformist approach, the communist manifesto of "To the Workingmen," and August Spies's anarchist self-defense could all allude to and adapt the ideas of the Declaration in order to further their particular agendas.

III. Immigration

Industrialization and the resulting social struggles were not the only prominent issues, however. Immigration and race relations were topics of discussion, too, and two documents in the anthology speak to the optimistic belief that racial issues, after the end of the Civil War and the passing of the Fourteenth and Fifteenth Amendments, were no longer contentious matters.[4] William Evarts's oration appraises both the new race relations and gives an historical evaluation. The "converging streams of immigration" made up of people who "came by choice and for greater liberty," Evarts argues, have been "knit together" and animated by the "spirit of the nation" (*KC*, 652-3). Evarts believes that immigration is an admirable feature of the nation, ultimately proving the strength of American political and social institutions, that "if we consider further the variety and magnitude of foreign elements to which we have been hospitable, and their ready fusion with the earlier stocks, we have new evidence of strength and vivid force in our population" (*KC*, 653).

Meanwhile, Thomas Nast's 1869 cartoon "Uncle Sam's Thanksgiving Dinner" (doc. 312) shows an idyllic image of the new post-war American society.[5] Under the steady and benevolent gaze of Presidents Grant, Lincoln, and Washington, the members of an imagined American family are gathered around a common, food-filled table, on which the twin bedrocks of universal suffrage and self-government support a classical temple of liberty that is reminiscent of Early Republic representative buildings, such as the White House and Capitol, and intended to mirror republican virtues. A part of the wall hangings are drapes containing the words "Fifteenth Amendment" and a picture with the legend "Welcome [...] Castle [...] Garden." Protected in America's castle and provided for by its gardens, the mixed community of whites, blacks, Natives, Chinese, and other nationalities reveals, in its depiction of the different cultures and races, much about the lingering stereotypes. However, it also illustrates the cheerful vi-

---

[4] The Fourteenth Amendment provided for the citizenship of "[a]ll persons born or naturalized in the United States" without reference to race, whereas the Fifteenth Amendment declared that the right to vote could not be "abridged [...] on account of race, color, or previous condition of servitude" (in Commager 1949, 147-8). Together, both amendments seemed to establish a racial equality that, post-Reconstruction, failed to materialize.

[5] A large-scale reproduction of the image can be found on the anthology's web site.

sion of the future that Nast had at this time, when the Amendments, the momentary subduing of Southern reaction during the Reconstruction, and the postwar economic boom seemed to have quelled all sources of intra-societal strife. Both documents, one in words, the other in images, affirm the traditional view of America as an immigrant-friendly society and hold out high hopes for the continuation of this tradition.

According to Roger Daniels, the Gilded Age is characterized by a great increase in the number of immigrants. Furthermore, he sees "a decided shift in [immigration's] sources and composition" that ultimately led to "the beginning of its effective restriction" (2007, 76). Immigration figures varied greatly over the course of the Gilded Age, their tendencies coinciding with the upswings and downturns of the economy,[6] so that "[m]ajor economic downturns in the United States soon resulted in lower levels of immigration" (Daniels 2007, 85).[7] Percentage-wise, the majority of the immigrants were still of those nationalities that had previously made up the larger part of new arrivals in the United States: mainly Germans, British, Irish and Scandinavians, contributing about two-thirds of all immigrants. But significantly, one third of the arrivals during the Gilded Age were natives of hitherto almost unrepresented cultures: Italians, Russians, Poles, and people of the heterogenous Austro-Hungarian empire (Carter 1997, C 89-119). It was primarily this new group of arrivals, and a group of even smaller numbers, the less than 200,000 Chinese that came to the United States between 1871 and 1901, that caused the severe outcry against immigration.[8]

---

[6] It is necessary to add a caution as to the figures provided here, and in fact most of the literature. Bernard Axelrod notes that "[t]he question to be considered is not how many immigrants came to this country but how many remained," a figure much more difficult to compute than the sheer number of new arrivals: "The difference between the total immigration (the accepted gain in population) and various estimates of the net immigration (the real gain in population) appears to be significant" (1972, 32). Quoting from an 1893 publication on arrivals and departures, Axelrod notes that real immigration gains are statistically about 16 percent lower than quoted in the historical statistics for the period from 1881 to 1890 (cf. 36). Since statistics for passenger departures from the United States only became available with the 1907 Immigration Act (cf. 38), it is very difficult to establish accurate net immigration figures. The figures used here are best seen as rough illustrations of overall trends.

[7] While between 1870 and 1873, prior to the first great post-Civil War depression, about 1.5 million immigrants reached the United States, in the five years of depression that followed, only about a million immigrants came. In the ten subsequent years, 1879 to 1889, 5.2 million immigrants arrived, and the numbers remained high until the next depression – between 1879 and 1894, only two years saw less than 400,000 immigrants, but after 1894 and to the end of the Gilded Age, immigration figures decreased slightly, with only 1900 and 1901 having more than 400,000 immigrants. Through the thirty years 1871 to 1901, over twelve million immigrants reached the United States – a nation that, in 1870, had only had about 40 million inhabitants (cf. Carter 1997, C 89-119, A 1-5).

[8] By numbers, immigration was primarily a concern of northern and Midwestern cities, from Boston to St. Louis. Almost every larger city between those two had a high percentage of non-native inhabitants: Indeed, "one-third of the population of the fifty-two American cities with

Immigration was a frequent concern throughout American history, largely connected with the idea of nativism, "a deep-seated American antipathy against internal 'foreign' groups of various kinds (national, cultural, religious), which has erupted periodically into intensive efforts to safeguard America from such perceived 'threats'" (Friedman 1967, 408). In the 1750s, the growing number of Pennsylvania Germans was felt to be a threat by English Pennsylvanians, including Benjamin Franklin, who feared a slow Germanization of the English heritage and a dulling of the pure white color of the English race. Legislative attempts to ban German immigration were, however, unsuccessful (cf. Friedman 1967, 412).

In the late 1840s and 1850s, larger numbers of Europeans immigrated to the United States, some because of economic reasons, such as the infamous Irish Potato Famine, some on political grounds, like the defeated revolutionaries of 1848. The perceived danger of the mass of new immigrants, combined with the demise of the Whig party, led to the formation of the Know-Nothing Party, which functioned as a secret society until the elections of 1854. Its members "believed in limiting Catholic and immigrant influence in the United States, blamed immigrants for the declines in income and status of American workingmen, and were antagonistic to established political parties. Violence was frequently associated with the party's activities," as Cohn notes (2000, 363), and it considered "only native-born Protestants [...] fit to hold political office." Even "[m]ost Know-Nothings," however, did "not [favor] a restriction on the volume of immigration" (Cohn 2000, 374). Interestingly enough, the combination of Know-Nothing political strength (over 70 members of the 1856/57 Congress belonged to the party) and the subsequent leniency towards anti-immigrant violence seems to have had a direct impact on immigration, which decreased during the second half of the 1850s. This ultimately made the Know-Nothing Party redundant and led to its demise: While the party had still fielded a Presidential candidate in 1856 (former President Millard Fillmore), it had passed out of the political arena by the 1860 Presidential election (cf. Cohn 2000, 374-80). The Know-Nothing Party's agitation against the Irish, the Germans, and Catholics in general, provides a first glimpse at some of the issues that played a role later on in the Gilded Age. While hostility towards Germans and Irish was no longer particularly prominent and shifted towards other immigrant groups, the reasons for nativist hostility remained the same, namely, their "otherness" in religion and complexion and their sameness in the search for scarce employment opportunities in a shifting economy. Indeed, the dedicated search for industrial jobs, instead of jobs in the agricultural sector, was one of the central features of the new immigration of the 1880s and 1890s. "More exclusively than most older immigrant groups, the new ones swarmed into the slums, the factories, and the mines," Higham notes, so that "[e]ither urbanites or industrial workers, and usually both, they played a

---

more than twenty-five thousand people" consisted of immigrants, with percentages ranging up to 40 percent in the largest cities such as New York and Chicago (Daniels 2007, 83).

role in American life that lend itself to nativist interpretation" (1993, 274). Living in ethnically delineated city districts, their apparent cohesion as a "class apart" made them the obvious targets of a renewed nativism in the 1890s, which, connecting race, social Darwinism, and nationalism, surfaced in many of the key documents of the time.

The concern with immigration that emerged during the Gilded Age, then, was not an entirely new phenomenon. Again and again in the debate on immigration, what James Phelan, San Francisco's turn-of-the-century mayor, called the "American question, affecting the perpetuity of our institutions and the standard of our civilization" (in Wong 1995, 6), was brought up to identify the main objections to continuing the policy of unlimited immigration. If "Come One, Come All," was the motto of Thomas Nast's cartoon (*KC*, 701), Josiah Strong's text "Perils – Immigration" (doc. 315) enumerates the reasons that detractors of free immigration saw for their beliefs. In this article, Strong compares the current waves of immigration hitting America with the historic invasions of the Goths and Vandals that led to the demise of Rome, thus referring back to the American self-understanding as heirs of Rome in the westward course of empire (cf. Hannemann in this vol., 221-5). Strong's military metaphors are then extended to the "advance guard of the mighty army" (*KC*, 703). Where William Evarts saw primarily the immigrant's easy inclusion into American society, Strong fears the "moral and political influence of immigration [...]. The typical immigrant," he argues, "is a European peasant, whose horizon has been narrow, whose moral and religious training has been meager or false, and whose ideas of life are low" (*KC*, 703). While Evarts stressed the knitting of the migrant streams into a coherent, American whole, Strong believes that "[n]o man is held upright by the strength of his own roots; his branches interlock with those of other men, and thus society is formed [...]. All this strength the emigrant leaves behind him" (*KC*, 703-4). He fears that new immigrants threaten the societal structure and laments that they are "sadly conspicuous in our criminal records" (*KC*, 704). However, the chief danger of immigration lies, in Strong's opinion, in its support for the political elements that run counter to the white Protestant American establishment that he implicitly considers genuinely American. Immigrants, by contrast, are "Americans [that] are not Americanized" yet, so that they may easily be manipulated by "demagogues" for their own political ends, for instance to support "the Mormon vote [...] the Catholic vote [... or] the Socialist vote" (*KC*, 704). Strong asserts that "[s]o immense a foreign element must have a profound influence on our national life and character" (*KC*, 703), and he believes this can only be a profoundly negative one. Immigration is equivalent to social vice in all its forms, whether it concerns personal behavior, as "affecting the morals of the native population" (*KC*, 704), a decline of national intelligence, or crime.

Of the various nationalities coming into the United States during the Gilded Age, the Chinese deserve special consideration. Although, as noted, only a miniscule percentage of immigrants actually were Chinese, not all of whom stayed permanently in the United States, the American reaction to this group of immigrants was much more negative than to the other ones; the reasons for this being both economic and racial. Chinese laborers came to the western port cities starting in the 1850s and found employment in manual labor such as railroad construction, farming, mining, and land-clearing. For US corporations and the US government, Chinese immigrants were a welcome source of cheap labor, especially for the construction of the Central Pacific Railroad. However, with the railroad complete and the general economic downturn of the mid-1870s setting in, public sentiment turned against what was called "coolie labor" (cf. Calavita 2000, 4). In due course, large numbers of Chinese migrated to the cities on the Pacific Coast, where they established businesses requiring low initial investments and a large labor force – the stereotypical laundries and restaurants. As Roger Daniels notes, some Chinese workers showed considerable entrepreneurial spirit, finding "unfilled spaces within the American economy and [filling] them" (2007, 85). But whether laborers or entrepreneurs, the Chinese population was quickly seen as detrimental to the whites, and opposition to Chinese settlement became vocal. Daniels points out that "[t]he Chinese, almost exclusively single males with a very low standard of living, did, in fact, consistently undercut prevailing wage scales" (Daniels and Black 1964, 114). At the same time, the Chinese were seen in terms of racial hostility. "Representations of the Chinese," writes Wong, "were often part of the larger racial and political agenda of promoting segregation and exclusion" (1995, 5). Even when segregated, however, the Chinese faced hostility. In 1876, during the California State Senate Hearings on Chinese Immigration, San Francisco Fire Marshal John L. Durkee commented:

> They [the Chinese] are within sight and hearing distance all around here, and very close to the business part of town. Property around here is constantly depreciating in value, because of the approach of the Chinese. The whites cannot stand their dirt and the fumes of opium, and are compelled to leave the vicinity. [...] Houses occupied by Chinese are not fit for white occupation, because of the filth and stench. Chinamen violate the fire ordinances, and unless we catch them in the act we cannot convict. [...] The only way I can account for our not having a great fire in the Chinese quarter is, that the wood is too filthy and too moist from nastiness to burn. It has too much dirt on it to catch fire. [...] They are more trouble than all the white people put together. (in Wong 1995, 5)

The creation of bonafide "Chinatowns" was the consequence of an effort on the part of those anti-Chinese groups which desired the elimination of the Chinese-American communities in the United States. They would, if they could not enforce removal, accept segregation, creating a situation where they would not have to take any interest in the Chinese nor have much of a relationship with them. The creation of Chinatowns occurred throughout the United States, but their existence was curiously contradictory. On the one hand, segregation allowed for control, especially over the movements of the Chinese immigrants. On the other hand, Chinatowns allowed Chinese to work within their own culture and traditions. In the common quest for racial and cultural purity, both the Chinese and the Americans assured each others' success (cf. Wong 1995, 3-11). Beyond economic reasons, it may have been this underlying irresolvable conflict between two societies that were equally determined not to integrate themselves, but whose different racial origins were clearly visible (unlike, for example, in the case of unintegrated Scandinavian settlers in the Midwest), that caused the comparative viciousness of anti-Chinese immigration campaigns.

The illustration *The Magic Washer – The Chinese Must Go* (doc. 316) gives an indication of the implicit acceptance of the Chinese as long as they benefited white Americans by filling their needs, in this case exemplified by the laundry business, but of course also applicable to the other occupations mostly filled by Chinese in California, i.e., mining and railroad working. This implicit tolerance, however, could easily be superseded by technological developments, such as the Magic Washer, or by the Chinese's own movement away from the tasks they were initially recruited for and into their own businesses. *The Magic Washer* takes up the slogan "The Chinese must GO!" that had been coined by the California anti-Chinese movement (cf. Daniels 2007, 90) and uses the symbolism of an oversized Uncle Sam kicking out the stereotypically-dressed and diminutive Chinese laborer onto a sailing junk that is supposed to carry him off to his home, represented by a setting sun with Asian features. The depiction of the Chinese in this cartoon affirms the racial superiority of the whites and extends it onto a symbolic level: Not only is it American ingenuity that has enabled the substitution of manual Chinese labor by the newly-invented Magic Washer, but both culturally, as exemplified by the traditional dress of the cartoon Chinese, as well as technologically, as exemplified by the sailing junk, Americans can affirm their progressiveness and superiority when contrasted with the Chinese.

Opposition to Chinese immigration was strongest, of course, in California, where the majority of Chinese lived (cf. Calavita 2000, 4). The efforts to curb Chinese immigration begun by the Californian government, part of which were the California Senate's hearings of 1876,[9] culminated in a US Senate comittee's finding in 1876 claiming that "there is not sufficient brain capacity in the Chinese race to furnish motive power for self-government. Upon the point of morals, there is no Aryan or European race which is not far superior to the Chinese" (in Calavita 2000, 4). On the "sound" basis of racial bias and economic concern, especially that of unions, grew the political will to exclude Chinese immigrants; not only in California, where an 1879 referendum saw 154,638 to 883 voters in favor of exclusion (cf. Daniels 2007, 91), but also in the entire United States. Nevertheless, it took until 1882 for Congress to pass, and the President to sign, a law prohibiting immigration of Chinese to the United States.

---

[9] The regulation of immigration had rested with the US Congress ever since the 1849 Passenger Cases, in which immigration was ruled part of "foreign commerce" and fell, therefore, under Congressional jurisdiction (cf. Daniels 2007, 89).

The dominantly economic purpose and justification of the Chinese Exclusion Act of 1882 (doc. 313) becomes immediately clear on a close reading of the document. It explicitly suspends "the coming of Chinese laborers" for ten years, under threat of penalty to "the master of any vessel who shall knowingly bring within the United States [...] any Chinese laborer." The penalties themselves were severe enough: Anyone judged guilty could expect "a fine of not more than five hundred dollars for each and every such Chinese laborer so brought, and may be also imprisoned for a term not exceeding one year" (*KC*, 702). The act defined Chinese laborers as "both skilled and unskilled laborers and Chinese employed in mining," and added that "hereafter no State court or court of the United States shall admit Chinese to citizenship" (in Commager 1949, 110-1). Like most other contentious issues in the Gilded Age, the line between supporters and detractors concerning the question of Chinese exclusion was drawn parallel to class lines. "Exclusion's key advocates," as Roger Daniels shows, "were workingmen, their allies, and politicians who needed their votes, while against it were chiefly the employers of labor" (2007, 90). Since workingmen saw the Chinese as competitors for unskilled industrial jobs, support for Chinese exclusion extended also to the labor unions that attempted to defend workers' interests.

The exclusion of Chinese laborers from the United States, in terms of numbers, was a modest enough success for the anti-immigration camp – at the time of the ban, there were perhaps 110,000 to 125,000 Chinese in the United States (cf. Daniels 2007, 91; Calavita 2000, 4). In the following ten years, Chinese immigration sank to about 10,000 but never to zero, thanks to various exception clauses in the Exclusion Act (cf. Carter 1997, C 89-119). But if the Chinese Exclusion Act did not affect a decisive part of the immigrants streaming into the country, it "was the hinge on which all American immigration policy turned" (Daniels 2007, 91). For the first time in its history, the United States had decisively limited the immigration of a group of people. Not even during the times of the Know-Nothings, when American nativism was strong enough to field a Presidential candidate, was political will sufficient to enact legislation. That it was powerful enough in 1882 probably owes to the labor unions' use of "the politics and rhetoric of race and culture" (Wong 1995, 6). The unions' use of the racial biases of the American population, as well as an increasing concern about America's status as a predominantly Anglo-Saxon, white, and Protestant society combined to pressure the US Congress into passing a law that ran counter to the principles of free immigration, which had previously dominated US policy.

IV. American Imperialism in the Gilded Age

"If foreign markets meant good instead of mediocre or poor profits for some industrialists, adequate markets abroad meant the difference between being solvent or bankrupt to many farmers," Walter LaFeber writes in his study *The New Empire* (1998, 10). If the changing nature of the economy decisively influenced the nature of the relationship between labor and business and the government and its people, it also influenced Americans' relations with the world at large. For three decades after the Mexican War (cf. Mackenthun in this vol., 251-3), Americans, absorbed by internal problems, had shown only limited interest in foreign affairs and commercial and territorial aggrandizement, although individuals like William H. Seward, Secretary of State under Lincoln and Johnson, aggressively advocated and even achieved territorial expansion. Besides Alaska in 1867, the United States acquired a number of small Pacific islands (cf. LaFeber 1994, 221), foremost among them Midway. By the middle of the Gilded Age, however, a new sentiment came to the fore, seeking to expand American influence throughout near and distant regions. Three principal justifications underlay this new striving for foreign opportunities: first, the new Manifest Destiny with its "unvarnished racism, its claim to scientific foundations," and its "dogma of Anglo-Saxon superiority" (De Conde 1963, 317-8). Second, the Christianizing mission that would yield a civilizing influence on the world, but especially a calming influence on the United States itself: Christianizing the world was seen by some, especially Josiah Strong, as a means of stabilizing the United States (cf. LaFeber 1998, 72-80). Finally, economic reasons played a decisive role in the American acquisition of new territory during the Gilded Age. With the closing of the frontier, claimed by Frederick Jackson Turner in 1893 (cf. doc. 185), "Americans [...] reacted in the classic manner of searching farther west for new frontiers, though primarily of a commercial, not landed, nature" (LaFeber 1998, 11). Indeed, economic reasons were almost always predominant in the shaping of US acquisitions abroad. Land was acquired for trade, and, although, as in the case of the Philippines, it may have been retained because of the presumed inability of the natives to govern themselves, markets for American products and produce were the primary goal for US expansion abroad.

None of the possible reasons for American expansion were foreseen by William Evarts. His America is already an "ample home for a nation" (*KC*, 653), and Americans are expected to find "scope for all [their] energies, rewards for all [their] ambitions, renown enough for all [their] love of fame" in peace and "its arts, its labors, and its victories" (*KC*, 654). Peace, however, was not the destiny of American foreign policy in the Gilded Age. One reason for the initial post-Civil War phase of territorial expansion was America's rapid economic growth. By the middle of the Civil War, the United States, even without the still-unconquered South, produced a large agricultural surplus, which was augmented even more by the growth of industry, transportation, and refrigeration in the course of the following twenty years. This was coupled with an industrial surplus, so that the demand of the home markets, with the frontier closed and no room for growth in sight, did not suffice to deal with the increase in supply (cf. Wehler 1982, 155-8). Of course, economic concerns "neither took precedence in nor dictated all Gilded Age foreign policy decisions, but over the thirty years after 1870 this objective was a consistent impetus toward a more assertive world view" (Fry 2007, 310). This world view was backed, like so many other Gilded Age theories, by social Darwinist ideas. Thus, when Josiah Strong, in "The Anglo-Saxon and the World's Future" (doc. 318), asserts that "the final competition of races, for which the Anglo-Saxon race is being schooled" is imminent, he goes on to argue that "'the survival of the fittest'" will inevitably lead to a "tremendous overbearing surge of power in the Christian nations, which, if the others are not speedily raised to some vastly higher capacity, will inevitably submerge and bury them forever" (KC, 709). Strong both prophesies and alarms: For him, speed is of the essence, unless in the inevitable struggle of races, others catch up to white, Western, Christian supremacy. "God [...] is preparing mankind to receive our impress" (KC, 710), he asserts, whether by the force of missionaries or the might of the entire American civilization: Indeed, Strong considers Americans to be especially suited to spread the Anglo-Saxon gospel, and especially needful of it. The spread of Christianity would necessarily be followed, he believes, by the victory of Western values – and, in turn, only if based on Christianity would American expansion prove possible. While Strong's vision of a common Anglo-Saxon dominance quickly ran into real world obstacles like Anglo-American conflicts over Venezuela, his ideas continued to exert an influence on the justification of US policies (cf. LaFeber 1998, 72-80, 100).

Arguments such as Strong's, which combined American exceptionalist ideas with the modern pseudo-science of social Darwinism, saw few actual results in policy formulation, especially at a time when a Democratic White House hoped to curb American expansion. What had more influence on American foreign policy decisions was the economy: Whenever Americans strove to acquire territories outside the continental United States, economic reasons were advanced. Increasing American commercial ties with Latin America, and interest in reciprocal trade commitments that would open Latin American markets for American goods, were a first step towards the extension of US foreign commerce in the 1880s, and American acquisition of modern warships, starting in 1883, helped to emphasize American interest in overseas trade and its protection. Under the administrations of the 1880s, this search for foreign markets remained peaceful: Harrison's and Hayes's Secretary of State James G. Blaine clearly stated that there would be no territorial expansion, although both administrations were tempted by such places as Hawaii (for the China trade) and Nicaragua (for the possibility of building a trans-isthmian canal there; cf. LaFeber 1998, 102-10).

The great depression of 1893 to 1897 finally convinced leading Americans that "foreign markets were necessary for the prosperity and tranquility of the United States" (LaFeber 1998, 150) and that it was good government policy to attempt to secure those markets. To some industrialists, foreign markets, especially China, looked vital: From 1887 to 1897, America textile exports to China rose by 120 percent, at a time when US production of almost all industrial goods was growing and the local markets were in depression (cf. LaFeber 1993, 21-44). In the immediacy of the crisis, American foreign policy was directed by the Democrat Grover Cleveland, whose interests, like that of Presidents Hayes and

Harrison before him, were still primarily aimed at Latin American markets. The opportunity of annexing Hawaii arose in early 1893 and was taken up by President Harrison in a treaty sent to the Senate, which agreed to the annexation. Cleveland, however, withdrew the treaty five days after coming into office. Nevertheless, the debate over the necessity of acquiring Hawaii led Carl Schurz to formulate a scathing indictment of both past American acquisitiveness and current dreams of expansion (cf. Mackenthun in this vol., 262-3).

In "Manifest Destiny" (doc. 317), written in 1893, Schurz seeks to undermine American efforts and hopes for an overseas empire by denying the validity of one of the great ideas of American foreign policy. "[M]anifest destiny meant an increase of the number of slave states," Schurz argues (*KC*, 706). He believes that the Civil War should have ended both this perfidious desire on the part of the South to add to their political strength and the overly naïve hope of Americans that "this republic, being charged with the mission of bearing the banner of freedom over the whole civilized world, could transform any country [...] into something like itself" (*KC*, 706). Schurz decries the need to utilize the old Manifest Destiny ideas as a cover for their new search for commerce and territorial acquisitions, but most importantly, he worries about the lack of selectiveness: There are "forces we find bent upon exciting the ambition of the American people whenever a chance for the acquisition of foreign territory heaves in sight" (*KC*, 706). For Schurz, territorial acquisitions should be contiguous, and more importantly, fit for inclusion into American society, much as Strong had argued when he said, "Bring savages into contact with our civilization, and its destructive forces become operative at once" (*KC*, 709-10). While the inclusion of a willing Canada would "not seriously change [the US's] character," indeed, would be the result of "the feeling of naturally belonging together" (*KC*, 707), the same cannot be said of Latin America, especially Caribbean nations, which Schurz fears are a target for acquisition. Their becoming part of the United States would "be fraught with incalculable dangers to the vitality of our democratic institutions," and would lead to "a rapid deterioration in the character of the people and their political institutions, and to a future of turbulence, demoralization, and final decay" (*KC*, 708). Schurz does not believe in the economic necessity of expansion and thus denies its being used as a justification: "[I]f we once are fairly started in the annexation policy for such purposes [of commerce], the appetite will grow with the eating. There will always be more commercial advantages to be gained" (*KC*, 707), while, by contrast, an annexation policy based upon mutual character traits, heritage, and race, would end with Canada. During the four years following the failed annexation of Hawaii, Democratic control of the Presidency ensured that Schurz's hopes of a more reserved foreign policy would be fulfilled. Indeed, American de facto control over Hawaii and its "interim" government of American revolutionaries who had ousted the reigning queen, as well as an intensive trade with the Caribbean countries, were, to President Cleveland, preferable to actual physical control of the islands.

Hawaii's internal problems were nothing that Cleveland cared to deal with, but it still loomed large in long term policy: It was a stepping-stone to the markets of Asia, and foreign, especially British and Japanese, interference would not be tolerated in Hawaiian affairs. To that end, Americans secured the right to use Pearl Harbor as a naval base. Samao in the southern Pacific was also secured, in a maneuver barely short of war and a three-nation treaty with Germany and Britain, explicitly to secure the southern flank of a transpacific trade route.

The entirety of American foreign policy in the Pacific Ocean was aimed at one overarching goal: China (cf. LaFeber 1998, 54-5), which was a market for both of the two central driving forces behind American imperialism, trade and the Christian mission. In both cases, it illustrated the fundamental discrepancy between the actual facts of American involvements abroad and the perception that underlay American policies. For although exports quintupled between 1865 and 1898, and although individual industries exported large shares of their production, exports made up only a little more than 7 percent of the total gross national product at any given time, and the vast majority of these exports went to Europe (cf. Fry 2007, 309-10).[10] Albert Beveridge could use this firm but mistaken knowledge of the need for new markets to justify his expansionist rhetoric: "[W]e are raising more than we can consume, making more than we can use. Therefore we must find new markets for our produce" (*KC*, 712). China also inspired missionaries, for the same 400 million Chinese that were being pursued as consumers of cigarettes, sewing machines, and other consumer goods were also heathens: "China is open to the Gospel now," one missionary claimed in 1890 (in LaFeber 1993, 100). So important did the idea of the China market become to industrialists and missionaries alike that, when war with Spain began in 1898, the country was second only to Cuba on the minds of the men who directed the war.

Cuba had been a major target of American investments since the early 1870s. In 1896, about 60 million US dollars were invested in the island, especially in sugar, and it was with considerable apprehension that American investors, and the US government, saw the outbreak of a pro-independence revolt on Cuba that same year, and with still greater apprehension that they followed the Asian crisis a year later – fear for the long established Open Door policy in China and for Cuban investments were the primary foreign political concerns of a new administration un-

---

[10] Indeed, in 1900, Americans held 2.5 percent of all foreign investments in China (cf. Hunt 1977, 278), and at no point before 1919 did exports to China exceed 100 million dollars in value – even then, only 2 percent of the total American exports. Between 1893 and 1900, exports to China accounted for between 1.5 and 2 percent of total American exports. The vaunted China market just did not exist (cf. Carter 1997, U 317-44). That it still figured so large in American thought of the time was owing to a simple calculation: 400 million Chinese made for a magnificent, if latent, market, and this, more than any real profits, inspired American business and political leaders: "[B]usinessmen and others believed that the Chinese market offered the opportunity for a vast future trade" (De Conde 1963, 360).

der William McKinley (cf. LaFeber 1993, 129-39).[11] When American efforts to negotiate a settlement between the Cuban rebels and the Spanish government, which still held colonial control of Cuba, failed, and, in February 1898, the combination of insulting correspondence by the Spanish envoy in Washington and the destruction of the battleship *Maine* (cf. Allen 1998) in Havana harbor dragged Spain and the United States down the road to war, it was the background of American expansion of trade and missionizing abroad that proved decisive. In the war itself, the United States, though less than adequately prepared for a military campaign, quickly defeated the Spanish fleet in the Philippines and off Cuba, then took Santiago. More critically than the war itself, the aftermath underscored the change in American foreign policy under the new quest for foreign markets.

The discussion of American imperialism in the anthology must be read against this background of missionary and industrialist interests in the Far East and Latin America, which explains some of the heated rhetoric and fierce disputes. Albert Beveridge's speech "The March of the Flag" (doc. 319) spells out several of the key ideas outlined above. "Shall the American people continue their march toward the commercial supremacy of the world? [... S]hall we reap the reward that waits on our discharge of our high duty; shall we occupy new markets for what our farmer raise, our factories make, our merchants sell [...]?" (*KC*, 711), are the questions uppermost in Beveridge's mind. But his rhetoric uses a different strategy: Although trade is the ultimate goal, moral responsibility is the lever. Beveridge combines the "mission" and the "duty" that are due to God's special Providence for the United States with the practical use of the Philippines: They are indeed "our duty and desire," the legitimate target of the "Anglo-Saxon impulse" (*KC*, 712) to strive for progress, commerce, and prosperity, as well as for the enlightenment of the people. How far removed the rhetoric of the expansionists was from the facts of the situation is evident especially in this repeated assurance that there are "peoples to be saved" (*KC*, 713), people who need "God's final and complete solution of the dark problem of heathenism," or even "unexplored lands and savage wilderness" still to be found (*KC*, 710). Indeed, since all the formerly Spanish colonies had been populated for centuries by largely Catholic populations, none of the American acquisitions of 1898 could well be called "unexplored," and American efforts at pacifying the resisting Filipino rebels, who had been struggling with Spain for a decade, cost 200,000 Filipino lives (cf. LaFeber 1993, 160, 165).

The discrepancy between the ideals of American liberty and the reality of the country's politics was not lost on others. William Jennings Bryan seems specifical-

---

[11] The Open Door policy had been instituted by several treaties between China and the Western powers in the aftermath of the Opium Wars and effectively held that all nations would have equal access to the Chinese market, especially where the payment of customs duties and access to inland waterways was concerned. It was a mainstay of US-China policy, as it absolved the United States from actually controlling the territory its trade was going to (cf. De Conde 1963, 229, 360).

ly to target Beveridge's speech when he notes that "[w]e have felt it due to ourselves and to the world, as well as to those who were struggling for the right to govern themselves, to proclaim the interest which our people have [...] in every contest between human rights and arbitrary power" (*KC*, 714). Bryan argues that Beveridge and his supporters "seek to confuse imperialism and expansion," a distinction he believes to lie in expansion's aim to form new states versus imperialism's rule over unwilling peoples. Like Schurz, Bryan believes Canada to be a perfectly viable target for expansion, a "land which [...] adds to our population people who are willing to become citizens and are capable of discharging their duties as such" (*KC*, 714), and scorns the imperialist belief in Manifest Destiny: "Destiny is the subterfuge of the invertebrate, who, lacking the courage to oppose error, seeks some plausible excuse for supporting it" (*KC*, 715).

In the case of Albert Beveridge's speech, ideas of exceptionalism, mission, Christian duty, and Anglo-Saxon superiority mingle in support of the trade motivation. Beveridge's talk of liberty is the means by which the commercial goals can be sold: Although "[w]e cannot retreat from any soil where Providence has unfurled our banner; it is ours to save that soil for liberty and civilization" makes for a stirring conclusion, it must be contrasted with the obvious injunction to "remember our duty to our homes," and the fact that "we do need what we have taken in 1898, and we need it now" (*KC*, 713, 712). Beveridge ties Christian morality and economic concerns into one apparently coherent whole, even in details of language: "Will you affirm by your [negative] vote that you are an *infidel* to American power and practical sense" (*KC*, 711; emphasis mine), he challenges his listeners. Being adverse to expansion and commerce is tantamount to treason against Christian morality.

American expansionism in the 1880s and 1890s, and American imperialism during the Spanish-American War and later, has been variously described as a break from previous expansionist and nationalist practices, or a continuation of them; an accident of history, or a premeditated effort to enlarge American influence; a question of economics or of manifest destiny (cf. Fry 2007, 307). Whatever it was, it propelled America onto the world stage, gave it responsibility extending over nearly half the globe, and influenced American foreign policy for the next fifty years.

V. Towards Progressivism

The Gilded Age ended in violence: On September 5, 1901, anarchist Leon Czolgosz gunned down President William McKinley. Theodore Roosevelt became President after McKinley's death, and thus the era of progressivism dawned. Roosevelt "believed that the McKinley administrations had represented the 'tyranny of money over principle,'" and he was "the best hope for progressives to pursue [...] national reform" (Flanagan 2007, 101). Indeed, after the thirty years of the Gilded Age, America was at a point where the alternatives seemed all too clear. Without reform, they "were socialism/anarchism or the continuing repression of democracy by the growing power of the wealthy industrialists" (Flanagan 2007, 102).

The problems of the Gilded Age, monopolism, conflicts between labor and capital, the integration of immigrants or the banning of further immigration, imperialism, as well as voter representation, were left unsolved as the Gilded Age concluded.[12] During Roosevelt's presidency, the establishment of a Department of Commerce and Labor, trust-busting activities, and regulation of railroads and food production alleviated some of the most immediate and troublesome aspects of the new industrial age (cf. Flanagan 2007, 104-5). By 1910, the public's perception of the social problems of the nation had reached such depths that Roosevelt could campaign on these issues against his successor William Howard Taft. Roosevelt's speech *The New Nationalism* (doc. 322) at Osawatomie, Kansas, combines idealism and political expediency into a whole that seemed to answer many of the Gilded Age's most egregious shortcomings. While Roosevelt's call for "the triumph of real democracy, the triumph of popular government" (*KC*, 717) mainly sought to secure the popular primaries that Roosevelt hoped would propel him to the Republican nomination in 1912, he picked up on a variety of popular issues that, in combination, would lead to a new kind of nationalism, in which the

> object of government is the welfare of the people. The material progress and prosperity of a nation are desirable chiefly so far as they lead to the moral and material welfare of all good citizens. Just in proportion as the average man and woman are honest, capable of sound judgment and high ideals, active in public affairs, – but, first of all, sound in their home life, and the father and mother of healthy children whom they bring up well, – just so far, and no farther, we may count civilization a success. (*KC*, 720)

Even more important than Roosevelt's motivation, which was a mix of the politically expedient and the morally right, was the final arrival of such an issue as "comprehensive workmen's compensation acts, both state and national laws to regulate child labor and work for women" (*KC*, 720) at the highest political stage. Roosevelt's New Nationalism neatly tied the belief in American exceptionalism with the changing nature of society, proclaiming that

> the history of America is now the central feature of the history of the world; for the world has set its face hopefully toward our democracy; and, O my fellow citizens, each one of you carries on your shoulders not only the burden of doing well for the sake of your own country, but the burden of doing well and of seeing that this nation does well for the sake of mankind. (*KC*, 717)

---

[12] Monopolies became stronger throughout the waning years of the nineteenth century, with the creation of U. S. Steel in 1901 symbolizing "the growth of industry, its consolidation, and its domination of the market" (LaFeber et al. 1992, 35). Anarchism killed McKinley. Socialists made their greatest inroads into the political system after the foundation of the Socialist Labor Party in 1901, and the Socialist Party of America fielded a presidential candidate in 1912 (to gain six percent of the vote) and as late as 1920 (cf. Flanagan 2007, 128, 138, 240). Immigration remained an unsolved problem; imperialism did not even start into full swing until the final years of the Gilded Age. Some of these problems were tackled, if not all of them solved, during the progressive era.

Although Roosevelt lost the Republican nomination to the party machine, and his Progressive Party the election of 1912 to the Democratic Party under Woodrow Wilson, Progressive ideas finally reached fruition (cf. Graubart 2004, 140-7). Changes to the political system drew off conflict potential that might have aided the socialists and defused some of the most problematic conflicts between labor and capital. "Universal white male suffrage [...] influenced segments of the working class to reject socialism in favor of reforming the state into a more democratic one that protected workers and labor interests," as Flanagan notes (2007, 50). Within a single decade, 1911 to 1920, four "progressive amendments," introducing income tax, the direct election of US senators, prohibition, and women's suffrage, addressed many of the most critical questions raised by Gilded Age problems. Other problems became worse: Immigration restrictions were added for Japanese in 1908 (cf. De Conde 1963, 371-2) and, in the aftermath of World War I, a series of Congressional acts ended mass immigration (cf. Brogan 1985, 512). Black Americans were segregated in 1896 through the Supreme Court's infamous *Plessy v. Ferguson* decision, and American troops were deployed to Honduras, Nicaragua, Panama, the Dominican Republic, and Haiti, besides the acquisitions from Spain, throughout most of the 1910s and 1920s (cf. LaFeber 1994, 283).

The Gilded Age was the stage on which the dawning of a new era could be witnessed. As the United States became a world power, its industrial, military, and political strength could now compete with the old powers, and in many cases superseded them. The key concepts that gained ground during the age, like socialism, imperialism, and the desire to alleviate the most immediate social disorders remained important for the United States throughout the decades to follow. In some cases, indeed, they would not begin to be solved until after World War II.

Instructional Strategies and Classroom Issues

I. Key Concepts and Major Themes

1. Social Darwinism (docs. 298-9, 308)
   A theory relating social phenomena to the ideas of Charles Darwin's 1859 book *The Origin of Species*. It generally holds that social phenomena, such as class standing, wealth, or success, can be described primarily in terms of what Herbert Spencer called "survival of the fittest," and thus come down to competition for scarce resources that some are better able to compete for than others. Social Darwinism was also influenced by, among others, Thomas Malthus. One must be careful in defining the term, because not all social Darwinists were also subscribers to Malthusian population policies or advocates of eugenics, or necessarily approved of the consequences of social Darwinist thought. Most of the authors presented in this essay should be considered social Darwinists only in so far as they accepted a naturally determined economic superiority of some members of society over others, but

they drew different conclusions as to the consequences for the individual's as well as society's behavior (cf. Bannister 1979).

2. Anarchism (docs. 299, 301, 304-6)
   A theory that supports the dissolution of government and the state in favor of other systems of society. Anarchist behavior in America can be traced to frontiersmen's necessary anarchism where no government existed, and can be found in the writings of Thoreau. Anarchism became a worldwide, violent phenomenon in the 1880s, in some cases fusing with communist ideas. Anarchist ideas remained influential until the First World War and then slowly died out, virtually ceasing to exist by 1940 (cf. Madison 1945).

3. Imperialism (docs. 317-321)
   Imperialism is generally used to denote the period of the "race for Empire" from the 1870s to the aftermath of the World War I. It saw the emergence on the colonial stage of such nations as Germany, Belgium, Japan, and the United States, who increasingly competed with the established colonial powers for territory. In American history, imperialism is a loaded term: Many historians deny that the United States has ever had an imperialist phase (cf. LaFeber 1998).

4. Urbanization (docs. 294-7)
   Urbanization, the trend towards a concentration of a nation's population in cities, increased the number of city dwellers in the United States from roughly 25 percent of the population after the Civil War to 40 percent in 1900, an even more significant development when considered against the backdrop of a major population increase. In the growing cities, mass transportation allowed for a larger area to be settled without a decline in cohesion, and dense city centers started growing vertically. The large populations of cities, often consisting to a significant degree of poor immigrants, led to the construction of increasingly squalid tenement housing and severe social problems, many of which would remain unsolved well into the progressive era (cf. Barrows 2005).

5. The Economy of the Gilded Age
   The most obvious development in American society during the Gilded Age was the immense growth of the economy, from which all the principal questions of the age stemmed. America's post-Civil War industrial revolution, especially the application of mechanical power to all fields of human enterprise, from office environments to farms and manufacturing, substantially increased production in all sectors. Railroads supported the geographical expansion of industry by making transportation to and from distant regions cheaper and easier and by spurring the production of steel for rails and engines. Government support of economic growth came in the form of weak regulation and the legal construct of the corporation.

Corporations were considered legal persons by the courts, allowing the extension of such personal rights as were codified in the Fourteenth Amendment onto them. Moreover, corporations implied a limited liability of shareholders in case of a collapse, stimulating investment. The growth of production and the contraction of money supply due to the gold standard (q.v.) led to a period of severe depressions. Working conditions, lack of job security, and income inequalities were aspects of the Gilded Age economy that were crucial to the social disturbances of the age (cf. Kerr 2005).

6. Gold Standard
Early in the Gilded Age, the American dollar was largely coined silver and gold bullion. In 1873, the coinage of silver was abandoned in an effort to stabilize the currency still bloated from the issuance of paper dollars during the Civil War, which the government sought to purchase and remove from circulation. The consequent deflation of the smaller amount of currency in circulation led to reduced real prices, a significant burden especially on farmers, who had mortgages to pay with less real income. Populist efforts to revive silver coinage or even the issuance of "greenback" paper dollars followed in the 1880s and 1890s. The dispute over silver and gold culminated in the election of 1896 and William Jennings Bryan's "Cross of Gold" speech, in which he postulated a dichotomy between Republicans, city dwellers and industrialists on the one hand and farmers, Midwestern and plains states, and Democrats on the other (cf. Bryan 1993, 176-80). Bryan's defeat by William McKinley ended the question in favor of gold – probably much to the nation's benefit (cf. Friedman 1990, Nugent 1970).

II. Comparison – Contrasts – Connections

Example: Docs. 131, 156, 166, 237, 256, 268-9, 276-7, 279, 298, 303, 306

Many documents from the Gilded Age refer to the Declaration of Independence in their arguments, quoting some of the central passages of its text in support of their various arguments. *The Declaration of Independence* (doc. 131), however, was not exclusively used during the Gilded Age; many texts from earlier sections of the anthology refer to it as well. This section will make the connection between the Declaration and the various documents using themes from it to show the unbroken appropriation of its ideals and rhetoric that climaxed during the Gilded Age. Students should learn to identify the persistence of the Declaration in many different social and political contexts.

Thomas Jefferson's Declaration is both a justification and explanation of societal upheaval as well as a document of war rhetoric and propaganda whose central ideas grew out of Lockean philosophy and English constitutional tradition (cf. Goetsch 1992). Jefferson's trinity of life, liberty, and the pursuit of happiness as "inalienable rights" is part of the universal preamble in which he argues that "when a long train of abuses and usurpations, pursuing invariably the same object, evinces a design to reduce them under absolute despotism, it is their right, it is their duty to throw off such government" (*KC*, 303). Jefferson's syllogism, concluding from the major premise of inalienable rights and the belief that "all men are created equal," and the minor premise that these rights have been ignored by the king, that it is the colonists' duty to create a new government, would prove to have a lasting influence on the adaptability of the Declaration's message. More important than Jefferson's list of "facts [to] be submitted to a candid world" (*KC*, 305), the Declaration's malleable phrases of equality, liberty, and its justification of violent revolution would again and again serve as the arguments of choice for people discontent with the existing system.

For several decades after 1776, the Declaration's identification as a primarily anti-British document caused it to figure rarely as a major argumentative tool. Although Charles Paine's Fourth of July oration in 1801 (doc. 155) echoed the phrase "and of right ought to be [free]" (*KC*, 366), in the first fifty years of its existence it took both the nationalistic mood of the period after the war of 1812 and the slow realization that the founding generation would soon be gone to revive interest in the Declaration (cf. Detweiler 1962, 571-4). Besides the obvious debt owed to it by the Texan revolutionaries in their own *Unanimous Declaration of Independence* (doc. 165), the malleable messages of the Declaration of Independence, its inscribed applicability to more than just the realm of international relations, required the emergence and voicing of intra-social conflicts. William Lloyd Garrison's text "Truisms" (1831, doc. 254) hits upon the issues that many after him would also attack, claiming that "[all] men are born equal, and entitled to protection, except those whose skins are black and hair wooly; or, to prevent mistake, excepting Africans, and their descendants" (*KC*, 577). Garrison's sarcastic adoption of Jefferson's central line became a powerful tool in the abolitionist arsenal:

> I am a believer in that portion of the Declaration of American Independence in which is set forth, as among self-evident truths, "that all men are created equal; that they are endowed by their Creator with certain inalienable rights; that among these are life, liberty, and the pursuit of happiness." Hence, I am an abolitionist. Hence, I cannot but regard oppression in every form – and most of all, that which turns a man into a thing – with indignation and abhorrence. [...] Convince me that one man may rightfully make another man his slave, and I will no longer subscribe to the Declaration of Independence. (*KC*, 609)

His phrasing of the "American Independence" gives notice to the fact that the Declaration did not differentiate internally between Americans and slaves – for Garrison, the Declaration could only apply to everyone. Indeed, Garrison's rhetoric fastens on the idea that the Declaration's language implies promises to the American people, and denounces the "guilty inconsistency" of celebrating national independence while keeping a significant part of the nation in fetters. "[N]otwithstanding our Fourth of July celebrations, and ostentatious displays of patriotism: in what European nation is personal liberty held in such contempt as in our own?" (*KC*, 609), Garrison asks, and wonders about what "becomes of the Declaration of Independence" if slavery remains in existence. Indirectly, Garrison also adopts the Declaration's justification of violent reform of an oppressive government: "The law that makes [man] a chattel is to be trampled under foot; the compact that is formed at his expense, and cemented with his blood, is null and void" (*KC*, 610).

The associations between individual liberty and the Fourth of July were also apparent to Frederick Douglass, whose own post-Independence Day speech *What to the Slave is the Fourth of July?* (doc. 268) elaborates the problematic relationship between the Declaration's ostensible goals and the realities of antebellum America. The Fourth of July, Douglass asserts, "is the birthday of your National Independence, and of your political freedom. This, to you, is what the Passover was to the emancipated people of God" (*KC*, 602). Like Garrison, he explicitly points out that it is impossible for him to celebrate American independence and equality. "You may rejoice, *I* must mourn. To drag a man in fetters into the grand illuminated temple of liberty," Douglass assures his audience, is "inhuman mockery" (*KC*, 605). Douglass, like Garrison, fastens on the "national inconsistencies" of the preamble, in which

> [y]ou declare, before the world, and are understood by the world to declare, that you "*hold these truths to be self-evident, that all men are created equal; and are endowed by their Creator with certain inalienable rights; and that, among these are, life, liberty, and the pursuit of happiness*;" and yet, you hold securely, in a bondage which, according to your own Thomas Jefferson, "*is worse than ages of that which your fathers rose in rebellion to oppose*," *a seventh part* of the inhabitants of your country. (*KC*, 607)

Douglass also affirms that from the Declaration stems the right to violent action to achieve change: "[T]he fathers of this republic [...] were statesmen, patriots, and heroes [...]. They loved their country better than their own private interests [...]. They were peace men; but they preferred revolution to peaceful submission to bondage" (*KC*, 604). Douglass is "drawing encouragement from the Declaration of Independence [and] the great principles which it contains," while Garrison refuses to accept the Declaration's validity in the face of evidence; for both, however, the Declaration's justification of revolution is an important part of their argument. They were not the last to use the argument: As social difficulties increased, the Declaration's role as a founding document of the nation and the consequent grounding of the nation in the right to abolish unjust government (which was the usual interpretation) combined to make it the natural document to refer to when justifying actions beyond the Constitution.[13]

---

[13] It was not only slavery that inspired antebellum reference to the Declaration. Although never as prominent a topic as slavery, women's rights were sufficiently contested, and the apparent contradiction between the Declaration's promise of equality and the actual legal standing of women was so grave, that recourse to the Declaration came easily. When the Seneca Falls Convention in 1848 sought to express its grievances in writing the *Declaration of Sentiments*

By contrast, the Constitution itself was the document of choice for the defenders of the status quo, as the case of the two contrasting Inaugural Addresses of Confederate Jefferson Davis and Federal Abraham Lincoln shows. Davis's *First Inaugural Address* (doc. 276) makes many of the same points that Garrison and Douglass had already made, though for different reasons. Davis suggests that it is "the American idea that governments rest upon the consent of the governed, and that it is the right of the people to alter or abolish governments whenever they become destructive of the ends for which they were established." When the Confederate States left the Union, Davis argues, "they merely asserted a right which the Declaration of Independence of 1776 had defined to be inalienable; of the time and occasion for its exercise, they, as sovereigns, were the final judges, each for itself" (*KC*, 627). By contrast, Abraham Lincoln's *First Inaugural Address* (doc. 277) manages to place the Declaration in a line of constitutive acts that, rather than pronouncing disunion between Britain and America, primarily affirms the colonial union; the union "was matured and continued by the Declaration of Independence" (*KC*, 629). Lincoln's inaugural address, moreover, stresses the Constitution's safeguards and its ability to cover all the grievances of the seceding states, noting that "[s]uch of you as are now dissatisfied, still have the old Constitution unimpaired, and [...] the laws of your own framing under it" (*KC*, 631). The difficult task of weighing between the Constitution's affirmation of perpetual union and the Declaration of Independence's inscribed acknowledgment of the validity of violent revolution was not solved.

The idea of a promise made by the Declaration of Independence remained influential through the aftermath of the Civil War and into the Gilded Age. With the abolition of slavery, this promise seemed fulfilled (cf. doc. 277). Again, however, the Declaration's call for equality and happiness was immensely adaptable to the claims of other groups that believed themselves oppressed by prevailing conditions and were prepared to fight to change their situation. For reformers such as Henry George, the Declaration's promises provided the basis on which

---

and Resolutions (doc. 237), it did so not only by the allusion of the title but by conscious imitation and copying of the Declaration of Independence. Women were, "by the laws of nature and of Nature's God" (*KC*, 531) as much entitled to equal position – and a revolution, if necessary – as their ancestors in the international arena. For the authors of the Declaration of Sentiments, it is therefore "self-evident: that all men and women are created equal" (*KC*, 531). The authors apply a minimum of changes to Jefferson's preamble and do so only when it becomes necessary again to affirm the special purpose of the Seneca Falls Convention: "Such has been the patient sufferance of women under this government" (*KC*, 532). More interesting than the necessary changes is the fact that the majority of Jefferson's preamble remains untouched, its message in its entirety applied to the new conflict without regard for the historical underpinnings of Jefferson's text. Because Jefferson had managed to completely separate his reasons for independence from his justification of the mechanism by which Americans sought to achieve it, he had essentially made his preamble timeless. Its universal truths could, with very little editorial work, be made to justify women's emancipation as easily as political independence: All that was necessary for the men and women at the Seneca Falls Convention was to change the list of grievances.

they could found an argument that, hopefully, would be undeniable by all Americans for whom the Declaration had become a cornerstone of their Republican values. What are George's proposed reforms, he asks in his 1879 treatise *Progress and Poverty* (doc. 298), but "the carrying out in letter and spirit of the truth enunciated in the Declaration of Independence – the 'self-evident' truth that is the heart and soul of the Declaration" (*KC*, 672). The many different forms of inequality in the Gilded Age, according to George, directly challenged the Declaration's promises. Four years afterwards, the pamphlet "To the Workingmen of America" (doc. 303) picks up on the idea that the Declaration of Independence's avowal of the right to armed rebellion also justified anarchist labor in its rebellion against the existing societal structures:

> FELLOW-WORKMEN: – The Declaration of Independence says:
> "[...] But when a long train of abuses and usurpations, pursuing invariably the same object, evinces a design to reduce them (the people) under absolute Despotism, it is their right, it is their duty to throw off such government and provide new guards for their future security."
> This thought of Thomas Jefferson was the justification for armed resistance by our forefathers, which gave birth to our Republic, and do not the necessities of our present time compel us to reassert their declaration? (*KC*, 682-3)

This same passage, which August Spies, one of the drafters of the pamphlet, also quoted at his trial (doc. 306), encapsulates many of the problems that the shifting interpretation of the Declaration of Independence's language brought. As interpreters of the Declaration's meaning, of course, Spies and his colleagues not only failed, they did not even attempt to actively tie its language to their situation. Although "To the Workingmen" enumerates the major grievances that, according to the Declaration, allow for a revolution, it does not actually work with the Declaration and its rhetoric to provide a visible parallel between the situations of the American Revolution and the Gilded Age's problems. It does not pick up on either "abuse" or "usurpation" or "despotism," and although it implicitly accuses the "propertied" of "exploitation," in the end the document takes recourse to misquoting Jefferson, who never wrote "[i]t is, therefore, your right, it is your duty, to arm" (*KC*, 685). In both Spies's speech and the pamphlet "To the Workingmen," quoting the Declaration is an act which taps into national mythology – an effort to provide an argument with an unarguable foundation to protect the rest of the discussion from closer scrutiny. The pamphlet's point that "[t]he Declaration of Independence says," (*KC*, 682), and Spies's statement that "[t]his is a quotation from the Declaration of Independence" (*KC*, 691) are, of course, true. And although they, by themselves, prove neither the correctness of the following or preceding interpretation nor the conclusions drawn, they poison the rhetorical well: Any argument against Spies's points is implicitly accused of being a denial of the Declaration itself.

Over the first century of its existence, then, the Declaration of Independence's language was first uncommented on, then increasingly revered as part of a national compact affirming all the principal values of the republic. The focus of commentators and readers shifted from the anti-British enumeration of grievances to the preamble, whose concrete meaning in Jefferson's age lost its specificity over time and became a national myth. In their growing unspecific loftiness, the preamble's premises became adaptable to virtually any cause.

III. Reading and Discussion Questions

1. Albert Beveridge, in "The March of the Flag" (doc. 319), refers to Thomas Jefferson as "the first Imperialist of the Republic" (*KC*, 711); William Jennings Bryan, in his "Imperialism" (doc. 320), denies that charge. With whom do you agree? In discussing this question, take care to study the definition of the term "imperialism" versus "expansionism." Compare also Carl Schurz's claim of the "conservative traditions of our foreign policy" (*KC*, 706) with Beveridge's enumeration of American imperialist ventures.

2. Outline the lines of argument that William Graham Sumner uses in his "The Challenge of Facts" (doc. 299), especially where they relate to the concept of social Darwinism. How does Sumner react to the threats posed by socialists, anarchists, and atheists? How does he manage to combine these three groups into one single threat? Examine the title.

3. Compare the various concepts of American exceptionalism as they appear in the anthology. How can you trace the basic idea of exceptionalism through the texts? How does the idea shift? Distinguish between religious exceptionalism and its secular forms. What traces of historical exceptionalism can still be found in Gilded Age texts, and what are some of the rhetorical strategies these texts use?

IV. Resources

a. Recommended Reading

Robert C. Bannister. *Social Darwinism: Science and Myth in Anglo-American Social Thought*. Philadelphia: Temple University Press, 1979. Bannister's study should be read critically by those interested in the issue of social Darwinism for its argument that rather than being a shaping and justifying force of laissez-faire capitalism, it was a myth created by anti-capitalist writers. Bannister believes that there were, in fact, almost no social Darwinists in the US. According to Bannister, William Graham Sumner's writings must be understood as stemming from older notions of political economy, rather than social Darwinist thought. Although persuasive in its effort to identify the evolution and definitional problems of the term social Darwinism, Bannister's reading of Sumner should be carefully compared with other sources, including Sumner's own writings.

Charles W. Calhoun, ed. *The Gilded Age: Perspective on the Origins of Modern America*. Lanham: Rowman and Littlefield Publishers, 2007. A collection of essays providing introductions to sixteen major topics of Gilded Age history. Each of the essays offers well-researched information on which one may base further research into Gilded Age topics. The lack of a more recent history of the Gilded Age than Sean Cashman's 1984 study makes this volume especially useful.

Sean D. Cashman. *America in the Gilded Age: From the Death of Lincoln to the Rise of Theodore Roosevelt*. New York: New York University Press, 1984. Cashman's narrative history of the Gilded Age is a well-illustrated and readable treatment of the era, covering all of the major problems and issues. Cashman's emphasis on the interconnectedness of the economic and the societal as well as both internal and external political developments offers a necessary comprehensive basis from which to delve further into the key issues of the age.

Walter LaFeber. *The New Empire: An Interpretation of American Expansion 1860-1898*. 1963. Ithaca: Cornell University Press, 1998. LaFeber's classic account of American imperialism in the Gilded Age stresses the importance of the economic impetus to expansion, and has therefore been called "Marxist" in its interpretation of American foreign policy. LaFeber argues that the Spanish-American War and the acquisition of overseas territories in its wake constituted not an aberration of American foreign policy, as had frequently been suggested, but rather the continuation of a long-standing tradition. This thesis has been very influential, but has also been strongly debated.

Alan Trachtenberg. *The Incorporation of America: Culture and Society in the Gilded Age*. New York: Hill and Wang, 1982. Trachtenberg's book analyses the changes that the growing professionalization and incorporation of American society had on culture and intra-societal relations during the Gilded Age. Trachtenberg argues that the growth of corporations coincided with the growth of secularization, individualization and bureaucratization and, in turn, changed the character of the nation.

b. Works Cited and Reading Suggestions

Allen, Thomas B. (1998). "What Really Sank the Maine?" *Naval History* 12.2, 30-40.

Arnesen, Eric (2007). "American Workers and the Labor Movement in the Late Nineteenth Century." *The Gilded Age: Perspectives on the Origins of Modern America*. Ed. Charles W. Calhoun. Lanham: Rowman and Littlefield Publishers, 29-52.

Axelrod, Bernard (1972). "Historical Studies of Emigration from the United States." *International Migration Review* 6.1, 32-49.

Bannister, Robert C. (1979). *Social Darwinism: Science and Myth in Anglo-American Social Thought*. Philadelphia: Temple University Press.

Barrows, Robert G. (2005). "Urbanization." *Encyclopedia of the Gilded Age and Progressive Era*. Ed. John and Joseph Buenker. Armonk: Sharpe, 35-43.
Brogan, Hugh (1985). *The Penguin History of the United States of America*. New York: Penguin.
Bryan, William Jennings (1993). "Cross of Gold Speech." 1896. *Major Problems in the Gilded Age and the Progressive Era*. Ed. Leon Fink. Lexington: Heath, 176-180.
Calavita, Kitty (2000). "The Paradoxes of Race, Class, Identity and 'Passing': Enforcing the Chinese Exclusion Acts, 1882-1910." *Law & Social Inquiry* 25.1, 1-40.
Calhoun, Charles W. (2007). *The Gilded Age: Perspectives on the Origins of Modern America*. Lanham: Rowman and Littlefield Publishers.
Carter, Susan, et al., eds. (1997). *Historical Statistics of the United States on CD-ROM*. Bicentennial Edition. Cambridge: Cambridge University Press.
Cashman, Sean D. (1984). *America in the Gilded Age: From the Death of Lincoln to the Rise of Theodore Roosevelt*. New York: New York University Press.
Cohn, Raymond L. (2000). "Nativism and the End of the Mass Migration of the 1840s and 1850s." *The Journal of Economic History* 60.2, 361-388.
Commager, Henry Steele (1949). *Documents of American History*. New York: Appleton Century Crofts.
Daniels, Roger, and Isabella Black (1964). "American Labour and Chinese Immigration." *Past and Present* 27, 113-115.
Daniels, Roger (2007). "The Immigrant Experience in the Gilded Age." *The Gilded Age: Perspectives on the Origins of Modern America*. Ed. Charles W. Calhoun. Lanham: Rowman and Littlefield Publishers, 75-99.
De Conde, Alexander (1963). *A History of American Foreign Policy*. New York: Scribner's.
Detweiler, Philip F. (1962). "The Changing Reputation of the Declaration of Independence: The First Fifty Years." *The William and Mary Quarterly* 19.4, 557-574.
Flanagan, Maureen A. (2007). *America Reformed: Progressives and Progressivisms 1890s-1920s*. Oxford: Oxford University Press.
Friedman, Milton (1990). "The Crime of 1873." *The Journal of Political Economy* 98.6, 1159-1194.
Friedman, Norman L. (1967). "Nativism." *Phylon* 28.4, 408-415.
Fry, Joseph A. (2007). "Phases of Empire: Late Nineteenth-Century US Foreign Relations." *The Gilded Age: Perspectives on the Origins of Modern America*. Ed. Charles W. Calhoun. Lanham: Rowman and Littlefield Publishers, 307-332.
George, Henry (1973). *Progress and Poverty: An Inquiry into the Cause of Industrial Depressions and of Increase of Want with Increase of Wealth*. 1873. Garden City: Doubleday, Page.
Goetsch, Paul (1992). "The Declaration of Independence." *The Fourth of July: Political Oratory and Literary Reactions, 1776-1876*. Ed. Paul Goetsch and Gerd Hurm. Tübingen: Narr, 11-31.

Graubart, Stephen (2004). *The Presidents: The Transformation of the American Presidency from Theodore Roosevelt to George W. Bush*. London: Penguin.
Higham, John (1993). "Nativism and the New Immigrants." *Major Problems in the Gilded Age and the Progressive Era*. Ed. Leon Fink. Lexington: Heath, 273-279.
Hunt, Michael H. (1977). "Americans in the China Market: Economic Opportunities and Economic Nationalism, 1890s-1931." *The Business History Review* 51.1, 277-307.
Kerr, K. Austin (2005). "The Economy." *Encyclopedia of the Gilded Age and Progressive Era*. Ed. John and Joseph Buenker. Armonk: Sharpe, 28-34.
LaFeber, Walter, Richard Polenberg, and Nancy Woloch (1992). *The American Century: A History of the United States Since the 1890s*. New York: MacGraw-Hill.
LaFeber, Walter (1993). *The Cambridge History of American Foreign Relations*. Vol. 2: *The American Search for Opportunity, 1865-1913*. Cambridge: Cambridge University Press.
– (1994). *The American Age: U.S. Foreign Policy at Home and Abroad*. Vol. 2: *Since 1896*. New York: Norton.
– (1998). *The New Empire: An Interpretation of American Expansion 1860-1898*. 1963. New York: Cornell University Press.
Madison, Charles A. (1945). "Anarchism in the United States." *Journal of the History of Ideas* 6.1, 46-66.
Montgomery, David (1980). "Labor and the Republic in Industrial America 1860-1920." *Le Mouvement Social* 111, 201-215.
Nugent, Walter T. K. (1970). "Money, Politics, and Society: The Currency Question." *The Gilded Age*. Ed. H. Wayne Morgan. Syracuse: Syracuse University Press.
Porter, Glenn (2007). "Industralization and the Rise of Big Business." *The Gilded Age: Perspectives on the Origins of Modern America*. Ed. Charles W. Calhoun. Lanham: Rowman and Littlefield Publishers, 11-28.
Raeithel, Gert (1988). *Geschichte der nordamerikanischen Kultur*. Vol. 2: *Vom Bürgerkrieg bis zum New Deal 1860-1930*. Weinheim: Quadriga.
Trachtenberg, Alan (1982). *The Incorporation of America: Culture and Society in the Gilded Age*. New York: Hill and Wang.
Twain, Mark, and Charles Dudley Warner (1901). *The Gilded Age: A Tale of Today*. 2 vols. 1874. New York: Harper's.
Wehler, Hans-Ulrich (1982). *Grundzüge der amerikanischen Außenpolitik 1750-1900*. Frankfurt/M.: Suhrkamp.
Weir, Robert E. (2000). *Knights Unhorsed: Internal Conflict in a Gilded Age Social Movement*. Detroit: Wayne State University Press.
Wong, K. Scott (1995). "Chinatown: Conflicting Images, Contested Terrain." *MELUS* 20.1, 3-15.

LIST OF KEY CONCEPTS

Abolitionism 352
America as second Eden 18
Anarchism 410
Anglo-Saxonism 267
Antinomianism 181
Colonizationism 352
Commemoration 239
Concept of improvement 18
Cultural alienation 293
Deism 181
Democracy 293
Denominationalism 181
Disunionism 352
Domestic dependent nation 44, 267
Ecocriticism 294
Economy of the Gilded Age 410
Emancipation 377
Enthusiasm 181
Equality 208
Evangelism 182
Exceptionalism 238
Federalism vs. Republicanism 238
Female education 323
Filiopietism 110
Frontier 267
Genius 293
Geographical predestination 266
Gold standard 411
Goodwife 322
Imperialism 410
Indian treaties 44
Interracial visions 378
Jeremiad 110, 208
Law of nature 266
Liberalism 208
Liberty 208
Manifest Destiny 266, 293
Millennialism 151, 152

Modernization 182
Nature religion 293
New Woman 322
Noble Savage 42
Postcolonialism 294
Postmillennialism 152
Post-romantic identity 293
Praying Indian 43
Predestination 79
Progress 237
Proslavery and racial discourse 352
Providence 18, 110, 266
Pursuit of happiness 208
Racial determinism 266
Racism as propaganda 378
Republican Mother 322
Republicanism 209
Resistance and violence 353
Romantic spirituality 293
Salvation 78
Savage 18, 42
Self-reliance 294
Separate spheres 322
Social Darwinism 409
Social reform 293
Transatlantic Puritanism 79
Translatio imperii 18, 237, 266
Triple world order 17
True Woman 322
Typological Indian 43
Typology 78, 110
Unionism 352
Urbanization 410
Vacuum domicilium 43
Vanishing Indian 43
Virtue 209, 238
Westward expansion 17
Wilderness 44, 293

INDEX

Abolitionism 332, 338-352, 357
Adams, John Quincy 220, 229-232, 240-241, 253, 256, 258, 261
  Oration Delivered at Plymouth, An 220, 229, 256
African Americans 332, 335-337, 341, 344, 346, 349-351, 352, 357; colonization 262, 335, 341-343, 352, 360
Agriculturalism 19, 252
Alcott, Amos Bronson 277, 292
American Revolution 143, 152, 155-156, 166, 177-178, 183, 192, 207, 221, 234-235, 318, 322, 332, 357, 415
Anarchism 391, 408, 410
Anglican Church 55, 57, 93, 100, 101, 127-128, 131, 145, 152
Anglo-Saxonism 263, 267, 270
Anon.
  Address of the People of South Carolina 365, 369
  "Female Influence" 313, 316
Antichrist 126-127, 129-131, 133, 141
Antinomianism 164, 166-167, 181
Antiquity 28, 30, 33, 46, 106, 201, 209, 231, 237-238, 251
Anti-Slavery Society 345, 349, 354
Apocalypse 26, 86, 90, 120, 128-130, 134, 140, 157, 159-160, 162
Aspasio 220-225
Autobiography 59, 62, 73, 80-81, 98, 104, 167-168, 178-179, 183-184, 356

Bancroft, George 277, 281, 286, 295, 298
Beecher, Catharine E. 309, 314, 320
Berkeley, George 23-26, 51-52, 54, 81, 83-84, 160, 232-233, 253, 268, 297-300, 302, 359-360
  "On the Prospect of Planting Arts and Learning in America" 147, 253, 268
Beveridge, Albert 46, 405-407, 416

Bible, The 12, 37, 43, 66, 110, 124-125, 136, 149, 168-169, 174, 176-177, 224, 265, 288, 320, 321, 322, 338, 350
Bradford, William 81, 88, 96-99, 100-101, 104, 113, 170, 177
  "Of Plymouth Plantation" 95-97, 100, 105, 184
Bradstreet, Anne 59, 66, 68-72, 79, 80, 167, 184
  "Flesh and the Spirit, The" 59, 68-69
  "To My Dear Children" 80, 184
  "Upon the Burning of Our House" 59, 69-70, 80
Brownson, Orestes A. 277-278, 281, 283, 287, 292
Bryan, William Jennings 406-407, 411, 416
  "Imperialism" 406-407

Calhoun, John C. 339-340, 352, 365
  "Slavery a Positive Good" 339-340
Calvinism 55-58, 63, 67, 79, 140, 147, 153, 163, 204, 287
Canaan 19, 155, 254, 266, 338
Cannibals 4, 16, 32, 340
Captivity narrative 38, 104
Carleill, Christopher 9, 37, 222
  "Concerning a Voyage" 37, 222
Carnegie, Andrew 44-45, 47, 391, 393
  "Wealth" 44, 45, 47, 393
Cass, Lewis 40, 250, 257-258
Catholicism 35, 55, 57, 131, 141, 145, 290
Centennial exposition 18-19, 47
Channing, William Ellery 34, 80, 172, 245, 255, 260, 277, 287, 296
Chattel slavery 331, 340, 365, 369, 371, 379
Chauncy, Charles 171-177, 179, 182, 184
  Enthusiasm Described and Cautioned Against 171-177

Christianity 4, 16, 32, 35, 37, 39, 46, 96, 124-126, 136, 141, 146, 157, 176-180, 235, 264, 266, 269, 275, 289, 342, 350, 403
Church of England, see Anglican Church
Civil War (American) 18-19, 250, 310, 332, 352, 358, 363-382, 387, 389, 395, 402, 404, 410, 411, 414
Colonization 2-17, 21, 22, 27, 37, 39, 49, 130, 234, 294
Columbia 19, 50, 155, 165, 222-225, 244, 249, 268-269
Columbus, Christopher 20, 29, 32, 35, 48, 250
Conversion narrative 79, 168-169, 171
Cotton, John 12, 37, 39, 74, 77, 82, 131-133, 137, 151, 257
   Churches Resurrection, The 131, 133
Cranch, Christopher Pearse 277, 296

Davis, Jefferson 365-366, 369, 414
   "First Inaugural Address" 365-366, 369, 414
Devil 4, 15, 32, 38, 44, 55, 67, 97, 108-109, 139, 145, 176, 199 (see Gog and Magog)
Domesticity 212, 249, 309, 316, 322, 328
Douglass, Frederick 207, 241, 348-351, 356-357, 365, 370, 373-374, 378, 380, 413-414
   "What the Black Man Wants" 370, 373
   What to the Slave Is the Fourth of July? 241, 350, 356, 370, 413
Dwight, Timothy 146-148, 268
   America 146-148

Early Republic 34, 150, 151, 212, 219-242, 243, 280, 287, 308, 312, 322-323, 327, 395
Ecclesiastical history 58, 90, 104-107, 128, 139
Eden 9, 11-12, 18, 241
Edwards, Jonathan 78-79, 81-82, 140-143, 147-148, 164, 167-176, 182-190
   Sinners in the Hands of an Angry God 164, 166-167, 184

Emerson, Ralph Waldo 80-81, 170, 194, 275-281, 285-290, 295-300, 325, 351
   "American Scholar, The" 275, 286-287, 296
   "Divinity School Address" 275, 278, 288, 290, 296
   Nature 275, 277, 289, 296
Empiricism 167, 168, 170, 177, 182, 284
Enlargement of Japheth 5, 17
Enlightenment 1, 38, 47, 78-80, 94, 122, 141-143, 150, 152-153, 156, 163-189, 192, 194-195, 197-199, 204, 208, 221, 235, 258, 265, 269-270, 294, 316, 318, 322, 335, 337, 352; deism 149, 177-180, 186, 188, 204; self-perfection (self-improvement) 143, 167, 291
Enthusiasm 140, 164-167, 171-173, 175-177, 181, 187-188, 236, 287, 386
Eschatology 120, 133, 140, 144, 153
Europe 3, 4, 8-9, 15, 17, 20, 29, 47, 51, 63, 102, 127, 131, 132, 146, 147, 180, 198, 199, 221, 222, 236, 238, 214, 245, 250, 255, 260, 263, 264, 266, 279, 285, 293, 343; Old World 2, 7, 9, 15-16,18, 20-22, 56-57, 59, 63, 79, 130, 134, 147, 237
Evangelism 163, 165, 169, 173, 177, 181, 182
Evarts, William M. 19, 386, 395, 398, 402
Exceptionalism 123, 153, 156, 233, 235-238, 240-241, 243, 407, 416 (see Manifest Destiny, Millennialism)

Federalists 220, 224-226, 229, 238-239, 241
Fessenden, Thomas Green 220, 223, 225-228, 240-241
   "Almighty Power: An Ode" 225-228
   "Ode, An" 220, 223
Fiske, John 253, 264
Fitzhugh, George 340-341, 355
Franklin, Benjamin 167, 171, 177-181, 183-184, 211-212, 235, 397
   Autobiography, The 167, 178-181, 183, 184
French Revolution 178, 225, 238, 284

Freneau, Philip 146, 148, 150, 153-155, 222, 268
"On the Emigration to America and Peopling the Western Country" 150, 153
On the Rising Glory of America 148, 156, 222
Frontier 41, 233-236, 245-246, 251-252, 267, 386, 402
Fuller, Margaret 34, 47-48, 277-279, 295, 321, 324-327
Summer on the Lakes 47, 277, 295

Garnet, Henry Highland 346-349, 356
Garrison, William Lloyd 166, 181, 343-349, 351, 353, 356, 412-414
"Address to the Slaves of the United States" 346-347
Geography of salvation 2-4
George, Henry 385, 388, 393-395, 414-415
Gilded Age 18, 44, 380, 385-419; class 388-389, 401, 409; economy 389, 399, 401, 410-411; Gold standard 387, 411; industrialization 388, 395; philanthropy 385-386; progress 385, 393-394, 408, 415 (see immigration)
Glorious Revolution 78, 108, 193
Gog and Magog 130, 139-140 (see devil)
Golden Age 28-35, 149, 151, 154, 224, 236
Goodwin, George 59-62, 66, 68, 71, 79, 80
Automachia, or The Self-Conflict of a Christian 59, 60, 68, 79, 80
Grand, Sarah 310, 321
Grayson, William J. 355-356
Great Awakening 159, 163, 165-167, 171-174, 184-188, 190, 287; denominationalism 181, 290; revivalism 176, 185, 187-188 (see religion)
Grimké, Angelina Emily 320-321, 327
Grimké, Sarah Moore 320-321

Hakluyt the Younger, Richard 2, 4-10, 15-16, 23, 25
Hancock, John 193, 200, 202, 209-210
Hariot, Thomas 10, 13-16, 24, 51
Briefe and True Report, A 2, 9-11, 14
Hawthorne, Nathaniel 81, 145, 277, 279

Hayes, Edward 6, 9, 37, 222
"Discourse Concerning a Voyage" 9, 37, 222
Historiography 48, 81, 87, 89, 94, 95, 106, 111, 114-115, 128, 155, 247, 270
Hooker, Thomas 61, 163
Hopkins, Samuel 133, 141-143, 156
Humphreys, David 146, 149-150, 268
Husbandry 12, 39, 247, 257

Immigration 16, 371, 386, 395-398, 400-401, 409
Imperialism 28, 38-42, 153, 237, 240, 246, 255, 258-259, 401, 405-409, 410
Indians, see Native Americans
Individualism 205, 208, 251, 267, 287, 288, 293, 323, 392, 393
Irving, Washington 34, 40, 48

Jackson, Andrew 40-41, 219, 248-250, 257, 259, 265, 268, 270
Jefferson, Thomas 38-39, 47, 178, 191, 195-198, 200, 202, 205, 207, 219, 226, 229, 231, 235, 238-239, 241, 246, 249-250, 254, 261-263, 335-337, 342, 395, 411-416
Declaration of Independence, The 20, 146, 178, 191-207, 213, 228, 239, 240, 275, 313, 319, 326, 332, 335, 341, 346, 349, 350, 357, 368, 369, 390, 391, 392, 394, 411-416
Notes on the State of Virginia 38, 47, 335, 336
Jeremiad 88, 101, 102, 103, 104, 110, 138, 156, 200, 208, 239, 350

Las Casas, Bartholomew de 35-36, 46
Legaré, Hugh Swinton 220, 228, 234-237, 241
Liberalism 192, 195, 197-198, 201, 204, 208, 213, 287
Lincoln, Abraham 206, 365-369, 372-374, 377-378, 380, 388, 395, 402, 414
Emancipation Proclamation 373-374, 377
"First Inaugural Address" 366, 368, 372, 414
"Second Inaugural Address" 367-368

Locke, John 12, 45, 168, 171, 177, 180, 191-192, 197-198, 208, 256-257, 282, 283-284, 308, 326
Lost Cause 369, 372, 380-382

Mandeville, John 3, 29-30, 32
Manifest Destiny 17-18, 43, 123, 147, 151, 153-154, 237, 241, 253-255, 259, 264-267, 270-271, 274, 293, 402, 404, 407
Marshall, John 41, 44, 247-249, 267, 270
Mather, Cotton 5, 17, 37, 48, 56, 58-59, 63-64, 66, 77, 79-80, 88-90, 102-109, 111, 113-115, 122, 134, 139, 140, 180, 184
   "General Introduction," *Magnalia Christi Americana* 17, 105, 106, 113
   Magnalia Christi Americana 58-59, 63, 80, 90, 102, 104-107, 109, 113, 139
   "Life of Sir William Phips, The" 106, 108, 114
Mather, Increase 38, 88, 94-95, 103-104, 108-109, 112-114, 116, 134, 137, 138, 156
   Day of Trouble is Near, The 137, 138, 156
   Doctrine of Divine Providence, The 94, 112
   Mystery of Israel's Salvation, The 137
Mather, Samuel 75, 135
Mede, Joseph 127-130, 132, 138-141, 152
Melville, Herman 114, 254, 277, 279
Mexican War 250, 262-263, 353, 402
Millennialism 32, 121-161, 235, 264, 287, 292, 294, 351; Book of Revelation (see Bible); civil millennialism 140, 144, 150, 152, 153, 155-156; postmillennialism 133, 141-142, 148, 150-152; Second Coming 124-125, 137, 142, 147, 150, 292
Monarchy 128, 158, 199, 238, 285
Morse, Jedidiah 253, 260

Nationalism 122, 152-153, 156-157, 183, 244, 259, 398, 408
Native Americans 4, 10, 12-18, 21-22, 27, 28, 30-49, 58, 62, 63, 73, 74, 76, 87, 103-104, 130, 139, 154, 156, 165, 206, 220, 231-232, 241, 248-250, 256, 257, 258, 267, 294-295, 334; Five Civilized Tribes 40, 44, 248, 258, 262; Indian captivity 35-38, 104; Indian removal 40, 248, 250, 262; Praying Indians 37-38, 43; ten lost tribes 37, 43, 139; treaty system 39-41, 44
Nativism 397-398, 401
Nature 34, 198, 255, 257, 259, 266
New England Way 38, 64, 100, 101, 103
New Jerusalem 37, 68, 75, 78, 105, 123, 132-134, 138-139, 142, 147, 148, 152, 155, 157
New Woman 306, 310-311, 321-322, 327-330
New World 1-25, 28, 30, 32, 36, 55-59, 61, 63, 77, 80, 82, 87, 90, 95, 96, 100, 102, 106, 113, 134, 139, 140, 151, 155, 170, 184, 196, 230, 233, 235-237, 247, 254
Noble Savage 33-35, 42-43, 54

O'Sullivan, John L. 153, 156, 255, 259, 266-267, 269
Oakes, Urian 94-95, 112-113

Paine, Thomas 177-178, 184, 192, 194, 198-199, 204, 258
   Common Sense 5, 144, 178, 194, 198-199, 204
Parker, Theodore 277, 289, 317, 351
Providence 19, 39, 64, 70, 71, 80, 87-119, 128, 154, 164, 179, 208, 226, 230-232, 236, 240-241, 255-256, 263, 266, 267, 406-407
Providential history 83, 95, 96, 100, 101, 107
Puritanism 17, 38, 55-85, 101, 105, 108, 110, 114, 124, 131, 133, 140, 143, 144, 156, 170, 177, 254; backsliding 97, 103, 134, 138, 167; chosen people 61-62, 79, 95, 97, 101, 104, 105, 106, 123, 132, 134, 155, 195, 254, 266, 338; congregationalism 165, 172; covenant 58, 64-66, 78, 80, 88, 95, 98, 101, 102, 113, 115, 116, 135-136, 138, 165, 294; covenant of grace 65, 78, 113, 165; elect 65, 105; errand into the wilderness 75, 122, 123, 145, 155, 254; filiopietism

110, 239; great migration 100-101, 130; Half-Way Covenant 78, 101, 102; separatists 57-58, 74, 95, 98; saints 66-67, 93, 96, 100, 104, 106, 109, 124, 126, 130, 132, 133, 135, 137, 140-142, 148-150; theocracy 57-58, 61, 75, 77, 78, 108-109, 128, 134 (see autobiography, jeremiad, New England Way, providence)

Quaker 199, 283

Racism 34, 42, 333, 339, 378, 402
Ramsay, David 199, 209-211
Reconstruction 19, 242, 358, 363-364, 369-371, 385, 396 (see Civil War)
Republicanism 121, 143, 144, 146, 153, 192, 195, 197, 201, 204-205, 208, 209, 220, 224, 238, 258, 318, 350, 392
Republican Mother 303, 306, 308-309, 311-313, 316, 322, 323
Revolutionary Period 152, 191-192, 197, 201-202, 204, 206-209, 212-214, 319, 327, 334, 337, 356
Revolutionary War 192, 220, 223, 241, 392
Richards, George 146, 147, 149-150, 154-155, 224, 225
Ripley, George 277-278, 288, 324
Ripley, Sophia 277, 323-327
Romanticism 279-280, 298-299
Roosevelt, Theodore 385, 388, 407-409
Rowlandson, Mary 38, 43, 54, 103-104, 116, 184
Rush, Benjamin 201, 224, 238, 313, 314

Sacred history 93, 101, 102
Savages 4, 18, 22, 29, 33, 34, 38, 42, 46, 47, 61, 70, 76, 231, 241, 256, 257, 262, 294, 295, 404
Savagism 26, 32, 33, 52
Schurz, Carl 404, 407, 416
Secular history 75, 89, 91, 93, 107, 231
Segregation 376, 378, 399
Seneca Falls Convention 319, 413-414
Separate spheres 303, 310-314, 316-318, 320-323, 325-328
Sewall, Samuel 17, 37, 139, 140, 160

Shepard, Thomas 59, 61, 62-63, 73, 80, 86, 167, 184
Sherwood, Samuel 17, 144-146
Slavery 145, 166, 197, 202, 212, 237, 241-242, 259, 270-271, 274, 276, 321, 331-362, 364-366, 369, 371-375, 377, 379-380, 413, 414
Smith, John 11, 16, 18, 21, 37, 47
Social Darwinism 42, 264, 392-394, 398, 403, 409, 416
Socialism 292, 386, 388, 391-392, 409
Spanish-American War 250, 407
Spies, August 44, 391, 395, 415
Stowe, Harriet Beecher 166, 309, 314, 351, 356
Strong, Josiah 17, 42, 264, 388, 398, 402-404
Sumner, William Graham 391-395, 416

Taylor, Edward 68, 72, 80, 114
Thoreau, Henry David 80, 170, 181, 184, 207, 233, 253, 258, 267-269, 276, 277, 279-281, 293, 295, 296
Walden 184, 253, 258, 268, 276, 277, 279-280, 296
"To the Workingmen of America" 390-391, 415
Transcendentalism 181, 275-301, 327; self-culture 291, 293, 323, 324, 326; self-reliance 276, 289, 291, 294, 321, 325; Transcendental Club 275, 276, 278-279, 324 (see empiricism, Unitarianism)
Translatio imperii 18, 147
True Woman 303, 306, 309-314, 322-323, 325
Turner, Frederick Jackson 41, 251-252, 267, 268, 295, 402
Turner, Nat 338, 345

Unitarianism 149, 172, 177, 287, 296

Vacant land 12, 18, 39, 43, 170
Vanishing Indian 28-35, 40, 43, 270
Vespucci, Amerigo 30-32, 45

Walker, David 342-343, 345, 349, 356
Warren, John 221, 227-228, 241

War of 1812 233, 239, 250, 412
Webster, Daniel 222, 367-368
Westward expansion 2, 14, 17, 232-233, 245-246, 264, 266, 267, 271
Whitaker, Alexander 18, 46, 48
Whitman, Walt 250-252, 274, 277, 279, 294-295
Wigglesworth, Michael 113, 294
Wilderness 8, 38, 39, 41, 44, 48, 75, 102, 122, 130, 134, 137, 144-145, 152, 154, 155, 168-170, 236, 251, 258, 262, 265, 266, 268-270, 276-277, 293, 295, 406
Williams, Roger 71, 74-76, 81
Williams, Samuel 200, 202
Winthrop, John 39, 57, 61-62, 72-73, 77, 88, 89, 96, 98-101, 104, 106-107, 114, 131, 173, 177, 235, 237, 257, 306-307
Winthrop, Robert Charles 154-155, 237